CANON AND TEXT

OF THE

NEW TESTAMENT

BY

CASPAR RENÉ GREGORY

Biblical Viewpoints Publications
16416 Sutters Lane Ct.
Northville, MI 48167

First printed by Charles Scribner's Sons, New York, 1907.

Canon and Text of the New Testament
International Standard Book Number: 1-890133-14-0
Reprinted by Biblical Viewpoints Publications
in the United States, 1997.
E-mail: haines@bibleviews.com

CANON AND TEXT

THE CANON AND THE TEXT

OF THE

NEW TESTAMENT.

———◆———

A GENERAL VIEW.

THE consideration of the canon and the text of the New Testament forms a preface to the study of what is called introduction. It is true that these two topics have sometimes of late years been remanded to the close of introduction, have been treated in a somewhat perfunctory way, and have been threatened with exclusion from the field. The earlier habit of joining them together and placing them at the front was much more correct. Now and then they were termed as a whole "general introduction." The rest of introduction, the criticism of the contents of the books in and for themselves, was then called "special introduction." The use of these names does not seem to me to be necessary. The introduction to the study of the New Testament is made up of three criticisms, of the critical treatment of three things.

The criticism of the canon tells us with what writings we have to deal, affords us the needed insight into the circumstances which accompanied the origin of these writings, and examines not only the favourable judgment passed upon these writings by Christianity, but also the adverse judgment that fell to the lot of other in a certain measure similar writings. This first criticism then rounds off the field for the New Testament student. Other writings he may touch upon by way of illustration. He need treat in detail of no others. It is true that a few scholars have thrust into the introduction to the New Testament a series of other books not belonging to the New Testament, and that a collection of such books was issued under the title of the "New Testament outside of the received canon." This proceeding is to my mind unnecessary, unwise, and contrary to the rules of scientific research. It produces confusion and relieves no difficulty.

The second criticism is the criticism of the text. The criticism of the canon settled upon large lines, drew a circle around, the object of study. If we take a given book in hand we know from the criticism of the canon all that we need to know of its external fate, and we know that it is a due object of our attention. But upon opening it, or during our work upon it, we may find that a certain section in it, possibly a section that has excited our interest and has led us to much expense of time and labour,—we may find that this section is really not a proper and genuine part of the book in question. Further, even if the book mooted contained no complete paragraph that was spurious, it would be possible that difficulties, and that of a serious nature, arise from a cause similar to the one just mentioned. We might form a certain conception of an important passage and base upon this conception a historical conclusion, a dogmatical theory, or an important theme in a sermon, only to learn at a later date that a phrase or a word which was vital to our point was not a part of the true text of the passage, that it had been the result of an unintentional or even of an intentional transformation, substitution, or addition long centuries ago. It is the criticism of the text alone that can save us from such trouble. The criticism of the text, if we may play upon the words, must do intensively that which the criticism of the canon does extensively; the canon touches the exterior, the text the interior. It must delve into the libraries, turn the leaves of the manuscripts, and determine for us what words and combinations of words make up each of the books to which we have to turn. Is the state of the text at any point uncertain, this criticism tells us about it, and gives us the materials for forming a judgment for ourselves.

The third criticism is the criticism of the contents of the books. It finds its way clear so soon as the two previous criticisms have done their work. It proceeds then to examine in detail all questions that affect the contents of the books. It is not exegesis, although, as in both of the other criticisms, the exercise of exegetical keenness will be necessary at every step. It would be hard to combat the declaration that the most searching, profound, and complete exegesis is of the greatest assistance to the work of the criticism of the contents. Yet the two are distinct, and the criticism of the contents must theoretically and practically precede exegesis proper, however certain it is that after completing the criticism of the contents and passing on to and completing the exegesis of the books, the scholar will return to all three of the introductory criticisms and modify the judgments there passed. It is the interweaving of all life. In the present work we have to do solely with the first two criticisms.

4

THE CANON

OF

THE NEW TESTAMENT

6

THE CANON.

INTRODUCTION.

THE first duty of a scholar is to secure a clear view of his aim
in taking up a given subject. In the case of a large number of
the writings which treat of the right that the New Testament
books have to a place in that collection, this duty has so far as
I can see been neglected. The discussions touching the proper
contents of the New Testament have been dominated by the
word canon. This word has, it may be imperceptibly, come to
determine the course of the inquiry. The general supposition is
that a canon exists. It is in approaching the subject taken for
granted as a thing long ago proved, or so certainly and well
known as to need no proof, that a certain canon was settled
upon at a very early date in the history of the Christian Church.
And the word canon in connection with this view means a
sharply defined and unalterable collection made, put together,
decided upon by general Church authority under the guidance
of the Holy Spirit. The long held theory of the inspiration of
every word in the books of the Bible needed as an accompaniment an inspired selection of the inspired books. For the
purposes, then, of the inquiring scholar the canon of the New
Testament is the book or the collection of the books of the New
Testament, and that of the New Testament precisely in the
extent and within the limits of the one that we use to-day.

From this starting-point it has been the custom to enter
upon the "history" of the canon. The canon is presupposed
as something that of right exists and is beyond all doubt. All
then that is to be done is to trace the various steps that led in
the early age of the Church to its formation and determination
or authorisation, that is to say, it is only necessary to write the

history of the canon, as though we should speak of the history of the Church or of the history of Greece. If in examining the subject one thing or another seem uncertain or not clear, it is no matter. That is a mere accident of history. The canon exists, that is plain, whether we know or do not know when and why, according to what rules and regulations, and by whom it was formed. The inquiry then serves merely to determine the question of more or of less in the contents of the canon, or of more or less in the testimony to the existence and contents of the canon. These things are all very well; they are right, and are of weight in clearing up the whole field. Nevertheless this is not the right aim, not the right way to put the question. The reason why it has done less mischief than it otherwise might have done, is that the larger number of the books of the New Testament were from a very early period beyond all doubt in the possession of and were diligently used by many Christians.

That way of opening the case was wrong. The first thing to be done is to determine whether or not there is a canon. For the moment we may here hold fast to the current use of the expression. The first duty of the inquirer in this field is to determine whether or not there existed at an early period in the history of the Christian Church a positively official and authorised collection of books that was acknowledged by the whole of Christendom, that was everywhere and in precisely the same manner constituted and certain, and that corresponded exactly to the New Testament now generally in use in Western Europe and in America. Compare the case with that of the word doctrine or dogma. A dogma is a doctrinal statement that has been officially, ecclesiastically defined, that has been determined upon by a general council of the Church. Were it not open to view that such official definitions are in our hands, the first aim of the dogmatician would be to inquire whether there were any dogmas in existence. We have now to ask, whether or not there is a canon of the New Testament. Our first aim is not the history of the canon, but the criticism of the canon. Should it be objected that we cannot criticise a thing that does not exist, the reply to this just observation is, that the criticism of the canon, in case a canon does not exist, resolves itself into the criticism of the statements about a presupposed canon, statements that have been rife for a long while. We have, on the one hand, to examine the traditionally accepted statements and declarations bearing upon the origin or the original existence of the books of the New Testament and upon the process by which they were gathered together into one collection. On the other hand, we have to seek in the surroundings of the early Church, in the early Church in so far as it occupied itself with the earliest books, in the early Church as the guardian of the earliest books,—we have to seek for signs of the combination of, the putting together of, the uniting of, two or more books in such a way that they were to remain together as forming a special and definite volume of a more or less normative character for the use of Christians and the Church. We say of Christians and of the Church. The two are not of necessity the same. It would be quite possible to think of the combining into one volume of various books which would be interesting and useful and even adapted to build up a Christian character, and which, therefore, would be desirable for Christians, which nevertheless would not be suited in the least for the public services of the Church. We shall see later that it was possible for some writings to be upon the boundary between these two classes, between the books for Christians in their private life and the books for use in church.

Should any one fear that it must be totally impossible to give a due answer to the question as to the existence of a canon before the whole field has been carefully examined, the difficulty or the impossibility must at once be conceded. As a matter of fact, however, the difficulty is hardly more than an apparent, or a theoretical, or a momentary one. For if we proceed upon the supposition that no canon is to be presupposed, that we are not to determine that there is a canon until we discover it in the course of our inquiry, the difficulty will be only apparent or theoretical. Our researches upon the lines already pointed out will continue unhampered, either until a canon offers itself to view, or until, having reached the present without detecting signs of a canon, we conclude that none ever existed. The answer to the question must come forth from the threads of the discussion. It is indifferent at what point. In so far as the fear alluded to proceeds from a solicitude for the dearly cherished canon of tradition, the difficulty may prove to be but temporary. For the current assumption is, that the canon is there almost from the first, that the books of the New Testament can scarcely be conceived of as all in existence for an appreciable space of time before the swift arm of ecclesiastical power and forethought gathered them from the four winds of heaven and sealed them in the official volume. Should we, then, in the earliest periods of the history of the Church find that the assumed canon fails to present itself to our view, there will, it is true, be a certain shock to be borne by those who have thus far held to the existence of the canon. But that will pass quickly by and leave a calm mind for the treatment of the succeeding periods.

In one case or another a question might emerge from the discussion that would perplex the inquiring mind. Should the testimony for a given book seem either to be weak in general or to offer special and peculiar reasons for uncertainty, the query would at once arise, whether it have had, and whether it still to-day continue to have or cease to have, a right to hold the place it actually occupies in the New Testament volume. Such doubt might even find a proper place in consideration of the rules which were either clearly seen to be, or which have long been traditionally assumed to be, the rules of the early Christians for accepting or for rejecting books. In such a case it would not be absolutely necessary to think of a false judgment, of a false subjective conception, on the part of the Christians of that day, of facts or of circumstances that stood and stand in fully the same manner at the command of the Christians then and of Christians to-day. For it is altogether conceivable that a scholar to-day should be able to gain a wider and more comprehensive view of the circumstances of that early time, as well as greater clearness and greater depth of insight into the mental movements of the period, than a Christian scholar of that very time could have secured. It may be possible or necessary to say that the decision at that time would have been rendered in another sense if the judges had known what we now know.

This question would in outward practice take the form of asking, whether or not we intend to-day either to limit or to extend the number of the books in the New Testament, whether, for example, we should like to leave out the Epistle of James because Luther did not like it, or the Revelation because it

is too dream-like, or the Epistle to the Hebrews because it is
not from Paul's mouth, or the Second Epistle of Peter because
it was so little known at the first, or the Acts of the Apostles
partly because it is not mentioned until a late date, partly because
it offers to us a great many puzzling questions, or the Fourth
Gospel because it does not say: "I, John the son of Zebedee,
write this present book and place my seal upon it, which shall
remain visible to every man to all eternity." Do we really
purpose to ask the Bible societies to publish the New Testament
without one or the other of these books? This question will
strike younger men as very strange. It will seem less singular
to the older ones who remember the apocryphal books of the
Old Testament in our common Bibles. These books had for
centuries in many circles maintained their place beside, among,
the books of the Old Testament. The Protestant Church looked
askance at some of them, condemned them all, and put them
out of the Bibles in common use, so that to-day it is not easy
for any but scholars to find access to them. It was scarcely
well-advised to turn those books out of the sacred volume ; for
they offered not only much valuable historical matter, but as
well religious writings suited to elevate the soul. They went far
to bridge over the gulf between the Old and the New Testament. From this—to return to the practical question just
put—it will at once be apparent to every one that we do not
cherish the wish to reduce the number of the books of the
New Testament.

The companion thought is just as possible. It may be
necessary to ask, whether after due consideration of the
circumstances it may become our duty to say that other writings
besides those that are found in our New Testament to-day are
to be declared worthy to have a place in it. Perhaps some
one may succeed in proving that if the Christians of that
day had had our knowledge touching a given book they would
have received it as a proper part of the New Testament collection.
This thought may assume the form, that we are in a position
to declare that a certain book, which in some circles was then
regarded as either belonging to the New Testament or as
being fully equal to the writings of the New Testament, would
certainly also on the part of the authoritative or ruling circles
of the time have met with a more favourable reception and have

been placed among the books of the New Testament had those
high circles had our present knowledge with respect to the book
in question. But we have no desire to increase directly the
number of the books in our New Testament or to add to it
as a second volume the so-called "New Testament outside of
the received canon."

Lest any one should be led by these observations to suppose
that it is our purpose to turn the whole of the New Testament
upside down, or at least to make it appear that the greater
part of it is of doubtful value, we hasten to state that we have
no such intention, and that we regard anything of that kind
as scientifically impossible. The books of the New Testament
are in general to be recognised as from an early date the
normative writings of the rising Christian Church. It is not
easy to see upon what ground a man could take his stand,
who should set out to prove, let us say, that only one Gospel
or only one letter of Paul's was genuine, or even that not a single
New Testament book was genuine. In that case Christianity
must have developed itself from a cell or a convolution in the
brain of a Gnostic of the second century, and also have unfolded
itself by a backward motion into the books of the so-called
New Testament. But, if the Church were prepared to accept
this, we may be sure that some one would at once call the
existence of that Gnostic, or of any and every Gnostic, in question. It is, then, not our purpose either to declare or to prove
that the New Testament is not genuine.

People, however, often treat the Bible, and in particular
the New Testament, as if they were fetish worshippers. They
refer to the books, to the paragraphs, to the sentences, and to
the words with a species of holy fear. They refuse to allow
the least portion of it to be called in question. They consider
a free, a paraphrastic use of its sentences to be something
profane. They hold that the words of the New Testament
are to be reproduced, quoted, used with the most painful accuracy
precisely as they stand upon the sacred page. They think
that anything else, any free use of the words, any shortening or
lengthening of the sentences, falls under the terrible curse
pronounced in the Revelation of John at the close of its
prophecies. It may readily be granted that the general thought

of those verses may in special cases find a fitting application within a limited circle, in order to keep thoughtless men from a trifling use of these books and of their words. As a curse, the words should be remanded to the time and the circle of the author of that particular book. It is never desirable, never admissible to use the truth and the words of the truth as a means of frightening the ignorant, and as little should we try to protect the words of the truth by a bugbear. The truth suffers, it is true, under every impure application of its contents, and as well under every less careful observance of, or every twisted and untrue use of, the form of its contents. The writings of the New Testament are not to be treated with levity. But they are just as little to be used in a mysterious way to frighten people.

It will be our duty here first of all to examine the somewhat kaleidoscopic word canon, since we shall otherwise stumble at every step in tracing its use in profane and ecclesiastical history. After that it will be advisable to cast a glance at the way in which the Jews treated their sacred books. The Jews stood as patterns to a certain degree for the men who gathered the books of the New Testament together, seeing that at the first these books were brought into close connection with the books of the Old Testament. As a matter of course no Jewish authority can have had a hand in the collection of the Christian books. Yet we must seek in Jewish circles for a clue to the thoughts that guided the Christian collectors. The question as to the freedom of travel and the ease or difficulty of communication between different parts of the known world of that day, or of the Roman Empire with its surroundings, might seem at the first blush to lie far aside from our inquiry. If I do not err, it really has much weight for our researches, and we shall devote a few moments to it. It will also be apparent to every one that we must give some attention in advance to the way in which books were written, given to the public, and reproduced in the early centuries of our era. These four points : the canon, the Jewish canon, intercommunication in the Roman Empire, and bookmaking, complete the necessary preparation for the work before us. We shall then describe briefly what it is to which we have to direct our attention in entering upon the examination of the early history and literature of the Church.

In the criticism of the canon itself, it would be most fortunate if we could, as is desirable in every treatment of historical matter, build our foundation or lay out the course of our researches concomitantly, not only according to time, but also according to place. Since that is, alas! impossible, it would be a good thing to pass through the whole field of this criticism twice, discussing everything the first time according to the succession of the years and centuries, and the second time according to the contemporaneous conditions in the several divisions of the growing Church, in the Churches of the different countries, peoples, and tongues. This would, however, exceed the limits of our space, and we shall therefore have to content ourselves with treating our subject according to time. We shall speak of six periods. The distinction of these periods is to a large extent not severely necessary, but it is convenient.

The first period extends from the year 30 to 90 after Christ, and may be termed the period of the Apostles. In it the most of the books with which we have to do were written. The second period, from 90 to 160, places before our eyes the earlier use of the books that are in the New Testament, and the gathering them together into groups, preparing for their combination into a single whole. This period is, as a matter of fact, by far the most important period in the course of our discussion. For it is during these years of this post-apostolic period that these books pass from a common to a sacred use. The third period, from 160 to 200, we may call the period of Irenæus. Here the Old Catholic Church is on a firm footing, and the life in several of the great national divisions of the Church begins to be more open and more confident. The fourth period, from 200 to 300, bears the stamp of the giant Origen, but brings with it many a valiant man, not least Dionysius of Alexandria and Tertullian of Carthage. The fifth period, from 300 to 370, the period of Eusebius, sees the opening of the series of great councils in the Council of Nice in 325. Eusebius himself, the quoter of the earlier literature of the Church, has done a vast deal for the definition of the canon. The sixth period, from 370 to 700, bears the name of the much defamed scholar, the great theologian Theodore of Mopsuestia, and brings us into the work of Jerome and of Augustine. By that time the treatment of the books of the New Testament has become to such a degree uniform in the different parts of the Church, or has, in case of the variation of some communities from the general rule, attained such a stability, that it is no longer necessary to follow it up in detail. Should a canon not be determined upon before the close of that period, should a given book not have won for itself a clear recognition by that time, there is but little likelihood that the one or the other ever will come to pass.

A. THE WORD CANON.

The word canon seems to spring from a Hebrew root, unless indeed this should be one of the roots that extend across the bounds of the classes of languages and may claim a universal authority. The Hebrew verb "*kana*" means to stand a thing up straight, and then takes the subsidiary meanings of creating or founding, and of gaining or buying. The first or main sense leads to the Hebrew noun "*kane*" that at first means a reed. Of course such a reed was for a man without wood at hand an excellent measuring-rod, and the word was applied to that too; and it was taken horizontally also and used for the rod of a pair of scales, and then for the scales themselves. In Greek we find the word "*kanna*" used for a reed and for things made by weaving reeds together, and the word "*kanon*" for any straight stick like a yard-stick or the scale beam. In Homer the latter word was used for the two pieces of wood that were laid crosswise to keep the leather shield well rounded out. The word "*kanon*," which we then write canon in English, found favour in the eyes of the Greek, and passed from the sense of a measuring-rod to be used for a plumb-line or for a level, or a ruler, for anything that was a measure or a rule for other things. It entered the mental sphere and there it also stood for a rule, for an order that told a man what was right or what he had to do. In sculpture a statue modelled by Polycleitos was called a canon, for it was so nearly perfect that it was acknowledged as a rule for the proportions of a beautiful human body. In music the monochord was called a canon, seeing that all the further relations of tones were determined from it as a basis. We call the ancient Greek writers classics, because they are supposed to be patterns or models in more ways than one ; the grammarians in Alexandria called them the canon. And these same grammarians called their rules for declensions and conjugations and syntax canons. In chronology the canons were the great dates which were known or assumed to be certain and firm. The periods in between were then calculated from these main dates. The word was thus very varied in its application ; it might mean a table of contents, it might mean an important principle.

A favourite use of the word was for a measure, a definition, an order, a command, a law. Euripides speaks of the canon of good, Aeschines of the canon of what is just. Philo speaks of Joshua as a canon, as we might say, an ideal for subsequent leaders. Before the time of Christ I do not know that it was applied to religion, but it was applied in morals. Other words were often used by preference for positive laws and ordinances, and canon was used for a law or a command that only existed in the conception of the mind or for an ideal rule.

Christians found good use for such a word. Paul used it in the sixth chapter of Galatians and the sixteenth verse, where after speaking of the worthlessness of circumcision and of non-circumcision and the worth of a new creation, he added : mercy be upon all those that walk according to this canon. And in the tenth chapter of Second Corinthians, verses thirteen to sixteen, he alluded to the measure of the canon, to our canon, and to a foreign canon. Our good women of to-day will not admire the phrase used in the letter of the Church at Rome to the Church at Corinth, the so-called letter of Clement, which speaks (1. 3) of the women " who are under the canon of obedience." The same letter also says (7. 2) : " Let us quit, then, the empty and vain cares and pass on to the glorious and honourable canon of our tradition." And in still a third sentence of it (41. 1) we find the words : " without going out beyond the set canon of his due service." Hegesippus (Eus. H. E. 3. 32) speaks of people " who try to corrupt the sound canon of the saving preaching" or of the proclamation of salvation. The author of the Clementine books finds the " canon of the Church " in that in which all Jews agree with each other, for he conceives of the Church merely as a spiritual Judaism. The Christian Church began to feel its union in a more distinct manner than at the first, and the Old Catholic Church began to crystallise during the second century. The Christianity of this movement was a development, but a development backwards, for, like the author just mentioned, it found its basis in the Old Testament. Christianity was no longer with Paul free from the law. It had put itself again under the law, even though with manifold modifications. For this Christianity our word was applied in a general sense; the ecclesiastical canon was the token of the union of the Old and the New Testament. Clement of Alexandria (Str. 6. 15) called "the ecclesiastical canon the harmony and symphony of both law and prophets with the covenant or the testament given when the Lord was here," while in another passage (6. 11) he refers to the "musical ecclesiastical harmony of law and prophets, joined also with apostles, with the gospel." He also speaks of the canon of the truth. Elsewhere (7. 16) he speaks of those who like heretics "steal the canon of the Church." Polycrates, the bishop of Ephesus, in writing to Victor of Rome appealed to the witness of men who followed after the canon of the faith. Origen, Clement's pupil, refers (de Pr. 4. 9) to the canon "of the heavenly Church of Jesus Christ according to the succession of the apostles." He still thinks of the canon as something which lies more in the idea; the ecclesiastical proclamation or preaching was, on the contrary, something actual.

Little by little the word canon came to be used in the Church for a concrete thing, for a definite and certain decision. This is in one way a return to the origin, only that it is no longer a foot-rule or a spirit-level, but an ecclesiastical determination. It was about the middle of the third century that Cornelius, the bishop of Rome, wrote to Fabian, the bishop of Antioch, about Novatus, and complained (Eus. H. E. 6. 43) that, after being baptized when he was ill, he had not done what, "according to the canon of the Church," was necessary. Firmilian seems to have the word canon in mind shortly after the middle of the third century, when he writes (Cypr. Ep. 75) about a woman who imitated a baptism so well "that nothing seemed to vary from the ecclesiastical rule"; he probably would have used the word canon if he had been writing in Greek instead of in Latin. In the year 266 a synod at Antioch (Mansi, i. 1033), in referring to Paul of

2

Samosata, declared one of his doctrines to be "foreign to the ecclesiastical canon"; the synod used the cautious expression "we think it to be," but added : "and all the Catholic Churches agree with us." The edicts of Constantine after 311 made the conception of Christianity upon which the Catholic and Apostolic Church was based, that is to say, the ecclesiastical canon of the Catholics, a recognised religion. Had it been a religion with a visible god, its god would then have had a right to a place in the Pantheon at Rome. Thus the ecclesiastical canon, the canon of the Church, had become a set phrase to denote the rule of the Church, the custom and general doctrine of the Church. Often merely the word canon was used The Synod of Ancyra in the year 315 referred to it as the canon, and so did the Council of Nice in 325 repeatedly. The plural appears to view first about the beginning of the fourth century. Perhaps in the year 306 Peter, the bishop of Alexandria, in writing of repentance calls the conclusions canons, and Eusebius speaks of Philo as having the canons of the Church. At first the decisions of councils were called dogmas, but towards the middle of the fourth century, in the year 341 at Antioch, they also came to be called canons. Thus far, as we have seen, the word has not been applied, in the writings which are preserved to us, to the books of Scripture. It would, however, appear that about the year 350 it gradually came to be applied to them, but we do not know precisely at what moment or where or by whom. It has been assumed that this application might well be carried back as far as the time of Diocletian, and to an imperial edict of the year 303 that ordered the Christian Scriptures to be burned ; but we have not the least foundation for such a theory. Felix, the official charged with the duty of caring for religion, and of preventing the worship and spread of religions that were not recognised by the State, said to the Bishop Paul : "Bring me the scriptures of the law," and Cæcilian wrote in 303 to Felix and alluded to the scriptures of the law. But this expression is so properly and so naturally suggested by the Old Testament and Jewish use of the word law, as to make it totally improper to argue that the word law here is canon. Much less does it seem to me to be admissible, until we receive evidence that is not now known, to attribute the use of the cognate words canonical and canonise in connection with the Scriptures to Origen. It is by no means certain that the word was not used earlier than I have suggested, but it is well to move cautiously. The first application of the term to Scripture that is thus far known is not direct, in the word canon, but indirect in cognate words like those just named. The fifty-ninth canon (Mansi, ii. 574) of the Synod at Laodicea of about the year 363 determines that "private psalms should not be read in the churches, nor uncanonised books, but only the canonical [books] of the New and Old Testament." And in the year 367, when Athanasius wrote the yearly letter (Ep. Fest. 39) announcing to the Church the due calculation of the day upon which Easter would fall, he said: "I thought it well . . . to put down in order the canonised books of which we not only have learned from tradition but also believe [upon the evidence of our own hearts?] that they are divine." Here we have nothing to do with the general contents of Athanasius' statement or of the canon of the Synod of Laodicea, but only with the technical term. Both use these terms canonical or canonise in such a way as to show that they were in common use, or had been so much used as to be generally understood. It may be granted that even if a reader of the festal letter did not happen to have met with the word before, he would have been able to gather its meaning from this letter itself without the least difficulty. Nevertheless, I suppose that it had been used before quite aside from the Synod of Laodicea, and therefore I attribute its rise in this sense to the middle of the century.

Having reached this use of the word for the Scriptures, we must ask in what sense they, the books of the Bible, were called canonical, for the word has two meanings that look in opposite directions. A given thing might be canonical because something had been done to it, that is to say, because it had been put into the canon, or it might be canonical because it had in and of itself a certain normative character. A clergyman was called canonical because he had been canonised, or in other words, not because he had been a saint and had been declared to be a saint, but because he had been written down in the list, the canon, let us say, the table of contents of the given bishopric. And he was also, though probably only later, called canonical because he was one of those who were bound to live according to a certain rule or canon. What was the case with a book of the Bible? It seems to me to be likely, in spite of the fact that we have no direct testimony to the custom as a custom, that Christian scholars and bishops before the time of Eusebius were in the habit of making lists of the books that they included in the Scriptures. There is one such list, containing some of the books of the New Testament, of which we have a fragment in the Muratorian leaves, and it may be as early as the year 170. Aside from that, the only list known to us by name before the time of Eusebius is one containing the books of the Old Testament which Melito, the bishop of Sardes in the third and fourth quarters of the second century, says that he had made ; he had gone to the East for the purpose of studying scripture history, and made the list of the Old Testament books after he had learned all about them. It may then well be the case that at least in some places the books of the New Testament were called canonical because they had been added to such a list, were found in such lists. Were any one in doubt about a given book, he could beg the bishop to tell him whether or not it stood in the list or canon. The use of the word in this sense does not in any way preclude its having been used in the other sense. It is in every way probable that the books of the Old Testament at first, and then later also the books of the New Testament at an early date, came to be called canonical in the sense that they contain that which is fitted to serve as a measure for all else, and in particular for the determination of faith and conduct. It was in connection with both meanings, but especially with the latter, that the thought of a totally finished and closed up collection of books was attached to the word, and that this thus limited series of writings was called the canon as the only external and visible rule of truth. Clement of Alexandria had mentioned the canon of the truth without binding it up with the Scriptures. Two centuries later Isidore of Pelusium referred to " the canon of the truth, the divine Scriptures."

B. THE JEWISH CANON

In order to secure a wide basis for comparison, it would be of interest to the Christian student, if space allowed, to look at other religions and ask what sacred books they have, and in what way these books were determined to be sacred. The

Brahmans have four Vedas, the Rigveda, the Samaveda, the Yajurveda, and the Atharvaveda, as well as supplementary parts called Brahmanas. The canonical works are the first three Vedas with their sections of the supplement. These were given by divine revelation and are therefore called "hearing"; God spoke and men listened. Other books are mere traditions, and are called "memory" as remembered tradition. The Rigveda, containing ten books with 1017 hymns, is supposed to date between 4000 and 2500 before Christ. Many Brahmans hold that the Vedas were pre-existent in the mind of deity, and therefore explain away all references to history and all human elements.

The canon of the Buddhists is different in different places. The canon of the northern Buddhists appears to have been determined upon in their fourth council at Cashmere in the year 78 after Christ, or four hundred and two years after the death of Buddha. If we turn to the late centre of Buddhism in Tibet, where it found acceptance in the second quarter of the seventh century after Christ, we find a canon of 104 volumes containing 1083 books; this is named Kanjur. The Tanjur supplements it with 225 (not canonical) volumes of commentary and profane matter. The collection of the canonical books is so holy that sacrifices made to it are accounted very meritorious.

In Egypt we find the Book of the Dead, which might almost be called a handbook or a guide-book for departed spirits, containing the needed information about the gods and the future world. It is called the canon of the Egyptians; but there is no great clearness in reference to the book in general, and its canonicity in particular. We know even less about the Hermetical Books, which are attributed to the god Thoth or Hermes Trismegistos. Clement of Alexandria counted forty-two of them, but Seleucus in Iamblichus speaks of 20,000, and Manetho of 36,525. It may be that these large numbers apply to the lines contained in the books; in that case the great difference between the numbers would be intelligible.

Rome honoured the Sibylline books. After the destruction, the burning, of the Capitol in the year 83 before Christ, the State ordered the books of the fates that were in private hands to be gathered together in order to replace the old books that had perished. Copies of the books were sought for all around, and especially in Asia Minor. It is said that above two thousand of these private books were on examination rejected and burned as worthless imitations. The renewed volumes were placed in the temple of the Palatine Apollo, and unfortunately ruthlessly burned by Stilicho in the fifth century. Here the notions of inspiration and canonicity do not seem to be strongly marked.

The Persian Avesta, as we have it to-day, offers a mere fragment of the original work, and does not seem to be surrounded by a special halo. of inspiration. The first part, called Jasna or Prayers, contains, among other matter, five Gathas or hymns, which are directly attributed to Zarathustra himself, who lived more than six centuries before Christ.

The Koran is supposed to be a product or an embodiment of the Divine Being, and only pure and believing men are to be allowed to touch it. It is uncreated. It lay on a table beside the throne of God written on a single scroll. In the night Alkadar of the month Ramadan Gabriel let it down into the lowest heaven, and it was imparted to Mohammed bit by bit according to necessity. Mohammed caused his secretary to write it down ; and he kept it, not in any special order, in a box. Later it was edited, rewrought into the shape in which we have it now.

Before we leave the realm of myth and uncertainty it may be well to recall the statement of the Talmud, that the law of Moses almost equals the divine wisdom, and that it was created nine hundred and seventy-four generations before the creation of the world, or a thousand generations before Moses.

According to the Jewish tradition, the law, the Tora, was written by Moses himself, even the last eight verses about his death. Some thought that it was put by God directly into the hands of Moses, and that either all at once or book by book. Among the Jews, questions as to the canonicity, or let us say as to the authenticity, and authority of one book or another have been much discussed, less, however, for the purpose of laying aside the book suspected, and more for the greater glory of the successfully defended book. A curious form of the debate is to be found in the question whether the book treated of soiled the hands. If it did, it was canonical. If not, not. This point is said to have originated in the time of the ark, and to have been devised, that is to say, the declaration that the canonical writings soiled the hands was devised to prevent people and prevent priests from freely handling the copy of the law kept in the ark.

Three classes of men attached especially to the law, the Sofrim or bookmen or scribes or the Scripture students, the lawyers, and the teachers of the law, the rabbis. Quotations from the Scriptures were introduced by the formula: "It is said," or, "It is written." So soon as the Jews, but that was at a late day, observed that the copying of the law led to errors, they instituted a critical treatment of the text, trying to compel accuracy of copying. They counted the lines, the words, and the letters, and they cast aside a sheet upon which a mistake had been made.

We may assume that some written documents were in the hands of the Israelites from the time of Moses, but we can in no way define them. They doubtless included especially laws, and then as an accompaniment traditions. When, however, we speak of the Israelites, it does not follow that all existing documents were to be found on one spot, and in the hands of one librarian or keeper of archives. It is a matter of course that the persons first to care for, to write, and keep such documents were the heads of families and the priests. Whether they were of a directly legal character like laws and ordinances, and deeds of gift or purchase, or whether they were of a more historical description like accounts of the original ages of the tribes, or of humanity, the recital of travel and of wars, and, above all, the birth lists of the great families,—it is a matter of course that the persons who had these would be the sheiks, the old men, the tribal heads. In many cases such a man in authority will have had his priest, who will at the same time have been a scribe, as a proper guardian of these treasures. In other cases the sheik will have been his own priest and his own keeper of the rolls. The documents will then have been largely local and of a limited general value. But it will have been a thing of common knowledge that one or two centres, I name Shiloh as a likely one, were possessed of particularly good collections. To these the more intelligent will have applied for copies of given writings, and the less well educated for information about their history, their family, and their rights. It is clear that in Hosea's day, in the eighth century before Christ, many laws held to be divine were known, even though he does not make it clear to us just what laws these were. And the Second Book of Kings shows the high authority conceded to the law at the time of Josiah, in the last quarter of the seventh century, in spite of the fact that the previous disappearance of the law, that the thought of its having been forgotten and having needed to be found again, gives a shock to those who would fain believe that the priests and all the laws were active and in force in all their vigour and extent from the time of Moses onward. We may date the authoritative acceptance of the five books of the law, or if anyone prefers to put it differently, the renewed acceptance, or the first clearly defined acceptance of that whole law, at the time of Ezra, about the middle of the fifth century before Christ. The "front" and the "back" prophets, or the historical books and the great prophetical works, may have been determined upon soon after that time, although it is suggested that they were not really of full authority before the second century before Christ. We do not know about it; nothing gives us a fixed date. The same is true for the third part of the Hebrew Bible. Book after book in it seems to have been taken up by the authorities, who now can have been none other than the scribes and lawyers in Jerusalem. Whether the process was one of conscious canonising or authorisation from the first for these books, or whether at first the writings were merely collected and preserved rather than authorised, it would be hard to say. The latter seems probable. So far as can be determined, no new book was added after the time of the Maccabees. But various books seem to have been called in question as late even as the first century after Christ.

We have as a result of this process, in describing which I have used the word canon and its cognates in the current sense, an Old Testament in three parts: Law, Prophets, Writings. The third part received then in Greek the name "Holy Writings." It is important for us at this point, in view of the close connection between the Old Testament and the New Testament, to ask: What is the definiteness and surety of the work of making or settling the canon of the Old Testament? This question is of all the greater interest because the time of the commonly assumed determination of the canon of the New Testament is not separated by any very great interval from the last of the dates above mentioned. Even in our rapid survey of the field— and a more detailed inquiry would only have made the uncertainties more palpable—every one at once perceives that the authoritative declarations as to the divine origin of the books leave much to be desired for those who are accustomed to hear the canon of the Old Testament referred to as if it were as firm as a rock in its foundations. We do, it is true, find a massive declaration for the acceptance of the law, in part in the seventh century, in part and finally in the fifth century before Christ. Yet even in that case we are not absolutely sure of the precise contents of the law, not absolutely sure even for Ezra, probable as it is that he had all or nearly all our Pentateuch. And then what a gap opens between the period of Moses, the lawgiver, and the time of Ezra, or even of Josiah. If we assume that Moses lived about the year 1500, and that Ezra led the exiles back to Palestine about the year 458 before Christ, a thousand years had passed between. But leave that point. For the second part, the Prophets, we have no such word of a definite authoritative proclamation as to its or their authenticity and dominating value. And for the third part, there is not only no word of an official declaration, but there is also every sign and token of a merely casual, gradual taking up into use of one book after another. It would be desirable, were it possible, to inquire closely into the special sense in which each book was accepted, and what the amount of divine authority was, that the men accepting it attributed to it. That is not possible. The so-called canon of the Old Testament is anything but a carefully prepared, chosen, and guarded collection in its first state. If, however, any one should be inclined on that account to find fault with the Jews, we must remember that they not only were in the work of " canonising " and of guarding their sacred books in those early times far superior to all other known peoples, but that they at a later date and up to the present have proved themselves to be unsurpassed, unequalled preservers of tradition written and unwritten. The Christian Church owes them in this respect a great debt.

The glimpse at other sacred volumes aside from the Bible has shown us that our collection of holy books is more concise, better rounded off, and, we might almost venture to say in advance of our present inquiry, better accredited than any others, save the Koran. But it has also made it plain to us that it has not been the custom of men in general to "canonise" their sacred books by a set public announcement; that sacred books have, on the contrary, usually found recognition at first only in limited circles, and have afterwards gradually but almost imperceptibly or unnoticed passed into the use of the religious community of the country. It will be necessary to bear this in mind when we come to examine the testimony for the divine or ecclesiastical authority of the books of the New Testament.

C. INTERCOMMUNICATION IN THE ROMAN EMPIRE.

It would be difficult to discuss intelligently the question of the spread and general acceptance of the books of the New Testament among the Christians of the various lands and provinces, without referring to the possibilities of travel then and there. Probably the majority of modern people who turn their thoughts back to the Roman Empire in the time of the apostles, think of those countries and their inhabitants as to a large extent unable to communicate easily and rapidly with each other, and they would be much surprised to learn that aside from railroads, steamers, and the electric telegraph, there would be little to say in favour of European means of communication, that a Roman in Greece or Asia Minor or Egypt would have been able to travel as well as most of the Europeans who lived before the year 1837. It is to be granted that at that time journeys to China, South Africa, and North America were not customary. But no one wished to go to these then unknown or all but unknown regions. Nowadays people are proud to think that they can travel or have travelled all over the world. At that time many people travelled pretty much all over the world that was then known. At the time of Christ the known world was little more than the Roman Empire. We might describe it as the shores of the Mediterranean, if we should take the northern shores to include the inland provinces adjacent to the provinces directly on the seaboard. That would carry us to the Atlantic Ocean across Gaul, to the Black Sea across Asia Minor, and to the Red Sea across Egypt.

The ease of intercourse depended in a large measure upon the ships of the Mediterranean. If the sailors then disliked winter voyages between October and March, there are not a few people to-day who avoid the sea during those months even when they can find luxurious steamers to carry them. With the ships that they used they were able to sail very fairly. For the voyage from Puteoli to Alexandria only twelve days were necessary ; and if the wind were good, a ship could sail from Corinth to Alexandria in five days. The journey from Rome to Carthage could be made in two ways, either directly from Ostia at the mouth of the Tiber, and that was a trifle over 300 miles or with a good wind three days,—or by land 350 miles to Rhegium (Reggio), across the strait an hour and a half to Messana, around Sicily to Lilybäum (to-day Marsala), and then with a ship in twenty-four hours to Carthage, that would be 673 miles in all. From Carthage to Alexandria by land was 1221 miles. The direct journey to the East led by land to Brundusium (Brindisi), from which a ship could reach Dyrrachium in a day or a day and a half. From Dyrrachium the road passed through Heraclea, Edessa, Pella, Thessalonica, Philippi, and on to Byzantium (now Constantinople), in all 947 miles. Starting in the same way and turning south to Athens the journey would be 761 miles. If the traveller had the Asiatic side in view he could in Thrace go to Gallipoli and in an hour cross over to Lampsacus, the starting-point for Antioch in Syria. From Antioch he could go east to the Euphrates or south to Alexandria. From Rome to Antioch was 1529 miles, from Rome to the Euphrates 1592 miles, from Rome to Alexandria 2169 miles. If a traveller chose, he could go all the way to Byzantium by land, going north and around by Aquileia, which makes 1218 miles for the trip. On the west from Rome to Spain, to Gades was 1398 miles.

The shipping came later to be, if it was not at the time of which we have to speak, to a great extent in the hands of certain companies, although not named as Cunarders or Hamburg-Americans. The freight ships were by no means very small, and they carried large cargoes of grain with the most punctual regularity. From Spain they brought the beautiful and spirited Spanish horses for the public games ; these horses were so well known that the different species were at once distinguished by the

Romans, who adjusted their wagers accordingly. We must of necessity suppose that the freight ships also carried people, the people who had time, and especially those who had not money to pay for better ships. Paul's journey as a prisoner from Cæsarea to Rome gives us a good example of a freight and passenger boat, and shows us how the winter affected the voyage and the voyagers. The quick and, of course, dearer passenger carrying trade was served by lightly built ships, and these fast ships will have certainly been often more adventurous than the freight ships, and have hugged the land less. Particular attention seems to have been paid to the ships that acted as ferries or transfer boats on the great lines of travel, since they were necessary to the use of the roads. For example, from Brundusium to Dyrrachium, from Gallipoli to Lampsacus, from Rhegium to Messana. It is likely that frequent vessels passed from the western coast of Asia Minor towards the north-west, keeping east of Akte (to-day Mount Athos), and reaching behind Thasos, the harbour of Neapolis, which was only 15 miles from Philippi.

Everyone has heard of the Roman roads. Beginning at Rome, they stretched through the whole empire. In a newly conquered land a Roman commander or civil governor hastened to lay out and to order the work on the roads that would be adapted to give the troops easy access to all parts of the country, and to allow of the utilising of the products of the different districts. Traces, remains, of such roads are to be seen to-day at many places from Scotland to Africa. Augustus had the whole empire measured by Greek geometers or civil engineers, and erected in the Forum at Rome the central pillar from which the miles were counted off to the most remote regions. Gaius Gracchus, 123 before Christ, was the first one to bring forward a law to set milestones at every thousand paces. The principal distances were given on the pillar itself. Besides that, Augustus caused a map of the world to be made and hung up in a public place, a map based on those measurements and on Agrippa's commentaries on them. Guide-books or lists of the places, and stations, and distances on the roads were prepared later; there may very well at once have been copies made for the chief roads. Greece is said to have been less carefully provided with roads, probably owing in part to the difficulty of making roads among the mountains, in part to the fact that the inhabitants in general caused no great trouble,—while Corinth and Athens were easily to be reached,—and in part to the circumstance that the sea was so near at hand that the roads were less necessary.

The travel on these roads, as on our roads to-day, was of four kinds, on wheels, in sedan-chairs or litters, on beasts, and on foot. Seeing that the roads were in the first instance made for the benefit of the government, the officials of every degree had the preference on the roads. They often acted brutally and barbarously in compelling the inhabitants to let them have their horses and oxen to draw waggons, and in urging these animals to greater speed ; and special orders were issued forbidding all such acts. Under given circumstances, travellers, and especially those in the public service, went very swiftly, changing horses at every station. Cæsar rode from Rome to the Rhone in his four-wheeled travelling carriage in about eight days, making 77 miles a day. In his two-wheeled light carriage he made 97 miles a day. The public post from Antioch to Constantinople in the fourth century went, including stops, in about six days, about 4 miles an hour. Private persons used, according to their means, private carriages, or rode on horses, mules, or asses, or went on foot. There were societies that let out carriages or riding horses just as to-day. The foot traveller was more independent on the road than anyone save the public officials.

Not infrequently do we hear modern travel spoken of as if it were an entirely new invention. It is presupposed that in the times of which we are now treating, the population was almost exclusively man after man tied close to the one spot on which he had been born. This conception of the case falls wide of the mark. A very large number of people were often under way, and many were never long at rest. We have had occasion to refer more than once to officials journeying. The condition of the Roman Empire, the methods by which the lands and districts were governed and were kept in order and were defended, required a constant flow of soldiers, of officers, of officials of every rank hither and thither. These persons had, so far as their station entitled them to use horses and carriages, the use of the imperial post, which was forbidden to private persons. They had therefore also the precedence in the often clashing claims for relays at the stations, and in the choice of accommodation at the inns. It is scarcely necessary to urge that high officials also often had a considerable staff of assistants or a numerous household as a travelling accompaniment. If these were weighty travellers they found a balance in the other extreme, in the actors and players who passed from place to place to afford the people diversion; doubtless they sometimes associated themselves closely with the higher and wealthier officials, lightening by their arts the cares of office, or amusing and thus occupying the thoughts of the populace and making them more content with the government. Precisely as to-day, countless invalids sought health far from home at baths, at healing springs, in milder or in cooler climes, and that not merely the wealthy, but also many a poor man. Rich Romans made excursions to their possessions in Gaul, in Spain, in Africa, and sometimes took a crowd of friends with them as well as a host of servants. Others travelled to see the peculiarities or the beauties of foreign peoples and foreign landscapes. Some went to consult oracles. Workmen went in numbers hither and thither, now driven like the wandering apprentice by the thirst for further knowledge of the secrets of their handiwork, now sent out by the rich at Rome or sent for by the rich abroad to ply their skilful arts in city houses or country houses in the provinces or in distant lands. Manufacturers, if we may use the term for those who rose above the level of the mere workman, also went from place to place, sometimes on compulsion, like Priscilla and Aquila who had to leave Rome, sometimes of their own will, to wit the journey which we may presuppose that Prisca and Aquila made previously *to* Rome, and their journey from Corinth to Ephesus. They were doubtless part makers and part sellers of tent cloth from camels' hair. Paul's own case is like that of the workmen, and he may at Corinth really have worked for Prisca and Aquila. It is not at all unlikely that he answered, or that he would have answered, an inquisitive policeman on reaching Corinth, that the purpose of his coming was to work at his trade in the bazaar. Reference to his mission would have been as unintelligible as it would have been suspicious in reply to such an official. Of course, merchants travelled. Many of them went with their goods on ships, others will have travelled by land, carrying their boxes and bales on waggons, on beasts, or on the backs of their slaves. An inscription tells us of a merchant in Hierapolis who travelled from

Asia Minor to Italy seventy-two times.   And learning will have caused many a journey.   Teachers went hither and thither to gather new classes of pupils, themselves gaining in wisdom by their new experiences.   And students sought at Alexandria, at Athens, at Antioch, at Tarsus, or at Rome itself the teachers needed for their special subjects.   Paul went to sit at the feet of Gamaliel at Jerusalem, and when he later went to Tarsus, his birthplace, again, it is likely that he visited the university.

The things shipped from and to a land afford an insight into an important part of its relations to other lands, and show how easily or with how much difficulty men and writings could pass from one country to the other.   It will suffice to limit ourselves to Palestine, for that is our centre.   Tunny-fish were brought thither from Spain, and Egyptian fish also, I suppose from the Nile.   Persia supplied certain nuts.   Beans and lentils came from Egypt.   Grits were sent from Cilicia, Paul's province.   Greece sent squashes.   The Egyptians sent mustard.   Edom was the source for vinegar.   Bithynia furnished cheese.   Media was the brewery for beer.   Babylon sent sauces.   Greece and Italy sent hyssop, it is said;—why this plant was sought from afar I do not know; perhaps it was a particular species.   Cotton came from India.   So much for the imports.   A word as to the exports of this little country.   The Lake of Tiberias produced salted and pickled fish; the town Tancheæ was the " Pickelries." Galilee was celebrated for its linen.   And Judea supplied wool and woollen goods; Jerusalem had its sheep market and its wool market.

This brief review makes it plain that the period before us is one of continual movement in all directions.   For the spread of Christianity and for the subsequent widespread scattering abroad of, and the universal acceptance of the cherished literature of the early Christians, this journeying and sending of men and of goods from one end of the empire to the other could not but be of the greatest importance.   Quite aside from the actual travel and the actual traffic, the mental attitude of men was one of calm consideration of, and not of suspicion or flashing hatred towards, all that came from another country.

D. BOOKMAKING OF OLD.

In considering the fates and fortunes of books, it is important to ask how they were made. Here we may touch upon a few points bearing more upon the criticism of the canon. Other points will come up in connection with the criticism of the text. In many cases those who speak of the books of the New Testament pay little regard to this matter. They discuss it almost as if they thought that books were then produced, multiplied, bought and sold much as they are to-day. This is the less blameworthy from the circumstance that the history of these things has thus far been much neglected, and that the sources for the history in Greek circles are still largely a thing of conjecture, not well-known and carefully studied documents. We know much more about Latin than about Greek bookmaking. Our information touching Greek work in this line must be searched for in the byways and hedges of ancient Greek literature, in chance observations made in some important historical or theological or philosophical writings, and in the bindings and on the fly-leaves of old books. Bearing in view the difficulty of finding the materials for a judgment, we shall not be surprised to learn that opinions upon this topic go to one of two extremes. Some seem to suppose that books at that time, and especially among the Christians, could only be made, this is to say, written, with great difficulty and at large expense. They think of books at that day as exceedingly rare and dear. Others swing the pendulum to the opposite point, and declare that books were then as plenty as grass in the East; the figure would perhaps be near the truth for one who should reflect upon the meagre herbage of those dry regions. Applying this to Christians and to the books of the New Testament, we are on the one hand liable to hear that these books were seldom in the hands of any but the wealthy and were at no time existent in great numbers, or on the other hand that families, to say nothing of Churches, —that families and individual Christians were in a position to get and keep and use freely the sacred writings.

Nothing would be more dangerous than a too free generalisation here. Time and place varied the circumstances. Time came into play, for the Christians were at first largely poor and largely or often viewed with distrust and dislike by their neighbours, and would therefore not be in a position to have books made for them easily. At a later date, when more and more people gathered around the preachers and the Christian Churches grew apace, when the Christians began to be drawn more from the better educated classes and to have a wider acquaintance with literature and a greater facility in literary methods, and when they had secured for themselves from their heathen surroundings rather respectful tolerance or even admiration than ill-confidence and disdain, they certainly could and undoubtedly did order and use more books. That the place, however, must be considered is a matter of course. That is true even to-day in spite of all printing presses and publishing houses. In large cities, and in particular in cities like Antioch, Tarsus, Alexandria, in which many scholars taught and learned, studied and wrote, books could be easily and quickly gotten. And in such cities, among scholars of various climes, tongues, opinions, religions, and habits, scribes would busy themselves less with an inquisitorial consideration of their customers, and be at once ready to copy any sheet, any book placed in their hands. In the provinces, in small towns and villages, in out of the way places it must have been usually difficult, very often impossible, to get books, impossible to have them made. That does not imply that people there could neither write nor read, ignorant indeed of these arts as the majority of them may have been. But there was a difference between writing a private letter or a business letter and a bill, and writing a book. The difference was similar to that found to-day between the usual writers in private life and in business circles, and the art-writers who prepare beautiful diplomas and testimonials for anniversaries.

In large towns the methods for the multiplication of writings that were used for profane books often could be and probably sometimes were applied to the books of the New Testament, and that especially as time progressed during the third and the opening fourth century. We have no exact information upon this point, and we are therefore left to conjecture. I am inclined to think that the usual bookmaking methods were seldom used by Christians. It does not seem to me to be likely that a heathen bookseller would, as a rule, apply himself with any great interest to the multiplication of Christian writings. The reasons that lead me to this conclusion are the following :

3

(*a*) It is worth while to cast a glance at the general position of the Christians. It is true that antique life, modified by the climate of those southern lands, was to a far greater extent than life in northern Europe to-day spent before the eyes of other and often strange men. The Italian in Naples carrying on his trade on the sidewalk, or in a shed, or booth, or room opening with its whole front upon the street, is a fair type of the Eastern tradesman. In consequence, the life of the Christians in the East was to a large measure a public life, a life seen and known of men. But they were nevertheless for long decades in many places not openly acknowledged and recognised as Christians. Here and there, doubtless often, they met with tolerance and forbearance or even good treatment from the hands of their neighbours and of the authorities of the district, town, or city. That, however, cannot screen the fact that they will in general have found it prudent and often strictly necessary to keep the signs of their faith in the background, not to allow them to attract open notice when it was possible to avoid doing so. For this reason, then, Christians will in many places have refrained from applying to heathen scribes to copy the books of the New Testament.

(*b*) The last phrase brings an important point. It would not be impossible that a scribe should become a Christian. But we may be sure that, as a rule, directly in connection with their daily bread,—remember, we have to do with book scribes not with everyday letter writers,—they will have been, and have been inclined to remain, heathen. Their work was the copying of heathen books. They copied for a living, it is true, and may often have not hesitated to take up Christian books. Nevertheless, they may well have preferred the heathen books that they knew and liked, especially if they were writers of "known" and not in general of "new" books. Then, too, the Christians may have hesitated to let heathen scribes copy the writings because they were so much prized by them, may have hesitated to place them before the eyes and in the hands of men who would despise and scoff at these precious books. And this hesitancy will not seldom have been rendered greater by the fear that these scribes could for lewd gain denounce them to the authorities as the possessors of forbidden books, and give over the books into the hands of their enemies.

(*c*) It must, in connection with the last sentence, be borne in mind that although these books were sacred books, books held in particular honour by a certain number of men, they were in those days not in the least public books. These two considerations were of moment, in particular, before the close of the first quarter of the fourth century. Let us pass beyond that date.

(*d*) After the greater influx of members in the early years of the fourth century, there probably were enough self-denying Christians at command who were able to write a book hand, and therefore to copy the Christian books. It is to be regretted that Eusebius, who caused fifty large manuscripts of the Bible to be copied for, at the command of, the Emperor Constantine, does not tell us to what scribes he entrusted the work. Had he been in Constantinople, in Constantine's town as they then began to name it, we should have turned our eyes to the regular book trade. For it is very likely that with the accession of Christianity to the throne many a public scribe, many a bookseller would have been led to embrace it, to take upon him the name that was no longer a badge of disgrace, but had become a claim to preferment. In Cæsarea the case is different. It was, it is true, a large city, and would have had at least some public scribes. But we must remember that we have positive knowledge of Christian scholarship here. Cæsarea had long been a centre of interest for Christian theologians, and had about a century before sheltered the great Origen within its walls. He received there his ordination as presbyter, and when the fanatical Bishop of Alexandria attacked him, he settled in Cæsarea and gathered many pupils around him. These Christians had a large library there, and we have in various manuscripts references to books in that library. Putting these things together, it seems fair to suppose that Eusebius had in his town Christian scholars at command, and Christian scribes, to write the fifty sacred volumes. Should any one say that the size of the probable school and the cultivation of the Christians there probably rendered the work of these Christian scribes a thoroughly well-appointed and business-like institution, not very different from and not inferior to the establishments of profane booksellers, I shall at once concede the point. If I am not mistaken, that is precisely the reason why Constantine ordered the books for his proud capital in that distant town in Palestine. He had doubtless made inquiries, and had learned that Eusebius not only had in the library of his deceased bosom friend Pamphilos, whose name he had added to his own, the finest known copies, the most accurately written copies, of the Bible, but that he also had at his command in his neighbourhood, and probably within the precincts of his episcopal residence, of the houses and grounds attached to his own palace, the best scribes that were to be found in all that region. If these surmises come near to the truth, that large book order on the part of the emperor is likely to have made that scriptorial establishment, that book-house, still more celebrated, and to have led to other orders of a less imposing extent. That is, so far as I can recall, the only case in early times in which we hear so directly about the making of Christian books, and therefore, to return to our point respecting the matter in general, we can only say that we have no knowledge of any business man, of any bookseller who occupied himself especially with making Bibles or New Testaments or single books out of the New Testament. Perhaps some scholar will one day find in an old manuscript new information on this subject.

Whatever may have been the real facts in earlier days, however near our guesses may come to the true state of the case, we know certainly that at a later date the copying of the books of the New Testament was a part of the work of ecclesiastics and of monks. Of the many, many volumes which contain a description of the position of the scribe who copied them, by far the larger number were from the classes named. In a great number of manuscripts the scribe is said to be just upon the point of becoming a monk. This remark is found so often that I am inclined to think that frequently it must have been the rule for a novice who was at the end of his probation and was approaching his tonsure as monk, to copy a part of the Bible, certain books of the New Testament, as a token of his proficiency in external letters and of his devotion to the sacred volume.

E. WHAT WE SEEK.

Setting aside for the moment our preliminary considerations touching the existence of a canon, it is pertinent at this point to try to define in detail what we must seek for. We are about to enter upon the field of early Christian history. What do we wish to look for in this field? We are not concerned now to examine the piety of the members of the various rising Christian societies. We are not going to ask in what rooms they held their meetings. We are not intending to find out how they appointed their leaders. All these things, and a great many other things in themselves equally weighty and interesting, must now remain untouched. Three objects call for our attention.

We must in applying ourselves to a view of the early Church, inquire for traces of the existence of the books that we have in our New Testament to-day. It is the existence that is first to be sought for, some sign that the given book *is*, and if possible that it is at a given place. In advance an ignorant man might take it for granted that no book could possibly be used by the Church without having been previously or at the time in question made the object of a rigid examination, and without a minute having been entered into the documents of the Church with regard to the said book. But the Christians of that day were not so critically inclined as that would indicate. At the very first there are no tokens of anything of that kind. In consequence we must be content with less clear evidence. We must search in the literature of the Church—we should search just as eagerly in profane literature if there were anything to be found in it—for signs that these books have been used even without their having been alluded to by name. A later treatise might show or seem to show by the things spoken of in it that the author of it had read some book now in the New Testament. He might lean towards or lean upon the material given in it. In some cases it might be possible to show by his style that he had used the said book. It is unnecessary to press the warning not to judge too hastily in a matter like this. The differences between use and non-use are sometimes extremely hard to be detected. A second stage in this inquiry after the existence of the books is the search for quotations from them, quotations giving their very words but not mentioning their names. Here the thing seems to be and really is much clearer. Yet even here great caution is needed, since sentences sometimes appear to be similar to each other or practically identical, which prove on closer examination to have no direct connection

with each other. The words may be from a third, a previous
writing, or they may be a saying that was long current in various
circles before the words with which we compare them were
written. The third and satisfactory stage of the search after
proofs of the existence of the books, is the search for direct
mention of the books by name. A mention by name, particularly
if it be accompanied by a clear quotation from the text of the
book, is the best evidence that we can ask for. Of course, we
should be on our guard lest the name should be an interpolation
by a later writer who had been led or misled by the real or only
apparent quotation. It is plain that these three stages in the
inquiry for tokens of the existence of the books are not to be
conceived of as only possible of separate consecutive examination,
looking in each single book first for the one and then for the
other stage. In taking up a later book we may find first of
all the third and highest stage of the evidence. We should,
however, in spite of that examine the whole document, seeking
as well for the other two less important stages as corroborative
evidence.

The second object for attention, proved or conceded the
existence of the books, is the search for signs of an especial
valuation of these books on the part of Christians, and, if that
may be distinguished, on the part of authorised or authoritative
Christians, men of a certain eminence. Here we may place five
kinds of evidence before our minds. The first kind would be
the discovery that these books of the New Testament or that
any one of them is in literary use preferred to other books not
in our New Testament. We might find, for example, that they
in case of quotation were particularly emphasised, that they
were more frequently mentioned and treated with greater respect
than other books, that they were spoken of as if they might
claim for themselves a special authority. Here we are again,
as we were at the first stage of the previous inquiry, looking for
something that may perhaps sometimes be rather felt than
directly seen, may lie in a turn of a sentence and not in a direct
statement. The second kind of evidence is that which in some
way shows that these books were settled upon as worthy of, or
were designated directly for, being read by Christians in private
life for their instruction, for their edification, or for their comfort
and consolation. The third kind of evidence is that which

proves their designation for public use in church. The weight of the evidence for this point must be characterised more closely. The difference between books for private reading and those for public use will be plain by a moment's comparison with books of to-day. To take an extreme example, it would be quite conceivable that a clergyman should recommend to a parishioner to read a certain novel of a specifically Christian tendency; it would not be conceivable that he should read this novel before the congregation. There is nothing double-tongued or hypocritical in this. The clergyman knows, on the one hand, that the person advised is capable of judging aright of the contents of the book, whilst he could not know who might hear and misunderstand it in the public assembly. But, on the other hand, he also knows that the Church by ancient custom admits no such literature to a place in the services. The fourth kind of evidence is that which places these books upon the same level as the books of the Old Testament. The importance of this point is clear. The books of the Old Testament—we are not able to say precisely which ones book for book—were accepted by the early Christians as in a peculiar way given by God to the Jews and through them to the Church. They were accepted as the one authoritative collection of documents revealing to men the mind of God. It must here be expressly stated that we have not the least indication that the early Christians were in any way inclined to inquire closely into the origin and authority of the religious books in their hands. Their attitude towards certain books not a part of the Old Testament proper goes to show either that the Old Testament was then scarcely clearly defined in its third division, or that the Christians freely used other books as equal to those in that third division. But this concession does not in the least alter the value of the point we have now in view. It is for us of the greatest moment if we can show that, or when we can show that, a book was considered as on a par with the books of the Old Testament. The fifth and last kind of evidence is that which directly calls these books canonical or declared them to be among the number of the canonised books. Just what that may mean is a topic for later consideration after we have reached that point.

At the first glance it might seem as if that were all that we had to do, as if no further steps were necessary to place the

books of the New Testament upon their proper and firm basis
of clear history, always supposing that we succeeded in finding
the best of the evidences just described. But this is not all.
If we stopped at this point the favorers and furtherers of what
they call "the New Testament outside of the received canon"
might come to us and claim that these books were in possession
of precisely the same evidence as that which we have discovered
in the case of the New Testament books. Now we have indeed
said at the outset that the books just referred to have no proper
place in New Testament introduction, and that still holds good.
But it is in no way possible to avoid an inquiry calculated directly
either to confirm or to annul the claim of these other writings
to be a part of the New Testament. This leads, then, to the
third object that claims our attention. We have sought after
signs of a special valuation of the books of the New Testament.
Are signs of such, of an equal, valuation to be found for any
other writings belonging to the early period of Christianity?
And if tokens of certain such signs can be pointed out for other
writings, have we other evidence, tokens of an opposite character
which force the conclusion that these writings are nevertheless
finally not to be considered as equal in authority to those of the
New Testament? Here we have to ask about other books, then,
the same questions as before, touching the way in which they
are quoted, whether they are named for private reading or for
public services, and whether they are placed in conjunction with
the Old Testament. Should we find that some of the questions must be answered in the affirmative, we must then inquire
whether the given books were in any way thereafter so treated
as to show that these previous signs were not of a general
and authoritative value. We may find that they were definitely
distinguished by official statement from the books of the New
Testament. The fact that they must be thus put aside places
clearly before our eyes how very near they must have been to
the New Testament. No one would need to say that Homer
was not a part of the New Testament. We may find that they
are termed apocryphal. That word was originally one of respect.
It pointed to a book containing a secret doctrine but a lofty
one, a matter that was too hard, too deep, too high for the
common run of men, something that was only adapted to the
initiated. As time went on the Christians came to a clearer

vision, and formed the opinion that these books, supposed to be so peculiarly valuable, were in reality much less valuable than the books of the Church that were not apocryphal. Therefore they used the word apocryphal at that later day as a term for books that were not what they purported to be, were not genuine, were not in the least as good as the publicly known and used writings. It will be our duty to examine the case carefully, and to decide whether or not we can approve of what they did.

These three inquiries exhaust in general our task in regard to the early ages of the Church. In pursuit of them we must endeavour as far as possible to distinguish between different times and as well between different places. Four warnings may be useful. The first is that we must strive not to mistake the nature of the given section of history and confuse earlier conditions with those of a later date. Imagine anyone's supposing that Schopenhauer's writings were as eagerly read and as much the object of public approval in the year 1819, when his great work was issued, as they became towards the year 1860, after Frauenstädt had urged them upon public notice. The second is that we must not let earlier conditions be made doubtful and less clear by statements made about them at a later date. Our means of judging of a period removed from the vision of an ancient writer are often better than his. The third warning prevents our incautiously making the conditions and circumstances in one country a certain measure for the conditions and circumstances in other countries. What is true of Egypt at a given time need not be true of Italy at the same time. Conceive of a writer in the future who should presuppose, in drawing historical conclusions, that the internal conditions in Spain were the same as those in Germany in the year 1907, that the workmen were equally intelligent and equally successful in securing their rights, and that the upper classes were equally free from the domination of the Roman Catholic clergy. The fourth draws a similar line within much narrower limits, and forbids us to suppose that the circumstances in out of the way places and districts are the same as in the large cities. For all our post-offices and telegraph, this remains largely true even to-day. There are small towns, sometimes curiously enough quite near to large cities, that preserve to-day many of their old characteristics. Such differences were in ancient times in the lands that we have in view often extremely great. There was often a gulf of race and speech, and therefore of character, education, and customs, fixed between the city and the villages around it.

If that is the course before us for the earlier ages, in which by far the greater part of our task has to be performed, the later periods will demand of us an account of the varying or unvarying consistency with which they keep to or depart from the decisions of their predecessors. It will perhaps sometimes be necessary for us to ask whether given nations or societies have from the first held to that which they at the present suppose that they have ever believed and cherished.

I.

THE APOSTOLIC AGE.

33–90 (100).

WHEN we approach the age of the apostles we must lay aside for the moment modern ways of thinking, and strive to put ourselves beside the first Christians as they went in and out of the temple and Jerusalem and Nazareth and Capernaum. It is hard for us to reduce ourselves to the simplicity of the time, of the places, of the country, of the circumstances in which this little but growing society found itself. For us, that was all the enthusiastic opening of the movement that was later to fill and possess the world of that day. For them, for those incipient Christians, there was, it is true, a certain outlook of a coming glory. But the death of their leader and the doubt and hesitation, the little faith of many of the brethren dampened and clogged the flight of their thoughts. The glad thought of the trumpet sounding at midnight the return of their Jesus, a return upon the clouds of light in the majesty of a king by the grace of God, a return that would herald them to the rest of the world as the favourites and confidential friends of this universal sovereign,—this glad thought must before the lapse of many years have given place to a quiet resignation, or at most to a modest and longing wishfulness. Like the Thessalonians, they saw one and another of their number recede into the darkness of the tomb, though all of them were men who had counted upon the open vision of that triumphant entry. They had thought that they had a draft on sight, not one payable in two thousand or ten thousand years. They were simple-minded people. What did they think about the writings of the New Testament when they were placed before their eyes? Let us consider the case.

We regard the word as of pre-eminent importance. We have

not heard Jesus speak.   Nor do we know anyone who has
heard Him.   Neither our fathers nor our grandfathers wandered
with Him over the hills of Galilee.   For us the written word is of
great weight; and of right, for it is beyond price.   But there is
something still more important than the written word.   Did we
wish, as some people unfortunately often do, to limit the sayings
and the deeds, the events in those years of the Church's infancy,
to what we find written down in the New Testament, as if it
were a precise chronicle of all that the Christians experienced,
we should go astray.   And we should err still more widely if we
refused to accept any testimony as to the written word in the
New Testament which we cannot read in so many sentences in
ecclesiastical authors.   The Christian Church is more than a
book.   Jesus was more than a word.   Jesus, the Logos, the
Word, was the Life, and the Church is a living society, a living
fellowship.   There is something sublime in such a fellowship that
passes through the ages in a living tradition.   Our connection
with Jesus, which reaches now over more than eighteen hundred
years, does not rest upon the fact that He wrote something down,
which one man and another, one after another has read and
believed until this very day.   So far as we know, He left no
writings, no notes behind Him.   We do not read that He ever
told anyone to take down His words so as to give them to others
in white and black.   We are not told that He ever wrote or
dictated even a letter.   He *lived* and He spoke.   Christianity
began with the joining of heart to heart.   Eye looked into eye.
The living voice struck upon the living ear.   And it is precisely
such a uniting of personalities, such an action of man on man,
that ever since Jesus spoke has effected the unceasing renewal of
Christianity.   Christianity has not grown to be what it is, has
not maintained itself and enlarged itself, by reason of books
being read, no, not even by reason of the Bible's being read
from generation to generation.   How many millions of the
Christians of past days could not read!   How many to-day
cannot read!   Christianity is first of all a life and has been
passed along as life, has been lived, livingly presented from age
to age.   The Christian, whether a clergyman or a layman, has
sought with his heart after the hearts of his fellow-men.   A
mother has whispered the word to her child, a friend has spoken
it in the ear of his friend, a preacher has proclaimed it to his

hearers, and the child, the friend, the hearers have believed and become Christians. Christianity is an uninterrupted life.

These considerations have certain practical consequences for the inquiries in the criticism of the canon. It is certain that the leaders of the Church, the more prominent men particularly in the earliest ages, wrote very few books. Our researches will probably show us that most of the books of the New Testament were written at an early date. But it is not in the least to be reasonably presupposed or expected that the Christians in the years that immediately followed spent their time in writing books that should convey to us what we wish to know about the criticism of the canon. It was a period of tradition by word of mouth. It was not tradition by book and eye, but tradition by mouth and ear, that occupied the minds of those Christians in their unresting, untiring efforts to spread the words of Jesus and the story of His work. We sometimes hear complaints about the scantiness of the literature that has been preserved to us, that are uttered as if those early days of the Church had been days of prolific literary activity, as if an exuberant literature had existed which has been lost. Nothing of the kind was, so far as we can see, the case. On the contrary, but little in comparison was written. But this circumstance—and that is the point of these remarks—cannot be turned into a good reason for doubting the existence and use of the books of the New Testament at that time. It was a time of busy proclamation of the gospel, and a time at which the near end—in spite of all disappointed hopes— was still looked for. Literary events, literary processes, literary activity were far from their thoughts. The members of the Christian Churches, of the little circles that were here and there linking themselves together in the bond of fellowship, were to a great extent poor and uneducated. The larger part of the first Christians were neither in a position to buy nor able to read books. They were in the habit of hearing, not of reading, news that was of interest to them. They had no newspapers to allure them from their unlettered state.

The Christians were, however, not all ill-educated. Their leaders will doubtless in most cases have been able to read and write. It might be supposed then that these leaders were eager furtherers of Christian literary effort. We have no indications that that was the case, and a little reflection, combined with what

has been already said about the making known of the good
tidings, will I think, lead to the conclusion that books and
literature were among the things farthest from their thoughts.
For we must not forget that these leaders were not trained
officials, not even trained as officials in general, let alone literature.
They had not been recruited from the number of the head men
of the Jews. They were taken from the rank and file. And in
especial they were not scribes and lawyers, not used to dealing
day by day with books, with the Jewish book of books, the Law.
If they could read a passage in the synagogue and say a few
words about it, that would be the utmost that could be required
or asked of them.

Just at this point, having reminded ourselves of the fact that
neither the common run of Christians nor those who had by age
or social standing or some personal quality been placed in a
position of a certain trifling authority had any special literary
inclinations, it will be pertinent to reflect for an instant upon the
uncritical disposition of the age. This was not a peculiarly
Christian failing. Men such as those we have just glanced at
could not be expected to examine cautiously and precisely every
grain of evidence for books presented for Christian use. It
would be very strange if they thought of such a thing. But the
whole world of that day was credulous to a high degree. Clement
of Rome, and even Tacitus in a way, appear to have half-believed
the myth of the phœnix, and the majority of the people were
ready to believe the most improbable stories. I have spoken of
that age as being credulous. I might have said that all men,
with very few exceptions, are credulous. Men are credulous to-
day. People of birth and education go to inane but cunning
spiritists and fortune-tellers. And the poor of all countries
devour eagerly the wildest fancies of a lying messenger. To
return : the age with which we have to deal and the persons with
whom we have especially to do was not and were not critically
inclined. We must keep this in mind when we reflect upon
their acceptance and approval of writings that may happen to
have been offered for their consideration.

If anyone had asked a Palestinian Jewish Christian in the
year, let us say, 35 in what language a book meant for the use of
Christians should be written, I have little doubt that he would
have replied : "In Aramaic," although he might have called it

Hebrew or Syriac in a slovenly way of speaking. The sacred books were indeed in good Hebrew, we might call it classical; and if the man questioned should have entertained the thought that the books referred to should be equivalent to the books of the Old Testament, he would, of course, have replied that they must be in classical Hebrew. Even to-day in Arabic-speaking countries the Arabic Christians wish the Scriptures read to them and the sermons preached to them to be in classical Arabic, even though the sermons, in fact, fall far short of any due classical standards. The Western scholars who sometimes are surprised by this fact and demur at it, should reflect that a Billingsgate fishwoman, a London omnibus-driver, a Berlin cab-driver, and a New York street arab would all alike be surprised, and I scarcely think pleased, to hear the Scriptures read and sermons preached in the jargon that they daily use. The Aramaic which Jesus spoke was not from the east, not a product in Palestine of the return from the exile in Babylon, but from the north, an importation made probably during the first half of the second century before Christ. It is likely that the same answer would have been given by some Christians even at a later date. Nevertheless we have every reason to believe that a large number of the Jewish inhabitants of Palestine understood and spoke Greek long before the time of Christ. The Aramaic population was encircled by and, if the expression be not contradictory, at least sparsely permeated by Greek-speaking inhabitants. The seacoast was chiefly Greek. Joppa, now Jaffa, where the Jews of the south touched the coast, was the scene of the Greek myth of Perseus and Andromeda. Cæsarea was Greek. Ptolemais or Akka was, like several cities on the other, the eastern side of Palestine, a Hellenistic city, and they all had been in existence for centuries. As for literature, Ascalon produced four Stoic philosophers. The Epicurean Philodemus was from Gadara, and so was the Cynic Menippos. Civil officials and military officers were stationed here and there. Heathen plays were well known, there being a theatre and amphitheatre at Jerusalem, a theatre, an amphitheatre, and a hippodrome at Jericho, a stadium at Tiberias, and a hippodrome at Taricheæ, the Pickelries. Add to that the movements of Greek-speaking traders and workmen. Consider, further, the proselytes, the synagogues of the Libertines, the Cyreneans, the Alexandrians, and the Cilicians named in

Acts. From all this hasty glimpse we see that Greek must have been in Palestine a very well-known language. The effect of the Greek elements, just alluded to, upon the Aramaic-speaking population can only be duly appreciated by taking into view the small extent of the country and the resultant compulsion the Arameans were under to meet and deal with Greeks. From Jericho to Joppa itself was not two days for a fast traveller. It is interesting to observe that the military governor, the colonel, in the twenty-first and twenty-second chapters of Acts, is surprised to find that Paul, whom he had taken for a wild Egyptian, can speak Greek, while in a reverse direction it is clear that the mob is surprised to hear him speak Aramaic. The interesting thing is that the mob had evidently expected to understand him, even if he had spoken Greek. So soon as Christianity began to address itself to the Greek-speaking Jews outside of Palestine, the first thought of any author of a letter or of a book designed for general circulation will have been to write it in Greek. For that language would reach almost all Jews, even in Palestine, saving a certain part of the poorer classes.

The Jews who heard Jesus and believed on Him, will at the first moment not have dreamed of the production of a literature, of a series of books for their own particular use and benefit. Then and long after that, probably so long as the temple continued to stand, they remained good Jews and did their duty, observed the rites due from them as Jews. If anyone had asked after their sacred books they would have pointed to the Old Testament without a thought that anything more could be desired. They had heard Jesus. They continued to be Jews in union with Jesus. They were fully satisfied with the Scriptures which they possessed. No one had asked Jesus to write a continuation of the Old Testament. What could be desired? Should a new law be drawn up? Jesus had declared that the old law should outlast the heavens. Should a new prophetical book be added? Jesus had announced the close of the prophecy: "until John." As time passed by there came, however, two literary movements, one in gathering at least fragments of the words of Jesus, the other in the supplying of certain needs of the Christians by means of letters from the apostles or other Christian leaders; but neither of these movements had at the first moment a trace of an intention to continue, to complete, or to supplement the sacred books of the Jews which were also the sacred books of the Christians. The earliest Christian authors did not for an instant suppose that they were writing sacred books.

If we go back in thought to these years in which the Christians are gradually growing more and more numerous, in which the many who had been in Jerusalem at that great Whitsunday were being multiplied not only in Palestine but also far and wide throughout the Roman Empire, we must be cautious in assuming for them too large a number of adherents at the first moment. Eastern people are poor counters, and easily exceed the facts with their tens and hundreds and thousands. The Churches were small gatherings, chiefly of not very well educated men and women. These Churches were not on the lookout for books. They had among them men who had seen and heard Jesus, or at least His apostles, the Twelve. Some of the Churches really had members of the inner circle, of those Twelve, among them It could not be otherwise, for the Twelve neither died nor were killed all at once at the time of the death of Stephen. Even at the time at which Paul wrote the First Epistle to the Corinthians—and that was probably in the year 53—it is clear that no Gospels were known to him. He says in that letter (1 Cor. 15³), speaking of his preaching, that he had passed on to the Corinthians, when he first went among them, that which he had received, namely, that Jesus died for our sins according to the Scriptures, and so on. He does not say that he had read this, but that he had received it and that is here that he had heard it. Ananias and others had told him about it. As little does he tell them to take up the Gospels in their hands and see for themselves whether his doctrine agrees with the books. It seems to me that this altogether does away with the opinion formed by some, that Paul spent his time in Damascus and Arabia immediately after his conversion in reading a Gospel written by Matthew. We have, then, no reason to suppose that Paul or the Corinthians, and therefore as little to suppose that Peter or the Christians at Jerusalem and Antioch, had in the year 53 Gospels before them. It would, however, be quite possible that somewhere about that time one and another Christian had begun to think of using his pen in a limited way.

Before inquiring what these possible writers probably would have written, I must touch upon one other matter, which I prefer to mention here, instead of giving it in connection with the Jewish

4

canon, because it will throw light upon the circumstances of the earlier Christian societies. We saw above that the Jews had sacred writings in three parts—Law, Prophets, Writings. It is, I think, important to emphasise the fact that we are by no means authorised to suppose that every Jewish synagogue had all the books of all three of these parts, of course in the third part all the books that at any given time belonged to this part. It is very easy to-day to buy an Old Testament and a New Testament and both may be in one volume. At that day the whole of the Old Testament filled several rolls of different sizes, and I feel sure that many a village synagogue will have been glad of the possession of the Law and the Prophets, and have not been able to buy all the other rolls. The Psalms they will probably have had. Even if anyone should hesitate to agree with me on this point in respect to the smaller Jewish synagogues, I think no one will fail to concede, that when we turn to the few Christians who at the first here and there separated themselves as Christians, for the purpose of having Christian worship, from the synagogues in their town or village, we must not think of them as able to have the Law, the Prophets, and the Writings. I say separated, it would perhaps be better for at least many places to say: were forced to leave the synagogues. In time the little circle will have succeeded in getting at least certain parts of the Old Testament for liturgical purposes, but it may often have been a long while before that was possible. Where they were still allowed to go to the synagogue they will still have continued to go to it on Saturday, on the Sabbath, and then have had their own special Christian services on the Lord's Day, on Sunday. It was this that led, I suppose, in the early Church, and I doubt not at an exceedingly early date, to Christian services on Saturday or the Sabbath,—we must quit the pernicious habit of calling the Lord's Day by the Jewish name for Saturday,—services that were only secondary to the Sunday services. It was this that led to the determination not only of Sunday but also of Sabbath Gospel lessons, and the two series are still to be found in the lesson books of the older Churches. To return to our point, the early Christian societies will often not have had all the books of the Old Testament at their command, and will therefore have had still less inclination to look beyond that for new books. What they heard about Jesus they heard from the living voice of the wandering preachers who were called apostles, and that was fresh, varied, interesting, something quite different from the rolls of the synagogue. It is a strange thought for us : Christians who had no written Gospels. To think that Paul the great apostle probably never saw a written Gospel ! He had heard the gospel, not read it ; heard it from Christians in Damascus, seen it in heavenly visions, not read it. What a preacher he must have been for all his weakness ! But he had not a sign of a commentary out of which to draw his sermons, much less ready-made skeletons of sermons, and not even a written text.

The words of Jesus and the story of Jesus' work were then the great thing. That was what men cared to hear. And when a Christian sharpened his reed pen and dipped it in the ink and began to write on a piece of papyrus, he probably first wrote down some of the words of Jesus. What would the curiosity-mongers give for that pen and for that first piece of papyrus with the first words of Jesus that were written down for future reading ? One Christian may have written down a parable which had especially pleased him. Another will have told with his pen of a miracle of Jesus. Another may have let his memory and his pen dwell upon a journey made with Jesus, from Nazareth to Tiberias, from Jerusalem to Jericho. Later other parables, miracles, and journeys will have been added. More than one such frail and fleeting little papyrus roll will have been written upon, of many of which we have never heard a word and of which we shall never see a line. Some wrote in Aramaic, probably the most of them at the first, for the most of the hearers of Jesus will have been Arameans. Is it not strange that the Twelve did not write down the words of Jesus ? But perhaps they did without our hearing of it. It is likely that one of them in particular wrote quite a book. That was Matthew. We shall hear more about it later. He doubtless wrote a book that contained a great many of Jesus' words, and told in between in scattered sentences what Jesus did as He went about Galilee preaching the gospel of the kingdom.

It was probably Paul who first wrote one of the longer books of the New Testament. But he did not begin with the very largest. We do not know when he began to write, and we do not know whether we have his first writings or not. One thing we are sure of—we have not all that he wrote. He began by trying to comfort and reassure the Christians in the little Church at

Thessalonica, perhaps in the year 48. And then he wrote to the Corinthians in the year it may be 53, and then to the Romans it may be in the year 54, and then to the Galatians, and so on. It is not entirely beyond the pale of possibility that Peter and that James the brother of Jesus wrote such a letter before Paul wrote to the Thessalonians. So far as we can judge from the very little that the books of the New Testament tell us about Paul, he stopped preaching and stopped writing letters and went to heaven about the year 64, and that book of Matthew that was referred to above may easily have been written somewhere about that time.

Matthew's Aramaic book, or the Aramaic book about Jesus in Galilee, whether Matthew wrote it or not, must before more than a year or two had passed, perhaps before more than a month or two had passed, have been translated into Greek. Now that the book was before the Christians' eyes, they will have wondered that no one had thought to write it at an earlier day. That book did not tell about the passion. The passion did not belong to Galilee. Before long it became clear that the Christians needed a more complete account of the words and deeds of Jesus. This need John Mark the Jerusalemite, the cousin of Barnabas, the friend of Paul and of Peter, seems to have felt and tried to supply in our second Gospel, written perhaps about the year 69. Someone else, we have not the most remote idea who it may have been, took up the story a few years later and wrote our first Gospel. Still later Luke wrote the third Gospel and the book of Acts. It was not till nearly the end of the century that the Fourth Gospel appeared.

We are at the close of the apostolic age. We see the numerous little Churches, that is to say, companies of Christians, scattered over the Roman Empire, meeting from week to week in private houses and exhorting one another to a firm faith, a good life, and a living hope. A number of books have been written that these Christians find particularly valuable. Part of them look a little like histories, part of them are simply letters, one of them is a book of dreams. But for all these writings the thing which holds the attention of the Christian Churches is still the living word, the weekly sermon, if the given Church be so fortunate as to have a preacher every week.

So far as we can see, there is as yet no collection of Christian books. That must soon come. We have nearly closed the first century. The apostolic age laps over on to the post-apostolic age. It closes about the year 100, but the post-apostolic age begins about the year 90. The reason for this double boundary lies in the wish to include in the former age the Fourth Gospel and in the latter age the letter of the Church at Rome to the Church at Corinth, the letter called Clement's of Rome.

Paul wrote to the Thessalonians in his second letter, 2 Thess. 2^{15}, that they should stand firm, and that they should hold fast to the traditions that they had been taught either by word of mouth or by a letter from him. That was the signature of the early age of the Church. It will still follow us into the second period. But a new principle is preparing, or the foundation is being laid for a new principle, that will recognise a crystallisation of the traditions. The enthusiasm of the simple Christian brethren of the first years is to fade into a cool and steady service under a new law and a new hierarchy. The living voice of the preacher, of the apostle hastening from place to place, is to give way to the words read from a written page and to uncertain comments thereupon.

Between the years in which the first books of the New Testament were written and the close of the apostolic period about a half a century had elapsed, which would be for us as far as from 1860 to to-day. During that time the books of the New Testament were probably most of them written. Before we leave this age, we should ask whether we can find any signs of what might be called self-consciousness in these writings of the New Testament. That is to say, we know of, or suspect the existence of but one book, outside of the books of the New Testament, that was probably or possibly written during this period. And therefore when we ask if there are any signs at this time of the existence of these books, it amounts to much the same as asking whether these books give any tokens of noticing their own existence, any tokens of a knowledge of any Christian literature. The passage already alluded to, in which Paul refers to the traditions which the Thessalonians received by word or from his letter, is scarcely more than a shadow of self-consciousness of these writings, since he there is speaking so thoroughly practically, and not in the least claiming book value and permanent value for his letter. But the phrase, the sentence, is nevertheless well worth remark, for in fact there lies at the back of this command to them the thought that what he has written to them is normative or that his letter is normative. The opening of the third chapter of the Second Epistle of Peter with its reference to the First Epistle and to the command of the apostles, and then the words about Paul and his Epistles, I pass over here because I do not think that this Epistle belongs to this age. Luke at the beginning of his Gospel mentions many other attempts at Gospels. That may refer in part to various private attempts such as we have already spoken of. It undoubtedly refers, if I mistake not, to the book of Matthew, the Aramaic one that was translated into Greek, and also to the Gospel of Mark, and it is possible although not very likely that it has in view, only by hearsay, our Gospel according to Matthew and the Gospel to the Hebrews. In no case is the word "many" here to be taken in the sense of a very large number, so that we should think of twenty or fifty Gospels. Many means more or less according to the thing spoken of, and here a half a dozen would be an abundant number. The one book mentioned a moment ago as possibly belonging to this period but not found in the New Testament is the Gospel of the Hebrews or to the Hebrews. We know, however, very little about it. It may very well be that Aramaic book by Matthew, in which case it is in the main or perhaps entirely to be found in our synoptic Gospels. It may be something quite different. It will probably come to light some day in Egypt or in Armenia or in Syria, and then we shall know more about it.

II.

THE POST-APOSTOLIC AGE.

90–160.

IN passing over to the age after that of the apostles, we need first of all to form for ourselves some conception of the way in which the Christians looked at the books which they found in their hands. We are interested to know, or at least to try to fancy, what they thought of them and why they kept them. It has been to such an extent the habit in the Christian Church to throw a cloud of glory about these books, that it is difficult to bring our minds down to what it is likely were the hard facts of the case. The guidance and care of the Holy Spirit has been emphasised so strongly that we must needs suppose that each book was from its day of writing definitely marked as a future member of the illustrious company, and was most scrupulously, we might say masoretically, guarded and transmitted to our day. We know, however, now that this has not been the course of things. If we turn back to the early days, we may calmly say that it is in every way probable that one or another letter of the apostles, that would humanly speaking have, or seem to have, afforded us as much instruction, comfort, and help as certain Epistles in the New Testament, has simply been lost. The early Christians had no thought of history, no thought of an earthly future. They were soon to cut loose from all their surroundings. Why should they then save up books, or rather save up letters. They had read and heard the given letter. That was all. They knew what was in it. No more was needed. Why keep the letter? Precisely the opposite may now and then have happened, namely that a little Church read a letter to pieces; unrolled the papyrus and rolled it up again until it fell apart, and that without setting about copying it so as to keep it in a new form. The letters that the apostles wrote to them were not "Bible." They were the letters of their favourite preachers. Some members of the Church were enthusiastic about the apostle, others were not, others liked another apostle or another preacher very much better. The very man in the little community who because of his better education came to have charge of a letter received might be a friend of some other preacher, and therefore neglect the letter of an apostle. In the case of the Epistles which we still possess, some were surely kept with the greatest care, read duly by the members of the Church, read in occasional meetings, lent to neighbouring Churches, copied off for distant Churches, and copied off for themselves as soon as they began to grow old and were threatened with decay. No one will have given a thought to the original the moment that a new copy was done.

The Gospels were different. They were not sent to Churches or to anybody else. No one got one unless he ordered it. And they did not convey to the reader merely the words of an apostle, but the words and deeds of Jesus. During the apostolic age there will not have been so very many copies of the Gospels made. For the Churches were poor, and books from which to copy may not have been anywhere near. Most of all, they then had the wandering preachers who told them about Jesus, and therefore the written Gospels were the less necessary.

Certainly, however, these writings came to be read in the public meetings. The word public has for this primitive time, it is true, a strange sense, since the groups were often so very small, and were always in private houses; but it was nevertheless, within the limits of the case and as the forerunner of the later services in Church edifices, a public reading, not the reading of one man for himself or for his room mate or for his family, but the reading of a book before a duly collected group of men and women. We must consider carefully this early reading of books in the Christian assemblies. If I am not mistaken, we shall in it see the process of authorisation of books from the first to the last step.

Going back to the beginning, to the first time that a letter from an apostle, let us say Paul, was received by a Church, let us say Thessalonica, we can imagine the stir it will have made. The little group will have been complete; no one will have stayed at home that evening. The letter was eagerly read and eagerly heard, and then they probably talked it over with each other. They perhaps read it again the next night and the next. The Church at Berœa and other Churches, possibly as far as Philippi, may have borrowed it or asked for copies of it, although we do not suppose that at this early moment the borrowing and copying were so common as they soon came to be. Gradually the letter will have been in a measure laid aside. The members of the company knew it almost by heart. The second letter may have reached them. That this letter was in any way secret, will not have entered their minds. The same thing happened in the other Churches that received letters from apostles. As time went on, as one apostle and then another passed away, some Churches here and there with a member or two who had a special liking for books or for documents, probably got all the letters they could reach copied for them and then kept them together, reading them as occasion might offer, either from beginning to end, or the particular part of the letter which appealed or applied to the moment.

During all this time, and doubtless well on into the second century at least in many districts, the word was still preached in the passing flight of the wandering preachers, the apostles. Little by little it will have become known that the Gospels had been written. These Gospels will at first have been circulated in the immediate neighbourhood of the place in which each was written, and then have soon struck the great lines, if they were not already on one of them, and have reached Rome and Jerusalem and Alexandria. Wherever a Gospel was received, Christians will have compared its tenor with that which they had heard by word of mouth. But for a while the living voice of the evangelising preacher will have been preferred to the dead letter in the book. Many Churches will for a long while have had no Gospel or only one Gospel, and only after much waiting have gotten more. Church after Church, group after group of Christians had then a Gospel and an Epistle or two, a few Epistles. The tendency of the intercourse between the Churches was towards an increase in the collection of books ; now one now another new one was added by friends to the old and treasured store of rolls. It is totally impossible to give any accurate idea of the rapidity of the accretion, totally impossible to say when it was that a number of

Churches secured all four Gospels and the greater part of the Epistles. Each one must make his own estimate. I am inclined to think that about the close of the first century or in the first twenty years of the second century—that is indefinite enough— the four Gospels were brought together in some places. The last Gospel to be written, the Fourth Gospel, must have been at once accepted, and that if I am not mistaken as the work of John from the Twelve, and have had great success.

Let us turn to the worship, the public worship of the Christians. It need only be mentioned in passing that there was nothing like a regular order of services that prevailed all over, in Palestine as well as in Spain. There will have been every description of order of exercises, from the silence of the Quakers of to-day to the more elaborate liturgy or order which we shall now mention. I am persuaded that the ordinary services consisted of four parts, comprising (*a*) that which men offered, said, laid before God; (*b*) that which God said to men; (*c*) that which a man said to men; and (*d*) a meal, the love-feast, closing with the breaking of bread, the Lord's Supper. The division (*a*), man to God, will have consisted of prayer, free if possible, often probably with much out of the Psalms, and, after the prayer, a hymn or a psalm. The division (*b*), God to men, will have consisted originally of the Scripture reading, and that, of course, from and only from the Old Testament. The division (*c*), man to men, contained the sermon or an address of some kind, an exhortation. This must have been in general the point at which the gospel was preached, at which the life, deeds, and words of Jesus were brought before the hearers. Then followed part four. Remember, I am not pretending to say that the order of services from instant to instant must have been (*a*) (*b*) (*c*) (*d*). All I am contending for is, that the services consisted of these four parts, of these four thoughts, if anyone prefers the expression, and that all that occurred during the course of the service, in whatever order, belonged under one head or another out of the four, and that anything new that might be introduced must vindicate for itself a place in some one of the four divisions. Now it is evident that the reading of letters from apostles, and, when the Gospels were there, the reading of the Gospels, must have taken place under the third part or (*c*), for that was all : "Man to Men." No one will object to the definition of this division for the Epistles, and every one will grant that the Gospels also belong here, so soon as I call attention to the fact that the traditions concerning Jesus always must have been given under this heading. No one had at that time thought of calling the Gospels or the Epistles a part of Holy Writ; the Old Testament was that. The Gospels were the written sermon, that is to say, the story of Jesus written down instead of merely being on the lips. The Epistles were an exhortation in writing. Whether the Christians at the beginning used the Jewish Parashahs and Haphtarahs, the old sections for the law and the prophets, or some new divisions of their own, does not concern us. All that we have to settle is that originally in the Christian Church the part (*b*), God to man, consisted solely of Old Testament lessons.

It was, if I do not err, during the post-apostolic age that this was changed, that the contents of the part (*b*) came to be enlarged. That can scarcely have come about in any other way than the following. The Gospels and the Epistles, such of each as the Churches had, were read gradually more and more regularly. The living tradition on the lips of wandering preachers or of more stationary clergymen, lost day by day in freshness as the years passed on and the age of the apostles receded into a dim distance. At last it became clear, at first it may be in one Church and little by little then in others, that the new writings had a meaning for Christian life which the books of the Old Testament did not possess. Were the Old Testament books authoritative, then must these also be authoritative. Did God speak through the old books, then must it be His voice that was heard in the new books. Thus it came about that the Gospels and the Epistles passed from the third part of the services to the second part. The word of God to men was to be found as well in them as in the Old Testament. In the third part of the services the sermon remained. Sometimes a bishop's letter, sometimes a letter from another Church was added in that place. That was: Man to Men.

It can scarcely have been at that time, but at a later date, which we are thus far not able to determine, that the Old Testament lessons were almost entirely excluded from the services of the Church on Sabbaths and on Sundays. Aside from a few, comparatively few, lessons on special days, they were remanded to the week days of the great fast, of Lent.

Before we really enter upon the examination of the literature of this period, it is desirable to say a word or two about doctrine, even if we are in the present inquiry not concerned with doctrinal questions. In discussing early Christian writings, objections are often raised touching the character, the genuineness, or the value of the testimony of a book because of an alleged one-sidedness in it. This objection takes in by far the greater number of cases the form of disparaging or distrusting or disowning what is alleged to be Pauline. It is declared or assumed that the ground story of the Christian Church was Petrine, and that only a peculiar connection with Paul personally or with his writings, and only a distinct aversion to Peter and as well an antagonistic attitude towards the old mother centre at Jerusalem can possibly lead, during the prefatory years to the Old Catholic Church, to any sentences or paragraphs or whole books that seem to agree with the views of the Apostle to the Gentiles. This is not the place to discuss this question, yet it appears to me to be important to emphasise at this point the opinion that I personally hold. It is my impression that the story of Paul's arrest at Jerusalem, while carrying out in the temple a vow suggested to him by the leaders of that one centre, thoroughly disposes of the notion that there existed any difference of doctrine between them that could conflict with the love that they will at Jerusalem have entertained for the man who kept bringing to them the gifts that he had got for them from the largely heathen-Christian Churches abroad. Further, it is to be considered that Paul was the only one who had with a facile pen spread out on broad lines a conception of Christian views as to salvation and as to life. The conclusion that I draw from this is, that this Pauline Christianity was, if I may so speak, the only Christianity of the time immediately preceding his death. Nevertheless, no one at that uncritical period will have thought of its being peculiarly Pauline. It was Christianity, and that was the end of the matter.

At the outset it is well for us to consider what we may justly look for in the books of this time that will be of use to us in proving the existence and defining the authoritative character of the writings of the New Testament. To put the extreme case, some critics seem to look for such a completeness of reference as the only due and acceptable testimony to the presence and valuation of the New Testament, that a writer of the post-apostolic age could only have met their demands by writing his own thoughts on the margin of a copy of the entire New Testament, Matthew to Revelation, prefacing his work : " Citing as in duty bound the whole of this sacred volume, I proceed to discuss . . ." Others are apparently surprised to find that any author fails to name or at least quote most accurately every solitary book in the New Testament, and they find the lack of both for any book a sure sign that the missing book was not then in existence or not then known to the writer. So far from that does the everyday literary habit diverge, that we must on the contrary be profoundly grateful when an early writer mentions any one of the books by name, and find great satisfaction and security even if he does not mention the name, if he offer us sentences which, even if rewrought with editorial licence, clearly point to the said book as their source. We should never forget that these writers did not write for the purpose of giving us proofs of the authority of the New Testament books. How many Christian essays might be found to-day that on ten or on thirty pages contain few or no quotations from the New Testament, and no mention of the author of a New Testament book ! And that leads me to emphasise the circumstance, that we must keep the thought of a direct quotation in many places in all our researches very much in reserve. If we do this we shall also hesitate to blame a writer for careless quotation, and be slow to suppose that slightly altered phrases point to other books or other texts than those which we have in hand.

It would be fitting to speak of three degrees of references to books. In the first and lowest degree the reference is to the speaker or writer, at least often, a latent, a sub-conscious, an unconscious reference. He has, at some time or other, read the book in question, and a phrase has pleased him, has fastened itself in his brain. Now that he comes to speak or to write upon the topic, this sentence appears on the surface. It is not clear to him whence it comes. Perhaps it does not even occur to him that the words are not his own. The words are, after all, not exactly the same as in the book referred to. Some of them are his. The phrase has a new cast. But for the man who knows the source the thing is plain. This kind of citing may grow so distant or so shadowy as to be little

more than an allusion.   In the second degree the act of quoting
may become quite clear to the writer.   He may, however, at the
instant not know precisely whence he has drawn the words or
precisely what the original sentence is.   He knows fully enough
to make with the phrase the point that he has in mind, and he
writes the words down without an instant's hesitation.   He is
not trying to quote, he is trying to express himself.   It is totally
indifferent to him whether the quotation be exact or not.   Let us
put it on high ground.   The other author has had a divine
thought, and has uttered it.   He has the same thought, and he
utters it too.   To whom the words belong, no one cares.   The
third degree is that in which the writer goes to the book and
copies the precise words down with painful accuracy, and names
the book and the passage.   We must always be thankful for
what we thus get, for the insight into the earlier writings.

    This post-apostolic age opens with a book that excites our in-
terest and calls for our admiration.   It is a letter, but not a letter
of one man to another.   The Church of God that is living in this
foreign world at the city of Rome, writes to the Church of God
living in this foreign world at the city of Corinth.   The Church
itself could not in its corporate character seize a pen or even
dictate a letter.   Tradition tells us that a Christian named Clement
wrote it.   A certain halo encircles him.   He is said by some to
have been from a Jewish, by others from a heathen family ; he is
fabled to have had imperial connections; he is claimed as a follower
of Peter and as a follower of Paul ; he is the representative of law,
of the specifically Roman characteristic, in the growing Church,
and a number of writings gathered around his name, claiming
for themselves his authority.   There is no very good reason for
doubting that he had himself heard the apostles, at least the two
great apostles.   This letter is probably from his pen.   Someone
in Rome wrote it, and we are bound to accept him till a better
suggestion can be made.   So far as appears, it was written about
the year 95.   The writer, in order to have been set to do this
task, is to be supposed to be one of the older men in the Roman
society.   He may have been fifty or sixty years old.   If only
fifty, he will have been about twenty years old when Paul suffered
martyrdom ; if he were sixty, he will have been thirty.   The
Roman Church claims him among her first bishops, and I do not
doubt that he was the most prominent or influential man in that

Church in his day, little as I suppose that anyone up to that time in that Church had received the title of bishop. Indeed this seems to me to be made plain by the letter itself. All in all, little as we know about him in detail, and much as was attached to his name by the fertile fancy of his admirers, he must have been an exceptionally strong and good man. His letter is an extremely valuable document. It is well written, and contains some beautiful passages. Further high opinion of Clement's literary powers is found in the fact that, as Origen relates, he was considered by some to be the author of the Epistle to the Hebrews.

The value of the testimony of Clement in this letter is enhanced by the fact that he is writing in the name of the Christians at Rome and to the Christians at Corinth. This causes his words to pass for both of these Churches. He knows about the Church at Corinth, and refers to their Church lessons, as we shall see. His letter shows no tokens of a bias towards one apostle or another, no inclination to use but a single series of the books of the New Testament. His language is that of the educated Greek Christian. Certain words were probably suggested to his mind by passages in the New Testament, now in Peter, now in Paul, now in John. We might say that various paragraphs or sentences seemed to be coloured by the cast of mind shown in New Testament writings, were it not that the style is so good and so vigorous that we have the feeling that the author in treating the points in question has of himself risen to the level of the authors who, in the New Testament, dealt with the same thoughts. In his exquisite chapter (ch. 49) on love he touches Proverbs, but through the medium of First Peter : "Love covereth a multitude of sins "; and at the same time he reminds us of James. With his plea for subjection to other Christians he coincides with Titus and First Peter and Ephesians. When he refers to what is pleasing, good, and acceptable, before Him that made us, he reminds us of First Timothy, though he may simply be using a common form of speech.

Again he writes (ch. 46) : "Or have we not one God and one Christ, and one spirit of grace shed upon us, and one calling in Christ ? " That is one of the cases of the use of words without direct quotation. Undoubtedly it was Ephesians and First Corinthians that led him to use these words, but no one of the passages in those letters would have fitted in precisely. In just the same manner he uses (ch. 35) Paul's words from the latter part of the first chapter of Romans : "Casting away from our-selves all unrighteousness and lawlessness, avarice, strifes, both malice and deceit, both whisperings and backbitings, hatred of God, pride, and insolence, both vainglory and inhospitality. For those who do these things are hated of God ; and not only those doing them, but also those agreeing to them." How absurd it would be for any one to say that that was a new text for the passage in Romans ! When Clement quotes (ch. 34), " Eye hath not seen," and so on, it is probably taken from First Corinthians. It is, at any rate, not drawn directly from Isaiah. Perhaps it comes from the Revelation of Elias, but we do not know. The most pleasing allusion to the Epistles is to that very Epistle to the Corinthians. Clement says (ch. 47) : " Take up the Epistles of Saint Paul the apostle. What did he first write to you at the beginning of the gospel ? In truth, he wrote to you spirit-ually both about himself and Cephas and Apollos, because even then there were parties among you." That is very good indeed. Observe how he calls Paul's message a gospel. Perhaps the thought may arise, that Clement only treated the Epistles in this free way, and that because he knew the apostles, had known them personally. Not at all. He quotes, and that clearly from memory, and mixes up into one, two passages from Matthew, one of which is also found in Mark and Luke. It is not another text, it is a free quotation, introduced by the words (ch. 46) : " Remember the words of Jesus our Lord : for He said : Woe to that man. It would have been better for him not to have been born than to offend one of My elect ; it would have been better for him to have been bound round with a millstone and have been sunk into the sea than to offend one of My little ones." In another place he makes a thorough combination of various verses from Matthew, partly found also in Luke. He introduces the passage thus (ch. 13) : " Especially remembering the words of the Lord Jesus, which he uttered while teaching meekness and long-suffering." It was indeed " re-membering," but not accurately. Clement continues : " For he spoke thus : Be merciful, that ye may be mercifully treated ; forgive, that ye may be forgiven. As ye do, so will be done to you. As ye give, so shall be given to you. As ye judge, so shall ye be judged. As ye show mildness, so shall ye be mildly treated.   With what measure ye mete, with it shall be measured for you." He then calls that a command and orders.   The most interesting thing about Clement is his close acquaintance with the Epistle to the Hebrews.   If we could only know all about it that he knew.   He uses its words, sometimes he quotes the Old Testament with its help, sometimes he follows its order of thought, sometimes he changes the thought round.   It was said a moment ago that Clement was suggested by someone before Origen as the author of the Epistle to the Hebrews.   The man who proposed that was doubtless impelled by the contemplation of this free and intimate use of that Epistle.   But we have no reason to suppose that Clement wrote it.   He knew the Epistle well and he liked it amazingly, as every Christian and every lover of brilliant writing should love it.   Do we find in this letter any traces of other writings that seem to have been of the same character as the New Testament books?   No.   There are several allusions to passages that we cannot verify, some of them at least closely attached to an "it is written," but they are probably from apocryphal books.   One is, for instance, attached to a passage from Exodus, another to a verse from the Psalms, although the context of the passages exhibits nothing of the kind.

What have we gained from this early work of a Christian who was in a position to know all that was going on in the Roman Empire and in the Christian Churches, who had in his hands at Rome the threads that ran out through the provinces, who stood in correspondence with the chief Church in Greece?   I hope that no one will say that we have gained but little, that Clement should have said more about the books of the New Testament. We stand with him at the close of the first period and at the opening of the second period.   He may almost be said to belong to both.   It is impossible at that time that he should think of making a list of the books of the New Testament for us.   And it would be absurd for us to think that he only knew of such of these books as he named or quoted.   We can only look for two great general topics that his letter may present to us in a way to satisfy our desire for literary testimony.   One is negative, the other positive.   The negative proposition which his letter might be suited to prove, or to favour so far as it goes, is that there were for him at the time of writing the letter no other writings

5

aside from those of our New Testament that he needed to or cared to quote. It is to be conceded that he might have known of a dozen without quoting them, just as he failed to quote the greater part of the New Testament books. Yet, nevertheless, the fact is that he does not show signs of knowing of other books that are Christian and of acknowledged value, and this is worth a great deal. We must not forget that Clement's Christian literature mirrors itself not merely in the few direct quotations. It lies back of his way of thinking, his way of putting things, and back of his language. Nothing in all this points to other writings of the given kind.

According to the theories which represent his time as one that overflowed with evangelical and epistolary literature, that would lead us to assume the existence of twenty or fifty Gospels and numerous letters, it would have been almost impossible for him to have written so much, so long a letter, without quoting here and there or betraying in passing a knowledge of the contents of Gospels and letters that are unknown to us. It is only necessary to remark, by the bye, that the unknown books which were quoted a few times all seem to have been such as belonged to the Apocrypha of the Old Testament. A negative is difficult of proof. The phenomenon here named proves nothing mathematically. But it goes to show that in the nineties of that first century other writings than ours were not held to be as valuable as ours were held to be. That is a very important point for the consideration of the criticism before us. The stream of Christian tradition is just forming, and it is in this respect what a defender of the high value of the present New Testament would wish it to be. If Clement does that for us negatively, he may also do much for us positively. It is possible that he shows direct acquaintance with James, First Peter, First Timothy, and Titus, although the quotations in view do not absolutely force this conclusion. He knows the Epistle to the Romans, to his own Church, and the Epistle to the Corinthians, to whom also he is writing, and the Epistle to the Hebrews, perfectly well, and he quotes our Gospels more than once. Above and beyond this his thoughts and his language, his sentences and his words, show in many places the influence of the books with which we are concerned. Thus Clement supports positively the existence of our New Testament. He does not mention all the books, but there are few that he does not seem to know. Again, we assert that the stream of tradition at this initial point is all that we could expect it to be. It can be claimed as full evidence for Matthew, Romans, First Corinthians, and Hebrews, and it fits in with the authenticity of the most of the other books. It disappoints no just expectations.

Clement was a member of a well-known Church, a member in good and regular standing. He might be called orthodox. There existed, however, even at that time men who combated Christianity or special forms of Christianity. In part they were old opponents of the apostles, or the successors of such opponents. They represented in many diverse shadings a Judaism that busied itself seriously with Christianity, and endeavoured to enforce the law among Christians ; and this phase of Judaism seems to have had its foundation in Ebionism. Another type had some roots reaching back before the birth of Christ to Philo. Philo, the Therapeutæ, and the Essenes were inclined to combine Judaism and Greek philosophy. Philo's way of starting was the, to him satisfactory, proof that all the valuable contents of that philosophy were borrowed from Moses. So soon then as Christianity began to spread, this Philonian movement became, or branched off into, what may be called Gnostic Ebionism or Ebionitic Gnosticism. In a genuine Jewish manner, this type also laid stress upon the law. A third type of the movements against orthodox Christianity, if we may use the modern term in passing, was found in a Gnosticism that proceeded from heathenism and was connected with the Samaritan astrologian from Gittæ. This Simon Magus, who may be found in the eighth chapter of Acts, must have been a man of some importance. Though we know little directly about him, we can trace the influence of his activity for a long while. He might be called a match for or a contrast to Clement. Clement became the typical Churchman in the traditions of the second century, and Simon was the typical heretic or opponent of Christianity. A book called the *Great Declaration* is attributed to Simon, but may be the work of one of his pupils.

We owe almost all our knowledge of these and many other heretics of the post-apostolic age to an anti-heretical book called the *Philosophumena*, that was probably written by Hippolytus of Rome, or rather Bishop of Portus, towards the close of the

first quarter of the third century. It is true that the quotations
from the heretical writings are alleged to have been furnished
to Hippolytus by some assistant, and not to be accurate or not
to be precisely what they purport to be. It is not likely that
they were manufactured out of the whole cloth. If they be
not exactly from each of the sources to which they are severally
attributed, they may have been extracted by a labour-hating
hand from a single book or from one or two heretical books that
were easy of reach. In the case of Simon, the quotations are
probably right. A curious but telling proof for the existence
of approved and much read Christian books is found in the
fact that Simon or his pupils went to work to write books in
the name of Christ and of the apostles in order to deceive
Christians. Simon's book quotes from Matthew or Luke the
axe at the root of the tree, from Luke the erring sheep, from
John the being born of blood, and from First Corinthians the
not being judged with the world. Of course, he quotes in an
off-hand way. Freedom in the use of the words lay nearer for
him than for Clement. If his pupil Menander wrote that book,
these remarks would apply to him. Otherwise we know nothing
of this Menander's views, since a reference to him in Irenæus
which has been connected with Second Timothy is entirely too
vague to be of use.

One of the Jewish opponents or heretics was Cerinthus,
apparently by origin a highly educated Egyptian Jew who
was fabled to have been — or was it true? — variously in
person an opponent of the apostles. Irenæus' story that John
rushed out of a public bath on seeing Cerinthus in it, crying
that the roof might fall in on such a man, looks like a true
story. Later tradition said that the roof did fall and kill
Cerinthus. However that may be, Cerinthus knew and used
at least the genealogy in Matthew and quoted from that Gospel
that it was enough for the disciple to be as his master. The
chief interest in Cerinthus attaches to Revelation. Although
he was taken to be a special antagonist of John's and of Paul's,
—because Paul belittled the law,—and to have opposed the
genealogy in Matthew to the opening words of John's Gospel,
he appears to have occupied himself particularly with Revelation.
Cerinthus' apocalyptic dreams and fancies were rewarded by
the attribution to him first of the book of Revelation itself

and then much later of the Gospel and the Epistles of John. This was criticism run wild. The connection of the Jew with the Revelation fits into the newer theory of the original Jewish basis for Revelation. But the upshot of the matter is that the Revelation is thrown back to a very early date.

We may mention here in passing two heresies or sects, one of which was partly the other almost wholly of Jewish extraction. The Snake Worshippers, also called Ophites and Naassenes, are perhaps the first sect that called itself Gnostic. They claimed to have gotten their doctrine from Mariamne, who got it from James the brother of Jesus. They quote or allude to Matthew, Luke, John, Romans, First and Second Corinthians, Ephesians, and Galatians, possibly also to Hebrews and Revelation. They also refer to the Gospel to the Egyptians and to the Gospel of Thomas. This was the Christian modification of an old, a heathen, belief. Their opposition to John places them on the list of those who prove the existence of the Fourth Gospel. The other sect is that of the Ebionites, who say that Matthew wrote a Hebrew Gospel. They seem to have used apocryphal acts of the apostles.

Another heretic named Basilides, from Alexandria, is quoted directly and fully by Hippolytus. He was a pupil of Menander's, and lived, so far as we can judge from the accounts, soon after the beginning of the second century. He wrote twenty-four books on the Gospel. It is clear that he accepts in general the books of the New Testament. He appears to know Matthew, and he quotes Luke, John, Romans, First Corinthians, Ephesians, and Colossians. He may have alluded to First Timothy, and have quoted First Peter. Now it is extremely strange that this heretic at that early date should do what no one had done before him, according to our literature, namely, quote the books of the New Testament precisely in the same way as the books of the Old Testament. For example (7^{22}): "And this is that which is spoken in the Gospels, He was the true light that lighteth every man that cometh into the world." He quotes (7^{25}) from Romans: "as it is written," (7^{26}) from First Corinthians: "about which the Scripture saith," from Ephesians: "as is written," from Luke: "that which was spoken," and (7^{27}) from John: "the Saviour saying." It seems very hard to believe that that was written in the opening years of the second century.

It has been suggested that he, the heretic, would be more likely
to emphasise the scriptural character of the new books than
a Christian, who would assume it silently; but I cannot see
the least reason for such a plea.   Since I know of no grounds
upon which I could assert it likely that a Christian of a later
day inserted the words mentioned, it seems to me to be the
best thing to suppose that Basilides wrote this himself.   But
I insist upon it then, first, that we must remember that the
life and activity of such a teacher is not likely to have been
confined within a very few years; and second, that Basilides,
if he did not write this book later, say than in the year 130, may
himself have at a still later date modified the form of quotation
according to the then prevailing custom of Christians.   Without
these formulas, Basilides confirms in general our New Testament
by exact quotations, supposing that the manuscripts are correct.
With these formulas he advances the question of the authority
of the books a long way.   Were he of Jewish descent, had he,
as some sentences touching him would seem to intimate, Jewish
connections and therefore habits, the use of "as it is written,"
and of "the scripture saith," would be the more natural for
him, would glide more easily from his pen.   But precisely
for a Jew or for a friend of the Jews, it would be less likely
that he should think of applying to these new books the formulas
that belonged to the sacred books of the Jews.   In connection
with Basilides, it is important to mention a contemporary of
his named Agrippa Castor.   We know very little about him,
but one thing marks him agreeably for us.   He is the first
man, so far as we know, who in a set book defended the Gospels
against a heretic, in his defence of them against Basilides.   He
is thought to have been a Jew.

These scattered opponents of Christians or of the gathering
Church have offered us no signs of other Gospels than those that
we have already considered, and as little do they point to other
Epistles than those in the New Testament.

Clement was in Rome, towards the West, and was combined
with Corinth.   The next step leads us to the East, to the second
capital of the Roman Empire, to Antioch in Syria.   This city
held the first place in Christianity after Jerusalem itself.   It was
Antioch in which the great missionaries Paul and Barnabas
sought their foothold for their journeys.   And Peter must have

spent much time there. It was a city not only of wealth and power, but also of learning, and its university was only second to that at Athens. Ignatius was the bishop there about the beginning of the second century. His death as martyr appears to have taken place after the year 107 and before the year 117. He wrote seven letters, so it is alleged, on his way to martyrdom at Rome,—seven letters addressed to the Ephesians, the Magnesians, the Trallians, the Romans, the Philadelphians, the Smyrnaeans, and to Polycarp, the bishop of Smyrna. An extended form of these letters is a piece of work from the fourth century. The shorter forms seem to be genuine. Should they be proved not to be from the hand or brain of Ignatius himself, —this has not yet been proved,—they would remain a very early and interesting monument of Christian literature. They afford what we might call a duly developed continuation of the Pastoral Epistles, and represent or place before our eyes a condition of affairs in the Churches which would appear to be the due sequence to that portrayed in those letters of Paul.

One of the things which strikes one strangely in his letter to the Smyrnaeans is his use of the word catholic for the Church, and that both for the general Church, the Church through the world, and for the special, single Church as of the universally accepted type. This objection to the authenticity of this and therefore of all the letters is to be met in two ways. In the first place, some one must have begun the use of these words that is current at a later time, and that some one may have been Ignatius at this early period, however few applications of the term we may find in the immediately succeeding literature, which had but little occasion to use it ; but it is used in more limited sense by the Smyrnaeans in their letter to the Philomelians. And, in the second place, nothing would be easier than to suppose that the word was in each of the six places in which it occurs an interpolation by a later hand. It seems to me that the word fits in well where it stands, and that it agrees with the style of the writer, but it might easily have crept into the text from marginal glosses in one of the early manuscripts.

It agrees with the style of the writer, and particularly with the circumstances under which the letters were written, that quotations are a rare thing, that they are short, and that they are evidently from memory. For our purpose it is

enough to observe that the author clearly knows our New
Testament in general. The Gospels of Matthew and John appear
to have been either his favourites or the ones better known to
him. He knew the Epistles of Paul well. But at one point he
is supposed to quote from an apocryphal book or from an otherwise unknown Gospel. He writes (Smyr. 3) : " And when he came
to those around Peter, he said to them : Take, touch Me, and
see that I am not a bodiless spirit." It may very well be from
the Gospel of Peter, his teaching, or his preaching, or from the
Gospel to the Hebrews as a parallel to the passage in Luke.
The word " take " is odd at that place. That is enough. It is
interesting and beautiful to read in the letter to the Philadelphians
the words (ch. 8) : " For me Jesus Christ is archives." This same
letter gives us for the first time the word Christianism as a parallel
to Judaism. It was appropriate that Christianity should get its
name from the city in which the word Christian was coined.
Ignatius, if genuine, agrees well with the stream that we conceive
to have flowed forth from the first century. If the letters be not
genuine, they give the same testimony for a period a trifle later,
perhaps at or soon after the middle of the second century.

An interesting piece of testimony to the Gospels must be mentioned here. Eusebius quotes in his Church History (3, 39) words
that Papias drew from a presbyter called John, who probably
lived about the turn of the century. This John says that Mark
wrote his Gospel according to what he heard from Peter, and that
Matthew wrote " Words " or " Sayings " in Hebrew, which means
in Aramaic. This must be examined closely. It reads : " And
this the presbyter said : Mark the interpreter of Peter wrote
down accurately, yet not in order, so far as he [Peter] told what
was said or done by the Christ. For he did not hear the Lord,
nor was he a disciple of His, but afterwards as I said of Peter,
who used to give lessons according as it was necessary, but not
as if he were making a collection in order of the Lord's words,
so that Mark made no mistake in thus writing down some things
as he remembered them. For he took care of one thing, and
that was, not to leave out anything he heard or to give anything
in it in a wrong way." This presbyter named John probably
lived at Ephesus at the same time that the Apostle John was
passing his last years there. He calls Mark the interpreter of
Peter. He might have said private secretary. The word

interpreter, however, need not be limited to the literary services here discussed, but may, if we consider the circumstances, have a further interest for us, quite aside from the story about Mark's Gospel. Peter the Aramaic Palestinian probably spoke some Greek in Galilee and Judea, but as an older man in the foreign capital it was doubtless desirable for him to have a younger man at hand to do any interpreting that was necessary. Whether that has anything to do with the Greek of First Peter, is a question for another place. What I have written "[Peter] told" may also be rendered "[Mark] remembered"; the sense remains the same; in each case Peter tells and Mark remembers. The giving of lessons, as I have written it, is, of course, his teaching, telling, explaining what Jesus said or did. That Peter did according as occasion offered, according to the needs of the occasion, or we may say, of the listeners. The reference to Matthew is as follows: "Matthew then wrote the sayings in Hebrew dialect, and each one translated them as he was able." The way in which Eusebius puts this makes it look as if this too came from that presbyter John. For my part, I have no doubt that these Aramaic sayings were the book that, after it was translated into Greek, became the chief source for Mark, and then for the writer of the first Gospel and for Luke.

Perhaps we may attach to the year 117 tentatively a few pages from the letter to Diognetus, which has by some been supposed to have been addressed to Marcus Aurelius' tutor Diognetus; we have here in mind the so-called first part of that letter; the second part is a totally different thing, perhaps thirty years later in date. This may be from Greece. We know little about it, but we see in it our stream of New Testament tradition, not in quotations, but in the whole contents. It places Paul's Epistles and John's Gospel clearly before us in its subjects and in its phrases and in its words.

When referring to Ignatius, I named his letter to Polycarp. Let us turn to him. Polycarp was probably born in the year 69, five years after Paul's martyrdom; and he himself was burned at Smyrna, where he was bishop, on February 23rd, 155. The stadion in which he was burned is still to be seen on the hill south of the city. He wrote a letter to the Philippians, Paul's beloved Philippians, in Macedonia, just after the martyrdom of Ignatius. Now I wish to lay special stress upon this Polycarp.

To use a figure that must not be forced, he is the keystone of the arch that supports the history of Christianity, and therefore of the books of the New Testament, from the time of the apostles to the close of the second century. To begin with, as was said, he appears to have been born about 69, and to have been converted by one of the apostles, perhaps by John, whose disciple he probably was. Irenæus, bishop at Lyons, who was born in Asia Minor, of whom we have to speak later, saw Polycarp when a boy. Irenæus it is who tells us that he was a pupil of John and bishop at Smyrna. To complete the matter, the Church at Philomelion in Phrygia asked the Church in Smyrna to tell them about the martyrs of that year—the year in which Polycarp was burned, and we actually have in our hands the account written by the Church of Smyrna for the Philomelians and for all Christians. Every Christian should know Polycarp's answer (ch. 9) to the governor's demand before the multitude in the stadion. The governor had tried to get him to swear by the emperor, but in vain. He cried out again: "Swear, and I release you. Revile Christ!" Polycarp said: "Eighty and six years do I serve Him, and He has never done me wrong. And how can I blaspheme my king that saved me?" It was a long fight. The governor did not wish to burn the old man who had willingly come up to the stadion to declare his faith. But soon the smoke of his fire curled up out of the stadion and was seen from the city and from afar upon that gulf, calling upon heaven and earth to witness to the death of a Christian. That is the keystone: A pupil of John, known to Irenæus, at Rome to discuss with the Bishop Anicetus the Easter question, proclaimed by his Church at his death.

A few words then about his letter to the Philippians. They and Ignatius too had asked him to send to them the letters of Ignatius, and he refers to their having sent their letters—or the one letter that they had received from Ignatius?—to him to be forwarded to Syria. In closing (ch. 13) he says that he sends with this letter the letters that Ignatius had sent to Smyrna: "and others as many as we had in our hands." That is an excellent example of what was said above about the intercourse between the Churches. Think of these few lines: Polycarp's surroundings connect Antioch in Syria where Ignatius was bishop, Smyrna where he himself was bishop, Philippi in

Macedonia to which he wrote, Philomelion in Phrygia to which his Church wrote about him, Rome where he conferred with Anicetus, and Lyons where Irenæus who had seen him died about 202. And this man connects through Irenæus alone the Apostle John who saw Jesus with the beginning of the third century. There may have been a dozen Christians besides who knew him, and who carried his traditions on to the third century. What did this Polycarp know about the books of the New Testament? His letter is full of the New Testament. It is plain that he had in his hands the Gospel of Matthew, and he probably had all four Gospels; he had all the Epistles of Paul, he had First Peter and First John, and he had that letter of Clement of Rome. I have no doubt that he refers to Acts in his first chapter. That he did not set about giving precise quotations is due to the habit of his time and to his way of writing. He is, if I may say so, saturated with Peter, but he is also Pauline to a very high degree. We shall not meet with a second Polycarp, but we do not need a second.

The next book that we have to look at is a new one. It is the Teaching of the Apostles, and was only discovered a few years ago. It may be dated in the form in which we have it about the year 120. It is, however, without doubt in part much older than that. One main source, or main part of it, is not Jewish Christian, but out and out Jewish in its origin. For this Teaching the Old Testament alone is Scripture. It contains over twenty allusions to New Testament books, or short quotations, of which a number are what we may call a free reproduction of Matthew. Three or four quotations seem to be a combination of Matthew and Luke. It shows no traces of a definitely other Gospel. It is in many thoughts and phrases much like John, but it does not quote him. One very interesting point has respect to the Lord's Prayer. Though we have little knowledge of the everyday life of the first Christians, we may feel sure that they were in the habit of using that prayer daily. The Jews had their " Hear, O Israel "; and John the Baptist gave his disciples a form of prayer; and precisely this latter instance led the disciples of Jesus to ask Him for a prayer, and brought forth from His lips this one. Now it looks as if the writer of the Teaching, or as if some scribe in copying it off, had not drawn the prayer from the text of Matthew, but had written it down as he remembered it from his own daily use of it. It will be observed that we cannot prove this, yet it seems to be likely that the various readings came from that source. We shall later find a peculiarity in this prayer in Tertullian, that perhaps was caused in the same manner. The older, originally Jewish opening part, the Two Ways, contains no direct quotation from the Old Testament, but the second, newer part gives us two, from Zechariah and Malachi. One is introduced by the formula, "as was spoken," and the other by the words, "For this is the (offering) named by the Lord." Four times we find in the second part mention of the Gospel with words drawn perhaps from Matthew. It is, however, possible that these quotations are a later addition. They are characterised twice: "as ye have in the Gospel" (to which "of our Lord" is once added), once: "as the Lord commanded in the Gospel," and once: "according to the dogma of the Gospel." Once we read (ch. 9): "About this the Lord hath said, Give not the holy thing to the dogs." But if we do not find direct quotations, we find plenty of sense and sentences that must have come from Matthew and Luke and John, and Paul's Epistles, and First Peter.

The writer knows the majority of our New Testament books, and uses their words as freely as if he knew them well from beginning to end. Of course he knows books that he does not happen to quote. He is busy with the thoughts and not with the duty of quoting all the books for the benefit of the criticism of the canon. The testimony of this Teaching is all the more valuable because it is such a convenient Christian handbook. It certainly was then used very widely, and it passed largely into later, more extended writings of the same general character. The question may present itself to some minds, how it comes to pass that here as elsewhere thus far, the words of the Gospel to so great an extent seem to be those or nearly those of the Gospel according to Matthew. I will say in advance that it does not occur to me to suppose that none of these early writers had written Gospels, that their allusions or similarities are due alone to oral tradition. But why so often from Matthew, so seldom from Mark and Luke? A definite answer is impossible. But we may reflect in the first place that even to-day many people read more of Matthew than of the other two. To-day its position at the opening of the volume makes it easier to reach.

In the second place, there is much in it that attracts the mind. The rich and full Sermon on the Mount, that the author combined for himself, draws all eyes to Matthew. Think, too, of the groups of miracles and parables. Think of the majestic effect of the: "This was done because it was written," and the impressive fulfilment of prophecy. The great preference of commentators for Matthew depends doubtless partly on its initial position, but these other thoughts will have been of moment. In manuscripts we sometimes find Matthew with a full commentary, [John with a full one], Luke with a commentary on passages not already treated in Matthew, and Mark with no commentary, or but a very short one, because its matter is found in Matthew and Luke.

Barnabas the apostle, but not one of the Twelve, is one of the most striking figures in the early days of Christianity. He stands out before us as the man who started Paul upon the great mission journeys, who said to him : Come with me. From Cyprus, long at Jerusalem, much at Antioch, no small traveller, he must have had a wide view of Christianity. He died, it may be, early in the sixties, before Paul. It would seem very appropriate that he should write a book of some kind for the Christians. Have we one from him? Perhaps so. But the book that bears his name, the so-called letter of Barnabas, is not from his pen. Sometimes it has been attributed to him, but wrongly. In connection with it, the question as to its having a right to a place in the New Testament, if it were really from Barnabas, has been mooted. For myself I do not doubt at all that it would have been one of the books of the New Testament if he had written it. But this statement must be accompanied by the remark that if he had written it, it would have been another, a different book. I do not mean to say that everything that an apostle penned would belong to the New Testament. A book by Matthew about the custom-houses in Palestine would not have been a part of the New Testament, whether written before or after his becoming an apostle. Just as little would a letter of Paul's about tent-cloth that had been ordered and woven have been added to his thirteen Epistles. At the same time, in spite of all I have previously said, we have no reason to suppose that the apostles were extremely inclined to write a number of books. And I doubt not that the most of what any

of them wrote after their joining Jesus, will have had some
connection with Him and His word and works and the life of
the Christians.

This letter of Barnabas is a work of the second century;
perhaps it was written about the year 130, and at Alexandria.
The temple had been long destroyed. Christians had begun
at that place, at the place where the writer lived, at least to
give up the observance of the Jewish Sabbath, and to confine
themselves to the Lord's Day. The letter is full of the
Old Testament, but it is the Old Testament, on the one hand
allegorised, on the other misunderstood, ill appreciated, run
down. He, the unknown author, is on the lookout for odd and
striking things. He agrees to the old tradition given by Suidas
as Etrurian, which counts six periods of a thousand years each
before the Creation, and six of the same length after the Creation.
The notion pleases him that Abraham's family of three hundred
and eighteen prefigured the name of Jesus and the figure of the
cross, because in Greek the number eighteen gives the letters
"Je" for Jesus, and the number three hundred the letter T,
which is clearly the cross. If he could only have known that the
first general council at Nice two hundred years later was going to
be attended by three hundred and eighteen Fathers, his happiness
would certainly have been much greater. Barnabas has two
quotations from Matthew. The sentences quoted are so short,
and are of such an easy kind to be remembered, that the oral
tradition might be supposed to have passed them directly on to
Barnabas, were it not that in the one case he directly writes:
"as is written," and thus shows that he knows of written Gospels.
This application of the phrase, "it is written," which is the
technical way of quoting the sacred books of the Old Testament,
may be the earliest case of this use of the New Testament books
as Scripture. In one place (ch. 7[11]) he quotes words of Jesus that
we have not in our Gospels. He has been telling about the goat
of the day of atonement, and that the reddened wool was to be
put upon a thorn-bush when the goat was driven out into the
wilderness. This he declares to be a figure for the Church in
reference to Jesus, seeing that if any one tries to get the wool
he will suffer from the thorns, and must be under stress to
become the master of the wool. "Thus," he says, "they who
wish to see me, and to attain to my kingdom, must be under

stress and suffering to take me." But these words may well be simply a combination of the author's and not be drawn from an unknown Gospel. They remind us of Paul's words in Acts on reaching Derbe, after being stoned and left for dead at Lystra. This letter has passages which remind us of Paul and of John. The written books are, however, still of less account than the tradition by word of mouth.

During the first half of the second century an Egyptian named Valentinus applied himself to the question of the origin of all things, and the sequence of the universe. He worked out an elaborate system of spiritual powers, starting from the original source of all things and running through thirty eons. From the last eon, the Mother, came Christ and a shadow. The latter produced the Creator and the devil, with their human races. Jesus then came as the fruit of all thirty eons, in a merely apparent body, and took the spiritual people, the children of the Mother, and the Mother herself into the spiritual kingdom. He alleged that his doctrine was connected with Paul through Theodas. The quotations of his writings that we have are scanty, and some of them are not of undoubted authority. Yet he is a witness for the body of the New Testament books. His whole system, the beings that he uses, or rather their names, are drawn from the Gospel of John. His first three names, after the original source of all things, are Mind, the Father, and Truth; and the following four are Word, Life, Man, Church. Of course, those are good words in common use; but their use in this way by a Christian points, I think, unmistakably to John's Gospel. But we have in the case of Valentinus a witness of high authority and credibility, namely Tertullian, and he says that Valentinus appeared to use the whole New Testament as then known. He did, it is true, or Tertullian thought so, alter the text, but he did not reject one book and another. Perhaps Valentinus only used a different text from Tertullian. In Clement of Alexandria we find a reference to Valentinus that looks interesting for the criticism of the canon. Clement makes Valentinus distinguish between what was written in the public books and what was written in the Church. That looks like a distinction between books that everybody, Jew and Gentile, might read, and books that only Christians were permitted to read. But we have no clue to the exact meaning of his words. Three of the books of the New Testament—Luke, John, and First Corinthians—are referred to by him.

From one of the pupils of Valentinus, Ptolemæus, we have a number of fragments which contain quotations from Matthew, Mark, Luke, John, Romans, First Corinthians, Galatians, Ephesians, and Colossians. We find, besides these fragments that Irenæus has kept for us, in Epiphanius an interesting letter written by Ptolemæus to a Christian woman named Flora; and he refers in it to Matthew, John, Romans, First Corinthians, and Ephesians. Irenæus storms at the Valentinians because they wrote a new Gospel called the Gospel of Truth; and Epiphanius tells of two other Gospels written by Gnostics, the Gospel of Eve and the Gospel of Perfection. Should we call these apocryphal Gospels if we had them in our hands, and place them beside the Gospel of the Infancy and the Gospel of Thomas, for example? I very much doubt it. I do not suppose that these Gospels offered an account of the life and works of Jesus and the apostles. They were probably more or less fantastic representations of the doctrines of the special Gnostic sects, the Gospel of Truth of the Valentinian sect, from which they proceeded. We have directly from the Valentinian school most important testimony, not only to the existence, but also to the high value of the Gospels which are in the New Testament; for Heracleon, a near friend of Valentinus', wrote upon the Gospels. Perhaps he wrote a commentary to one or all of them, perhaps he commented particular passages that seemed to him to be more interesting. We cannot tell. Origen quotes his comments on John; and Clement of Alexandria mentions a comment of his on a passage in Luke. And the quotations give references to Matthew, Romans, First Corinthians, and Second Timothy. All that shows that these branches of Christianity held to the main books of the New Testament. Nothing shows that they dreamed of putting their books upon a level with the books that became afterwards a part of our New Testament. Heracleon quoted the Preaching of Peter, but we do not know that he considered it scripture. One branch of the followers of Valentinus, the pupils of a Syrian named Mark, are said to have written, to have forged Gospels, but they went back, so far as we can see, only to our four Gospels, not to any unknown or apocryphal Gospels.

We must now turn to a man who claims a great deal of attention. His name is Marcion. His father was the Bishop of Sinope on the coast of Paphlagonia. He is in every way the most active and influential man, bearing the name of Christian, between Paul and Origen. The position of the Christian Church towards the Scriptures of the Old Testament seemed to him to be totally false. He quarrelled with his father and went to Rome. At Rome he quarrelled with the Church and left it. Polycarp called him "Satan's firstborn." In spite of all difficulties he set about founding a Church of his own about the year 144, and he succeeded. Churches of his sect were to be found in Syria as late as the fifth century. The thing that interests us about Marcion in the criticism of the canon is the fact that he set to work to make a New Testament for himself. That is to say, not that he wrote the books, but that he decided upon them, passed judgment upon their merits, their value, their right to a place in a Christian collection. Here we find in fact, so far as the authority of this Church founder could be said to determine anything duly, a canon. Here for the first time in the history of the Christian Church a clear cut, definitely rounded off New Testament offers itself to view. He was led in his selection of the books by his opinions about the course of history. The usual supposition that the God of the Old Testament and the Messiah of the Old Testament were the God and the Christ of the Christians was wildly wrong. The God who made the world was the Demiurge; he was just, in a way, but only just, not good. He was in the Old Testament hardhearted and cruel and bloodthirsty. Jesus let Himself be called the Messiah simply to fit in with the thoughts of the people. He was not the son of a virgin, because that was impossible. He simply came down from heaven and afterwards went back to heaven. Of course, then, Marcion cast the Old Testament aside. A Jewish Gospel like Matthew was nothing for him. Why John did not suit him it is hard to say; probably the author was too Jewish for him, and besides it joined Jesus directly with the creation of the bad Demiurge's world. He chose for himself the Pauline Gospel according to Luke, and omitted from it what his unerring eye knew to be from the wrong sphere, the sphere of the Demiurge. Acts had too much of Peter in it. The Epistle to the Hebrews, it is hardly necessary

6

to say, was altogether impossible. The Pastoral Epistles were probably too local.

In the end, then, his New Testament, we may say his Bible, consists of the Gospel part or the Gospel of Luke, and of the Apostle part or the ten Epistles of Paul; he called Ephesians the Epistle to the Laodiceans. His Gospel began perhaps with these words: " In the fifteenth year of Tiberius Cæsar, in the times of Pilate, Jesus descended into Capernaum, a city of Galilee." Therewith he had disposed of all birth accounts and genealogical tables. Towards the close the Crucifixion must have been omitted. And the identification of the person of Jesus may have been joined directly to the thought that He really was an "appearance," a "spirit." His Apostle began with Galatians, after which the Epistles to the Corinthians, Romans, and Thessalonians followed. Then came the Epistle to the Ephesians, but named Laodiceans. Colossians, Philippians, and Philemon finished the book. What would the Church have been if this headstrong man had succeeded in carrying out his plans, if that were our whole New Testament? Doubtless Marcion was moved by lofty thoughts. It was certainly nobler to condemn the bloodthirstiness that Israel attributed to its God than to condone it. But his influence, though it held out long, did at last fade away. It seems likely that many of the Christians in his Churches, partly from indifference or from ignorance out of mere accident, came, as years passed by, to use other books of the general New Testament of the Church. The whole Marcionitic movement has its great value for the criticism of the canon in its testimony, which is undoubtable, to the mass of the New Testament books. Marcion's books were a selection from the books of the Church. In the second place, it shows with the clearness of daylight that up to that moment no canon had been determined upon by the general Church. And, in the third place, it shows how tenaciously the Christians clung to what books they had, when the stormy and vigorously generalled Marcionitic movement, with its arraignment of the remaining books, succeeded after all in making no lasting impression upon the general contents of the New Testament.

If any title for a book destined for Christians could be appropriate, it is that of the Shepherd. Jesus called Himself the good Shepherd. A brother of Pius, the bishop of Rome, wrote it. Pius was bishop probably about from 141 to 157. A threefold tradition says that his brother wrote the Shepherd while Pius was in the chair. It contains eight visions, twelve commands, and nine parables communicated to him by the Church and the Shepherd. The tenth parable is the closing section of the book, and contains the rules given to Hermas how to order his life from henceforth. It will be at once clear that a dream-book of this kind cannot be expected to contain quantities of quotations from sheerly practical writings like the Gospels and the Epistles in general. I suppose that people seldom quote in dreams. The ecstatic condition makes the writer all in all, without books. From the contents of the whole composition it seems plain that the author knew at least one of our synoptic Gospels; the knowledge of all three is not to be proved from the text. For myself, I do not doubt that all three Gospels, all four Gospels, were well known at Rome before that time. This author had no mission to speak of them in detail. It seems certain that he knew the Epistle to the Ephesians. The other Pauline Epistles do not come to the front. Some things remind us of Hebrews, but we need not press the similarity. The Epistle of James is discernible partly in its matter, in the thoughts and things mentioned in it, and partly in the words used. Of course, the book of Revelation fitted best of all into Hermas' ideas.

He is one of the organisers of the renewal of the Old Testament, and of the law in the Old Catholic Church that is beginning to knit together. But it is not the more open Jewish manner with the notion that the Church is merely Judaism perfected. It is a Christianity that takes to itself serried legal forms. This kind of Christianity cannot be called Mosaic, but it is just the kind of Christianity that must commend itself to a mind that had been brought up under severely Jewish influences. We should not, however, fail to observe where we stand. If I do not err, the reason for the growth of this kind of religion then and there is to be sought, not in the Old Testament and not in Ebionitic fancies of the movers, but in the spirit of the people in which the new religion had now been present for nearly a century. To dispose of Ebionism, it was the tendency of this spirit that led the movers to Ebionitic thoughts, not Ebionitic teaching which warped them from a description of Christianity that lay nearer to their hearts. The early Christianity at Rome was by the time of the Epistle to the Romans of a heathen Christian cast. It could not at that time be well other than Greek. It remained Greek in language even beyond the time with which we are now dealing. But as years passed by the Roman element grew stronger and began to think for itself. The soul of Rome was law. And that law, that sense of law and for law, must needs be impressed upon the form that Christianity finally assumed in the eternal city. The growth of the Old Catholic Church is not merely to be charged to a general human perversity, and its leaning towards the Old Testament is not alone a token of a new life in Jewish-Christian circles in the second century, and its centring and vast strength in Rome was not solely the consequence of the enormous influence of the capital of the world. The crystallisation of this Church was the necessary consequence of the action of the spirit of the Roman people upon the Christian Church. For those Christians, little as they overcast the whole sphere to reach such a conclusion, the new form of Christianity was not one of the retrograde steps, returning to the used-up bottles of the Old Testament, but a step forward. It was not a Judaising, but a Romanising of Christianity. It was not conceived of as a limiting of Christianity, much as it would block heresy, but as a development and opening out of its capabilities.

At the close of the second vision we have a chance to see how a good book would then be started on its way in the Church. The elder woman, the Church, asks Hermas whether he has already communicated to the elders a book that he had borrowed from her to copy off. When he replied No, she says that it is all right, she wishes to add something: "When, then, I shall finish all these words, they shall be made known by thee to all the elect." The process was to begin with the making two copies, so that three books should be available: "Thou shalt write, then, two little books,—that is to say, two copies,—and thou shalt send one to Clement and one to Grapte. Clement will then send out to the cities outside, for that is charged upon him. And Grapte will put in mind the widows and the orphans. You, however, will read it in this city with the elders who stand at the head of the Church." Is not that a pretty window looking in upon the literary habit in Christian Rome? In the rest of the visions the Church bids him again and again to "tell" the saints what she says. The word of mouth is still powerful. But in the commandments the Shepherd who takes charge of him again enjoins him repeatedly to write. Thoroughly Pauline is (Vis. 3, 8) the putting Faith at the head of the seven women who bear the tower, the Church: "The first one of them, the one clasping her hands, is called Faith. By this one the elect of God are saved. The next one, the one girt up and holding herself firmly, is called Self-mastery. This is the daughter of Faith." Later follow, each the daughter of the preceding: Self-Mastery, Simplicity, Purity, Holiness, Understanding (or Insight), and Love. "Of these, then, the works are pure and holy and divine." In the ninth parable (ch. 15) the Shepherd calls them virgins, and there are twelve of them: "The first Faith, and the second Self-mastery, and the third Power, and the fourth Long-suffering, and the others standing in the midst of these have the names: Simplicity, Purity, Chastity, Cheerfulness, Truth, Insight, Concord, Love. The one who bears these names and the name of the son of God will be able to enter into the kingdom of God." The Christianity that this beautiful dream depicts is from the beginning to the end a Christianity that lives upon our New Testament and not on books of which we know nothing.

We have a sermon, a homily, written soon after Hermas, and at Rome. It is even barely possible that the Clement whom Hermas above mentions wrote it. We cannot tell. It would have been in that case all the more easy for it to be attributed, as it was for centuries, to the same Clement as the one who wrote the good letter from the Church at Rome to the Church at Corinth. Curiously enough this sermon gives several quotations that do not agree with our Gospels. Undoubtedly it is possible in one or two passages that the writer merely gives the words at haphazard from memory, as has been done even in modern sermons. In other cases the author probably had a Gospel that we do not know the text of, perhaps the Gospel of the Egyptians. He used Old Testament books. That we do not in the course of a single sermon find allusions to the mass of the New Testament, is nothing strange. He, the writer, says (ch. 4), where he is speaking of the Lord: "For He saith, Not every one saying to Me Lord, Lord, shall be saved; but he that

doeth righteousness." That may be from an unknown Gospel,
but it may be his homiletical way of using Matthew's account.
The following, however, gives a new turn (ch. 4): "The Lord said,
If ye were gathered together with Me in My bosom and should
not do My commandments, I will cast you out and say to you,
Begone from Me, I know not whence ye are, workers of lawlessness." If it be not a confused and rewrought shape of several
Gospel passages, we do not know whence it comes. It is good,
plain sermon quotation of our Gospels when he says (ch. 5): "For
the Lord saith, Ye shall be as lambs in the midst of wolves."
If anyone could have called his attention to the words of Jesus:
"Behold, I send you as lambs in the midst of wolves," he would
at once have replied: "That is just what I said, Ye shall be
as lambs in the midst of wolves." For a mind of that kind in
a sermon a general approach in thoughts and words is more
than enough to justify the phrase: The Lord saith. In another
place he uses words which we find in a like form in Irenæus
and in Hilary. They are in a measure a rounding off of a
passage in Luke, and they may have stood in the original
book of Matthew of which we spoke at the outset: "For the
Lord saith in the Gospel, If ye keep not that which is little,
who will give you that which is great? For I say unto you
that the one faithful in the least is faithful also in much." One
of the phrases used by this sermon-writer confirms for us his
careless way of writing, yet it throws light upon the position
which the New Testament books were then beginning to take
as of a similar value to the Scriptures of the Old Testament, and
it at the same time uses them as of authority: "I account you
not ignorant that the living Church is Christ's body . . . and
that the books and the apostles [say] the Church is not from
now but from before." The books are the Old Testament, it
is the Bible; and the apostles are here the New Testament.
There is not the least reason to suppose that this preacher used
any other New Testament than ours, in spite of his quotations
from a strange Gospel or so. We know that a few such books
were in existence, and that they were occasionally used. Nothing
indicates that the strange Gospel was to supplant one of the
four Gospels.

A few lines, in two chapters, make up the second part of
what is called above the Letter to Diognetus. Nothing betrays

to us the origin or purpose of these few lines distinctly, if the close may not be supposed to be the close of a sermon. The style is florid but lofty. The author describes clearly for us (ch. 11) in one well turned sentence his Bible and its union with the Church: "Then the fear of the law is sounded abroad, and the grace of the prophets is made known, and the faith of the Gospels is grounded, and the tradition of the apostles is guarded, and the grace of the Church leaps for joy." There we have the law, the prophets, the Gospels, and the apostles. The word tradition used for the apostles no more points away from the books to the living tradition by word of mouth than the grace of the prophets applies to something not in the Old Testament. The author refers (ch. 12) to First Corinthians: "Knowledge puffeth up, but love buildeth up." The Word appears everywhere in this fragment, and the writer must have known John.

It appeared from what we said above that the great spirit, even if the somewhat unmanageable one, between Paul and Origen was Marcion. He passed through the Church and the Churches like a storm, tearing much down here and there, building some things up, and certainly inspiring many souls with loftier thoughts of God and with more intense devotion to purity of personal life than they had cherished before. Justin the Martyr was of a totally different character. His name fills, nevertheless, a very large place in the annals of the early Church, in the chronicles of the second Christian century. He was born probably about the year 100, near Jacob's Well, for the Greek family from which he sprang lived at Nabulus, Flavia Neapolis, old Sychar, Sichem. The Greek Samaritan was of cooler metal than the Paphlagonian, and instead of starting out with a certain thesis that alone was truth, he set out to seek the truth among the philosophers of his day, and he closed his eventful life at Rome as a martyr probably in the year 165.

The order and success of his quest is very interesting. He tells Trypho the Jew about it in his dialogue with him (ch. 2). "I at first . . . handed myself over to a Stoic. And I having spent enough time with him, since nothing more was imparted to me about God (for he neither knew himself, nor did he say that this was a necessary object of study), I changed from him and came to another called a Peripatetic, in his own opinion a keen man. And this one, after enduring me the first few days, wished me then to name his fee, so that the intercourse should not be with-out benefit for us. And him I left for that reason, not thinking him to be in the least a philosopher. My soul was, however, still all aglow to hear the genuine and lofty side of philosophy, and I went to a very celebrated Pythagorean, a man who laid great store in philosophy. And then as I conversed with him, wishing to become a hearer and close pupil of his: What then? Art thou at home in Music and Astronomy and Geometry? Or dost thou think that thou canst perceive any of the things that conduce to happiness, if thou hast not first learned these things which draw the soul from the things of sense and prepare it to use the things of the mind?" Justin was rather discomfited when the Pytha-gorean sent him away. But he thought of the Platonists, and went to them. They pleased him. The theory of the ideas gave wings to his thoughts, and he soon became so puffed up that he thought he might hope soon to see God. Wishing to consider some things quietly he went out towards the sea (perhaps from Ephesus). There a very old and mild and holy man met him and asked him about philosophy only at last to tell him of Christ. Remember what was said above about Chris-tianity as a life. Justin relates (ch. 8): "I took fire at once in my soul, and a love seized me for the prophets and for those men who are Christ's friends. And considering with myself his words, I found that this was the only safe and useful philosophy. Thus and therefore am I a philosopher." Carping souls have sometimes suggested that Justin remained to the end more a philosopher than a Christian. His story of this first acquaintance with Christianity is not marked by a lack of warmth. Must every Christian be as hotheaded as Marcion? And Justin went about in his philosopher's robe persuading men with tongue and pen that Jesus was better than all the philosophers.

Were we not sure that our four Gospels were by this time as a simple matter of ecclesiastical and literary necessity long domiciled at Rome, long known on all the main roads and in all the chief towns of Christian frequence, Justin would be the one to assure us of it. The examination of his testimony will be in more than one way instructive. The great question in respect to any author who quotes texts is, how he quotes. We wish to know whether he gets down a roll every time he wishes to refer to a sentence, or whether he writes down the general sense and the words as they occur to him in dashing them off with a quick pen.   There are so many quotations in Justin that we are not at a loss for material to examine.   Now these quotations are to a large extent from the Old Testament.   There we are on neutral ground.   There no one can think that we are trying to save the appearances of a canonical Gospel or to avoid the words of an uncanonical one.   The first remark to be made is the curious one that Justin in various quotations from the Septuaginta translation of the Old Testament agrees strikingly with Paul in words which do not coincide with those in the common text. Now this is not to be explained by the theory that Paul and Justin both happened to make precisely the same deviations in trying to give the same verses.   The reason seems clearly to be this, that Justin knew the Epistles of Paul so well that all the passages from the Old Testament in them took for him the form that Paul had clothed them with.   Justin says to Trypho the Jew (ch. 39): "It is nothing marvellous, I continued, if you hate us who know these things, and denounce your ever hard-hearted mind. For Elias, too, begging for you to God, says: Lord, Thy prophets have they slain, and Thy altars have they torn down ; and I alone am left, and they seek my life.   And He answers him, I still have seven thousand men who have not bent their knee to Baal."   In the main point that is Paul's way of quoting this passage in Romans.   And, the one difference of a few words is probably due to a slip in Justin's memory.

Another check is to be found in the passages that Justin quotes more than once, for we find in a large number of cases that he does not give precisely the same words each time.   It is not singular, after we are thus sure that he is quoting out of his head, that we find him naming the wrong author for a passage, Jeremiah for Isaiah, or Hosea for Zechariah.   If he names the passage more than once, he may have the name right in one place and wrong in another.   Sometimes he combines various passages that fit together into the thought and expression.   Sometimes he warps the words to suit his point.   And ever and ever again, by the sovereign right of a writer to give the sense without regard to words, he quotes the Greek Old Testament in such a way that if it were the text of the Gospels many an investigator would be inclined to call it a quotation from an unknown Gospel.   If that be the way in which

Justin cites the Scriptures of the Old Testament, we may in advance feel sure that he will not act in the least differently when he refers to the words of the New Testament. Strange that we so often berate men for cleaving to the letter in their words, and that we in this case because of a modern view of the holiness and intangibility of the words of the Bible, a view based partly on the post-Christian Jewish Masoretic habits, are so much discontented with these ancient worthies who strike at the heart of the matter and think nothing of the form. Do we, when we feel stirred against the writers and preachers who quote carelessly,— do we ever reflect upon the fact that we are not able to say what book of the Wisdom of God Jesus refers to towards the end of the eleventh chapter of Luke? "On this account also the Wisdom of God said, I will send to them prophets and apostles, and some of them they will slay and will persecute, in order that the blood of all the prophets that was shed from the founding of the world should be demanded of this generation, from the blood of Abel till the blood of Zacharias, who was slain between the altar and the house." If Jesus could quote God's Wisdom so that we cannot verify His words, much more may late writers like Justin allow themselves a certain freedom in the use of Gospel texts.

Before we enter upon the examination of his use of the words of Jesus, we must refer to the name that he employs for the books from which he draws these words. He does not usually call them Gospels. We must bear in mind that the title Gospel was not at first attached to each of the books. In Justin's three genuine works which have been preserved, the two (one) Apologies and the Dialogue with Trypho, we find references to the Gospel in the singular, Trypho speaks thus, and to the Memoirs or Memorabilia which are Apomnemoneumata precisely like Xenophon's Memorabilia. Eight times he calls these memoirs: "Memoirs by the Apostles." Four times he calls them only: "Memoirs." Once he calls them: "Memoirs composed by the Apostles of Christ and by those who followed with them." In this latter case he quotes Luke. And once, in quoting Mark on the name Jesus gave Peter and on the name Boanerges for James and John, he calls them: "Peter's Memoirs," doubtless in allusion to the account in Papias that Mark wrote down Peter's words. The writers of the Gospels, that is to say, of these Memoirs, Justin calls Apostles in one place, for he says : "the Apostles wrote," and adds a point given in all four Gospels. He refers to these writers (Apol. 33) as : "those who have written memoirs of all things concerning our Saviour Jesus Christ whom we believe."

Justin also tells us something else about these books, something that is very important and that will take our thoughts back to the usages and habits in the divine services in the early Christian Church. It is well on in his Apology for the Christians to the heathen emperor (ch. 67), and he describes the weekly worship of the Christians : "On the day called the day of the Sun a gathering takes place of all who live in the towns or in the country in one place, and the memoirs of the apostles or the writings of the prophets are read, so long as the time permits. Then the reader stops and the leader impresses by word of mouth, and urges to imitation of, these good things. Then we all stand up together and send forth prayers." Here it is plain that in the circles that Justin was acquainted with, these Memoirs, whatever they were, were not regarded as being upon a very different plane from the Scriptures of the Old Testament. It is true that he does not speak with great exactness. It would be possible for him to say what he says, even if the Memoirs were still regarded as human books, were only read in the public services under the heading of : Man to Men. Nevertheless, after making every allowance, it must be granted that when he names the Memoirs before the Old Testament Scriptures, he really places them not merely on a level with them, but above them. Of course, the writings of the prophets must here include the Law. He is only giving a general description.

The fact that Justin causes Trypho to speak of the Gospel in the singular has nothing to do with the use of one Gospel book instead of the four Gospels. Even to-day, a writer or orator does not hesitate to speak of what we find in the Gospel, meaning merely in the Gospel story of Jesus, and totally irrespective of the point whether the matter in question happens to stand in only one of the four Gospels or in two or in all four. And whatever may happen to-day, we have many a writer of the time following that of Justin who says Gospel in the singular ; for example, Theophilus of Antioch, Irenæus, Clement of Alexandria,

Origen, Hippolytus, and Tertullian. Thus far, then, we have found that Justin speaks of the Gospel, of the Gospels, but especially of the "Memoirs of his Apostles," a form used five times,—a form in which "his" can refer to no one but Jesus. Let us count it up : Justin, who as a Christian philosopher has passed through many lands, knows books telling of Jesus, written by His apostles and by those who followed with them, called Gospels. He calls them Memoirs. Has the name Memoirs any particular value for Justin or for anyone else ? Scarcely. It was probably a mere philological fancy of Justin's that was born with him and died with him. It undoubtedly fitted well into his discussions with men of classical training to be able to use thus Xenophon's word as an introduction for the written story of Jesus. Otherwise the word was not of the least importance. We may therefore let the word Memoirs pass and take up the word Gospels, for Justin says they are also called Gospels.

Does anything go to show that Justin had among the number of these Gospels a Gospel that we do not possess among our four Gospels ? He speaks of Christ as born in a cave, of the Wise Men as from Arabia, and of Christ's making ploughs and yokes as a carpenter, all of which is not in our Gospels. But then that is not in other serious Gospels, and it is nothing to us whether Justin got it from verbal tradition or from some current apocryphal Gospel. We certainly have no ground to expect in advance that he would name for our special benefit every New Testament book that he knew of. He does mention one book besides the Gospels, and that is the Revelation. It is in the Dialogue with Trypho (ch. 81) : " And then, too, a certain man of our number, his name was John, one of the apostles of the Christ, prophesied in a revelation made to him that those who believed in our Christ would spend a thousand years in Jerusalem, and that after this the general and, in a word, the eternal resurrection of all like one man would take place, and the judgment." That is the only other book of the New Testament that he names.

When we examine the words that he quotes from the Memoirs and ask ourselves whether or not they could be, could have been drawn from our four Gospels, we must at once recall what we learned from the examination of his quotations from the Old Testament. It is not the habit of Justin to take down a roll and copy off a sentence carefully when he wishes to quote it.   He reproduces a passage from the Old Testament just as it comes into his thoughts, and we may be sure that he will do exactly the same with the New Testament.   Ezra Abbot examined this matter and placed the results, as follows, far beyond the reach of doubt.   In the sixty-first chapter of the Apology Justin describes baptism : "Those who are persuaded and believe that these things which we teach and say are true, and promise to be able to live thus, are taught to pray fasting and beseech God for the remission of the former sins, we praying and fasting with them.   Then they are led by us to a place where there is water, and in the manner of new birth, in which we ourselves also were new born, they are born again.   For in the name of the Father of all things and Master God and of our Saviour Jesus Christ and of Holy Spirit they then undergo the washing in the water.   For the Christ also said : If ye be not born again, ye shall in no wise enter into the kingdom of the heavens.   But that it is impossible for those who have once been born to enter into the wombs of those who bore them is clear to all."   Now in the third chapter of John we read : "Jesus answered and said to him— that is, to Nicodemus— : Verily, verily, I say unto thee, Except a man be born anew, he cannot see the kingdom of God. Nicodemus saith to Him : How can a man be born when he is old?   Can he enter a second time into his mother's womb, and be born?   Jesus answered, Verily, verily, I say unto thee, Except a man be born of water and the Spirit, he cannot enter into the kingdom of God."   For a man who did not already know how Justin quotes, the difference between the words in Justin and those in John might in truth seem to exclude the suggestion that Justin was really quoting from John.   Careful investigation shows, however, in the first place, that pretty much all the omissions made here and there by Justin have also been made by well-known Church writers of a later date, and who certainly quoted John.   As for the changes in words, so that the sense rather than the form of John is reproduced, these changes are to be matched in similar later writers, some of them ten times, some of them twenty times, some of them sixty times.

The last touch of proof for the thorough nothingness of the claim that Justin was here using some unknown apocryphal Gospel, is given by a comparison of the use of this text in the writings of the famous English clergyman Jeremy Taylor, who died in 1667. He quoted this passage at least nine times. It scarcely need be said that he got it from the English version of the Gospel of John and not from an unknown Gospel. Now Jeremy Taylor writes every time "Unless" instead of "Except"; that is so uniform, it must, of course, be another Gospel. He writes six times "kingdom of heaven" for "kingdom of God"; that is a great difference; the kingdom of heaven is like Matthew. Once he says merely "heaven" instead of "kingdom of God." He writes four times "shall not enter" instead of "cannot enter." He writes the second person plural "ye" twice instead of the third person singular. He writes once "baptized with water" instead of "born of water." He writes once "born again of water" instead of "born of water." He writes once "both of water and the Spirit" instead of "of water and of the Spirit." He omits "of" before Spirit six times. He adds "holy" before Spirit twice. We see that in spite of the ease with which an English clergyman in the seventeenth century could refer to the text of a Gospel passage, he did not do it. What wonder that Justin did not do it in the second century, when he would have had to unroll a roll and look around for the words. Even the Book of Common Prayer quotes this passage twice alike, and wrong. That one passage shows of itself that Justin used the Fourth Gospel. He probably used all four Gospels.

The thought that Justin did not know our Gospels, but used apocryphal ones, finds a very good blocking-off in a single passage. In speaking of Jesus' baptism (Dial. 103), Justin gives as addressed to Him the heavenly words: "Thou art My Son. This day have I begotten Thee." These words are in some of our witnesses to-day for the passage in Luke. Now Justin does not attribute these words to the Memoirs, but adds after these words that in the Memoirs of the Apostles the devil is then described as having come to Him and tempted Him. He appears to distinguish between the Memoirs and the source of that addition. It was seen above that Justin said that the Memoirs were from the apostles and from those who followed them. That looks as if Justin had in view Matthew and John as apostles, and Mark and Luke as followers of apostles. A passage in the Dialogue (ch. 88) appears to confirm this thought by referring to something given alone by Matthew and John, as written by the apostles; it is the only passage in which Justin says the apostles have written: "And then when Jesus came to the river Jordan, where John was baptizing, as Jesus went down into the water also fire was kindled in the Jordan; and when He came up from the water, like a dove the Holy Spirit flew upon Him, wrote the apostles of this our Christ." It is that last part for which Justin appeals to the apostles as if meaning that that was told by Matthew and John, in whose Gospels it is.

In telling Trypho of the vast love of God and His readiness to take men who are willing to come to Him, Justin gives us a word, a saying of Jesus that is not in our Gospels. It may have passed from the tradition by word of mouth to the Gospel of the Hebrews. After quoting Ezekiel, Justin continues (ch. 47): "For this reason also our Lord Jesus Christ said: In whatsoever things I shall light upon you, in these also I shall judge you." We might instead of "light upon" say directly "catch" you. In another passage in the Dialogue (ch. 35), Justin quotes two passages from Matthew, and in between them the words: "And there shall be schisms and heresies." This occurs in another form in the Clementines. It may be a word of Jesus. But it may also be a vague deduction from some words of Paul that came to be attributed to Jesus. That is all that Justin gives us from possible other Gospels. It is not much.

What Justin says about Jesus is then almost without exception precisely what our Gospels gave him, and we may be positively sure that he got it out of no other Gospels. He exaggerated it may be, as when he writes that Herod killed all the male children in Bethlehem; but that might befall a writer at any date who liked strong statements. In like manner he declares that the first Jewish calumniators of the Christians at the resurrection sent picked men out into the whole world denouncing the theft of the body of Jesus and the false story of the resurrection and ascension. That was a very easy stretching of the story in Matthew. A story-teller would regard it as altogether legitimate. In some passages we may hesitate whether to suppose that he himself was the author of a certain addition to or an exegesis of Gospel words, or whether to assume that he had heard them from others as he travelled about. Some of them may have been rabbinic Jewish interpretations which had passed over into Jewish Christian and Christian circles. For example, it makes us think of the writer of our Gospel of Matthew when we read that Justin first quotes Moses (Apol. 54): "A ruler shall not fail from Judah. . . . And he shall be the longing of the Gentiles, binding to the vine his foal," and, as he recounts the fulfilment of all the details of the prophecy, assures us: "For a certain foal of an ass stood in a byway of the village bound to a vine." He may just as well here be following Jewish commentators on Messianic passages. The writer of the Gospel of Matthew would scarcely have failed to add that vine, if he had thought of it, and have declared: "That took place in order that the words might be fulfilled."

Justin's books are full of scripture, full of gospel matter. The gospel matter is from our four Gospels precisely as we must look for it to be. Justin is a witness for widely separated countries and Churches, from Palestine to Rome. The philosopher has been of no less value to us than the Paphlagonian spiritual giant and stormy reformer. Justin quotes from memory. He sometimes quotes much at random. He adds to one book words from another. He combines two or three passages into one unwittingly. But in all he shows that the gospel history for him is precisely the history that we have in our four Gospels; he has nothing to add to it and nothing to take away from it. This circumstance is the more noteworthy because we know that he was so widely travelled and so well informed. He cannot but have known of some of the Gospels that are sometimes named, the Gospel of the Hebrews and the Gospel of the Egyptians, for example. But, if he knows of them, he does not bother about them. He does not search out for peculiar statements about Jesus and the words of Jesus in them in order to lay them before us as curiosities. And now it is worth while to observe that Justin's writings were probably written before the year 165, his Apology before the year 154. The best opinion thus far is that he died about the year 165. Supposing that the original ante-evangelical book that we conjecture to have been written by Matthew was written about the year 67, there would have elapsed from it to the year 154 only ninety years. If we regard it as likely that Justin became a Christian by the year 133, that would have been little more than sixty years, and within those sixty years we should have to place the writing and the earliest using of our four Gospels. That is no large margin of time for the preparation of and the spreading abroad of a number of unknown books which should have filled the places later held by our Gospels. Justin had every chance to know all that was before the eyes of Christians in the Roman Empire shortly before and ten years after the year 150, and he betrays no knowledge of books highly valued by them and neither to-day in our New Testament nor known to us.

Just after referring to the letters of Ignatius, we had occasion to speak of certain words that Papias had related as from a presbyter John. It is now time to speak of Papias himself. He must have been born long before the year 100, for he was apparently an older contemporary of Polycarp, and we may suppose that he was born about the year 80.

He may have been a heathen by birth. His name rather points to that. And the name fits well for a boy born at Hierapolis. Eusebius speaks slightingly of his mental calibre, but we do not need to think less of him on that account. Eusebius was one of the cool scientific people who looked back to the great Alexandrian and Syrian schools with pride. He had little patience with the fancies of the millenarians in Asia Minor. Eusebius writes, then (H. E. 3. 39), of Papias in the following strain, after he has given various things out of Papias : " And the same [writer] adds further other matter as if it had reached him from an unwritten tradition, both some strange parables of the Saviour and strange teachings of his, and some other things rather of a mythical kind. Among which he also says that the kingdom of Christ will exist bodily upon this very earth a thousand years after the resurrection from the dead. Which I think he assumed through misconception of the apostolical explanations, not having himself seen what was told to them mystically in certain signs. For he appears to have been exceedingly small in mind, as can be put forth so to speak from his own words. Besides, he has been the chief cause (Eusebius would say: of the absurd opinions) also for the most of those churchly men after him of a like opinion with himself, they hiding themselves behind the great antiquity of the man, as, for example, Irenæus, and if there is any other that has come to light thinking the like things. And he hands down also in his book other discussions of the word of the Lord by Ariston, the one above alluded to, and traditions

7

of the presbyter John, to which remanding those eager to learn, we shall here of necessity add to the former words presented [from his book] a tradition which, alluding to Mark who wrote the Gospel, is put forth in these words. And this the presbyter said : Mark the interpreter of Peter wrote accurately as many things as he [Peter] related, yet not in order, of the things said or done by the Christ. For he neither heard the Lord nor followed with Him, but afterwards as I said with Peter, who gave teachings according as they were necessary, but not as setting forth a connected system of the Lord's words. So that Mark made no mistake, writing down some things thus as he remembered them. For he gave attention to one thing, not to leave out anything that he heard or to say anything false among what [he gave]."

Papias' whole neighbourhood was millenarian, and he could not suspect that a Church historian two hundred years later would throw that up to him. For our purpose Papias' five books, the Explanations of the Lord's Sayings, would, we think, be invaluable. They may still be found in some corner of the East. Irenæus refers thus to the fourth book (Eus. H. E. 3. 39) : " This Papias the hearer of John, and the companion of Polycarp, an ancient man, testifies in writing in the fourth of his books." " Papias himself, however, (Eusebius continues) shows in the preface to his Words that he was in no wise himself a hearer and beholder of the holy apostles, and he teaches in the following words that he received the things of faith from those who were the acquaintances of them : ' I shall not hesitate to weave together with the comments for thee such things as I at any time learned well from the elders and kept well in memory, since I am convinced of their truth. For I did not take pleasure, as most people do, in those who say a great deal, but in those that teach the true things ; and not in those who relate foreign commandments, but in those [who relate] the commandments given to faith by the Lord, and coming from the truth itself. If, forsooth, also someone came who had followed with the presbyters, I sought after the words of the presbyters ; what Andrew, or what Peter said, or what Philip, or what Thomas or James, or what John or Matthew, or what any other of the disciples of the Lord, and what both Aristion and the presbyter John, the disciples of the Lord, say. For I did not account it that the things from the books were to me of so much profit as the things from a living and remaining voice.' Where also it is worthy of note, that he counts the name John twice, the former of which he combines with Peter and James and Matthew and the rest of the apostles, clearly aiming at the evangelist; and the other John, interpunctuating his discourse, he orders among the others who are aside from the number of the apostles, putting Aristion before him, and he clearly names him a presbyter. Thus also by this we have a proof that the history of the two who are said to have had the same name is true, and it is also said that at Ephesus in Asia there are tombs still to-day for each one of the Johns. To which also it is necessary to pay attention. For it is likely that the second, unless someone should wish that it were the first, saw the revelation that is in our hands said to be of John. And this Papias now before us confesses that he received the words of the apostles from those who followed with them, but says that he himself was an own hearer of Aristion and of the presbyter John. Accordingly, often referring to them by name in his books, he lays before our view their traditions. And this shall not be said to us for no profit. It is also worth while to add to the words of Papias presented, other sayings of his in which he relates some paradoxical things, and other things as if they had reached him by tradition. The fact then that Philip the apostle together with his daughters lived at Hierapolis is made known by the forefathers. And Papias being at that [place] relates that he received a miraculous story from the daughters of Philip, which is noteworthy. For he relates that a resurrection of a dead man took place in his day, and again another paradoxical thing that took place about Justus the one called Barsabas, as drinking a poisonous medicine and experiencing nothing disagreeable by the grace of the Lord."

Eusebius tells us that Papias quotes First John and First Peter, for he is looking up the witnesses for the books that are less well attested. He also mentions that Papias has the story of the Adulteress, which he says is also in the Gospel of the Hebrews. That does not in the least make us sure that that story belonged to that Gospel. It may have been thrust into it, just as it was thrust into the Gospel of John. The story is doubtless good tradition, wherever it started. Irenæus gives us a good view of what was possible in the way of millennial exegesis at the hands of a Papias, and we need not remark that Irenæus as a millenarian was well contented with it.

Irenæus quotes (5. 33) the words of Jesus from Matthew: " I will not drink henceforth of the fruit of this vine, until that day when I drink it new with you in My Father's kingdom," and insists upon the earthly, the terrestrial character of this kingdom, because real wine could only be drunk by real men. After referring to sayings of Jesus touching the rewards that those who have done or have suffered for Him shall receive in a clearly mundane sphere, he states that the patriarchs had a right to look for the fulfilment of the promises to them in a solid earthly form, and not in vague heavenly blessings. Here he then draws from Papias. " As the presbyters recounted, who saw John the disciple of the Lord, that they had heard from him, how the Lord used to teach about those days and to say : The days will come in which vines shall grow, each one having ten thousand shoots, and on each shoot ten thousand branches, and on each branch again ten thousand twigs, and on each single twig ten thousand clusters, and in each single cluster ten thousand grapes, and each single grape when pressed shall give twenty-five measures of wine. And when any one of the saints shall have taken hold of one of the bunches, another will cry out : I am a better bunch. Take me. Bless the Lord through me. In like manner also a grain of wheat shall bring forth ten thousand heads, and each single head will have ten thousand grains, and each single grain will give five double pounds of fine pure flour. And the rest, apples and seeds and grass, according to the same manner. And all the animals using these things for food which are received from the earth will become peaceful and ready each in its place, subject to men in all subjection. And those things also Papias the hearer of John and the companion of Polycarp, an ancient man, testifies in writing in the fourth of his books. For he put together five books. And he added saying : These things are credible to those who believe. And Judas, he said, the traitor not believing but asking : How then shall such growths be brought about by the Lord? the Lord said : Those will see who shall come to these [times]."

We can easily imagine how Eusebius, who was no millenarian, despised a writer who delighted in these fancies ; but we shall nevertheless not regard these fancies as enough to put Papias into the class of weak-minded men. Papias was clearly a wideawake man, ready and eager to learn from any and every source. Can we form any judgment as to what the sayings of the Lord were about which Papias wrote his comments? Put the question differently. Does anything that we learned in Eusebius or in Irenæus about Papias and about his comments give us a chance to suspect that in those five books he considered words of Jesus that are not to be found in our Gospels? Were his comments framed upon the Gospel to the Hebrews, or on the Gospel to the Egyptians, or were they based upon all sorts and descriptions of single sayings of Jesus that he had gathered together? We have no reason to think of anything of that kind. How eagerly would Eusebius have told us of the contents of the book had that been its description! How would Anastasius of Sinai in the sixth century have revelled in a book with new words of Jesus! No. Papias' book may well have here and there reproduced an unknown saying of Jesus, as, for example, in the supposed reply to Judas a moment ago. But his five books were probably a collection of all manner of traditions out of those early years which would answer many a question that we should like to have answered, but give us twice as many new questions to answer.

Papias' Comments will probably in no special way increase our knowledge of the direct words of Jesus. But we should like to have them nevertheless. The importance of Papias for the criticism of the use of the books of the New Testament lies not only in his having lived before the death of the Apostle John, and in his having lived until the middle or ten years after the middle of the second century. That stretch of years is extremely interesting, it is true, but Polycarp has already given us the beginning of the period and carried us well towards the end of it. Papias' weight for us is increased because he comes from another and that an important town, Hierapolis, in another province, Phrygia, and indeed from a town that has for us another trifling memory of interest.

For the evangelist Philip, one of the seven chosen in the sixth chapter of Acts, and who in the twenty-first chapter was at Cæsarea, after went to Hierapolis and died and was buried there; and Papias appears to have seen Philip's daughters with his own eyes. That is a new proof for the way in which Christians travelled in those days, and a new hook for the fastening of the genuineness of the books and of the lives of the apostles and of the followers of the apostles. It is not the case that a great gap separates the time of Paul from the time of Papias, for example. The years were closely interwoven with the threads of human lives.   Paul stayed several days in Philip's house at Cæsarea, and Philip's four prophesying, virgin daughters must then have been more than mere children, else they would not have prophesied. At least two ·of the daughters and perhaps all four lived later with Philip at Hierapolis.   Can we suppose that they forgot that Paul had spent several days at their house at Cæsarea?   They may well have spoken of Paul to Papias, if Papias when he saw them was more than a little boy.   This is not to be called playing with earnest things.   This is scientific consideration of the facts of personal intercourse, which go to connect the earliest period of Christianity with the beginnings of a more definitely tangible and in a literary way more firmly based history in the middle of the second century.   Whether or not Philip had seen Jesus, we do not know.   It is possible that he had seen Him.   It is further to be kept in mind that Papias was not a mere lay member of the Church at Hierapolis, but its bishop, one, therefore, who will have had every opportunity and every right to have searched out carefully all the memories of the past in those circles.

Papias refers to presbyters, to elders who had furnished him with valuable information from former times.   That was due and proper tradition.   We have a similar reference to presbyters in Irenæus, and it will be worth our while to see what these presbyters to whom Irenæus refers have to tell us touching the books of the New Testament.   Irenæus writes, for example: " As I heard from a certain presbyter, who had heard from those who had seen the apostles and from those who had learned (who had themselves been apostles?): that for the older circles in the case of things which they did without the counsel of the spirit, the blame was enough which was taken from the Scriptures.   For since God is no respecter of persons, He placed a fitting blame on things not done according to His decree."   After giving examples from David and Solomon, Irenæus continues: " The scripture bore hard in upon him, as the presbyter said, so that no flesh may boast in the sight of the Lord.   And that for this reason the Lord went down to the parts below the earth, preaching the gospel of His coming also to them, there being a remission of sins for those who believe on Him.   But their deeds—the deeds of the great ones of the Old Testament—were written for our

correction, that we should know first of all that our God and
theirs is one, whom sins do not please, even when they are done
by great men ; and in the next place that we refrain from evils.
We should not therefore say that the elders were proud, nor
should we blame those of old times, but ourselves fear, lest by
chance after having recognised Christ, doing something that does
not please God, we should have no further remission of our
offences, but should be shut out from His kingdom. And that
therefore Paul said : For if He did not spare the natural branches,
lest He by chance spare not thee, who being a wild olive was
inserted in the fat olive and wast made a companion of its
fatness : and similarly seeing that the prevarications of the people
are described, not because of those who then transgressed, but
for our correction, and that we should know that it is one and
the same God against whom they then used to sin, and against
whom some now sin who say that they have believed. And that
the apostle had most clearly shown this in the Epistle to the
Corinthians, saying : I would not that ye should be ignorant . . .
let him see to it that he fall not."

"The presbyters used to show that those were very senseless
who from the things which happened to those who of old
did not obey God, try to introduce another father." This
is evidently pointed at men who like Marcion condemned
the cruelty of the God of the Old Testament and explained
that the New Testament and Christ proceeded from a totally
different God who is a loving Father. Irenæus proceeds
with the presbyters : "On the contrary, placing over against that
how great things the Lord's coming had done for the purpose of
saving those who received Him, pitying them. But remaining
silent as to His judgment and as to what shall happen to those
who have heard His words and have not done them, and that it
were better for them if they had never been born, and that it will
be more tolerable for Sodom and Gomorra in the judgment than
for that city which did not receive the word of His disciples."
Against similar deprecation of theft commanded by the God of
the Old Testament another passage is directed : " Who, moreover,
blame it and reckon it [for evil] that the people when about to
set out, by the command of God received vessels of all kinds, and
robes from the Egyptians, and thus departed, from which things
also the tabernacle was made in the desert, not knowing the

justifications of God and His arrangements they prove themselves [bad] as also the presbyter used to say."

Another passage aims at the same false views, and brings a phrase that particularly interests us: "In the same manner also the presbyter, the disciple of the apostles, used to discourse about the two Testaments, showing that they were both from one and the same God. For neither was there another God besides Him that made and shaped us, nor had the words of those any foundation who say that this world which is in our day was made by angels or by some other power or by some other God." The calling the presbyter a disciple of the apostles is probably a slip of Irenæus', or it may be of his translator's, for this is only extant in Latin. The great point here for our purpose is that Irenæus makes the presbyter speak of the two Testaments, that is to say of the Old and the New Testament. This fits in with what we shall in a moment relate about Melito of Sardes. Unfortunately, however, in an account of this remote kind we cannot tell whether the presbyter himself really used the expression Testaments or not. He may have used it. But it is (1) presbyter, (2) Irenæus, (3) translator before it reaches us. In another place Irenæus does not write the word presbyter, but "one of those who went before": "And as a certain one of those who went before said, [Christ] by the (divine) stretching forth of His hands was bringing the two peoples together to the one God." That is a beautiful thought for the crucifixion.

In another passage we simply have an unknown earlier author whom Irenæus quotes, how much earlier does not appear. "God does all things in measure and in order, and there is with Him nothing unmeasured, because there is nothing unnumbered. And someone said well that the unmeasured Father Himself is measured in the Son. For the Son is a measure of the Father, since He also receives Him." Once Irenæus says that the earlier Christians were better than those of his day: "Wherefore those who were before us and indeed much better than we, nevertheless could not sufficiently reply to those who were of the school of Valentinus." Our Lord's age Irenæus knows from tradition: "But that the first age of thirty years is the youthful disposition and reached up to the fortieth year, everyone will agree. From the fortieth, however, and the fiftieth year it declines already towards the older age, in possession of which our Lord used to teach as the Gospel and all the presbyters testify, who came together with John the disciple of the Lord in Asia, that John handed this down." It is likely that the source for these references of Irenæus to the presbyters was Polycarp. "But certain of them saw not only John, but also other apostles ; and they heard these same things from them, and witness to an account of this kind." All this shows us the living fulness of these years for the Christians. It is totally false to suppose that the books of the New Testament were during all these years living a merely tentative life, and that they were not in the common possession of the mass of Christians.

Polycarp was bishop at Smyrna, Papias was bishop at Hierapolis, Melito was bishop at Sardes. We mention him here in the post-apostolic age as standing near to the other two earlier bishops with whom he probably had much to do. Melito presented his Apology to Marcus Antoninus probably in the year 176, but other writings of his are of an earlier time. Onesimus asked Melito to make what we might call an anthology, a bunch of flowers, from the Law and the Prophets touching the Saviour and the faith in general, and apparently asked him to give what we might name an introduction to the Old Testament, that is to say, some explanations, presumably for Christians who had been originally heathen, about the old books. Melito took the matter seriously and went to the East to make researches about the books and the events. "Melito to Onesimus the brother, greetings. Since thou often didst in thy zeal for the word demand that selections should be made both from the Law and the Prophets about the Saviour and all our faith, and thou, moreover, didst earnestly take counsel to learn the details about the old books, how many their number and what their order might be, I hasten to do this, understanding thy zeal for the faith and thy love for learning about the word, and because thou placest before all things these questions in thy longing towards God, striving for eternal salvation. Having therefore gone to the East and reached the place where [it all] was preached and came to pass, and having learned exactly the books of the Old Testament, I have sent a list of them." Of course when Onesimus asked about the old books, he must have had new books also in mind. And when Melito sent him a list of the Old Testament books, he must have thought of a New Testament as the other side. But we have no list of New Testament books from him, although we know that he wrote a book on the Revelation.

After the list of the books Melito said to Onesimus : " From which also I made the selections, dividing them into six books." I confess to a certain surprise in the thought that Melito of Sardes really went to Palestine in order to search out the names of the books of the Old Testament and to make the selections from them.   I had altogether forgotten that he thus appears to show that the books of the Old Testament were not in their entirety at his command in Sardes.   To reflect upon the matter, I have been inclined to think that in the larger synagogues in the great cities of the Roman Empire the Jews had in their hands, as a rule, all or the most of the books of the Old Testament.   It is true that Melito's case does not directly clash with this thought, since it would have been possible, conceivable, that at Melito's day the authorities in a Jewish synagogue would refuse to show their holy books to a Christian bishop.   Yet possible as this may be, I do not regard it as likely.   The Jews are not known as book concealers.   I am the rather inclined to assume that Melito's words find their point in the two thoughts, first that the number of the books was differently given by different Jews ; and second, that Melito wished both for authoritative certainty as to the number, which he thought most properly to be sought in the East, and for an authoritative text from which to make the selections desired by Onesimus.   Further, I think that the greater knowledge of the exegete who has been upon the ground, was a special object of Melito's in his journey.   In any case we must use this lateral testimony of Melito's to repress our inclination to think that each great Christian Church must have of necessity had a complete set of the books of the Old Testament.   The great Churches will probably have had the Law and the Prophets and the Psalms.   It is not impossible that many a Jewish synagogue in the diaspora had no more of the Old Testament than this.

Melito seems to have been a very prolific writer for his time, although but little has been preserved to our day.   We find in his writings quotations from all the books of the New Testament save James and Jude and Second and Third John.   He gives (Fragm. 15) a summary of the life of Jesus in his book on Faith. He writes with an impetus : " From the Law and the Prophets we gather those things which are foretold of our Lord Jesus Christ, so that we may demonstrate to your charity that He is the perfect mind, the Word of God. It is He Himself who was born before the light, He Himself is the Creator with the Father, He Himself is the former of man, He Himself it is who was all things in all: it is He who was the Patriarch in the patriarchs, in the law the Law, among the priests the Chief Priest, among the kings the Ruler, among prophets the Prophet, among angels the Archangel, in voice the Word, among spirits the Spirit, in the Father the Son, in God God, King to the ages of ages. For this is He who to Noah was the Pilot, He who led Abraham, He who was bound with Isaac, He who wandered with Jacob, He who was sold with Joseph, He who was Leader with Moses, He who with Joshua the son of Nun distributed the inheritance, He who through David and the prophets foretold His sufferings: He who in the Virgin became incarnate, He who was born at Bethlehem, He who was swathed in swaddling-bands in the cradle, He who was seen by the shepherds, He who was praised by the angels, He who was worshipped by the wise men, He who was heralded by John, He who gathered together the apostles, He who preached the kingdom, He who healed the lame, He who gave light to the blind, He who raised the dead, He who was seen in the temple, He who was not believed in by the people, He who was betrayed by Judas, He who was seized by the priests, He who was judged by Pilate, He who with nails was fixed to the cross, He who was hung upon the wood, He who was buried in the earth, He who rose from the dead, He who appeared to the apostles, He who was borne above to heaven, He who sits at the right hand of the Father, He who is the Rest of the dead, the Finder of the lost, the Light of those who are in darkness, the Redeemer of captives, the Guide of the erring, the Refuge of the mourning, the Bridegroom of the Church, the Charioteer of the cherubim, the Chief of the army of the angels, God of God, Son from the Father, Jesus Christ King to the ages. Amen." We feel as we read that, that Melito had at least in general our New Testament books. His summing up brings no element that is strange to us.

We have passed by the middle of the second century. The time of the Old Catholic Church is at hand. Christianity is consolidating itself. Among orthodox Christians, among the general body of Christians in the great Church, there is nothing like the violent rending into two parties which was suggested by some scholars in the former century, the nineteenth century. It has sometimes been suggested that Papias, whose writings give very little from Paul, was an opponent of Paul. I should rather take it that Papias did not fully comprehend the difference between his point of view and that of Paul. And I regard it as likely that the fact that we do not see Paul's writings in his text, depends in a large measure upon his dreamy fanciful way of thinking and writing that had no special hold in Pauline Epistles. The Church is essentially one, aside from the great sects, aside from Gnostics, and Marcionists, and Montanists, let us say. But the size of the Church begins to be appreciable. The Christians feel more and more strongly how many men there are, east and west and north and south, for whom they are in a measure responsible, whose opinions are charged to them. And they see in the growing sects a danger for themselves, a danger for the Church. The natural simplicity of the first Christian Church is gone beyond recall. The Churches have already certainly sometimes, like the Church at Smyrna, begun to pray for "peace for the Churches through all the world."

During this period Christianity has had the great task of expansion. It had had the duty laid upon it to go out into all the world and preach and baptize and make disciples. It had through all these years the need of defending itself, of holding its ground against the Jews. But that task has gradually begun to vanish. The Jews have no longer their determining import for the position and acceptance of the Christian communities on the great roads of the Roman Empire. Here and there in remoter corners a little of the old combination of Jew and Christian confuses the gaze of officials from time to time. That is all. Christianity has ever in increasing measure found itself compelled to justify and declare itself over against heathenism. Now an official was suspicious, now one was curious, now one was indifferent, now one was overbearing and cruel. For all their duties the Christians found that the written word was the least important thing for them. Their first and great duty, the preaching, was the continuation of the preaching of the apostles. And that was anything and everything but preaching from texts. It was the heralding of the kingdom of God, the kingdom of the heavens. It was the preaching of the Son of Man, the Son of God. This preaching was not preaching upon the Gospels or out of the Gospels or about the Gospels. It was a Gospel itself. It was such a segment of a Gospel as the time and the place permitted the speaker to lay before his hearers. As for the apostles, the Christians busied themselves less with their words and more with their thoughts. The Greek language, the common language of the Roman Empire, played its part in all this. It was the language of the greater number of the preachers. In it the books of the New Testament were first written. Most of all the Christians asked about the facts, the events of the life of Jesus, less about the notes that had been written down about that life.

But that is beginning to change. The written reports are beginning to excite more interest. The power of tradition by word of mouth is fading gradually away. We see thus far, if we close our eyes to the rough work of Marcion, nothing that looks like the exercise of careful critical judgment in efforts to determine the nature of Christian writings or their origin or their value for the Church, or their possible danger for the minds of the unlearned. No one has thus far come forth with the assumed or with the imposed mission to settle questions about books that should be used for one purpose or another. Marcion alone has taken up these points for his followers, but that is of no interest for the rest of the Christians. The books have had to care for themselves, to make their own way, fight their own battles, lead their own retreats. That does not, however, in the least mean, that the early Christians took, hit or miss without looking at it twice, any book that was thrust into their hands. Far from it. The first books arose in small circles in which each man knew each other. None needed to ask who brought forward the given book. Everyone saw and knew whence the book came. If the book came from afar, from Rome to Corinth or to Ephesus or to Tarsus or to Antioch, each Christian knew again who had brought it, and whence he had brought it, and why he had brought it.

Little by little during all this post-apostolic age the written treasures of the Churches had been growing and gathering. The great Churches in the great cities on the great roads of travel will have at a very early time gotten by far the larger part of what we now have in the New Testament. City after city and Church after Church will have sent in its contribution to the list. In the provinces and in the villages the process will have spread but slowly. There was too little money and too little education to secure for the small places for decades that which had long been in the hands of the large Churches. The same influence wrought in a like manner in reference to other books, to books that were not to the same degree acceptable to the Churches. A certain uncertainty and a vacillating determination will here and there have played a part in helping a book upwards into the more treasured, or downwards into the less favoured regions of Christian literary liking. No authority saw to the due criticism. The book rose or fell. It was more used, it was less used. But one thing was gradually going forth from the process of writing and of preserving and of valuing the books, and that was the general acceptance of the mass of the books of the New Testament as books that were of peculiar value to Christians. This peculiar value showed itself in their being placed with or even placed before the books of the Old Testament. The equality of the two series of books came most distinctly to view in the public services of the Churches. On the other hand, the lack of value that showed itself in the case of other books, was seen more clearly than anywhere else in the fact that these other books were not allowed in the public services of the Churches to claim for themselves the first rank, to reach the point at which they could be read at the chief place in the Church as the expression of words which God had to say to Men.

III.

THE AGE OF IRENÆUS.

160–200.

In the post-apostolic age we found Christians from widely distant lands meeting and crossing each other's paths, and giving witness on one side and on the other to the oneness of the great body of Christians, to the undisturbed sequence of Christian tradition, and to the silently presupposed existence of the more important books of the New Testament. The period to which we now direct our gaze will uphold the character of early Christianity in respect to widely spread Churches, and in respect to men of letters who journeyed afar, and who were therefore able to give practical examples of ecclesiastical unity, who in their journeys did much to knit more closely the bonds of fellowship which united the Churches to each other, and who in their discussions or in their works did much to prepare or to usher in the first great literary and scientific period of the growing Church. We have therefore to do especially with Hegesippus who carries us to Palestine but does not leave us there, to Tatian who draws our eyes towards Syria only to send us back to the West, to a curious fragment of a list of the books of the New Testament, to the Bishop Dionysius of Corinth and to the Bishop Pinytus of Cnossus on the Island of Crete, to Athenagoras of Athens, then to the East again to the Bishop Theophilus of Antioch, then far to the West to the letter written by the Churches of Vienne and Lyons in Gaul. Irenæus, the bishop of Lyons, binds the East to the West, for he came from Smyrna. A heathen named Celsus will call for a word or two. And we must cast a glance at one and the other of the versions into which the early Church translated her sacred books so as to make them more easily accessible in wider circles.

Hegesippus is a very interesting man, and he will be still more interesting when someone draws forth his book from a Syrian or an Armenian or a Coptic library. He was probably born in Palestine. Eusebius, referring to his use of Semitic languages, adds : "showing that he himself had come to the faith from the Hebrews." Sometimes people have proceeded from that observation of Eusebius to reason that Hegesippus was a rabid Jew of the Ebionitic Christian group. There is, however, not only no proof of anything of that kind, but there is plenty to show that precisely the opposite was the case. For we shall see that he was a Christian in good and regular standing, and that he ever bore himself accordingly. He should by rights have been born at an early date, seeing that Eusebius declares that he "was of the first succession of the apostles." That phrase cannot, however, well be taken very exactly, unless—what no one reports—Hegesippus lived to be extremely old. Hegesippus is the author who has given us at length the story of the martyrdom of James the brother of Jesus, and I shall give it here as a guarantee for Hegesippus' knowledge of the early Church, but as well as an example of the Jewish character of the Christianity of James and of his friend the Apostle Paul, who had taken a vow at Jerusalem a few years before, but escaped immediate death owing to his Roman citizenship.

James showed himself a man (Eus. H. E. 2. 23): "The brother of the Lord, James, receives the Church in succession with the apostles, the one who was by all called the Just from the times of the Lord till our day, since many were called James. This one was holy from his mother's womb. He drank no wine nor spirits, nor did he eat meat. A razor did not go up upon his head, he did not anoint himself with oil, and he used no bath. For him alone it was allowed to go into the Holies. For he wore no wool but only linen, and he alone went into the temple, and was found lying on his knees, and begging for the remission [of the sins] of the people, so that his knees were hardened off like the knees of a camel, because of his ever bending them praying to God and begging remission for the people. And by reason of the exceeding greatness of his righteousness he was called Just, and Oblias, which in Greek is bulwark of the people and righteousness, as the prophets make plain touching him." Here I must make a parenthesis. In another place (Eus. H. E. 4. 22) Hegesippus tells about seven heresies or diverse opinions among the Jews, and this I must put here: "And there were different opinions in the circumcision among the sons of Israel, of which these were against the tribe of Judah and of the Christ: Essæans, Galilæans, Hemerobaptists, Masbotheans, Samaritans, Sadducees, Pharisees."

Now we go back to the story of James: "Some, then, of the seven heresies among the people, of those that I wrote of above in these memoirs, inquired of him what the door of Jesus was. And he said this was the Saviour. From which circumstance some believed that Jesus is the Christ. And the aforesaid heresies believed not that there is a resurrection, or that each man will have to return [judgment] according to his works. But as many as believed, it was because of James. Many then also of the rulers believing, there was a tumult of the Jews and scribes and Pharisees saying, that the whole people is in danger of awaiting Jesus the Christ. Therefore coming together with James, they said: We beg you, hold the people back, since it is going astray to Jesus, as if He were the Christ. We beseech thee to persuade all those coming to the Day of the Passover, about Jesus. For all obey thee. For we bear witness to thee, and all the people [bears witness] that thou art just, and that thou dost not respect persons. Persuade thou, then, the people not to go astray about Jesus. For all the people and we all obey thee. Stand, therefore, on the pinnacle of the temple, so that thou mayest be visible from above, and that thy words may be readily heard by all the people. For on account of the Passover all the tribes have come together, also with the Gentiles. So the aforesaid scribes and Pharisees stood James upon the pinnacle of the temple, and cried to him and said: O Just One, whom we all ought to obey, since the people goes astray behind Jesus the crucified, announce to us what the door of Jesus is. And he answered with a loud voice: Why do you ask me about Jesus the Son of Man, and He is seated in Heaven at the right hand of the Great Power, and He is going to come upon the clouds of Heaven. And many were receiving these words and rejoicing at the testimony of James, and saying, Hosanna to the Son of David. Then again the same scribes and Pharisees said to each other: We did

8

ill affording such a testimony for Jesus. But let us go up and throw him down, so that fearing they may not believe in him. And they all cried: O! O! even the Just One has gone astray. And they fulfilled the scripture written in Isaiah: Let us take away the Just One, for he is unprofitable to us. Therefore they shall eat the fruits of their works. And going up they cast down the Just One, and said to each other: Let us stone James the Just. And they began to stone him, since in falling down he had not died. But turning he kneeled saying: I beseech thee, Lord God Father, forgive them: for they know not what they do. And thus they stoning him, one of the priests, of the sons of Rechab the son of Rachabim of those witnessed to by Jeremiah the prophet, cried, saying: Stop! What do ye? The Just One is praying for you. And one of them took a fuller's bar with which they beat the garments, and brought it down on the head of the Just One. And thus he became a martyr. And they buried him in the place by the temple, and his pillar still remains there by the temple. This one became a true martyr both to Jews and Greeks, that Jesus is the Christ. And immediately Vespasian besieges them."

That shows us how the early Christians lived and died, and how well Hegesippus knew about them. That is taken from the fifth book of his Memoirs. But Eusebius shows us in another passage that Hegesippus also saw and wrote of what the heathen did. Eusebius (H. E. 4. 7, 8) recounts the heathen Gnostics, and observes: "Nevertheless then the truth again brought up, against these whom we have mentioned, and set in the midst of the fray several of her champions, warring against the godless heresies not alone by unwritten debates but also by written proofs. Among these Hegesippus was well known, from whom we have already quoted many sayings, as presenting from his traditions some things from the times of the apostles. So then this [Hegesippus] in five books giving the memoirs of the unerring tradition of the apostolic preaching in the most simple order of writing, notes for the time alluded to (or for the time that he knew about) touching those who at the beginning founded the idols, writing about in this way: To which they set up cenotaphs and temples as up to this day, among whom is also Antinous the slave of the Emperor Hadrian, where also the Antinous game is held, lasting up to our time, for he also built a city named for

Antinous, and (instituted?) prophets." Eusebius (H. E. 4. 21) shows us how highly he valued Hegesippus by the list in which he places him at the head in referring to that time : " And there flourished at that time in the Church not only Hegesippus whom we know from what was said above, but also Dionysius the bishop of the Corinthians, and Pinytus another bishop of the Christians in Crete, and, further, Philip and Apolinarius and Melito, both Musanos and Modestus, and above all Irenæus, from [all of] whom also the orthodoxy of the apostolical tradition of the sound faith has come down to us in writing. Hegesippus therefore, in the five [books of] Memoirs which have reached us, has left behind him a very full minute of his own opinion, in which he sets forth that he held converse with a great many bishops on his journey as far as Rome, and that he received from all the same teaching. It is fitting to hear him, after he has said something about the letter of Clement to the Corinthians, adding the following : And the Church of the Corinthians held fast to the sound word until Primus who was bishop in Corinth, among whom I conversed as I sailed to Rome, and I spent no few days with the Corinthians, during which we were refreshed with the sound word. And coming to Rome, I stayed there till the time of Anicetus, whose deacon was Eleutherus. And Soter followed Anicetus, after whom Eleutherus. And in each bishopric and in each city things are as the Law heralds and the prophets and the Lord." Observe Hegesippus' expression. Everything is in order in all the bishops' sees and cities that he has visited, because it all agrees with what the Law demands and the prophets and the Lord. He does not speak of the New Testament books. The Law and the Prophets are books. But he does not place other books over against them but simply the Lord, and that is, what the Lord said.

Hegesippus (Eus. H. E. 4. 22) gives us further word of what happened in the earliest Church at Jerusalem, and describes the first steps of unsound doctrine. "And the same [Hegesippus] describes the beginnings of the heresies of his day in these words : and after James the Just had died as martyr with the very same saying as the Lord,"—that was, the : Father forgive them : for they know not what they do,— "again Simeon the son of his uncle Clopas was appointed bishop, whom all pressed forward as being the second cousin of the Lord.   Therefore they called the Church a virgin.   For it was not yet corrupted with empty speeches.   But Thebouthis begins to corrupt it because he was not made bishop, being from the seven heresies (and he was among the people), from whom was Simon, whence the Simonians, and Cleobios, whence the Cleobians, and Dositheus, whence the Dositheans, and Gorthaeus, whence the Gorathenians, and Masbotheus, whence the Masbotheans.   From these the Menandrianists and Marcionists, and Carpocratians and Valentinians, and Basilidians and Satornilians, each separately and for themselves introduced their own view.   From these [came] false Christs, false prophets, false apostles, who divided the unity of the Church with corrupt words against God and against His Christ."

No one can say that Hegesippus was not awake to the movements of the times.   His journey to Rome fell in between the years 157 and 168, seeing that it was under Anicetus, but he seems to have remained there or to have been there again, in case he moved about among the cities of the West, until somewhere between 177 and 190 during the time of Eleutherus. It was under Eleutherus that he wrote his Memoirs.   He is said to have died under Commodus, and that is to be understood as between the years 180 and 192.   Eusebius uses Hegesippus as a witness for the condition of affairs in Corinth at the time that the letter of Clement was written, and gives us at the same time a glimpse of the conditions of exchanging or distributing books among the Churches.   After referring to Clement, Eusebius (H. E. 3. 16) says: "It is well known then that a single letter of this Clement is in our hands, both great and wonderful, which is represented as from the Church of the Romans to the Church of the Corinthians, there having been just then an uproar at Corinth.   We know that this letter was also used publicly before the assembly in very many Churches, not only in old times, but also in our own very day.   And that at the time aforesaid the things of the uproar of the Corinthians were stirred up, Hegesippus is a sufficient witness."   Hegesippus had, as we saw above, spent some time at Corinth, and had learned, therefore, all about this letter and the conditions there.   We cannot at all tell from all the stray fragments of Hegesippus' Memoirs that are before us what kind of a book these Memoirs were.   They cannot have been a chronologically disposed history, because we are directly told that the story about the death of James given above was in the fifth book, whereas James stood at the beginning of the Church.

We have given much from Hegesippus that does not bear directly upon the criticism of the canon, but which was calculated to give us insight into the character, position, advantages, and information of the man. It seems to me to be clear that few men of all that time can have been in so good a position to give us in words and without words a notion of the attitude of the Christians towards the books of the New Testament. In the first place, Eusebius (H. E. 4. 22) gives us a few words about Hegesippus : " And he writes many other things, part of which we have already mentioned above, putting them exactly where they belonged in the times of the history. And he not only gives us some things from the Gospel according to the Hebrews, but also from the Syrian and especially from the Hebrew dialect, showing that he himself became a believer from among the Hebrews. And he refers to other things as if from a Jewish unwritten tradition. And not only this one [Hegesippus], but also Irenæus and the whole chorus of the ancients called the proverbs of Solomon all glorious wisdom. And speaking of the books called apocryphal, he relates that some of them were falsely concocted in his times by some heretics." Here we have an account of certain sources from which Hegesippus drew.

He used the Gospel to the Hebrews. That is, of course, the book to which reference has been so often made. The connection makes it quite clear that Eusebius regards it as a book written in a Semitic language. It is probably not the little collection of the sayings of Jesus that Matthew made, but another book more like a full Gospel; and it is quite possible that the name has misled Eusebius, and that the Gospel as Hegesippus knew it was a Greek Gospel and not in the Aramaic tongue. Then Eusebius says that Hegesippus quotes some things from the Syrian and especially from the Hebrew dialect. What can these two be ? The Syriac so close upon the Gospel to the Hebrews might be a Syriac Gospel, and the Hebrew dialect also points to a Gospel. But I am upon the whole not inclined to think that that is the meaning. The sentence bristles with Semitic wisdom, and it would not have

been in the least out of the way for Eusebius, the bishop of
Cæsarea in Palestine, to have had some knowledge of Syrian and
Aramaic.   If we tried to distinguish between the Syriac and the
Hebrew dialect, we should be forced to suggest that the Syriac
was perhaps a North-Syrian dialect, say from the district near
Aleppo, and that the Hebrew dialect, as no one then spoke
Hebrew, was the Aramean used at and near Jerusalem, which
had itself a century or two before come down from northern
Syria.   But I do not think for a moment that Hegesippus has in
view a Syrian or a Hebrew Gospel in the two latter expressions.
Had he given "some things" from the Gospel according to the
Hebrews and some things from a Syriac Gospel and some things
from a Hebrew Gospel, it is scarcely conceivable that he should
not have given some characteristic traits from the words and
deeds of Jesus which are not to be found in our Gospels.   And
it is as little conceivable that a mass of such material should
have been passed in utter silence by Eusebius, who is ever on the
watch for new things.

Instead of wishing that we had no one knows what from
those "Gospels," we only need to take the matter up from
the other end and ask ourselves what Eusebius really gives us
from Hegesippus.   And we may feel sure that the things which
Eusebius found worth transferring from Hegesippus' pages to
his own were at least in part things that he drew from the
Syrian and Hebrew that Eusebius mentions with such impressive-
ness.   If there were any Christians anywhere who used a
Semitic dialect that could by some play of fancy, according to
the inaccuracy of all these dialect designations in Semitic
countries, be called a Hebrew dialect, it was the Christians in
southern Palestine, the Christians in Jerusalem, or those expelled from Jerusalem and living as they could somewhere in that
neighbourhood.   What has Eusebius drawn from Hegesippus
that might be taken from such a source?   Precisely the story
of the death of James.   There is "something" that may have
come from the Syrian or the Hebrew, let us say from the
Aramean of Judah.   James and his followers are the Jewish
Christians by way of eminence.   But I am actually going to give
another long quotation from Hegesippus.   The story of James'
death brought the tradition of the New Testament squarely down
to the year 70.   After James' death : "Straightway Vespasian

besieges them." The passage that I am going to give now
stretches this tradition down about to the end of the century,
perhaps over into the beginning of the second century ; and this
is, again, a passage that must have come from Jerusalem, that
could have come from nowhere else, and that, therefore, was
probably from the Hebrew dialect.   We shall see how the meshes
of the net of tradition are being woven more and more securely
together.   There will probably in the end be no place for a book
to slip through to get away from the grasp of the Church.   Before
I begin the story from Hegesippus I must call attention to the
fact that the persons to whom our attention is first to be called
are the descendants of Jude.   The Epistle of Jude interests us.
It interests us to know that down to the second century there
were men of his family in view and known.

Hegesippus (Eus. H. E. 3. 20) says : " And there were still
left some from the family of the Lord, grandsons of Jude, of
the one called His brother according to the flesh, who were
charged by hostile men with being of the family of David."
A moment before Eusebius had said that it was some of the
heretics who accused them of being of the family of David and
of the family of the Christ.   Hegesippus continues : " These,
then, Ivocatus led to the Emperor Domitian.   For he feared
the coming of Christ just as Herod did "—that points to the
second chapter of Matthew—"and he asked them if they were
from David, and they said Yes.   Then he asked them what possessions they had or how much money they were masters of."—
He clearly wished to know whether they would be in a position
to pay for troops and to bribe people in general to help them.—
" And they both said they only had nine thousand denars, half
belonging to each of them.   And they said, this they had in
money, but in the reckoning up of the land they had only thirty-
nine acres, and that the taxes had to come out of that, and that
they made their living cultivating the land themselves.   Then
also they showed their hands, the hardness of their body being
a witness for their working themselves, and showing the wales
imprinted on their own hands from the unceasing labour.   And
when they were asked about the Christ and His kingdom, of
what kind it would be and where and when it would appear,
that they answered, that it was not of the world and not earthly,
but heavenly and angelic, and that it would be at the end of the

age, at which time He coming in glory will judge living and dead, and will give to each one according to his works. Upon which Domitian, not having anything against them but despising them as poor people, let them go free and stopped by decree the persecution against the Church. And that they then dismissed became leaders of the Churches, on the one hand as witnesses" —they had stood before the emperor—"and on the other hand as from the family of the Lord. And that they, there being peace, continued to live up to the time of Trajan. This Hegesippus relates."

" After Nero and Domitian, at the point of which we are now searching out the times,"—thus writes Eusebius (H. E. 3. 32), —" it is related that here and there and city by city by reason of uprisings of the common folk, the persecution was excited against us, in which, as we have received word, Simeon the son of Clopas, whom we have shown to have been appointed the second bishop of the Church in Jerusalem, laid down his life in martyrdom. And of this that very same one is a witness of whom we have before used different statements, Hegesippus. Who then telling about certain heretics, adds the relation that therefore at this very time enduring accusation from these, the one named as a Christian [Simeon] having been tortured many days and astonishing not only the judge but also those about him in the highest degree, was finally borne away almost with the passion of the Lord. But there is nothing like hearing the author relating these very things word for word about thus: Some of these, namely of the heretics, accused Simeon the son of Clopas as being from David and a Christian, and thus he becomes a martyr, being one hundred and twenty years old, while Trajan was emperor and Atticus was consul."—That was probably about the beginning of the second century, perhaps around the year 104.—Eusebius continues: " And the same [Hegesippus] says that then also it came to pass that his [Simeon's] accusers, the ones from the royal tribe of the Jews, being sought for, were taken prisoners as being from it. And by a calculation anyone would say that Simeon also must have been one of the personal seers and hearers of the Lord, using as a proof the length of the time of his life and the fact that the scripture of the Gospels makes mention of Mary the wife of Clopas, from whom also above the account showed that he was born."

"More than this the same man [Hegesippus], relating these things about the ones mentioned, adds that until those times the Church remained a pure and uncorrupted virgin, those trying to corrupt the sound canon of the saving preaching, if there were any such, until then remaining concealed as in some obscure darkness. When the holy chorus of the apostles received a various end of life, and that generation passed by of those who had been held worthy to hear the very utterances of the divine wisdom, then the system of the godless delusion took its start, through the deceit of the teachers teaching other doctrines, who also, inasmuch as no one of the apostles was longer left, now with uncovered head tried to herald abroad the falsely so-called knowledge (Gnosis) against the heralding of the truth." The great point of the Simeon story for us is the age of Simeon. He was a hundred and twenty years old at the time of his martyrdom. We do not know in what year that was, save that it was between 98 and 117, and I have suggested 104 because of the fact that an Attius, which is almost Atticus, was then consul. But let us go to the year 117. If Simeon happened to be martyred in the last year of Trajan's reign, with his hundred and twenty years he would have been born three years "before Christ," that is to say, a single year later than Jesus. How much he must have known of the life of Jesus from the very first and how much he must have seen and heard of the life of the Christians between the crucifixion and the reign of Trajan!

But to return to Hegesippus: the remark of Eusebius about the books that are called apocryphal deserves attention. It is true that Eusebius gives no names of books, and it is possible that Hegesippus mentioned no names. Yet when he says that Hegesippus relates that some of these were fabrications of heretics of his own day, we feel sure that with that word the genuine books of the New Testament are placed for Hegesippus beyond all doubt as from the time of the apostles. The passage of Christians hither and thither, and the interchange of thought and of life, were far too incessant to admit of the successful fathering of books that were not genuine upon the apostles. When we reflect upon Eusebius' words about Hegesippus and the Hebrew and the Syriac and the Jewish tradition, we shall at once understand that it is not the intention of Eusebius to say that Hegesippus did not know our New

Testament books. He calls attention to the unknown, the uncommon in Hegesippus; the common, the every day part, has no special interest for him. When we get Hegesippus' five books, we shall see what he calls apocryphal. As the name of Jude occurred above, when we read of his grandsons who were such plain everyday farmers or small peasants, the thought may have arisen, that these grandsons scarcely point to a grandfather who could have written the Epistle of Jude. To that is to be observed first, that we do not with mathematical certainty know who wrote the letter; second, that the letter purports to be from this Jude whose grandsons are alive at the end of the century; third, that Jude might have dictated the letter to a man who could write Greek; and fourth, that even in this enlightened twentieth century there may be found grandsons of facile authors who are themselves not able to write books. So far from it that Hegesippus did not know our New Testament books, Hegesippus will undoubtedly have known the mass of our New Testament books. If there were some of them that he had not known in Palestine, he will have become acquainted with them at Corinth and surely at Rome, towards which all flowed. But he probably knew the most of them before he travelled westward. He probably had the Scriptures partly in view when he spoke or wrote of the unity of the Church, only that still for him the tradition by word of mouth seemed to be the weighty thing.

If we try to gather together the fragments of knowledge that Eusebius' words about Hegesippus and out of Hegesippus' five books of Memoirs have given us, we shall find that the harvest is large, although not yet in every point precise. Dying between 180 and 192, we may regard it as likely that Hegesippus had come to be seventy years old or thereabouts, and had been born therefore about 110; were he sixty years old he would have been born about 120. Taking the earlier date with the statements as to his reaching Rome, which do not precisely agree with each other, we may conjecture that he came thither about 160, being fifty years of age. A certain ripeness of experience might be looked for from a man who set out to take a general account of stock in the Christian Church. A very young man would not be likely to conceive the thought of searching through the lands for correct teaching and for due tradition.

And the Churches would easily have viewed with suspicion a young man who came to them upon an errand of that kind. Hegesippus may well have begun his journey then as a man high up in the forties. Regarding it as certain that before Hegesippus reached Corinth and Rome the mass of our New Testament books were in common use in those two cities, we look upon the absence of any note of surprise or of dissent from him in respect to these books as a sign that he was accustomed to the use of the same books. Eusebius has with the greatest good sense not thought it necessary to give indefinite proofs for the generally accepted books, seeing that with his clear view of the early history of Christianity he felt sure that these books had from the first been in the undisturbed possession of the members of the great Churches. Had he found in Hegesippus signs of dissent from the books used by the Church, he would have told us of it. We may rely upon that. We have no reason thus far to think that Eusebius did not play fair with his sources.

If Hegesippus in all probability came from Palestine, Tatian came from Assyria. We do not know very much about him save that he was brought up as a Greek, and that he eagerly studied the various philosophies, and was initiated into various of the heathen mysteries. Perhaps Syrian or Armenian manuscripts will some day give us more. He went to the West, to Rome, as a heathen. While there, probably under the influence of Justin Martyr, he became a Christian. He was very much devoted then to his teacher Justin, who died perhaps in the year 165. Tatian attributes his conversion to Christianity to writings. This may well be a figure of speech, in so far as he may have been led by the exhortations of Christians to the Scriptures. But it is interesting to see him put the Scriptures in that place. He tells in his Speech to the Greeks, that is to say to the heathen, how hollow and foul he had found their philosophy and their religious mysteries to be. And then (ch. 29) he says: "Coming back to myself, I sought around in what way I might be able to find out that which is true. And while I was turning over in my mind the most earnest questions, it so fell out that I lighted upon certain barbaric writings,"—everything is barbaric that is not Greek,—"more ancient in comparison with the opinions of the Greeks, and more divine in comparison with their error. And it came to pass that I was persuaded by these books because of the modesty of the way of writing and the artlessness of those who spoke and the comprehensibility of the making of all things and the foretelling of things to come and the propriety of the precepts and the oneness of the rule over all things. And my soul being thus taught of God, I understood that those things (the heathen things) had the form of condemnation, whereas these things do away with the servitude in the world and free us from many rulers and from ten thousand tyrants, and give us not what we had not received, but what, having received under the error, we were prevented from keeping." Those books were the books of the Old Testament certainly; possibly he also had the Gospels in view.

Tatian was not one of the men who go half-way. He had been much displeased by the looseness and corruption that he had found everywhere in heathenism, and he was eager to go to the greatest perfection possible in Christianity. Under Justin he remained a member of the Church. The heathen philosopher Crescens attacked both Justin and Tatian. After Justin's death Tatian taught in Justin's place. It may have been about the year 172 or 173 that he finally broke off his more direct connection with the Church. Some say that he never completely broke away from it. At any rate he went back to the East and became a leader—to speak in modern terms—of a monastic body. That is to say, he did away with marriage and with eating flesh and with drinking wine. But there were then no monks. These people were Selfmasters. One thing that he did strikes directly into our criticism, and goes very far to prove the many claims I have made to the continued unquestioned existence and use of the books of the New Testament in the Church up to this date. For Tatian made a Harmony of the Gospels. Now what Gospels did he use? The Gospel to the Hebrews, or a Syriac or a Hebrew Gospel? The whole subject is still somewhat lacking in clearness. But Tatian appears to have made his Harmony in Greek. That he made it in Greek fits also well with the name which he himself appears to have given the work. He called it the Through Four, which is a name taken directly from the four Gospels. The Greek name is Diatessaron. But what four Gospels did he use? Our four Gospels. The four Gospels of the Church. The only one of the four that anyone would have been inclined to have doubts about, would have been the Gospel of John, and Tatian began precisely with verses from that Gospel.

He appears to have known well pretty much all our New Testament books, and I affirm that an educated Christian at Rome at that time could not help knowing them. Of course, Tatian could not go into scripture quotations out of either Testament in his Speech to the Greeks. He would not have found much in them of the heathen systems and gods that he holds up before their eyes in derision and scorn. He certainly used many of the Epistles of Paul. He is said to have rejected the Epistles to Timothy, probably because of the advice to take a little wine. He insisted upon it, however, that Titus was genuine.

Eusebius (H. E. 4. 29) gives from Irenæus some account of the group of heretics of which Tatian became one, and speaks at the same time hardly of Tatian, as became a good orthodox man who was the pink of propriety and who attacked by reason of office all heretics. I do not mean to say that Irenæus was a bad man. But he was a heresy hunter. He says : " From (coming from) Satorninus and Marcion those called Selfmasters preached no marriage, setting aside the ancient creation of God, and calmly denouncing the making of male and female for the generation of men. And they introduced continence on the part of those among them whom they called the full-souled ones, displeasing God who made all things. And they deny the salvation which is from the first Creator. And this now was conceived by them, a certain Tatian first leading in this blasphemy, who having been a hearer of Justin's, so long as he was with him brought nothing of this kind to the light, but after his martyrdom leaving the Church, made overweening with the notion of being a teacher and puffed up at the thought of being different from the others, he grounded a special kind of school, mythologising about certain unseen eons like those from Valentinus, and proclaiming that marriage was corruption and whoredom, almost like Marcion and Satorninus, and making a proof from the salvation of Adam by himself. This much then from Irenæus. A little later a certain Severus, laying hold of the name of the aforesaid heresy, became the cause for those who started from it of the name drawn from him of Severians. These, then, use the Law and the Prophets and the Gospels, interpreting in their own way the thoughts of the sacred writings. And blaspheming Paul the apostle, they do away with his Epistles ; nor do they receive the Acts of the Apostles. Their former leader, Tatian, putting together a certain connection and collection, I do not know how, of the Gospels, attached to it the name Diatessaron, which also still now is in the hands of some. And they say that he dared to change some of the sayings of the apostle, as correcting the syntax of their expression."

Eusebius then tells us that Tatian wrote a great deal, and he praises his Speech to the Greeks, which deduces all the wisdom of the Greeks from Moses and the prophets. In all this account from Irenæus and Eusebius we see the spirit which at once accuses a man, even one who takes up an ascetic thought, of bad motives, the spirit which has in every age disgraced Christianity. The combination of the Law and the Prophets and the Gospels is striking. That the Severians interpreted in their own way was a matter of course. Neither Irenæus nor Eusebius did anything else. But observe the fact that these people do away with Paul's Epistles. That can have only one single sense, and that is, that the Church all around and for long years before this time, let us say it up and down since the days of Paul had treasured his Epistles. It is almost worth a mild heresy to get in this negative way the confirmation of what we have all along insisted upon. These Epistles of Paul were not just at this time coming into use, and these Severians did not merely say: "No! we do not agree with it. We shall not accept these Epistles." The Epistles were there long before the Severians were, just as the Epistle of James was there long before Luther called it "a straw letter." And it is very good, too, that Eusebius tells us that they did not receive the Acts of the Apostles. That book of Acts was there, too, years before. But their rejection of it makes its presence visible again precisely here.

Eusebius' statement that Tatian was charged with changing some of the sayings of the apostle as if he were bettering the syntax, needs looking at. In the first place, the apostle is, of course, Paul. In the second century "the apostle" is pretty much always Paul. In the next place, if Tatian really did try to improve the Greek of some of Paul's wild sentences, it would not be very strange, and it would agree with the work which not at all unorthodox Alexandrian grammarians are suspected of having done at a later date. But, in the third place, it is in reality quite likely that the good people who spread this accusation were people who were not enough versed in the history and condition of the text of the New Testament. It is quite possible that what they thought were changed, corrected sentences, were simply manuscripts with other readings, or simply signs that Tatian had used manuscripts with other readings. And we may further add that the readings which Tatian had may just as well here and there, or even in general, have been better readings than the ones that his opponents supposed to be the right readings. These are the theoretical possibilities. What the precise state of the case was, we could only tell by receiving the two sets of readings.

If we remember that books were at that time rolls, and that the four Gospels will have been four rolls, which must have been both dear and bulky and troublesome to compare with each other passage for passage, it will be easy to see that Tatian's condensing of the four Gospels into one convenient Harmony in one book must have met what a bookseller with modern views would call a pressing need of the day. The success of the book showed that the Church appreciated the work. It was translated into Syriac, supposing that we are right in assuming that it was originally Greek, and it passed in some shape or other, or much misshapen, into other languages. Now a Greek bishop about the middle of the fifth century gives us a view of the way in which this book had by that time come into vogue in his parts. It is Theodoret, who became bishop of Cyrus on the Euphrates in Upper Syria in the year 423. He writes (Hær. Fab. 1. 20) : "And Tatian the Syrian became at first a sophist,"—that is Theodoret's short way of giving a heretic a not very nice title, and getting round the fact of the wide philosophical and heathen religious researches of Tatian,—"and thereafter was a pupil of the divine Justin the martyr. This one also put together the Gospel called Diatessaron, not only cutting away the genealogies, but also the other things so far as they show that the Lord was born from the seed of David after the flesh. And not only the people of his society used this, but also those who follow the apostolical dogmas, not having known the evil tendency of the composition, but using it in simplicity as a short book. And I found more than two hundred such books held in honour in the Churches among us, and gathering them all together I put them aside, and introduced instead of them the Gospels of the four evangelists."

Long after that time copies of the book itself and of commentaries on it were found in some places. We should be glad if we could find a genuine copy of it to-day. From Theodoret's description it is perfectly clear that only our four Gospels were used in the Diatessaron. He would have pounced like a vulture on any sign of an apocryphal Gospel in it. We have another reference to this Diatessaron from the Syrian side of Syria, Theodoret having given us the Greek side. Somewhere about the middle of the third century it is likely that the apocryphal book called the Teaching of Addai was written, and perhaps in or near Edessa. This book says that the early Christians in Edessa heard the Old Testament read, and with it " the New [Testament] of the Diatessaron." We know further from Dionysius Bar Salibi, who wrote near the close of the twelfth century, that Ephræm the Syrian, a deacon in Edessa, who died in the year 373, wrote a commentary on the Diatessaron, parts of which commentary we now have from an Armenian translation. We also have an Arabic translation from a Syriac text ; but this and a Latin form especially are not accurate reproductions of the original, the Latin being not in the least from the real text of the Diatessaron. Tatian's book did a long service, and will certainly not have corrupted the Christianity of any reader, much as Theodoret was exercised about its use in the Churches near him.

Tatian has placed before our view a man who grew up a heathen, affording a contrast to Hegesippus, who appears to have been of Jewish descent. Like Hegesippus he was a man of travel, and like him he visited Rome. Hegesippus had the practical unity of the Church in view. Tatian regarded purity as an aim that preceded unity. His heretical ideas have in no way injured or lessened his value for our criticism. He had as a good orthodox Christian the most of our books, and he only made their existence the more clear when he as a heretic discarded some things that he had before used. He holds an altogether unique position in the history of the New Testament.

Aside from his Diatessaron, no other book of such importance ever gained such a foothold in the Christian Church. One point should not be overlooked, namely, the fact that Tatian did not hesitate to pare away from the New Testament the parts which he did not consider good. We have no information as to whether in this he was led by the influence of Marcion or not. The likeness of some of the views attributed to him to views of Marcion's would make Marcion's example seem all the more probable. Should any one, however, be desirous of concluding from Tatian's treatment of the Gospels that the Church then, the Church of his day, did not hold the Gospels to be equal to the divine Scriptures of the Old Testament, we have only to recall the two facts, first that a heretic freed himself from the opinion of the Church, and second that Tatian as well as Marcion seems to have thought the God of the Old Testament creation to be an inferior God. The trend of these two facts goes nevertheless to show that the whole question of religious, of sacred books was not regarded as one of very strict importance, or as one that had been definitely and once for all settled, even for the Old Testament.

We now come to a remarkable fragment of an old book that is extremely valuable for the criticism of the canon. It is called the Muratorian fragment, after the name of the Italian historian and librarian Muratori who first published it. Muratori found the fragment in the Ambrosian Library at Milan. He seems to have thought that it would not be prudent to publish it as a fragment that bore upon the canon, seeing that its statements are sometimes peculiar. He therefore printed it as a specimen of the very careless way in which the scribes in the Middle Ages copied manuscripts. The actual writing is of the eighth or perhaps even of the seventh century, but the contents are several centuries older. It is sometimes thought to be of the third century. I still incline to date it about 170. It is written in Latin. Some have regarded it as a translation from the Greek. Should it have been written at Rome at the date named, it would presumably have been written in Greek, for Greek continued to be the Christian literary language at Rome until well into the third century. But this argument is not of great weight, in so far as we do not know what the extent of the book or the essay was to which the fragment belonged. Caius

9

and Papias and Hegesippus have been named by different scholars as the probable authors. We have no clue whatever to the name of the writer, and as little to the character of the book from which it was drawn. It may have been an apologetical book. In this fragment, were it complete, we should have the earliest known list of the books of the New Testament, although we do not find this designation in it. We cannot doubt that the full copy contained the books of the Old Testament, of which, as we have already seen, Melito had drawn up a list.

The beginning of the list of the books of the New Testament is lost. It is, however, to be presupposed that the Gospel according to Matthew was named first, and that the first of the eighty-five lines preserved refers to Mark. The mutilated sentence probably said that Mark gave the account of tradition which Peter related to him and then, referring to the presence of Mark after the crucifixion, said that, nevertheless, Mark put down for himself the narrative of the occurrences which he himself saw as an eye-witness. It should not, it seems to me, be thought that Mark, who lived at Jerusalem, had positively not seen Jesus before the crucifixion. He was certainly a young man, perhaps very young, and his merely seeing Jesus and hearing Him speak in passing would not be a thing of which the least notice would have been taken at that time. There were many men of mature age who had had much intercourse with Jesus. It did not in the least lie in the habit of the time and the land to ask around exactly and to chronicle carefully the name of every child that had been in the presence of Jesus. That there were four Gospels, and only four, is clear then when we find in the second line that Luke is given as the third. And there is not a shadow of a reason for thinking that the first and second were anything but Matthew and Mark. Luke is designated as a physician, and then described as one who after the ascension was attached to Paul as a student of the law. That does not mean that Luke gave up medicine and turned law student under Paul, as Paul had studied under Gamaliel. It points to the need that Luke as a heathen by birth had to take up the study of the Old Testament. The fragment seems to allude to the fact, which every one feels, that Luke was more independent as an author than Mark was. It agrees that he did not see the Lord in the flesh. It adds, however, that he wrote in his own name and as well as he could follow the events, and that he began with the birth of John.

The account of the way in which John came to write his Gospel is interesting. The fellow-disciples of John and his bishops—one might think of the bishops in Asia near Ephesus —appear as having urged him to write a Gospel. John replied to them : "Fast with me three days from to-day on, and let us tell each other whatever may be revealed to each one. That same night it was revealed to Andrew the apostle that John should write everything in his own name, and that they all should look his work through." That is a pretty story, but is in all probability a late invention. Then the author tells us that though the Gospels have each an own principle, as going forth from different authors, they nevertheless present no differences for faith, since they all proceed from the one chief spirit, relating the birth, the passion, the resurrection, the conversation with His disciples, and His double coming, the first time in humility despised, which is past, the second time glorious in royal power, which is to come. Marcion rejected all the Gospels but Luke, and attested thereby the four of the Church. Tatian witnessed to the four in his Harmony. And this Muratorian fragment has the four Gospels. They have been together for years before we have happened to receive these glimpses of the state of the case. They probably were brought together very soon after, it may be immediately after, the writing of the Gospel according to John.

The author of the fragment continues by observing that it is then not strange that " John gives the details so firmly also in his Epistle, saying : What we ourselves have seen with our eyes and heard with our ears and touched with our hands, these things we have written to you. For he thus declares himself to be not only a seer but also a hearer, and also a writer of all the wonderful things of the Lord in order." In these words we have, then, an early instance of the way in which the First Epistle of John was closely bound to the Gospel in tradition. The Second and the Third Epistles may very well have still been lying quietly in the hands of the private persons who first received them, at the time at which the custom of joining the First Epistle to the Gospel was started. Next follows the book of Acts, which the author of the fragment, without the least propriety but in accordance with the carelessness of early times and in accordance with other

Christians, calls the Acts of all the Apostles. He says that they
are written in one book. How many books would the acts of
all of the apostles have filled? How much there must have
been to tell about Peter and about John! Here the author
thinks that Luke had personal knowledge of the details. He
agrees that Luke omits Peter's death and Paul's journey to
Spain, and we may conjecture that it is because he was not
present at either event. As for Paul's Epistles, they themselves
declare to those who wish to know it from what place and for
what reason they were written : "First of all to the Corinthians
forbidding the heresy of schism, then second to the Galatians
about circumcision, but to the Romans he wrote more at length,
declaring the sequence of the Scriptures, and that their head
and chief is Christ. About these things we must say more.
Inasmuch as the blessed Apostle Paul, following the order of his
predecessor John, writes by name only to seven Churches in the
following order : to the Corinthians first, to the Ephesians
second, to the Philippians third, to the Colossians fourth, to
the Galatians fifth, to the Thessalonians sixth, to the Romans
seventh. But to the Corinthians and Thessalonians for reproof
he writes a second time. Nevertheless it is made known that
the one Church is diffused through the whole round of the earth.
And John, although he writes in the Revelation to seven Churches,
notwithstanding speaks to all. But one to Philemon and one
to Titus and two to Timothy for love and affection. Yet they
are sacred to the catholic Church in the regulation of Church
discipline." The way in which that remark is added, looks
almost as if the author had in mind some people who did not
accept or like these Epistles to the separate persons.

Then the fragment alludes to two Epistles that are not among
ours : "There is also an Epistle to the Laodiceans, another to the
Alexandrians forged in Paul's name for the heresy of Marcion,
and many others which cannot be received in the catholic
Church, for it is not fitting to mingle gall with honey. The
Epistle of Jude and two with the name of John are held in
honour in the catholic Church, and Wisdom written by the
friends of Solomon to his honour." The way in which these
two small Epistles of John are named seems odd. The author
alludes to them almost hesitatingly. Or is it only because they
are so very short? Two Revelations are known to this writer,

but the second is of questioned acceptance : "The Revelation of John and of Peter only we acknowledge, which (I think this applies only to Peter's Revelation) some of us do not think should be read in church."

At this last sentence our thoughts must turn back to the discussion of the reading in church, and the words that follow will bear upon the same point. They refer to that book of Hermas of which we spoke above : "The Pastor, however, Hermas wrote lately in our day in the city of Rome, his brother Pius the bishop being seated in the chair of the Roman Church. And therefore it is fitting that it be read. But to the end of time it cannot be read publicly in the church before the people either among the finished number of the prophets or among the apostles." There we have a clear distinction, I think, between the books that are : Man to Men, and those that are : God to Men. The fragment closes with references to heretical books. The names are partly so much corrupted that we cannot tell just what they are : "But of Arsinous or Valentinus or Miltiades we receive nothing at all. Who also wrote a new book of Psalms for Marcion, along with Basilides, Assianos the founder of the Cataphrygians." That is a rich fragment in spite of all its defects. We have the four Gospels, Acts, the Epistles of Paul, the Epistles of John, Jude, the Revelation. So far as the fragment goes, it brings neither James nor the Epistles of Peter nor Hebrews. Of course, in the case of a copyist who was so extremely careless, there remains the possibility that in some place a line or several lines have been omitted. These Epistles are, however, Epistles that would be likely at first to be read more in the East than in the West. But we have seen that the Epistle to the Hebrews was known at Rome as early as about 95. There may have been some special reason for its omission in this fragment. Perhaps the author of the fragment thought, as Tertullian did, that Hebrews was written by Barnabas, and he may have not been inclined to put it into the list on that account.

We have thus far in this period touched Palestine, Syria, and Assyria, and ever again Rome. Now we must turn to Corinth, and to the Bishop Dionysius of that city. Dionysius was in one respect like the Apostle Paul and like Ignatius, namely, in writing letters to the Churches. He wrote to the Christians of the Churches, not to the bishops. He was probably bishop at the time of Justin's martyrdom, perhaps in the year 165, and it is likely that he died before 198. He was perhaps the successor of Primus whom Hegesippus mentions. He must have been a man of great note, since the brethren demanded that he write to them. We gain from the few words about him and from his pen, that Eusebius (H. E. 4. 23) has preserved for us, quite a picture of the Churches of his day in his neighbourhood. He names several bishops, Palmas in Pontus, Philip in Crete, Pinytus in Crete, Soter at Rome, Puplius and his successor Quadratus at Athens. We know of seven of his letters : to the Lacedæmonians, to the Athenians, to the Nicomedians, to the Gortynians, to the Amastrians, to the Cnossians (Cnossos was a little east of Candia on the island of Crete ; its position was settled by Arthur John Evans and his friends in 1900), and to the Romans. Eusebius gives a short characteristic description of his letters, which Eusebius calls " catholic letters to the Churches," as if he thought of the Catholic Epistles in the New Testament. He calls the letter to the Lacedæmonians a catechetical letter of orthodoxy, and a reminder of peace and unity. The letter to the Athenians is an awakening letter for faith and for the manner of life taught in the Gospel, and he reproves those who forget that life, and points to the example of their Bishop Puplius who became a martyr in the persecutions then. He also praises the zeal and chronicles the success of the Bishop Quadratus who followed Puplius. Thereat he refers to Dionysius the Areopagite led to the faith by Paul, and as the first one taking the oversight of the parish at Athens. The letter to Nicomedia was written against the heresy of Marcion, and stands fast in the canon of the truth. Writing to the Church living in this foreign world, " parishing," at Gortyna and to the rest of the Churches on Crete, he praises the Bishop Philip, and tells him to guard against heresy. In the letter to Amastris and the rest in Pontus, written at the request of Bacchylides and Elpistos, he "adds explanations of divine scripture." It would be interesting for us to have these comments of such a high age. The subjects touched upon in this letter show how wide a range a bishop then dared to take in writing to the Christians under another bishop. " He exhorts them at length about marriage and purity,"—we might almost think he were passing on to Amastris

the good thoughts that Paul had written to his own Church,—
"and he tells them to receive again those who return again
from any fall, whether a sin in general or whether a heretical
error."

The letter to the Cnossians on Crete and to their Bishop
Pinytus displays still more plainly the fact that Dionysius, we
might almost say, takes the place of a pope or of a patriarch
towards these bishops and their sees. Precisely this letter gives
us a New Testament background, for in it "he begs Pinytus
the bishop of the parish not to place upon the brethren a heavy
burden of necessity concerning purity, but to consider the
weakness of the many." This doubtless points to a wish on the
part of Pinytus to bring into use ascetic rules. "In replying to
which Pinytus admires and accepts what Dionysius says, but
begs him in return some time to impart firmer food, nourishing
the people under him in the future with more complete letters,
so that they may not by spending their time with milk-like words
in the end discover that they had grown old in an infant method
of life." We could not wish for any more practical portrayal of
the application of Paul's word to Church questions. "Further,"
says Eusebius, "we have a letter of Dionysius also addressed to
the Romans." "He writes as follows: For from the beginning
this is your habit to bestow kindness in various ways upon all
the brethren, and to send provisions for the journey,"—remember
that the Christians are all living in this foreign land, are all
pilgrims to the heavenly home, and hence need the money or
other provision for the way,—"here refreshing the poverty of the
needy, and by the money for the journey which you have sent
from the beginning affording support to the brethren in the
mines, ye Romans thus preserving the custom of the Romans
handed down from the fathers, which your blessed Bishop Soter
not only kept up but also increased, not only bestowing the
abundance distributed to the saints, but also like a warmly-loving
father comforting the desponding brethren like children with
blessed words." That was Dionysius.

Eusebius adds for our special benefit: "In this very letter he
also makes mention of the letter of Clement to the Corinthians,
bringing to view that the reading of it before the Church was
done from old times by an ancient custom." He says then:
"To-day then we passed the Lord's day a holy day, in which we

read your letter, which we ever hold and keep in mind by reading it, as also the one formerly written to us by Clement." The point of these things for the canon, lies first of all in the active intercourse between the Churches. We have seen that Rome must have long since had the body of our New Testament books. Now we see this same Rome sending its riches to the poor in various Churches, and to the Christians working as prisoners in mines and quarries. And, moreover, Soter sends not only money, but also comforting words. It seems to me that no rational person will be inclined to think that these Churches and these scattered Christian prisoners were totally ignorant of the New Testament books, the fulfilling of the precepts in which was bringing them these bountiful provisions for the hard places in their earthly journey. And in the reading of Soter's letter and of the letter of Clement we have examples of the way in which the division Man to Man in the service was partly filled up. It will remain to be seen later whether we should in the case of the letter of Clement suppose that it was read at Corinth from the point of view of God to Man. For the moment it will certainly be granted that the mention of it in connection with the letter of Soter does not point to that. Further is to be observed that the reading of the books of the New Testament in Corinth as in Rome is to be presupposed although it is not mentioned here. This is not a thoughtless assumption. It is the only conception of the situation that is scientifically possible.

Dionysius has not yet exhausted his stores for us. He gives us a glimpse of the way in which some Christians treated letters at that day. Eusebius writes : "And the same [Dionysius] speaks as follows of his letters as being treacherously treated : For when the brethren asked it of me that I should write letters, I wrote them. And these the apostles of the devil have mingled with tares, taking some things out and putting some things in. For whom the Woe is waiting. It is then not strange if some have laid their hands upon the work of treating the writings about the Lord treacherously, seeing that they have taken such counsel against letters that are not such as those are." Last of all, Eusebius tells that Dionysius wrote a letter to a most faithful sister Chrysophora, "in which, writing to her of the things that belong to her duty, he imparts also to her logical food," food of the word we may say, or reasonable food. The expression recalls

Paul's words in Romans, "your reasonable service," or Peter's words, "the reasonable guileless milk."   Dionysius has carried us to Asia Minor on the east and to Rome on the west, and has set the Church before us in constant intercourse between its parts. His letters themselves display a kind of interchange between Churches that we should not look for to-day in circles in which bishops rule.   The Bishop of Rhode Island of the Protestant Episcopal Church would scarcely like it if the Bishop of Illinois should take occasion to write to his diocese about their duties. The Bishop of Durham would certainly not be pleased if the Bishop of Lincoln should be asked to write and should write to his diocesans about marriage and chastity.   The explanation lies partly in the simple conditions of that day, in the comparatively undeveloped notion of the duties and rights of bishops,—would that the notion had remained undeveloped,—partly in the high position of Corinth as a city in which Paul had lived and to which he had sent two letters, and partly without doubt in a certain gracious fatherly disposition on the part of Dionysius himself, possibly coupled at the close with the glory, the halo of a patriarchal age on the part of Dionysius that made bishops and people eager to bask in the light that reflected alike from a remote past of Christian tradition and from a near future when he should stand before the throne of God.   Dionysius' distinction between writings about the Lord—the Greek phrase is really "Lordly writings," the word Lord meaning here surely Jesus—and his own letters "that are not such," emphasises for us the difference alluded to between the writings which belong in the service to the part God to Man and those which belong to the part Man to Man.   Probably Dionysius has at first in view the Gospels as especially pertaining to the Lord.   Inasmuch, however, as he is speaking of his own letters, it is altogether possible, and I think it probable that he also thinks of the Epistles of the Apostles as belonging to these writings respecting the Lord.

At the beginning of the last quarter of the second century, probably from the year 177, we have a trifling yet not unwelcome testimony to Matthew, and John, and Romans, and First Corinthians, and Galatians, from the pen of Athenagoras an Athenian philosopher, who wrote an Apology, addressed to Marcus Aurelius and Commodus, and soon after that an essay on the Resurrection from the dead.

Antioch, which gave us Ignatius, offers us here Theophilus, who was bishop there somewhere about the years 181 to 190. He wrote three books to Autolycus which are preserved, and among many other, lost, books was a Harmony of the Gospels and a commentary on the Harmony. Eusebius declares that Theophilus quotes the book of Revelation in his book against the heretic Hermogenes. Describing Theophilus, Eusebius observes how very corrupt heresy then was, and how the shepherds of the Church warded the heretics off like wild beasts from the sheep of Christ: "On the one hand with warnings and admonitions to the brethren, and on the other hand by placing them naked and unclothed before them, not only face to face with unwritten discussions and refutations, but now also by means of written reminders setting straight forth their opinions with the most exact proofs." Eusebius adds that Theophilus wrote a good book against Marcion which was then still preserved. The three books written by Theophilus to his friend Autolycus, a heathen,—and Theophilus was himself by birth a heathen,—are not strictly connected with each other, having been written, the first as an account of a discussion with Autolycus, the second at the request of Autolycus, and the third as a thought of Theophilus'.

In the closing chapter of the first book, Theophilus tells how he himself had been converted by reading "the sacred writings of the holy prophets," who had foretold the future. Like Justin and the earlier Aristobulus and Philo, he declares that the heathen writers drew their wisdom from the prophets. In the second book he calls the prophets "spirit-bearers of the Holy Spirit" inspired and made wise by God, and quotes the Old Testament as: "teaches us the Holy Spirit by the prophets,"—"teaches the divine scripture,"—"the divine scripture,"—"the divine Scriptures." In one passage he writes: "Whence the holy Scriptures and all the spirit-bearers teach us, of whom John says: In the beginning was the Word, and the Word was with God, showing that at first God only was and in Him the Word." Then he says: "And God was the Word: all things were made by Him; and without Him nothing was made." This passage is said not to imply the equal value of the books of the New Testament with those of the Old Testament. I insist upon it that so far as these words of Theophilus have any meaning at all, they place John the evangelist and his words in a distinctly exceptional position. They call John one of the " spirit-bearers," and that is precisely the designation which, as we saw a moment ago, Theophilus applied to the prophets who were the writers of the divine Scriptures of the Old Testament. When, then, the holy Scriptures and all the spirit-bearers are mentioned together and John is declared to be one of them, the purpose of this juxtaposition is not to say that John is less than the prophets, but to put him on a par with the prophets. The same thing if not more appears from the contents of the quotation from John. What is quoted is not a saying of Jesus, but the saying of the evangelist. And this evangelical spirit-bearer does not here make some general indifferent remark such as that idolatry or whoredom or what not is a sin. On the contrary, this Gospel writer gives the fundamental statement touching God and the Word : " In the beginning was God, and the Word was with God." It seems to me that no observation upon the difference made between a prophet and a spirit-bearer can in any way overbalance the use here made and made by name touching John. It is, besides, the first time that John is thus named as the evangelist. Theophilus also knows very well indeed the Epistles of Paul and First Peter. In the third book, after dealing with the prophets, he says (3. 12) : " Moreover also as to righteousness of which the law speaks, we find that similar things are con- tained in the [writings] of the prophets and of the Gospels,"—the word " Gospels " may very well be an error for " evangelists,"— " because all the spirit-bearers have made their utterances with the one spirit of God." He then quotes the Gospels repeatedly ; for example (3. 13) : "And the gospel voice teaches in the strongest manner about chastity, saying "—not to look at a woman with evil thought, and not to put away a wife. Then he writes (3. 14) : " And those doing what is good it [the Gospel] teaches not to boast, that they may not be men-pleasers. For let not your left hand, it says, know what your right hand does. Moreover also about the being subject to powers and authorities and praying for them, the divine word commands us that we should lead a calm and quiet life, and teaches to render to all, all things ; to whom honour, honour ; to whom fear, fear ; to whom taxes, taxes : to owe no man anything, save only to love all."

A great deal too much has been made of the fact that Theophilus in writing these three books brings in comparison so little from the New Testament and so much from the Old Testament. The fact is that Theophilus in the first place quotes extraordinarily often all manner of heathen books, not, of course, as Scripture, high as he rates the Sibyl. And then he quotes a great deal from the Old Testament precisely because Autolycus wishes to be informed about God and about man from an Old Testament point of view. He quotes, for example, at one breath about three pages from the first chapter of Genesis, and a little later he brings another three pages. For the larger part of the three books only the Old Testament gave him the massive sentences about God that he wanted. Furthermore, it has been said that he quotes the New Testament very freely; but so he does also the Old Testament when he does not need to get down a roll and write off a long paragraph. For example, Isaiah writes (40^{22}): "He that sets up as a chamber the heaven and stretches [it] out like a tent to inhabit." Theophilus introduces this most formally, but writes (2. 13): "*God this one* (This God [I wished to represent the Greek words]), the one *making the heaven like a chamber*, and stretching [it] out like a tent *to be lived in.*"

As to the use of the Old Testament, even in the third book it is to be urged that one main point of that third book, as the first chapter shows, is the refutation of the opinion of Autolycus that the books of the Christians are new. It seems to me to follow directly from this opinion of Autolycus, that he had heard of altogether new Scriptures of the Christians. Indeed the weight of this statement goes rather to show that these newer books were the ones upon which the Christians laid the greatest stress. Of course, then, in opposing such views Theophilus must quote more Old Testament than New Testament, and must emphasise the value of those old books from which he deduces the wisdom of the heathen poets and philosophers. And there he cites Moses and Isaiah and Jeremiah and Ezekiel, whose very names produce an atmosphere of antiquity and of mystery. The words given above as the strong command of the Gospel voice about chastity are the intensifying of a word from Solomon. But that does not in the least signify that Theophilus did not account the Gospel as equal to Solomon. It is only a part of Theophilus' plan to give first those old writings which he is straining every nerve to commend as ancient and reverend to his heathen friend.

The very way in which he nevertheless represents the Gospel as giving a more commanding statement as to chastity, permits us to see that he himself is more inclined to place the Gospels above than below the Old Testament Scriptures. And then we are told that Theophilus does not account Paul's writings of high value, or as equal to those of the Old Testament. Now it is not well to be all too wise about shades of difference. I confess that I do not feel sure that Theophilus regarded the prophets as exactly equal to the law. In the same way it must be conceded that Theophilus may have thought that the letters of Paul were not quite equal to the words of Jesus. But a concession of this kind is of no extraordinary importance. For, if I am not mistaken, in spite of all doctrines of the equality of the holiness of the books of the New Testament, only very few Christians in this twentieth century would fail to feel that a statement backed by direct words of Jesus had a higher authority than one merely confirmed by an Epistle of Paul or any other apostle. When, however, we find that Theophilus quotes Old Testament passages with varying degrees of freedom and with indefinitely varying introductory words, we must not ask too much for the New Testament words. Look, for example, at the following series. Theophilus (3. 14) quotes Isaiah, and introduces the words by : "Isaiah the prophet said." Directly after the verse from Isaiah he quotes Matthew, using the introduction : "And the Gospel : Love ye, it saith," and so on. He brings here two or three passages from Matthew together. And then he passes to the Epistle to Titus in this manner : "And further also about the being subject to powers and authorities and praying for them, the divine word commands us that we should live a calm and quiet life. And teaches to render to all, all things"; see above. The prophet said, the Gospel saith, it says (used in one of the quotations from Matthew), the divine word commands us. That series shows to my mind no special decline in its reverence for Paul when it says of his words : "the divine word commands us." His words are words of the divine word, and they command us.

It seems to me that that places Paul's words just as high as the words of Isaiah. We must, however, remember that Theophilus' main point against his heathen friend is the age of the writings. Shortly after the above quotation he writes (3. 16):

"But I wish to show thee now more accurately, God granting, the things which pertain to the times, so that thou mayest understand that our word is neither new nor mythical, but older and more true than all the poets and writers, of those writing in uncertainty." Of necessity, then, he must go back to Moses and the prophets as predecessors of Homer and Plato and the rest of the heathen poets and philosophers. And this third book then continues to the close the comparison of Jewish and heathen history. There is to my mind not the shadow of a doubt that Theophilus had the bulk of our New Testament books, and that he regarded them in general as all of them equal in authority to the books of the Old Testament.

From Antioch and the East we must now pass far over to the West, to Gaul, and visit the Churches of Vienne and of Lyons. Vienne is the place to which Herod was sent as an exile with Herodias after the murder of John the Baptist. Josephus the Jewish historian says so. It lies thirty-one kilometres to the south of Lyons, and contains still a temple of Augustus and Livia. Lyons itself, where Augustus resided several years, is to-day the third city of France. Eusebius opens the fifth book of his Church History by a brilliant paragraph upon the martyrs who suffered under Antoninus Verus, that is to say, Marcus Aurelius, and that in the seventeenth year of his reign, about the year 178–179. He relates that these persecutions were stirred up by the populace in the cities here and there through the world ; and he offers to give as a specimen the story of those martyred in one special country, because he is so fortunate as to have a written account of their sufferings, which were worthy of imperishable remembrance, being not victories won by blood and tens of thousands of murders of children, but most peaceful wars for peace of the soul, not even for the native country, but for the truth and for godliness. And then he points to Gaul and to those cities in the valley of the Rhone.

The document to which he refers is a letter of the two Churches of Vienne and Lyons. The very address of this letter reminds us again of the close union between the Churches in distant lands, for it is addressed to the Churches in Asia and Phrygia. It was less strange that the same Churches also sent at the same time a letter to Rome, borne by Irenæus, to whom we have already referred, who was then a presbyter in the Church at Lyons.

They began the former letter thus: "The servants of God dwelling in this foreign world at Vienne and Lyons in Gaul, to the brethren in Asia and Phrygia who have the same faith and hope of redemption as we have, peace and grace and glory from God the Father and Christ Jesus our Lord." Declaring that they could not duly describe nor writing contain an exact account of all they had suffered, they wrote: "But the grace of God led the fray against them and strengthened the weak, and set up firm pillars able by their patience to draw upon themselves the whole impetus of the evil one, who also met him together, standing all kinds of contumely and punishment, who also thinking the many [ills] were but few hurried on to Christ, showing, in fact, that the sufferings of the present time are not worthy to be compared to the glory which is going to be revealed to us." It is clear that they knew the eighth chapter of Romans (ver. 18). And they told of the first valiant young martyr who laid down his life for the defence of the brethren: "For he was and he is a genuine disciple of Christ, following the Lamb wherever He may go." They therefore were at home in the fourteenth chapter of the Revelation. Ten, alas! yielded to the wiles of the evil one.

Some of their heathen servants came out and denounced them as cannibals and as committing other horrible crimes, and then the people attacked them still more furiously: "And that was fulfilled which our Lord said: That the time will come in which every one slaying you will think he is offering a service to God." The sixteenth chapter of John was therefore in their hands. One of the men tortured was Attalos, who was from Pergamon; and a woman, Blandina, endured torture from early morn until the evening, so that her persecutors confessed themselves conquered, for they did not know what they could do more to her; and they were amazed that she still lived, with her whole body rent and open. But she still held out, and she cried: "I am a Christian, and no evil deed is done among us." Sanctus, who was tortured in the extreme, then took up a single answer; and whether they asked his name, or his race, or his native country, or whether he was bond or free, replied to all questions by saying in Latin the words: "I am a Christian." The governor was furious, and they put fiery plates of brass upon the tenderest spots in his body. It burned his flesh, but he remained firm:

"Cooled and strengthened by the heavenly spring of the water of life going forth from the body of Christ." We see how the Revelation and John are combined in that expression.

Potheinos the bishop, who was over ninety years of age, was brought before the governor, who asked him who was the God of the Christians. After all the questions and answers that the governor had put and heard in these days, Potheinos regarded this question as mere trifling, and he replied to the governor: "If you were worthy, you would know." And then the crowd hit and kicked and threw things at the old man, and he was carried away almost lifeless to the prison, where he died in two days. The beasts were let loose upon them in the amphitheatre, but in vain. The greater part of those who had from fear renounced Christianity, returned to a joyful martyrdom. One of the most valiant martyrs was Alexander, a physician from Phrygia, who had been many years in Gaul, another witness for the union of West and East. When they put Attalus on the heated iron chair, he cried out to the crowd in Latin: "This that you are doing is eating men. We do not eat men, nor do we do anything else that is bad." The firmness of the martyrs only infuriated the governor and the mob, and the Church wrote of them in the words of Daniel and of Revelation: "That the scripture should be fulfilled: Let the lawless one be lawless still, and let the just one be justified still." Knowing of the doctrine of the resurrection, the heathen watched the corpses of the martyrs night and day, and allowed no Christian to hold a burial service over them or to take them away for burial. After six days they threw what was not eaten by the dogs or burned up by fire into the Rhone. And they cried in an unconscious imitation of the spectators around the cross of Jesus: "Now let us see whether they will rise again, and whether their God is able to help them, and to draw them out of our hands."

The letter called the Christians who had been tortured not once or twice only but often, and who were full of burns and sores and wounds, and who nevertheless neither called themselves martyrs nor wished the others to call them martyrs,—the letter called them zealous followers and imitators of Christ, "who,"— in the words of the second chapter of Philippians,—"being in the form of God, did not think that the being equal to God was a thing that He should seize." We see in that the way in which they understood that passage, and, of course, we see that they knew well that Epistle. A little after that they used a phrase from First Peter, saying of the martyrs that "they humbled themselves under the mighty hand [of God]." And then they allude to the book of Acts: "And they prayed for those who brought these fearful things upon them, like Stephen the perfect martyr: Put not this sin upon them." And they add beautifully: "But if he prayed for the people who stoned him, how much more for the brethren." That letter warmed and cheered and spurred on to like deeds many a Christian heart in those days. For us it is a monument of the unity of the Church, and a witness to the use of books of the New Testament.

No one will undertake to deny that Potheinos, dying as bishop in 178 at more than ninety years of age, stretched back with his memory to the end of the first century, seeing that he must have been born before the year 88. We know of Potheinos the bishop, over ninety years old, and of Polycarp, who was martyred as bishop, eighty-six years old, in the year 155. How many other bishops and Christians wove the long years with long bands in one, whose names we do not know, because they were not martyrs, or because the story of their martyrdom has not reached us! Who that has any appreciation of historic sequence and of historic contemporaneity can speak of the early Christian Church as if it were a disjointed, ill-connected series of little societies that knew little of each other and less of the past, and were a ready prey for every and even the most unskilful forger of Scriptures?

It was about this time apparently, somewhere about the year 178, that a heathen named Celsus wrote a book against Christianity and called it The True Word. In it he first produces a Jew who refutes the externals of Jesus' life. Then he attacks it from the general point of view of a heathen philosopher, and endeavours to refute it in detail by arguments drawn from the history of philosophy; and then he tries to persuade the Christians to turn heathen. One thing is plain, and that is that he in general uses for the purpose of refuting them precisely our New Testament books in the main. He regards them as for Christians authoritative. At the close of his first part, in which a Jew has been bearing hard against Christianity, he shows clearly his position, his attitude towards the Scriptures. He writes: "Thus much, then, for you from

10

your own writings, on the basis of which we need no other witness, for they refute themselves." He was of the opinion that the different Gospels arose from a different conception of the facts which led different people to change the one original Gospel into the forms of the four Gospels. He scourges the inclination of Christians to divide up into sects seeking novel opinions, and declares that if all other people came to desire to be Christians, the Christians would not care to be Christians any longer. He says that at the beginning there were only a few of them, and these were of one mind ; but that after they had increased and were spread abroad in great numbers, they divided and separated themselves from each other, and each wished to have his own party. He says that in the end they only have the name Christian in common, but in reality hardly that. He presses hard upon the belief of the Christians : "All this great effect is made by faith, which is determined in advance for something or other. And so the faith, which has taken possession of their souls, procures for the Christians the great attachment to Jesus, so that they account Him, who came from a mortal body, for God, and suppose they are doing something holy in thinking this." Celsus' book, so far as we can judge of it from the plentiful quotations which Origen gives in refuting it, was simply full of the New Testament, of the New Testament in general as we have it in our hands. What he finds strange, stupid, base, that is what we read in the New Testament. He is also well acquainted with the history of the Christians, and with the way in which certain heretics treated the Gospels and Epistles.

We have named the period which is now occupying our thoughts, the age of Irenæus. Irenæus is another of the living bonds between the East and the West, between Smyrna, we may say in general Asia Minor, and Lyons or Gaul. It is to be agreed that we do not know positively that he was born and grew up in Asia Minor. He himself did not think it worth while to make any precise statements upon this subject. I think, however, that his reference to Smyrna and to Polycarp and to Florinus, a friend or at least an acquaintance of his boyhood, all point to a stay of some years in Smyrna ; and nothing seems to speak against his having been born there, save the tradition, almost isolated tradition, that he was by birth a Syrian. We know of nothing that in any way seems to favour his coming originally from Syria. In one special way there would be no obstacle to Syrian birth, if, namely, like Tatian, he should have been brought up in Syria as a Greek. However, I regard it as most likely that he was born and lived through his boyhood at least in Asia Minor, and probably in or near Smyrna. Thus far we can only guess at the date of his birth. He was probably born between the years 135 and 142.

As a boy he saw Polycarp at Smyrna, and he appears to have been younger than Florinus whom he also saw, also during his own boyhood, at Smyrna and in the presence of Polycarp. Irenæus speaks in no wise as if he had been a pupil of Polycarp's, but only as if he remembered seeing the distinguished old man as any boy stands and admires an old and reverend bishop. It is humanly speaking a mere accident that furnishes us with that minute touching Polycarp. Florinus, who was a presbyter in the Church at Rome, became a heretic, took up the Valentinian Gnosticism while Victor was bishop, and therefore after 189 or 190. And Irenæus, who has been finding that Florinus' heretical books are spreading that heresy in Gaul, not only writes to Victor and begs him to suppress Florinus and his writings, but also writes to Florinus himself, and begins as a way of catching at a favourable point in Florinus' feelings by recalling his having in boyhood seen Florinus playing a distinguished part in the imperial chambers and before Polycarp. Whether the allusions to royalty imply a visit of an emperor or not, is not so clear as to make that point valuable for dating the meeting of Irenæus with Florinus. Irenæus says the most flattering thing he can to Florinus, and gives us at the same time a glimpse of his own early life. He tells that he remembers just where and how Polycarp sat and preached to the multitude, and how he told of his intercourse with John and with others who had seen the Lord, and of some things he had heard from them about the Lord and about His miracles and teaching, and how, having received [it] from those who themselves had seen the life of the Word, Polycarp announced all things in unison with the Scriptures. Here we see the combination of the two elements, of the tradition by word of mouth and of the written books. It is fitting that Irenæus should lay stress upon this point, for it is especially with him that we begin to feel as if we had a certain literary basis for Christian life and Christian doctrine.

He continues the appeal to Florinus (Eusebius, H. E. 5. 20):
"And these things then by the grace of God that was granted
to me I heard eagerly, storing them up for memory not on
paper but in my heart, and I do ever by the grace of God
chew the cud of them in their genuineness." And then he
applies this all to his friend: "And I am able to bear witness
before God that if that blessed and apostolic presbyter had
heard some such thing as this [Florinus' heresy], crying out
and stopping his ears and saying his accustomed phrase: 'O
good God, until what times hast Thou preserved me, that I
undergo these things,' he would also have fled from the place
sitting or standing in which he had heard these words." And
he confirms this his verbal tradition by adding the reference to
Polycarp's letters: "And this can be made plain from his letters
which he sent either to the neighbouring Churches strengthening
them, or to some of the brethren admonishing them and urging
them on." We thus have here the whole round of our field:
(1) the teaching of the Lord; (2) the words of those who saw and
heard the Lord; (3) the living words of Polycarp preaching to
the people what he heard from those who saw the Lord; (4)
Irenæus' account of the preaching of Polycarp as agreeing with
the Scriptures; (5) and at last Polycarp's letters as conveying
the same things as his preaching. The Scriptures play in this
an important part. The value of the testimony from the eye-
witnesses is undisputed, and this testimony is brought to bear to
confirm the sacred books of the Church.

Irenæus was then no stranger to the Church at Rome, for
he had about ten years before as a presbyter of the Church
at Lyons carried the letter of that Church and of the Church
at Vienne about the persecutions to the Church at Rome, and
his Church gave him a high and warm recommendation to the
Church in the imperial city. The two Churches wrote to
Eleutheros the bishop at Rome (Eusebius, H. E. 5. 4):
"We have encouraged our brother and partaker [in our cares]
Irenæus to bear this letter to thee, and we beg thee to be kind
to him as being zealous for the covenant of Christ." It is
interesting to observe that Irenæus in his effort to draw Florinus
back to the Church also wrote to him a treatise on the Eight,
the Ogdoas of Florinus' Valentinian system. Irenæus' great
work was his Refutation of the Heresies in five books. Un-

fortunately the original is to a large extent lost, so that we are compelled to use for much of it the Latin translation.   It must have been written between the years 181 and 189, and it may be called our first large Christian treatise in the series of Church writers that continues from his day to the present in an almost unbroken series.   A bishop of his day, one combining the traditions of Asia Minor, of Rome, and of Gaul, cannot but have had the bulk of our New Testament.   He uses distinctly the four Gospels, the book of Acts, First Peter, First John, all the Epistles of Paul save Philemon,—how easily that could happen not to be quoted,—and the Revelation.

Irenæus' words about the four Gospels have passed into the literature of the Church in the closest connection with the Gospels, for they are used in a very large number of manuscripts as a brief preface to the Gospels.   After giving through many pages a full description of the four Gospels, he writes (3. 11. 8): "But neither are there more Gospels in number than these, nor does it receive fewer.   Since there are four directions of the world in which we are, and four general winds, and the Church is dispersed through all the earth, and the pillar and confirming of the Church is the gospel and spirit of life, it is fitting that it should have four pillars, breathing from all sides incorruption, and inflaming men.   From which it is clear that the Word, the maker of all things, the one sitting on the Cherubim and holding all things together, having been revealed to men, gave us the Gospel fourfold, but held together in one spirit. . . . For the Cherubim are four-faced, and their faces are images of the activity of the Son of God.   For the first living being, they say, is like a lion, characterising his practical and leading and kingly office. And the second is like a calf [or an ox], showing forth the sacrificial and priestly order.   And the third having the face of a man, denoting most clearly His presence in human form.   And the fourth like a flying eagle, making clear the gift of the Spirit flying down to the Church.   And therefore the Gospels agree with these, in which Christ sits.   For that according to John relates His princely and effective and glorious generation, saying : In the beginning was the Word. . . . And that, according to Luke, [telling] what is of the priestly character, begins with Zacharias the priest sacrificing to God.   For the fatted calf is already prepared, about to be slain for the finding again of the younger

son.   And Matthew heralds His birth according to man, saying :
The book of the generation of Jesus Christ, son of David, son of
Abraham.   And : The birth of Jesus Christ was thus.   Therefore
this Gospel is anthropomorphic.   And Mark made his beginning
from the prophetic spirit, that comes upon men from on high,
saying : The beginning of the Gospel of Jesus Christ as is written
in Isaiah the prophet, showing the winged image of the Gospel.
And for this reason he made the message short and swiftly
running, for this is the prophetic character. . . . For the living
beings are fourfold, and the Gospel and the activity of the Lord is
fourfold.   And for this reason four general covenants were given
to humanity.   One of the Flood, with Noah with the sign of the
rainbow.   And the second Abraham's, with the sign of circumcision.   And the third, the giving of the law under Moses.   And
the fourth, the Gospel, through our Lord Jesus Christ."

Then Irenæus goes on (3. 11. 9) to berate the empty and unlearned and bold men "who put aside the idea"—that is to say,
the proper notion and preconception—"of the Gospel, and bring
forward either more or fewer than the above mentioned forms of
the Gospel.   Some of them so that they may seem to have found
out more of the truth, the others setting aside the things arranged
by God."   These words look, at the first glance, very interesting.
It seems as if we might here, say in the year 185, have a representation of unknown apocryphal Gospels, or perhaps a description
of various Gospels that were just as good as, and in some places
quite as well accepted as our four Gospels, but that did not
survive because they had not the good fortune to be added to the
four Gospels.   Whom has Irenæus thought of?   Who had less
or more Gospels?   Irenæus goes on : "For Marcion rejecting
the whole Gospel, or to say it better, cutting himself off in fact
from the Gospel, boasts that he has a part of the Gospel."   We
see at once what that means.   The rejecting the whole Gospel is
simply Marcion's cutting himself off from the Church and setting
up Churches for himself.   And the boasting that he has part of
the Gospel is not Marcion's, but Irenæus' way of putting it, or is
rather a mixture of Irenæus and of Marcion.   Marcion would
not have boasted and did not boast that he had a "part" of the
Gospel.   According to his conception of the case, what he had
was the Gospel and the whole Gospel.   What he rejected and cut
out, that was not Gospel at all.   Marcion therefore boasted that

he, and that he alone, had the pure and genuine Gospel, without adulteration and corruption, in that Gospel which he had won from the ore in the Gospel of Luke. But that was for Irenæus a mere butt end of a Gospel, a miserable excuse for a Gospel, and hence he puts it as he does, that Marcion boasts that he has a part of the Gospel. That was, then, one effort to reduce the number of the Gospels, or we might term it, to lessen the amount of the Gospel.

The second is of a different character: "Others, however, in order to make the gift of the Spirit ineffective, which in these last days by the decree of the Father is shed abroad upon the human race, do not admit that form which is the Gospel according to John, in which the Lord promises that He will send the Comforter, but reject at the same time the Gospel and the prophetic spirit. Wretched men, indeed, who wish to be false prophets,"—again a word of Irenæus', for they regard themselves, of course, as true and genuine prophets,—" but repel the prophetic grace from the Church. . . . We are given to understand, moreover, that such men as these as little accept the Apostle Paul. For in the Epistle which is to the Corinthians, he spoke most diligently of prophetic gifts, and knows of men and women prophesying in the Church. By all these things therefore, sinning against the Spirit of God, they fall into the sin that cannot be forgiven." Who are these people who reject the Gospel of John? They appear to be certain Christians whom a later writer, Epiphanius, calls Alogians, or people who were against the Logos, the Word. We might call them No-Worders. Singularly enough, we know very little about them. With them Irenæus has exhausted his catalogue of the people who are content with fewer than the four Gospels. The great point for us is, that these two sets of people bring in no new Gospels. They had our four Gospels in their hands, and they chose on the one hand to content themselves with a mutilated Luke, and on the other hand to be satisfied with Matthew, Mark, and Luke, and to let John go. Marcion did have great influence, as we have seen. These others, the rejecters of John, appear to have had as good as no influence, for we find almost no traces of them. They are celebrated as being about the only persons in ancient times who were so lacking in judgment as to give up that Gospel. We cannot, however, discover any tokens that their

notions found favour in wide circles. We are at a loss to place
them. But what does the remark about the Epistles of Paul
mean? We cannot tell. Nothing of that kind is to be found
elsewhere attached to the special rejection of John. It is
possible that the thought is simply a conclusion of Irenæus':
They reject the spiritual Gospel. They therefore reject spiritual
gifts. First Corinthians praises spiritual gifts. Therefore—which,
of course, would not in the least follow by any logical necessity—
these people reject the Apostle Paul.

If those two sets of people had fewer Gospels, who had more?
Here again we are eager to learn of some new Gospel. We shall
be disappointed: "But those who are from Valentinus, being
again beyond all fear, bringing forward their own writings,"—
we might almost say concoctions; they are things that the
Valentinians have "written together," have "scraped together in
writing" for themselves,—"boast that they have more than the
Gospels themselves are. In fact, they have proceeded to such
boldness, that they call that which was written by them not very
long since the Gospel of truth, which does not agree at all with
the Gospels of the apostles, so that they cannot even have a
Gospel without blasphemy. For if that which they bring forward
is the Gospel of truth, and this is moreover unlike those (Gospels)
that have been handed down to us by the apostles, as anyone
who cares can learn, as is clear from the Scriptures themselves,
then that which is handed down from the apostles is not the
Gospel of truth." This gives us nothing new. We have an
inkling of the state of the case with the Valentinians. The
Valentinians had and used our four Gospels. They—or some
one of them—wrote a book upon the ideas of their system, and
they unfortunately took a fancy to call it a Gospel. So far as we
can see, they did not for a moment purpose to put it in the place
of any one of the Gospels or of all four Gospels. It was a totally
different thing. At the same time the use of the word Gospel
made it easy for Irenæus to decry their action in the above way.
It would further not be at all impossible that other uninformed
people, and let us concede it, even some less informed Valentinians, might have taken the title Gospel in the same sense, and
have supposed that the book was meant to be a proper Gospel.
We should not fail to observe that on the one hand this use of
this title indicates a high valuation of the name Gospel in the

circles in which Valentinus lived.   Far more important, however, is the observation, that the isolation in which this use of the word by the Valentinians stands is really, if I mistake not, in itself a most thorough refutation of that view of the second century and of our Gospels, which represents the century, and especially the former half of it, as deluged with all manner of Gospels, some bad, some indifferent, but a large number quite good, which Gospels then disappeared of a sudden, because the Church had arbitrarily settled upon our present four.

Irenæus' high appreciation of scripture, and that of the New Testament as well as of the Old Testament, shines forth in a few sentences (4. 33, 8) which we shall understand better when we some day find the original Greek words for the whole ; now we have the Greek only for the first sixteen words :   " True knowledge "— Gnosis—" is the teaching of the apostles and the ancient system of the Church through all the world, and the sign of the body of Christ according to the successions of the bishops, to whom they "—the apostles—" gave over the Church which is in each single place, [and] the fullest use of the Scriptures which have reached us in [careful] custody without corruption, consenting neither to addition nor to subtraction, and the text "—reading— " without corruption, and the legitimate and diligent explanation according to the Scriptures both without peril and without blasphemy, and the chief duty of love, which is more precious than knowledge, more glorious, moreover, than prophecy, and supereminently above all the rest of the graces."   Here we behold as one of the main points of right Christian knowledge the most extended use of the Scriptures.   These Scriptures, he says, have been handed down to us in watchful care " without fiction."   I have written above " corruption " as a general term. I take it that the fiction here warded off is on the one hand the fictitious composition of new books, and on the other hand the fictitious or corrupting and changing or mutilating treatment of known books.   In neither case does true knowledge allow of addition or of curtailment.   The following sentence has at least two possible senses.   It may mean a guarding of the text in the books from falsification.   But it may refer to the reading the Scriptures in church, and would then mean that the reading is to be a direct reading, keeping exactly to the words of the text, not changing or paraphrasing them.   If that sentence refers thus to the public reading, then the following would fit well with homiletic commentating on the text. The explanation of the text must be legitimate and diligent, without running into dangerous questions or doctrines, and as well without blasphemy ; but it must above all be according to the scripture, that is to say, that scripture agrees with itself, and that scripture must interpret scripture. It seems to me that the opening with the teaching of the apostles and the closing with the First Corinthians' view of love, compels us to take the words scripture here as applying to the New Testament as well as to the Old.

Before leaving Irenæus we must read a few words that Eusebius has saved for us from the close of one of his books. It was that book About the Eight that, as we saw above, he sent to the heretical friend Florinus who had turned Valentinian. Eusebius writes : " At which place, at the end of the book, having found a lovely note of his, we must of necessity add it here in this book. It reads thus : I adjure thee who dost copy this book by our Lord Jesus Christ, and by His glorious coming, in which He comes to judge living and dead, that thou compare what thou copiest, and that thou correct it carefully, according to this original, from which thou hast copied it, and that thou likewise copy off this oath and put it in your copy " (H. E. 5. 20). It was a much too small matter for the use of the oath by Christ and His glorious coming, but that lay in the method of thought of these dreamy and fiery representatives of an apocalyptic cast of Christianity.

Irenæus has done well by us. He has given us a most full use of the New Testament, quoting even the book of Acts at great length. And he has discussed for us in a very welcome manner the state of the question as to the valuation of the Gospels in his day. It is true he writes in the years between 181 and 189, but his view of the books of the New Testament is not one that he first conceived of while writing. His view of the case in the year 155 was probably precisely the same.

We have, it is true, thus far moved freely and far in the Church and in the Roman Empire, passing repeatedly from Syria in the East to Gaul in the West. Nevertheless we have to a great extent had more to do with the Greek language and with Greek writers than with other languages and with those who used them. The question arises whether or not we can find at this early time witnesses from some of the other literatures, from Churches using other languages. I personally am inclined to think that we can. Others think not. Let us begin with Syria. When did Christianity gain a foothold in Syria? Remember the character of Antioch in Syria as a second capital of the Empire, with the wealth and the trade of Syria pouring into it, and with an important university. Consider, further, the Christian constellation there, and the part played by Antioch as a starting-point for mission journeys. Barnabas, Paul, Peter, and how many other eminent Christians of that time we know not, spent much time there. Of course the city was largely **Greek**, but the Syrian element was not, could not be, lacking.

The free intercourse between Palestine and Antioch was shown distinctly at the time of the questionings about Gentile and Jewish Christians that found a solution on the occasion of the visit of a committee headed by Barnabas and Paul to the mother Church at Jerusalem. Now the very fact of the occurrence of such a question at Antioch, and the circumstance that Paul at Antioch openly reproved Peter for changing his habit of life at the coming of certain Jewish Christians from Jerusalem, seem to point to the presence there of at least a number of Aramaic-speaking Christians. Their Aramaic, if they came from Jerusalem, was closely related to the language of the north, for it had come from there. It seems to me then in every way probable that at that early date, speaking roughly, before the year 70, there were in Antioch Aramaic-speaking Christians. Edessa was not far from Antioch, not as far from Antioch as Damascus was. Nisibis was not far, not as far again beyond Edessa. If we should go down towards the south-east, Babylon was not three times as far from Antioch as Damascus was. Enough of that about distances. We find a reference to Peter's being at Babylon. It is the custom with some scholars to insist upon it that that was Rome and not Babylon. To me it appears to be only reasonable to suppose that Peter and other Christians who spoke Aramaic did some mission work, going out from Antioch to Edessa, Nisibis, and, we add because it really is named for Peter himself, to Babylon.

I have no doubt, although I have not a word about it in books, that there were Syrian Christians in Syria itself in the three cities named, before the death of Paul. If anyone chooses to put it

all thirty years later, he will have Christians there in the year 100.
The next wing in this castle in the air is the statement that these
Syrian Christians of the year 70, or even of the year 100, may be
supposed by the year 150, or at latest 170, to have reached such
a number, and to have attained so much education and so much
insight into the value of the Greek Gospels and Epistles, as to have
made not merely verbal, but also written translations of them.
In spite of the lack of external testimony, I regard the opinion
that the Syriac version of the bulk of the New Testament books
was in existence, say in the year 170, to be a very modest one.
So far as we can tell, this Old Syriac translation contained all the
books of our New Testament except the Revelation and the four
Epistles, Second and Third John, Second Peter and Jude.   The
Revelation was at that time chiefly used in the West.   Second
and Third John were more private letters, and Second Peter was
scarcely generally known before the close of the third century.
That Jude should be missing seems strange.

The Old Latin translation arose probably in North Africa.
Rome and Southern Italy in Christian circles were too thoroughly
Greek at first to need a Latin text.   It appears to have been
made at or soon after the middle of the second century, and to
have been used, for example, by the translator of Irenæus.
Tertullian, who began to write at least in the year 190, tells us
that before the close of the second century the Christians filled
the palace, the senate, the forum, and the camp.   I think we may
count upon the existence of this translation as early as the year
170 at the least.   It seems to have contained the four Gospels,
the book of Acts, thirteen Epistles of Paul, First Peter, First,
Second, and Third John, Jude, and Revelation.   Perhaps it
included Hebrews, with the name of Barnabas as author, or
without a name at all.   James and Second Peter do not show
themselves.   We may remark, that First Peter does not seem to
have been read much in the Latin Churches.   It does not, however, appear to have been called in question.

The Coptic translations I am inclined to date also from the
last quarter of the second century, but some Coptic scholars think
them to be much later.

When we find that the Syrian and Old Latin and Coptic
witnesses are more rare and less profuse in the second century
than the Greek witnesses, we should never fail to recall the cir-

cumstance, that the persistence and preservation of the latter witnesses by no means forces or even permits us, then, to conclude from the present lack of the former witnesses, that Christianity did not flourish in those lands under those races, and that there were no written monuments in those tongues.   Greek was the common language then, and the number of people who spoke, read, and wrote Greek was, it is true, very large.   This had its effect upon the number of books that were written in Greek. Whoever wished to reach a wide circle of readers was impelled to write Greek.   And this had its effect also upon the number of Greek books that were preserved.   A greater number of people took an interest in Greek books, and cared to have them copied off and handed down.   That seems to me to be quite certain. Nevertheless, I do not in the least doubt that from a very early date, possibly not only in Syria but also in Northwestern Africa and in Egypt, there were many Christians, and at least a few Christian writings.   But Syriac and Old Latin and Coptic Christian writings were on the one hand less, much less, plentiful than Greek Christian writings, because there were not so many people who could read them, and who therefore would order them to be copied off.   These writings were in the next place, by reason of the limited range of their circulation, not so well prepared by the survival of chance copies in one place and another to outlive the general vicissitudes of literature.   In the third place, the separatistical movements in those Churches did much to sever their few books from the use of the Church.   And in the fourth place the political turmoils, with the attendant destruction of cities and libraries, committed much greater havoc among these limited books and places ; this is the reverse of the second point.   Could we imagine that the centre of Christianity for the time from Paul's first missionary journey down to the year 350 had been in Babylon, or even in Edessa or in Nisibis, we should certainly have had a far different literary Christian harvest from those years.   More would have been written in Syrian, and more would have been preserved.

We are nearing the close of the second century.   The Age of Irenæus closes with the year 200.   It is pertinent at this point to take a review of what we have thus far seen.   At this time we find in the hands of the Church, in the hands of the larger number of great Churches upon the usual lines of travel, the larger part of the New Testament books.   The four Gospels, the book of Acts, the First Epistle of Peter, the First Epistle of John, thirteen Epistles of Paul, the Epistle to the Hebrews, and the book of Revelation.   It is not strange that in one place or another the scanty amount of Christian literature does not supply us with a sign of life for one book or another.   That is not necessary. When we are doubly and triply assured, from the letter of Clement of Rome from the year 96, that the Epistle to the Hebrews was then known, valued, and almost learnt by heart by an eminent and ready writer in the capital of the Empire, it really does not make very much difference to us if we find that one man or another towards the close of the century has failed to use that book in what is preserved to us of his writings.   When we find that that same Clement of Rome in the year 96 uses the Epistle of James, and that Hermas the brother of the Roman bishop Pius uses it profusely about the year 140, we know surely that it was at home at Rome early and late in this period, and it is a matter of supreme indifference to us when this short letter fails to put in an appearance in one writer or another in between or later.   Those authors did not write in the first place chiefly for the purpose of telling us what books they had in their New Testament.   We must here, then, observe that the series of books named above does not present itself to us at the close of this age of Irenæus as a new thing.   The fact is, that no single sign has been found that any book has been added to the list during this period.   On the contrary, from the first to the last every Christian writer and even the heretical ones are clearly of the opinion that the writings which we now have, and which they then received or rejected, were on hand long before that time.   If Marcion rejected Matthew, Mark, and John, it was not because they were young, but because they did not suit him.   He rejected the books of the Old Testament which he acknowledged to be still older.   He rejected the Creator God not because He was a young God, but because according to the history of Israel He was a bad God, cruel, brutal, and bloodthirsty.

We have from this period, probably from the year 196, an interesting example of the way in which the Churches passed letters from one to another.   Eusebius relates (H. E. 5. 25) that the Palestinian bishops Narcissus and Theophilus, and with them Cassius, bishop of Tyre, and Clarus, bishop of Ptolemæis, had a meeting with others to pass resolutions about the apostolical tradition touching the celebration of Easter. "At the close of the writing"—that is to say, of the utterance of these bishops, and that probably determined especially by the skilled and practical writer Theophilus of Cæsarea—"they add to their words the following: Try to distribute copies of our letters to each Church, so that we may not be guilty in respect to those who recklessly let their own souls go astray. And we make known to you that at Alexandria they celebrate on the same day on which we celebrate. For letters have reached them from us and us from them. So that we celebrate the holy day with one voice and together." These letters about Easter are a premonition of the later following Festal Epistles of the patriarch of Alexandria announcing the proper day for Easter. And the distribution of the letters Church by Church shows how readily then written material could be produced and sent about among Christians.

THE POSSIBILITIES OF TRADITION.

We have now reached, naming the year 190 as doubtless later than the composition of Irenæus' great work against the heresies, a date that is about one hundred and sixty years distant from the death of Jesus, one hundred and twenty-six years from the death of Paul, and perhaps a little over ninety years from the death of John, probably not ninety years from the death of Simon the son of Clopas, who was possibly born about the same time as Jesus. We have repeatedly taken occasion to call attention to the way in which a long life has made a bridge for us between extremely distant points of time. Now we shall do another thing. The long lives of which we have spoken have in part come to our notice more by chance than by any necessity of the historical recital, in that some small incident, like Irenæus' need of writing to the heretical friend of his youth, has called forth the story. Now I wish to say a word or two about tradition in general, and to point to the possibilities of tradition, taking examples from modern life. I wish to show the possibility of a much more compact and far-reaching net covering this early field of Christian history.

Let me begin with a soldier, Friedrich Weger, who in 1901

was living at Breslau eighty-nine years old, still fresh and hale
in body and mind. He was born in 1812, served in the years
1834–1836, and took part in a parade before the Prussian King
Friedrich Wilhelm III. and the Russian Emperor Nicholas I.
sixty-one years before 1901. — Another veteran celebrated in
sound health his hundredth birthday on March 14th, 1901.
His name was Hermann Wellemeyer, and he was a house-
carpenter in Lengerich in Westphalia. He served in the years
1823–1825, but he remembered distinctly the marching of the
French and Russian and Prussian troops through Lengerich, and
the general joy at the victory over Napoleon at Leipzig in 1813.—
In the year 1899 there were living in Silesia in Schwientochlowitz
a working woman named Penkalla who was one hundred and
four years old, and in Domnowitz the widow of a veteran, Rosina
Nowack, who was one hundred and seven years old, and who
told with pleasure what she had seen as a child.—And in
the year 1904, Andreas Nicolaievitch Schmidt, a former orderly
sergeant, was still living at Tiflis and able to go about by himself,
although he was one hundred and twenty-two years old. He
fought in 1812 at Borodino, and was wounded in 1854 at
Sebastopol. In 1858 he was sent to Siberia because he had
let a political prisoner escape.—In a parenthesis the curious
case may be mentioned of Sir Stephen Fox's daughters. He
married in 1654, and his first child, a daughter, was born and
died in 1655, three years before the death of Cromwell. After
losing several married children, he married late in life, and his
youngest daughter was born in 1727, seventy-two years after her
oldest sister. This daughter lived ninety-eight years, and died in
1825, when Queen Victoria was six years old. Thus there passed
one hundred and seventy years between the deaths of these two
sisters.

But it may be objected that these are all isolated cases.
Of course they are. Yet such isolated cases are occurring all
over the world. In many cases it is the merest accident that
brings such an old man to public notice.—In the year 1875,
referring to the sixtieth anniversary of the battle of Waterloo, the
Times newspaper in London gave the names of *seventy-six*
Waterloo officers who were still alive.—A man named Johann
Leonhard Röder, who was at the battle of Waterloo as a boy of
fifteen, was still living at Quincy, Illinois, in January 1907.—In

the year 1899, King Albert of Saxony celebrated at Dresden the fiftieth anniversary of his first battle on the 13th of April 1849. At that celebration there were drawn up before him, in the park of his villa at Strehlen near Dresden, *seven hundred* veterans from that year 1849. They were all more than seventy years old. The king's military instructor, the oldest orderly sergeant, named Schurig, was there eighty-five years old and gave a toast to the king at lunch. There were seven hundred men whose memory as grown men reached back fifty and largely more years. Two such men would stretch over more than a century.

The most interesting case that I know of is connected with Yale College. In the year 1888 a clergyman named Joseph Dresser Wickham, who was in his ninety-second year and still hearty in body and mind, was at the Alumni meeting. He had entered college at fifteen, in the year 1811. In that year 1811 he saw and heard an alumnus who had left college in 1734, seventy-seven years before. That alumnus was twenty-six years old when he left Yale, and was one hundred and three years old when Wickham saw him in 1811. In the year 1716, eighteen years before that alumnus left Yale, and when he was a boy eight years old, the college was moved from Saybrook to New Haven. The changing the place for the college caused much stir and excitement, and the eight-year-old boy remembered the change very well. Thus two men carried a tradition of a special occurrence over the space of one hundred and seventy-two years. Should we put that back into the second century, Irenæus the bishop could reach from the year 178 back to the sixth year of our Lord. Irenæus at the year 150 would reach back to 22 B.C. Justin the martyr, who was no longer young in the year 150, would also reach back to 22 B.C. Do not forget Simon the son of Clopas dying a martyr at one hundred and twenty years. And if ninety-two and one hundred and three are rare old ages, eighty and eighty are less rare, and eighty and eighty make, from the twentieth year of each, one hundred and twenty years. Observe, however, the single persons. One of the alumni reached back seventy-seven years with his memory, the other ninety-five years. Take again the year 150 for Irenæus and the older Justin. Seventy-seven years would carry them back to the year 73, and ninety-five years to the year 55.

It is furthermore not to be forgotten that that time was a

11

time at which tradition was cultivated in a much higher style than it is to-day. They did not have our newspapers and chronicles and books. Tradition was almost all they had, and they were used to thinking of it. They practised it carefully. They narrated. They listened. They studied it over. They told it then to younger men. Now I wish to lay stress upon two things. In the first place, we know very well of a number of lines of tradition, for example the grandson of Jude, Simon the son of Clopas, the daughters of Philip the evangelist who had seen Paul for several days at their father's house in Cæsarea, and whom Polycarp saw at Hierapolis, and Polycarp himself who probably saw John. That is enough for the moment. In the second place, however, if we are scientific enough to consider the whole growing Church from Jerusalem and Antioch to Ephesus and Smyrna and Thessalonica and Corinth and Rome and Vienne and Lyons in Gaul, and to conjure up to ourselves the occasional Christian societies in countless places in between,—if we consider this large field, and I shall now not say the possibility, but the necessity of there having been many men and women of seventy and eighty, and some men and women of ninety overlapping each other, we shall be ready to concede that the course of Christian tradition has not been in the least a frail and weak passage from Paul to Irenæus, from John to Clement of Alexandria. A judicial view of the field—the writer of any given statement is always to his own way of thinking judicial—will refuse to suppose that at Antioch (Alexandria?), Smyrna, Corinth, and Rome, as representatives of great provinces of Christianity, there were any gaps in the living and seething life of the Church between Paul and Irenæus.

Testimony for Separate Books.—Matthew.

In approaching thus the year 200, what have we before us in the way of clear use of the books of the New Testament? We have in advance presupposed that the most of them were in existence, and where we do not hear of anything to the contrary, anything that excludes their early existence and proves their later composition, we go upon the theory that they are in use. Nevertheless, what do we positively and directly know about

their use before the year 185, before Irenæus' great work?
Let us take up the books.   The Gospel according to Matthew
was quoted apparently in the Great Declaration written by Simon
Magus or by some close pupil of his.   Hippolytus (6. 16) gives
the words thus : " For somewhere near, he says, is the axe to the
roots of the tree.   Every tree, he says, not bearing good fruit, is
cut down and cast into the fire."   No one will be surprised that
he quoted loosely.   We have seen how loosely good Christians
quoted, and Simon Magus could not be expected to be more
careful than they.   For the followers of Cerinthus, and it doubtless holds good also for Cerinthus himself, Epiphanius tells us
(28. 5) directly that they used this Gospel.   He says : " For they
use the Gospel according to Matthew in part and not the whole
of it, because of the birth list according to the flesh " ; and again
(30. 14) : " For Cerinthus and Carpocrates using for themselves,
it is true, the same Gospel, prove from the beginning of the
Gospel according to Matthew by the birth list that the Christ
was of the seed of Joseph and Mary."   He may well have
had a Gospel with a different reading in the first chapter of
Matthew.

The Ophites also used this Gospel.   "This, they say, is what
is spoken (Hippolytus, 5. 8 ; p. 160 [113]) : Every tree not making
good fruit is cut down and cast into fire.   For these fruits, they
say, are only the reasonable, the living men, who come in through
the third gate."   From the seventh chapter they quote (5. 8 ;
p. 160 [114]) : " This, they say, is what he saith : Cast not that
which is holy to the dogs, nor the pearls to the swine, saying that
the words about swine and dogs are the intercourse of a woman
with a man."   And again from the same chapter, turning the
words around in memory (5. 8 ; p. 166 [116]) : " About these
things, they say, the Saviour spoke expressly : That narrow and
strait is the way leading to life, and few are those entering in
to it ; but broad and roomy is the way that leads to destruction,
and many are they that pass through by it."   And still from
the same chapter (5. 8 ; p. 158 [112]) " And again, they say, the
Saviour said : Not everyone saying to me, Lord, Lord, shall
enter into the kingdom of the heavens, but he that doeth the
will of My Father which is in the heavens."   They give (5. 8 ;
p. 160 [113]) the parable of the Sower from the thirteenth chapter
just as anybody might quote it from memory : " And this, they

say, is what is spoken: The one sowing went forth to sow. And some fell by the wayside and was trodden down, and some on rocky ground, and sprang up, they say, and because it had no depth withered away and died. And some fell, they say, on good and fit ground, and made fruit, one a hundred, another sixty, another thirty. He that hath ears, they say, to hear, let him hear." One of their quotations brings a quite intelligible loose combination or confusing of two verses in the same thirteenth chapter. It is a capital specimen of a wild quotation (5. 8; p. 152 [108]): "This, they say, is the kingdom of heaven lying within you like a treasure, like leaven hid in three measures of meal."

Just of the same kind is the following from the twenty-third chapter (5. 8; p. 158 [112]): "This, they say, is that which was spoken: Ye are whitened tombs, filled, they say, within with dead bones, because the living man is not in you." And thereupon they recur to the twenty-seventh chapter: "And again, they say, the dead shall go forth from the graves, that is to say, the spiritual, not the fleshly ones, being born again from the earthly bodies." The Sethians quote from the tenth chapter (5. 21; p. 212 [146]): "This is, they say, that which is spoken: I came not to cast peace upon the earth, but a sword." Basilides knew this Gospel. It is the merest chance that the little we have from him touches Matthew, just touches it. He was speaking of everything having its own time (7. 27; p. 376 [243]), and mentioned thereat: "the wise men who beheld the star." How easily could he have failed to use that example, or could Hippolytus have failed to quote the five words! The so-called letter of Barnabas uses, as was mentioned above, the technical phrase "it is written" for a quotation from this Gospel (ch. 4): "Let us give heed, lest, as it is written, we should be found: Many are called, but few are chosen." These words might have been, yes, they may have been a common proverb in the time of Jesus, and the author of this letter could have quoted them as a well-known everyday proverb. But he does not do that. He quotes them as scripture, and doubtless has Matthew in view. When he writes (ch. 19): "Thou shalt not approach unto prayer with an evil conscience," he may have the words of Jesus in Matthew in his mind, but it is not necessary that he should. His words (ch. 19): "Thou shalt not hesitate to give, nor when thou givest shalt thou murmur ; but thou shalt know who is the good payer back of the reward," looks very much like a reference to the sixth chapter of Matthew.   He quotes Matthew, but takes a curious view of the apostles when he writes (ch. 5) : "And when He chose His own disciples, who were going to preach His gospel, they being beyond all sin the most lawless ones, that He might show that He did not come to call righteous but sinners, then He manifested Himself to be a Son of God."   One of his short summing-ups (ch. 7) seems to have Matthew's account of the trial before Pilate as a basis : "And they shall say : Is not this the one whom we once crucified, deriding and piercing and spitting (upon Him) ?   In truth this was the one who then said that He Himself was a Son of God."

We have very little of what Valentinus wrote, and nevertheless Clement of Alexandria (Strom. 2. 20. 114) has, as men say, happened to save up for us a beautiful passage from him which gives us a few words from Matthew.   Valentinus quotes and then comments upon the thought.   I give his first sentence and then a later sentence which appears to show us what his text was here, what reading he had : "And one is good, whose revelation was openly through the Son ; and through Him alone could the heart become clean, every evil spirit being thrust out of the heart. . . .   In this manner also the heart so long as it does not reach wisdom, being impure, being the dwelling-place of many demons ; but when the only good Father turns His eyes upon it, it is made holy and beams with light ; and he is blessed who has such a heart, for he shall see God."   Is not that beautiful ? And it tells us that Valentinus knew and valued Matthew.

Epiphanius (33. 8) has given us some quotations from Ptolemæus, Valentinus' disciple, including a letter written to a Christian woman named Flora ; and in this he shows clearly that he uses Matthew.   Ptolemæus is explaining the state of the Law to Flora : "Thus, therefore, also the law confessed to be God's is divided into three parts, on the one hand into that which was fulfilled by the Saviour ; for the word : Thou shalt not kill, thou shalt not commit adultery, thou shalt not swear falsely, is comprised in the neither being angry, nor lusting after, nor swearing. And it is divided into that which is finally done away with.   For the word : Eye for eye and tooth for tooth, being woven about with unrighteousness and having itself something of unrighteousness, was annulled by the Saviour by the opposites. And the opposites annul each other : For I say unto you, Resist not evil at all. But if any one strike thee upon the cheek, turn to him also the other cheek." There we have both a quotation from Matthew and a summary based upon Matthew. And the same text that we found above in Valentinus is used again by Ptolemæus in this letter, saying : "And if the perfect God is good according to His own nature, as He is,—for the Saviour declared to us that one alone is the good God, His own Father,— then the one of the opposite nature is characterised not only as bad, but also as wicked in unrighteousness."

For another of Valentinus' pupils, the very little known Heracleon, we have in Origen's commentary (13. 59) on John a pair of sentences that point to Matthew. In one he uses the phrase : "Supposing that both body and soul are destroyed in hell." In the other : "He thinks that the destruction of the men of the Demiurge is made plain in the words : The sons of the kingdom shall go out into outer darkness."

Among the many who indulged in the fancies of Valentinus' system was a man named Mark, apparently a Syrian, and his followers, who were called Marcosians. They are said to have written spurious Gospels. Yet it is plain that they used and treasured highly our four Gospels. For Matthew we may take the following which Irenæus brings from them (1. 20. 2) : "And to the one saying to Him : Good teacher, He confessed the truly good God, saying : Why dost thou call Me good ? One is good, the Father in the heavens. And they say that the heavens are now called the Eons." Again Irenæus writes : "And because He did not answer to those who said to Him : With what authority doest Thou this ? but confounded them by His return question, they explain that He by so speaking showed that the Father was un-utterable." Then Irenæus places before us their use of the treasured verses in the eleventh chapter : "And again saying : Come to Me, all ye that labour and are heavy laden, and I will give you rest. And learn of Me, (they say) that He announced the Father of the truth. For what they did not know, they said, this He promised to teach them. . . . And as the highest point and the crown of their theory they bring the following : I confess Thee, Father, Lord of the heavens and of the earth, that Thou hast hidden (these things) from the wise and prudent, and hast revealed them to babes. Thus, O Father, because grace was granted Me before Thee. All things were given over to Me by My Father. And no one knows the Father except the Son, and the Son except the Father, and to whomsoever the Son may reveal Him." This, as Irenæus then explains, they apply to their notion that the God of the Old Testament had not the least in common with the good God of the New Testament: "In these words they say that He shows most clearly that the Father of truth whom they have also discovered, was never known to anyone before His coming. And they wish to insist upon it that the Maker and Creator was ever known of all men, and that the Lord spoke these words of the Father who was unknown to all, whom they set forth." They base thus their main theory on the Gospel according to Matthew in this point, in which they undoubtedly followed in the footsteps of Valentinus. And we see, in spite of all that is said about other Gospels, that these are their real Gospels, these are their foundation and tower.

We have already shown above that Justin Martyr appears to have known the Gospel according to Matthew. To make assurance doubly sure, we find in the Dialogue with Trypho the second chapter of Matthew used and discussed more than once. He impresses it upon the Jew that Herod got his information from the Jewish presbyters (ch. 78): "For also this King Herod learning from the elders of your people, the wise men then coming to him from Arabia and saying that they knew from a star that appeared in the heaven that a king was born in your country, and we are come to worship him." Justin continues the story at length, combining it with Isaiah. It is in connection with this that he speaks, as given above, of Herod's slaying all the boys in Bethlehem. More than twenty chapters later (ch. 102) he returns to this chapter again. Here he again reverts to the journey into Egypt, and offers a possible objection: "And if anyone should say to us: Could not God have rather slain Herod? I reply: Could not God at the beginning have taken away the serpent that it should not exist, instead of saying: I will put enmity between him and the woman, and his seed and her seed? Could He not at once have created a multitude of men?" And he again reverts to this a chapter later (ch. 103). Then he gives the etymology of Satan from *sata*, an apostate, and *nas*, a serpent— *Satanas*, and continues: "For this devil also at the same time that He went up from the river Jordan, the voice having said to Him: Thou art My Son, I to-day have begotten Thee, in the memoirs of the apostles it is written, coming up to Him also tempted Him so far as to say to Him: Worship me, and that Christ answered him: Go behind Me, Satan, the Lord thy God shalt thou worship, and Him alone shalt thou serve." Again he writes (ch. 105): "For also urging on His disciples to surpass the method of life of the Pharisees, and if not that they should understand that they will not be saved, that He said, this is written in the memoirs: Except your righteousness abound above the scribes and Pharisees, ye shall not enter into the kingdom of the heavens." At another place he writes (ch. 107): "And that He was going to rise on the third day after being crucified, it is written in the memoirs that men from your race "—that is to say, Jews, like Trypho—"disputing with Him said: Show us a sign. And He answered to them: An evil and adulterous generation seeketh a sign, and a sign shall not be given unto them "—unto the people of that generation—"save the sign of Jonah." In the fragment on the Resurrection (ch. 2), Justin quotes Matthew: "The Saviour having said: They neither marry nor are given in marriage, but shall be like angels in the heaven." Of course he quotes here as elsewhere loosely.

We have already seen what Papias says about the work of Matthew in writing the Sayings of the Lord in Hebrew. I am inclined to suppose, as I have already explained, that that refers to the book which lies at the basis of the three synoptic Gospels. It may be that Papias as well as Eusebius, supposed that Hebrew book to have been accurately translated in and to be precisely our Matthew. The knowledge of Hebrew was not so widespread as to compel us to suppose that the assumption that the Hebrew book agreed with our Matthew was correct. Nothing indicates in the least that Papias did not have and hold and treasure our four Gospels.

As for Athenagoras, he quotes Matthew loosely, possibly bringing in a word or two from Luke. He writes (ch. 11): "What then are the words on which we have been brought up? I say unto you: Love your enemies, bless those who curse you, pray for those who persecute you, so that ye may be sons of your Father in the heavens, who causes His sun to rise on the evil and good, and rains upon just and unjust." One of his summaries (ch. 11) seems also to point certainly to the same Sermon on the Mount: "For they do not place before us words, but show good deeds: being struck, not to strike back, and being robbed, not to go to court, to give to those who ask, and to love the neighbours as themselves."

Theophilus, in the passage above touched (3. 14), gives Matthew thus: "But the gospel: Love ye, it saith, your enemies, and pray for those who revile you. For if ye love those who love you, what reward have ye? This do also the robbers and the publicans. And those who do good, it teaches not to boast, that they may not be men-pleasers." The following (2. 34) points doubtless to Matthew: "And all things whatsoever a man does not wish to be done to himself, that he should neither do to another."

Tatian seems to have used Matthew in a very strained way to back up his asceticism. Clement of Alexandria describes the agreement of the Law and the Gospel in reference to marriage, and then gives the forced interpretation of Tatian (Strom. 3. 12, 86 and 87): "Saying that the Saviour spoke of the begetting of children, on earth not to lay up treasures where moth and rust destroy." And a few lines farther on: "And likewise they take that other saying: The sons of that age, the word about the resurrection of the dead: They neither marry nor are given in marriage."

But we have given enough passages to show that, during the time that we have thus far paid attention to, the Gospel according to Matthew was used freely and in circles widely distant from each other, and as a book that had a position out of the common run of books. Let me say at once that we should not look for such a general application of Mark and Luke. The position of Matthew as the first of the four Gospels, and perhaps the naive character of the history of the birth and temptation of Jesus in it, have secured to it at all times, and, if I am not mistaken, still secure to it to-day, a frequency of perusal that the two other synoptic Gospels cannot equal. Matthew is read more than the others, save perhaps by the people who with heroic consistency compel themselves to pay like honour to every part of scripture, and who therefore read in unvarying course from the first chapter of Genesis up to the last chapter of the book of Revelation.

MARK.

For the Gospel of Mark we shall have little to bring forward, for the reason just given.   There is a curious coincidence with Mark in Justin Martyr's dialogue, which shows us that he knew and used this Gospel.   Only this Gospel gives us the name of Sons of Thunder for the sons of Zebedee, and it gives it to us in the same list of the apostles in which it tells us that Jesus called Simon by the name Peter.   Justin writes (ch. 106): "And the saying that He changed the name of Peter, one of the apostles, and that it is written in his"—"his" memoirs is here then the Gospel according to Mark which was regarded, as we have seen, as based partly on what Peter told Mark—"memoirs that this took place, and that with him also others, two brothers, who were the sons of Zebedee, were supplied with the new name Boanerges, which is Sons of Thunder, this was a token that He was that one by whom also the name Jacob was given to Israel and to Auses Jesus"—Joshua.   Perhaps Justin has the close of Mark in his thoughts in the following passage in the fragment about the Resurrection (ch. 9), although he also brings near the beginning words that recall to us Matthew: "Why then did He rise with the flesh that had suffered, were it not for the purpose of showing the fleshly resurrection?   And wishing to confirm this, His disciples not believing that He had truly risen in the body, while they were gazing and doubting, He said to them: Have ye not yet faith? He said: See that it is I.   And He permitted them to touch Him; and He showed them the prints of the nails in His hands.   And when they had recognised him from all sides, that it was he and in the body, he begged them to eat with him, so that by this they should learn certainly that He was truly risen in the flesh. And He ate honeycomb and fish.   And thus having shown them that it was truly a resurrection of flesh, wishing to show them also this—as is spoken: your dwelling is in heaven—that it was not impossible even for flesh to come up into heaven, He was taken up into heaven as He was in the flesh, they gazing at Him."   As for Papias, we have already seen how very definitely he described the writing of the Gospel by Mark in connection with what Peter had told him about Jesus.   And we have seen that the Muratorian fragment seems to give the same or a like view of the case.

LUKE.

The Gospel of Luke is more largely used. It was a fuller and more attractive book than Mark. The Ophites refer to it. Hippolytus speaks of their mentioning both Assyrian and Phrygian mysteries, and joins to the latter (5. 7 ; p. 140 [100, 101]): "The blessed nature of things past and things present and things to come, which is at one and the same time concealed and revealed, which he says is the kingdom of heavens sought within a man. Then they quote the apocryphal Gospel of Thomas. The words in Luke are: "For behold the kingdom of God is within you." We know how readily the kingdom of heaven or the heavens is written for the kingdom of God. That is one of the instances of the influence of the Gospel according to Matthew. A similar citation of the same text by the Ophites was given above. One passage that they use (5. 7 ; p. 142 [102]) looks a little like the seven times sinning of the brother as given by Luke: "And this is that which is spoken, they say, in the scripture: Seven times the righteous will fall and will rise again." If they have not this place in view, it is hard to say what had induced the form of the sentence. A few lines later they give the verse we have so often found in use among the heretics: "This one they say is alone good, and about him they said that was spoken by the Saviour: Why dost thou say that I am good? One is good, My Father in the heavens, who causes His sun to rise upon just and unjust, and rains upon saints and sinners." The fact that they tie the words from Matthew on to the words from Luke only shows how carelessly they quote from memory. Another passage or two in Luke seem to be touched in the following phrase (5. 7 ; p. 144 [103]): "Like a light [not] under a bushel, but put on the candlestick, a sermon preached upon the houses, in all streets and in all byways and at the houses themselves."

Basilides interprets Luke's words of the angel to Mary in the sense of his system (7. 26 ; p. 374 [241]): "The light came down from the Seven, which came down from the Eight above to the son of the Seven, upon Jesus the son of Mary, and He was enlightened, having been enkindled by the light shining upon Him. This is, he says, what was spoken : Holy Spirit shall come upon thee, the spirit from the sonship having passed through the boundary spirit to the Eight and the Seven as far as Mary, and power of the Most High shall overshadow thee, the power of judgment from the peak above [through] the Demiurge down to the creation, which is to the Son." The same passage is used by Valentinus (Hipp. 6. 35): "When, then, the creation came to an end, and it was necessary that the revelation of the sons of God, that is to say, of the Demiurge, should take place, [the uncovering of] the hidden condition in which the psychical man was hidden and had a veil over his heart; when, then, the veil was to be taken away and these mysteries were to be seen, Jesus was born of Mary the virgin according to the word spoken: Holy Spirit shall come upon thee. Spirit is the Wisdom. And the power of the Most High shall overshadow thee. The Most High is the Demiurge. For which reason that which is born of thee shall be called holy."

Heracleon seems to allude to Luke in his reference to a most original way of branding the sheep in the Christian flock. It is Clement of Alexandria who tells us of it. Clement says (Ecl. Proph. 25), in speaking of John the Baptist's words, that the one coming after him would baptize "with spirit and fire. But no one baptized with fire. Yet some, as Heracleon says, marked with fire the ears of those who were sealed"—"baptized." Irenæus and Epiphanius say of the Carpocratians that they branded their ears. Clement of Alexandria also quotes the passage from Luke: "And when they shall bring you before synagogues," and then tells us directly that Heracleon comments on it (Strom. 4. 9. 71): "Heracleon, the most approved of the Valentinian school, explaining this passage, says word for word that confession is on the one hand in faith and in manner of life, and on the other hand with the voice. The confession, then, with the voice takes place also before the authorities, which, he says, many in an unsound way regard as the only confession; but even hypocrites can confess this confession." There is, then, no room for doubting that Heracleon knew and valued Luke. It does not, however, follow from this passage that he wrote a commentary on the whole Gospel. He may have treated this and other passages singly in connection with discussions upon the Valentinian system. Luke was one of their books. The wide spread of that system and of its many branches and side

developments makes the acknowledgment of our four Gospels
upon the part of the Valentinians of extreme importance for the
general acceptance of these Gospels in all Christian circles before
the time of Valentinus.   He did not invent or write these books
He found them in stated use, and used them too.

Justin Martyr gives us two allusions to Luke in one breath,
and continues the sentence with a phrase from Matthew.   Let
us look at the passage (Dial. 103) carefully.   " For in the
memoirs, which I say were composed by His apostles and by
those who followed with them "—those who followed with them
refers here directly to the same Greek word as the one used by
Luke of himself at the beginning of his Gospel, refers directly to
Luke himself who is the only one to give us the phrase that is
pointed out—" that sweat flowed down in blood drops "—here
the word blood, which Luke puts in, is left out, but the Greek
word used for drops is especially used for drops of blood, half
congealed—" He praying and saying : Let this cup, if it be
possible, pass by." The words of this petition are rather the
words of Matthew than the words of Luke. We have, however,
no reason to think that Justin meant to change from one Gospel
to another. He is full of his theme, and totally regardless of
trifles of expression. He goes to the point, and he gives the
point aright. It should be observed, that his drawing these
words unconsciously from Matthew here, although he begins with
Luke, is not to be used as a sign that his manuscript of Luke
here had a reading of Matthew in it. Justin did not look at the
text of either Gospel. He quoted from memory. The fact that
he brings in Matthew is only another proof of the prevailing,
certainly unconscious, tendency to which attention was called
above, to use Matthew more than the other synoptic Gospels.

Again, Justin cites Luke and follows it up with various words
from Matthew. We have here to do with Luke alone. He
writes (Apol. 1. 16): "And about being ready to endure evil
and to be servants to all men and to be without anger, what He
said is this : To him that striketh thy cheek, offer also the other
one, and thou shalt not forbid the one taking thy garment or thy
coat." It is hardly necessary to say that that is loose quoting
and from memory. We are now accustomed to this habit of
Justin's. In a like hapless way he joins Mark and Luke (Apol.
1. 76): " For if through the prophets in a hidden way it was

announced that the Christ would be a suffering one and after that ruling over all, still even then that could not be conceived of by anybody until He moved the apostles to herald these things clearly in the Scriptures.   For He cried before being crucified : It is necessary that the Son of Man suffer many things, and be rejected by the scribes and Pharisees, and be crucified ; and on the third day rise again."   Here we have directly from Justin the statement that what the apostles wrote, that is to say, that not only the Old Testament, but also the New Testament, was scripture.   And that was spoken, moreover, to Trypho the Jew. Justin quotes the same passage or rather passages twice besides this in his Dialogue, and the words are each time a trifle different. It is head work, not out-of-book work.   Just before the last quotation he gives another passage from Luke and puts centipedes in, which is certainly still more vivid : " And again in other words He said : I give you power to tread upon snakes and scorpions and centipedes, and upon every might of the enemy." He could " remember " a fitting word right *into* the text without the least difficulty.   As for Hegesippus, we have already seen that in his account of the death of James the Just, the last words of James agree with the words of Jesus in Luke asking God to forgive his murderers.   We saw that Theophilus of Antioch had chiefly to do with the Old Testament, but he knows and uses Luke.   He writes (2. 13) : " And the power of God is shown in this, that at the first He makes what is, out of things not existing and as He wills.   For what is impossible with men is possible with God."   It is clear that the Gospel according to Luke is in wide use in the Church.

JOHN.

Thus far we have found that the three Gospels called the synoptic Gospels, Matthew, Mark, and Luke, were in use in the Church, and we have understood why the Gospel according to Mark was less frequently quoted than the other two.   The Gospel according to John stands by itself.   It was undoubtedly, I think, written after the other three, and probably towards the close of the first century.   If we remember that the Christians of the earliest years sought eagerly the accounts of Jesus' life, we might suppose, on the one hand, that Matthew, Mark, and Luke would be preferred to John because they give so many little details of what Jesus did and so many short and striking utterances of Jesus ; and, on the other hand, that John would be slighted because he gives so little of Jesus' movements, and such long and lofty discourses. And we should not be surprised if the late origin of John should cause it to be less used and to have less authority than the other three. Let us see.

Simon Magus in speaking of the beginning of all things as infinite power, appears to refer to the preface to John. Hippolytus writes (6. 9 ; p. 236 [163]), that Simon, after pointing to the habitation in which the book of the revelation of voice and name out of the intelligence of the great and infinite power is found "Says that this habitation is the man born of bloods ; and he says that the infinite power dwells in him, which is the root of all things." The reference to John is there all the more likely because Simon is speaking of the beginning. In another place Simon may possibly refer to Jesus' words to the Samaritan woman, when he says (6. 19 ; pp. 254, 256 [175]) that Jesus "seemed to suffer in Judea, not having suffered, but having appeared to the Jews as Son, and in Samaria as Father, and among the rest of the nations as Holy Spirit ; and that He suffered Himself to be called by whatever name men chose to call Him." I do not think that that needs to be a reference to John.

The Ophites quote John more than once. We begin with the preface to John (5. 8 ; p. 150 [107]) : " For all things, they say, were made by Him, and without Him nothing was made. And what was made in Him is life." They referred also to the water made wine (5. 8 ; p. 152 [108]) : " And this is the water, that in that good marriage, which Jesus turning made wine. This, they say, is the great and true beginning of signs which Jesus made in Cana of Galilee, and revealed the kingdom of the heavens." The kingdom of the heavens is the phrase of Matthew. The third chapter and the conversation with Nicodemus are clearly known to them (5. 7 ; p. 148 [106]) : " For mortal, they say, is all the birth below, but immortal that which was born above ; for it is born of water alone and Spirit, spiritual, not fleshly. But that which is below is fleshly. This is, they say, that which is written : That which is born of the flesh is flesh, and that which is born of the Spirit is spirit. This is according to them spiritual birth." Again, they name the living water of which Jesus spoke to the Samaritan woman (5. 7; p. 140 [100]): "For the announcement of the bath is according to them nothing else than the leading into unfading joy the one bathed according to them in living water and anointed with an unspeakable anointing." Someone might be inclined to think that this phrase had nothing to do with John; but just as as if to prove the point they refer to the living water in another place (5. 9; p. 174 [121, 122]): "And we are, they say, the spiritual ones, those who choose for themselves the habitation from the living water of the Euphrates flowing through the midst of Babylon, walking through the true gate, which is Jesus the blessed." Observe the allusion to John in the last phrase too.

But we must add further for the living water the direct quotation of the verse,—a quotation which is all the more valuable because it, in its freedom, does not give the word living alone, but also the word welling up, springing up, and yet leaves out everlasting life. Speaking of the river Euphrates (5. 9; p. 172 [121]): "This, they say, is the water which is above the firmament, about which, they say, the Saviour spoke: If thou knewest who it is that asketh thee, thou wouldst have asked from Him and He would have given thee to drink living water welling up." In another passage they follow up the Samaritan story (5. 9; p. 166 [117]): "For a spirit, they say, is God. Wherefore, they say, neither in this mountain nor in Jerusalem shall the true worshippers worship, but in spirit. For spiritual, they say, is the worship of the perfect ones, not fleshly. And the spirit, they say, is there where the Father is, and is named also the Son, being born from this Father." The quotation is free enough, but it is beyond doubt a quotation from John.

A like freedom is shown in the following from the fifth chapter of John (5. 8; p. 154 [109]): "This is, they say, that which is spoken: We heard His voice, but we did not see His form." From the sixth chapter (5. 8; p. 158 [112]): "About this, they say, the Saviour spoke: No one can come to Me, unless My heavenly Father draw some one." And they add: "It is altogether difficult to receive and accept this great and unspeakable mystery." From the same chapter the following words are drawn, but they are mixed up with other words from John and from the synoptists (5. 8; p. 152 [109]: "This, they say, is

what the Saviour spoke: If ye do not drink My blood and eat
My flesh ye shall not enter into the kingdom of the heavens.
But even though ye drink, He says, the cup which I drink,
whither I go, thither ye cannot enter in." Then they combine
the ninth and the first chapter of John (5. 9; p. 172 [121]):
"And if anyone, they say, is blind from birth, and not having
beheld the true light that lighteth every man that cometh
into the world, through us let him look up and see. . . ."
Again they quote from the tenth chapter, using the word gate
instead of door. At this point the word is the more fitting
because they had just cited Genesis (5. 8; p. 156 [111]): "This
is none other than the house of God, and this is the gate of
heaven. Therefore, they say, Jesus saith: I am the true gate."
The Peratæ say (5. 16; p. 194 [134]): "This is the great
beginning, about which it is written. About this, they say, it is
spoken: In the beginning was the word"—and so on until—
"what was made in him is life. And in him, they say, Eve
was made, Eve is life." Again they say: "This is that which is
spoken (5. 16; p. 192 [134]): And as Moses lifted up the
serpent in the desert, so must the Son of Man be lifted up."
They quote the following freely (5. 12; p. 178 [125]): "This is,
they say, that which is spoken: For the Son of Man did not
come to destroy the world, but that the world should be saved
through Him." They contrast to the Father in the heavens,
from whom the Son comes, the evil Demiurge (5. 17; p. 196
[136]): "Your father is from the beginning a manslayer, he
speaks of the ruler and Demiurge of matter, . . . for his work
worketh corruption and death." They quote aright the door
(5. 17; p. 198 [137]): "This, they say, is that which is spoken:
I am the door."

The Sethians give a long and complicated explanation of the
birth from water, and combine with it a coming down from above
on the part of God and spirit and light, and they continue that
the perfect man not only must needs enter into the womb of the
virgin, but also that he then was cleansed from the impurities of
that womb, and drank the cup of living water welling up, which
it is in every way necessary that the one should drink who is
going to put off the servant form and put on the heavenly
garment." Hippolytus quotes also the same verse from the
Gnostic Justin, whom he discusses immediately after the Sethians,

12

and apparently as one of them.   Justin says that the earthly and
psychical men are washed in the water below the firmament, but
the spiritual living men in the living water above the firmament,
and he refers to the book of Baruch and to the oath of "our
father Elohim."   After this Father had sworn and had seen what
no eye had seen (5. 27 ; p. 230 [158]): "He drinks from the
living water, which is a purifying bath to them as they think,"—
I take it, to the Sethians—"a spring of living water welling up."
In an extremely disagreeable connection reference is made to
the scene in which Jesus entrusts Mary to John, and synoptic
words are united closely to those drawn from John (5. 26;
p. 228 [157]): "Woman, thou hast thy Son, that is the psychical
and earthly man"—that which was left upon the cross,—"and
He, placing His spirit in the hands of the Father, ascended to
the Good."   The Greek text seems to demand the rendering:
placing or taking in His hands the spirit of the Father, as if this
spirit were the medium of the power to ascend.   We have already
given above two passages in which the noted Gnostic Basilides
quoted John.

Ignatius the Antiochian bishop speaks to the Magnesians
of God (ch. 8): "Who revealed Himself through Jesus Christ
His Son who is his Word, going forth from silence"—a Gnostic
phrase,—"who was well-pleasing in every respect to Him that
sent Him."   That gives us at once two plain allusions to John.
To the Philadelphians (ch. 7) he writes: "The spirit"—this is
here Ignatius' own spirit—"is not led astray, being from God.
For he knoweth whence it cometh and whither it goeth, and
reproves the things which are hidden."   He tells the Romans
(ch. 7): "The ruler of this world wishes to make a prey of me,
and to corrupt my thought of God."   Just after that he refers
to the living water: "For living I write to you, wishing to die.
My longing is crucified, and there is no fire in me loving matter.
But there is water living and speaking in me, saying within
me: Come to the Father!"   And a line later: "I wish for
God's bread, which is the flesh of Jesus Christ, the one from
the seed of David, and I wish the potion His blood, which is
His love incorruptible."   He speaks to the Philadelphians (ch. 9)
of the high priest: "He being the door of the Father, through
which Abraham and Isaac and Jacob and the prophets and the
apostles and the church enter in."   It is plain that Ignatius is

full and running over with the Gospel of John, even if he does
not copy off whole paragraphs of it for us.

Valentinus the Gnostic shows us that he knows the Gospel
of John very well. We saw above that his whole system seems
to proceed from this Gospel. Hippolytus, condensing Valentinus's
words, writes (6. 35): "Therefore all the prophets and the law
spoke forth from the Demiurge," from a foolish God, he says,
fools knowing nothing. On this account, he says, the Saviour
saith: "All who came before Me are thieves and robbers."
Ptolemæus quotes from the preface to John in his letter to Flora
(Epiph. 33): "Moreover He [the Saviour] says that the making
of the world was His own, and that all things were made by
Him and that without Him nothing was made." And Irenæus
gives us another quotation of his from the same preface (Hær.
1. 8. 5): "And he says that the Son is truth and life, and that
the Word became flesh. Whose glory we beheld, he says, and
His glory was such as that of the only begotten, which was
given to Him by the Father, full of grace and truth. And
He speaks thus: And the Word became flesh and dwelt among
us, and we saw His glory as of the Only-Begotten by the Father,
full of grace and truth. Exactly therefore he also showed forth
the Four, saying: Father and Grace and the Only-Begotten and
Truth. Thus John spoke about the first Eight and the mother
of all Eons. For he said: Father and Grace and Only-Begotten
and Truth and Word and Life and Man and Church." The
name John is doubtless put in by Irenæus. And Irenæus refers
to the attempt to show Jesus' distress or perplexity (Hær.
1. 8. 2): "And His consternation likewise, in that which was
spoken: And what I shall say, I know not," which points to the
twelfth chapter of John.

As for Heracleon, whom Origen calls an acquaintance of
Valentinus', and whose commentary on John he often quotes in
his own commentary on that Gospel, Origen says, for example
(2. 14 [8]): "He adds to the not one"—that is: and without
him was not one thing made which was made—" of the things
in the world and in the creation." Origen charges him with
forcing interpretations, and that without testimony to back up
what he says. How sharply he looked at Heracleon's words we
can see by another passage (6. 15 [8]): "The difference 'the
prophet' and 'prophet' has escaped many people, as also it did

Heracleon, who says in just so many words: that then John
confessed not to be the Christ, but also not a prophet and not
Elias." And he adds that Heracleon ought to have examined
the matter more carefully before he said that. Origen tells us
(6. 40 [24]) that Heracleon read Bethany and not Bethabara
for the place where John was baptizing. Again he writes (6. 60):
"Heracleon again at this passage, without any preparation and
without bringing references, declares that John spoke the words:
Lamb of God, as a prophet, and the words: That taketh away
the sins of the world, as more than a prophet," and Origen continues to describe Heracleon's explanation of the verses. We
need nothing more than that to prove that Heracleon was
thoroughly at home in John.

We have not, so far as I know, any reference to John in
what is left of Marcion's words. We know that he only
accepted the Gospel of Luke. Nevertheless we find a word or
two in Hippolytus' account of Apelles, a disciple of Marcion's
which can scarcely have come from any other source than
John. The curious and the interesting thing is that Apelles
combines this with words from Luke. Perhaps he thought he
was only quoting Luke, although he was adding what he had
really read in John. I give parts of the passage (7. 38):
"And that Christ had come down from the power above and
was its Son, and that this one was not born of the virgin, and
that the one appearing was not fleshless he says, . . . and that
after three days having risen He appeared to the disciples,
showing the marks of the nails and of His side, persuading them
that it was He and not a phantasm, but that He was in the
flesh. . . . And thus He went to the good Father, leaving
behind the seed of the life to the world to those who believe
through the disciples." The prints of the nails and the side
are from John, and the expression the seed of the life sounds
much like John.

As for Hermas, we have seen that dreams are not fields
for quotations, yet he seems to have used John. He writes,
for example: "It was necessary for them, he says, to go up
through water, that they may be made alive, for they could not
otherwise enter into the kingdom of God." The allusion in the
latter part seems to be to the conversation with Nicodemus,
and then the words through water and be made alive remind

us of the being born again.   Explaining to Hermas the rock
and the gate the shepherd tells him (Sim. 9. 12): "This rock
and the gate is the Son of God."   And again: "Therefore
the gate was new, so that those about to be saved should
enter in by it into the kingdom of God."   That is the
word of Jesus: "I am the door," John 10[7.9].   Speaking of
the sheep he says (Sim. 9. 31): "But if He shall have found
some of these scattered, woe shall be to the shepherds," 10[12.13].
Jesus receives commands and power from the Father (Sim. 5. 6):
"He then having cleansed the sins of the people showed them
the paths of life, giving them the law which He received from His
Father.   Thou seest, he says, that He is Lord over the people,
having received from His Father all power."   The homily, which
used to be called Second Clement, appears to point to John's
preface when it says (9. 5): "If Christ the Lord who saved us,
being at the first spirit, became flesh, 1[14], and thus called us,
so also we shall in this flesh receive our reward.   Let us love
each other, 4[7.12], so that we may all come into the kingdom
of God."

We have already seen that Justin Martyr used the story
about Nicodemus, and we have besides learned how recklessly
he quotes from memory.   He calls Jesus the Word (Apol.
1. 63): "The Word of God is His Son," 1[1.18].   And again
(Apol. 1. 63): "These words have become a proof that the Son
of God and apostle Jesus is the Christ, who was formerly the
Word, . . . now, however, by the will of God become man
for the human race," 1[1.14].   He approaches in the following
the only [begotten] (Apol. 2. 6): "And His Son, the one
called alone by way of eminence Son, the Word being with
Him and begotten before the creatures, when at first He
created and ordered all things through Him."   That is from
John, 1[1-3.18], through and through.   In another place he writes
of certain opinions of the Jews (Apol. 1. 63): "For those
saying that the Son is the Father are proved to be men who
neither understand the Father nor who know that there is a
Son unto the Father of all things, who is the Word and the
first born of God, and is God," 1[1.18].   Again he says (Apol.
1. 32): "And the first power after the Father of all things
and ruler God is also a Son the Word, who in what manner
being made flesh He became a man, 1[14.18], we shall say in

the following." That can only be from John. Again (Apol.
1. 32): "He declared that Christ has blood, but not from the
seed of man but from the power of God, 1¹³." Again (Apol.
1. 5): "The Word being formed and becoming man and being
called Jesus Christ, 1¹⁴." Again: "And Jesus Christ alone was
born particularly a son to God, being his Word and first born
and power, 1¹⁸." Justin says that the heathen philosophers
and poets and writers (Apol. 2. 13): "Each uttered it clearly,
seeing something related to them from the part of the divine
Word which was scattered abroad. . . . As many things therefore as are well spoken by all belong to us the Christians, for
we worship with God and love the Word from the never born
and unutterable God, since also He became man on our account,
1¹· ¹⁴." Again he writes (Dial. 105): "For as I showed before,
this one was the Only-Begotten to the Father of all things, 1¹⁸,
Word and power sprung especially from Him, and afterwards
becoming man by the virgin, as we learned from the Memoirs."
The Gospel of John must have been one of the Memoirs. He
writes of John the Baptist from the Gospel according to John
(Dial. 88): "The men supposed that He was the Christ; to
whom also He cried: I am not the Christ, but the voice of one
crying, 1²⁰· ²³." Jesus says that He only does what the Father
teaches Him, what pleases the Father, and Justin writes (Dial.
56): "For I say that He never did anything except what He
that made the world, above whom there is no other God,
wished Him to do and to speak, 4³⁴ 5¹⁹· ³⁰ 7¹⁶ 8²⁸· ²⁹ 12⁴⁹· ⁵⁰"
(comp. Dial. 56). That covers a number of passages in John.
Justin speaks twice of the man blind from birth, whom we
find only in John 9¹⁻⁴¹. We saw in the Muratorian fragment
that the First Epistle of John was mentioned with the Gospel.
A phrase in Justin (Dial. 123) reminds us both of the Gospel
and of the First Epistle and in the Epistle of a singular
reading: "And we are called true children of God and we
are, those who keep the commandments of the Christ, 1 John
3¹· ²²." Justin must have known the Gospel of John very well.

As for Papias, who gave us such clear statements about
Matthew and Mark, we are compelled to take a second-hand
witness. But it speaks so definitely that it can scarcely invent
the fact. A short preface to John in a manuscript in the Vatican
Library says that Papias speaks of John at the close of his five

books, and declares apparently that Papias himself wrote it at John's dictation. That is probably a mistake for Prochorus. Again we come to the First Epistle, for Eusebius tells us that Papias quotes it. Hegesippus, as we have already observed, appears to refer to John in naming the door of Jesus. Athenagoras says (Suppl. 10): "But the Son of God is the Word of the Father in idea and energy. For of Him and by Him all things were made, the Father and the Son being one. And the Son being in the Father and Father in Son, in oneness and power of spirit, mind and Word of the Father, the Son of God, $1^{1.\ 18}$." In another passage he seems to paraphrase a verse in the seventeenth chapter (Suppl. 12): "And we are furthered on our way alone by knowing God and the Word with Him what the oneness of the Son with the Father is, what the communion of the Father with the Son is, what the spirit is, $17^{3.\ 21}$." Theophilus was the first one to mention this Gospel of John by name, the first one of the writers whose books have reached us. Tatian beginning his harmony of the Four Gospels with the beginning of John and the fragment of Muratori, with the attempt to explain the origin of the Gospel, close our series worthily. We have found that John was not at all less open to quotation because it did not give details of the life of Jesus in great masses. And nothing has pointed to an inclination to give this Gospel the go-by because it was written at a late date. The Christians who accepted this book so quickly are likely to have had good authority for their view that it was closely connected with the Apostle John.

ACTS.

We now come to the book of Acts. It is a matter of course that it cannot have had for the early Christians the same value as the Gospels. The inclination to write and to read history as such was at the beginning of Christianity extremely small. The eyes of all were directed to the near future in which the world would close and the new, the heavenly life, would begin. Nevertheless we know that this book was in the hands of the churches at an early date—we may leave the date for the moment indefinite—and we find occasional references to it. The letter to

Diognetus refers to it (ch. 3): "For he that made the heaven and the earth and all things that are in them and supplies us with all things that we need, doth Himself lack none of the things which He supplies to those who think that they give [to Him], Acts $17^{24, 25}$." Polycarp of Smyrna quotes Acts directly (ch. 1): "Who endured for our sins up to meeting death, whom God raised up, loosing the bonds of Hades, Acts 2^{24}." Hermas appears to have Acts in view when he writes (Vis. 4. 2): "Believing that thou canst be saved by no one except by the great and celebrated name, Acts 4^{12}." The Exhortation to the Greeks which is associated with the works of Justin Martyr seems to have Acts in mind when it writes of Moses (ch. 10): "But he was also regarded worthy to share in all the education of the Egyptians, Acts 7^{22}." Hegesippus, whom we quoted, seems to refer to Acts when he speaks of James as being a true witness to both Jews and Greeks that Jesus is the Christ, Acts 20^{21}. The letter of the churches of Vienne and Lyons refers to the story of Stephen the first martyr, Acts 6^8–7^{60}. And finally, the fragment of Muratori names the book regularly, while Irenæus quotes and paraphrases many paragraphs from it. Irenæus is a witness to the opening of a new time. We found that the early Christians did not lay great stress upon history. Irenæus does, and therefore makes much of Acts.

The Catholic Epistles.

In approaching the Catholic Epistles we come upon something new, something that is very different from what we have thus far had before us. The Four Gospels and the book of Acts were large books. The Gospels claimed a special authority and value as accounts of the words and work of Jesus. The Acts seemed to busy themselves with the whole of rising Christianity, and were often supposed to include the acts of all the apostles, as, for example, the fragment of Muratori said. These five large books were not to be overlooked. If a church or a private man had bought one of them, he had had to pay well for it. The papyrus, or the parchment, and the work of writing these books had their equivalent in a round sum of money. The Catholic Epistles were on the contrary small books; in a New Testament lying at hand the book of Acts, for example, takes about ninety four pages, and James, the longest of the Catholic Epistles, only about ten pages. Now, a little letter like that would, on the one hand, be easily copied off, so that if there had been a great demand for it it could have been easily distributed widely through the churches. But such a little letter could, on the other hand, without difficulty escape notice. The purchaser would not need to pay so very much for it, and would therefore in so far be less conscious of having it. It would the more readily pass out of his thoughts because it had cost him little.

These letters could then, as short letters, have been easily and comparatively cheaply copied had people wanted them. Did many Christians wish for them? At the first blush a modern Christian would say: Yes, they did wish for them. James was the first bishop of Jerusalem and the brother of Jesus, Peter was the great apostle, the leader of the twelve, John was the beloved disciple, and Jude was the brother of Jesus. On the face of it, that seems plausible. But we must try to get away from our conception of the value of these Epistles. We must ask what the Christians of that day probably thought of them. To begin with James and Jude, they were, it is true, brothers of Jesus, and if their letters were genuine they should have been treasured by the Church. Yet we must agree, in the first place, that we know of no mission work on their part that impressed their names, their personalities, and their influence upon those circles of Christians to whom the greater part of the books of the New Testament were entrusted. They were doubtless active in some way, but we find no great signs of their activity in western and in Greek-speaking districts. And in the second place, the longer of the two, the letter of James, was addressed to the twelve tribes in the diaspora, and appeared therefore, however generally intended, to be particularly Jewish in its aim, while the two or three pages of Jude's letter, if really from Jude, Jude being named as a brother of James, were full of the Old Testament and of Jewish fables, and must therefore have appealed to the Jewish more than to the Greek Christians. These two letters were therefore not good candidates for a wide circulation among the Christians west of Palestine.

First Peter claims for us consideration because of the name of the chief of the twelve. When, however, we go back to early times we see at once that the whole trend of the greater number of Christians was towards Paul and not towards Peter. During the second century, as we have seen, "the Apostle" was Paul. It did not occur to anyone that Peter was the great apostle. Paul was the great apostle. We must not forget that this trend towards Paul is not a splitting of the Church into Pauline and Petrine Christians. Far from it. The Christians who could be expected to be Petrine are almost without exception, and without having any thought of being peculiar, Pauline Christians. The greatest division in the early Church, that became for a while in a sense independent, was the split caused by Marcion, and that was in the other direction. That threw everything Jewish overboard. The upshot of this is, then, that a letter from Peter could in no wise offer a particular rivalry to the letters of Paul. And therefore this letter too was not likely to be so widely copied and read. Second Peter I do not regard as genuine, and I see no reason to suppose that it should have been known at this time. As for the Epistles of John, we have already observed that the first one was apparently closely attached to the Gospel, almost as if it were an appendix to it, so that it has a peculiarly good stand. I do not suppose that the Second and the Third Epistles emerged from the obscurity of private possession long before the point of time at which we now are, and if that supposition be just, it is not strange that they should not be quoted. Besides their private character, their limited size, their small contents made the possibility of quoting the less. They are in comparison not quoted very much to-day.

JAMES.

The Epistle of James is perhaps the basis for Clement of Rome when he writes (ch. 10): "Abraham, named 'he friend, was found faithful in his becoming obedient to the words of God." This seems more likely to be taken from James 2^{23} than from Isaiah 41^8, or 2 Chronicles 20^7. Hermas' Shepherd is simply full of James, full of the spirit, the thoughts, and the words of James. The ninth commandment begins: "He says to me: Take away from thyself doubt," and gives then a long development of James 1^8, which runs on with variations into the following two commandments. The doubter and doubt are scourged in many passages as of the devil. In the eighth parable the shepherd says to Hermas (ch. 6): "These are the apostates and betrayers of the Church, and who have blasphemed the Lord in their sins, and moreover also have been ashamed of the name of the Lord which was named upon them," referring to James 2^7. He touches James 3^{15-17}, putting faith in for wisdom (Mand. 9): "Thou seest then, he says, that faith is from above from the Lord and has great power. But doubt is an earthly spirit from the devil, having no power." The rich who cheat their labourers are warned as in James 5^{1-6} (Vis. 3. 9): "See to it then, ye that luxuriate in your wealth, lest those who are in want groan, and their groaning shall go up to the Lord, and ye shall be shut out with your good things outside of the door of the tower." In another place he draws from James 4^{12} (Mand. 12. 6): "Therefore, hear ye me and fear Him that is able to do all things, to save and to destroy, and keep these commandments, and live to God." So far as we can judge of the Old Syrian translation it contained the Epistle of James. One would look for this Epistle in the East.

First Peter.

The First Epistle of Peter is referred to by Basilides. Clement of Alexandria tells us where (Strom. 4. 12, 81): "And Basilides in the twenty-third book of his commentaries speaks about those who are punished as martyrs as follows in these very words: For I say this, that so many as fall under the so-called afflictions, whether having sinned by carelessness in other faults they are led to this good by the mildness of him who guides them, being really accused of other crimes by others, that they may not suffer as condemned for confessed wicked deeds, neither reviled as the adulterer nor the murderer, but as being Christians, which will comfort them so that they will not seem to suffer. And if anyone comes to suffer who has not sinned at all in the least, which is rare, not even this one shall be moved against the will of might, but shall be moved as also the infant suffered that seemed not to have sinned." That is 1 Peter 4^{14-16}. The first part of the letter to Diognetus adds 1 Peter 3^{18} to Romans (ch. 9): "He gave His own Son a ransom for us, the holy one for the lawless ones, the guileless one for the wicked ones, the just one for the unjust ones, the incorruptible one for the corruptible ones, the immortal one for the mortal ones."

Polycarp in his letter to the Philippians touches here and there about ten verses of First Peter. He quotes 1 Peter 1⁸ most loosely (ch. 1) : "In whom not seeing ye believe with joy unspeakable and glorified"—and continues with an allusion to 1¹²,— "into which many desire to enter." A few words later 1¹³ comes in : "Therefore girding up your loins serve God in fear and truth,"—from which he passes to 1²¹ :—"Leaving the empty vain talk and the error of the many ; having believed on Him that raised our Lord Jesus Christ from the dead, and gave Him glory and a throne at His right hand." The following belongs to 1 Peter 2¹¹ (ch. 5) : "For it is good to be cut off from the desires in the world, for every desire wars against the spirit," even though 1 Peter has a different Greek word. Later we find 1 Peter 2¹² (ch. 10): "When ye can do good, do not put it off, for mercy frees from death. Be ye all subject to one another, having your conversation blameless before the heathen, so that from your good works also ye may receive praise and the Lord may not be blasphemed in you." He quotes 1 Peter 2²⁴. ²² of Jesus (ch. 8) : "Which is Christ Jesus who bore our sins in His own body on the tree. Who did no sin, nor was guile found in His mouth, but He endured all for us, that we may live in Him." Again he quotes and enlarges 1 Peter 3⁹ : "Not returning evil for evil, or reviling for reviling, or blow for blow, or curse for curse." And we find also 1 Peter 4⁷ (ch. 7): "Let us return to the word that was handed down to us from the beginning, being sober unto prayers and holding out in fastings." That is a very abundant use of First Peter for Polycarp's short letter.

Among the few fragments of Theodotus, of the Valentinian eastern school, that are preserved we have a quotation from 1 Peter 1¹² with Peter's name (Frag. 12) : "Into which angels desire to look, Peter says." Hermas alludes (Vis. 4. 3) to 1 Peter 1⁷ in describing the four colours on the head of the beast : "And the gold part are ye who flee from this world. For as the gold is proved by fire and becomes good for use, so also are ye proved who dwell in Him." Again (Vis. 4. 2) he quotes 1 Peter 5⁷, "Well didst thou escape, he says, because thou didst cast thy care upon God and didst open thy heart to the Lord, and didst believe that thou couldst be saved by none except by the great and glorious name." Irenæus quotes (1. 18. 3) from the Marcosians a phrase that reminds us of First Peter: "They say that the arrangement of the ark in the flood, in which eight people were saved, most clearly pointed to the redeeming Eight." That looks like 1 Peter 3^{20}; it uses the same Greek word for "saved." As for Papias, Eusebius, in a passage already quoted, says that he uses proof passages from First Peter. It may be that Theophilus has 1 Peter 1^{18} in mind when he writes: "Believing in vain doctrines through the foolish error of an opinion handed down from their fathers." The allusion to First Peter is the more likely because Theophilus a few lines later in a list of sins uses two designations given in 1 Peter 4^3, one of which only occurs there in such a list. We have already read above words from First Peter in the letter of the churches at Vienne and Lyons; this Epistle had reached the far west. Irenæus (4. 9. 2) quotes and names First Peter: "And Peter says in his Epistle: Whom not seeing, ye love, he says, in whom now not seeing ye have believed, ye will rejoice with joy unspeakable." That is 1 Peter 1^8. The sentence is curiously twisted. The word for unspeakable means rather "untellable." The Old Syriac translation appears to have contained First Peter.

FIRST JOHN.

When we turn to First John we must remember how much testimony we have already had for it as bound fast to the Gospel. The letter to Diognetus (ch. 10) refers to 1 John 4^{19}: "Or how wilt thou love the one who thus loved you before?" Polycarp (ch. 7) quotes, but freely, 1 John $4^{2.3}$, and perhaps 2 John 7: "For every one who shall not confess that Jesus Christ is come in flesh, is antichrist. And whosoever does not confess the testimony of the cross, is of the devil." Possibly First John moved Valentinus (Hipp. 6. 29; p. 272 [185]) to write: "For he was entirely love. But love is not love, if there be not the thing loved." We have already seen that Justin Martyr and the Muratorian fragment knew this Epistle, and it appears to have formed part of the Old Syriac translation.

Second and Third John.

The two smaller Epistles of John do not find a place at the first directly beside the Gospel and the First Epistle.   They were doubtless treasured highly and preserved carefully in the family or families to some member of which they were originally sent. Finally, as time went on, the Christians began to have a little more thought for history, for archæology, for personal reminders of the apostles.   Then the owners of these two letters gave them to the Church in general, placed them in the circles over which they had any influence, or handed them over to the circles nearest to them.   The clear reference to them in the fragment of Muratori gives us no distinct view of what the author of the work from which it was taken really thought about them.   The text is at that point so corrupt that we can only guess at its possible meaning.   We may, I think, say this about it.   It is in the first place of importance that these letters are named at all at this early period.   In the second place, it is of weight that they are not abruptly rejected as fictions or as not genuine.   In the third place, the sense of the passage as originally written may have been to the effect that these letters were held in honour in the Catholic Church, meaning that they were regarded as being just as good, just as genuine as, even if much less important than, the First Epistle of John or the Epistles of Paul.   In the fourth place, the mere fact of their not being mentioned at the same time with the First Epistle would seem to assign to them a lower value than to it, although the separation might be due alone to the contents.   We might give this thought the turn, that the peculiar contents of the First Epistle may well have induced the otherwise unusual union of it with the Gospel, and thus its separation from the two other letters. And in the fifth place, the original sense of the uncorrupted sentence may have been, that these letters were not regarded as of equal worth with the other Epistles, but that they were recommended or perhaps only endured and allowed as writings that could be read for general information and comfort, but as void of all authority.   In that I suppose these letters to have been mere private letters, this species of depreciation, if the sentence should some day be actually proved to have had this turn, would not be of any great importance.   The two letters might seem to be the dictation of one growing feeble and inclined to repeat phrases coined before by himself.

JUDE.

The Epistle of Jude has a general address.   Yet it must, as said above, if genuine, have appealed especially to Jewish Christians, and therefore have been less likely to be met with in other circles.   Up to this time the only mention of it is found in the fragment of Muratori where it is joined to the Second and Third Epistles of John of which we have just spoken.   What was said of them holds good for Jude, all but the reference to the private character of those two letters.

THE EPISTLES OF PAUL.

When we turn our thoughts to the writings of Paul we have to keep in mind some general considerations.   It is not uncommon to find people point to 2 Thessalonians 2^2, where Paul says that the readers shall not let themselves be alarmed by a letter that may purport to be from him, but, as is suggested, is not from him at all, but from some one who is trying to deceive them by forging.   It is not out of place, then, to ask at this point whether or not we should suppose that a large number of letters forged in the name of Paul were current in the early Church, and whether it be likely that any such letters have succeeded in winning a foothold among the Epistles which the Church assigns to Paul. If, as I assume, Second Thessalonians be genuine, it is of a comparatively early date among the Epistles of Paul, and if we should be forced to concede that from that time onward until the death of Paul, or even until still later, forgers, the same ones or others, had continued this nefarious work, there certainly would be room for a whole series of Epistles attached to Paul's name, but totally opposed to his person and to his spirit.

Two reflections seem to me to make it altogether unlikely that such Epistles continued to be forged.   On the one hand, the very reference to the frauds here made by Paul would have the tendency both to check the activity of the deceivers and to make it hard or useless for them to try to palm off their fabrications upon the

churches.   And on the other hand, the long missionary work of
Paul, his passage from city to city, at least as far as Rome, the large
number not only of his acquaintances, but also of his intimate companions and helpers, who knew what he had written and what he
had not written, and the large number of Epistles that he wrote,
must have made it exceedingly difficult for forgers to start their
fabrications upon a voyage of deceit throughout the Church
and very hard to prevent anything, that they might perchance
have succeeded in starting, from being detected, exposed, and
denounced in a dozen places that had the most accurate information as to what he had written.   Paul wrote so much that
forgers would have had too limited a field for action.   Paul's
personal acquaintances were too numerous and too widely
dispersed throughout the Church to leave any districts of importance unprotected from unscrupulous writers.   It is therefore from
the outset not likely that a number of spurious Epistles bearing
the name of Paul were in the hands either of the great churches
in the cities or of the smaller churches in the provinces and in
remote districts.

ROMANS.

The Epistle to the Romans meets our eyes at the very
beginning in the letter of Clement of Rome.   Of course, Clement
quotes freely, not from the roll before him but from memory.
To the question, how we may come to find a place among those
who await the Father and his gifts, he replies (ch. 35), among
other things : " If we seek out what is well-pleasing and acceptable to him.   If we accomplish the things that pertain to his
blameless counsel and follow the way of the Truth, casting away
from ourselves all iniquity and lawlessness, avarice, strifes, both
evil habits and frauds, both backbitings and slanders, hatred of
God, both pride and boasting, both vain glory and lack of
hospitality.   For those doing these things are hateful to God, and
not only those doing them but also those who agree with them."
That is Rom. 1^{29-32}.   And it was quoted thus at Rome about
the year 95, and quoted to the Corinthians, the people living
where Paul had been when he wrote Romans.   The Ophites
(Hipp. 5. 7 ; pp. 138, 140 [99, 100]) quote Rom. 1^{20-23} and $^{26.\ 27}$.
It is clear that they quote this long passage, from the roll before

their eyes.   They attribute the words to the Logos, the Word,
and appear to say that Paul writes them.   Basilides (Hipp. 7. 25 ;
p. 368 [238]) quotes Rom. 8[19. 22], but turned about and mixed up.
He says: "As it is written: And the creation itself groans (with
us), and is in travail awaiting the revelation of the sons of God."
In another place (7. 27 ; p. 374 [241, 242]) he uses this very same
passage, but still more freely.   He says: "When then all sonship
shall come and shall be above the boundary, that is the spirit, then
the creation shall be treated mercifully.   For it groans until now,
and is tortured and awaits the revelation of the sons of God, so
that all the men of the sonship may come up thence."   Again
(7. 25 ; p. 370 [238, 239]) he touches this passage in this shape,
uniting to it Eph. 1[21] : "Since then it was necessary, he says,
that we the children of God should be revealed, about whom,
he says, the creation groaned and travailed awaiting the revelation, and the Gospel came into the world and passed through
all might and authority and lordship and every name that is
named."   In another place (7. 25 ; p. 370 [238]) he refers to
Rom. 5[13. 14] from memory, and mixes the two verses together in
the sentence: "Therefore until Moses from Adam reigned sin,
as is written."   That is enough for Basilides.

The letter to Diognetus (ch. 9) bases a long paragraph on
the two "times" of Paul, as, for example, in Rom. 3[21-26].
In that paragraph it quotes Rom. 8[32] which I gave above
in connection with 1 Pet. 3[18], and refers as follows to the
verses opening with Rom. 5[12] : "In order that the lawlessness
of many should be hidden in one just one, and the righteousness
of one should justify many lawless ones."   Polycarp of Smyrna
(ch. 6) quotes Rom. 14[10. 12] : "For we are before the eyes of the
Lord and God, and we must all stand before the judgment-seat
of the Christ, and each one give account for himself."   This is
the constant loose quoting of those early days, which is after all
so very much like the loose quoting that is often to be heard
and to be read in these modern days.   Valentinus (Hipp. 6. 35)
quotes Rom. 8[11] : "This, he says, is that which is spoken: He
that raised Christ from the dead will also make alive our mortal
bodies or psychical [bodies].   For the earth came under a curse."
Ptolemæus (Iren. 1. 8. 3) touches Rom. 11[16] : "That the Saviour
received the first-fruits of those whom He was about to save,
[they say that] Paul said: And if the first-fruits are holy, so also

13

is that which is leavened (or the baking)." He may have Rom.
11[36] in mind when he says (1. 3. 4): "All things are unto Him
and all things are from Him."

Heracleon refers (Orig. on John, vol. 20. [38 30]) to Rom.
13[4]: "The one seeking and judging is the one revenging me,
the servant set for this purpose, who does not bear the sword in
vain, the revenger (the attorney or the judge) of the king." He
alludes (Orig. on John, vol. 13. 25) to Rom. 12[1], and in so
doing gives us an example of the way in which the second
century calls Paul "the apostle": "as also the apostle teaches,
saying that such piety (or service of God) is a reasonable service."
Again he points to Rom. 1[25], when he blames (Orig. on John,
vol. 13. 19) the former worshippers who worshipped in the flesh
and in error the not-Father: "So that all those who worshipped
the Demiurge alike went astray. And Heracleon charges that
they served the creation and not the true creator, who is Christ."
Theodotus (Fragm. 49) gives us in like manner Paul as "the
apostle," and quotes Rom. 8[20]: "Therefore the apostle said:
He was subject to the emptiness of the world, not willingly but
because of Him that subjected Him, in hope, because He also
will have been freed when the seed of God are gathered together." He uses (Fragm. 56) also Rom. 11[24] freely: "When
then the psychical things are grafted in the good olive tree unto
faith and incorruption, and partake of the fatness of the olive,
and when the heathen shall enter in, then thus all Israel shall
be saved." Again he writes down (Fragm. 67) Rom. 7[5]:
"When we were in the flesh, says the apostle, as if already
speaking outside of the body."

The presbyter whom Irenæus cites (4. 27. 2) alludes to
Rom. 3[23]: "For all men are lacking in the glory of God, but
they are justified not from themselves but from the coming of
the Lord, those who await His light." And again (4. 27. 2)
he quotes Rom. 11[21] and [17] from memory curiously combined:
"And that therefore Paul said: For if He did not spare the
natural branches, lest He perchance also spare not thee, who
though thou wast a wild olive, wast grafted into the fat of the
olive and wast made a companion of its fatness." Justin Martyr
(Dial. 47) refers to Rom. 2[4]: "For the mildness and the
philanthropy of God and the unmeasuredness of His riches
holds the one who repents from his sins, as Ezekiel says, for just

and sinless." Perhaps he has Rom. 12⁶ half in mind when he (Dial. 40) writes of Christ as of a paschal lamb : " With whose blood according to the word (or the measure, perhaps) of their faith in Him they anoint their houses, that is to say themselves, they who believe in Him." We have already seen that the churches in Vienne and Lyons knew this Epistle. And Theophilus of Antioch, writing to his friend Autolycus, gives (1. 14) a loose quotation of Rom. 2⁶⁻⁹, putting into the middle of it 1 Cor. 2⁹ and 6⁹· ¹⁰, evidently altogether from memory. It is a typical quotation : " Paying each one according to deserts the wages. To those who in patience through good works seek incorruption He will give freely life everlasting, joy, peace, rest, and abundance of good things, which neither eye hath seen nor ear heard nor hath gone up into the heart of man. But to the unbelieving and despisers and those not obeying the truth, but obeying injustice since they are kneaded full of adulteries and fornications and sodomies and avarices and the forbidden idolatries, shall be wrath and anger, tribulation and straits. And at the end eternal fire shall take possession of them."

First Corinthians.

The First Epistle to the Corinthians had a rare testimony to its genuineness in the letter of Clement of Rome quoted above : "Take up the Epistle of the sainted Paul the apostle. What did he write to you first in the beginning of the Gospel?" After that we could almost dispense with later witnesses. Simon Magus (Hipp. 6. 14 ; p. 244 [168]) uses 1 Cor. 11³² : "This," he says, "is that which is spoken : That we may not be condemned with the world." The Ophites (Hipp. 5. 8 ; p. 158 [112]) bring us 1 Cor. 2¹³· ¹⁴ : "These, they say, are the things that are called by all unspeakable mysteries : which [also we utter] not in learned words of human wisdom, but in [words] learned of spirit, judging spiritual things by spiritual, and the natural (psychical) man does not receive the things of the spirit of God, for they are foolishness to him. And these they say are the unspeakable mysteries of the spirit, which we alone know." In another place (5. 8 ; p. 160 [113]) they play on the word for "ends" in 1 Cor. 10¹¹, using it also in the sense of "customs" : "For tax-gatherers, they say, are those taking the customs of all things, and we, they say, are the tax-gatherers : Upon whom the customs (taxes, instead of ends) of the ages have fallen." And they go on to discuss the word. The Peratæ quote (5. 12 ; p. 178 [125]) again 1 Cor. 11[32] and call it Scripture : " And when the Scripture saith, they say : That we may not be condemned with the world, it mentions the third part of the special world." Basilides (6. 26 ; p. 372 [240]) quotes also 1 Cor. 2[13] and calls it Scripture. Ignatius in writing to the Ephesians (ch. 18) refers to 1 Cor. 1[20] : " Where is a wise man ? Where is one making researches ? Where is the boasting of those called intelligent ? "

The letter to Diognetus (ch. 5) points to 1 Cor. 4[10-12] when it says of the Christians : " They are dishonoured and glory in the dishonourings. They are blasphemed and are justified. They are reviled and they bless. They are insulted and do honour." Polycarp, writing to the Philippians, names Paul (ch. 11) and quotes 1 Cor. 6[2] : " Or do we not know that the saints shall judge the world, as Paul teaches." Again (ch. 5) he quotes 1 Cor. 6[9. 10] : " And neither whores nor effeminate men nor sodomites shall inherit the kingdom of God, nor those doing unseemly things."

Valentinus gives us 1 Cor. 2[14] again (6. 34 ; p. 284 [193, 194]) : " Therefore," he says, " the natural man does not receive the things of the spirit of God, for they are foolishness to him, And foolishness, he says, is the power of the Demiurge, for he was foolish and without understanding, and thought he was working out the world, being ignorant that Wisdom, the mother, the Eight, works all things in him for the creation of the world without his knowing it." The Valentinians (Iren. 1. 3. 5) quote 1 Cor. 1[18] : " And they say that Paul the apostle himself refers to this very cross "—they insisting upon it that the fan for purging the threshing-floor was the cross—" thus : For the word of the cross is to those who perish, foolishness, but to those who are saved, the power of God." They bring forward (1. 8. 2) also 1 Cor. 15[8] with 11[10] in this way : " And they say that Paul spoke in the [Epistle] to the Corinthians : And last of all as to the untimely born, he was seen also by me. And that he in the same Epistle manifested the appearance to the Achamoth with the contemporaries of the Saviour, saying : It is necessary that the woman have a veil on her head because of the angels.

And that when the Saviour came to her, the Achamoth put on a veil for modesty's sake." Again (i. 8. 3) they combine 1 Cor. 15[48] and 2[14. 15]: "And [they say] that Paul, moreover, spoke clearly of earthly men, natural men, and spiritual men. In one place: Such as the earthly one is, so also are the earthly ones. And in another place: And the natural (psychical) man does not receive the things of the spirit. And in another place: The spiritual man judgeth all things. And they say that the phrase: The natural man receiveth not the things of the spirit, is spoken of the Demiurge, who being psychical did not know either the mother who is spiritual, or her seed, or the sons in the pleroma."

Heracleon (Orig. on John, vol. 13. 59 [58]) seems to refer to 1 Cor. 2[8] when he speaks of: "The kingly one of the rulers of this age." He gives 1 Cor. 15[53. 54] thus (13. 60 [59]): "And Heracleon does not regard the soul as immortal, but as having need of salvation, saying that it is the soul which is meant in the words: Corruption putting on (clothed in) incorruption and mortality putting on immortality, when its death is swallowed up in victory."

Theodotus, speaking of "the apostle," which, of course, is Paul—a few lines farther he calls Peter, Peter—quotes (Fragm. 11) from him 1 Cor. 15[40] in this enlarged way: "Another glory of the heavenly ones, another of the earthly ones, another of the angels, another of the archangels." Then a little later (Fragm. 14) he turns to 1 Cor. 15[44]: "Therefore the apostle: For it is sown a natural (psychical) body, but is raised a spiritual body." And again (Fragm. 15) he gives us 1 Cor. 15[49] and 13[12]: "And as we bore the image of the earthly, so also shall we bear the image of the heavenly, of the spiritual, being perfected by degrees. But he says image again, as if there were spiritual bodies. And again: Now we see through a mirror in an enigma, but then face to face." In another passage (Fragm. 22) he quotes 1 Cor. 15[29]: "And when the apostle says: 'Since what will those do who are baptized for the dead?' For in our behalf, he says, the angels were baptized, of whom we are parts." This he discusses at length. Like the Valentinians, he also (Fragm. 44) gives us 1 Cor. 11[10]. The passage is thoroughly Oriental. Wisdom sees Jesus Christ, runs with joy to meet Him, and worships Him: "But beholding the male angels sent out with Him, she was ashamed and put on a veil. Because of the mystery Paul commands the women : To wear power on the head because of the angels." How absurd that the great Wisdom should be represented as feeling the Eastern feminine reluctance to be seen, to have her face seen, by male persons, yes, by male angels. Another remarkable passage (Fragm. 80), the last from Theodotus, I must give in full, for it reaches from Nicodemus to Paul : "He whom the mother bears to death is lead also to the world, but whom Christ bears again to life is changed off to the Eight. And they will die to the world, but live to God, so that death may be loosed by death, and the corruption shall rise again. For he who has been sealed by Father and Son and Holy Spirit cannot be seized by any other power, and is changed by three names of all the Trinity (?) in corruption. Having borne the image of the earthly, it then bears the image of the heavenly," 1 Cor. 15^{49}. Of course that means that the corruption rises in incorruption, and is changed from corruption to incorruption.

Hermas (Sim. 5. 7) seems to have 1 Cor. 3$^{16. 17}$ in mind when he writes that the shepherd says to him : "Hear now ; keep thy flesh pure and unspotted, in order that the spirit dwelling in it may bear witness to it, and thy flesh may be justified. . . . If thou soilest thy flesh, thou wilt soil also the Holy Spirit. And if thou soil the spirit, thou shalt not live." Justin appears (Apol. 60) to allude to 1 Cor. 2$^{4. 5}$ in saying that the Christians were largely humble, unlearned men, and adding : "So that it may be understood that these things did not take place by human wisdom but were said by the power of God." It would be possible that Justin (Dial. 38) thought of 1 Cor. 1$^{19. 24}$, or 2$^{7. 8}$ when he wrote : "I know that the Word of God said : This great wisdom of the Maker of all and the all powerful God is concealed from you." He quotes (Dial. 111) plainly 1 Cor. 5^{7} : "For the passover was the Christ, who was sacrificed afterwards." Perhaps we may see 1 Cor. 5^{8} in his words (Dial. 14): "For this is the sign of the unleavened bread, that ye do not do the old works of the evil leaven." Justin (Dial. 35) puts in, as if they were words of Jesus, the phrase : "For He said : There will be schisms and heresies." But it is not impossible that the words are in momentary forgetfulness assigned to Jesus, and that they really are the reproduction of the impression made by 1 Cor. 11$^{18. 19}$. When Justin

(Dial. 41) speaks of the Lord's Supper his phrase recalls 1 Cor. $11^{23, 24}$. He says that the offering of flour for the one who had been cleansed from leprosy: "Was a type of the bread of the eucharist, which Jesus Christ our Lord handed down to us to do in remembrance of the passion, which He suffered for the men who were cleansed as to their souls from all wickedness." At another place (Dial. 70) he alludes to the same passage as follows: "It is clear that in this prophecy"—from Isaiah—[reference is made] "to the bread which our Christ commanded us to do in memory of His having been made body for the sake of those who believe on Him, for whom also He became a suffering one, and to the cup which He commanded us to do, giving thanks, in memory of His blood." Finally, Justin seems to be thinking of 1 Cor. 12^{12} when he writes (Dial. 42): "Which is what we can see in the body. The whole of the many numbered members are called and are one body. For also a community and a church being many men as to number are called in the one calling and are addressed as being one thing."

The essay on the Resurrection, whether from Justin Martyr or not, refers (ch. 10) naturally to 1 Cor. 15^{42} or ^{50} or ^{53} and ^{54}. It is an interesting passage which proceeds from the thought that Jesus, if He had only preached the life of the soul, would have done no more than Pythagoras and Plato: "But now He came preaching the new and strange hope to men. For it was strange and new that God should promise, not to keep incorruption in incorruption, but to make corruption incorruption." The Exhortation to the Greeks turns in its freedom 1 Cor. 4^{20} thus (ch. 35): "For the operations of our piety are not in words but in works." Instead of operations of piety we might say simply: our religion.

Tatian is not content with 1 Cor. 7^5. Clement of Alexandria (Strom. 3. 12. 85) tells us about it: "Therefore he writes word for word in what he says about the state of mind according to the Saviour: Symphony therefore fits well with prayer, but the communion of corruption"—by which he means the marriage bed—"destroys the supplication. And then he forbids it in a repelling way through the agreement. For again he declared that agreements to the coming together were because of Satan and of a lack of temperance, about to persuade to serve two masters, through symphony God and through not symphony intemperance and whoredom and devil. And this he says explaining the apostle, and he treats the truth sophistically, building up a lie by means of a true thing." In another place (3. 23. 8) Irenæus tells us that Tatian used 1 Cor. 15^{22}: "Since in Adam we all die." The fragment of Muratori places the letters to the Corinthians at the head of the list of Paul's letters, or names the Corinthian church as the first of the seven churches to which Paul wrote. We know, however, that the apostle wrote to the Thessalonian church first, and that from Corinth where he was founding a new church. Athenagoras in his essay on the Resurrection (ch. 18) quotes 1 Cor. 15^{53}: "What remains is clear to every one, that it is necessary according to the apostle that this corruptible and fleeting should be clothed in incorruption." He used a less common Greek word in substituting in his memory fleeting for mortal.

Theophilus in writing to his heathen friend Autolycus (2. 1) gives us a touch of 1 Cor. 1^{18} or ^{21} or especially ^{23}, and a living proof of it. He says: "Thou knowest and rememberest that thou didst suppose that our word"—that is here as much as: our religion—"was foolishness." He uses the same passage later of heathen who look down upon Christians. He may have 1 Cor. $2^{7. 8. 10}$ in mind in writing (2. 33): "That shows that all the rest have gone astray, and that only we Christians have given place to the truth, who are taught by Holy Spirit that spoke in the prophets and announced all things beforehand." At another place (3. 2) Theophilus appears to have 1 Cor. 9^{26} in mind. He writes: "For in a certain way those who write what is not clear beat the air." The word he uses for not clear is the one that Paul uses for the manner of his running in the preceding phrase. Again (1. 13) he alludes to 1 Cor. 12^{11}: "All these things worketh the wisdom of God." So also (1. 13) he quoted 1 Cor. $15^{36. 37}$: "For if, for example, perchance a grain of corn or of the other seeds should be cast into the ground, first it dies and is dissolved, then it rises and becomes an ear." He brings 1 Cor. 15^{50} as the close of the following sentence (2. 27): "For God gave us a law and holy commandments, which every one who doeth can be saved and obtaining the resurrection inherit incorruption." And he also cites 1 Cor. $15^{53. 54}$ briefly (1. 7): "When he shall put off that which is mortal and put on immortality, then he shall see God according to his deserts." This collection of quotations from First Corinthians made by Theophilus shows us that, in spite of all his need of using the Old Testament, he knows well and knows how to apply the New Testament books.

SECOND CORINTHIANS.

When we turn to Second Corinthians we need not look for such a free and full use of it as of the First Epistle. It did not contain so much that was striking. I question very much whether it is read so often to-day as the First Epistle. So far as I can judge it is less frequently made the object of university lectures. The Ophites say (5. 8 ; p. 158 [112]) in the words of 2 Cor. 12²⁻⁴: "This gate Paul the apostle knows, opening it in a mystery and saying : That he was snatched by an angel and came as far as the second and third heaven, to paradise itself, and saw what he saw, and heard words unspeakable, which it is not permitted to man to speak." Basilides quotes ver. 4 at another place (7. 26 ; p. 374 [241]) in direct words : "I heard unspeakable words which it is not permitted to man to speak." The letter to Diognetus (ch. 5) touches 2 Cor. 10³: "Being in flesh, but not living according to flesh." And again (ch. 5) the first part of 2 Cor. 6¹⁰ comes in : "Being punished they rejoice as being made alive," and just before it the second part : "They are poor and make many rich. They want many things and abound in all things." Polycarp approaches 2 Cor. 4¹⁴ when he writes to the Philippians (ch. 2) : "And He that raised Him from the dead will also raise us if we do His will and walk in His commandments and love what He loved." In another place (ch. 6) he combines 2 Cor. 5¹⁰ with Rom. 14¹⁰·¹², just as other writers did, and puts Christ instead of God as judge : "And we must all stand before the judgment-seat of Christ, and each one give account for himself." That is a very natural change.

GALATIANS.

The Epistle to the Galatians is quoted by the Ophites. They say (5. 7 ; p. 138 [99]) of their Attis after Gal. 3²⁸ and 6¹⁵ :

"He has gone over to the eternal nature above, where, they say, there is neither female nor male, but a new creation, a new man, who is male and female." At another place Adamas is named as male and female. Explaining a passage of the Psalms they say (5. 7 ; p. 148 [106]) : "That is from the confusion below to the Jerusalem above which is the mother of the living," as in Gal. 4[26], which reads : our mother. Justin the Gnostic (Hipp. 5. 26 ; p. 226 [155]) reproduces Gal. 5[17], but puts the soul, the psyche, instead of the flesh : " For this reason the soul is drawn up against the spirit and the spirit against the soul." Polycarp, just after mentioning Paul and his letters to the Philippians, calls faith (ch. 3), in the words of Gal. 4[26] about Jerusalem, our mother : "Which is the mother of us all." And in the words of Gal. 6[7] he writes (ch. 5) : " Knowing that God is not mocked, we should walk worthily of His commandment and glory." Theodotus writes (Fragm. 53) from Gal. 3[19] : "And Adam had unknown to himself the spiritual seed sown into his soul by Wisdom, ordered by angels in the hands of a mediator. And the mediator is not of one, but God is one." In another place (Fragm. 76) he touches Gal. 3[27] : "For he that is baptized into God is taken up into God." It is a vague remembrance of Galatians that shapes his phrase.

The Oration to the Greeks, possibly Justin Martyr's, gives us Gal. 4[12] in a call of Christ's (ch. 5) : "Come! Learn! Become as I am, for I also was as ye are." And a few lines farther on he takes up Gal. 5[20, 21] in passing : "Thus the Logos drives away from the very corners of the soul the frightful things of sense, first desire, by means of which every frightful thing is born, enmities, strifes, anger, contending passions, and the things like these." In two passages (chs. 95, 96) in his Dialogue with Trypho, Justin Martyr quotes Deuteronomy in a form that is not like the text of the Septuagint, but is just like the form of the same passages given in Gal. 3[10] and [13]. It is not absolutely impossible that both Justin and Paul quoted from some third source, some collection of Old Testament passages, which gave the verses in the shape found. We know, however, nothing of such an anthology, and it is therefore the only proper thing to suppose that Justin quoted the passages from Galatians, or rather quoted the passages in the words which Galatians had impressed on his memory. Athenagoras (Suppl. 16) uses words from Gal. 4⁹, when, having stated the view of the Peripatetics that the world was God's substance and body, he writes : "We fall away to the poor and weak elements."

EPHESIANS.

The Epistle to the Ephesians 1⁴ doubtless moved Clement of Rome to write (ch. 64) : "Who chose our Lord Jesus Christ and through Him us to be a special people." In another place (ch. 32) he has in mind Eph. 2⁸ and 1⁵ : "Therefore they all have been glorified and enlarged not through themselves, or their works, or the righteous deeds that they have done, but through His will." Again (ch. 46) he brings in Eph. 4⁴⁻⁶ : "Or have we not one God and one Christ and one spirit of grace poured out upon us and one calling in Christ?" Probably he thought of or was guided by Eph. 4¹⁸ in referring to the darkened understanding (ch. 36) : "Through this One (Christ) our foolish and darkened mind flowers up into His wonderful light." The following passage (ch. 49) reminds us of Eph. 5² : "In love the Master took us up. Because of the love that He had towards us Jesus Christ our Lord gave His blood for us by the will of God, and His flesh for our flesh and His soul for our souls." In two places (ch. 2 and 38) he returns to Eph. 5²⁷ : "Ye were all humble-minded, boasting not at all, subjected [to others] rather than subjecting," and : "Let our whole body be saved in Christ Jesus, and let each one be subjected to his neighbour as also he was set in his grace." The Ophites quote Eph. 3¹⁵ turned about (5. 7; p. 136 [97]) : "In order that the Great Man above may be perfectly set in His might : From whom, as they say, every fatherhood is constituted on earth and in the heavens." As to the resurrection they say (5. 7; p. 146 [104]) with Eph. 5¹⁴ : "Rise thou that sleepest and stand up, and Christ will enlighten thee."

Basilides uses Eph. 1²¹ when he writes (5. 20; p. 356 [230]) : "For also that which is not unspeakable is not named unspeakable, but is, he says, above every name that is named." He speaks also (7. 26; p. 374 [241]) of : "The mystery which was not made known to the former generations, as it is written, he says : According to revelation the mystery was made known to me." That points to Eph. 3^3 and ^{5}. It is not out of place to recall again here Ignatius' exaggeration, in which in writing to the Ephesians he declares that they were people who had been as initiated into the mysteries, companions of Paul: "Who makes mention of you in Christ Jesus in every Epistle." The letter to Diognetus (ch. 2) takes up the thought and in part the words of Eph. $4^{21\text{-}24}$: "Come now, cleansing thyself from all the considerations that held thy mind fast before, and putting off the habit of mind which deceived thee and becoming as from the beginning a new man, as also of a new way of thought, as thou indeed thyself hast confessed, thou wilt be a hearer." Polycarp writes (ch. 12): "Only as is spoken in the Scriptures: Be angry and sin not, and, let not the sun go down upon your wrath," adding to the psalm Eph. 4^{26}. Barnabas (ch. 6) seems to refer to Eph. 3^{17} and 2^{22} in writing: "For He was about to appear in the flesh and to dwell in you. For my brethren the dwelling of your heart is a temple holy to the Lord." The Valentinians (6. 35 ; p. 284 [194]) quote Eph. $3^{9.\ 10}$. "And the apostle: The mystery which was not made known to the former generations." Again (6. 34; p. 284 [193]) they quote Eph. $3^{14.\ 16\text{-}18}$: "This is, they say, that which is written in the Scripture: For the sake of this I bend my knees to God, and the Father and the Lord of our Lord Jesus Christ, in order that God may give you that Christ may dwell in your inward man, that is the psychical not the bodily, that ye may be able to know what is the depth, which is the Father of all things, and what is the breadth, which is the Cross, the boundary of the pleroma, or what is the length, that is the pleroma of the ages."

Theodotus (Fragm. 19) quotes Paul by name for Eph. 4^{24}: "And Paul: Put on the new man the one created according to God." Again he writes (Fragm. 43): "The Saviour himself ascending and descending, and that he ascended, what is it but that he also descended? He himself is the one going down into the lowest parts of the earth and going up above the heavens." That is Eph. $4^{9.\ 10}$. He quotes also (Fragm. 85) Eph. 6^{16}: "Therefore it is necessary to be armed with the weapons of the Lord, having the body and the soul invulnerable with arms able to quench the darts of the devil, as the apostle says." Finally, we have from him (Fragm. 48) Eph. 4^{30}: "Wherefore also the apostle saith: And grieve ye not the

Holy Spirit of God in which ye have been sealed." Hermas
(Sim. 9. 13) used Eph. 4⁴: "Thus also those who believed on
the Lord through His Son and are clothed in these spirits shall
be unto one Spirit and unto one body and one colour of their
garments." In another place (Mand. 3) he touches apparently
Eph. 4³⁰: "For thou must needs as a servant of God walk
in truth and not cause an evil conscience to dwell with the
spirit of truth, nor bring grief upon the sacred and true spirit."
Theophilus (1. 6), speaking of the Pleiades and Orion and of the
rest of the stars: "In the circle of the heavens, all of which
the much varied wisdom of God called by their own names,"
refers to the wisdom mentioned Eph. 3¹⁰. This he again
alludes to (2. 16): "And on the fifth day the living creatures
came forth from the waters, by which also in these the manifold
wisdom of God is displayed." He seems to use Eph. 4¹⁸ when
he writes: "And this befell thee because of the blindness of
thy soul and the hardness of thy heart."

PHILIPPIANS.

As for the Epistle to the Philippians, the Sethians (5. 19;
p. 206 [143]) quote Phil. 2⁷ saying: "This of the beast is the
form of the servant, and this is the necessity for the Son of God
to come down into the womb of the virgin." The letter to
Diognetus (ch. 5) refers to our citizenship as in Phil. 3¹⁸⁻²⁰:
"They spend their time on earth, but they are citizens in
heaven." Polycarp in writing to the Philippians says (ch. 3):
"For neither I nor another like me can follow up the wisdom
of the blessed and glorified Paul, who being among you in
person before the men of that day taught accurately and
most certainly the word about truth, who also, when far from
you, wrote Epistles to you, into which if ye look, ye shall be
able to be built up in the faith given to you." That sentence
is not only of interest as a testimony to the existence of at
least one letter of Paul's to the Philippians. It tells us in so
many words something that plain common sense must have
told us long ago. We know that the Philippians were allowed
by Paul to send him money for his personal support, and that
they sent money to him repeatedly and even while he was at

Rome. Now no one could dream that Paul did not repeatedly write to them to say that he had received their gifts, and to thank them for these gifts. And here Polycarp tells us that Paul wrote letters, not merely one letter, to them. The people who think that our Epistle to the Philippians really consists of two or more such letters combined into one have not yet convinced me that they are right in this view. It is likely that the said letters were short and chiefly personal, we might almost say chiefly occupied with the business side of the matter, and that therefore they were not saved for the general use of the Church. Again Polycarp (ch. 11) refers to the one letter of Paul to the Philippians, in reproving a presbyter who had gone astray : "And I perceived no such thing among you, nor heard of it, among whom the blessed Paul laboured, who are in the beginning of his Epistle. For he boasts of you among all the Churches, which alone then knew God, and we did not yet know [him]."

Theodotus (Fragm. 19) quotes Phil. 2^7: "Whence also he is said to take the form of a servant, not only the flesh according to his coming, but also the nature from the being subject, and the nature of the servant as able to suffer and subject to the powerful and lordly cause." Again (Fragm. 35) he alluded apparently to the same verse : "Jesus our light, as the apostle says, having emptied Himself," that is according to Theodotus coming to be outside of His boundary, "since He was an angel." The essay on the Resurrection, attached to Justin Martyr's works, quotes (ch. 7) Phil. 3^{20}: "We must next oppose those who dishonour the flesh, and say that it is not worthy of the resurrection or of the heavenly citizenship." It gives it a second time a little later thus (ch. 9) : "As it was spoken : Our dwelling is in heaven." Theophilus (1. 2) uses the phrase : "Proving the things which are different" which occurs both in Rom. 2^{18} and Phil. 1^{10}. He speaks in another passage (2. 17) in the words of Phil. 3^{19}: "Of some men who do not know or worship God, and who think earthly things and do not repent." He is evidently thinking by means of Phil. 4^8 when he writes (2. 36): "Because then these things are true and useful and just and agreeable to all men, it is clear also that those doing ill shall of necessity be punished according to the measure of their deeds."

COLOSSIANS.

For the Epistle to the Colossians we have first to point to the Peratæ, who quote Col. 2⁹ and say (5. 12; p. 178 [124]): "This is what is spoken: All the fulness"—the pleroma— "pleased to dwell in him bodily, and all the Godhead of the thus divided Trinity (?) is in Him." Basilides seems to touch Col. 2³ and 1²⁶˙²⁷, perhaps with Eph. 3⁵, when he writes (7. 25; p. 370 [238]): "This is the mystery which was not known to the former generations, but he was in those times king and lord, as it seems of all, the great prince, the Eight." Theodotus (Fragm. 19) gives us Col. 1¹⁵: "And still more clearly and exactly in another place he [Paul] says: Who is the image of the invisible God, then he adds: "Firstborn of all creation," and he proceeds to discuss the passage. In another passage (Fragm. 43) he brings Col. 1¹⁶˙¹⁷ thus: "And becomes head of all things with the Father. For all things were created in him, seen and unseen, thrones, lordships, kingships, godheads, services."

Justin cites Col. 1¹⁵ apparently (Dial. 84): "That is that through the virgin womb the first begotten of all creations having been made flesh became truly a child." In another place (Dial. 85) he gives the title better: "For according to His name, this Son of God and firstborn of all creation." Again (Dial. 125) he gives it: "Child firstborn of all creatures," using altogether different Greek words. But there is no question about it that he has this passage in his mind. And still again (Dial. 138) he writes: "For Christ being firstborn of all creation, became also a beginning again of another race, the one born again by Him through water and faith and wood, which has the mystery of the cross." And once more (Dial. 100) he says of Jesus: "Therefore He revealed to us all things as many as we have understood from the Scriptures by His grace, we knowing that He is firstborn of God and before all creatures, and son of the patriarchs, since He was made flesh through the virgin from their race." He seems to have had Col. 2¹¹˙¹² in mind when he wrote (Dial. 43) of our receiving the spiritual circumcision: "And we received it through baptism on account of the mercy which is from God, since we had become sinners, and it is permitted to all to receive [it] likewise." It may be that we should see in the Exhortation to the Greeks (ch. 15) an allusion to Col. 1^{16} in a discussion of an Orphic verse: "He names voice there the Word of God by whom were made heaven and earth and the whole creation, as the divine prophecies of the holy men teach us, which he also in part having perceived in Egypt, knew that all creation took place by the Word of God."

Theophilus also (2. 22), like Justin Martyr, quotes Col. 1^{15}: "And when God wished to make what He had determined upon, He begot this forth-proceeding Word, a firstborn of all creation, not that He was emptied of His Word, but that He begot a Word and converses ever with the Word." Speaking of the just (2. 17) he uses Col. 3^{2}: "Like birds they fly upward in their soul, thinking the things which are above and being well-pleasing to the will of God."

First and Second Thessalonians.

First Thessalonians comes to view in Ignatius' letter (ch. 10) to the Ephesians, where he touches 1 Thess. 5^{17}: "And for the rest of men pray without ceasing." Polycarp brings the thought of 1 Thess. 5^{17} in writing to the Philippians (ch. 4) when he says of the widows that they: "Should intercede without ceasing for all." We gave above Dionysius of Corinth's words to the Church at Rome in which he reverted to the thought of 1 Thess. 2^{11}, comforting the distressed as a father his children. Polycarp quotes directly Second Thessalonians in speaking (ch. 11) of the erring presbyter Valentus and his wife. He writes: "Be ye therefore also moderate (sober) in this matter, and do not regard such people as enemies, but call them back as suffering and erring members, so that ye may save your whole body," see 2 Thess. 3^{15}. Justin Martyr (Dial. 110) applies 2 Thess. 2^{3,4}: "Two of His comings are announced: the one, in which He is preached as suffering and without glory and dishonoured and crucified; and the second, in which He will come with glory from the heavens, when also the man of the apostasy, who also speaks lofty things to the Most High, will dare upon the earth lawless deeds against us the Christians."

HEBREWS.

The Epistle to the Hebrews is the book of the New Testament that comes before our eyes in such abundance in that first great letter of the generation following upon the time of the apostles, in Clement of Rome. Quoting Heb. 1^3, Clement writes (ch. 36): "Through this one"—Christ—"the Master wished that we should taste of the undying wisdom, who being the reflection of His greatness, is so much greater than the angels, as He inherited a more excellent name [than they]." Yet the quotation is a very free one. We know that nothing else is to be looked for. Immediately afterwards he gives the Old Testament quotations found in Heb. 1^5 and 7 and 13, and we must presuppose that he takes them from that Epistle and not directly from the given psalms. See how freely Clement (ch. 17) quotes Heb. 11^{37}: "Let us become imitators also of those who walked about in goatskins and sheepskins heralding the coming of Christ." Hermas (Vis. 2. 3) touches Heb. 3^{12}: "But the not departing from the living God saves thee, and thy simplicity and much temperance."

Justin Martyr shows that he knows this Epistle, and that 3^1, by the way in which he in his Apology calls Jesus an apostle, for He is only called so in that verse. In one passage (ch. 12) Justin writes: "For He foretold that all these things should come to pass, I say, being our teacher and the son and apostle of the Father of all and ruler God, Jesus Christ, from whom also we have our being named Christians." In another passage (ch. 63) he says: "And the Word of God is His Son, as we said before. And He is called angel and apostle. For He Himself announces whatever needs be known, and is sent proclaiming whatever is declared, as also our Lord Himself said: He that heareth Me heareth Him that sent Me." Theophilus (2. 25) refers to Heb. 5^{12}, which we saw that Pinytus the bishop of Cnossus on Crete used in writing to the Bishop Dionysius of Corinth. Theophilus says: "For also now when a child has been born it cannot at once eat bread, but is brought up at first on milk, then with advancing years it comes also to solid food." He applies that then to Adam. Only a few lines farther on he gives us Heb. 12^9: "And if it be necessary that children be subject to their parents, how much more to the God and Father of all."

14

FIRST AND SECOND TIMOTHY.

Clement of Rome knows First Timothy. He touches 1 Tim.
2³ and 5⁴ in writing (ch. 7): "And let us see what is good and
what is pleasing and what is acceptable before Him that made
us."   Polycarp (ch. 4) quotes 1 Tim. 6¹⁰ and ⁷: "And the
beginning of all ills is the love of money.   Knowing then that
we brought nothing into the world, but neither have we anything to take out [of it]."   But we see how freely he quotes from
memory. We could imagine that Basilides (7. 22 ; p. 360 [232])
was guided in his words: "Increasing them by addition, especially at the necessary times," by 1 Tim. 2⁶, since, although he says
"necessary times," he uses for "especially" the word attached by
Paul to "times."   The letter to Diognetus (ch. 4) reminds us of
1 Tim. 3¹⁶: "Do not think that you can learn from men the
mystery of their especial godliness."   Barnabas quotes (ch. 12)
from the same verse: "Behold again Jesus, not a son of man
but a son of God, and by a type revealed in flesh."   The essay
on the Resurrection (ch. 8) touches 1 Tim. 2⁴: "Or do they think
that God is envious?   But He is good, and wishes all to be
saved."   Athenagoras closes his apology (ch. 37) to Marcus
Aurelius and Commodus most fitly by quoting 1 Tim. 2²: "And
this is what suits us, that we may pass a calm and quiet life,
and we ourselves will obey eagerly all that is commanded."   In
another place (ch. 16) he uses two words from 1 Tim. 6¹⁶: "For
God Himself is all things to Himself, light unapproachable, a
perfect world, spirit, power, word."   We saw above that Theophilus quoted 1 Tim. 2². Barnabas quotes (ch. 7) 2 Tim. 4¹:
"The Son of God being Lord, and going to judge living and
dead."   Heracleon (Cl. Al. Strom. 4. 9. 72) quotes 2 Tim. 2¹³
in his most exact discussion of denial: "On which account He
can never deny Himself."

TITUS.

Titus is quoted by Clement of Rome (ch. 2): "Be not ready
to repent of any kind deed, ready to every good work," Titus 3¹.
Perhaps he afterwards thinks of Titus 2¹⁴ in writing (ch. 64): "Who
chose our Lord Jesus Christ and us by Him to be a peculiar

people." As for Tatian, we have direct testimony from Jerome that he insisted upon the genuineness of Titus. Perhaps Titus 2¹² guides Theophilus in writing of God (3. 9): "Who also teaches us to act justly and to be pious and to do good." In another passage (2. 16) he takes God's blessing the beasts from the waters on the fifth day as a sign that: "Men were about to receive repentance and remission of sins through water and bath of the new birth, those approaching in truth and born anew and receiving blessing from God," Titus 3⁵.

PHILEMON.

Of course, we cannot look for many references to the tiny letter to Philemon. There is, however, a curious likeness, even in some of the words used, between a paragraph in Ignatius' letter to the Ephesians (ch. 2) and the letter to Philemon (7. 20).

REVELATION.

We have reached the last book, the book of Revelation. The strange fate of this book must be dealt with again. Here we have at first to recall what was above said as to the way in which it was connected with Cerinthus. Cerinthus would, so far as we can see, have written an entirely different book, and it is even probable that he wrote one or more books in imitation of this book. Nevertheless it was conjectured in the third century that he was the author of it itself. This was early criticism. But it was too late to be informed. Perhaps the Ophites drew from Rev. 2²⁴. Hippolytus (5. 6; p. 132 [94]) says of them: "After this they called themselves Gnostics, saying that they alone knew the depths." I am not inclined to think that they got the words from this passage. It would in the same way be possible to connect the twenty-four angels of Justin the Gnostic with Rev. 4⁴, and the twenty-four elders. Justin the Gnostic says (Hipp. 5. 26; pp. 218, 220 [151]): "Of these four-and-twenty angels the fatherly ones accompany the Father and do all things according to His will, and the motherly ones the mother Eden. And the multitude of all these angels together is paradise."

Hermas describes the Church (Vis. 4. 2) in words drawn from Rev. 21^2: "After the beast had passed me and had gone on about thirty feet, behold a virgin met me adorned as going out from the bridal chamber." He often uses the thoughts and the words of Revelation. The Marcosians, speaking of the descent of the dove at the baptism of Jesus, say (Iren. 1. 14. 6): "Which is Omega and Alpha." In another place (1. 15. 1) they again insist upon the connection of the number of the dove with Alpha and Omega. The Greek letters of the word for dove count up to eight hundred and one, and that is the numerical value of Alpha and Omega. They probably drew the two letters from Rev. 1^8. We observed above that Justin Martyr named John as the author of Revelation. He quotes Rev. 20^2 as follows in his Apology (ch. 28): "For with us the chief of the evil demons is called serpent and Satan and devil, as also you can learn, searching out of our writings." Eusebius tells us that Theophilus quoted from Revelation. Irenæus (5. 35. 2) quotes Rev. 20^{15}: "And if anyone, it says, is not found written in the Book of Life, he is sent into the lake of fire." He adds then 21$^{1-4}$. Just before he names John as author of the Revelation, and quotes three other passages.

We have approached the end of the second century and we stand at the year 190, or between 190 and 200. We have seen that, with varying exactness or with varying freedom and looseness, the writers of these early years of Christianity have shown that they knew and treasured many of the books of the New Testament. We have already by thoroughly unimpeachable witnesses shown that the greater part of the books of the New Testament are at this time in general use in the Church, and that the use made of them assigns to them a special value. Not only the writers who are in positions of authority in many of the scattered societies of the regular Christians, but also a number of those who are leaders in groups of Christians, who for different reasons have separated themselves from or have been declared foreign to the usual, general line of churches and Christians, have shown by the way in which they name, or allude to, or copy as models, or quote these books, that they consider them as of a peculiar as of the highest religious authority. In so far as anyone may be inclined to lay stress upon the fact that the quotations are often loose, and may wish to draw the conclusion that the books were not highly valued, it is pertinent to point out that we have found a like looseness also in quotations from the books of the Old Testament, the normative value of which was supposed to be certainly fixed.

We saw some distance back that the first books used in the Christian churches for public reading were the books of the Old Testament, and that these alone could lay claim to be read as of divine authority, as writings that speak from God to man. The question now arises for us, whether we can at this point discover any change in the books read in church, whether we can detect any change in the way in which given books are read. At the earlier period the liturgical division : God to Man, contained only these books of the Old Testament, and it was even a question whether all of them were really firmly settled as authoritative. The books of the New Testament at that time were read in the division, the liturgical division : Man to Man, had the same right to be read as a sermon, a letter by a bishop, or any instructive Christian treatise. No one thought of them as standing on a line with the books of the Old Testament, which claimed an unimpeachable divine authority. It is above all clear that we have nowhere during the course of our investigations seen any tokens of an official declaration touching the public reading. But it is also clear from the slight hints here and there as to the reading of books, and from the now distinct attachment to the books of the New Testament of the words "it is written," "it is spoken," or "scripture," that these books are looked upon as fully equal to those of the Old Testament. Going back to the beginning, we must, if I am not mistaken, conceive of the process in the following way, not forgetting that we are reasoning from common sense and not drawing from documents, but also insisting upon it that the documents say nothing which makes this view of the process impossible or even improbable.

The churches which received the Epistles of Paul read these Epistles in their gatherings, ever and again as part of the division : Man to Man. The supposition that they read such Epistles but once or at most two or three times is manifestly absurd. It is absurd because of the importance of the Epistles, the lack of much other matter, and the need of material for the weekly or even more frequent services. And it is absurd from the view of the documents. For if the letter of Clement of Rome was repeatedly read at Corinth, and was read in other churches as well, of course as : Man to Man, much more will the letters of Paul to the Corinthians and to other churches have been repeatedly read before the assembled Christians. Precisely how often they were read and re-read cannot be determined. We have no reason to suppose that at the first any rule was made as to this point.

It may be observed here in a parenthesis that the Old Testament was probably read originally in the Christian assemblies about in the same way as in the synagogues. That is the only reasonable supposition. The earliest Christians were largely Jews, and may even often have continued to visit synagogues after becoming Christians. They were used to reading given books at given times in given quantities, and the natural impulse will have been still to do the same. Moreover, it is likely that this habit, the habit of reading the Old Testament as the Jews did, passed over to such Christian communities, where there were such, which were entirely of heathen birth. The given thing was to do as the others did. The apostles and preachers who brought the Gospel to them will certainly have proceeded according to their custom, and have handed down this custom to the newly planted churches.

To return to our main topic, the division God to Man contained the Old Testament. The division Man to Man contained a verbal proclamation of the Gospel. This may have been by a passing apostle—a wandering preacher, but must in the larger number of cases have been by a man from the given church. In very many cases this last, merely local preacher will have had little to say, or there will even have been no one in the church who could pretend to speak to the rest. Here a letter from an apostle like Paul will have often been used, as soon as the church could get possession of one. So soon, however, as the Gospels were written, these accounts of the words and deeds of Jesus must have been eagerly welcomed in such smaller communities as were unable to find regular speakers for their meetings, and as were able to buy a Gospel. This Gospel will then have been read, as the Epistles of Paul were read, in the part: Man to Man. It will have replaced or been used as a substitute for the not available wandering preacher who brought word of Jesus. This is the first stage of the public use of the books of the New Testament, to which we called attention above.

The number of churches increased rapidly, and the size of the churches in the great centres grew. The consequence was that the number of apostles, of wandering preachers, was no longer in a position to supply the calls for their services. And, since we have no reason to suppose that a large succession of such wandering preachers — much as Eusebius presses the missionary spirit at the time of Pantænus—, such missionaries, continued and enlarged their sphere, these preachers will have become more and more rare. Thus the demand increased, whereas the supply diminished. This forced the Christian communities to lay more stress upon the written Gospel, to secure for themselves in some measure words of Jesus and words of the apostles to fill up the part of the church services denoted as Man to Man. The intense interest attaching to this newer literature, and the wish to have variety in it and to possess it in all its fulness, will have led to the interchange of books between the churches, to the sending of copies of books to churches that did not own any or precisely the given books. With the increase in the amount of this newer literature its peculiar value began to dawn upon the Christian mind.

What the Christians wished to know of, to hear of, to discuss, was not the Messiah of the Old Testament who was in the Old Testament future, but the Jesus of the New Testament who had already come, and the Christ who was still and soon to return to earth and to them who belonged to Him. Therefore the reading of the new books demanded and secured more and more attention, and this reading assumed in the weekly services a more and more important position. This was, I take it, an absolute necessity, and need not in the least be placed in connection with thoughts of a violent opposition to or of a dislike to Judaism and a consequent turning away from the Jewish books. From the middle of the second century onwards Judaism loses its weight as an opponent of Christianity, in so far as it had not lost it immediately after the destruction of Jerusalem. Justin Martyr's discussion with Trypho may be taken as a combination of his and that Jew's philosophical and rabbinical disposition to debate upon the questions common to them, or as a treatise due from the Greek Neapolitan to his Hebrew countrymen, or as a first Christology of the Old Testament with the vivid background offered by Trypho and his friends, but not as a sign that at that day the relations of Christianity to Judaism as such filled an extremely large space in Christian thought and life.

All in all it seems to me to be likely that before the middle of the second century the books of the New Testament in general, and I may name the four Gospels and the Epistles of Paul in particular, had passed over from the liturgical division Man to Man into the division God to Man. That in some places doubts should have arisen as to whether one book or another belonged within or without the peculiarly sacred books was not strange. It was the less strange because even then some of the books of the Old Testament were scarcely fixed in their position of strictly normative value.

A single suggestion is here in place. It is constantly argued, from the presence of other than New Testament books in the Sinaitic, the Vatican, and the Alexandrian manuscripts of the Greek Bible, that the said books were at the places at which those manuscripts were written regarded as fully equal to the books of the New Testament. It seems to me to be a question whether at that early date this conclusion is valid. As regards the Sinaitic and the Vatican manuscripts, I think it likely that they are among the earliest leaf-books and among the earliest complete Bibles, among the earliest books which brought together the many rolls which till then had contained the Scriptures. Under these circumstances I think it possible that the other books were added to the books of the New Testament for convenience in use in the church services, without an intention on the part of those who inserted them in the manuscript to say that they were divine Scripture. This is, I think, possible. But it is necessary to insist upon the point urged above, that uncertainties and doubts as to various books are under such circumstances thoroughly natural and to be looked for.

It should at this place be observed, that the number of books that were written up to this time was not very great, but it is still more important to emphasise the fact that so few of those written have been preserved to us. Had we more books, even heretical ones, we should have more testimony.

It is clear that the question as to the existence of a New Testament book is not to be confounded with the question as to its general acceptance and authoritative valuation. The three synoptic Gospels found their way gradually into general use. The Gospel of John must have found immediate acceptance. The book of Acts was unquestionably in existence at an early date, but may not have become generally used before the middle of the second century. First Peter gradually found acceptance. First John doubtless accompanied, or followed close upon the heels of, the Gospel. The other Catholic Epistles we have still to deal with. The Epistles of Paul found severally and locally immediate acceptance, and probably at a very early date general spread and acceptance. The Epistle to the Hebrews is, as we have seen, testified to before the close of the first century, yet it found, as we shall see, difficulty in some quarters at a later time. The book of Revelation was curiously enough generally accepted at an early date, but fell afterwards into discredit in some districts, and will therefore again attract our attention.

The last point that we need to allude to is the important fact that up to this time, up to the time of Irenæus, up about to the close of the second century, we have not found the least sign of anything like an official declaration as to the canonicity of any one book or of a number of the books of the New Testament.

Leaving this period, we advance to a new one in which we no longer have to search with a lantern for signs of the presence and use of the books of the New Testament in general. Our eyes will now be directed to three things. We shall seek for signs, first, of a certain and sure act making the books of the New Testament canonical; and secondly, of the use and appreciation of seven books that have thus far failed to attain such general recognition as the rest; and thirdly, of the use and appreciation of other books, be they totally apocryphal or be they nearly equivalent to the acknowledged books.

IV.

THE AGE OF ORIGEN.

200–300.

In passing from the second to the third century we enter into a totally new scene. The landscape, the persons, the movements in the new age are of an entirely different character from those in the period left behind. Between Clement of Rome in the year 95, and Irenæus in the year, say, 185, in Lyons, we had to flit about from Antioch to Smyrna, from Nabulus to Ephesus, from Philippi to Rome, and to Lyons. And no orthodox or regular writer was with certainty to be fixed in Africa. Now we have in the main to do with Africa alone, although we may make some excursions into other lands. The persons who attracted our attention during the second century were out of very different lands, but all of them wrote Greek. The five men whom we have to discuss during the third century are all of them, at least by residence if not by birth, Africans, and two of them are Latin writers. The men treated of before were of varied occupations, though largely officials of a more or less definite standing in various churches. Justin Martyr wore the robe of a philosopher. Hegesippus was a traveller. Turning to the third century, we have to do with three professors of theology, with one lawyer, and with a single bishop. And the movements that occur are of another description. Those schools of Gnostics find no rival in the new period. No heretic arises to outdo Marcion. No one vies with Tatian in harmonising and condensing the four Gospels into one.

Our aim now is to be on the watch for signs of any action canonising books, to examine most closely all that pertains to the use and the Church standing of the seven books,—James, Second Peter, Second and Third John, Jude, Hebrews, and Revelation,—and to mark what books approach in use and valuation the books of the New Testament, and how they are treated. The first of these three points calls for no recapitulation. As to the second, we found already for James a possible testimony in Clement of Rome, a sure one in Hermas, and a probable one in the Old-Syrian translation,—for Second Peter no particle of testimony,—for Second and Third John the testimony of the fragment of Muratori,—for Jude also Muratori,—for Hebrews the abundant testimony of Clement of Rome, and that of Justin Martyr, of Pinytus, bishop of Cnossus on Crete, and of Theophilus of Antioch,—and for Revelation the testimony of Hermas, of the Marcosians, and of Theophilus and Irenæus, possibly of Papias and Melito ; while Justin Martyr expressly names John as its author. The recapitulation for the third point we leave until the close of this period, where we shall sum up all that needs to be said of these companions to the books of the New Testament, and of their fate in the Church from the beginning until to-day.

If we only knew more of Pantænus we should probably have to place him at the head of the line of scholars in this age. He was towards the close of the second century the teacher, the director, of the theological school in Alexandria, and had, it is likely, before taking charge of the school, gone as a missionary to the East, reaching India and finding that the Apostle Bartholomew had preceded him there, and had left behind him the Gospel according to Matthew in Hebrew. His pupil Clement succeeded him in the school. The school has been supposed by some to date from the time of Mark's stay in Alexandria. We have not any reliable ground for that statement, yet it is quite possible that Pantænus had known disciples of the apostles.

Clement, to whom we now have to turn, tells us of his own teachers, including Pantænus, and shows us that the frequency and the extent of the intercourse among the churches and Christians of his day was no less than that which we have become acquainted with during the previous period. It is at the beginning of his great work called the Carpets. He writes of this work : " And now this affair is not

a book artistically composed for show, but it treasures up
memories for me for old age, an antidote for forgetfulness, an
image without art, and a picture of those real and soulful saintly
men, and truly worthy of praise, whose words I had the honour
of hearing. Of these one was in Greece, the Ionian, and one
in Great Greece (Southern Italy), another of them was from
Cœle-Syria, and one from Egypt, and others throughout the
East, where one was from the Assyrians, one in Palestine by
origin a Hebrew, and meeting the last one—this one was in
power the first—I stopped, having hunted after hidden things in
Egypt. The bee, in reality Sicilian, harvesting the flowers both
of the prophetic and of the apostolic meadow, implanting a
true thing of knowledge in the souls of his hearers. But they
preserving the pure tradition of the blessed teaching directly
both from Peter and James, both from John and Paul of the
holy apostles, son receiving it from father—but few were those
like unto the fathers—came then with God also to us sowing
those ancestral and apostolical seeds." It is a pity that Clement
did not name his teachers. Nevertheless the testimony for the
wide acquaintance of Clement with scholars from all parts of the
empire, and for the frequent communication between distant
countries, remains.

The information that we wish for from Clement we get
through Eusebius, who describes Clement's work, named
Sketches, as follows (H. E. 6. 14): "And in the Sketches,
speaking briefly, he makes short comments on all the testament-ed Scripture,"—on all the books in the two Testaments,
one would think, seeing that he treated at least of some Old
Testament books,—"not passing by the books that are spoken
against, I mean the Epistle of Jude and the rest of the Catholic
Epistles, and both Barnabas and the Revelation called Peter's.
And he says that the Epistle to the Hebrews is Paul's, and was
written to the Hebrews in the Hebrew tongue; and that Luke,
having translated it carefully, published it for the Greeks, for
which reason the same colouring is found in the translation of
this Epistle as in the Acts. And that the usual, Paul the
Apostle, was not written at the beginning of the letter, probably,
he says, because, writing to the Hebrews, who had taken a
prejudice to him, and suspected him, he, with thorough prudence,
did not at the outset rebuff them by putting in his name.

Then he (Clement) adds farther on : " And as even the blessed presbyter " — he seems to mean Pantænus — " said, since the Lord, being the Apostle of the Almighty, was sent to the Hebrews, in his modesty Paul, as sent to the Gentiles, does not write himself down as apostle of the Hebrews, not only because of the honour due to the Lord, but also because of its being a superfluous thing to write also to the Hebrews, seeing that he was a preacher and apostle of the Gentiles."

Photius refers to the Sketches, and says (Cod. 109) : " Their whole purpose is, as it were, explanations of Genesis, of Exodus, of the Psalms, of the Epistles, of the divine Paul, and of the Catholic [Epistles], and of Ecclesiastes." As Clement only commented on four of the Catholic Epistles, leaving out James and Third John, Photius is merely speaking generally in naming the Catholic Epistles without any limitation. In the sixth century Cassiodorius of Calabria, prime minister of Theodoric's, and others, and then founder of a monastery in Bruttia (Calabria), wrote a general theological handbook for his monks, in which he says (de inst. 8) : " In the canonical "—that is for us the Catholic—" Epistles, moreover, Clement, an Alexandrian presbyter, who is also called the Carpet-er," — from that book the high-coloured Carpets,—" explained in Attic language the First Epistle of Saint Peter, the First and Second of Saint John, and James,"—but James is a mistake, probably of some copyist ; it must read Jude. Then Cassiodorius translated some of these comments, including some on Jude, none on James.

It is perhaps enough when we say that Clement commented on these four Epistles, but we may add the following quotations for the sake of being sure. It is not strange that we find no quotation from the short Second John. That Clement fails to mention Third John may be because he did not know of its existence, although he might have thought it scarcely worth mentioning because of its shortness and of its similarity in some phrases to Second John. As for Jude, however, Clement refers to the verses 8 to 16 thus (Strom. 3. 2. 11) : " About these, I think, and the like heresies Jude spoke prophetically in his Epistle : ' Nevertheless, these also likewise dreaming—for waking they attack the truth—as far as : And their mouth utters swelled-up things.' " Now it may be that Clement wrote that just so, with " as far as " instead of giving all the verses.   But it is possible that a lazy copyist put in "as far as" and left the verses out.   In either case it is a large quotation, and fixes Clement's use of Jude, which he quotes several times besides.   Clement often quotes Hebrews.   It is enough to mention one passage.   He gives us Heb. $6^{11\text{-}20}$, precisely in the same way as those verses in Jude (2. 22. 136): "And we desire that each one of you show the same zeal unto the fulness of hope, until: Being a high priest to eternity, according to the order of Melchisedek."   Out of the several quotations from Revelation I take this free one (5. 6. 35): "And they say that the seven eyes of the Lord are seven spirits resting upon the staff flowering up out of the root of Jesse."   That is an odd confusion of memory for Rev. 5^6.   However, we have gotten from Clement of Alexandria clear testimony to Second John, Jude, Hebrews, and Revelation; but nothing for James, Second Peter, or Third John.

From Alexandria we now pass towards the west, and we find at Carthage the lawyer Tertullian.   He is not a petty advocate, but a man of note and influence, one whose business may call him to Rome.   He is a lawyer, but a Christian.   He is not half a Christian, but a whole one.   He may write sometimes a not very polished Latin, but he knows how to put life and fire into the words.   He burns and it burns within us.   We must quote a section from his work against Marcion in which he shows himself a believer in tradition.   And when we reflect how short the course of tradition from the apostles to him was, his words have great weight for us.   He writes (4. 5): "In short, if it be agreed that that is truer which is earlier, that earlier, which is even from the beginning, that from the beginning which is from the apostles, it will also likewise surely be agreed that that was handed down from the apostles which has been sacredly preserved among the churches of the apostles. Let us see what milk the Corinthians drank from Paul, according to what rule the Galatians were reproved, what the Philippians, the Thessalonians, the Ephesians read, what also the Romans from our neighbourhood proclaim, to whom both Peter and Paul left the Gospel and that sealed by their blood.   We have also churches cherished by John.   For although Marcion rejects his Revelation, yet the series of bishops traced to its source will rest upon John as their founder.   Thus also the high birth of the rest is recognised. And therefore I say that among them, and not only among the apostolic churches but also among all the churches which are confederated with them in the fellowship of the oath (sacrament), that Gospel of Luke which we defend with all our might stands fast from the moment it was published, but Marcion's [Luke] is unknown to the most, known, moreover, to none without being at once condemned."

We have then to ask, what this Tertullian thinks of our seven books. Four of them : James, Second Peter, Second and Third John, he does not appear to know at all. It might merely be questioned as to the two last, whether he simply passed them by as short and without thinking that they were not genuine. The ease with which they might have been, may have been overlooked will be clear from the case of Jude. Jude he mentions by name as apostolic. Now, interestingly enough, he mentions it (de cultu fem. i. 3) at the close of a discussion of the canonicity of the book of Enoch. He suggests that the Jews may have refused Enoch a place in their closet because it spoke of Christ, and agrees that it is no wonder that they reject a book that spoke of Him, seeing that they did not receive Him speaking before them. He concludes : "To this comes the fact that Enoch possesses testimony in the Apostle Jude." Just nine words give us his view of Jude. The sentence is a mere trifle. As men say : he happens to add the thought. And were it not for this trifle we should know nothing of his valuation of Jude. How easily, then, Second and Third John may have escaped his pen. How about the two other books ? Tertullian is perfectly well acquainted with the Epistle to the Hebrews, but he only quotes it once. He writes (de pud. 20): "Nevertheless I wish in a redundant way to adduce also the testimony of a certain companion of the apostles, fit to confirm of next right the discipline of the masters. For there exists also a writing of Barnabas to the Hebrews, a man sufficiently authorised by God, whom Paul placed beside himself in the matter of abstinence : Or have I alone and Barnabas no right to work. And would that the letter of Barnabas were rather received among the churches than that apocryphal Shepherd of the adulterers. And so admonishing the disciples, leaving all beginnings behind to stretch forward rather to perfection nor again to lay the foundations of repentance from the works of the dead. For it is impossible, he says, that those who have once been enlightened and have tasted the heavenly gift," . . . and he continues the quotation to the end of the eighth verse.

For myself I accept Tertullian's opinion as to the authorship of Hebrews. But the interesting thing is, that he does not accept it as equal to the mass of the books of the New Testament. For him it is not New Testament at all. It is as he says, like a lawyer, a title, it is an enunciation, a letter, a book, and it is quite a respectable book, but it is not scripture. It was not written by a Twelve-Apostle and not by Paul, and not by a brother of Jesus. It is better than Hermas. On that point he has a definite opinion. But it is not apostolic. I accept Tertullian's author, but I put the book fairly into the New Testament, as he did not. One book remains: Tertullian is thoroughly convinced that the Revelation was written by the Apostle John, and he refers to it constantly as an authoritative book. He writes: "For also the Revelation of John," "For also the Apostle John in the Revelation," "Also in the Revelation of John," quoting verse after verse. For Tertullian and for Carthage we have thus testimony touching Jude and Revelation, and testimony of a second-class intention for Hebrews.

We return now to Alexandria and to the old theological school, and to Clement's pupil and successor the giant Origen. He personifies the intercourse between distant churches and the intense eagerness of what may with justice be called scientific theological research in the Church of his day. Origen knew not merely Alexandria, but as well Rome and Antioch and Arabia and Athens and Cæsarea. His testimony has for us a high value. He was an exegete. He knew the books of the Bible. Eusebius tells us (H. E. 6. 25) that: "Also in the fifth book of the commentaries upon the [Gospel] according to John, the same [Origen] says this about the Epistles of the Apostles: Now he who was enabled to become a servant of the new covenant, not of letter but of spirit, Paul, who caused the Gospel to abound from Jerusalem and around as far as Illyria, not only did not write to all the churches which he taught, but also sent [but] a few lines to those to which he wrote. And Peter, upon whom the Church of Christ is built, against which hell's gates shall not prevail, left behind him one Epistle that is acknowledged, possibly a second, for it is called in question. What need to speak of the one reclining on Jesus' breast, John, who left behind him one Gospel, confessing that he could make so many that not even the world could contain them? And he wrote also the Revelation, having been commanded to be silent and not to write the voices of the seven thunders. And he left behind also an Epistle of altogether few lines. It may be also a second and a third. Since all do not say that these are genuine. But both are not of a hundred lines."

In his homilies on Joshua (7. 1), which unfortunately are only preserved in a translation, Origen takes fire at the sound of the priestly trumpets moving around the walls of Jericho at the command of that earlier Jesus: "But our Lord Jesus Christ coming, whose advent that former son of Nun pointed out, sends as priests His apostles bearing well-drawn trumpets, the magnificent and heavenly doctrine of preaching. First Matthew sounded with priestly trumpet in his Gospel. Mark also, and Luke, and John sang each with their priestly trumpets. Peter also sounds with the two"—one reading says: from the three—trumpets of his Epistles. James also and Jude. None the less does John also here still further sing with the trumpets by his Epistles and the Revelation, and Luke describing the deeds of the apostles. Latest of all, moreover, that one coming who said: I think, moreover, that God makes a show of us newest apostles, and thundering with the fourteen trumpets of his Epistles he threw down to the very foundations the walls of Jericho and all the contrivances of idolatry, and the dogmas of the philosophers." We may remain in doubt at this, whether he himself wrote "fourteen" Epistles for Paul, calling Hebrews his, or whether the translator changed thirteen to fourteen. In his homilies (13. 2) on Genesis he calls the apostles the sons, the servants, the boys of Isaac: "Therefore Isaac also digs new wells, rather the sons of Isaac dig. The sons of Isaac are Matthew, Mark, Luke, and John. His sons are Peter, James, and Jude. His son is also the Apostle Paul. Who all dig the wells of the New Testament. But for these"—for the possession of these new wells—"contend those who like earthly things, nor suffer new things to be instituted nor old ones to be cleaned. They oppose the Gospel wells. They war against the apostolical wells."

15

Hebrews he discusses at length. He quotes it more than two hundred times, sometimes saying: The Apostle, or the Epistle to the Hebrews, or Paul, or Paul in the Epistle to the Hebrews. He wrote homilies on it after the year 245, and in these homilies he gives us the following judicious account of the Epistle, which Eusebius (H. E. 6. 25) has saved for us: "About the Epistle to the Hebrews he presents these words in his homilies on it: Everyone who understands how to distinguish the difference of phrases would agree that the character of the style of the Epistle entitled as that to the . Hebrews has not in its wording the peculiarities of the apostle, who confessed that he was an unlearned man in speech, that is in the phrasing, but that the Epistle is more thoroughly Greek in the composition of the wording. And again, moreover, that the thoughts of the Epistle are wonderful and are not inferior to those of the writings that are acknowledged to be apostolical, and this every one giving heed to the reading which is apostolical would say with me to be true. After other things he adds to this, saying: Speaking freely, I should say that the thoughts were of the apostle, but the wording and the composition were of some one drawing the apostolical things from his memory, and as it were of one who wrote notes upon what had been spoken by the teacher. If then any church holds this Epistle as Paul's, let it be content with this thought. For the men of old did not in vain hand it down as Paul's. But who wrote the Epistle, the truth God knows. The account has come to us of some who say that Clement who became Bishop of Rome wrote the Epistle, and of others [who say] that Luke, the one who wrote the Gospel and the Acts, [wrote it]."

In his commentary on the Psalms (Ps. 30) we read a reference to James as a proof that the word spirit is applied by Scripture sometimes to the soul, the psyche: "As in James: And as the body without the spirit is dead," James 2[26]. In another place, in his commentary on John (vol. 20. 10), he speaks as though some would not take what James said for authoritative: "This would not be conceded by those who receive the saying. Faith without works is dead," James 2[20]. But the weight of the words "who receive" as a questioning of the authority of the Epistle is diminished by the fact that Origen immediately continues: "Or of those hearing," and quotes Romans   It is further interesting to see that he does not use the reading "vain" or "ineffective," but draws the word "dead" from v.[17]. In the same commentary on John, a little earlier (vol. 19. 23 [6]), he calls it a letter that is in circulation, as if it were not a genuine letter: "And if faith is alleged, but chance to be without works, such is dead, as we have read in the current Epistle of James." It is further to be observed that in his commentary on Matthew, when he speaks at length of the brothers of Jesus, he mentions James, but says nothing of his Epistle.

As for Jude, we may begin precisely at that point. In that commentary on Matthew (vol. 10. 17) he says: "And Jude wrote a letter but of few lines, yet filled with hearty (or strong) words of heavenly grace, who spoke in the preface: Jude a servant of Jesus Christ, and brother of James." At a later point (vol. 17. 30) the phrase used for Jude is less definite: And if anyone should also bring in the letter of Jude, let him see what follows the word because of the saying: And the angels, those not keeping their first estate but leaving their own dwelling, he has kept in lasting bonds under darkness unto the judgment of the great day." We have already given above his unqualified allusion both to James and Jude in his general statements, and as well a qualified and an unqualified one to Second Peter; the lack of qualification may in the latter case be due to the translator. In the case of the Epistles of John the mere plural would not distinguish between two or three Epistles, but we may keep to three because he mentions them in the first general statement. The book of Revelation we have found in the general summings-up, and we may add a single quotation from among many (on John, vol. 1. 14): "Therefore John the son of Zebedee says in the Revelation: And I saw an angel flying in mid-heaven," Rev. 14[6], and he quotes to the end of v.[7]. We have, then, from Origen firm testimony for Jude, Hebrews, and the Revelation, and wavering testimony for James, Second Peter, and Second and Third John.

His pupil, Origen's pupil, Dionysius of Alexandria, took charge of the school there probably about the year 231, became Bishop of Alexandria about the year 247, and died about 265. He was twice banished. He was a live man, just such a one as the best pupil of Origen could be expected to make, and he was in constant intercourse with Rome, of course with Cæsarea, and with Asia Minor. He wrote a vigorous but short letter to Novatus to leave the church at Rome in peace and save his soul. Indeed, he reminds us with his letters of his less gifted namesake Dionysius of Corinth nearly a century earlier. He wrote not merely to the Egyptians, and, when banished, to his Alexandrian sheep, but also to Origen and to Laodicea, where Thelymidres was bishop, and to Armenia, where Meroudsanes was bishop, and to Cornelius, Bishop of Rome. He was called upon by Elenus, the Bishop of Tarsus in Cilicia, and the rest of those with him, by Firmilian in Cappadocia, and Theoctistus in Palestine to stand up against the followers of Novatus at the synod of Antioch. But that is enough to show his influence.

The following paragraph from a letter of Dionysius' shows his view of the harmonious state of the Church in general, the persecutions having ceased and the Churches having given up their love for Novatus (Eus. H. E. 7. 5): "And now, brother, know that all the Churches throughout the East and still beyond, that were torn apart, are united. And all the leaders everywhere are of one mind, rejoicing exceedingly at the peace which has come against expectation,—Demetrianos in Antioch, Theoctistus in Cæsarea, Madzabanes in Aelia, Marinus in Tyre, Alexander having fallen asleep, Heliodorus in Laodicea. Thelymidres having gone to his rest, Elenus in Tarsus and all the churches of Cilicia, Firmilianus and all Cappadocia. For I have named only the more illustrious of the bishops, lest I should add length to the letter or undue heaviness to the discourse. Nevertheless all the Syrias and Arabia, to each of which ye give aid and to which ye now wrote, and Mesopotamia, both Pontus and Bithynia, and to speak briefly all everywhere rejoice in oneness of mind and in brotherly love, glorifying God."

Dionysius quotes the Epistle of James (Galland, vol. 14. App. p. 117 E): "For God, he says, is not tempted by evils." He also refers (Eus. H. E. 6. 41) to Hebrews as written by Paul: "And the brethren turned aside and gave place (to their persecutors), and they received with joy, like those to whom also Paul bore witness, the plundering of their goods," Hebrews 10^{34}. And in his discussion of the book of Revelation he shows plainly that he regards the Second and Third Epistles of John as his, and we see that he claims their anonymity as a sign of John's inclination to write anonymously: "And not even in the Second and Third Epistles of John which are in our hands, although they are short, does John appear by name, but the presbyter writes anonymously." In the same connection, however, thirty lines later, he speaks of "the Epistle" more than once, and the Catholic Epistle, meaning the First Epistle, as if John had only written one. But we find a like numberless reference to the Second Epistle by Aurelius of Chullabi in the seventh council of Carthage, which was held in the year 256 during the lifetime of Dionysius (Routh, 3. p. 130): "John the apostle commanded (laid it down) in his Epistle saying: If anyone come to you and have not the teaching of Christ, refuse to admit him into your house, and do not greet him. For whoever shall have greeted (welcomed) him takes part in his evil deeds," 2 John [10, 11]. The quotation is loose enough. We then have Dionysius' testimony for James, for Second and Third John, and for Hebrews, but nothing for Second Peter or Jude. As for the book of Revelation, we must give his words at length.

Dionysius of Alexandria's discussion of the authorship of the Revelation is the first scientific discussion of the kind in the early Church that has been preserved until our day. It offers in its way for the criticism of the books of the New Testament a parallel to Origen's criticism of the text of certain passages. Eusebius (H. E. 7. 25) gives us first Dionysius' account of the way in which some Christians had previously treated Revelation: "For some then of those before us rejected and cast aside the book in every way, and correcting it chapter for chapter, and, showing that it was ignorant and unreasonable, declared that the title was forged. For they say that it is not from John, and that it is not even a revelation, being covered with the heavy and thick veil of ignorance, and that not only no one of the apostles, but not even any one of the saints or of those belonging to the Church, was the maker of this book, but Cerinthus, backing up the heresy called after him the Cerinthian, and wishing to set a name worthy of credence at the head of his own fabrication. For this is the dogma of his teaching, that Christ's kingdom will be earthly, and in this he dreams that it will consist in those things which he himself longed for, being a lover of the body and altogether fleshly, in satisfyings of the belly and of the things below the belly, that is in feastings and drinkings and marriages, and in the things by means of which he thought that he would succeed in getting these things under more acceptable names, in feasts and offerings and sacrifices of sacred animals. But I should not dare to reject the book, since many of the brethren hold it with zeal, and I accept as greater than my consideration of the book the general opinion about it, and regard the explanation of the details in it for something hidden and most wonderful. For even if I do not understand, yet I presuppose that a certain deeper sense lies in the words. Not measuring and judging these things with a reasoning of my own, but attributing them rather to faith, I have thought that they were too high to be apprehended by me, and I do not reject these things which I have not seen with the rest, but am rather surprised that I have not also seen them." Thus Dionysius.

Eusebius continues: "Thereat putting to the test the whole book of Revelation, and having shown that it is impossible to understand it according to the common conception, he adds, saying: "And having finished the whole prophecy, so to speak, the prophet blessed those who keep it, and so also himself. For blessed, he says, is he that keepeth the words of the prophecy of this book, and I John the one seeing and hearing these things. I have then nothing to oppose to his being called John, and to this book's being by John. For I agree that it is by some one holy and inspired, yet I should not easily suppose that this was the apostle, the son of Zebedee, the brother of James, of whom the Gospel according to John and the Catholic Epistle bear the name. For I judge from the bearing of each, and the shape of the discourse, and the outcome of the book, that it is not the same. For the Evangelist nowhere writes his name, by the bye, nor heralds himself, either by means of the Gospel or by means of the Epistle. Then a little farther on he says this again: And John nowhere neither as about himself nor as about another[?]. But the one writing the Revelation at once in the beginning sets himself at the head: Revelation of Jesus Christ which He gave to him to show to His servants speedily, and He signified it sending by His angel to His servant John, who bore witness to the Word of God and to His testimony, to as many things as he saw. Then also he writes a letter: John to the seven churches which are in Asia, grace to you and peace. But the Evangelist did not even write his name before the Catholic Epistle, but without needless words began with the very mystery of the divine revelation: That which was from the beginning, which we heard, which we saw with our eyes. For on occasion of this very revelation also the Lord called Peter blessed, saying: Blessed art thou Simon bar Jonah because flesh and blood did not reveal it to thee, but my Heavenly Father. But not in the Second that is circulated of John, or in the Third, although they are short Epistles, does John appear by name, but the presbyter writes namelessly. But this one did not even think it enough, having named himself once, to relate what follows, but he takes it up again: I, John, your brother and sharer with you in the suffering and kingdom and in patient waiting for Jesus, was on the island called Patmos because of the Word of God and the testimony of Jesus. And then also at the end he says this: Blessed is he that keepeth the words of the prophecy of this book, and I, John, who see and hear these things. That therefore John is the one who writes this is to be believed himself saying it. Which one, however, this is, is not clear. For he did not, as often in the Gospel, say that he himself was the disciple loved by the Lord, or the brother of James, or the one who had been a self-seer and a self-hearer of the Lord. For he would have said something of these things that were made clear beforehand if he wished to display himself clearly."

Dionysius then speaks of the many Johns: "As also Paul was much named, and Peter among the children of the believers," that is, that many boys were called Paul and Peter. He mentions John Mark, but thinks him unlikely to be the author. Then he refers to the other John in Ephesus, who appears to be more likely to have written it. He gives at length a view of the way in which the author of the Gospel and the First Epistle writes, and turning to the Revelation says: "But totally different and foreign to all this is the Revelation, neither joining on to nor approaching this in any way, almost so to speak not even having a syllable in common with it. And neither has the Epistle any reminder or any thought of the Revelation (for I let the Gospel pass), nor the Revelation of the Epistle, whereas Paul refers in passing by his Epistles also to his revelations which he did not write out by themselves. And further also the difference of the language between the Gospel and the Epistle over against the Revelation is to be emphasized. For the former are written not only faultlessly as regards the Greek speech, but also most logically in the phrases, the arguments, the composition of the explanations. It goes very hard to find in them a barbarous sound, a solecism, or any personal peculiarity. For he had, as it appears, each of the two words, the Lord having granted them to him, the word of knowledge and the word of diction. But that this one saw a revelation and received knowledge and prophecy, I do not deny ; nevertheless I see his dialect and his tongue not Grecising accurately, but using barbaric idioms and occasionally also committing solecisms."

Dionysius was a great and a learned and an influential man. He was not like Origen, for years before his death the object of ecclesiastical hatred in Alexandria. Yet nevertheless his discussion of the Revelation in this way seems to have had but little effect upon his surroundings or his successors, although it certainly may have had a share in the shaping of the general fate of the book of Revelation of which we have still to treat. Dionysius stands for James, Second and Third John, Hebrews, and for the Revelation as from an unknown John, but not for Second Peter or Jude, so far as we can see.

Now we turn again to the West, again to Carthage. This time we have to do not with a lawyer but with a bishop. Cyprian was born at Carthage in the year 200, and taught rhetoric there. He was baptized in 246, became presbyter and in 248 bishop of Carthage. In the Decian persecution he fled for safety to the desert, and under Valerian he was banished, but then beheaded in 258 in his native city. Cyprian gives no signs of having known anything about James, Second Peter, Second and Third John, Jude, or Hebrews. He is a great quoter of Scripture, and gives something from all the other books of the New Testament, saving Philemon and those just named. Of course, there is the bare possibility that he passed over one or the other short Epistle merely by accident, as doubtless was the case with Philemon, because it was short and offered little occasion for reference. Singularly enough, we have a reference apparently to Second Peter in a letter of Firmilian's, the bishop of Cæsarea in Cappadocia, which we find in Latin among the letters of Cyprian (Ep. 75), to whom it was addressed. It will be remembered that Dionysius mentioned Firmilian. Firmilian appears to have the second chapter of Second Peter in mind when he writes to

Cyprian that Peter and Paul, the blessed apostles, "have in their Epistles execrated the heretics and admonished us to avoid them." Cyprian, however, knows well the Revelation, and uses it freely.

The heresy of Paul of Samosata, who was bishop of Antioch from 260 to 272, although excommunicated in 269, secures us a reference to Hebrews and perhaps one to Jude. The Synod at Antioch in the year 269 wrote a letter to Paul, and quoted Hebrews under the introduction (Routh, 3. pp. 298, 299): "According to the apostle," which means according to Paul, and as the accompaniment to two quotations from First Corinthians: "And of Moses: Reckoning the shame of Christ greater riches than the treasures of Egypt," Heb. 11^{26}. The allusion to Jude is less clear. It is in the letter which Malchion, a presbyter at Antioch and the head of a Greek school there, wrote in the name of the bishops and presbyters and deacons of Antioch and of the neighbouring cities and the Churches of God, to Dionysius, bishop of Rome, and Maximus, bishop of Alexandria. Malchion (Routh, 3. p. 304) describes the Bishop Paul as one: "Denying his own God, and not keeping the faith which he also himself formerly had." That may be connected with Jude [3] and [4].

So we see that the great theological writers of this third century give us divided testimony as to the seven books to which we have especially directed our attention. James is supported by Dionysius of Alexandria, and in an uncertain way by Origen. Second Peter only has an uncertain testimony from Origen. Second John is supported by Clement of Alexandria and by Dionysius of Alexandria, but receives from Origen only an uncertain note. Third John rests here on Dionysius and on uncertain testimony from Origen. Jude is supported by Clement of Alexandria and by Tertullian and by Origen, the first of our seven books to find faith in the West. Hebrews can only appeal to the three Alexandrians: Clement, Origen, and Dionysius. Tertullian sets it aside as not a part of the New Testament, although he thinks it a very fair book. Revelation again, like the Epistle of Jude, finds support both East and West, for it is accepted by Clement and Origen at Alexandria and by Tertullian and Cyprian at Carthage, while Dionysius of Alexandria accepts it, it is true, but insists upon it that the current belief of its having been written by the Apostle John is altogether baseless.

Our task for this period consisted of three parts. One is completed by the simple observation that we have nowhere found any signs of a canonization of the books of the New Testament, and with a single somewhat indistinct exception of a movement on the part of any synod to say just what books were genuine or what books were to be read, or what books were not to be read. The second task is completed by the review of the seven books just given. The third remains, the question as to the books which are not in our New Testament and which yet appear at or up to his time, during this period or during an earlier period, to have held a place near to the books of the New Testament.

This question may be divided into two, in so far as we may ask on the one hand what books were in good and churchly circles associated with the books of the New Testament, and, on the other hand, what books anyone may have tried to forge in the name of the apostles. We must in advance make our minds up to one thing, namely, to the difficulty in many or in almost all cases of being perfectly sure in just what sense the churches, and with the churches the authors whom we have to consult, regarded the books in question. Further, it must be observed that in cases of doubt we have not the office to insist upon it that the given books must of necessity have been held by the churches to be equal to the books of the New Testament. Be there doubt, we have a right to suppose that what was the case elsewhere or before or after may be used to decide the case in favour of a distinction between the doubtful books and those that were certainly acknowledged.

Still further is to be observed, that the happy-go-luckiness with which, the reckless way in which we have seen that the writers of the early literature, which we have had to examine, quote not only the books of the New Testament but also those of the Old Testament, permits us to argue that they certainly will not in every single case have paused to reflect whether or not in their rapid flight they should write or should not write : " As it is written," " As it is spoken," " The Scripture saith," or not. Should anyone urge that that will be true of cases touching the New Testament books, and that they may have been by these errors of flightiness and carelessness denoted as Scripture by writers who upon sober reflection would not have thus designated them, we must concede it. But the error in the other cases is the error that is to be looked for, and we have a right, it is our duty in this examination, to be especially upon our guard against it. At the same time we may declare in advance, from human necessity or from the consideration of the inevitable consequences of human frailty, that certainly one book or another will really have been quoted or used as canonical, although it is not in our New Testament, simply because the boundaries were not settled, because there was no definite boundary line between canonical and non-canonical books.

Inasmuch as the question as to the valuation of a given book is largely combined with the question as to its being read in the assemblies of the Christians for public worship, it is necessary that we revert for a moment to what was said above on this point. What was read in the public meeting was read either under the head of : God to Man, or under the head of : Man to Man. It must not be overlooked that this is by no means a Christian innovation. For the Jews read before the time of Christ, so far as we can conjecture, various writings in the synagogue which were not as yet determined to be authoritative. Without doubt in some cases such public reading led the way to the authorization of the said books. Under God to Man at the close of the third century only the books of the Old Testament and the books of the New Testament which were current in the given church could be read. At the middle of the century Cyprian had already placed the words of Jesus above those of the prophets, like the keynote to the Epistle to the Hebrews. And these words of Jesus were the words written in the Gospels (Cypr. de dom. orat. 1) : " Many are the things which God wished to be said and to be heard through the prophets His servants, but how much greater are those which the Son speaks."

Whether the view of all the churches as to what was New Testament coincided with our view or not, is what we have here to examine. But no book could be read as from God to Man which had not then and there attained to this right of being considered a part of the New Testament. Under Man to Man might be brought first of all a sermon attaching to the passage or one of the passages read, or it may be

to a special text. Of course, this sermon was originally, as we
saw above, not attached to a text, but was a presentation of
something verbal that corresponded to a written Gospel.   This
verbal Gospel had been succeeded by the written Gospel, which
in the third century had already passed on to the division God
to Man.   The letters of the apostles were at first read here, but
had now also passed on to that higher division.   Finally, there
might be read here a letter from a bishop, which makes us think
of the letters of Dionysius of Corinth and of Dionysius of
Alexandria, or a letter from another church.   Nor was that all.
It will not seldom have been the case that a preacher could not
be had.   Nowadays in Saxony in such a case the school teacher
may be appointed to read a sermon written by the clergyman, or
a printed sermon.   In those early ages it was often desirable
to have something to read in the place of the lacking sermon.
Here then any good book, any book fitted to build up the
listening assembly in Christian life, could be read.   What
should be read was at the first moment not determined by a
synod of bishops.   The single churches will have acted as the
leading men in them decided.   And it is to the books that we
discover thus to have been read that we have now to give
especial attention, and to try to decide whether they reached
this distinction of public reading by right of the assumption that
they were an utterance of God to Man, or whether they were
merely regarded as good books which spoke for Man to Man as
a sermon would speak.

The first book that we have to consider is the letter of
Clement of Rome to which we have already so often alluded.
It is a book about whose origin at Rome, and by the hand of
Clement a prominent Christian there, and probably about the
year 95, there can be no reasonable doubt.   We read above
that Hegesippus stayed some time at Corinth on his way to
Rome.   Eusebius gives us, then, Hegesippus' testimony for this
letter by adducing his statement that, as the letter presupposes,
there really had then been an uproar, an unusual dissension, a
revolution in the church at Corinth.   Much more clear is the
account, given above, from Dionysius, the bishop of Corinth,
who mentions this letter in writing to the church of Rome or to
Soter, the bishop of Rome, perhaps just before 175.   Now his
words are of great moment for the whole question touching the

public reading of these non-apostolic books in the churches. He says (Eus. H. E. 4. 23): "To-day then we are passing the Lord's holy day, on which we read your letter, which we shall ever have, reading it now and then to keep it in mind, as also the former one written to us by Clement." Remembering what was said above about the point of view from which different writings might be read in church, we have in the first place to observe that Dionysius does not make a shadow of a distinction between the reading of the lately received letter of Soter's and the reading of the letter of Clement that had reached Corinth eighty years before.

We must conclude from his words that Soter's letter was read as Clement's was, or reversed, that Clement's letter was read for the same reason, from the same standpoint, that Soter's was. I see no possible way of escaping this conclusion. But no one can for an instant think of supposing that the letter of Soter that had just come was read to the church at Corinth under the heading: God to Man, that it was read as if it were to be valued as highly as Paul's letters to the Corinthians. And therefore that must be the case with Clement. Here at Corinth, at the place from which the copies of the letter of Clement were sent out to neighbouring or even to distant churches, the letter of Clement of Rome was read as a letter of Man to Man, was read in the second, not in the first division of the writings used in public worship. This circumstance must have in general been of determining character for the other churches which received this letter from the Corinthians in a copy. And this fact will have to be borne in mind when we come to other similar writings. There may have been here or there a misconception as to the proper valuation of the letter, there may have been churches that took the decision in their own hands and declared this letter for the equal of the Pauline Epistles, but the decision of Corinth will certainly have been the chief and overwhelming decision for the case that anyone raised the question.

Irenæus speaks of Clement as having heard the apostles, and says (Eus. H. E. 5. 6): "At the time, then, of this Clement, there being no little dissension among the brethren in Corinth, the church in Rome sent a most powerful letter to the Corinthians gathering them together unto peace and renewing their faith." That he calls it a most powerful letter does not

suggest anything like canonicity. The word that he uses for
letter is the word for scripture, but it is totally impossible to
take it here in the specific sense of scripture. The sentence
demands its being taken in the general sense of "writing," which
I have given as "letter." Besides, Irenæus uses the same adjective
"most powerful," and the same root for written, only this time
in a participle, in speaking of Polycarp's letter to the Philippians.
So there is no thought of its being scripture in the mind of
Irenæus. Clement of Alexandria quotes his namesake often
and with respect, but does not use his letter as scripture. The
words : "The scripture saith somewhere," which begin a long,
loose quotation from Clement of Rome in one place, belong to
Clement of Rome himself, save that Clement of Alexandria has
put in the word scripture because the first sentence is from
Proverbs. He calls his namesake "the apostle Clement," but
he also with the New Testament calls Barnabas an apostle, "the
Apostle Barnabas." Origen calls him a "disciple of the apostles,"
and in one place "the faithful Clement who was testified to by Paul."

As for Eusebius, it is curious that in one place (H. E. 6. 13)
he puts it with the books that are disputed, saying of Clement of
Alexandria that he uses "quotations also from the disputed
writings ('scriptures,' it would be in a different connection), both
from the so-called Wisdom of Solomon and that of Jesus Sirach
and of the Epistle to the Hebrews, both from Barnabas and
Clement and Jude." Yet in the following chapter Eusebius
describes Clement of Alexandria's Sketches as explaining all the
"testament-ed" scriptures, not even passing by the disputed ones,
that is to say, Jude and the other Catholic Epistles and the letter
of Barnabas and the Revelation bearing the name of Peter,"
leaving Clement out altogether. And when Eusebius gives the
list of genuine, disputed, and spurious books he does not mention
Clement at all, although he names a number of the less known
books. He does in one passage (H. E. 3. 16) say of it : "And
we know also that this is read publicly before the people in very
many churches, not only of old, but also in our very own day " ;
yet it is plain, taking all this together, that he does not think it
to be scripture. Athanasius does not think it necessary to name
it when he, at the close of his list of the books of scripture,
excludes from that list the Teaching of the Apostles, which was
attributed to Clement, and the Shepherd of Hermas.

Succeeding Church writers quote it, but never in such a way as to indicate that it occurs to them to regard it as scripture. A reference to it among the books of the New Testament in the Apostolic Canons (Can. 85) of the sixth century is probably an interpolation, difficult as it is to imagine who would have put the words in. The Greek text has : " Of Jude one, of Clement two Epistles, and the Constitutions addressed to you the bishops by me Clement, . . . and the Acts of us the apostles." The Coptic text reads : " The Revelation of John ; the two Epistles of Clement which ye shall read aloud." In the Alexandrian manuscript of the Greek Bible the two letters, that is to say, this letter and the homily called Second Clement, stand after the Revelation. Had they been conceived of as regular books of the New Testament they should have stood with the other Epistles and before Revelation. The same manuscript contains three beautiful Christian hymns, which no one so far as I know supposes to be a part of the New Testament. A list of the scriptures added to Nicephorus' Chronography of the early ninth century put this letter among the Apocrypha. In the twelfth century Alexius Aristenus, the steward of the Great Church at Constantinople, refers to that list in the Apostolic Canons, and mentions the two letters of Clement as scripture, but he stands alone in this. The amount of it all is, that the letter of Clement of Rome may here or there possibly have been read as scripture, but that it never in any way approached general acceptance as anything more than a good Christian book. It does not appear to have been translated into Latin, so that there is not even a question as to its scriptural authority in the Latin Church.

In the letter that bears the name of Barnabas we again find a name that occurs in the New Testament, and that the name of a man who plays a large part in the early Church and holds a more important position than either Clement or Hermas. Clement, however, may perhaps have been Paul's Clement, whereas neither the one nor the other of these other writers had anything to do with the times of the New Testament. The letter of Barnabas was probably written about the year 130. Whether its author really happened to bear the name of Barnabas or not we do not know, for we know nothing about him aside from his book. The book itself is certainly very interesting. We find that it was especially valued and used in

Alexandria. Clement of Alexandria quotes it often, naming the author simply (2. 15. 67 and 18. 84) Barnabas, or (2. 6. 31 and 7. 35) "the Apostle Barnabas." Once he writes (5. 10. 63): "Barnabas who also himself preached the word with the apostle according to the service of the heathen (in the mission to the heathen)." Again he says (2. 20. 116): "I shall need no more words when I add as witness the apostolic Barnabas, who was of the Seventy and a fellow-worker of Paul's, saying word for word here. . . ." Origen quotes this letter also. For Tertullian we may draw a very fair conclusion from his view of the Epistle to the Hebrews, which we gave above. He thought that Hebrews was quite a good book, and he was certain that it was written by the real Barnabas, the companion of Paul, yet it did not occur to him to regard it as equal to scripture. How much less would he have thought that this "Barnabas" was scripture.

The name Barnabas in the Stichometry in the Codex Claromontanus is probably to be used as a proof that it was in good standing in Egypt at about the beginning of the fourth century. Eusebius places it in his list of books among those which are spurious, between the Revelation of Peter and the Teachings of the Apostles. In the Codex Sinaiticus of the Greek Bible it stands after the Revelation. As a part of the New Testament it would have taken a place among or with the Epistles, and before the book of Revelation. Jerome says that it is an apocryphal book, but that it is read. Its being read is simply no sign of its being scripture. It is read as: Man to Man, as a good book, but not as an equal of the apostolic books. In the list in Nicephorus' Chronography, Barnabas stands among the disputed books. We may say, then, of Barnabas that it shows far less signs of wide use than Clement of Rome's letter does, but we may take it for granted that, like Clement's letter, it will here or there have been accepted as equal to the books of the New Testament. But that can have occurred but rarely. After the fourth century it seems gradually to have faded out of the thoughts of the Church.

We now come to a book which secured to itself a host of readers and friends. The Shepherd, written by Hermas the brother of Pius the bishop of Rome, probably about the year 140, is a beautiful book of Christian dreams, putting to flight every assault of doubt, and urging the faithful to endurance and to patience in certain hope of the future glory. The fragment of Muratori gives us over seven lines upon this book, and furnishes the only account of its origin. It says: "The Shepherd, moreover, Hermas wrote but very lately in our times in the city of Rome, Pius the bishop his brother being seated in the chair of the Roman church, and therefore it should be read, but it cannot until the end of time be published (that is: read as if it were scripture) in the church before the people, neither among the completed number of the prophets nor among the apostles." That tells us that two kinds of scripture books were then read in the church, prophets and apostles. The "prophets" include Law, Prophets, and Books, the whole Old Testament, and the author of this list is sure that the list of those books is completed. That is an announcement that the Old Testament canon was closed for him at least. He does not say that the list of the apostolic books has been closed, and the inference from the contrast is that it is not yet closed as far as he is concerned. But be that as it may, one thing is settled, Hermas may be read as a good book, yet it may never to the end of time be accounted a part of scripture. That is a strong statement.

The essay on the Dice-Players, written by we do not know whom towards the end of the second century, calls the Revelation and Hermas scripture, but does not name the words of Jesus and the apostles scripture. Hermas is quoted by Irenæus as scripture (4. 20. 2): "Well spoke therefore the scripture which says: First of all believe that one is God, He that created all things and wrought them out and made all things from that which was not, into being." The word "scripture" seems there to be used in its proper and full sense. It would be possible to suggest that it was a momentary slip of the memory on the part of Irenæus, were it not for the fact that the words stand in a prominent place in Hermas. The words sound scriptural enough. If anyone should quote them to-day to a good Christian, who was not a Scotchman or a Würtemberger that knew every verse from Genesis to Revelation, he would be very likely for the moment to accept the quotation as a good one, and to blame his memory for thinking that it sounded after all a little odd. It is also fair to remember that we found Justin Martyr mistaking the book in which a quotation was, and here Clement does not name Hermas. Immediately afterwards he

16

names Malachi.   We are led to make all these excuses because
the case seems so strange.   When Eusebius quotes this passage
from Irenæus, in giving an account of the literature used by
Irenæus, he used himself the word "writing" in the general way,
not as of scripture.   He says (H. E. 5. 8, 7) : "And he not only
knows but also receives"—that must mean as scripture—"the
writing of the Shepherd saying : Well spoke, therefore, the scripture which says," etc.   Enough about the one passage which is
from a prominent writer, and which assigns to a book not in the
New Testament the rank of a New Testament book.   Clement
of Alexandria quotes Hermas nine times, but never as scripture.
He usually refers not to the author, but to the one who has
spoken to Hermas : "For the power that appeared in the dream
to Hermas," "The shepherd the angel of repentance, speaks to
Hermas," "Divinely therefore the power, uttering according to
revelation the visions to Hermas, says."

Tertullian, our Carthaginian lawyer, is clear in his mind
about Hermas.   It has often been said that he called Hermas
"scripture" while he was still a Catholic, but that he condemned
the book after he had become a Montanist.   The fact is, that
he mentions the book twice, once contemptuously and briefly
while he was a Catholic, and once at length and violently
after he had left the Church.   He says in his wonderful essay
on prayer (ch. 16) : "For what, then, if that Hermas, whose
book (writing, scripture) is inscribed something like Shepherd,
after he had finished praying had not sat down on the bed,
but had done something else, should we also insist upon it
that that was to be observed?   Not at all."   There is nothing
but contempt in his allusion to "that Hermas" whose book
was perhaps called Shepherd, perhaps something else.   But
Tertullian had not time then to busy himself with Hermas.   The
time for Hermas came when Tertullian wrote his treatise on
Modesty.   In one place in it (ch. 20, see above at the Epistle
to the Hebrews) he says, would that that Epistle were more
common among the churches : "Than that apocryphal Shepherd
of the adulterers."   In another place (ch. 10) he delivers himself
as follows : "But I should yield to you, if the writing (scripture) of
the Shepherd, which only loves adulterers, should have been
worthy to fall into the divine instrument (instrument is testament),
if it had not been condemned by every council of the churches,

even of yours, among the apocryphal and false (books or things), an adulteress (the word for writing being feminine) both herself, and thence a patroness of her companions, from whom also you would initiate others, whom that Shepherd perhaps would defend, whom you depict on the cup, himself a prostituter of the Christian sacrament, and deservedly the idol of drunkenness and the asylum of the adultery about to follow upon the cup, from which thou wouldst taste nothing more gladly than the sheep of a second penitence. But I draw from the scriptures of that shepherd who cannot be broken. This one John (the Baptist) at once offers me with the bath and office of penitence, saying: Bring forth fruits worthy of repentance."

That is a rich passage. We learn that the Churches often had a shepherd on the communion cup. We learn, what we thus far know from no other source, that more than one, doubtless several, synods had discussed the question as to the admission at least of Hermas, and probably of other books, to the number of the New Testament books. And we learn that the Shepherd had been strictly and everywhere condemned, not only in synods of heretical, of Montanist clergymen, but also in regular synods of the Catholic Church. How widely spread these synods were does not appear. They may have been only in Africa, in the province about Carthage. We should expect to hear or to have heard something about them if they had also been held in Italy or in eastern Africa.

Perhaps we should know a little more about what the churches in eastern Africa and Palestine thought of Hermas if we had the Greek original of Origen's commentary on Romans. The Latin translation of the commentary on Rom. 16[14], where Hermas is named, reads: "Yet I think that this Hermas is the writer of that little book which is called the Shepherd, which book (writing, scripture) seems to me to be extremely useful and, as I think, divinely inspired." That seems all very well. But it does not sound like Origen, and the translator Rufinus tells Heraclius, to whom he wrote on finishing the translation of this commentary, what an "immense and inextricable labour had weighed upon him" in the translation of this very commentary, in supplying what Origen had omitted, which means, in making a good orthodox book out of the work of that wild Origen. These words are therefore no guide to Origen's view touching Hermas. In his commentary on Matthew, while discussing Matt. 19[7] [9] at great length, he says: "And if it be necessary venturing to bring in a suggestion from a book (writing, scripture) that is current in the Church, but not agreed by all to be divine, the passage could be drawn from the Shepherd about some who at once when they believed were under Michael." He gives the passage. But he says at the close: "But I think that this is not proper," so that he does not seem to have any great opinion of Hermas after all.

Eusebius places it among the spurious books. He names as the first of these the Acts of Paul, then the book called the Shepherd, and then the Revelation of Peter. It stands in the Codex Sinaiticus with Barnabas after the Revelation, and it was still copied in Latin Bibles as late as the fifteenth century; it stood in them between Psalms and Proverbs, a strange place for a book that was like neither the one nor the other of the two. Athanasius, in his letter announcing the date of Easter, the thirty-ninth letter, of the year 367, names it at the end with certain non-canonical books that are allowed to be read, namely, the Wisdom of Solomon, the Wisdom of Sirach, Esther, Judith, Tobit, the Teachings of the Apostle, and the Shepherd. It is the last of all. Jerome has been supposed to refer to Hermas in one passage as: "That apocryphal book to be condemned of stupidity"; but as he elsewhere quotes it with respect and regards it as a churchly book, and as one useful to be read, he probably has in that passage some other book in view.

In the manuscript of the Pauline Epistles named Claromontanus, which is supposed to be of the sixth century, we find, before the Epistle to the Hebrews, a Stichometry, a list of the books of the New Testament which is very old, probably much older than the manuscript itself. In this list we have at the close Revelation, Acts, then the Shepherd, and after it the Acts of Paul and the Revelation of Peter. Here it is placed in contact with the New Testament, yet it takes its character also from the two books which follow it. The fact of its being in that list at that point can scarcely be considered as a certain testimony to the canonicity of Hermas at that time and in that place. But though the manuscript was undoubtedly written in the West, and though this list is a Latin list, the approach to canonicity, or if any one please the canonicity claimed for it here, is part and parcel of the same thing that we saw in the case of Clement of Alexandria. The list appears to be of Egyptian origin, although it may be connected with Eusebius. It probably dates from the beginning or middle of the fourth century. Hermas is supposed to have ceased to be used, or to be read in church in the East, where it had happened to be so read, in the fourth or fifth century.

We have already mentioned Polycarp's letter to the church at Philippi. It was not singular, when we consider the important position held by, and the wide influence exercised by, Polycarp, not only in his immediate neighbourhood but also through widely distant provinces, that this letter should be highly prized and repeatedly read in the churches that secured copies of it. Jerome, in speaking of Polycarp, says (de vir. ill. 17): "He wrote to the Philippians an exceedingly useful letter which is read in the Church of Asia until to-day." The expression is not definite. It points, however, not to Philippi in Macedonia but to Asia. It is to be presupposed that at least in Philippi itself, if not in other churches in Macedonia, the letter also continued to be read. The phrase "in the Church of Asia" cannot be used of a single congregation. It means the Church in Asia. Yet it need not be supposed that every single church used the letter, and there is not the least reason for taking the word Asia in anything more than the most general sense. In other words, we do full justice, I think, to Jerome's statement if we suppose that a few of the churches in western Asia Minor at his day still continued to read this letter. It was certainly read as: Man to Man, and not as equal to the books of the New Testament. Nothing indicates the latter. It stands on the same basis as the letters of Dionysius of Corinth.

One book that now seems to stand very near to the Gospels, and again moves further away from them, demands particular attention. But we shall scarcely reach any very definite conclusion about it. It is like an *ignis fatuus* in the literature of the Church of the first three centuries. We cannot even tell from the statements about it precisely who, of the writers who refer to it, really saw it. Yes, we are even not sure that it is not kaleidoscopic or plural. It may be that several, or at least two, different books are referred to, and that even by people who fancy that there is but one book, and that they know it. This is the Gospel according to the Hebrews, or the Gospel of the Hebrews.

Let us first name the possibilities, say what may have been alluded to under this designation. Every reader will at once turn in thought to the "previous Gospel" or to the "sayings of Jesus" that we have referred to as having probably been written by the Twelve-Apostle Matthew and in Hebrew or Aramaic. Nothing would be easier than for any or every one who saw, read, or heard of that book, either and particularly in its original Semitic garb or even in its Greek dress in the form under which the writers of our Gospels used it, to call it the Gospel to the Hebrews, the Gospel according to the Hebrews, or the Hebrews' Gospel. The second possibility I must mention, although I hold it myself to be an impossibility. For those, and there are doubtless still scholars who hold the opinion, who think that our Gospel according to Matthew was at first a Hebrew book, the name Gospel according to the Hebrews might well have attached to it. Not only the language but also the many references to the fulfilment of prophecy, the close connection of the whole with the Old Testament, would seem to justify the use of this title. The third possibility is that this designation has nothing to do with our Gospels or with their sources, but that it properly attaches to a real Gospel, that is to say, to a full account of the words and deeds of Jesus from the beginning of His ministry to His death and resurrection, which was written in Hebrew or Aramaic. The date of this Gospel may have, almost must have, been quite early, seeing that after the composition and distribution of copies of our Gospels one would look for a translation of one of them rather than for the preparation of a totally new Gospel. This third possibility regards the Gospel as one from the circles that were in touch with the general Church.

The fourth possibility passes this line, and regards this Gospel as the product of some branch, sect, offshoot from the central form of Christianity at that day, as the Gospel of some Ebionitic or other Jewish Christian group, for the language limits the search to Jewish lines. This Gospel need not then have been at all an autochthon gospel, one that arose independently from a root of its own upon Palestinian soil. It may have been a revamping within still more narrow Jewish limits of what our Gospel according to Matthew contains, or its author may have had the three synoptic Gospels before him. Yet even in this case it would be to be expected that the author or composer should add to what he found in writing before him many a trait and many a saying attributed justly or of no right to Jesus in the Palestinian group to which he himself belonged. A fifth possibility, not a probability, would be that some Christian from one of the more exclusively Jewish groups had written this Gospel, not in Hebrew but in Greek, intending it for the Jews in the Diaspora, and thus offering an evangelical parallel to the Epistle to the Hebrews. These possibilities will suffice for the moment. It may be added here that, as a matter of course, such a Gospel, whatever the circumstances of its origin may have been, the moment that it presented matter foreign to what our Gospels bring, must have been used as a source for interpolations, for the addition of words, sentences, sayings, paragraphs to our Gospels. One might almost suppose that the readers of our Gospels who knew and read that Gospel, either in Aramaic or in a Greek translation, would scarcely fail to insert in the synoptic text, or later in the text of the Fourth Gospel, all important additions, all that seemed to them worth while to record, that the Gospel to the Hebrews contained, and therefore that if we should find some day this Gospel, it would prove to be almost entirely familiar to us out of our own Gospels and their interpolations, the fragments put into them.

In passing now to the examination of the references to some such Hebraic Gospel we must be ready in advance to find allusions which cannot with certainty be ascribed to the one or the other of the possibilities mentioned. First of all, we must recur to Papias, of whom Eusebius says that he has the story of a woman, apparently the adulteress of John 7^{53}–8^{11}, which the Gospel according to the Hebrews contains. But Eusebius does not say, evidently is not sure, that Papias drew it from that Gospel. Then we must turn to those words about Hegesippus, who as Eusebius tells us brings material "from the Gospel according to the Hebrews." Perhaps it was in this Gospel that he found the following words, which must have been taken from 1 Corinthians 2^9, which again is based upon Isaiah 64^4: "That the good things prepared for the righteous neither eye hath seen nor ear hath heard nor has entered into the heart of man." Stephen Gobarus, as quoted by Photius (cod. 232), declares that Hegesippus, in the fifth book of his Memoirs, decries

these words as false, and quotes Matthew 13[16] as right : " Blessed
are your eyes that see and your ears that hear," etc.   But it may
be that Hegesippus really is combating a heretical application of
these words.   It has also been suggested that they are even not
taken by Paul from Isaiah, but from an apocryphal book, and that
Hegesippus has this apocryphal author in view and not the Gospel
to the Hebrews.

In Justin Martyr (Dial. 103) we have a quotation that might
very well come from this Gospel.   He writes of Jesus after the
baptism : " For also this devil at the time that He came up
from the river Jordan, the voice having said to Him : Thou art
my Son, I have begotten Thee to-day, in the Memoirs of the
apostles is written coming up to Him and tempting Him so far as
to say to Him : Worship me."   Now Justin does not give the
Memoirs for these words of the voice.   We must observe further
that it would be very fitting for a Jewish writer to apply these
words of the Second Psalm to Jesus here at the baptism.   And
we find, oddly enough, that these words have been put into
the passage in Luke 3[22] in the manuscript of Beza, Codex D,
which represents the text that was wrought over by many busy
hands in the second century.   And Augustine tells us that some
manuscripts in his day had these words there in Luke, although
they were not to be found in the older Greek manuscripts.   It
was said above that this Gospel might have, for example, Ebionitic
connections ; it is therefore interesting to observe here that
Epiphanius gives this saying for the voice at the baptism as
contained in the Ebionitic Gospel according to Matthew.   We
must revert to that again in a moment.

Justin, referring in another passage (Dial. 88) to the baptism,
touches another point that may be from this Gospel.   He says :
" When Jesus came down to the water a fire was also kindled in
the Jordan."   Here that Ebionitic Gospel (Epiph. 30. 13) says
that after Jesus came up from the water, and after the voice had
spoken : " And at once a great light shone about the place."
From this difference it would at first not seem possible that
Justin's source and the Ebionitic Gospel could be the same.
But when we reflect that Justin is not quoting but telling about
it, and when we remember how loosely Justin quotes even when
he does quote, it would appear to be quite possible that he had
here put a fire for a great light.   The general thought remains

the same. However, the time of the phenomenon is different. Justin's story lets the Jordan burn as Jesus enters into it, whereas the Ebionitic account assumes that the light is a heavenly accompaniment as a confirmation of or corollary to the words of the voice. This light also appears in a Latin, an old Latin manuscript which may also here stand as a representative of that re-wrought text of the second century.

Justin may have found another saying of Jesus in this Gospel. He writes (Dial. 47): "Wherefore also our Lord Jesus Christ said: In what things I take you, in these shall I also judge you." That can hardly be, as some have thought, another form for John 5^{30}: "As I hear, I judge." Clement of Alexandria gives the same phrase, only a trifle altered (Quis Dives, 40): "At what I find you, at these also I shall judge," and he does not give an author for it. The Sinaitic monk John of the Ladder attributes it to Ezekiel. Justin may have it from the Gospel to the Hebrews. There is then one other saying of Jesus, also already mentioned above in another connection when we spoke of Justin. He says in between two quotations from Matthew (Dial. 35) as all three spoken by Jesus: "There will be schisms and heresies." It is possible that these words simply offer us a combination of two of the kinds of error we have found to occur in Justin, loose quotation and reference to a wrong book, and that they are only a "Justinian" form for 1 Corinthians $11^{18.19}$. But they may be from the Gospel to the Hebrews. The Clementine Homilies combine these words with the quotation from Matthew which follows them in Justin, so that they appear to have used Justin and to have confused what Justin kept at least that far apart. Nevertheless they write: "As the Lord said."

Eusebius says that the Ebionites use only the Gospel according to the Hebrews, and think that the other Gospels are not worth much. The question for us is, whether we should combine this with what we observed above as to the similarity between the text of the Ebionites and the singular passages in Justin, or whether we should suppose that Eusebius thought that the Ebionites used a Hebrew Gospel that was the equivalent of our Greek Matthew. When Eusebius makes his list of the New Testament books he gives the accepted books, then the disputed ones, then the spurious ones, tacking on the Revelation doubtfully, and finally he adds (H. E. 3. 25): "But some also reckon among these the Gospel according to the Hebrews, in which especially the Hebrews who have received Christ take pleasure."

Epiphanius says (Hær. 30. 13) that the Ebionites use the Gospel of Matthew: "not, however, full and complete, but spoiled and cut down (mutilated), and they call this the Hebrew [Gospel]." Now here again we must ask whether Epiphanius is right in thinking that this is Matthew mutilated, or whether the Gospel that they used was that shorter Gospel which we suppose Matthew to have written, and which was then used in the composition, for example, of our Matthew. Of course, it would look like a mutilated Matthew although it were precisely, on the contrary, a Matthew that had not yet been bolstered out from other sources. In another passage (Hær. 30. 3) Epiphanius says: "And they also receive the Gospel according to Matthew. For this they also, as also those who follow Cerinthus and Merinthus, use alone. And they call it: according to the Hebrews, as in truth it is to be said, that Matthew alone in the New Testament made a representation and proclamation of the Gospel in Hebrew and in Hebrew letters." Now, when Epiphanius speaks of the Nazarenes (Hær. 29. 9) he says: "And they have the Gospel according to Matthew most complete in Hebrew. For with them clearly this is still preserved as it was written from the beginning in Hebrew letters. But I do not know whether they have taken away the genealogies from Abraham till Christ." The last words show that he really knows nothing about this Gospel. It may also be the short preliminary Gospel. That only impresses more strongly the thought just urged, namely, that Epiphanius may in his ignorance have confused reports of the usual Gospel according to Matthew with those of the previous preliminary Gospel.

Clement of Alexandria quotes this Gospel simply with the formula "it is written" (2. 9. 45): "In the Gospel according to the Hebrews it is written: He that admires shall rule, and he that ruled shall cease." Origen quotes it, for example, thus (on John, vol. 2. 12 [6]): "And if anyone approaches the Gospel according to the Hebrews, where the Saviour Himself says"; and again he quotes precisely the same passage, saying: "And if anyone accepts the words." In his Theophany (4. 13) Eusebius quotes a Hebrew Gospel, in discussing the parable of the talents, thus: "But the Gospel which has reached us in Hebrew characters fastened the threat not upon the one who hid away, but upon the one who lived luxuriously." That may have been merely a Syriac copy of our Gospels, but it may have been the Gospel according to the Hebrews in one of its chameleon phases. Theodoret's remarks on the Ebionites and this Gospel are clearly a poor condensation of what Eusebius says.

Jerome knew this Gospel well, and translated it into Greek and Latin (de vir. ill. 2), and said that Origen often used it. He tells us that it was written in the Chaldee and Syrian language, but in Hebrew letters, and that it was still used in his day by the Nazarenes, and he names it also (adv. Pel. 3. 2) "according to the Apostles, or as many think according to Matthew, which also is in the library at Cæsarea." The use of Hebrew letters for Syriac was nothing strange. The Jews write and print to-day in various languages, using Hebrew letters. I have a German New Testament printed in Berlin nearly eighty years ago in Hebrew letters. Jerome (de vir. ill. 3) seems to have copied this Gospel from a manuscript which Nazarenes in Berœa (Aleppo) possessed. The vague way in which he speaks of it shows that he did not regard it, or at any rate that he was perfectly sure that others would not regard it, as apostolic. He says of its authority (adv. Pel. 3. 2): "Which testimonies, if you do not use them for authority, use them at least for age (antiquity), what all churchly men have thought." Bede, who died in 735, counted it among "the churchly histories," because Jerome had used it so often. In the list given in the Chronography of Nicephorus it stands as the fourth of the four disputed books: Revelation of John, Revelation of Peter, Barnabas, Gospel according to the Hebrews. That is the great Gospel that lies outside of our New Testament. We shall doubtless some day receive a copy of it in the original, or in a translation. It may have contained much of what Matthew, Mark, and Luke contain, without that fact having been brought to our notice in the quotations made from it. For those who quoted it did so precisely in order to give that which varied from the contents of our four Gospels, or especially of the three synoptic ones.

It will not be necessary to treat at length of other Gospels. None of them approaches the importance of the Gospel according to the Hebrews. The Gospel of the Ebionites and that of the Nazarenes doubtless were taken by some authors to be the same as the Gospel according to the Hebrews, and may have

been closely related to it. It should not be forgotten that, just
as the text of our Gospels was much re-wrought during the
second century, so also these Gospels or this Gospel, if the three
should happen to be one, will surely have been re-wrought.   In
consequence of that it will be possible that differences that
appear in the form are due to different recensions and not to
different books.   In discussing asceticism Clement of Alexandria
refers to things supposed to have been said by Jesus to Salome.
He says (3. 9. 63): "It stands, I think, in the Gospel according
to the Egyptians."   In another place, writing against the leader
of the Docetæ, Julius Cassianos, who had urged some of the
Salome passages, he says (3. 13. 93): "First, then, we have not
this saying in the four Gospels that have been handed down to us,
but in that according to the Egyptians."   Origen, in the discussion of the first verse of Luke, says: "The Church has four
Gospels, the heresies a number, of which one is entitled according to the Egyptians, another according to the twelve apostles.
Even Basilides dared to write a Gospel, and to put his name in
the title."   Epiphanius writes of Sabellius and his followers
(Hær. 62. 2): "But they have all their error, and the power
of their error from some apocrypha, especially from the
so-called Egyptian Gospel, to which they gave this name."
None of these references implies an equality of this Gospel to
our four.

In the passage on Luke 1^1 Origen named not only the two
given above, but also one according to Mathias.   The Latin
translation speaks also of the Gospel of Thomas before that of
Mathias, but it may be a later addition.   To the Gospel of
Thomas might be added the name of another of the later
Gospels, the Gospel of the Infancy, and perhaps, too, that of
Nicodemus.   The Gospel of Nicodemus was in Canterbury,
chained to a pillar, as late as the time of Erasmus.

A Gospel or a teaching and acts and a revelation were adorned
with the name of Peter.   Ignatius seems to refer to this when
he writes to the church at Smyrna (ch. 3): "And when he came
to those about Peter, he said to them: Take, touch me and
see that I am not a bodiless demon.   And immediately they
touched and believed, joined with his flesh and his spirit."
Serapion, who was ordained bishop of Antioch about 191, is
said by Jerome to have written a book about the Gospel of

Peter and to have addressed it to the church at Rhossus in Cilicia, which had turned aside to heresy by reading it (the Gospel of Peter). This book was probably a letter.

Eusebius quotes from it (H. E. 6. 12) as follows: "For we brethren also receive Peter and the other apostles as Christ. But the books falsely written in their name, we as experienced men reject, knowing that we [of old] have not received such. For when I was with you, I supposed that ye were all united in the right faith. And without reading the Gospel produced by them in the name of Peter I said, that if it be this alone that seems to afford you modesty (or lowliness of soul), let it be read. But now learning from what has been said to me that their mind has been cherishing a certain heresy, I shall hasten again to be with you. Therefore, brethren, look for me soon. . . . For we were able from others of the ascetics to borrow this very Gospel, that is, from the successors of those who began it, whom we call Docetæ (for the most of the thoughts are of their teaching), and to read it. And we found that much of it was of the right word of the Saviour. But some [other] things were added, which also we have noted for you below."

Clement of Alexandria quotes it thus (Strom. 1. 29. 182): "And in the Preaching of Peter thou wouldst find the Lord proclaiming law and word." Again he writes: "Peter in the Preaching says," and: "Therefore Peter says that the Lord spoke to the Apostles," and (6. 6. 48): "At once in the Preaching of Peter the Lord says to the disciples after the resurrection," and (6. 15. 128): "Whence also Peter in the Preaching speaking of the apostles says." He quotes a great deal from it, and clearly with great respect. Once he writes: "Declares the Apostle Paul speaking in agreement with the preaching of Peter," but here he may refer to the preaching as by word of mouth. Still, he is quoting the book in the neighbourhood of this passage, so that the reference to it is more likely.

Origen speaks of it very differently and very decidedly in the preface to his work on Principles: "If, moreover, anyone may wish to quote from that book which is called Peter's Teaching, where the Saviour seems to say to the disciples: I am not a bodiless demon. In the first place, it is to be answered to him that that book is not held among the Church

books, and to be shown that the writing (scripture) itself s
neither of Peter nor of anyone else who was inspired with the
Spirit of God." In another place (on Matt. vol. 10. 17), speaking
of the brothers of Jesus, Origen mentions it merely in passing :
"Going out from the basis of the Gospel entitled according to
Peter or of the book of James, they say that the brothers of
Jesus were sons of Joseph by a previous wife who had lived with
him before Mary." Gregory of Nazianzus writes in a letter (Ep. 1)
to his brother Cæsarius : "A labouring soul is near God, says
Peter, somewhere speaking wonderful words." He does not say
from what book it is taken. The saying is beautiful. The
Revelation of Peter is mentioned in the Muratorian fragment
immediately after the Revelation of John. The writer adds of
the Revelation of Peter : "Which some of us do not wish
to be read in church." That shows that others did wish
it to be read in church. Eusebius tells us that Clement of
Alexandria wrote comments on it in his Sketches, as well as on
Barnabas.

Eusebius himself placed it in his list among the spurious
books, between the Shepherd and Barnabas. In another place
(H. E. 3. 3) he wrote : "As for the Acts called his [Peter's],
and the Gospel named after him, and the Preaching said to be
his, and the so-called Revelation, we know that they are not
at all handed down among the catholic [writings], because no
Church writer, neither of the ancients nor of those in our day,
used proof passages from them." He evidently had forgotten
or overlooked Clement of Alexandria. Macarius Magnes, probably from near Antioch and of the middle of the fourth
century, gives (4. 6) a quotation from the Revelation thus :
" And by way of superfluity let that be said which is spoken
in the Revelation of Peter." But he at once proceeds to show
that he does not in the least agree with the quotation.

A spurious Third Epistle of Paul to the Corinthians was long
preserved, and is now well known, especially from the Armenian
version of it ; with it the forged letter of the Corinthians to Paul
is also still in existence. An Epistle to the Laodiceans is found
in Latin. The oldest copy known is of about the year 546, in the
Vulgate manuscript written for Victor the Bishop of Capua, and
now for centuries at Fulda in Germany. It is of no value, but
it is found in a number of Vulgate manuscripts.

We may leave these books now. We have seen that the letter of Clement of Rome was much read, but we have no token that it was read as scripture. Irenæus named Hermas in that one passage scripture, and Clement of Alexandria quoted the Preaching of Peter in a most respectful way. That is all very little.

V.

THE AGE OF EUSEBIUS.

300–370.

In turning to a new age our problem becomes still more simple. We have already disposed of the books that are not in our New Testament. We only have the two questions left, touching the canonization of the books of the New Testament and touching the view held as to the seven disputed books : James, 2 Peter, 2 and 3 John, Jude, Hebrews, and Revelation.

One man must be mentioned at the outset from whom we should probably have received much had he lived to a good age. But he did much for the books of the Bible in spite of his shortened life. His name was Pamphilus. He was born at what is now called Beirut in Syria, the old Berytus. He studied at Alexandria under Pierius, and became presbyter at Cæsarea under the Bishop Agapius. He died as a martyr in the year 309. Eusebius was closely united to him, and is called therefore the Eusebius of Pamphilus. Eusebius wrote his life. A fragment lately discovered has been supposed to refer to a life of him by his teacher Pierius, but I am inclined to interpret the words as pointing to help given by Pierius to Eusebius in writing the life. Pamphilus wrote with Eusebius an Apology for Origen. His great merit for us lies in his extraordinary care for the library at Cæsarea. It is likely that Origen did much to enlarge this library, and it may have contained his own books. We still have in some Greek manuscripts of the Bible notes, subscriptions, telling that they or their ancestors were compared with the manuscripts in Pamphilus' library at Cæsarea, thus attributing to the manuscripts there a certain normative value as carefully written and carefully compared with earlier manuscripts. In one of the older manuscripts of the Epistles of Paul, which unfortunately is but a fragment, we read: "I wrote and set out (this book) according to the copy in Cæsarea of the library of the holy Pamphilus." In some manuscripts is added: "written by his hand," showing that he himself had shared in the work of writing biblical manuscripts. Such subscriptions are found not only in Greek, but also in Syrian manuscripts.

Pamphilus's friend Eusebius is of great weight for us. He has already shown his value for the criticism of the Canon in the mere preservation of fragments of earlier writers. To him we owe a large part of our knowledge of the first three centuries of Christianity. But the criticism of the Canon owes him a special debt, because much of his Church History is devoted to the observation of the way in which the churches and the Christian authors had used and valued or not valued the books of the New Testament which were of doubtful standing, and the other books which had secured for themselves a certain recognition and were to be found in manuscripts and in Church use in the immediate neighbourhood of the acknowledged books of the New Testament. His Church History was written at a mature age. He was probably born between 260 and 265, was Bishop of Cæsarea before 315, and he died probably in 339 or 340. He wrote the history apparently in sections, and with revisions between the years 305 and 325. We must give his statements in full. They are the chief discussions of the Canon in the early Church.

In the third book of his Church History, Eusebius tells first where the various apostles preached, drawing from Origen, then he mentions Linus as in charge of the church at Rome after the martyrdom of Paul and Peter, and takes up the Epistles of the Apostles (H. E. 3. 3): "One Epistle then of Peter, the one called his former [Epistle], is acknowledged. And this the presbyters of old have used often in their writings as undisputed. But the second one that is current as his, we have received not to be testament-ed (a part of the testament, canonical we should say to-day). Nevertheless, having appeared useful to many, it has been much studied with the other writings (books, scriptures). But the book of the Acts called his and the Gospel named after him, and the so-called Preaching and the so-called Revelation, we know are not in the least handed down among the Catholic (books, or among the Catholic churches), because no Church

17

writer either of the ancients or of those in our day has used proof passages from them.   And as the history goes on I shall make a point of calling attention along with the lines of succession [of the bishops] to such of the Church writers at each period as have used which (any) of the disputed books, and both to what is said by them about the testament-ed and acknowledged writings, and to as many things as are said about those that are not such (are not acknowledged).   But those named of Peter are so many, of which I know only one Epistle as genuine and acknowledged by the presbyters of old.   And of Paul the fourteen [Epistles] are open to sight and clear.

It is not just to ignore the fact that, however, some set aside the [Epistle] to the Hebrews, saying that it is disputed in the church of the Romans as not being Paul's.   And I shall chronicle at the proper time what has been said about this by those who were before us.   Nor have I received the Acts said to be his among the undisputed [books].   And since the same apostle in the greetings at the end of the Epistle to the Romans makes mention with the others also of Hermas, of whom they say there is the Book of the Shepherd, it must be known that this too is disputed by some, on account of whom it could not be placed among the acknowledged books, but by others it is judged to be most necessary for those who have especial need of an elementary introduction [to the faith].   Whence also we know that it is also read publicly in churches, and I have observed that some of the oldest writers have quoted it.   So much may be said to give an idea both of the divine writings that are not spoken against, and of those that are not acknowledged by all."

Twenty chapters later, after bringing from Clement of Alexandria a delightful account of John's reclaiming a robber, he again takes up the question of Church books by alluding to those of John (H. E. 3. 24 and 25) : "And now also let us make a note of the writings of this apostle that are not spoken against.   And indeed, first of all let the Gospel according to him be acknowledged by the churches under Heaven.   That verily with good reason at the hands of the ancients it was placed in the fourth division of the other three, in this would be clear.   The divine and truly godworthy men, I speak of the apostles of Christ, cleansed thoroughly in their life, adorned with every virtue in their souls, untaught in tongue, but full of courage in the divine and incredible power bestowed upon them by the Saviour, on the one hand neither knew how nor tried to make known the lessons of the teacher by skill and by rhetorical art, but using alone that which the Divine Spirit working with them set forth, and the miracle-working power of Christ brought to an end through them, proclaimed the knowledge of the Kingdom of the Heavens to all the inhabited world, giving little thought to the study of the way in which they should write it down. And this they did as being fully devoted to a service that was very great and beyond man."

" Paul then, who was the most mighty of all in array of words and most able in thoughts, did not put in writing more than the very short letters, although he had thousands of things and unspeakable to say, having attained unto the visions as far as the third Heaven and having been caught up in the divine paradise itself, and been held worthy to hear the unspeakable words there. Therefore also the remaining pupils of the Lord were not without experience of the same things, the twelve apostles and the seventy disciples and ten thousand besides these. Nevertheless, then, out of all Matthew and John alone have left us memoirs (notes) of the teachings of the Lord, who also are said to have been forced to come to their writing. For Matthew having formerly preached to Hebrews, as he was about to go also to others, putting in writing in his mother tongue the Gospel according to him, filled up by the book the void of his presence to these from whom he was sent. And Mark and Luke having published (made the edition) of the Gospels according to them, John they say having used the whole time an unwritten preaching, finally also came to the writing for the following reason."

Then Eusebius shows how the other three had left out the due beginning of the Gospel, what Jesus did before John the Baptist was cast into prison, and that John had to supply this in his Gospel. He also tells how Luke had reached a certain independence of judgment for his Gospel by his intercourse with Paul and others. Eusebius then takes up John again: "And of the writings of John, besides the Gospel also the former of the Epistles is acknowledged as undisputed both by the men of to-day and by those still ancient. But the other two are disputed. But the opinion as to the Revelation is still now drawn by the most toward each side (that is: for and against). Nevertheless this also shall receive a decision at a fit time from the testimony of the ancients. Being at this point, it is fitting that we should sum up the writings of the New Testament that have been mentioned."

[I] " And we must set first of all the holy four of the Gospels, which the writing of the Acts of the Apostles follows. And after this we must name the Epistles of Paul, and in connection with them we must confirm the current First Epistle of John and likewise the Epistle of Peter. In addition to these is to be placed, if that appear perhaps just, the Revelation of John, about which we shall in due time set forth what has been thought. And these are among the acknowledged books."

[II] " And of the disputed books, but known then nevertheless to many, the Epistle of James is current and that of Jude, and the Second Epistle of Peter and the Second and Third named for John, whether they happen to be of the Evangelist or of another of the same name with him. Among the spurious [books] is the book of the Acts of Paul to be ranged, and the so-called Shepherd, and the Revelation of Peter, and besides these the current Epistle of Barnabas and the so-called Teachings of the Apostles. And further still, as I said, the Revelation of John, if it seem good, which some as I said set aside, and others reckon among the acknowledged [books]. And even among these [I do not think this means among the "acknowledged " but among the "spurious " books], some have counted the Gospel according to the Hebrews, in which especially the Hebrews who have received Christ take pleasure. And these would then be all of the disputed books (Eusebius here brings the disputed and the spurious together as "disputed "). But of necessity, nevertheless, we have made the catalogue of these, distinguishing both the writings that are true according to the Church tradition and not forged and acknowledged, and the others aside from these, not testament-ed but also disputed, yet known by most of the Church [officials?], that we may be able to distinguish these very books, and "

[III] " those brought forward by the heretics in the name of the apostles, containing either Gospels, as of Peter and Thomas and Mathias, or also of some others beside these, or Acts, as of Andrew and John and the other apostles, which no man of the Church [writers] according to the succession ever held worthy to bring forward for memory in any way in a book. And further, in a way also the character of the language which is different from the apostolic habit, and both the opinion and the aim of what is brought in them which are as widely as possible from agreeing with true orthodoxy, clearly place before our eyes that they are forgeries of heretical men. Hence they are not even to be ranged among the spurious [books], but to be rejected as totally absurd and impious."

The great question for us here is the precise opinion of Eusebius as to the seven books for which we are seeking witness. He has them all in his list. James and Second Peter, and Second and Third John, and Jude are all among the disputed books, but in the first part of them, the good part, and not among the spurious books of the second part. Hebrews is squarely treated as one of Paul's Epistles. The book of Revelation is indeed put down among the acknowledged books, but it has a doubtful vote attached to it, and it, it alone of all the books, appears a second time, and that not in the first but in the second, the spurious part of the disputed books.

As for James, after telling of his martyrdom he continues (H. E. 2. 23) : "Such also is the affair touching James, of whom the first of the Epistles that are named Catholic is said to be. It must be understood that it is regarded as spurious—not many then of the ancients mentioned it, as also not the so-called [Epistle] of Jude, it also being one of the seven called Catholic,—yet we know that these also are read publicly with the others in very many churches." There he says that it is regarded as spurious, which, however, is not the case in the list, which stands at a later point in his history. If we turn to his other works we find that Eusebius does not hesitate to quote James, calling him "the holy apostle," or the words themselves "scripture." I know of no quotations from Second Peter, Second and Third John, and Jude. Hebrews, as we have seen, is fully accepted, and that as Paul's, even though in one place in speaking of Clement of Alexandria's Carpets, and observing that he quotes from the disputed books, he names as such the Wisdom of Solomon, and that of Jesus Sirach, Hebrews, Barnabas, Clement [of Rome], and Jude. It is, by the way, interesting that he here calls Clement of Rome disputed, although he does not give it any place at all in that exact list which we have just read over.

As for Hebrews there, one might almost think it was a momentary slip. At any rate, Eusebius quotes it often, and as Paul's : "The apostle says," "the wonderful apostle." Paul had written it, Eusebius thought, in Hebrew, and perhaps Luke, but more likely Clement of Rome had translated it into Greek. The book of Revelation evidently remained for him an object of suspicion. The swaying hither and thither in his list showed that his opinion was also "drawn towards each side," now for now against the authority of this book. In one place (H. E. 3. 39) he writes, speaking of the report that two graves of John were said to be known at Ephesus: "To which it is necessary to give heed. For it is likely that the second, unless anyone should wish the first, saw the Revelation which is current in the name of John." Curious it is that he even thrusts in as a parenthesis the choice again of the apostle. He really in this case either did not know his mind or had a dislike to stating too bluntly an opinion which he knew that many would not like. The fact that he quotes it less frequently than might have been expected looks as if he were not inclined personally to accept it, and the same conclusion follows from his form of quotation. We find for it not "the wonderful apostle," but merely "the Revelation of John," or "John." Eusebius then, in the first great list of books that we have, gives us our New Testament of to-day, but with verbal doubts as to the disputed book James that are pretty much invalidated by his quoting it as if thoroughly genuine,—with no verbal or quoting lessening of the disputed character of Second Peter, or of Second and Third John,—with a slight confirmation of the disputed character of Jude,—with a practical acceptance of Hebrews by most reverent quoting of it,—and with a hesitating use of Revelation which agrees better with its being disputed than with its being genuine, and which agrees with the tentative assigning of it to the presbyter instead of to the Apostle John.

The Council of Nice in 325 does not appear to have determined anything about scripture. It is true that Jerome states that it "is said to have accounted Judith in the number of the sacred scriptures," but he only gives hearsay for his statement, and it may have been a misconception that led to the supposition. During the discussions the scriptures served as the armoury and munition store for all the members of the council. Of the seven disputed books, only Hebrews seems to have been quoted, and that as Paul's, in an answer of the bishops, to a philosopher, by Eusebius (Migne, P. G. 85. 1276 A): "As says also Paul the vessel of choice, writing to Hebrews," and he quotes Hebrews 4$^{12, 13}$.   Hebrews is quoted not rarely in the Acts of this council.   The only other reference that might touch the disputed books is the naming of the "Catholics," meaning the Catholic Epistles : "And in the Catholics John the evangelist cries," and Leontius, the bishop of Cæsarea in Cappadocia, who is speaking, quotes (MPG 85. 1285) 1 John 5^{6}.   A chapter or two later (MPG 85. 1297 C) he writes : "For he who has not the Son, as it says in the Catholics, neither hath he the Father."   That is a very loose way of rendering : "Every one who denieth the Son, neither hath he the Father," 1 John 2^{23}. But this reference to the "Catholics" does not at all say surely that all seven Catholic Epistles are in the collection.   It is quite likely that they are all in Leontius' hand and heart.   Nevertheless it would be possible for a man to speak in this way who only had two Catholic Epistles, First Peter and First John.   Moreover, at a time at which the opinions about these seven books were still somewhat uncertain, it would be perfectly possible for some one member of the council to quote a book that some other members would not have quoted, just as one might of set purpose not quote a book that others would have quoted.   But the council, as far as we can see, did not think of settling what books belonged to the New Testament and what did not.   It had other work to do.

A few years later Constantine the emperor commanded Eusebius to have fifty Bibles copied for him, of which we shall speak when we come to the Criticism of the Text.   He had not probably any thought of a canonical determination of a series of books.   He merely wished to have some handsome and appropriate presents for a few large churches.   We have to-day parts of two manuscripts of the Bible that may perhaps have been among those fifty.   However that may be, they were probably written about that time.   One of them is the Codex Sinaiticus, of which the New Testament part is at Saint Petersburg, although forty-three leaves out of it, containing fragments of the Old Testament, are at Leipzig.   This manuscript contains the four Gospels, fourteen Epistles of Paul—because Hebrews is placed as a Pauline Epistle between Thessalonians and Timothy,—the book of Acts, the seven Catholic Epistles, Revelation, Barnabas, and a fragment of the Shepherd.   Therefore we find in it all the books of our New Testament, and in addition Barnabas and Hermas.

It is even not impossible that some other books were originally in it after Hermas. As observed above, Barnabas would probably have been placed before Revelation had the one who caused it to be copied intended to have it regarded as a part of the New Testament. And Hermas, although of a somewhat dreamy, apocalyptic nature, would probably also have been placed before Revelation. I suppose that these two books were added because they were often read in church as from: " Man to Man," and because it was convenient to have them thus at hand. We must return to this under Text. The other manuscript is the Vatican manuscript at Rome. It contains in the New Testament the four Gospels, the book of Acts, the seven Catholic Epistles, the Pauline Epistles as far as Thessalonians, and Hebrews to 9^{14}, where it unfortunately breaks off. Of course, it originally had the pastoral Epistles after Hebrews, and it doubtless contained also Revelation. Whether other books were in it or not we cannot tell.

Cyril of Jerusalem, who was born in 315 and died in the year 386, probably wrote his Catechetical Lectures about the year 346. In them he naturally enough speaks of the divine scriptures. The passage (4. 33–36) shows us at the same time how he treated his hearers and readers, what tone he struck in trying to fit their ears: " Learn then with love of wisdom also from the Church what are the books of the Old Testament and what of the New. The apostles and the ancient bishops were much more prudent and better filled with foresight than the leaders of the Church who handed these scriptures down to us. Thou then, child, do not treat falsely the determinations of the Church. And of the Old Testament, as is said, study the twenty-two books, which if thou are diligent to learn hasten to store up in memory as I name them to you." Then he gives the books of the Old Testament. "And of the New Testament the four Gospels alone. And the rest are forged and hurtful. The Manichæans also wrote a Gospel according to Thomas which by the fine sound of the gospel name attached to it corrupts the souls of the more simple. And receive also the Acts of the Twelve Apostles. And in addition to these also the seven Catholic Epistles of James and Peter, John and Jude. And the seal upon all, and the last thing of disciples the fourteen Epistles of Paul. And the rest let them all lie in a second place. And as many as are not read in churches, these neither read thou by thyself as thou hast heard." The books that are not part of the New Testament, but which may be read, are not named. The book of Revelation is not one of the books of the New Testament. That is the state of things at Jerusalem just before the middle of the fourth century.

Up to this time, that is to say until well into the fourth century, we have found no signs of a determination of a list of the books of the New Testament by any gathering of Christians. Marcion did make a list. But he was a single person and a heretic. The nearest that we have come to it was Tertullian's declaration that every council of the churches had judged the Shepherd to be among the apocryphal and false books. That looks as if these councils must have, or at least might have, at the same time made a definite statement as to what was not apocryphal and false, but in fact authoritative, public, and genuine. But this conclusion is by no means necessary. For the condemnation of the Shepherd may well have been uttered in connection with special doctrinal or disciplinary determinations, and have had nothing to do with the question of what books belonged in general to the New Testament. At the first glance it looks as if we were now to have at last a decision of a council. The council of apparently the year 363 held at Laodicea in Phrygia Pacatania, is sometimes urged as the first council that made a list, published a list, of the books which properly belong to the New Testament.

The name Council of Laodicea sounds very well, and the untutored reader might imagine to himself an imposing array of bishops, perhaps as many as the three hundred and eighteen of the Council of Nice. Far from it. There were, we are told, only thirty-two members of this council, and another reading says only twenty-four. It can only have been a local gathering, and in spite of the authority of the bishops in the fourth century I should not be surprised if among the thirty-two there had been some presbyters. It would seem likely that this little council or synod was summoned to meet by a bishop of Philadelphia named Theodosius, and that Theodosius had the most to do with the determining the canons of the council. He called the council then, and swayed it. He is said to have been an Arian, but that was of no particular moment for the questions of order which were laid, and of course laid by him, before the synod for decision.

The canon which interests us is the very last one, the fifty-ninth. It begins thus : "That psalms written by private persons must not be read in the church, nor uncanonized books, but only the canonized ones of the New and Old Testament." Thus far the canon is found in all accounts of the council with but trifling variations. Of course, the "reading" of a psalm might be the "singing" of the psalm. Such psalms are not to be uttered in church. That is a decision akin to the old-time rules of some Presbyterian Churches that nothing but the psalms of the Old Testament should be sung in church. The words uncanonized and canonized as applied to books remind us of the word "testament-ed" that we have already sometimes met. Now thus far we have no list of the books. But in some sources for this canon it goes on : "How many books are to be read : of Old Testament : 1. Genesis of world. 2. Exodus from Egypt. 3. Leviticus. 4. Numbers. 5. Deuteronomy. 6. Jesus of Nave. 7. Judges, Ruth. 8. Esther. 9. First and Second Kings. 10. Third and Fourth of Kings. 11. Chronicles, First and Second. 12. Ezra, First and Second. 13. Book of hundred and fifty Psalms. 14. Proverbs of Solomon. 15. Ecclesiastes. 16. Song of Songs. 17. Job. 18. Twelve Prophets. 19. Isaiah. 20. Jeremiah and Baruch, Lamentations and Epistles. 21. Ezekiel. 22. Daniel. And those of the New Testament : Gospels four : according to Matthew, according to Mark, according to Luke, according to John. Acts of Apostles. Catholic Epistles seven, thus : of James one ; of Peter, First, Second ; of John, First Second, Third ; of Jude one. Epistles of Paul fourteen : to Romans one ; to Corinthians, First, Second ; to Galatians one ; to Ephesians one ; to Philippians one ; to Colossians one ; to Thessalonians, First, Second ; to Hebrews one ; to Timothy, First, Second ; to Titus one, to Philemon one."

There we have a fair catalogue. All of the books of our New Testament are in it save Revelation. If the Synod of Laodicea, the thirty-two men, settled upon that list, it would be no great thing, but it would be a little beginning of a fixed, a settled, a decreed Canon. Unfortunately, when we examine the various sources we must decide that this list was not a part of the canon of Laodicea. It was not very strange that the list should be added.

This was the last canon. We might almost suppose that the man who first added the books did not dream of really making his catalogue a part of the fifty-ninth canon. He may have said to himself, considering the canon: "What must we read then? Let me see. In the Old Testament there are these. In the New Testament these." And writing them down there, the next scribe who came to copy a manuscript from that one, again thought no harm, thought innocently enough that all that really belonged to the fifty-ninth canon, and copied it accordingly. We are therefore still without a canon approved by a synod or a council. But we can have almost at once a proclamation of a list that is so very public, so very authoritative that it may for the time replace a synod which we cannot yet get.

It was the habit of the Bishop of Alexandria to announce the day on which Easter would fall by an Epistle. In the year 367, as it appears, Athanasius of Alexandria wrote his 39th Festal Epistle, and gave a list of the books of the Bible. "But since we have referred to the heretics as dead, and to us as having the divine scriptures unto salvation, and as I fear, as Paul wrote to the Corinthians, lest some few of the simple may be led astray by deceit from simplicity and purity by the wiles of men, and finally may begin to read the so-called apocrypha, deceived by the likeness of the names to those of the true books, I beg you to have patience if in alluding to these things I write also about things that you understand, because of necessity and of what is useful for the Church. And now about to recall these"—the scriptures—"I shall use as a prop for my boldness the example (another reading is: the passage, the verse) of the evangelist Luke, saying also myself: Since some have turned their hand to draw up for themselves the so-called apocrypha, and to mingle these with the inspired writ, concerning which we are informed fully, as those handed it down to the fathers who were from the beginning directly seers and servants of the word, it seemed good also to me, urged by true brethren, and having learned from time gone by, to set forth in order from the first the books that are canonized and handed down and believed to be divine, so that each, if he has been deceived, may detect those who have misled him, and the one remaining pure may rejoice at being put in mind of it again. So then the books of the Old Testament are in number all told twenty-two. For so many, as I heard, it is handed down that there are letters, those among the Hebrews. And in order and by name each is thus : first Genesis, then Exodus, then Leviticus, and after this, Numbers, and finally, Deuteronomy. And follow- ing on these is Jesus, the son of Nave and Judges, and after this Ruth, and again following four books of Kings, and of these the first and second are counted in one book and the second and third likewise in one, and after these First and Second Chronicles, likewise counted in one book, then First and Second Ezra, likewise in one, and after these the book of Psalms and following Proverbs, then Ecclesiastes and Song of Songs. In addition to these is also Job and finally Prophets, the Twelve counted in one book. Then Isaiah, Jeremiah, and with him Baruch, Lamentations, Epistle, and after him Ezekiel, and Daniel. As far as these stand the books of the Old Testament."

"And those of the New we must not hesitate to say. For they are these : Four Gospels, according to Matthew, accord- ing to Mark, according to Luke, according to John. Then after these Acts of Apostles and so-called Catholic Epistles of the apostles seven thus : Of James one, but of Peter two, then of John three, and after these of Jude one. In addition to these there are of Paul fourteen Epistles, in the order written thus : first to the Romans, then to the Corinthians two, then also after these to the Galatians, and following to the Ephesians, then to the Philippians, and to the Colossians, and to the Thes- salonians two. And the Epistle to the Hebrews, and following to Timothy two, and to Titus one. And again John's Revela- tion. These are the wells of salvation, so that he who thirsts may be satisfied with the sayings in these. In these alone is the teaching of godliness heralded. Let no one add to these. Let nothing be taken away from these. And about these the Lord shamed the Sadducees, saying : Ye err, not knowing the scrip- tures or their powers. And he admonished the Jews : Search the scriptures, for it is they that testify of Me. But for greater exactness I add also the following, writing of necessity, that there are also other books besides these, not canonized, yet set by the Fathers to be read to (or by) those who have just come up and who wish to be informed as to the word of godliness : the Wisdom of Solomon, and the Wisdom of Sirach, and Esther, and Judith, and Tobit, and the so-called Teaching of the Apostles, and the Shepherd.   And nevertheless, beloved, those that are canonized and these that are to be read [are recommended to us, but] there is nowhere any mention of the apocryphal books.   But they are an invention of heretics, writing them when they please, and adding grace to them and adding years to them, so that bringing them out as old books they may have a means of deceiving the simple by them."

The point of Athanasius' recounting the books of the Bible is seen at the beginning and at the end.   He is not in any way trying to block off what Eusebius had published in his Church History.   He has the heretics and their writings in view who concocted these books, as Athanasius thinks, to catch the souls of simple Christians.   The word "simple" is one of those nice words which in debate can always be applied to the people who do not think as you do.   Tertullian was not a simple man, an unlearned man easily to be led astray by any chance wind of doctrine, but he became a heretic.   And what shall we say of the great Origen?   But no matter.   Athanasius wishes to protect the simple from the snares of the heretics.   The heretics write apocryphal books.   He tells us what is "inspired scripture." With this list in his hand the simple man can at once settle the dispute with the heretic in favour of orthodoxy.   We find in the list our whole New Testament.

The notable advance upon Eusebius is, that now not a single one of these books remains as a disputed book.   They are all on one level.   Now that may be merely the Alexandrian view of the case.   In Cæsarea doubts may still prevail, or in other churches.   But for Alexandria the case is clear. Clear as a bell is it also that Athanasius does not lay claim to a decision of any general council for the canonizing of these books.   It would be possible, but it would not be likely, that he should know of the decision of some small council in favour of his books, of the books which he regarded as the true ones, and yet not mention it.   This consideration makes it all the less likely that the Council of Laodicea had four years earlier put forth the list that we looked at a few moments ago.   Athanasius accepts the Epistle to the Hebrews as Paul's.   It seems almost curious that a great bishop should for the moment leave the preaching, the proclamation of the Gospel by word of mouth, the living and breathing side of Christianity, so far out of sight.   It is

the heretics that force him to it.   Do the orthodox preach, so do
the heretics.   But these divine books, they are something that
heresy cannot touch.   Their imitation scriptures are of no avail.
These now called canonized books are the wells of salvation.
And now the process of choosing books has come to an end.

Perhaps Athanasius thinks of the words at the close of the
Revelation.   He knows that the New Testament is full and
complete.   No one may add anything to these books.   Nothing
is to be taken away from them.   And then he proceeds to add
something to them, but on a lower plane as second-class books.
Look at them : the Wisdom of Solomon, the Wisdom of Sirach—
which is by the way an exceedingly worthy book—Esther, Judith,
Tobit, the Teaching of the Apostles—which may be one of two
or three different books—and the beautiful dreams of the
Shepherd of Hermas.   Strange, however, it is that a bishop
should say that this medley of books : Esther, Judith, Tobit
among them, should be especially commended to be read to or
by the new-comers.   One would think that the new Christians
would need before all others the pure milk of the word.   Yet this
part of the letter of Athanasius has a moral for us touching the
earlier times.   Just such a statement as to second class books,
reaching back as far as Sirach, justifies my contention that the
Christians, like the Jews, have been reading all along in church,
as in the synagogue, books that were : Man to Man, not : God to
Man.

What books have now fallen away as compared with
Eusebius ?   Turning to the spurious books of Eusebius, we miss
the Acts of Paul, the Revelation of Peter and Barnabas.   The
letter of Clement, a letter scarcely inferior to some of the Epistles
of the New Testament, and fully equal to, or rather far above, the
Shepherd has fallen on all hands completely out of sight.   How
is it that Athanasius has reached this point?   Has there been
since Eusebius, and before Athanasius, any great discovery made
of new sources from the first or second century throwing a flood
of light upon the whole literature of the Christians, and enabling
Athanasius to say that all the Catholic Epistles are genuine, and
that Revelation is genuine, and that the other books are very bad
indeed?   Not at all.   It is even quite possible that Athanasius
would have written just thus if he had published this letter in the
same year in which Eusebius published his Church History—

only that he was not then bishop. Alexandria was not far from Cæsarea, and had been of old tied to it by many a bond. But there had also been fierce battles between the two places, and Alexandria had its own opinions, both in doctrine and in letters. Nor must we forget that Alexandria, even through and in those battles, had itself changed. That shows itself in Athanasius's list in the total omission of Barnabas, which had once been so much liked at Alexandria.

Twenty years ago Theodor Mommsen found a singular canon in a Latin manuscript of the tenth century. It probably belongs to an earlier date than Athanasius, but I let it stand here by way of comparison. It appears to be from Africa. In the Old Testament it counts the Wisdom of Solomon and the Wisdom of Sirach among the books of Solomon, and it has Esther, Judith, and Tobit, so that in that far it has a likeness to our Athanasius list, though the latter put those books in an appendix. It differs from Athanasius in adding Maccabees. In the New Testament it goes its own way, and an odd way it is. Hebrews is altogether lacking. Paul's Epistles number only thirteen. But the Catholic Epistles appear in the following form, save that I omit the number of the lines : the three Epistles of John, one only, the two Epistles of Peter, one only. Those are in the manuscript in four lines, in a column, divided by commas here. What does it mean? Of course, if we were positively determined to get from this catalogue the seven usual Catholic Epistles we should say that James was meant by the "one only" after John, and Jude by the "one only" after Peter. That would indeed be an extremely mild way of putting the scriptural character of James and Jude before a reader. No other instance like it occurs in the list.

The words look like the expression of two opinions in the list, for it is totally impossible to imagine that the scribe copying the list found a double mutilation, one for James and one for Jude, each before "one only" and each without the number of verses after "one only," and that he had no idea of what two Epistles might belong there, and therefore left them nameless. So ignorant a scribe among Christians is not to be thought of. The scribe may have found the names of James and Jude in the list, seeing that three Epistles of John and two of Peter are there. But if he found them there he left them out because he did not think they belonged there. He found then three Epistles of John, with the number of verses in them. He did not, however, believe at all that there should be three Epistles of John. He thought that only First John was scripture. Why did he then write "three Epistles," why did he not write "one Epistle" and be done with it? The reason lay in the number of the verses. He had the number for the three Epistles together, and he could not tell precisely how many were to be subtracted if he left out Second and Third John. Therefore he wrote the three Epistles of John, and added the number of the lines. But in order to save his conscience from the stain of calling Second and Third John biblical he added "one only." The case was then probably the same with the two Epistles of Peter. He only acknowledged First Peter, and could not separate its lines or verses from those of Second Peter. And thus he again wrote two Epistles of Peter with their verses, and doggedly added there below: "one only." We do not know, but it looks like that. Now we see in what way this list has a certain claim to a place at this point. It appears to give us a glimpse of a little skirmish in the war of canonical opinions. The scribe had, it seems, before him a manuscript which even may have had Hebrews in it as a fourteenth Epistle of Paul, but which at anyrate had three Epistles for John and two for Peter, and therefore probably James and Jude as well. He is himself one of the strict old school, and, if there were fourteen Epistles for Paul before him, he took his pen and wrote thirteen, he dropped James and Jude, and he only granted John and Peter one Epistle each.

What will the future bring? Will Eusebius' full list and that of Athanasius now have full sway? Will a general council settle the books of scripture? Will all doubt and all difference cease?

VI.

THE AGE OF THEODORE OF MOPSUESTIA.

370–700.

THE circle seems to be closing. We have a pair of full catalogues of the New Testament books in our hands, one with a few doubts clinging to it, one quite definite and sure. Now we must advance through the years and ask what the writers and what the Churches do in this matter. Whether they accept the full lists or whether they demur; we must have their vote, if we can find out what it is. And we must look for a decision of a general council, settling the matter for all Christendom.

Divisions overlap. We cannot cut up the lives of the authors according to our divisions, arbitrary divisions. The first writer whom we have to take up is Gregory of Nazianzus. The son of a Bishop Gregory of Nazianzus, he studied at Cæsarea in Cappadocia, at Cæsarea in Palestine, at Alexandria, perhaps ten years at Athens, was once for an instant Bishop of Sasima, and again for an instant Bishop of Constantinople as elected by the general council of the year 381, and died in 389 or 390, having been one of the very first rank as a Christian poet, orator, and theologian. His opinion of scripture he uttered in a poem (I. 1. 12). After the Old Testament he goes on: "And now count [the books] of the New Mystery. Matthew wrote to the Hebrews the wonders of Christ, and Mark to Italy, Luke to Greece, but to all John, a great herald, walking in heaven. Then the Acts of the wise apostles. And ten of Paul, and also four Epistles. And seven Catholic, of which of James one, and two of Peter, and three of John again, and Jude's is the seventh. Thou hast all. And if there is anything outside of these, it is not among the genuine [books]. That recalls to us the list by Cyril of Jerusalem. All our books are there again, save the Revelation.

18

Gregory may stand for Asia Minor, but we see how wide a basis he had in the long years of study in such widely separated cities. If we turn to his writings there appear to be no references to Second Peter, Second and Third John, and Jude, but he refers four times to James, eight or nine times to First Peter, and twice to First John. First John he names (Log. 31. 19): "What now John saying in the Catholics [the Catholic Epistles] that: Three are those who bear witness, the spirit, the water, the blood." In a dozen places Gregory quotes Old Testament passages which are given in the Epistle of James and in First Peter, and he probably quotes them because they are familiar to him from these Epistles, yet I let them pass, in order not to appear to press the matter unduly. First Peter 2^9 would have to be named seven times. First Peter and First John are also named here because it has been supposed that Gregory did not use them. He refers very often to Hebrews. The Revelation he quotes once, and in another place he may have taken an Old Testament quotation from it. In one place he names it thus (Log. 42. 9): "As John teaches me by the Revelation." We see then that in general Gregory's quotations may be brought into harmony with his list, for it is not at all strange that he should not happen to refer to Second and Third John, and not very strange that he should have passed by Second Peter and its mate Jude. Before leaving Gregory of Nazianzus it should be observed that his poems fill a large part of his works, and that these are not adapted to quotations.

The great friend of Gregory of Nazianzus was Basil the Great, the Bishop of Cæsarea in Cappadocia. We might look for a precisely identical use of scripture from these two. Certainly one of them will often have used the books belonging to the other. As for the seven books that were formerly disputed, Basil quotes James twice, and Second Peter once, and the Revelation twice ; of the two times, he once points to it as John's (To Eunom. 2. 14): "But the evangelist himself in another book (or another 'word') of such a kind, saying 'was' showed what was meant : He that is and was and the almighty." He is discussing the tense of "was" in John 1^1 at length. Hebrews he quotes freely. I have not noticed any quotations from Second or Third John or Jude. That would not be strange, even if he had them in his hands. But it is important to emphasise the difference between these two friends

in the use of First Peter and First John. Basil uses them often.
Gregory not often. The difference may be caused in part by
differences in topics treated, closely as the two were associated
with each other, not merely personally but also theologically.
Yet it may well be the case that the difference lies partly in what
I might term loosely a personal equation. I do not mean,
however, by that, that one of them would react at the chance
of a quotation more quickly than the other, but that one of them
may well have had, not precisely other likes and dislikes, but
other inclinations towards given books. The application of this
is that Gregory, although he had these books and accounted
them scripture, simply did not lean towards them so much as
Basil did, and therefore quoted them less frequently. The wider
application is, that we must be cautious in supposing that failure
to quote a book, however pat its sentences may seem to us to be
for an author's purpose, denotes that a writer does not know
of or directly refuses to quote the given book. Basil quotes
Second Peter once, where he had occasion to quote. The
occasion or his wish to intensify a preceding quotation might
easily have been lacking, and we should have heard suggestions
that he did not approve of this book.

Basil's brother, Gregory of Nyssa, will certainly have agreed
with his brother, and with their friend Gregory of Nazianzus in
the reception of the books of the New Testament. In his writings
I have not noticed any quotations from James, Second Peter,
Second and Third John, and Jude (I saw ten from First John
and twelve from First Peter). Hebrews he uses freely. He
appears really to quote the Revelation twice. Once he says of
it (Antirrh. 37): "As says somewhere the word of the scripture,"
and quotes from Rev. 21^6 or 22^{13}, or from a various reading of
1^8. In the other case he writes (Address at his ordination): " I
heard the evangelist John saying in apocryphal (here probably :
in lofty words, hard to understand) to such by an enigma, that
it is necessary with great accuracy always to boil in the spirit,
but to be cold in sin : For thou shouldst have been, he says,
cold or hot," Rev. 3^{15}.

Amphilochius, a Cappadocian by birth, a lawyer, and then
Bishop of Iconium in Lycaonia, wrote several books, but very
little of what he wrote has reached us. A poem to Seleucus,
which is sometimes found among the poems of ₍Gregory of

Nazianzus (2. 7), was probably written by him : "Moreover, it much behoves thee to learn this. Not every book is safe which has gotten the sacred name of scripture. For there are, there are sometimes, books with false names. Some are in the middle and neighbours, as one might say, of the words of truth. Others are both spurious and very dangerous, like falsely stamped and spurious coins, which yet bear the inscription of the king, but are not genuine, are made of false stuffs. On account of these I shall tell thee each of the inspired books. And so that thou mayest learn to distinguish well, I shall tell thee first those of the Old Testament. The Pentateuch has the Creation [= Genesis], then Exodus, and Leviticus the middle book, after which Numbers, then Deuteronomy. To these add Joshua and the Judges. Then Ruth, and four books of Kings, and the double team of Chronicles. Next to these First Ezra, and then the Second. Following I shall tell thee the five books in verses, of Job crowned in strifes of varied sufferings, and the book of Psalms, a harmonious remedy for the soul ; and again, three of Solomon the Wise, Proverbs, Ecclesiastes, and the Song of Songs. To these add the twelve prophets, Hosea first, then Amos the second, Micah, Joel, Abdiah, and Jonah the type of His three days' passion, Nahum after them. Habbakuk, then a ninth Sophoniah, both Haggai and Zachariah, and the double named angel Malachi (double named because the Septuaginta put the translation of Malachi—" angel "—in and let Malachi stay also). After them learn the four prophets : the great and bold-speaking Isaiah, and Jeremiah the merciful, and the mystical Ezekiel, and last Daniel, the same in works and words most wise. To these some add Esther. It is time for me to say the New Testament books. Receive only four evangelists : Matthew, then Mark, to whom add Luke a third, count John in time a fourth, but first in height of teachings, for I call this one rightly a son of thunder, sounding out most greatly to the Word of God. Receive Luke's book, also, the second, that of the general (Catholic) Acts of the Apostles. Add following the vessel of election, the herald of the Gentiles, the Apostle Paul, who wrote wisely to the Churches twice seven Epistles, of Romans one, to which it is necessary to join on to the Corinthians two, and that to the Galatians, and that to the Ephesians, after which that in Philippi, then the one written to the Colossians, two to the Thessalonians, two to

Timothy, and to Titus and Philemon, one to each, and to the
Hebrews one. And some say that the one to the Hebrews is
spurious, not saying well, for the grace is genuine. However
that may be, what remains? Some say we must receive seven
Catholic Epistles, others three alone,—that of James one, and one
of Peter, and that of John one. And some receive the three
(that is of John), and in addition to them the two of Peter, and
that of Jude a seventh. And again some accept the Revelation
of John, but the most call it spurious. This would be the most
reliable (the most unfalsified) canon of the divinely inspired
scriptures." Here we have a bishop in Asia Minor, a mate of
the Gregories and of Basil, and yet he appears inclined to reject
Second Peter, Second and Third John, and Jude, and almost
certainly rejects Revelation. He himself accepts Hebrews, but
he knows that others do not. Here we have the word "canon"
used directly.

Didymus of Alexandria, who died about the year 395, wrote a
commentary to all seven of the Catholic Epistles, of which, however, only fragments, and that mostly in a Latin translation, have
been preserved. James he appears to have fully accepted. He
calls him an apostle of the circumcision like Peter. But he produces in the discussion of 2 Peter 3^{5-8}, which does not suit him,
a condemnation of the Epistle which seems to be drawn from
Eusebius, whom we above quoted (Migne, P. G. 39. 1774): "It
is therefore not to be overlooked that the present Epistle is
forged, which, although it is read publicly, is yet not in the
canon." He quotes James, and he refers to the Revelation
repeatedly as John's, so that he probably did not suppose that
another "John," but that the Apostle John, wrote it. Dionysius'
criticisms do not seem to have been accepted in his own town.

Epiphanius, the Bishop of Constantia or Salamis on Cyprus,
who died in the year 403, gives us a somewhat careless list which
undoubtedly contains all our books, although he does not say
precisely seven Catholic Epistles. He adds to the New Testament thus (Hær. 76): "Revelation, and in the Wisdoms I say
both of Solomon and of the son of Sirach, and simply in all
the divine scriptures." He seems really to account these two
books as scripture. In his refutation of the heretics whom
he calls Alogi, he speaks several times of the Revelation as
from John the Evangelist.

A council at Carthage in the year 397 decreed a canon about the reading in church (Can. 39): "It is also settled that aside from the Canonical Scriptures nothing is to be read in church under the name of Divine Scriptures. Moreover, the Divine Scriptures are these." Then follow the books of the Old Testament, including Tobit, Judith, Esther, and Maccabees, and the books of the New Testament. I call attention to the fact that nothing else is to be read in Church under the name of scripture, and recall the distinction between: God to Man, and: Man to Man. We must further observe the use of "canonical." In the records the following is attached to this canon: "Let this also be made known to our brother and fellow-priest Boniface, or to other bishops of those parts, for the sake of confirming this canon, because we have received from the fathers that these are to be read in Church. It is, moreover, to be allowed that the passions of the martyrs be read when their anniversary days are celebrated." The reference to Boniface, who did not become Bishop of Rome until 418, is probably due to the person who superintended the codifying of the canons of a series of the Carthaginian councils, possibly in the year 419. The other statement, that the acts of the martyrs may be read on their days, confirms what was said a moment ago. That was: Man to Man. It did not come under the name of Divine Scripture.

Lucifer of Cagliari on Sardinia, who died in the year 370, does not, so far as I have observed, quote James or Second Peter or Third John or Revelation, but then he also fails to quote Mark and Philemon, so that the lack of quotations proves nothing. He does quote Second John three times (Migne, P. L. 13. 780–790). Once he says: "So also when the blessed John orders," and again: "Therefore also the apostle says in this Second Epistle." He quotes Jude four times close together, and that fourteen verses out of Jude's twenty-five. And he quotes Hebrews as Paul's (MPL 13. 782–784): "Showing an example of whose reprobation Paul says to the Hebrews," and there follow fourteen verses, and then three more. He does not happen to give us anything from the Revelation, but his pupil or adherent Faustinus does. Faustinus refers to Hebrews three times as a letter of Paul's, and he also calls it Divine Scripture. He quotes the Revelation by name (De trin. 3. 1): "But also the Apostle John says this in the Revelation."

Pacianus quotes Hebrews as Paul's, and so does Pelagius. Hilary of Rome quotes it in connection with other matter from Paul, but does not say exactly that it is his; doubtless he thought so. Julius Hilarianus about the year 397 quotes the Revelation by name. Zeno of Verona quotes apparently Second Peter, and possibly Hebrews. The Revelation he names as John's. Optatus, the Bishop of Milevis, in Numidia, who flourished about the year 370, quotes curiously enough an Epistle of Peter by name, but the words are not found in the Epistles bearing Peter's name. They are more like James 4^{11} than anything else. He writes (De schisma Don. 1. 5) : "Since we have read in the Epistle of Peter the Apostle : Do not judge your brethren by opinion." That may serve as a warning against treating quotations too strictly. No one will think of saying that Optatus here intends to declare some apocryphal book to be scripture. It is interesting further to see that he in more than one place uses the word Testament apparently for both Testaments : "The Divine Testament we read alike. We pray to one God."

John Chrysostom, the golden-mouthed preacher from Antioch who became Bishop of Constantinople, was preëminently a man of the scriptures. Even his homilies show his philological carefulness and his clear insight. His testimony stands properly for Syria, where he did his first work. He was born at Antioch in 347, and died in the year 407. But he wielded also in and from Constantinople during his brief and eventful work there a wide influence. His homilies are by far the most diligently copied works of the early and of the late Greek Church. If we see to-day in a library of Greek manuscripts a fine folio volume, if we find in the binding of a manuscript a beautifully written parchment leaf, the first thought of an experienced scholar is : It is probably Chrysostom. It usually is. He refers to the Epistle of James "the Lord's brother," but he appears not to make any use of Second Peter, Second and Third John, and Jude. Hebrews he considers to be Paul's. The Revelation he does not quote. Notwithstanding this failure to cite from five of the seven doubted books, Suidas says, when speaking of the Apostle John, that "Chrysostom receives both his three Epistles and the Revelation." I must confess that I do not lay any great stress upon this testimony of Suidas. A line or two before he lets the Apostle John live a hundred and twenty years, a totally improbable statement, one without the least foundation in the known traditions of the early Church, and one which would without doubt have been commemorated if true in the Church of Asia Minor, and have been known to thousands before Suidas published it in the tenth century. I could much more easily believe that Chrysostom received all three of the Epistles of John and the Revelation than I could believe that John had lived to be a hundred and twenty years old without its being mentioned by Polycarp or Papias or some one else in the second century. But I put no great faith in one or the other statement.

There is not the least reason, that I can see, to think that Chrysostom quoted Second Peter in his homilies on John. The words are much nearer the passage in Proverbs. At the same time we have in the bishop of Helenopolis—the birthplace of Constantine's mother—Palladius, a friend of Chrysostom's, who wrote a dialogue "On the life and conversation of the sainted John, bishop of Constantinople, Golden Mouth," and in this work he quotes both Third John and Jude. He writes (Galland, 8. 313): "About which things Jude the brother of James says," and adds Jude [12]. And again (Gall. 8. 322): "As the blessed John writes in the Catholic Epistles to Gaius," and he quotes 3 John [1-3] and [9, 10, 11]. That is Asia Minor. And on the other side of the Antioch line we find in a chain—a catena— that Eusebius of Emesa, now Homs, about 150 kilometres north of Damascus, quoted Second Peter (Wolf, Anecd. Gr. 4. 96): "Wherefore the apostle says in the Catholic (Epistle): Speechless beast," 2 Peter [2:16]. It is interesting that merely those two apparently indifferent words should have caused the reference to that Epistle, and should have been handed down to us through that chain. A Synopsis of scripture which is placed in the editions of the works of Chrysostom gives a very full descriptive list of the Old Testament books, and then disposes of the New Testament books as well known quite briefly. It gives fourteen Epistles of Paul, four Gospels, Acts, and three Catholic Epistles. That last can only be applied to James, with First Peter and First John.

We mentioned above a bishop of Asia Minor, a friend of Chrysostom's. There is still another and a more important one,

namely Theodore.   He was born at Antioch about the year
350.   At first a priest in Antioch from 383 onwards, he was
made Bishop of Mopsuestia in Cilicia in 392 and died in 428.
He was what would be called to-day a historical critical exegete,
and the Church condemned him as a heretic, and did all it could
to remand his valuable writings to oblivion, although he was the
most important scholar who had appeared since the days of
Origen.   He wrote commentaries on Matthew, Luke, John, and
the fourteen Epistles of Paul.   These books he acknowledged.
It is hard to say with certainty what his position was with respect
to the Catholic Epistles.   Summing up as well as can be done,
in view of the fragmentary condition of his literary remains, it
seems likely that he rejected James, Second and Third John,
Jude, and Revelation, and accepted First Peter and First John.
Another bishop, Theodoretus, was also born at Antioch.   He
was the bishop of Kyros on the Euphrates.   So far as we can see
he agreed with Chrysostom.

We have from Junilius—who has been supposed to be an
African bishop, but who now appears to have been by birth an
African, and by office one of the highest members of state in
Constantinople—an account of the view of the New Testament
books at Nisibis in the sixth century.   Junilius died soon after
550.   He gives at first only First Peter and First John as
Catholic Epistles, but says afterwards that a great many people
accept also James, Second Peter, Jude, Second and Third John.
Hebrews stands as Paul's.   And of Revelation he says that it is
a matter of much doubt among the Orientals.

If Junilius was really a statesman we can cap him with
another, and that a greater one.   Cassiodorius was prime minister
under Theodoric, and then devoted himself to his monks in his
monastery, Vivarium in Bruttium, in Calabria.   In his handbook of
theology for his ascetes he gave three differently arranged lists of
the New Testament books in three succeeding chapters.   The
first one is said to be from Jerome, though we do not find it in
Jerome's works, the second is from Augustine, and the third is from
what Cassiodorius calls the "old translation."   This third list does
not name Second Peter or Second and Third John.   It probably
includes Hebrews silently as Paul's, and it has Revelation.
This book was apparently much used in the West, but that
omission or those omissions of the third list will probably not

have had the least influence upon anyone. The "old translation" may not have had those books in Cassiodorius' volumes,
but the books were in vogue in the current translation, and that
was enough for the thoroughly uncritical mind of the average
monk or priest.   The Codex Claromontanus gives us in the list
above referred to James, Second Peter, Second and Third John,
Jude, and Revelation.   The omission of Philippians, First and
Second Thessalonians, and Hebrews is probably merely a clerical
error of a copyist.

Two men in the West call for special remark : the one because
of his intense occupation with the scriptures, the other because
of his importance in the Church of his day and of the following
centuries.   These are Jerome and Augustine.   Jerome was not
of the great mental power of Theodore of Mopsuestia, for
example, but he was of good parts, travelled widely, studied
diligently, owned his debt to his distinguished predecessors from
whose works he drew, and he worked enormously.   Augustine
was locally and in his studies much more limited, but he made
up for that by a keenness of perception, a breadth of mental
range, a fixedness of purpose, and a force of communicating his
thoughts which have made him the leader and the resource of
Western Christianity from the fifth century to the twentieth.

Jerome was by birth of a Christian family in Pannonia, and
saw the light about the year 346 at Stridon.   He studied at
Rome, then travelled north as far as Trier, then to the East, where
in the year 373, as one of the consequences of a severe illness, he
determined to devote himself to the study of the scriptures.
After spending five years in the desert, having been ordained
presbyter at Antioch in the year 379, having visited Constantinople
to hear Gregory of Nazianzus, and having stayed three years
(382–385) at Rome, he returned to the East, to Antioch, to Egypt,
and finally to Bethlehem, where he passed the rest of his life :
386–420.   What concerns us most is his revision of the Latin
translation of the New Testament, of which he handed the
Gospels to the Bishop of Rome, Damasus, in the year 384.
Perhaps he completed the rest—he did not do it so carefully as
the Gospels—a year later.   This New Testament contained the
books which we use, and as it little by little came to be the chief
Latin copy, its books became the accepted books of the Western
Church.   Nevertheless, with his encyclopædic view of Christi-

anity he knew very well the doubts that had been raised as to some books, and he referred to them upon occasion.

Oddly enough, he shows by a most trifling circumstance that he considered Barnabas almost if not quite a New Testament book. That came about as follows. With his knowledge of Hebrew he drew up at Bethlehem in the year 388 a list of the Hebrew names in the scriptures, giving their meaning, book by book. Therefore every book in the New Testament comes into the list, save Second John, which does not happen to contain any name; Third John is in the list sometimes called Second John, because it here is the second Epistle of John's that is mentioned. Of course, that does not mean that he rejected Second John. And then at the end of the New Testament he gives thirteen names from Barnabas, winding up with Satan. That was or is almost a canonising of Barnabas for him. He was a great defender of Origen's, and therefore closely bound to Alexandria, and this high estimation of Barnabas was probably a result of his imbibing the Alexandrian special valuation of that book.

Here and there we can find references to the case of the seven doubtful books. Speaking of James, "who is called the brother of the Lord," he says (De vir. ill. 2): "He wrote only one Epistle, which is one of the seven Catholics, and which very letter is asserted to have been published by somebody else under his name, although by degrees as time goes on it has gained authority." As for Second Peter, he has a special suggestion (Ep. 120): "Therefore he [Paul] used to have Titus as his interpreter"—interpreter here means also scribe,—"just as also the sainted Peter had Mark, whose Gospel was composed by Peter's dictating and his writing. Finally also, the two letters of Peter's which we have differ from each other in style and character and in the structure of the words. From which we perceive that he used different interpreters." And in another work, speaking of Peter he says (De vir. ill. 1): "He wrote two Epistles which are called Catholic, of which the second is by many denied to be his because of the difference of style from the former." Second and Third John do not seem to him to be from the apostle. He does not state, as in the case of James, Second Peter, and Jude, that the given author "wrote" them. In his account of John he says (De vir. ill. 9): "But he wrote also one Epistle, . . . which is approved by all churchly and very learned men. But

the other two . . . are said to be from John a presbyter." He
writes of Jude (De vir. ill. 4) : "Jude, the brother of the Lord,
left behind a little Epistle which is of the seven Catholics.   And
because it quotes the book of Enoch which is apocryphal it is
rejected by a great many.   Yet by age even and custom it has de-
served authority, and it is reckoned among the sacred scriptures."

The remaining two books are spoken of by Jerome in a letter
to a patrician, Claudianus Postumus Dardanus, written in the
year 414, and the passage is very instructive, in view of the
opposition to Hebrews in the Western Church (Ep. 129):
"That is to be said to our friends, that this Epistle which is
inscribed to the Hebrews is received not only by the Churches of
the East, but also by all Church writers of the Greek tongue
before our day, as of Paul the Apostle, although many think that
it is from Barnabas or Clement.   And it makes no difference
whose it is, since it is from a churchman, and is celebrated in the
daily reading of the Churches.   And if the usage of the Latins
does not receive it among the Canonical Scriptures, neither indeed
by the same liberty do the Churches of the Greeks receive the
Revelation of John.   And yet we accept both, in that we follow
by no means the habit of to-day, but the authority of ancient
writers, who for the most part quote each of them, not as they
are sometimes accustomed to do the apocrypha, and even also as
they use rarely the examples of the profane books, but as canonical
and churchly."   Twenty years earlier, in a letter to Paulinus, about
the study of the scriptures, Jerome said (Ep. 53): "Paul the
Apostle wrote to seven Churches, for the eighth to the Hebrews
is put by many outside of the number."   That is less decided.
He had become more clearly in favour of the authenticity between
394 and 414.   Jerome was no incisive critic.   He was in general
a vain and quarrelsome man, but he acquiesced calmly in the list
of books for the New Testament which were then in use.   The
nearest approach to personal dissent seems to be the view of
Second and Third John.   But those Epistles were on the one
hand minimal quantities, and on the other hand they might well
come under the delightfully liberal rule for canonisation that
Jerome gives in speaking of Hebrews.

Jerome's friend Augustine, who was born in the year 354 at
Tagaste in Numidia, and after a wild youth and a heretical and
half-heathen early manhood was baptized at Milan in 387,

returned to Africa an ardent Christian, and became assistant Bishop of Hippo in 395. He too accepted in a way the books now in our New Testament. He said that the Christian must read them, and at first know them at least by the reading even if he cannot comprehend them, but only the books called canonical. The other books are only to be read by one who is well grounded in the faith of the truth. But he shows after all that he recognised grades in value among the canonical books. The Christian reader (De doctr. Chr. 2. 12): "Will hold fast therefore to this measure in the Canonical Scriptures, that he place in the front rank those which are received by all Catholic Churches before those which some do not receive. Among those, moreover, which are not received by all, let him prefer those which more and more important Churches accept to those which fewer and less authoritative Churches hold. Should he, however, find some to be held by very many and others by very weighty Churches, although this cannot easily happen, yet I think that they are to be regarded as of equal authority."

In his list of the books he puts James at the end of the Catholic Epistles, thus giving Peter the first place. But all the seven doubtful books stand unquestioned in his list. It is perfectly clear that he has a certain feeling of hesitancy with respect to the Epistle to the Hebrews. He says in the list, it is true, that there are fourteen Epistles of Paul's, and Hebrews follows as the fourteenth after Philemon. But when he quotes it, it turns out that in his later works he avoids with painful accuracy saying that Paul wrote it. He quotes it and therefore he doubtless thinks it canonical, and he once calls it directly "Holy Scripture," but he does not know who wrote it. He says: "As we read in the Epistle to the Hebrews," "As is written," "Which is written," "Who writing to the Hebrews said," "Tell it to him who wrote to the Hebrews," "This, moreover, therefore said the author of that sacred Epistle," "In the Epistle to the Hebrews which the distinguished defenders of the Catholic rule have used as a witness." Curiously enough, Julian the Pelagian, against whom Augustine writes, does ascribe Hebrews to Paul (Aug. contr. Jul. 3. 40): "The Apostle understood this type of speech, who spoke as follows to the Hebrews." As for the Revelation, Augustine (Serm. 299) once suggested the possibility that his opponent, a Pelagian, may not accept it: "And if by chance thou who likest these [heretical] things shouldst not accept this scripture [a quotation from Revelation], or, if thou accept, despise and say : They are not expressly named."

Jerome and Augustine settled the matter of the number of the books of the New Testament for the orthodox circles in the Western Church so far as there may have lingered in it here and there doubts as to some of the books. But we shall see in a moment that in heretical circles other opinions ventured to continue. We saw above that certain books which do not belong to our New Testament were long favoured in the West even in thoroughly churchly provinces. In Spain, after the reconciliation of the Western Goths with the Church, their dislike to the Revelation evidently continued to show itself. In consequence the Council of Toledo, in the year 633, declared that the ancient councils stood for the authorship of the Revelation on the part of the evangelist John. It added in a sentence, which neverthe- less appears to be of doubtful authenticity, that many regard it as of no authority and refuse to preach from it. The decree of the council was (Mansi, 10. 624) : " If anyone henceforth either shall not have accepted it, or shall not have preached from it from Easter to Whitsuntide at the time of mass in the church, he shall have the sentence of excommunication."

Here we may close our view of the criticism of the canon. The one great result is that which has not come to the surface during the whole discussion. We have not said anything about a determination of the books which belong to the New Testament on the part of a general council of the Christian Church. We could say nothing about such a determination, because there never was one. Now and then a local or partial council ratified the statements of some preceding Church writer.

The criticism of the canon shows, then, that in the sense in which the word used to be understood, and is by some to-day still understood, there never was a canon. At no period in the history of Christianity did the necessity make itself apparent to the whole Church to say just what was and just what was not scripture. Tertullian mentioned synods, which can only have been small local synods, that rejected the Shepherd of Hermas, but he spoke of none which had stated what the books of the New Testament were. He spoke of the Jews as rejecting

certain things in the Old Testament "which sound out Christ,"
and gave thus a pleasing rule for the correctness of biblical
literature.   But he did not lay this down as a canon, or say that
it had been universally and authoritatively sanctioned.   Augustine,
the sound churchman, declared that the scriptures depend from
the Church.   He even went so far as to say in the contest against
the half heathenish Manichæans : " I indeed should not believe
in the Gospel, if the authority of the Catholic Church did not
press me to it."   It is true that Christianity is a life, and that
this life lives on in the Church.   Yet this life is the Gospel.   It is
nothing without the Gospel.   It seems to me, therefore, that this
excited word of Augustine's was all in all a frivolous word.   It is
upon a par with the foolishness of those Christians who to-day
declare in theological controversy that if the contention of their
opponents, Christian opponents, be proved true, they will give
up the Bible.   And yet even this Augustine could not point to
an authoritative deliverance of the whole Church touching the
books of scripture.   More than that, although he, with Jerome,
proved in a way the surcease of doubts as to books now in our
New Testament, he nevertheless really put down two points which
are altogether incompatible with the notion that, let us say, by
the time of Irenæus the canon of the New Testament was for all
good orthodox Christians a definitely settled fact.

The first point touches, in the first place, the fact that he does
not regard the books of the New Testament as all of equal
authority, as having each and all of them the same right to be in
the collection.   In the second place, it decides definitely that
they have not each and all equal authority and value.   In the third
place, it does not refer the decision upon the quality, character,
authority, and canonical standing of the separate books to ancient
and acknowledged councils and their decrees.   In the fourth place,
it refers the decision to a majority vote, a vote which combines
numbers and authority.   In the fifth place, the judge who is to
decide is not a council then in session, or soon to be gathered
together, but the Christian reader.   In the sixth place, he puts
before our eyes, taken strictly, five classes of books.—*A*. The
books accepted by all churches.   *B*. The books rejected by
some churches.   *A*. remains a class for itself.   *B*. is divided into
four possible classes, although he scarcely thinks that the two
last classes will really come into consideration.   *B.a.* contains

the books that many and important churches accept. The "important" churches in Augustine's eyes are those that have apostolical bishops' seats : Alexandria, Antioch, Rome, and those that received Epistles from apostles. *B.b.* comprises the books that are accepted by fewer and by less important churches. *B.c.* comprises the books that are received by a great many,—that is to say, by the majority of the churches, but without the important churches. Whereas *B.d.* includes the books that but a few, it is true, yet those the important churches, accept. According to Augustine's view, of course, the *A.* class is to be accepted and to be regarded as of the highest authority. The *B.* class is to be thought less authoritative. Going to the under-divisions of the *B.* class, *B.a.* is to be accepted, the books in *B.b.* are to be rejected. The case is more difficult between *B.c.* and *B.d.*, between multitude and knowledge or insight. Augustine knows how to solve the problem. The decision is : " I think they are to be held to be of equal authority." That is a curiously indefinite canonical decision for the fifth century. That is the first point. The second point is the great one, but it demands no discussion. It is the fact that Augustine thus really tells us that he regards the number of the books in the New Testament as not yet settled. It is still a question whether this or that book belongs to the fully authoritative New Testament or not. There is no canon in the technical sense of the word.

But we have a New Testament, and the Christian Church of Europe and America supposes it to consist in all parts of the world of the same books, of the books, of course, which we use. That supposition is the result of what might be called a half-unconscious process of closing the eyes to the testimony of history.

When the great mental upturning of the fifteenth and sixteenth centuries took place, many Christians saw clearly how precarious the standing of the seven disputed books was, of James, Second Peter, Second and Third John, Jude, Hebrews, and Revelation. Ever prudent Erasmus aimed his judicious questionings—which were interwoven with assurances of willing acceptance of the books—at Hebrews, Second and Third John, and Revelation. Luther declared freely that five books, John, Romans, Galatians, Ephesians, and First Peter, were enough for any Christian ; yet, while he received the books of the New

Testament in general, he boldly put Hebrews, the "straw-like" James, Jude, and Revelation in a lower class. Karlstadt made three groups of books. The Gospels formed the first. The second consisted of the thirteen Epistles of Paul with First Peter and First John. And the third contained the seven disputed books. Oecolampadius stated that James, Second Peter, Second and Third John, Jude, and Revelation were not to be compared to the rest, which was equivalent to putting them in a much lower second class. Calvin discussed the disputed books quite freely. He actually accepted everything in a way. Nevertheless he showed that he was not overmuch pleased with James and Jude, and not much pleased with Second Peter. And in his commentary he left out Second and Third John and Revelation, and called First John "the Epistle of John." Grotius, who died in 1645, accepted Hebrews as probably written by Luke, and James and Revelation as John's. But he regarded Second Peter as a brace of Epistles—the first = chs. 1. 2, the second = ch. 3—written by James' successor, Simeon, the second bishop of Jerusalem. He did not think that Second and Third John were from John. And he supposed that Jude had been written by a bishop of Jerusalem named Jude, who lived under Hadrian.

That was all very well. Such discussions showed progress and not a retrograde movement. They revivified tradition. But there were, on the other hand, motives rife which made a greater definiteness seem desirable. Rome and her offshoots sought for decisions. It was to them immaterial whether or not they were true to history. They wished a firm basis for their arguments in an immovable Word.

Rome wished on her part to stand up for that Word which the Reformers were placing in the foreground, and desired to sanction a form of it agreeable to herself. Therefore the Council of Trent, on the 8th of April 1546, made the Old Testament, including the now fully normative Apocrypha, and the complete New Testament a matter of faith. It even went so far as to make the Latin text, which its leaders used, the "authentic" text of the Bible. The insufficient insight of those who guided that decision was shown by the fact that the papal edition of that "authentic" text was so bad as to need speedy and shamefaced replacement by a somewhat better though far from excellent

19

papal edition. We must remember, however, that the Council
of Trent was no general council. So much for the Church of
Rome. Its position received a curious side-light from Sixtus of
Siena twenty years after the council. Sixtus in the year 1566
put the seven disputed books as well as three sections of the
text of other books into a second-class canon. Antonio a Matre
Dei of Salamanca followed Sixtus in the year 1670 and added
another passage to the list.

It might have been thought that the Churches of the Re-
formation would retain a free position over against the criticism
of the canon. Not at all. It is true that they did not allow
the great authority of the Church to compel their acceptance of
the books. They declared that the free spirit of the Christian
recognised the genuine work of the Divine Spirit in these holy
books and in their use. Yet they were not content to leave the
books to care for themselves. They followed the lead of Rome
and declared the whole New Testament for undoubted scripture,
as, for example, the Westminster Assembly of 1643 and the Swiss
Declaration of Faith of 1675. The latter went so far as to say
that in the Old Testament the Hebrew consonants and even—
imagine it—the Masoretic vowel-points (or at least their force)
were inspired. Thus everything was slurred over. The seven
disputed books had become indisputable. From that day to this
the questioning of the authenticity of one of the New Testament
books has even in Protestant circles called forth the Anathema
set by the Council of Trent upon that crime.

In spite of all that, there never was an authoritative,
generally declared and generally received canon. To the
supposition that a canon exists is to be said : firstly, that
the supposed state of affairs is, strictly taken, not the real state
of affairs ; and secondly, that the thing which produced the
actual, not the supposed, state of affairs was no single circumstance, no historical single event, but a series of causes working
in one district in one way, in another district, land, church in
another way.

The supposed state of affairs is not the real state of affairs.
In the Ethiopic Church, for example, we find in the manuscripts
for the number of the books of the Bible : eighty-one. Of these,
forty-six belong to the Old Testament, which does not now
concern us. The New Testament consists of thirty-five books,

or of our twenty-seven and of eight which come under the head of Clement and the Synodos. That is a surplus. In the Syrian Church, Second Peter, Second and Third John, Jude, and the Revelation were practically no part of the New Testament. Here we have a minus. That is of itself enough. But it is generally supposed that at least the great Greek Church, the mother of all Churches except the Church in Jerusalem, had and has the whole of our New Testament. In a way that might be affirmed. The Revelation stands in the lists of books on many a page. And it has been commented upon at least by two Greek authors, hard put to it as we are when we try to say precisely when Andrew and Arethas of Cæsarea lived, one probably at the end of the fifth century, the other possibly at almost the same date, but using his predecessor's book. But as a matter of fact the Revelation belongs, of course not to the Gospel, but just as little to the Apostle of the Greek Church, and only what is in the Gospel and the Apostle is read in church as Holy Scripture. Turning that around and putting it blankly, the Revelation has never had, has not to-day, a place among the Bible lessons of the Greek Church.

Further, it is to be urged in the same direction that the Revelation in a large number of cases in the manuscripts which contain it does not stand among the books of the New Testament. There are a few, comparatively a very few, Greek manuscripts which contain our whole New Testament,—that is to say, which contain the other books and the Revelation. But the other books are commonly copied off without the Revelation. The continuation or the other side of this circumstance is to be found in the fact that Revelation often stands in the middle of volumes that have no other biblical contents. We do not often find the four Gospels or the Acts, or the Catholic Epistles, or the Epistles of Paul in volumes of profane, that is to say, not scripture literature ; but we do often find the Revelation in such volumes. For example, one manuscript contains lives of saints, the Acts of Thomas, and then theological treatises, and Revelation stands between the life of Euphrosyne and an essay of Basil's on love to God. Various of the manuscripts which contain only the Revelation are the quires containing Revelation taken out from the middle of some such general theological book (see pp. 369, 383).

It would, I think, be no great exaggeration to say that the

printing of the Greek New Testament formed the most important step for the practical association of the Revelation with the other books of the New Testament.   But that remark must not be supposed to have effect with the Greek Church.   The printed New Testaments of Western Europe had, have had, have to-day, so far as I can judge from actual vision, very little or almost nothing to do with the Church of the East.   The printed Gospels and Apostles have held the ground there, neither one of them with the Revelation.   And it is pertinent to mention here another thing which recalls our earlier allusions to the reading in the churches. During all the centuries and still to-day a number of books which form no part of our New Testament are read in church in the Greek Church under our division : Man to Man.   Some of them, certainly one of them, for I remember at this moment John of the Ladder, are read yearly at a given time, the Ladder during Lent.   But enough of this.   The supposed state of affairs is not the real state of affairs.   The British and Foreign Bible Society and the Roman College for Propagating the Faith are gradually spreading abroad our New Testament.   But neither the one nor the other is a General Council authorised to settle the canon.

No single historical act or event brought about the supposed but not actually universal determination of the books which we have in our New Testament as constituting, they alone and they all, the second part of Holy Scripture.   No apostle, not even the Nestor John, settled the canon.   There was no settled canon at the time of the consolidation of the Catholic Church shortly after the middle of the second century.   No fixed canon guided the scriptural studies of the three hundred and eighteen Fathers who composed the Council of Nice.   And all the few and scattered statements and lists of books accepted and disputed and spurious failed in reality to secure one universally acknowledged New Testament of exactly the same contents. Nevertheless the truth, the Church, Christianity cannot be said to have suffered by this lack.   Even fewer books than the Syrian Church recognised would have been enough to herald the teaching of Jesus and to sustain, so far as it was desirable that written records should sustain, the life that has flowed in an unbroken stream from Jesus until to-day.

Let us for an instant press this thought.   The books that we call New Testament were certainly for the most part in existence before the year 100. The Gospels and the letters of Paul form the two greatest divisions of this collection. One or more of the Gospels or a combination of all four of them,—which was the most decided recognition of the four,—and some of the letters of Paul were at an early date, long before the year 200, to be found in the Church of every Christian district. The multiplication of the books, both the recopying repeatedly of one book and the addition in church after church of a new book, an Epistle or a Gospel, or the Acts or the Revelation, was not taken in hand by a Bible society or a council or a synod, or even so far as we can see by a single bishop, much as we may easily imagine that one and another bishop took especial interest in having his books, the books used in his church, spread abroad through other churches, and in having as many books as possible added to those already in use in his own church. Something of that kind we saw in the case of the letters of Ignatius and the letters about copies of them between Philippi and Smyrna and Antioch. Little by little the list of the books in each church grew.

The Church did not at first consider it necessary to issue decrees about the books. The books were something subsidiary. They were all good enough. They were like daily bread, and like rain for the thirsty land. But it was not necessary to decree anything about them. Finally, one and another really reflected upon the matter, and some lists were made. Some of the earlier lists tried to be very precise and to determine best books, a trifle less good books, poorer and poorest books. And then in later time followed lists that aimed at fulness. The list that is named after Gelasius and then after Hormisdas might be entitled: a list of the books which should form the library of the Christian. Inasmuch, however, as few Christians had the money to buy such a large library, we could name the list: a catalogue of the books from which the Christian should choose his library. There was then no formation of the canon in the sense that a general council took up the question. The number of books in the New Testament simply grew. When anyone had the question as to the sacred character of a book to decide, he was very likely to ask whether it was from an apostle or not. We see that Tertullian, like others before him, succeeds in agreeing

to Mark and Luke by the connection of the one with Peter and
of the other with Paul. And this same Tertullian, much as
he likes Hebrews, lets it stand aside because its author, whom
he may well have rightly thought to be Barnabas, was not a
Twelve-Apostle and not Paul the special apostle. Many another
reason came into play at one time and at another, in one place
and the other. A book favoured Gnosticism, therefore it
certainly was not sacred. A book used an apocryphal book,
therefore it could not be received. There was no general rule
that everywhere held good.

At the present time, with our clearer view of ancient history,
it is necessary to make a distinction between the contents and
meaning of three terms: truth, inspiration, canon. Many
Christians have nailed themselves to the word canon, and to
the thought that in some mysterious way during the early second
century the Spirit of God gathered precisely our New Testament,
from Matthew to Revelation, into one single volume,—a large
roll that would have made,—and that since that time the whole
Christian Church has held fast to just this book. We have seen
that this notion has not the least basis in history, that the facts
were of a totally different character. Such persons are not a
little inclined, if one calls attention to the state of the case,
to fall back upon the thought of inspiration. Their theory is
that God caused these words to be written, and that by a positive
necessity of the course of events He then took care that they
should be gathered together into the one collection. This
theory is as a theory beautiful, and it has been a comfort to
many a Christian. But it fails to agree with what really took
place. We see by turning back the pages of the years that
God simply did not, in the way supposed, have the books
collected. We say: Man proposes, God disposes. We might
here say: Man imagines, God did. I believe that God watched
over every step in the paths of the early Christians, but He had
no thought of this theory of inspiration and of canon. If anyone be then inclined to say that this puts an end to all faith
in the Scriptures, he may reassure himself with the reflection
that when God makes nuts, the point is not the shell of the nut,
but the kernel. If God sends the truth to men, the thing that
He cares for, the thing that His Spirit watches over, is the truth.
He saw to it that the early Christians, through all the

vicissitudes of their earthly fortunes and in spite of all their own human weakness and fallibility, got the truth and passed the truth along to us.   The great thing for us is, not to become excited about diverging views as to a canon and canonicity, but to take the truth and live in the truth, and live the truth and impart it in its purity to others.

296

THE TEXT

OF

THE NEW TESTAMENT

THE TEXT.

———◆———

I.

PAPYRUS.

As a general rule the mass of people take things as they are. They are also likely to think, or at least to go upon the supposition, that things always have been as they now are. They can buy a New Testament, a nicely bound one, for a mere trifle. It rarely occurs to them that six centuries ago that would not have been possible. Perhaps there are men who would be surprised to learn that Paul and even Peter and John and James did not each carry a little New Testament in his girdle. Yet it is not strange that the knowledge of just what Christians in the early ages were and did and had, should not be the common property of the unlearned. Externals are not the main thing.

Let us go back to the first century, to the days of Jesus. The only time that we hear of Jesus writing is in the story about the woman taken in adultery. He wrote upon the ground, as if He did not know that the scribes and Pharisees were near Him and were talking. He looked up and spoke to them, and again He wrote upon the ground. Perhaps He only drew circles and made figures of various forms with His fingers in the sand. It has been thought that He may have written the sins of the accusers. But we do not know. If Jesus ever wrote anything, He may have written as the Arabs write to-day, simply holding a piece of paper in His left hand and writing as we do with the right hand. However that may be, Jesus did not write the New Testament. So far as we know, He did not write a word of it.

It is not only not impossible, but it is even quite likely that various people had written down some things that are in our Gospels before the authors of these Gospels began their work. We do not need to deal with them. We have enough to do with the books of the New Testament. It is possible that some of Paul's letters were the first documents that were written that we now have in our New Testament. Here we must observe how strangely history repeats itself in varying forms. The older men of to-day grew up at a time at which most men wrote for themselves what they wished to entrust to paper. To-day, however, everyone is eager to have a stenographer with a writing machine, or to tell his thoughts to a grammophone and hand that over to his type-writing clerk. At Paul's day, much as is the case to-day in the East and in the South, even men who could write were in the habit of having scribes to do the drudgery of writing for them. If a man were not rich, he might have a young friend or a pupil who was ready to wield the pen for him. It comports less with the dignity of age in the East to write. The old man strokes his beard and dictates his words to the scribe. That is what Paul did, although I do not know whether or not he had the beard which Christian art gives him. He had a good reason for using another's hand, for his eyes were weak. The Epistle to the Galatians was an exception. His delicacy forbade him to dictate such a scolding letter. That was a matter between him and the Galatians alone. Let us turn to the Epistle to the Romans. For our purpose one Epistle is as good as another, and which one could be better than this chief Epistle? It was Tertius who wrote it, if the sixteenth chapter belongs to it. Timothy and Lucius, and Jason, and Sosipater were probably all sitting around Paul and Tertius at Corinth or at Cenchrea when Tertius wrote their greetings in 16[21], and he added his own before he went on to name Gaius.

When Paul told Tertius that he wished to write a letter by Tertius' hand, the first thing that Tertius had to do was to get pens and ink and paper. He may well have had ink at hand, possibly hanging in his girdle, a bottle of ink made from oak-galls. If he could find them, he certainly prepared three or four pens so as not to keep Paul waiting while he mended pens. Of course, these were not steel pens. The metal pens in ancient times were probably chiefly intended to make a fine show on a rich man's table. For actual work a reed pen was used. A scholar once wrote that the bad writing in a certain New Testament manuscript was probably due to its having been written with a reed pen instead of with a stylus. But you cannot write with ink with a stylus, and our most exquisite manuscripts were written with reed pens; and some people draw daintily to-day with reed pens. Tertius will therefore have cut half a dozen reed pens and laid them at his side ready for use.

The paper that he got was what was called papyrus, which is only the word paper in another shape. The reeds for the pens came from the marshes or river or sea edges, and the paper came from the marshes and rivers too. Papyrus is a plant that one can often find in well appointed parks. In the parks it is four or five feet high. If I am not mistaken I saw it fifteen feet high at the Arethusa spring at Syracuse. It has a three-cornered stem which is of pith, with vertical cell-pipes, and the sides are covered by a thin green skin. There are no joints. At the top is a large inverted tassel of grass-like hair like the crest for a helmet. The great place for papyrus in ancient times was Egypt, although European rivers, for example, the Anapo near Syracuse, also produced it. The pith stem was cut crosswise into lengths of fifteen or twenty centimetres according to wish, and then cut lengthwise into thin flat strips like tape. These tape-like strips were laid vertically to the edge of the table side by side till there were enough for a leaf of the desired size. Then other strips were laid across them, that is to say, horizontally, or running with the edge of the table. Between the two layers was a thin glue or paste. These leaves were pressed, so that the strips should all stick flat together, and left to dry. The drying is easy in Egypt. Things dry almost before they have come to perceive that they are wet. The dried leaves were a trifle rough. For the thread-like walls of those longitudinal cells often rose above the surface. For nice paper the surface was then smoothed off, it may be with pumice-stone or with an ink-fish's bone, or it was hammered. It was a very good surface to write upon, not unlike birch bark, which many readers will know from the Adirondacs or Maine or Canada.

It has sometimes been supposed that all papyrus leaves, that is, all leaves of paper made from papyrus, were of the same size. That was not the case. A scholar explained that Second John and Third John were just that long, because no more would go upon the papyrus leaf on which they were written. That theory neglected the size of the writing. I write on a half foolscap page, 21 × 16.3 centimetres 1200 or even 1700 or 1800 words, whereas people who write larger put fewer words on such a page, perhaps 200 or 300. But that theory also failed to observe that the papyrus lengths could be cut at will; and as for that, as we shall see in a moment, if a man had wished for a papyrus leaf six metres each way it would have been easy to paste the leaves together and reach those dimensions. Let us go back to Tertius. Paul will have told him that he intended to write a long letter, and Tertius will have bought a number of good-sized leaves, not ladies' note-paper, but a business quarto probably. It is even possible that he bought at once a roll that was about as large as he thought would be necessary. If so, that roll was made, as he could have made it himself, by pasting the single leaves together. If the roll proved too long he could cut the rest of it off. If it were too short, he could paste as many more leaves on to it as he liked. Tertius began to write at the left end of the roll, if he bought the leaves ready pasted together. That is to say, when he began to write he turned the roll so that the part to be unrolled was at his right hand. If Paul had wished him to write Hebrew,—Paul could have written Hebrew, I question whether Tertius could have,—he would have turned the roll upside down and begun to write with the part to be unrolled at his left hand. He probably wrote in columns that were about as broad as a finger is long. That is an uncertain measure. So is the breadth of the columns. But when the roll was already made up and had its curves set it was not so easy to write a broad column. And, besides, the narrow columns were easier to read.

So Tertius began: "Paul a servant of Jesus Christ, called to be an apostle." That Epistle was not written at one sitting. It is much more likely to have been written at twenty or thirty sittings. In the East there is less hurry than in the West. And Paul had to weave his tent-cloth. But at last the end came: "To whom be glory unto the ages of the ages. Amen." One would like to know whether Tertius appreciated that Epistle. Doubtless he did, as well as one could then. But he could not value it as we do after these centuries, during which it has instructed and warned and chided and comforted hundreds of thousands of Christians. And after it was done Phœbe carried it to Rome, always supposing that the sixteenth chapter was written at the same time with the first fourteen, a question which does not now concern us. It is not hard to look in upon the Christians at Rome when the Epistle reaches that city. Phœbe gives it to one of the chief men among the Christians. At the first possible moment, probably on a Lord's Day—for they would not think of calling that day by the Jewish name of Sabbath, as some English-speaking people do ; Sabbath is the name of Saturday—on the Lord's Day, because on that day everybody, or at least many of the Christians, could take the time for a long meeting, they read the Epistle before the assembled Church. Did they read it all through at one meeting? It seems to me likely that they did. They will have wished to know all that Paul had to say.

The next question that arises for us is not, whether the Roman Christians then proceeded to take to heart all the good advice that Paul gave them. That belongs to another department of theology. What we wish to know is, what they did with the Epistle, with this long letter, after they had read it that first time. One thing is clear. They did not then tear it up and throw it away because, as people to-day so often say of letters just received and at once destroyed, they knew all that was in it. It is actually possible to read in scientific books that doubtless the early Christian Churches read the letters sent to them by the apostles once or twice and then put them away. The impression given is, that they then perhaps for months and years did not read them again. To my mind it is not easy to find anything more unreasonable and improbable than that.

The early Christians were largely poor people, many of them not well educated, many of them certainly with no more education than the school of hard living and hard work had bestowed upon them. There were then no newspapers. What men knew of the events of the day had to be gained almost altogether from hearsay. There were also, and particularly for poor people, even if they knew how to read, but few books to be had. And there were still fewer Christian books. Christians who could write books were still few. The Christians had as yet no great motive for writing books. One thing filled their thoughts : It will soon be Heaven. They did not think that this earth had still a long lease to run. If we could imagine that one of them had said : I am going to write a big book, we should at once also imagine that his brother said : What is the use ? The trumpet will sound before you are half done. And, further, there were not many preachers. It is true that Paul's advice to the Corinthians seems to imply an extremely eager participation of anybody and everybody in the church services. Yet churches are different in such respects. Every city had not such enterprising rhetorical and prophetical and ecstatic members as Corinth had. And times differ. Corinth may well afterwards have had its periods of greater quiet on the part of the single Christians in the church gatherings. Summing it all up, the early Christian churches will certainly have welcomed new reading matter, new writings that they could read in church. That does not imply that they looked upon this letter and such letters as equivalent to the Old Testament. Not in the least. This letter was a message to them all from a well-known preacher, and therefore it could be read in church. A part of this letter would have been, will have been, for them like a sermon from Paul.

It is not to be supposed that they will every Sunday from that first Sunday onwards have read the whole Epistle through. Nor can we be sure that on every single Sunday they read some parts of it. But it seems to me that we may set down two things as quite certain under such circumstances. One is, that at the first, as a necessary following up of the first reading, the church at Rome will have soon and repeatedly read and discussed given parts of the Epistle. The other is, that even after time had passed, especially after Paul had been there twice and had died as a martyr, a year, two years, ten years later they will at least occasionally have again read this Epistle, section after section. That thought presents, how-ever, various further considerations for us touching the text. We are not now studying directly Church history, but book history. If you please, it is the book division of Church history. We are to fix our eyes on that roll of papyrus. It is a very fair sized roll, for Tertius in writing a letter that was to be read to the church was not likely to use a diamond size of handwriting. And, besides, only one side of the roll, the inside, was written upon. That was what we may call the "right side" of the papyrus. It was the side on which the strips of papyrus ran across the page from side to side, and not up and down the page from top to bottom.

One of the things to be considered is the fact that in a large city like Rome, even at that early date, the groups of Christians will have been somewhat scattered. The Christians to whom Paul wrote in this Epistle are evidently for the most part not Jewish Christians but heathen Christians, Christians who had before that time been heathen. Therefore they will not have all been living close together in the Jewish quarter of the city, as might have been the case if they had all been born Jews. In consequence of this there will have been meetings of ten or twenty or fifty who lived near each other on the week-day evenings, on Wednesday and Friday as a rule. Now it is in every way to be supposed that sometimes Paul's letter was carried to one and another of these little meetings, so that it could be read, that some passage from it could be read and discussed there. We can hear the man who had the roll saying to the one who carries it away from him to the little meeting: Take care of it. Do not let it be torn. Be sure to bring it back in good order. That was very necessary, for papyrus is a frail stuff.

We pass over a year or two and look at our roll. That papyrus, as we saw, was made of tape-like strips of vegetable fibre laid crosswise, at right angles to each other. When it dried, the fibre was, of course, stiffer than when green. The members of the church kept the book dry, and the fibres will have only grown the more stiff and the more set in their ways, in their curled-up way in the roll. The Epistle had to be kept dry, for it would have grown mouldy if allowed to be damp, and the ink would have been spoiled or printed off on the papyrus against the columns. The roll has been unrolled and rolled up again. When the reader read the beginning of it and went on towards the middle he rolled up with his left hand the part he had read, so as to able to hold it well for the further reading. When, as must often have happened, the part read was well on in the roll, there was quite an amount of unrolling with the right hand and rolling up with the left hand to be done before the passage was reached. If the roll had been lying still in the room of a careful scholar, who only unrolled it at rare intervals and then always with great care, it might have lived out these two years without much change. Instead of that it had been carried to the meetings. It had been often opened and re-rolled, and certainly often not with the greatest care. Curious people, even the unlearned who could not read, will in the small meetings have fingered the roll. There are many people, even people who can read and write, who do not think they have seen a thing until they have put their fingers on it, as if they were blind ; in this way our roll has been felt and pinched by many hands.

Here and there one of the stiff fibres, you might call it a tiny stick, has broken when it was rolled up, like a piece of wood broken across your knee. Another fibre has broken at the edge when somebody pinched it, or perhaps when the reader grasped it too firmly while busy rendering the impassioned sentences of Paul. No wonder that the reader forgot the papyrus while reading, let us say, what we call the eighth chapter of Romans, for Tertius will not have numbered any chapters. But it was also no wonder that then those little papyrus fibre sticks broke. Papyrus breaks rather than tears. Another fibre breaks alongside of the first one, and after a few have broken in the direction of the writing, the first thing you know some of the up and down fibres break and very soon there is a rough hole like a little square or a parallelogram in the letter. If that happens in the vacant space between two columns of writing, it does not do much harm for the moment. If, however, it happens in the middle of a line, then a part of a word or even a whole word may be lost, so that the reader will have to guess at it from the sense of the rest.

In time the leading men of the church see that if they wish in the years to come to know what the letter contains, they must copy it off before it falls altogether to pieces. And there may before this time have been another reason for copying the Epistle. A Christian from Corinth or Ephesus or Alexandria may have been at Rome on business and heard of this letter and heard or read it, and then have wished to take a copy of it back with him for the church at home. Thus in one way or the other the letter comes to be copied off for Rome or for another church. The Epistle is written again. This time Paul is not dictating, but the man writing has a roll before his eyes. And this man writing is not Tertius, but some one in the church at Rome. He will doubtless make some mistakes in copying, but we shall not trouble about them at this moment. We wish to know what becomes of the original letter. From the point of view of an antiquarian or of a relic hunter of to-day, one would say that the papyrus roll which Paul had sent to Rome would have been treasured most carefully by the church. As a matter of fact, nothing of that kind is likely to have happened.

Let us put the matter down as precisely as possible, remembering all the while that we have no exact knowledge of the details, and that the years may be quite different. Paul probably dictated Romans to Tertius at Corinth in the year 53 or 54. He was probably for the first time a prisoner at Rome about 57 to 59. Whether carried a second time as a prisoner to Rome from the West or from the East, or whether he was arrested while visiting that city, he appears to have died there as a martyr in the year 64. Considering the frailty of papyrus, it is in every way likely that the Epistle was copied off long before the death of Paul. Let us, however, give it, the original, a long life, and say that it was copied off for the Romans again shortly after Paul's death. We heighten thereby the value of that original. Yet we must again say, that the original was probably totally neglected so soon as the new copy was done. Paul was one of the greatest men, was the greatest man, among the Christians in those years. But he did not stand in the position that he now does. Further, however, so far as we can see, the reverence for relics had not yet begun among the Christians. There was enthusiasm and zeal, yet they were directed more to the future than to the past. The Christian was then bent on doing or on hoping, not upon looking back to worthies of the past. We might almost say that the gaze of the Church was fixed less upon Jesus of Nazareth and more upon Jesus the Prince that was soon to return. The original letter written by the hand of Tertius to the Romans was probably laid in a corner and soon entirely forgotten. It was old and time-worn. Papyrus, if much used, is soon time-worn.

We have spoken of a letter of Paul's. Of course, the case would have been much the same with a letter of James' or Peter's or John's or Jude's. It will be clear that in Rome, during the time to which we have referred, there may have been copies received of one or more of the letters that Paul

wrote to churches farther east, just as we supposed that copies
of Romans might have been made for churches in the East.
If such letters reached Rome, the leaders of the church will
probably have kept the various rolls in some one place. Some
one man is likely to have been charged with the care of them,
though it would be conceivable that separate persons kept
separate rolls. It is in no way to be supposed that anyone
in Rome will have thought of changing any words or cutting
any out or putting any in, in the original of Paul's letter. So
long as the original existed and was legible, the church had
in its hands precisely the words that Paul had dictated to
Tertius.

There are, however, in the New Testament, books that are
not letters. There is, for example, the Revelation, to which
I am still inclined to attribute an early date. It is a question
whether or not we should here think of dictation. Were the
book issued by John in the nineties of the first century, should
that some day be proved, then we should at once say that
the old man had dictated it. But if it was written before the
year seventy, there is more possibility that it should have been
written directly by the author. Yet that does not matter.

Whether dictated or whether written by its author, this book
of Revelation does not seem to have been a book written
from beginning to end fresh from the brain of the man who
thought it all out, who imagined the scenes depicted in it.
It is apparently made upon the basis of a Jewish book. The
author of the Christian book found that the dreams of the
Jewish book were good, and he made a Christian introduction,
an acceptable beginning for the book, and a like ending, and
he added or took away or rearranged and modified the Jewish
accounts to suit Christian needs. The Jewish Christians at
Jerusalem before the year 70 doubtless fulfilled, like James
and Paul, their religious duty as Jews. They were still good
Jews although they were Christians. They still looked upon
Christianity as the normal continuation of Judaism. For them
Judaism was Christianity. The Jews who were not Christians
simply failed properly to understand what Judaism was and
should be. Thus, then, the Christian who published this book
seems merely to have made an enlarged and corrected and
re-wrought edition of an existing Jewish book. The book is

not a whit the worse for that. The figures and scenes are as
vivid and the descriptions are as telling whether first conceived
by a Jew who was still only an old-fashioned Jew, or by a
Jew who had become a Christian. So or so this book of visions
and dreams is written upon a roll of papyrus.

Tertius wrote Romans for Paul for the Christians at Rome.
This book of Revelation was written by some one named John
for seven churches in Asia Minor : Ephesus, Smyrna, Pergamon,
Thyatira, Sardes, Philadelphia, and Laodicea. It would, of
course have been possible for John to write but a single copy
and to send it around to the seven churches like a book
from a circulating library, leaving it, let us say, four weeks in
each church, so that in twenty-eight weeks, a little more
than half a year, all would have had it. The churches are
not so very far apart. I went with the train from Smyrna to
Ephesus in $2\frac{1}{2}$ hours and returned in the afternoon. A slow
little steamer carried me from Smyrna in a few hours to
Dikeli, from which place I walked during the evening, and,
after a night on the sand, by seven o'clock the next morning
to Pergamon. From Pergamon a half a day's walk took me
to Soma, where a train passing through Thyatira returned
me to Smyrna in a little more than half a day. The other three
cities lie only a little to the east of these four. John could
easily have sent the letter around in a single copy. We might
think that that was meant by the words in Rev. 1^{11} "Write
what you see into a book, and send it to the seven churches."
And the fact that the letters to the seven churches all follow,
Rev. 2^1 to 3^{22}, might point to the same thing.

It would be possible to suppose that if a copy were written for
each church, if seven copies were written, each copy would have
had but one letter in it, the copy for Ephesus only the letter
to Ephesus, and so for the other churches. If, however, we
reflect upon the fact that these letters are not merely letters
for seven churches, but that they also under the guise of
the seven churches are directed towards the needs of Christians
in general and the needs of individual Christians in every
church, it will, I think, at once appear that it would not occur
to John to send the book with but a single letter to each church.
The seven letters are a mosaic pattern of Christian life
and belong together. No one will imagine, further, that only

those letters and not the book of Revelation were to be sent to the churches, for that verse says that John is to write in the book what he sees, that is to say, the visions which follow, and send it to the churches. The short letters are not visions, but messages. And, besides, word would have passed quickly from the first church that received the roll, had there been but a single one, and the other six churches would not have wished to wait for weeks and months to know what was addressed to them as well as to that first church. We must therefore suppose that John prepared at once seven copies of the Revelation and sent one to each church. Should any one insist upon it that John as the author merely wrote one copy and then left the book to its fate, no one would conceive it possible that the seven churches did not have copies made at once.

We therefore are now after this long discussion in a different position from that which we held in the case of Romans. There we saw at the first and for a while but one letter, one book, in the hands of one church. Here we have a book in seven copies addressed to seven churches of varying moods and characters. The situation is slightly different from the point of view of the criticism of the text. For Romans there was, so far as we know, for a time but one authentic copy which made its definite impression of words and phrases and paragraphs upon the minds of the Christians in a large city. Many of the Romans will have known very exactly just what the Epistle said touching one point and another. Here there are seven authentic copies, if John himself sent out the seven. And if the churches had the copies made, there are almost at once seven copies of the book. That will of itself have had perhaps an effect upon the exactness of the text. Copying a book looks easy, just as translation seems easy to people who know nothing about it. It is difficult to copy a common letter of four pages straightway and quickly without making a mistake. After one has discovered how easy it is to make mistakes in copying, he will be ready to believe that it is not beyond the realm of possibility that the text even in these first seven copies showed trifling differences. We leave the book of Revelation for the moment and turn to other books.

There remain the four Gospels and the book of Acts.

Matthew, Mark, and Luke with Acts all show in one way a
certain resemblance in their origin to the book of Revelation.
Every one of them was written upon the basis of an earlier
book, or of two or three earlier books. But they all used the
earlier matter in, it appears, a much more independent way
than Revelation used its basis. They gave more of their
own and impressed their personality upon the books more
decidedly. Mark was doubtless written first. It is the smallest
of the four books. It may very well have been written at Rome,
and may also, as ever busy tradition relates, have had some
connection with recollections of Peter's which he related to
Mark. Yet if it had such a connection we are nevertheless
not able to lay our pointer upon the words that depend upon
Peter's memory. Paul's Epistles were sent to the churches
here and there, the Revelation was given to the seven churches.
It would be very interesting to know to whom Mark gave his
Gospel. Perhaps to the church at Rome.

But to whomsoever he gave it, it probably met almost at
once with an accident, a bad accident. I think it most likely
that in the very first copy of it, which was probably on papyrus,
the last two or three columns were broken off or torn off or
cut off and lost. We shall come back to that at another
place (see pp. 511–513).

Matthew's Gospel, or better, the Gospel according to Matthew,
was written in its current form by someone who had Mark's Gospel
and perhaps a book by Matthew, and it may be still some other
book in his hands. He was, this author was, himself by origin an
ardent Jew, and kept referring to the Old Testament. But that
does not suffice to tell us where he wrote or to whom he gave his
Gospel. Perhaps he wrote somewhere in Asia Minor. Asia
Minor, that Paul had so vigorously missionised, was a stronghold
of Christianity. Both Mark and Matthew are likely to have
been at once copied in order to be carried to other churches
besides the one that first received each. There was nothing
in either work to limit its address or its use to a single
community.

In the case of Luke we find a pleasing personal turn. We
might say that the author was too modest to offer his work
to a church or to the Church in general, but ventured to
send it to his friend Theophilus, always supposing that this friend

the God-Lover or the one Loved-of-God was not a roundabout
address to any and every good Christian. Luke is so evidently
a skilled writer, that we must suppose him to have caused his
book to be copied a number of times in spite of the address
to a private person. Where he first issued it we do not know.
The former suggestion of Asia Minor for Matthew might very
well also be made for Luke. The book of Acts Luke wrote
doubtless a few years later. Now the three former books were
crystallisations of the gospel that was preached. They are
connected with each other through their basis, through the
writings used in their composition, so that they in general place
before our eyes the same phase of and largely the same incidents
in the life of Jesus and the same words of Jesus, and they
therefore support each other. The churches of the latter
part of the first century that learned of the existence of these
Gospels will have desired to have them, so far as their means
permitted them to buy the rolls. We are forced to suppose
that they were often copied and were sent hither and thither
among the churches, and in particular to the churches near
the place at which they first appeared, and to the churches in
the chief cities. These larger churches both heard more quickly
by means of the frequent travellers of the issue of new books,
and were more capable of paying for good copies of them.

It seems to me not to be reasonable to suppose that these books
lived a retired, violet like existence, remaining long unknown
to the mass of the churches. It does not seem to me to agree
with the first principles of scientific hypothesis to imagine that
these Gospels did not exist in towns from which we have received
no treatise quoting them. We cannot look for inscriptions for
every town in which Christians had Christian books, giving
every ten years from 70 to 200 the catalogue of those at
command. That means for textual criticism that we must
assume before the end of the first century the widespread
existence of a number of copies of Matthew, Mark, and Luke.
The interest in the book of Acts will have been by no means
so great as the interest in the Gospels, and it will not have
been copied anything like so often.

The Gospel of John stands by itself. The question as to
its author cannot here be treated at length. I am of the opinion
either that John the Twelve-Apostle dictated it to a disciple

shortly before his death, or that some such disciple who had been most intimately allied to John wrote the Gospel soon after the death of the apostle.   Now it is interesting to observe that in this case we have a tradition that upon the face of it does not look improbable.   Tradition says that John dictated the Gospel to a disciple of his named Prochorus.   We see this tradition given pictorially in a clear way in many a manuscript containing this Gospel.   In one of the upper corners, usually in the one at the right hand of the picture, either a hand or rays come forth from a cloud to indicate the presence and activity of the Divine Spirit.   John stands before us raising his left hand towards that divine manifestation in order to receive the heavenly inspiration, and stretching his right hand down toward Prochorus, who is seated at the left hand and writing the Gospel: " In the beginning was the Word."   There is nothing like this that often occurs in the manuscripts for the other evangelists.   I know of nothing thus far that should make it more impossible for Prochorus to have written the Fourth Gospel at John's dictation than for Tertius to have written Romans at Paul's dictation. But we have no positive knowledge of the fact.

This Gospel has, further, another peculiarity in reference to its authorship, for it contains at the close one (or two) verses evidently added by another hand.   John 21^{24} (and ^{25}) look as if they had been added by the chief men in the church which first received this Gospel.   In modern phrase, these would be the elders or the clergy of the church in which John worshipped.   In the verses before these the Twelve-Apostle John has been mentioned as the disciple whom Jesus loved, about whom Peter asked. Thereupon the twenty-fourth verse adds: " This is the disciple who testifies touching these things, and who wrote these things : and we know that his testimony is true."   The twenty-fifth verse says : " And there are many other things which Jesus did, which, if they were written one by one, I do not think that the world itself would hold the books written."   Now this verse might be from John.   That twenty-fourth verse might have been originally added by the elders at the side of the column near v.^{23} and then have been put into the column itself before v.^{25} by a later scribe.   Those words are almost like a receipt for the Gospel on the part of the community.   For textual criticism this declaration gives in a way a surety for careful attention to the words of the Gospel in that first church. We shall find that the text of this Gospel is in some ways in better condition than that of Matthew, Mark, and Luke, because it stood alone, and because it was not so much dependent upon written sources.

Ancient Handwriting.

It is not uninteresting to ask what kind of writing was probably used in the first copies of those New Testament books. At that time the main kinds of handwriting were two : uncial writing and cursive writing. We could call them capitals and a running hand. The capitals were used for books that were well gotten up, for fine editions. In such books the words were all written in capital letters, word joined on to word without break, much as if we were to WRITEINENGLISHTHUS. It was then easy enough to tell what the letters were, but it required a quick eye and a good head to tell quickly at some places just how the words were to be divided off, what belonged together and what was to be separated. At the first moment a Christian, thinking of the pretty editions of the Bible that we have, would say that Tertius when he wrote Paul's letter to the Romans must surely have used these large and fine letters. But those who know what people at that day were likely to write would say no. That was a letter that Tertius was writing, even if it was a very large letter. It was an essay, a treatise, an article ; but it was the habit then, as it often has been since, upon occasion to write such an essay in the form of a letter. And such a letter would not be written in the formal stiff capitals, but in the running hand. A running hand was just what the name says, handwriting written at a run, written in a hurry, as so many people write to-day. The letters were at first, we might say, just like those capital letters. But the swiftness of the strokes had impaired the form of the letters. If we look at many a handwriting that we see to-day and ask how much a *d* or an *m* or a *u* looks like the printed form of those letters or like the forms given in copy-books, we may understand that in the same way the writing that Tertius wrote in all probability contained many strange looking letters. The letters will often have been written close together, and all joined together without respect to the division between words. We

cannot at all tell how well Tertius was able to write. We do not
know whether he wrote a clear hand or whether he wrote a bad
hand. The chances are that he wrote well. That is, it may be,
the reason why he, and not Timothy or Lucius or Jason or
Sosipater, who were all there at the time, was asked to do the
writing.

From what we have already seen, it is clear that we cannot
look for the originals of the books of the New Testament among
the books of our libraries. One could dream of possibilities.
We might fancy that one of the little letters of John had been
slipped into some box or laid away in a diptych, a little double
wax tablet like two slates hinged together, and that the box or
the diptych was to be discovered to-morrow by the Austrian
scholar who is unearthing Ephesus. But there is not the least
likelihood of anything of that kind. The probability is that every
vestige of the original writings had vanished long before the time
of Eusebius, the most of the writings before the year 200, and
many of them before the year 100. A knavish fellow brought
some leaves of papyrus to England more than forty years ago
and sold them to an English merchant who trusted his word for
it that they were out of the original Matthew and the original
James and the original Jude. The material really was papyrus.
There was upon the leaves a real writing of a late century that
had nothing to do with the times of the New Testament. And
then there were some big but rather dim letters upon the papyrus
containing passages from Matthew and James and Jude, and
the rascal who sold them declared that these passages were a
previous writing on the papyrus, and had been written in the first
century of our era by those three authors. It was not strange
that the rich man who believed this paid a large sum to gain
possession of such wonderful treasures. When, however, the
experts came to examine the leaves they saw at once that the
pretended old writing was a mere piece of cheating. They could
clearly see that this writing, which was alleged to be of the first
century, had not at all been written at first upon the papyrus,
before that very much younger writing, but that it was on top of
the writing centuries younger. That man had written it there
himself to make money   He was really a very learned man, and
it was a great pity that he in this as in some other cases proved
untrustworthy. We cannot expect to find remains of the original

copies of the books of the New Testament. God did not hand these books down from heaven. He caused men to write them. And when each book had lived its day He allowed it to vanish away like other frail human fabrics. He did not have regard to the letter but to the spirit, not to the outside of the book or the roll but to the inside of it in the inward sense, not to something perishable but to something eternal.

II.

PARCHMENT.

WE saw that at Rome the time had come at which the leaders of the Christians there were persuaded that if they did not wish to lose the letter of Paul to them they must have it copied. The question that now arises refers to the way in which it was copied. If the church had been a poor little group of men who could only with great difficulty scrape together a small amount of money, the new letter would have been to all intents and purposes the counterpart of the old letter. It would have been written on papyrus again and in a running hand. It would have been written upon papyrus because that was the common writing material, the paper, of that day, whether at Alexandria or at Antioch or at Rome. If a man put a handbill up at Rome, he wrote it on a big piece of coarse papyrus. If he wrote a delicate note to his wife or his mother, he wrote it on a little piece of fine papyrus. Papyrus was their paper.

But I do not think it is probable that the Romans caused this Epistle to be copied on papyrus. The church at Rome had then many members. It was perhaps the largest and most wealthy Christian community in existence. If any church could afford to have a nice book written, it was the church at Rome. It was not a mere matter of pride or luxury, however, and not merely the desire, the very proper desire, to do honour to a letter of the Apostle Paul, that was calculated to lead them not to use papyrus. The papyrus was not very durable : we have seen why it was not. As time went on the Christians must have felt that they could depend less upon the immediate return of Jesus, that they must arrange the Church and its belongings for a longer stay in this wicked world. They still wrote as we saw above in the letter of Clement : "The church living in this foreign world at Rome," and they still looked to heaven as their real home. Yet they began to treat themselves more calmly, to make themselves more "at home" here. That meant for the books of the New Testament that they must put them upon the most durable book-material that they could find.

Now they might have had them written on leather. The Jews in ancient times often had their sacred books on leather. Leather is, however, not very nice for books. It is too thick and too heavy and too dark-coloured. The written words are soon not much blacker than the leather itself. There is something better than leather, and that is parchment. Parchment is called in Greek "pergamini" after the city Pergamus where it is said to have been invented. I suppose it was merely very well made there, so that the name of the city was given to the best kind. To make parchment, usually sheepskins or goatskins or calfskins are used. The skin is stretched out tight and dried, and then scraped off on both sides and then rubbed with chalk. In the East I am inclined to think that goatskins are most frequently used, when they can be had. They are better than sheepskins, because there is not so much oily matter in them. We shall return to parchment again and tell more about it.

Probably the Romans had Paul's letter copied off on to a parchment roll. Now they knew how long it was, and they could tell how long the roll must be. The textual critic must know all about book-making, not for races but for literature. We are at Rome. In this great city there were plenty of well-trained scribes. It is quite likely that some scribes had already become Christians. If not, there would be Christians who knew scribes upon whom they could rely, who would treat the Christian books carefully. The scribes were paid according to the amount of writing of course, and they often gave the measure of a book at the end of it. Then the man who had ordered the book would know how much he had to pay. And if anyone wished for a new copy he could at once tell the scribe how long it was, and learn the price. In England and America a printer who sets up a book is paid by the number of *m*s, which are called ems, because *m* is square and therefore makes a good measure. The Greek scribes were paid by the "line," called a stichos. It would never have done to leave the measuring "line" to vary according to the book. Therefore once for all, for all kinds of books, whether sacred or profane, whether prose or poetry, a line that was about as long as a line or verse of Homer, a hexameter line, was used. Such a line contains about thirty-six letters on an average. If a trained scribe were summoned to write Romans off, he would count the number of lines and then write them down at the end of the Epistle. If the Epistle has remained just as he had it before him, he must have written "nine hundred and twenty or fifty lines" or thereabouts. And this trained scribe will now probably not have used the running hand for his work. The Epistle was no longer a letter that someone wrote here and sent thither. It was a little book that these Christians wished to keep and read. The scribe wrote it doubtless in pretty capital letters, in comparatively narrow columns. That would be much clearer and easier to read, whether in private or in the meetings in church. The scribe we shall assume wrote the Epistle anew. If some simple Christian who could only write the running hand really wrote it off the first time, then the trained scribe came later. He came. He could not but come, so soon as the church wished for a pretty copy.

We must here mention another matter in passing, something also connected with book-making. There is one of the most interesting problems in the realm of New Testament research that attaches to the last two chapters of the Epistle to the Romans. The problem itself belongs rather to the criticism of the books than to the criticism of the text. But one or two of the solutions of the problem rest upon a possibility in textual criticism, upon a possibility in the copying off of books. For my own part I am inclined to accept in the case of these two chapters, and I may say especially in the case of the last, the sixteenth chapter, a solution which belongs precisely at this point, at which we are leaving the original letter as Tertius wrote it and passing on to a new copy written by an unknown scribe. Here we must be short. It is not impossible that Romans at first closed with chapter fourteen. If that was the case, then these two other chapters were probably written separately by Paul, and at Rome placed for good keeping in the roll of Romans. It must not be forgotten that, among the accidents which occasionally happened to papyrus rolls, the tearing across the whole roll sometimes took place. This circumstance would make it easy for a scribe to suppose on finding a couple of loose pieces that they were a part of the Epistle. He may even have thought that the original author of the Epistle had written, or dictated, them and laid them in the roll without taking the trouble or having the paste to stick them on to the end of the roll. It is, however, not even positively necessary to imagine a misunderstanding of that kind. It could have been done in all honesty and of set purpose.

Let us go back to Rome. The leader of the church who handed the roll to the scribe may have known very well that the pieces of papyrus, on which what we call the fifteenth and sixteenth chapters were written, had been received by the church apart from Romans. But he may have said: "Here are these two short communications from Paul. If I leave them lying around they will soon be lost. The best thing will be to write them into the new roll at the end of Romans. Here, scribe, copy these at the end of the roll. They are from Paul too." A Christian could then very well have spoken and acted thus. That would have been for him a thoroughly practical and perfectly proper way of disposing of such small letters. It was no forgery. Paul had written it all. And this Christian did not for a moment think of the critics in coming centuries who would rack their brains to discover what was the matter with these chapters. And even from the advanced standpoint of to-day we must confess that if this really be the state of affairs it does not do the least harm. No one's salvation, and I think no one's peace of mind, depends upon our knowing just how these chapters came to stand where they do (see pp. 521–526).

We have now reached the point at which Romans has been copied off in a literary hand on parchment. We pass over a few years. It is not easy to say just how many. The church at Rome has one by one at last come into possession of a number of the Epistles of Paul. Many or all of them may have reached Rome on the cheaper paper, papyrus, and written in the common running hand. It is not impossible that the church caused them some day to be copied together into one large roll. In like manner the four Gospels were at first on separate rolls and may later have been put into one roll.

We have fastened our gaze on Rome. There we have the most favourable conditions possible for the careful preservation of the books and for their re-copying whenever it may be desirable. At Corinth, at Smyrna, at Antioch, at Alexandria the general conditions for Christian books are not so very different from those found in Rome. Every one of these cities had a prosperous church, and that church was, like the one at

Rome, Greek, and used the New Testament in its original language. Such large churches were, we may be sure, the first to gather the books together. In smaller towns and in the villages, so far as Christianity had reached them, the circumstances were in many varying degrees different from those in the cities named. The cities that any of the Twelve-Apostles or that Paul had visited were in name and certainly to a large extent in fact ahead of the others, particularly those to which the apostles had written Epistles. They prided themselves on their distinction, and the other towns looked up to them with feelings akin to envy. In the villages the number of New Testament books at command must long have remained minimal. Often the copy of an Epistle or of a Gospel that a preacher brought with him from a neighbouring town, in order to read from it during the Sunday service, may have been the only such book that the Christians there saw from one week to another. In some cases we may hold it likely that the village churches received old and damaged rolls which the city churches had cast aside on securing new and better copies, precisely as it sometimes to-day happens that city churches send old Bibles or hymn-books or prayer-books to churches on the frontiers of civilisation. In other cases it is sure to have come to pass that Christians who could write but a very poor script succeeded in borrowing a roll and in copying a book for their town or village.

There was no standstill in all this. Everything was moving on. The mind's eye might have seen the books gradually going out and gradually multiplying from place to place like the leaven going through the lump, like a lichen spreading over a rock, like an ivy covering a wall. To this slight sketch of the growth in the number of the manuscripts of the books of the New Testament nothing need be added until the fourth century. There came now and then indeed, sad to say, times of reverse. A governor of a province or the ruler of a city occasionally took it into his head to check the progress of Christian effort by forcing the Christians under him to give up to him the writings which they so much cherished. The various cases differed much from each other. Sometimes they were told to bring their books, and the officials did not scrutinise the number or the character of the books handed over. In other places the officials rudely demanded all books, and searched

21

every nook and corner to find them. Yet in spite of such reverses the word was sowed broadcast. Such times of reverse served to sieve out the nominal Christians from the real Christians, the lovers of and the doers of the word from those who only "heard" it.

Leaf-Books.

As we approach the fourth century I must describe a theory of mine. It is a mere theory, a hypothesis, a fancy as to what may have happened. Should we some day or other come to know the facts, they will perhaps not agree with the theory at all. For the moment, however, the facts lie hidden and the theory may boldly stalk abroad. We have already remarked that the books in the times of which we have spoken were not leaf-books, not squares or parallelograms an inch or a few inches thick with a number of leaves to be turned over, but were rolls. At the close of the fourth century the books appear to have been almost altogether leaf-books, at least that is my impression. We do not yet know at what precise moment the change from rolls to leaf-books was made. It was a great change. How different a library of rolls would look from a library of leaf-books! How much more easy it is to hold, to read, to find anything in a leaf-book from what it is to hold a roll, to read it, or to find anything in it! At present, with all that I have heard and seen, I am inclined to think that this change was made about the end of the third or the beginning of the fourth century, or ± 300. We do not know. That is the best guess I can now make. A new papyrus may to-morrow show that the change came earlier.

The theory touches the person or persons who made this change, who invented leaf-books. I am ready to believe that leaf-books are due to a Christian; that a Christian was the first one who felt the need of a change, and who effected the change. The reason for the theory is this. No one had such need as the Christian to seek different passages in great numbers in widely separated places in large books. There were several classes of scholars. There were heathen classical scholars, who had a comparatively limited library of Greek and Latin works, among which Plato and Aristotle were perhaps with Homer the ones represented by the largest number of rolls. There were Jewish philosophers and

Jewish rabbis who both dealt with the Old Testament books, the philosophers also using the writings of the classical world. And finally appeared our latest generation the Christians, who knew and used the writings of the classical world, and who were compelled in debate with Jews and with heathen and with Christians to turn swiftly from Genesis to Revelation, from First John to Daniel, from Isaiah to Paul. No others needed to turn to so many books and so quickly. Here is the hold for the theory. I think this difficulty may have brought some Christian scholar, proceeding from the heathen diptychs or double wax tablets, to suggest or to prepare leaf-books. I am further ready to believe that two old manuscripts of the Bible, which we have now in Europe, were among the earlier leaf-books.

Sides of Parchment.

Now, however, that we are coming to the leaf-books we must mention another thing. Parchment has two sides. It is skin. It has a side that was on the outside of the animal and was covered with goat's hair or sheep's wool. And it has a side that was against the flesh, that covered the ribs. We may call them the hair side and the flesh side. The hair side is in comparison with the flesh side of a darker shade, and when the parchment grows old the difference in colour is more clearly visible, particularly in parchment made out of sheepskin. In the second place, the hair side is rougher than the flesh side. This difference is often very slight, but it is usually there. Once I was speaking with a parchment maker, and I asked him which side of a certain piece of fine parchment was which. He said he could not tell without a careful examination. I took hold of it and said to him what I thought the sides were, and it proved when he examined it that I had felt right. The parchment maker had never tried to tell the sides by feeling. That was not of the least use in his business. But I had for years been feeling parchment leaves just for this purpose. I do not doubt that some parchments would be too fine to be thus distinguished by feeling, but I am not sure. I question whether I could feel the difference between the sides in the great Vatican manuscript; I cannot remember about it as to this point. In the third place, the hair side is not only darker and rougher, but it is also more thirsty than the flesh side, and it drinks up the ink much more eagerly and drinks it in more thoroughly.   The result is that if a manuscript has grown old and the leaves have been much rubbed against each other or rubbed by men's hands, the writing on the flesh side may in the places that have been most rubbed vanish away completely so that no vestige of the letters can be seen.   On the hair side, on the contrary, the ink sinks in so deep into the pores of the skin that it is often no easy matter for a scribe to erase a word on it with his knife.

The reason we have to speak of the sides of the parchment is this : the quires are made according to a certain law.   Even if it be not important, I like to tell about this law because I discovered it.   A quire in a Greek manuscript of respectable family consists, like a quire in an ordinary modern octavo printed book, of four double leaves or eight single leaves.   It is called a four-er, and the name usual is a quaternion ; but those ten Latin letters say no more than the six Saxon letters : fourer, only you must know that the latter word comes from four or else you will not pronounce it right.   And these eight leaves must begin with a flesh side and end with a flesh side, and there must be two flesh sides in the middle of the quire, and every two pages that open out together must both be flesh sides or both be hair sides.   If a man does not know the law, he is likely to make a poor manuscript.   But infringements of the rule that the sides, the pages, that come together must be both alike are rare.   We have at Leipzig a small manuscript made without regard to this law, and it looks ugly, ill-bred, and generally disreputable.   If a roll be made of parchment, the flesh side must be the inside of the roll, the side that receives the writing.   For it is the most beautiful side, makes the best appearance, even if it does not retain the ink so well.

It is further to be remarked that if a Greek manuscript does not observe the above law as to the number of leaves in the quire, if instead of being a fourer it be a fiver, a quinio (not, as the books often write, a quinternio), made of five double leaves and therefore having twenty pages, or have any other number of leaves regularly in the quires, then it is not of pure Greek origin.   This conclusion is especially justified if the manuscript be well gotten up, like that great Vatican manuscript which was mentioned a moment ago, and which shows others signs of a non-Grecian descent. Indeed we can take up that very point precisely here. That beautiful manuscript has very old leaf-numbers. That is not Greek. Greek manuscripts do not number their leaves. A Greek manuscript numbers only its quires. If one happens to find numbers for the leaves in a Greek manuscript, that is to say numbers that belong to ancient times, that have not been put in in the West and in the fifteenth to the twentieth century, he may be sure that a stranger has written them in.

Parchment, to go back to the material written on, is of different thicknesses, just as paper is. But it is not possible, as I used to think it was, for the parchment makers to pare down or grind off or do anything else to make the parchment thinner. A certain skin, every skin, has its body of parchment, if the expression is intelligible. The sharp scrapers of the workmen go just so far and not farther. If they go beyond the proper point the skin is spoiled. Therefore a fine thin parchment can only be made from a thin skin, and that thin skin can only be a young skin. To go at once to the greatest extreme known to me, there is in the City Library at Leipzig a manuscript of the Latin Bible written upon parchment made from the skin of unborn lambs. It is exquisite parchment, and thinner than most thin papers are, I should think. On the other hand, we sometimes see parchment that is very thick and stiff, almost like so much pasteboard.

Parchment was really necessary for the leaf-books as contrasted with papyrus or with leather. If a leaf-book were made out of leather, the leaves would be likely to curl over at the top when the book was opened upon the reading-desk. The parchment leaves are usually more stiff and lie or stand well. Papyrus would have given no trouble in this respect, for it was stiff enough. But it is at once clear that papyrus with those little fibres so easily broken would not be fitted to stand the opening and shutting and the turning over of the leaves, but must if much used soon go to pieces. Parchment was, on the contrary, very durable, and could be bent and used at will. Reasonable use of a parchment book has no appreciable effect upon its condition during long years. The defects in parchment manuscripts are sometimes due to rough usage on the part of those who read them, but they are usually due to outrageous treatment on the part of ignorant people who have thrown them about and trodden on them and torn them. Good parchment was, I think, dearer than papyrus, but it was much more beautiful and indefinitely more durable, and when the rolls were exchanged for leaf-books the day of papyrus for literature began to wane.

Constantine's Manuscripts.

We now take our stand in the fourth century, and Christianity had up to the fourth century been growing apace in spite of all efforts to repress it. At last an emperor determined to be a Christian. There are people who think that this emperor, Constantine, took up Christianity rather as a matter of business than as a matter of religion, that it was State policy and not devotional feeling that guided his steps. Be that as it may, it is not easy for us after nearly sixteen centuries to go back to the city which he renamed after himself as Constantine's City, Constantinople, and try his heart and reins; and he did his royal duty towards the Bible at least in one case. It was in the year 331. Eusebius, the bishop of Cæsarea in Palestine, was a very learned man, a great book man, and an active prelate. He wrote a life of Constantine in which he displayed no little skill as a flatterer. In that year, 331, as Eusebius tells us in this life, Constantine conceived the idea of making a great present to the chief churches near him. He wrote to Eusebius about it, for Eusebius was not only very learned, but he was also the bishop of the city with the most celebrated Christian library. I like to think that that library contained many of Origen's own personal books, for he lived and taught there for years. Constantine knew then that first-class biblical manuscripts were there, and first-class scribes to copy new ones. He told Eusebius to have fifty fine copies of the Bible made, and to send them to him at Constantinople. He promised even to reward handsomely the deacon whom he asked Eusebius to send to Constantinople as a guard for the costly manuscripts on the long journey. It would be very nice if we could find some of those manuscripts.

Unfortunately Eusebius knew nothing of the burning wishes of textual critics in the twentieth century, and did not describe these manuscripts in detail. He told just one thing about them, and we, alas! do not know what his words mean. We can only guess at their meaning. He says that he wrote them by threes and fours, or "three-wise and four-wise." Eusebius knew what he meant. Would that we did. This must have been a technical expression in making books. Some scholars have thought that Eusebius referred to the quires, and that he said that he had written them on quires of three double leaves and on quires of four double leaves, on ternions and quaternions. This suggestion does not commend itself to me, for two reasons. In the first place, so far as we know, no Greek manuscript was ever made up in quires of three double leaves. We have seen that the rule was four double leaves. And, in the second place, the quires and the number of leaves in the quires are things that do not strike the eye when a man looks at a book. If a man to-day takes up an uncut printed book he may see the quires in a certain individuality, but even thus the number of leaves in a quire does not impress itself upon him unless he directs his mind to that point. But the Greek manuscripts were never uncut, and the moment a volume was bound, the man who opened it at hazard would in no way be forced to see how many leaves there happened to be in the quires. My theory about it is that "by threes and fours" attaches to the number of columns on a page. If a man opens a book he cannot help seeing instantly whether the page before his eyes has one or two or three or four columns. I think that Eusebius meant to say or did say by those mystic words that he had the fifty Bibles written in pages of three columns and in pages of four columns.

It is a practical reason that leads me to this theory. If I am not mistaken, we have one or two of these manuscripts to-day in our hands, or, to put it still more tentatively, we have one or two manuscripts that may as well as not have been among these fifty that were sent to Constantine from Cæsarea by Eusebius. We have two manuscripts of the Bible written in large part, one in four, the other in three columns. The poetical books of the Old Testament do not count, because they had to be written in two columns on account of their verses. And these two manuscripts are palæographically and theologically apparently to be referred to the fourth century. Perhaps they made that journey with the deacon from Cæsarea to Constantinople. No record is known of the churches to which Constantine gave the new Bibles. Those in Constantinople itself probably got the greater part of them, since Constantine mentioned them in writing to Eusebius. Yet he may have sent one or another to a more distant church of importance in order to honour the bishop who presided over it.

III.

LARGE LETTER GREEK MANUSCRIPTS.

The Codex Sinaiticus.

THE manuscript written in four columns is the Codex Sinaiticus, known by the Hebrew letter Aleph א, and we now turn our attention to it. In the year 1844, Constantine Tischendorf, a privatdozent then in the university at Leipzig, visited the monastery of St. Catharine at Mount Sinai. While there he found in a waste basket forty-three leaves of an old manuscript, and the monks let him have them. He also saw some more leaves that they refused to give him, but he copied one of them off. People have sometimes derided the story of his finding the leaves in waste basket. They did not know how manuscripts used to be treated in the East. These forty-three leaves Tischendorf brought to Leipzig and named them the Codex Friderico-Augustanus, after the King of Saxony, Frederick Augustus. These leaves contain parts of the Old Testament. Of course, Tischendorf did not say where he had found them, for he wished to return and get the other leaves. Nine years later he returned to the monastery, in the year 1853, but he only found a fragment of Genesis. He thought that someone else had secured the remainder. As, however, several years passed by and no one published the text of any such manuscript, he again went to Mount Sinai in the year 1859 to look for it.

He spent some days there but could not find it. He had already ordered the camels to be ready to take him away upon the following morning. The great steward of the monastery asked him to come into his room to pay him a visit. While he was sitting there the steward took down from the shelf some old leaves that he had lying there and showed them to him. He saw at once that this was just what he had been looking for all these years, save that there was much more of it than he had supposed to exist. That was not a disagreeable difference. The steward let Tischendorf take it to his room, and he found that it contained the whole of the New Testament, much of the Old Testament, and the letter of Barnabas, which up to that time was not known in Greek, and the Shepherd of Hermas. He spent the night copying the letter of Barnabas, for he did not know whether he should ever see the manuscript after the next morning, and he thought it a duty to Christendom to secure the original text of this letter. The next morning Tischendorf tried to get the monks to let him have the manuscript. They voted upon it, but there was a majority of one against him, so that he could not have it. Thereupon he left the monastery and returned to Cairo, where the monks of Sinai have also a small monastery.

We see now how absurd it is when people say that Tischendorf took the manuscript away from the monastery by stealth. For he did not take it away from the monastery at all. He went away from the monastery and left it there. At Cairo the head monk sent an Arab sheik to Mount Sinai to bring the manuscript to Cairo. The sheik brought it and gave it to the monks, not to Tischendorf. Tischendorf had a conference with the monks, and it was agreed that they should let him have it quire by quire to copy off. He was to give a receipt for eight leaves, the four double leaves of the fourer, the quaternio, and when he brought them back he was to have the next eight. Two Germans who happened to be at Cairo, an apothecary and a bookseller, helped him copy, and Tischendorf revised most carefully what they copied. Just then the highest place of authority among the monks of Sinai was vacant. The monks did not feel as if they could dispose of the manuscript until they had a new abbot. The abbot has the title of archbishop. The election took a great deal of time. In between Tischendorf went to Palestine. He had discovered the manuscript on the 4th of February 1859, and it was not until the 28th of September of the same year that it was placed in his hands.

So far removed were the facts from the favourite description of Tischendorf's envyers, who think that he slipped it into his breast-pocket in February and vanished unseen from the monastery. Try to slip into your pocket unseen three hundred and forty-six leaves of parchment which are forty-three centimetres long and thirty-seven centimetres broad. But besides that, on the 28th of September 1859 Tischendorf did not take it away from the monks at Cairo by stealth, with or without the necessary and necessarily gigantic breast-pocket. For it was given to him in all due form by the head monk in the presence of the others who were at Cairo, and in the presence of the Russian consul, who, of course, made an official minute of the whole proceedings. The monks delivered over the manuscript to Tischendorf in order that he should take it to Leipzig and publish it, and then present it to the Russian emperor in the name of the monks.

According to Western habits in reference to presents, that would be enough. If the monks sent it as a present to the emperor, very well. That is the end of the thing. But we know from the Bible that in the East a gift demands a return, and that this return may under given circumstances be extraordinarily like a good round price paid for the nominal gift. The twenty-third chapter of Genesis shows us how Ephron gave Abraham the field with the double cave in it as a family tomb, but Abraham paid him four hundred ounces of silver for it nevertheless. After Tischendorf had published the manuscript he carried it to Russia according to the bargain, and gave it to the Czar at Zarskoe Selo on the 10th of November, in Russian the 29th of October, 1862. But the Russian emperor, who had such a number of Eastern peoples under his rule, knew all about "presents" from the East, and it did not occur to him to put this manuscript into his library before he had arranged for the return present. Instead of that he sent it to the Russian Ministry of Foreign Affairs, so that it might remain as a foreign object until the necessary business arrangements had been made. At that time the journey from St. Petersburg to Mount Sinai was not so easy as it is to-day, and consumed much more time. Further, it used to be the case—modern diplomacy has doubtless more speedy methods —that diplomatic agents moved very slowly, took things up slowly, wrote and copied letters slowly, and sent them away most slowly of all. And, on the other hand, the monks of the East can far outdo all diplomatists in slow movement. An Eastern monk thinks he is doing an enormous day's work if within twenty-four hours he does as much as an ordinary European would do in twenty minutes.

In consequence of this it was not until the year 1869 that the business was brought to an end, and the manuscript was carried from the Ministry of Foreign Affairs and placed in the Imperial Library at St. Petersburg, where it now is. We must be very precise in all this, because it is constantly said, and has more than once been printed, that Tischendorf or the Russian Government promised to pay for the manuscript, but finally did not do so. Sometimes the narrative takes the dramatic form that a sum was offered but indignantly refused, and that the monks demanded the return of the manuscript. That is all wide of the mark. The business was regularly brought to a business-like close.

The monks at Mount Sinai received seven thousand rubles and the monks at Cairo received two thousand rubles, say six thousand seven hundred and fifty dollars, or more than thirteen hundred and fifty pounds sterling. That was for that time a high price to pay for the manuscript. So far from refusing to take the money, the monks took it and gave receipts for it which are in the hands of the Russian Government. And that was not all. The decorations referred to above are valued in the East even more highly than they are in the decoration-loving circles in Western Europe, and the monks received a number of these decorations.

The explanation for the fact that the monks give such totally incorrect accounts of the acquisition of this manuscript by Tischendorf, or to put it differently, of the gift of this manuscript to the Emperor of Russia, is to be found, I think, in two circumstances. On the one hand, as I found during a stay of eight weeks at Mount Sinai, there does not appear to be a shadow of anything like what may be called a firm and interested tradition in the monastery. The history of the monastery, apart from one or two general statements for the benefit of visiting pilgrims, did not seem to have any charm for the monks. It was of no importance to them that I noted in the history of the monastery occasional points, dates which I found in manuscripts. The result of this is that no one in the monastery, as far as I could find, had the least knowledge of what had passed the forty and odd years ago when Tischendorf was there. On the other hand, not clashing in the least with the foregoing, the monks think over the matter for themselves, connecting it with what they hear, but do not understand, about the value of the manuscript, and then project their fancy, as to what they from their present standpoint would do if the case were presented to them, into the past. Hereupon they assert with all the naïveness of ignorance that their predecessors did this and that, which in fact they did not do at all.

This manuscript is in its appearance, when it is thrown open, much like a piece of an old roll. If someone could give us eighty-six centimetres of a corresponding parchment roll it would look just so. The columns are very narrow. In a roll it was convenient to have the columns narrow. For then it was not necessary to open so much of the roll at once, to fill out so much space with it when reading or when copying a quotation from it. The fact that the columns are so narrow makes it appear more likely that this manuscript is among the earlier large books that were written on leaves instead of in a roll. It is as if the scribes still clung to their accustomed narrow columns for a fine book. At the same time, if what was said about Eusebius' use of the terms " by threes and by fours " for three and four columns on a page should happen to be right, it would go to show that the leaves in books, instead of a roll, were not just then new, that they had been in use for awhile. Therefore I am inclined at present to suppose that the change from rolls to leaf-books was made about the year ± 300 as above stated.

Of the 346½ leaves, the New Testament and Barnabas with Hermas fill 147½. The columns contain forty-eight lines. The parchment is good and is fairly thin. Tischendorf thought that it was made from antelope skins. I do not know with certainty what parchment made from antelope skins would look like. I fear that Tischendorf argued from the gentle grace of a swift antelope to a thin skin. Perhaps the size of the leaves led him to think of a larger animal. There can scarcely have been anyone in the East capable of telling him anything else than fanciful imaginings about what skins gave what parchments. It is hard to believe that there are no parchment makers to be found in Cairo or at Damascus, but I tried in vain to find them. At Jerusalem I discovered a Jewish parchment maker, but it is my impression that he was not a native of Jerusalem ; he had a German name, and was probably from Austria or Russia. The point is that there appears to be no one there who can say what kind of parchment comes from what kind of skin. And then, if I were to judge of antelope skin from the vigour and strength of the animals, I should not be inclined to suppose that it would be especially thin and fine; but that is sheer theory; I know nothing about it.

But a practical reason seems to me to stand against the use of antelope skins. Here are three hundred and eighty-nine and a half leaves, for we must, of course, add the forty-three leaves of the Codex Friderico-Augustanus which are from the same volume, and as a great many leaves of the Bible are further lacking, the volume must have been much larger. Neither at Sinai nor at Jerusalem nor in Egypt, so far as I can see, is there any reason to suppose that the supply of antelopes was such as to make it easy to obtain so many leaves of antelope parchment within a reasonable number of years. If my judgment as to the quality of antelope skins be not at fault, only young animals could give such fine parchment, and this question of age would further limit the supply. Here my knowledge or my suppositions as to the parchment end.

The ink is a pale brown, so pale that it might almost be called brownish, a suspicion of something brown. The letters in the lines are not very large. Perhaps they could be compared to the capital letters in this book, only that the old forms tend to a greater breadth, so that a round letter is a circle, not an oval, and a rectangular letter about fills a square. The words have no accents or spiritus signs. The apostrophe occurs sometimes. A period is occasionally used. In some places the sign > is found at the end of a line, showing that what follows is closely connected with what precedes. In other places it is used to fill out a line. There are often little short strokes, horizontal lines, that project a trifle from the column between two lines, or that are in the margin near the column, to show the beginning of a paragraph. Sometimes a paragraph is indicated by the fact that the first letter projects a mere trifle into the margin. It is one of the signs of the high age of the manuscript that these projecting letters are not larger than the rest of the text. The same remark holds for the small letters that occasionally occur. They keep to the full round or square form. Certain abbreviations occur frequently, such as the following: $\overline{\theta s}$ for $\theta \epsilon \acute{o} s$, $\overline{\kappa s}$ for $\kappa \acute{\nu} \rho \iota o s$, $\overline{\chi s}$ for $\chi \rho \iota \sigma \tau \acute{o} s$, $\overline{\pi \eta \rho}$ for $\pi \alpha \tau \acute{\eta} \rho$, $\overline{\mu \eta \rho}$ for $\mu \acute{\eta} \tau \eta \rho$, $\overline{\nu s}$ for $\upsilon \acute{\iota} \acute{o} s$, $\overline{\delta \bar{a} \delta}$ for $\delta \alpha \nu \epsilon \acute{\iota} \delta$, $\overline{a \nu o s}$ for $\mathring{a} \nu \theta \rho \omega \pi o s$, $\overline{\iota \eta \lambda}$ for $\mathring{\iota} \sigma \rho \alpha \acute{\eta} \lambda$, $\overline{\iota \lambda \eta \mu}$ for $\mathring{\iota} \epsilon \rho o \upsilon \sigma \alpha \lambda \acute{\eta} \mu$, $o \upsilon \nu o s$ for οὐρανός, σηρ for σωτήρ, and σρς for σταυρός.   In old times these abbreviations were termed a sign of age, but they are found even down to the youngest manuscripts and therefore mean nothing, give no token of high antiquity.   It is also an abbreviation when, as often occurs in this manuscript, the numbers are not written out, but are represented by the Greek letters which take the place of our Arabic numerals.

Owing to what is called itacism, certain vowels are not seldom replaced by others.   Itacism denotes the fact that in Greek to-day, and probably at least from the time of Alexander the Great, the vowels ι, η, υ and the diphthongs ει, οι all sound like an English e, and are often interchanged in the manuscripts. In a similar way ο and ω are both usually short and may be confused with each other, and αι and ε sound both like ε.   In this manuscript ει and ι are often written instead of each other, and then αι and ε.   The confusion of υ with οι, η with ει, and ο with ω, occurs here less frequently.   Certain grammatical forms, which are often incorrectly termed "Alexandrian," are often found in this manuscript.

One source of error depends upon the occurrence of the same word or words, or of words that look alike and end or begin with the same letters, more than once on the page from which the scribe is copying.   Looking away from the original to write down the words just read, the scribe in turning his eyes back to the original strikes the other line, the one in which the same or similar words are found, and copies further from that point, leaving out thus by accident the words in between.   It is, of course, not impossible for the scribe to return by this careless vision from the second occurrence of the words to the former place at which they occur, and thus to repeat a second time that passage.   This, however, does not happen so readily, because the scribe usually observes at once that he has just written that passage down.   This mistake is called homoioteleuton or "like ending," because the like close of a line or of the words causes the confusion.

This manuscript contains certain small sections that are of use to show in what way the Gospels agree with each other, that is to say, the Greek letters that give the numbers of these sections are written along the side of the columns.   Under the number of each section stands the number of a canon or list in which the corresponding sections of the other Gospels may be looked up. It was another scribe, not the one who wrote the text, who put in these numbers of sections and canons, but he did it probably at the same time. The titles and the subscriptions to the books are very short, which is a sign of high age ; for example, Matthew has at the beginning and at the end and over the pages simply "according to Matthew," the two Greek words κατὰ μαθθαῖον. We shall not recount the fragments of the Old Testament, that this manuscript contains, verse by verse. They are from Genesis, Numbers, First Chronicles, Second Ezra, Nehemiah, Esther, Tobit, Judith, First and Fourth Maccabees, Isaiah, Jeremiah, Lamentations, Joel, Obadiah, Jonah, Nahum, Habakkuk, Zephaniah, Haggai, Zechariah, Malachi, Psalms, Proverbs, Ecclesiastes, Song of Solomon, Wisdom, Sirach, Job. The New Testament is complete, and is arranged as follows : the Gospels, the Epistles of Paul in which Hebrews stands immediately after Second Thessalonians, Acts, the Catholic Epistles, and the Revelation. After Revelation, Barnabas and the Shepherd of Hermas are added.

Four scribes wrote this manuscript. One of the four, whom Tischendorf called A, wrote First Chronicles, First Maccabees, the last four leaves of Fourth Maccabees, the whole New Testament save seven leaves, and Barnabas. Without doubt this same scribe wrote also some of the books that are missing. The fourth scribe, named D, wrote Tobit, Judith, the first three and a half leaves of Fourth Maccabees, and the seven leaves in the New Testament not written by A. These seven leaves are the tenth and fifteenth in Matthew, the last in Mark, the first in Luke,—these two are leaves 28 and 29 of the New Testament,—the second leaf of First Thessalonians or leaf 88, the third leaf of Hebrews or leaf 91, and perhaps the beginning of Revelation on leaf 126*. It is odd that another scribe should have written seven scattered leaves. It looks as if there had been mistakes on the leaves and he had supplied more correct ones. Another curious circumstance is the fact that, according to Tischendorf's view, this scribe D seems to have written all that we have of the New Testament in the great Vatican manuscript of which we shall soon have to speak. Should this view be right it would fit in very well with the supposition that the two manuscripts both proceeded from the same place and were among the fifty of Constantine.

The text in this manuscript is very good, and often agrees with the text of the Vatican manuscript. Westcott and Hort said that it was altogether pre-Syrian, or that its readings had not been altered by the Syrian scholars who appear in the third and in the fourth century to have busied themselves with the text. In the Gospels, especially in John and to a certain extent in Luke, and perhaps in Revelation, it contains Re-Wrought readings which Westcott and Hort called Western. It also has some Polished or so-called Alexandrian readings. Many scholars have felt it necessary to decry the text of this manuscript. That is wrong. Tischendorf may well have rated his great find a trifle too high. He would have been more than human if under the circumstances he had not done it, seeing that he for three years ate, drank, and slept this manuscript. Had he lived, he would surely here and there have modified his predilection for its readings. But it is, nevertheless, a very exceptional manuscript. Westcott and Hort, who praise B, the Vatican manuscript, highly, declare that this manuscript is far better than any of the manuscripts except B. It used also to be the fashion to say that the Sinaitic manuscript was very badly written, was full of clerical errors, and therefore less trustworthy. And the Vatican manuscript was supposed to be very correctly written. When, however, the Vatican copy came to be better known, it was found that in this respect there was not much choice between the two. The scribe who wrote the Vatican often leaves out or repeats words and letters. The scribe of the Sinaitic errs less frequently in that way, but has his own faults, proceeding like those errors from swift writing; he sometimes puts a different Greek word in.

Tischendorf thought that seven several correctors had put their pens to this book. The one he named with the letter a seemed to be of the same date as the original scribe, and at any rate of the fourth century. The corrector b was of about the sixth century, and only corrected a few passages, aside from the first pages of Matthew. The corrector c was probably of the beginning of the seventh century, and is often not clearly to be separated from the next corrector, who is of the same century. When the two can be distinguished from

22

each other, c is ca and the other is cb. It is clear that the next corrector, named cc, had the manuscript in his hands for a long while. His changes may be seen easily in Rev. $1^{9.\ 11.\ 19}$ and 2^2. The next one, named cc*, was also of the seventh century, and corrected a little in Rev. $11^1\ 3^8\ 12^6$ and 18^9. The last corrector, named e, was of the twelfth century, and corrected but little; see, for example, Matt. 19^3 and 1 Tim. 3^{16}.

The following reasons may be urged to support the view of Tischendorf that this manuscript was written in the fourth century. In the first place, the parchment is very fine. In the second place, the four columns on a page, eight on the open double page, approach the form of the text as written on a roll. In the third place, the forms of the letters are old. In the fourth place, the column with no large initial letter thrust out into the edge is old. In the fifth place, the rarity of the punctuation speaks for age. In the sixth place, the less pure forms in spelling and grammar point to a high antiquity. In the seventh place, those short titles and subscriptions are old. In the eighth place, the larger chapters in the Gospels are not noted. In the ninth place, the Epistles of Paul are placed directly after the Gospels, as if in a near memory of the very great respect paid to Paul, and at a time at which the thought that it was most correct to place most of the apostles—as if Acts gave the deeds of all the apostles—and the Twelve-Apostles before Paul, had not yet crystallised. In the tenth place, the end of Mark (16^{9-20}) is not there, which fact points to a time at which the false ending, vv.$^{9-20}$, had not yet been generally attached to that Gospel. And in the eleventh place, the addition of Barnabas and Hermas carries us back to the early period at which they were still read in the Church. For all these reasons, uncertain as all such datings are, it is proper palæographically and theologically to assign this manuscript to the fourth century.

It will be remembered that Eusebius' Pamphilus was named some distance back, and his library at Cæsarea. At the end of the book of Esther is a subscription which refers to the comparison and correction of this manuscript with a manuscript of Pamphilus', which is called "very old." Adolf Hilgenfeld in Jena found that this manuscript was much too badly, too incorrectly, written to be of the fourth century, and he declared that if this manuscript and its corrector looked up to a manuscript of Pamphilus'—Pamphilus died in the year 309—as very old, it could not possibly itself be of the fourth, but must be of the sixth century. In urging this latter argument, Hilgenfeld overlooked the fact that that subscription to Esther was probably written as late as the seventh century, at which time the corrector might well call Pamphilus' manuscript very old. And as for the incorrect writing, Hilgenfeld regarded the Vatican manuscript as of the fourth century, and it was as bad as the Sinaitic. Dean Burgon, of Chichester, named a number of points which seemed to him to make the Sinaitic appear to be surely younger than the Vatican, whether fifty or seventy-five or a hundred years. But Ezra Abbot, of Harvard, showed that the reasons given were either founded upon imperfect observation, or were of no weight for the proof of the dating desired by the dean. A palæographer, Victor Gardthausen, of Leipzig, stated that the forms of the letters found in the Sinaitic manuscript showed that it had been written about the year 400 ; and he urged in support of this statement particularly a few words written with a brush on the wall of a cell. To this it may be freely acknowledged, that if there were good reasons for thinking that the Sinaitic manuscript was written in the year 400, the forms of the letters would scarcely place any bar in the way. But the reasons seem to point to an earlier date, and the letters offer no bar to that. It may, in fact, be asserted that all the palæographical material that we to-day have in hand does not allow us to distinguish definitely between forms of letters possible in 331 and forms possible in 400. And, finally, it is really not easy to comprehend how a palæographer can for a moment entertain the thought of comparing the forms used by a scribe writing with a fine pen on good parchment for a good copy of a sacred book, with the forms dashed with a brush on the wall of a cell.

I insist upon it that we do not know when the Sinaitic manuscript was written, yet at the present showing of the evidence it seems to me that the best tentative date to work upon is the year 331 named above. We or our successors are going to know more about all these things than we now know.

Tischendorf when he returned from the East in 1859 set to work to prepare the great edition of the manuscript. I do not think that any large manuscript before or since was ever edited with such extraordinary pains and accuracy. Nor do I think that so much pains ever will be expended again upon a manuscript. For photography and photographic printing now render type-setting in such a case unnecessary. He caused five different sizes of type to be cut, and he endeavoured so far as possible to render in the edition even the distances between the letters. It was his intention to publish it as one of the monuments to commemorate the thousandth anniversary of the Russian Empire; but a curious, one might say inexplicable, piece of jealousy on the part of some of his enemies in Russia caused that to be forbidden. It appeared in four volumes in the year 1862. The second and third volumes contain the fragments from the Old Testament, and the fourth volume the New Testament with Barnabas and Hermas, all three of which volumes are, it is true, printed, yet as just said so carefully printed as to be almost as good as facsimiles. The first volume contains the preface, the commentary of phenomenal accuracy and fulness, and twenty-one lithographic plates made from photographs, or, in the case of a few things from other manuscripts brought in for comparison, from the most accurate tracings at command. This edition placed scholars in a position to examine the manuscript independently, and it was interesting to observe that Ezra Abbot, of Harvard, discovered and used in answering Burgon some facts that Tischendorf himself had not happened to notice in reference to one of the scribes. This edition the Russian emperor presented to many of the great libraries. He allowed Tischendorf to have a number of copies. In the year 1863, Tischendorf published the New Testament in a quarto volume, in the four columns, but in ordinary Greek type, and with one facsimile. In the year 1864 he also issued a New Testament "from the Sinaitic manuscript," dated 1865; but the text that he gave in this was neither the Sinaitic text nor a good New Testament text, and was therefore of no proper use to anybody. In the year 1867 he published a brief appendix for the Sinaitic, the Vatican, and the Alexandrian manuscripts, a large page folio.

THE CODEX ALEXANDRINUS.

The next manuscript to be taken up is that Alexandrian manuscript that was just referred to. It is called A, and was the first manuscript to receive thus a large letter as its designation.

That set the fashion for the use of capitals to denote the manuscripts of the New Testament in the large or uncial writing. So far as we can judge, this manuscript was probably written in the last half of the fifth century, and in Egypt. The first historical note touching it is that it was presented to the patriarch of Alexandria in the year 1098, and the name "Codex Alexandrinus" is given to it because of this fact. In Egypt the belief was that Saint Thecla had written it with her own hand, as an Arabic note in the first of the four volumes states. We cannot be sure how the story arose. It may be that the manuscript was written in a monastery dedicated to Thecla. Tregelles made, however, another suggestion that looks quite plausible. The New Testament volume has long been mutilated, and begins now in the twenty-fifth chapter of Matthew, in which chapter the lesson for Thecla's Day stands. Tregelles thought that Thecla's name might have on this account been written in the margin above, which has been cut off, and that therefore the Alexandrians or Cairenes or other Egyptians imagined that Thecla had written it. Such stories arise very easily. It is not a year since I visited a women's monastery in the East in which the abbess assured me that their beautiful manuscript had been written by an ancient saintly woman, whereas I found in it the name, and I think the date of the man who wrote it.

In the seventeenth century, Cyril Lucar had this manuscript at Constantinople where he was patriarch. As he had previously been patriarch of Alexandria, one would suppose that he had carried it with him to the new chair. It has, however, been thought by some that the manuscript was sent to Constantinople from Mount Athos. We do not know about that. We do know what was done with it in the year 1628, for Cyril Lucar then sent it as a present to the king of England, Charles the First. It is now in the British Museum, where the New Testament volume lies open in a glass case so that everyone can see it. This manuscript is like the Sinaiticus, the Vaticanus, and the Codex Ephræmi, a manuscript of the Bible, although a few leaves are lacking. The four volumes number 773 leaves. It is the fourth volume in which the New Testament is to be found. It contains 143 (144) leaves; the extra leaf is a new one with a table of contents.

This volume gives, besides the New Testament, the letter

of Clement of Rome and the homily which is called Second
Clement, and which was probably sent from Rome to Corinth
during the second century. The leaves are 32 centimetres
high and 26·3 broad. The writing is in two columns of from
forty-nine to fifty-one lines each. The uncial letters are small
and neat and simple. The greater part of the third volume of
the Old Testament is in a different hand from the rest of the
manuscript. There are only a few accents in the first four lines
of the two columns at the beginning of Genesis, and they seem to
be by a later hand. Occasionally a spiritus or an apostrophe is
used. The period sometimes occurs ; sometimes a vacant space
serves as punctuation. The paragraphs are marked by a much
larger letter, which is put in the margin. We are accustomed to
see the first letter of the first word of a paragraph thus enlarged
and put in the margin. It is therefore surprising to observe that
this is often by no means the case in the manuscripts, and not in
this fine manuscript. The new paragraph begins in the line
where it happens to fall; and has the usual size of letter. But
the first letter of this new paragraph that strikes the next line is
enlarged and placed in the margin. For us that is much like
wriTing a word thus. At the beginnings of the books a few
lines are written in red for ornament. Certain leaves, leaves 20
to 95, from the opening verse of Luke as far as 1 Cor. 10[8]
are on a coarser parchment, and appear to be from another
hand. As for the itacistic errors, they are often to be met with ;
for example, $\alpha\iota$ being exchanged for ϵ, $\epsilon\iota$ for ι or η for ι. The
sign > on the margin calls attention to the quotations from the
Old Testament.

The Eusebian sections and canons, which were mentioned in
connection with the Sinaitic manuscript, are also found in this
manuscript. It has also the larger chapters, and at the beginning of each Gospel the list of the chapters in each with the
title of each chapter. The title of each chapter belongs also in
the margin of the page on which the chapter is found, but an
English bookbinder cut a large part of them off. The subscriptions are simple, but not so simple as in the Sinaitic, since, for
example, we read at the end of Matthew $\epsilon \dot{v}a\gamma\gamma\dot{\epsilon}\lambda\iota o\nu$ $\kappa a\tau \grave{a}$ $\mu a\tau\theta a\hat{\iota}o\nu$
instead of merely $\kappa a\tau \grave{a}$ $\mu a\tau\theta a\hat{\iota}o\nu$. A few verses are lacking at four
places in Genesis, a little over a chapter in First Samuel, and
about thirty psalms. The New Testament begins, as was stated,

with Matt. 25^6, and there is a gap in John 6^{50} to 8^{52}, and in
2 Cor. 4^{13}–12^7. One leaf is lost in the letter of Clement,
and the last two leaves of Pseudo-Clement are gone. It is
important to have the testimony of so old a manuscript in
respect to the story of the adulteress, John 7^{53}–8^{11}. Happily we
can surmount the difficulty offered by the fact that John 6^{50} to
8^{52} is lost. For by counting the lines we can prove that it was
not in the book. There is not room for it. By means of the
table of contents above referred to, we see that the eighteen
psalms of Solomon used to stand at the end, after Pseudo-
Clement. Karl Gottfried Woide published the New Testament
from this manuscript in the year 1786, and B. H. Cowper in 1860,
and E. H. Hansell, with three other manuscripts, in 1864. Finally,
the British Museum issued a photographic edition in 1878 and
again in 1880, and then the three volumes of the Old Testament.

THE CODEX VATICANUS.

The Vatican manuscript of the Bible is B. It is in one
thick volume. The leaves used to be somewhat larger ; now
they are about twenty-seven centimetres square. Seven hundred
and fifty-nine leaves are preserved, and a hundred and forty-two
of these belong to the New Testament. The three columns
on each page contain forty to forty-four lines each, but in the
New Testament forty-two lines. The parchment is very fine, and
is in a measure like vellum. The parchment looked to me like
Western parchment. I wish I were able to see it again, for I
have seen and studied parchment a great deal since 1886, when
I examined this manuscript. The letters in which the text is
written are small uncials, simple, and without breaks between the
words. The original scribe did not add spiritus and accents, but
there is occasionally in the New Testament an apostrophe. As
we said for the Sinaitic manuscript, so we must here emphasise
the fact that the paragraphs are not marked by larger letters. In
some cases the initial letter is pushed out a little, a trifle, into
the margin. The small letters sometimes used at the end of a
line keep to the old forms. The sign > is used for the quotations from the Old Testament, just as in the Alexandrinus.
There are plenty of the itacistic faults, especially the exchange

of ει for ι.   The later forms, so-called "Alexandrian" forms, are used often.

In the Gospels we find a chapter division that only occurs besides in a fragment at London.   The book of Acts has two different divisions into chapters.   The more singular of these two divisions seems to be noted in part in the Sinaitic manuscript, thus offering another indication of some kind of a connection between these two books in the days of their making.   A very interesting observation attaches to an old division found in the Epistles, for it does not appear to take any notice of Second Peter, and seems therefore to be the work of someone who rejected that Epistle.   Still another chapter phenomenon must be noted.   The Epistles of Paul have chapter numbers, as now and then happens in the manuscripts, that do not begin afresh with each Epistle, but continue from Romans to the last Epistle in one series.   In this manuscript Hebrews follows Thessalonians.   And, nevertheless, these chapter numbers show that in the book in which they were originally given to the chapters, Hebrews stood immediately after Galatians.   The titles and subscriptions are very simple. The manuscript is less neat than it otherwise would be, because a later hand went over the pale letters and added spiritus and accents.

A little way back I called attention to the fact that this manuscript has, a great exception in Greek manuscripts, ancient numbers for the leaves.   That these numbers are not from a Greek but from a Semite is shown by the circumstance that they are not on the recto but on the verso of the leaves, where the Semites put their numbers.   These numbers give us a chance to determine the, probably, original condition of the manuscript, the original number of the leaves at the beginning of the book, even if nothing tells us how many leaves are lost at the end.   There were apparently at first eight leaves at the beginning of the manuscript, before the text began.   For manuscripts, just like modern books with the numbers of the pages, begin to count their regular quires with the regular text.   Prefaces and the like at the beginning of the volume do not belong to the body of the quires.   The lines drawn in the parchment are in some respects peculiar, but it was not possible for me in 1886 to complete my examination of them.   They probably betray the hands of different workmen.   There is an amusing circumstance to be mentioned touching this manuscript.   On many of the leaves a sharp eye can detect the myriad lines that we sometimes see in paper and which I suppose are due to the wires upon which the paper is made. Of course, parchment has no such lines. A hasty observer might declare this fine parchment to be paper. But if that sharp eye should look still more closely it would in some places find Italian words, printed backwards, it is true. At some time or other, without doubt when the manuscript was bound in the present binding and was to be pressed, paper was put in between the leaves to prevent them from printing the old Greek letters off upon each other. Under such conditions, with such a sacred and costly manuscript, it should have been a matter of course to use for this purpose clean thin paper. Instead of that the profane binder put in ordinary everyday newspapers, hence those marks.

This manuscript contains both Testaments, but does not appear to have included the books of the Maccabees. There are three vacant spaces. At the beginning almost forty-six chapters of Genesis are lacking. Nearly thirty-two psalms are gone. And the end of Hebrews from 9^{25} has disappeared with First and Second Timothy, Titus, Philemon, and Revelation. The close of Hebrews and the Revelation were supplied in the fifteenth century out of a manuscript belonging to the Cardinal Bessarion.

Tischendorf distinguished three scribes in this manuscript. One of them wrote the whole New Testament and apparently those seven leaves of the Sinaitic manuscript. The Sinaitic was often corrected. The Vatican was corrected once, doubtless at the time of writing, and once, so Tischendorf thought, in the tenth or eleventh century. The Roman editors placed this second corrector in the fifteenth century.

This manuscript is supposed, as we have seen, to have come from the same place as the Sinaitic manuscript. I have said that these two show connections with each other, and that they would suit very well as a pair of the fifty manuscripts written at Cæsarea for Constantine the Great. Yet I have not failed to call attention to the apparently Western parchment of this Vatican manuscript, and I have seen some writing belonging originally to Italy which seems much more akin to the Vatican hand than to the hand that wrote the Sinaitic. We must wait and examine further.

The Vatican Library possessed this treasure before the first catalogue, which was made in the year 1475. It was not, however, until the nineteenth century that the real value of the manuscript was discovered. The discoverer was the learned Roman Catholic professor Leonhard Hug, who long taught in Tübingen. It was the fortunes and the misfortunes of war that made it possible for Hug to examine the book. The French troops annexed the manuscript treasures of Italy—the stamp of the République Française may still be seen in many of the great Italian libraries. Thus this volume was in 1809 at Paris. Hug dated it at the middle of the fourth century.

But it was then years before the manuscript could be freely used by scholars. And that was due to an unfortunate piece of work on the part of the learned Cardinal Mai, who published so many valuable manuscripts. This manuscript was worthy of his highest efforts, and for some unknown reason it was the worst thing he ever did, and he knew it. It was a pity that he did not burn the printed sheets and begin over again. I like to think that he wished to do that, and that he was not allowed to do it. Yet perhaps he could not bring himself to destroy the work done. His edition was printed in an unconscionably slovenly manner in the years from 1828 to 1838, but not then issued. Tischendorf went to Rome in 1843 and spent some months there, but was only allowed to study this manuscript for six hours on two days. He made the most of those few hours, collating important passages and tracing four facsimiles. Tregelles spent five months at Rome in the year 1845, and could not get permission to examine the manuscript at all. He remembered, however, some readings which he observed while looking at the manuscript as any traveller might. And all the while that edition of Mai was lying stowed away. Finally, Mai died in the year 1854. His edition had then reached the age of sixteen. It was nineteen years old before Carlo Vercellone actually issued four volumes of the Old Testament and a fifth containing the New Testament. Although this edition was about as bad as bad could be, it was notwithstanding possible to learn something about the hidden manuscript from it. In the year 1859 a slim little volume was published by Vercellone, which was not very accurate, but which gave the

New Testament from this manuscript far better than the five thick volumes had done.

After Tischendorf had published the Sinaitic manuscript, he conceived the plan of reproducing the Vatican manuscript in the same way. It was a great pity that the then pope did not allow him to do it. We should even to-day know far more about the manuscript, had he received permission. But finally he gained permission to examine the volume for two weeks, three hours a day, I suppose the library hours. While examining it he either wrote twenty pages off in the three columns or he noted just where the lines began on these pages, so that he knew precisely how they stood. It was an unsatisfactory and hasty way of working, but it was better than nothing. Upon the basis of that work he published a quarto edition, giving those twenty pages in the columns and lines, and for the rest merely giving each column as a paragraph. It was perhaps a part of the bargain for that work, that Tischendorf should allow the pope to have a set of his excellent old uncial types. With these types the Roman scholars began an edition. Carlo Vercellone and Giuseppe Cozza were the first two. When Vercellone died Cajetano Sergio took up the work. And Henrico Fabiani replaced Sergio after his eyes had grown too weak. The volume with the New Testament appeared in 1868, and the closing volume with the preface in the year 1881. The distinction between the different hands is not so accurate as is desirable. Giuseppe Cozza - Luzi published a photographic edition in the year 1889.

This Vatican manuscript is considered by a great many scholars to be the best of all the New Testament manuscripts. The Sinaitic and the Vatican are, from the standpoint of the history of the text as thus far known, by far the two best witnesses for the oldest text. Wherever they were written and at whatever date, they represent, it would appear, as both Tischendorf and Westcott and Hort thought, good manuscripts of the second century. The word good is to be emphasised here. If the given view be correct, they represent not the current re-wrought, worked over manuscripts of the second century, but such as retained in an eminent degree the text which had come to that century from the hands of the original writers. The Vatican manuscript shows in the Epistles of Paul a few readings from those current manuscripts of the second century, but not very many.

The Codex Ephræmi.

We have still one great manuscript of the whole Bible that we must look at, that is to say, a manuscript which at first contained both the Old and the New Testaments. But it is, alas! very far from its first estate. It is like a man who has been maimed in the wars. Its beauty and its fulness are departed. In the first place, the original writing had faded away. Let me observe at this point that we probably should assume that all the inks, the common inks used in the manuscripts, were at first black, or as nearly black as the makers of each ink could compass. We are told that the parchment of the old manuscripts was washed off and pumiced off in order to remove the writing. Some manuscripts show signs of such a treatment. Yet I think that in a large number of cases the ink became with time so pale, that, although a scholar examining it closely would be able to make out the words, it nevertheless offered no particular obstacle to a new use of the parchment with fresh and black ink. To return to this manuscript, we must first say that it is in the National Library at Paris, and add that its name is Codex Ephræmi, or in full Codex Ephræmi Syri, the manuscript of Ephraim the Syrian, and its sign is the large letter C. This name tells a tale. That fine old manuscript of the Bible had been pulled to pieces in its pallid old age. Much of it had either been lost or was now laid aside. The original had perhaps been written in Egypt before the middle of the fifth century, had been corrected, it may be, in Palestine in the sixth century, and again corrected in the ninth century possibly in Constantinople, and was in the twelfth century thoroughly used up. Thereupon someone wrote thirty - eight treatises of Ephraim the Syrian on it, but in Greek. I say on it, I should say on fragments of it, or on what was left of it.

There are now only 209 leaves, of which 145 belong to the New Testament. With this manuscript we reach a page of a single column. The Sinaitic has four columns, the Vatican

three, the Alexandrinus two, and the Ephraim one.   There are
usually forty-one lines in a column, but we find also forty, forty-
two, and four times there are forty-six lines.   The parchment is good and is fine.   The uncial letters are a trifle larger
than those in the three manuscripts just named.   There are
no spiritus or accents, and the apostrophe does not often
occur.   There is but little punctuation.   A colon is used,
and after it a space as wide as a letter is left free.   In this
manuscript the larger letters are frequently used, and that
not merely where paragraphs begin.   One ornamental part
of the writing of this manuscript was unfortunate for a little of
the text.   Much like the Alexandrinus, the first three lines
of each book were written in red.   That was very effective.
The red fluid, however, is not an ink, but an acidless preparation of colour, and the consequence is that anything written
in red has but the slightest, the most superficial hold on the
parchment, and with time, if the given leaves be much thrown
about, it vanishes almost entirely.   In case a leaf of parchment
is washed and pumiced, of course that is the end of colours in
the text.   The catalogues of the chapters were placed at
the beginnings of the books, and the little chapters or the
Eusebian sections were noted on the margin.   We do not
find the numbers of the Eusebian canons under the numbers of
the sections, but that may very well be because they were
written in red and have vanished.   Only the Gospels have
chapters.   The Acts, the Catholic Epistles, and the Epistles
of Paul have not the Euthalian chapters, and Revelation has
not the chapters of Andrew of Cæsarea.   The subscriptions are
very simple.

No one will be surprised to learn that in a manuscript
that has been so much buffeted about, words or letters are
often lacking, and the upper black writing covers many a
letter.   It is under such circumstances the merest lottery, what
may happen to be left over.   As a fact every book of the
New Testament is represented save Second John and Second
Thessalonians.   This manuscript is closely connected with
Tischendorf's early work, and gives a proof of his attention to
words written by Lachmann.   The latter said in a note to an
article in a theological journal that "Parisian scholars could
win immortal merit in reference to the criticism of the New

Testament by printing the royal Codex Ephraim and the Claromontanus." The moment that Tischendorf had habilitated, that
is, had won his place as a privatdozent in the theological
faculty at Leipzig, he started off to Paris and set about this
work. That was in 1840, and in 1843 the fragments of the
New Testament appeared, accompanied by a careful commentary on about 1500 passages that were doubtful or that had
been corrected, as well as an essay on 1 Tim. 3^{16}. The Old
Testament fragments were issued in 1845, and thus this old
writing, which Pierre Allix, who died in 1717, had discovered,
was given to the world by Saxon industry. It has sometimes
been said that Tischendorf spoiled this manuscript by using a
bad reagent to draw forth the old letters that had grown so pale.
That was a mistake. Simonin put Gioberti tincture on some of
them with the librarian's permission in 1834, and that was the
year at which Tischendorf left school and went to the university.

So much for the four great manuscripts of the Bible that stand
forth in the history and work of textual criticism like David's
mighty men. Yet the other manuscripts that give us but parts
of the New Testament are not to be despised. Some of them
are of very great importance.

The Codex Bezæ.

The Vatican manuscript recalled to us the vicissitudes of
times of war. The next one, it may be with a companion,
came to light amid similar scenes. We have two manuscripts
for which we use the sign D. One of them is the "Codex
Bezæ," or Beza's manuscript, in the University Library at
Cambridge, England, and the other is the "Codex
Claromontanus" in the National Library at Paris. Both these
manuscripts belonged to Théodore de Bèze, the celebrated
Frenchman who passed over to Switzerland and became the
successor of Calvin as leader of the Genevan Church. He said,
when he in the year 1581 gave the former manuscript to
the University of Cambridge, that it had long lain in the dust in
the monastery of St. Irenäus at Lyons, and that it had been found
there during the civil war in 1562. Just at that time, between
1561 and 1563, Bèze had returned to France because

Protestantism was apparently gaining due recognition. In the last edition of his notes on the New Testament in the year 1598, however, he called this manuscript " The Codex Claromontanus." And on the back of the title of the manuscript now at Paris, Bèze wrote that it was found in the monastery in Clermont-en-Beauvoisis, to-day the chief city of the department Oise. Clermont probably then still belonged to the Condés, so that he may well have gotten the books through the mediation of some officer or soldier from Condé's guards. It does not make much difference whether he got one from Lyons and the other from Clermont, a hundred and thirty or forty kilometres distant, or both from Clermont. The manuscripts doubtless belonged together originally. There are among other possibilities two worth mentioning, namely, on the one hand, that the reference of the Lyons manuscript to Clermont was merely a momentary slip of the memory ; or, on the other hand, that Bèze learned after 1581 that this manuscript was not as he had previously supposed from Lyons, but from Clermont. Perhaps the trooper had forgotten exactly where he had picked them up, and Bèze may later in some way have gotten surer word of the place.

Both manuscripts are of the sixth century, both are Greek and Latin, and both place the text before us that appears to have been most widely spread during the latter part of the second century, the Re-Wrought Text, the text that was worked over anew by many a hand. It would perhaps be better to say, not the text, but, one phase of the text current. For that text was in a way chameleon like, ever changing, and varying doubtless provincially as well. The Cambridge manuscript is 26 × 21.5 centimetres, and contains 409 leaves (or 415 with nine new ones). Originally it must have contained at least 510 leaves. Each page has one column ; the Greek is on the left-hand page. The column numbers thirty-three lines. The letters are of about the same size as those in the Ephraim manuscript. The Latin letters are in a way assimilated to the Greek letters, being rounded off like the latter. The words run together, save in titles and subscriptions. Here we meet a text that is not written straight ahead, out which is cut up into lines according to the sense. These are the oldest sense-lines for this part of the New Testament. The first letter of a section is thrust into the margin, but is usually of the same size as the other letters. A larger letter is in some places put in to show a division of sense in the middle of a line.

This manuscript contains the four Gospels and the Acts, but there are a few gaps in it. The Gospels are in the order Matthew, John, Luke, Mark, with the two Twelve Apostles first and the friends of apostles following. There is a singular chapter division which assigns to Matthew in Greek so far as this Gospel is preserved 583 chapters, in Latin 590, to John 165 and in Latin 169, to Luke 136 and in Latin 143, to Mark 148, and to Acts 235 chapters. Each book has the first three lines in red letters, and red and black lines alternate in the subscriptions. The Catholic Epistles apparently used to be in this volume. They present us a problem. In the first place, it is curious that they should have stood before and not after Acts. We find before Acts the last five verses of Third John, but only in Latin, and the subscription follows : " Third John closes, the Acts of the Apostles begins." That assures us that they were before Acts, and it shows us that Jude either was left out or must have stood at some other place than its usual one after Third John. But it is possible after all that the Catholic Epistles were not all here, for Wilhelm Bousset calculates that there is just room for the Revelation and the three Epistles of John. If the Gospel of John had been at the close of the four Gospels as usual, instead of following upon Matthew, such a position for Revelation and 1, 2 and 3 John would have given us John all in one. Frederick Henry Ambrose Scrivener published this manuscript in 1864, and in the year 1899 a fine photographic edition was issued in two volumes at the expense of the University.

Scrivener thought that fifteen different hands corrected this volume. The most important of these were the first four. The first one made about 181 changes in a careful beautiful hand in the sixth century. The second was probably of the seventh century, and made about 327 changes, besides adding some spiritus and accents and other signs. The third, it may be towards the end of the seventh century, made 130 changes ; and the fourth, of the same age, 160 changes, chiefly in the Acts. This manuscript was probably written in the West. The relation of the Greek to the Latin text has been much discussed. The Greek has been thought independent, and has been thought dependent upon an Eastern version, and has been also thought to be dependent upon

the Latin text at its side.   Curiously enough some Latin forms
have been introduced into the Greek text.   For several years
there has much been written about the text represented by this
manuscript, which used to be called the "Western Text," a
totally false name.   The effort was made to place it in value
before the Sinaitic and the Vatican manuscripts.   The real
state of the case, so far as the material in our hands permits
a decision, seems to be that this text is the current corrupted
text of the later second century.   Be this the case, then it
is clear that we may often find in passages that are not corrupted
an agreement with the two great manuscripts just named, and we
do find such agreement in many cases.   The Latin text was
probably modified so as to accord better with the Greek text.

In a parenthesis it may here be observed that there are in
the usual lists of the uncial manuscripts of the Gospels some
manuscripts that never should have been there.   The most
absurd case is that of the manuscript with the sign F^a, which
is an Old Testament manuscript that merely has a few scattered
verses of the New Testament on the margin.   And then there
are eight manuscripts, all but one clearly psalters, which contain
the three Canticles from the first and second chapters of Luke or
parts of them.   These belong among the lesson-books, not
among the uncial manuscripts of the Gospel text.

E G H I I^b K L.

The uncial manuscript of the Gospels known by the letter
E is at Basel in the University Library, and is of the eighth
century.   There are various gaps in the original text of Luke,
some of which a later hand supplied.—The manuscript F is at
Utrecht in the University Library, and is of the ninth or tenth
century.   A great many passages are missing. — The two
manuscripts G and H have each a half a leaf in Trinity
College at Cambridge.   They belonged once to the celebrated
Hamburg pastor and scholar Johann Christoph Wolf, and he
sent these fragments to Bentley, as a cloth merchant sends a
pattern of cloth, simply to let him know what the manuscripts
looked like.   The former manuscript, G, is now in the British
Museum.   It is of the ninth or tenth century.   The latter, H,

23

is in the City Library at Hamburg, and is also of the ninth or tenth century.—The letter I denotes twenty-eight leaves at St. Petersburg, in the Imperial Library, that are of the fifth century, and were written anew with a Georgian text in the tenth century.—The letter I[b] stands for two good leaves of the fifth century from Egypt, containing parts of the thirteenth and sixteenth chapters of John. These leaves were faded or the Greek was rubbed off in the ninth century, and Syriac was written upon them, and then in the tenth or eleventh century that had faded or was rubbed off, and Syriac, hymns of Severus', appeared as the third writing. Thus they are doubly palimpsest.— The manuscript for the sign K is in the National Library at Paris, and is of the ninth century. It was written by a monk named Basil and bound by a monk named Theodulos, and as they besought the Virgin Mary and Saint Eutychius to accept it and to pray for them, it was doubtless written for a church or a monastery, which would then mean the Church of the Monastery, dedicated to St. Eutychius.—The manuscript L is a particularly good one. It is also in the library at Paris, and stands there just before the manuscript K. It is of the eighth century, and has coarse and thick parchment. It is not well written, and it may be that the scribe who copied it did not understand Greek. There are five small gaps in it. Now this is one of the best later copies of the four Gospels. Its text is extraordinarily good, and often agrees with the text of the great Vatican manuscript.

M N O P Q.

The letter M stands for a Parisian manuscript of the end of the ninth century that doubtless came from the East, for it has Arabic writing in it.—The manuscript marked N has had a varied fate. There were two leaves at Vienna, four at London, and six at Rome. Then thirty-three turned up on the island of Patmos, and a few years ago the Russian ambassador at Constantinople, now at Paris, succeeded in getting 182 leaves more, which have been placed in the Imperial Library at St. Petersburg. That later part of the manuscript lived an exciting life for a few years before it was thus purchased. It was in the village Sarumsachly, about forty kilometres north of Kaisarie, in

Cappadocia that was. Once the bishop of the diocese is said to have caused it to be stolen. The villagers, however, got wind of the robbery and chased the thieves. When they caught them they gave them a sound beating, dusted their garments in the Connaught fashion, and carried the book back home again. This is a purple manuscript, and was probably written at the close of the sixth century. The leaves are 36 × 26·5 centimetres, and now 227 leaves are known. The pages have two columns of sixteen lines each. The text is written in silver letters, and the names of God and Jesus are in gold. In the time of the Roman emperors purple manuscripts were the noble books. They were not practical, but they cost a great deal, and they looked distinguished. A letter written by Theonas, who is supposed to have been bishop of Alexandria a little before the year 300, refers to them. He wrote to a Christian named Lucian, who had been made the overseer having the closer attendants of the emperor under his care. Theonas told him, in speaking of the librarian, that this official should not make a point of writing whole manuscripts on purple parchment and in gold letters, unless the monarch specially asked to have it done. The text offers many good readings. H. S. Cronin published the text in 1899.—There are in the library at St. Petersburg two fragments also on purple parchment, and also written probably in the sixth century, but with golden letters. — The letter O signifies eight leaves of John, of the ninth century, apparently written in the monastery of Dionysius on Mount Athos. They are now at Moscow in the library of the Synod.—At Wolfenbüttel, where Lessing was once librarian, there is a manuscript of the "Origins" of Isidore of Sevilla, Isidorus Hispalensis. Its chief value, at least for us, lies beneath the words of Isidore. For three old manuscripts contributed leaves to this volume. One contained Wulfila's Gothic translation of Romans, and the two others, which we call P and Q, contain Gospel fragments in Greek.—The one named P is of the sixth century, and consists of forty-three leaves, with two columns and twenty-four lines in each column, containing fragments from all four Gospels. Tischendorf published the text in 1869. The text is fairly good.—The other fragments, Q, are confined to Luke and John. There are thirteen leaves of them, with two columns and twenty-eight lines in the column.   These are of the fifth century.   The text is also fairly good.

R S T U V.

The letter R offers us a manuscript of the sixth century in the British Museum, having forty-eight leaves, with two columns and twenty-five lines in a column.   There is a thick and black Syriac text, writings of Severus of Antioch, written in the ninth century over the Greek, and making the reading of the ancient text more difficult.   This volume was brought to the British Museum in the year 1847 from the monastery of the Virgin Mary, a Coptic monastery in the Nitrian desert, seventy miles north-west from Cairo.   William Cureton read and published four thousand verses of the *Iliad* that were under the Syriac text, and Tischendorf published the fragments of Luke in 1857. — The letter S presents to us the first manuscript in our review which has a hard and sure date. It is in the Vatican Library, and was written just before the middle of the tenth century, in the year 949.   It was written by a monk named Michael.—The letter T represents, with a series of small letters to distinguish the different manuscripts, a number of fragments, some larger some smaller, of the centuries from the fourth (or the third?) up to the ninth or tenth.   This group is connected with Egypt and with Coptic scribes.—The letter U represents, like K and M, a complete manuscript of the four Gospels.   It is of the ninth or tenth century and is in the library of St. Mark at Venice.   The text is of a late cast.—The manuscript known as V is in the library of the Synod at Moscow, and is of the ninth century.

W X Y Z.

Somewhat like T, the letter W brings again many fragments of the Gospels in various libraries, dating from the seventh to the ninth century.—The letter X is one of the manuscripts that have an uncial text combined with a commentary written in minuscles.   It is in the University Library at Munich, and is of the tenth century.   The order of the Gospels is Matthew,

John, Luke, Mark. The Gospel according to Matthew is furnished with a full commentary drawn from Chrysostom, and so is the Gospel according to John. The commentary to Luke contains many references to what has already been discussed above in Matthew. By this time the whole contents of the Gospels have been treated, and therefore Mark has no commentary at all.—There are fourteen leaves in the Royal Library at Munich, of the ninth or tenth century, which are denoted by X^b. They contain the beginning of Luke, and have a commentary in small or minuscle writing. — Under the letter Y we find six leaves of the eighth century in the Barberini Library at Rome. The text is from John and is good. — In Dublin we have the manuscript Z in Trinity College, a sixth century palimpsest with an extraordinarily good text of fragments of Matthew. It agrees with the Sinaitic especially, but also with the Vatican and with the Codex Bezæ. It was published by John Barret in 1801, and again by Thomas Kingsmill Abbott in 1880, with three very fine facsimiles.

Γ—The Codex Δ.

Now we come to Greek letters as signs, and begin with Γ, which is partly in the Bodleian Library at Oxford and partly in the Imperial Library at St. Petersburg. There is a tantalisingly imperfect date in it, so that we are almost as wise without it as with it. It is probably of the ninth or tenth century. The text is of a late cast, but it sometimes has fairly good readings. Tischendorf brought it in two parts from an Eastern monastery.—The next manuscript, Δ, in the library of the Stift at St. Gallen in Switzerland, is in many ways interesting. It is of the ninth or tenth century, and contains 198 leaves of one column, with from seventeen to twenty-eight lines on the page. The text is both Greek and Latin. The Greek uncial letters are rough and coarse, and the Latin is in small writing between the lines. The writing is not very straight, so that the whole appearance of the manuscript is a little uncouth. There is sometimes a large letter in the middle of a line, showing that it was copied from a manuscript written in sense-lines. Almost everywhere we find a period or a point after each Greek word, but the words are sometimes not rightly divided. We can see clearly that the scribe was more used to writing Latin than Greek. He sometimes confused letters that looked alike; for example, N and Π, Z and Ξ, P and the Latin R. The larger letters are rather smeared over than painted with different colours. The titles for the chapters stand often in the middle of the text. There are Greek notes here and there, which mention Godeschalk, who died in 866, and a later hand names Aganon, who died in 941, whereas we are more accustomed to find the names of Origen and Basil and Chrysostom in the manuscripts.

One interesting thing about this manuscript is, that it seems to have been written by an Irish monk, and perhaps at St. Gallen itself, in the ninth or tenth century. Thus here for the second time Northwestern Europe appears in our review of the manuscripts. Further, this volume is, if I am not mistaken, one of a group of three, probably written by the same monk at the same time. One of the other manuscripts is at Dresden, and we shall have to describe it among the manuscripts of the Epistles of Paul as G. And the third is a psalter, which I saw at the library at St. Gallen. But another thing in Δ points us back to a much earlier period. There was a time, as we have seen, at which each Gospel was written on its own roll. I say "roll," because we do not suppose that this individualising, or this continued separate life of the single Gospels, lasted up to the years in which leaf-books were made. Now so long as the Gospels thus existed separately, each could have its own experiences, its own good or evil fortunes. Each could wander quite alone into this or that province, and be corrected and copied off without reference to the others. And conversely each could come into any province and exist there in a form different from that found usually in the given province. We could even imagine it possible that a Christian should have happened to become the possessor of four separate rolls, one of each Gospel, no two of which came from the same place, and contained the same cast of text.

Let us now suppose, however, a more likely case, namely that a man had three Gospels in the style of text usual in his neighbourhood, and that his fourth roll with the remaining Gospel was from another province; that it had been bought by him when on a journey, or brought to him by some strange Christian from afar. Taking a further step we observe that this possessor of three rolls of one cast of text, and of a fourth roll of a different cast of text, determines to have his four Gospels all copied off into one roll, or, if the invention of leaf-books has been made in between, to have them copied into a single leaf-book. The consequence is, that we at once see the difference between the kinds of text. This is what happened to the manuscript now under consideration. Matthew, Luke, and John are in it of a rather late kind of text, and give us but rarely old readings. Mark, on the contrary, offers to us a text that is more like the text of the Ephraim manuscript, and of the manuscript that has the sign L, and has many a good reading, many an old one. Therefore when Δ is quoted for a reading in the gospel according to Mark, it has a much greater value than when it is quoted for Matthew or Luke or John. H. C. M. Rettig published this manuscript in facsimile in the year 1836, in a most excellent manner. I can recall no edition of a New Testament manuscript before the exceptional editions of Tischendorf and of his day that could be compared in exactness to this edition by Rettig.

Θ—Λ AND 566.

Under the letter Θ we have, distinguished by added small a, b, etc., eight fragments of Gospel manuscripts, all but part of one at St. Petersburg. They range from the sixth to the ninth or tenth century.—The manuscript Λ is at Oxford in the Bodleian, and is of the ninth or tenth century. It offers a curious problem. It contains Luke and John. Now the small letter, minuscle, manuscript numbered 566 seems to be the first part of this very volume. That a man should, in the years which were on the margin between capital or uncial letters and small or minuscule letters, begin a manuscript in the older way in the large letters and then at the end of Mark say: Now I must try the new letters:—that would not be strange. But it is strange that he should write Matthew and Mark in the new small letter and then say: I am tired of that. I shall go back to the old, large, and fine letters. It is like the wine at Cana. The scribe has kept the good letters for the end. This manuscript has a good pedigree and one that is down in writing, although we must take the beginning of it from that former small letter part. At the end of Matthew we read in curt translation : " Gospel according to Matthew : written and corrected from the ancient manuscripts in Jerusalem : those kept in the holy mountain : in 2514 lines, 355 chapters." At the end of Mark we read : "Gospel according to Mark : written and corrected likewise from the carefully prepared ones in 1506 lines, 237 chapters." At the end of Luke : "Gospel according to Luke : written and corrected likewise in 2677 lines, 342 chapters." At the end of John : "Gospel according to John : written and corrected likewise from the same copies in 2210 lines, 232 chapters."

In the East it is hard to get the scholars to accept these inscriptions as applying to the holy mountain in Jerusalem. The name holy mountain would, of course, apply also to Mount Sinai, which is always called the "mountain trodden upon by God." And what could be more biblical, or sound more Davidic, than going up to the holy mountain, even Jerusalem, Mount Sion. But now for centuries Akte, Mount Athos, has been the one great Hagion Oros, ἅγιον ὄρος, Holy Mountain of Greek, Slavic, and Georgian Christendom, and it is hard for Eastern theologians to believe that anything else has been thus named. We do not know how far back this inscription reaches. It would be possible that this manuscript itself was thus written and corrected in Jerusalem. I see no difficulty in the supposition that the manuscripts kept in the holy mountain were manuscripts kept somewhere at Jerusalem, even if I cannot say precisely where. Those lines given at the end of the Gospels are the space lines I spoke of, and the chapters are the small chapters called the Eusebian sections. It must be conceded that this manuscript belongs to the younger class of manuscripts. Its text is, however, much better than that of the general run of younger books, and contains many old readings.

Ξ.

Our next manuscript is a very exceptionally good one, and it is a pity that there are only eighty-six and three half leaves of it in our hands. It is at London, and belongs to the British and Foreign Bible Society. It is extremely fitting that this great and incomparably useful society should have a fine manuscript of the Bible. The society is worthy of the greatest manuscripts. But keeping manuscripts is not the work of this society, and this manuscript is not in the proper place there. I hope that some day the society will ask Sir Edward Maunde Thompson to have the manuscript most carefully rearranged according to the ancient and precious text, by a competent scholar, say Frederic G. Kenyon, and then to bind it in the bindery of the British Museum, and then to keep it in the Museum, perhaps placing it in a glass case and writing upon it that it is the property of the British and Foreign Bible Society, put there on eternal deposit. It is denoted by the letter Ξ, and is of the eighth century, 35·8 × 28·7 centimetres. The text is written in large uncial letters, and is accompanied by a chain or combination commentary in small uncial letters. It is the oldest manuscript with a chain. The chapter division is the same as the singular one in the Vatican manuscript B. It contains fragments from the first eleven chapters of Luke. The text is extraordinarily good, and agrees with the oldest manuscripts. There is a second writing on top of this good ancient text, and we may be glad that there is, since we should certainly otherwise never have seen these leaves. They would have been thrown away centuries ago. The later writing is a lesson-book of the Gospel, probably of the thirteenth century. It does not often occur that biblical manuscripts are written upon leaves that have been used before, and still more rare is it to find biblical texts upon biblical texts. Samuel Prideaux Tregelles published the text in 1861. I think that some slight additions could be made if the leaves were entrusted as above suggested to the revivifying care of the British Museum.

II Σ.

The manuscript II is of the ninth century, and is in the Imperial Library at St. Petersburg, having been given to the Russian emperor by Mr. Parodi, of Smyrna, in the year 1859. —The next manuscript recalls the one named N, for it is on purple parchment, and contains Matthew and Mark. Its sign is Σ, and it lies in the strong chest of the archbishop at Rossano, at the southern end of Italy. It is of the sixth century. The writing is, as in N, silver, and the names of God and Jesus are in gold. The text is not especially good, and agrees largely with the text of N. The charm of this volume lies in the fact that it contains a series of pictures illustrating scenes from the Gospels : the raising of Lazarus, the driving of the traders out of the temple, the ten virgins, the entry into Jerusalem, the foot-washing, the last Supper, the Lord's Supper in two scenes, Jesus before Pilate in two scenes, the healing of the man born blind, the cursing of the fig-tree. There is also a picture of the evangelist Mark, by whom a figure stands, probably Wisdom. The late Oskar von Gebhardt and Adolf Harnack, now in Berlin, discovered this manuscript in the year 1878, and wished to make a fine edition of it, but were forbidden to do so by the Chapter. They published a short description of it in 1880, and Gebhardt published the text of the two Gospels in 1883. In the year 1898, Arthur Haseloff gave a photographic edition of the pictures, and in 1907 Antonio Muñoz an edition in coloured photography.

Φ Ψ Ω ℶ.

In the year 1885, Pierre Batiffol went from Paris to Berat in Albania, and found another purple manuscript of the sixth century, Φ, also containing Matthew and Mark in silver writing. This manuscript contains the strange long addition to Matt. 20²⁸. Batiffol published the text in 1887.—In the year 1886 I found, in the monastery called the Laura of Athanasius, on Mount Athos, a manuscript of the eighth or ninth century, containing a part of Mark, the whole of Luke, John, Acts, and the Catholic Epistles, and the Pauline Epistles and Hebrews down nearly to the end of the eighth chapter. Its sign is Ψ. It contains the short end of Mark. In the Catholic Epistles, First and Second Peter are put before James, showing a Western influence apparently.—In the same week I found in the monastery of Dionysius on Mount Athos, a complete manuscript of the four Gospels of the eighth or ninth century. Its sign is Ω.—In the same week I found in the monastery of St. Andrew on Mount Athos, a manuscript of the four Gospels of the ninth or tenth century, written entirely in pages or columns shaped like

a cross ≡≡≡≡. There are four gaps in it. Its sign is ב.—Under

ר we have seven fragments at Mount Sinai, found and published by J. Rendel Harris. They are from the fifth to the ninth century. That is enough for the present in regard to the manuscripts of the four Gospels, and we may turn to the other books, beginning with Acts.

MANUSCRIPTS OF ACTS.

The manuscripts attached to the letters אABCD we have already spoken of above. The next manuscript of Acts, E, is at Oxford in the Bodleian. It contains almost the whole of Acts in Greek and Latin. It is of the end of the sixth century. The lines in this manuscript are sense-lines and are very short, containing only two or three Greek or Latin words. It was written in the West, and it may have been written in Sardinia. At any rate it was once in Sardinia, for a later hand wrote at the end a ducal decree. If all signs do not fail, it was in England, and was used by the Venerable Bede, who died in 735. In an essay of his bearing on Acts he gives seventy and more readings, all of which are in this manuscript, and often only in this. It belonged to Laud the archbishop of Canterbury, and Chancellor of the University of Oxford, and he gave it to the University with many other manuscripts in the year 1636. Thomas Hearne published it in the year 1715, yet not very exactly, and then Hansell in the year 1864, and Tischendorf in 1870.—The fragment of Acts named G was taken by Tischendorf from the wooden cover of a Syrian manuscript; it is of the seventh century, and the text is not bad. It is in the Imperial Library at St. Petersburg.— The Vatican Library owns G^b, which is of the ninth century, and consists of six leaves. Hymns were written over the old text in the thirteenth century. The volume was once in the monastery of Grottaferrata. Giuseppe Cozza published five of the leaves in 1877; I found the sixth in 1886.

The manuscript H is in the Este Library at Modena. It contains the Acts in uncial writing of the ninth century, and the Epistles in minuscle writing of the tenth century.—Like the Gospel fragments marked I, there are three fragments of Acts at St. Petersburg also marked I. They are of the fifth and seventh centuries.—A manuscript marked by the letter K, is of the ninth century, and is in the library of the Synod at Moscow. It contains the Acts with a chain, and the Epistles of Paul with the notes of Johannes Damascenus. It was formerly in the monastery of Dionysius on Mount Athos.—The next manuscript, L, is at Rome in the Angelica monastery of the Augustinian monks. It was written in the ninth century, and contains a large part of Acts, beginning with 8^{10}, the Catholic Epistles, and the Epistles of Paul, closing with Heb. 13^{10}.—The manuscript P is in the Imperial Library at St. Petersburg, and is of the ninth century. It contains, with many gaps, the Acts, the Catholic and Pauline Epistles, and Revelation. In the Acts and in First Peter the text is not so very good, and is much like that in the later uncials such as H and L. In the rest of the Epistles, however, and in the Revelation the text is very good. Sometimes it agrees with א, the Sinaiticus, and still more frequently it accompanies the Alexandrinus and Ephraim, that is to say, A and C. The old text was covered in the year 1301 by Euthalius' commentary to Acts and to the Pauline Epistles. The volume contains some fragment of Fourth Maccabees; they are not palimpsest. Tischendorf published this manuscript in two different volumes of his "Sacred Monuments" in 1865 and 1869.—The next manuscript, marked S, I found in 1886 in the Laura on Mount Athos. It is of the eighth or ninth century, and contains Acts, the Catholic Epistles, and fragments of the Epistle of Paul.—A Vatican manuscript, which receives the letter ב, was discovered by Pierre Batiffol in 1887. It is of the fifth century, and is palimpsest. There are fragments in it of Acts, and also of the Catholic and Pauline Epistles. It was until the end of the seventeenth century in the monastery of St. Mary of Patire near Rossano in Calabria, and passed thence into the monastery of St. Basil, where Montfaucon discovered them. Cardinal Mai also discovered them. And finally Batiffol came upon them while studying the Patire manuscripts in the Vatican, and they were made known.

MANUSCRIPTS OF PAUL.

In proceeding to the manuscripts of the Epistles of Paul it must be remembered that we have already said various things about the Codex Claromontanus at Paris while speaking of its companion, the other D, the Codex Bezæ at Cambridge. This D contains the Epistles of Paul with only trifling exceptions. The text is very good. Tischendorf distinguished ten correctors. One of the objects of interest in this volume is a so-called stichometry. I mentioned a little way back, in speaking of the manuscript Λ and of the manuscript 566, certain lines given in the subscriptions to the four Gospels in those manuscripts, and I said that they were space lines. This stichometry gives a list of the books of the Old and the New Testaments with the number of these space lines that each contains. It was necessary to refer to this list several times while treating of the canon, because it gives with the New Testament books, Barnabas, the Shepherd of Hermas, and the Revelation of Peter. Whether written at the same time as the rest of the manuscript or not, this list is certainly very old. Bèze used this manuscript in the second edition of his Greek New Testament in the year 1582. Once this manuscript met with a misfortune even after being placed in the Royal Library at Paris. A thief named Jean Aymont stole thirty-five leaves in the year 1707 and sold them in foreign parts. But happily the leaves came back. A Dutchman named Stosch gave one back in the year 1720, and Count Harley's son gave back thirty-four in the year 1729. Tischendorf published this manuscript in the year 1852.

In the next manuscript, E, we have a rare chance to see clearly how a manuscript was copied in the ninth century, for this E is in the Greek a copy of the Claromontanus after it had been corrected by several hands. Really this should not have a letter; it should be attached to D. The way in which the fact of the copying from D can be proved is very interesting. For example, D had in Rom. 4[25] δικαιωσιν. One corrector put the accent in δικαίωσιν. Another corrector aimed to change the word into δικαιοσύνην, and he put νην for that last ν but did not change the accent. In consequence of this we find in E δικαίωσινην. In Rom. 15[29] D had πληροφορια.

A corrector changed this to πληρώματι. The scribe of E accepted the change, but thought well to keep also ρια from the word πληροφορια, and therefore we find in E the touchingly beautiful word πληρώματιρια. In First Corinthians the Claromontanus had at first in 15⁵ μετα ταυτα τοις ενδεκα. A corrector changed it to ειτα τοις δωδεκα. The scribe of E shook the two up in a bag and wrote μετα τανειτα τοις δωενδεκα. Heb. 10⁸³ had at first in the Claromontanus ονιδιζομενοι. A corrector put an obelus on the first and last letters to show that the word was to be considered as expunged, and then he wrote above it θεατριζομενοι. The scribe of E did really leave out the two obelised letters and then wrote νιδιζομενοθεατριζομενοι. One thing this E can do. It can tell us what D had in Rom. 1¹⁻⁷.

F G.

The next manuscript is at Cambridge, England, in Trinity College. Its name is Codex Augiensis, from the monastery Augia Maior or Dives, which means Reichenau, a rich meadow; this monastery was on an island in Lake Constance near Constance. It receives the letter F. It is of the end of the ninth century, and contains the Epistles of Paul, without Hebrews (except in Latin), and with a few gaps. With it we reach another member of a group of Greek-Latin manuscripts of which we have already seen three representatives in the Codex Bezæ, the Claromontanus, and its St. Petersburg son. This is a beautiful book. The scribe that wrote it liked to write. In the Greek a point stands between every two words so that the Latin monk may, at least, know where each word begins and ends. That reminds one of old inscriptions. The Greek text is good. Frederic Henry Ambrose Scrivener published it in the year 1859. I shall have to return to it in a moment in connection with the following manuscript.

A former Leipzig professor, Christian Friedrich Börner, once possessed a manuscript, and it is therefore named the Codex Bornerianus. From Börner it passed at his death to the Royal Library at Dresden. The letter for it is G. Börner lent it to Bentley, who kept it five years and longed to buy it, and had a copy made of it which is in Trinity College at Cambridge. Also of the ninth century, like F, it also contains the Epistles of Paul but not Hebrews. Of the six gaps in it, four are also found in F. Aganon, whose name we have already met, and Goddiskalkon, which is Gottschalk, are mentioned in the margin, and at one point there are some Irish verses. Christian Friedrich Matthäi published it in 1791, and did his work very well. Now the Augiensis and the Bornerianus are surely related to each other, closely related. Some think they are brothers, and some think that one of them is the father of the other. In spite of minor differences they are much like each other. Among other agreements they both have the curious word ἀστιζομενος, which is no Greek word at all, but merely the result of misreading Λ as A, —O as C,—and Γ as T, the proper word being λογιζομενος. Should the Greek text of each of them not have been drawn from a common original, then the Greek in F would appear to have been taken from G. The æsthetic difficulty is the chief one here. For the Bornerianus is, as we said above of its mate Δ in St. Gallen, a rough coarse uneducated-looking book, whereas the Augiensis looks very dainty and well-bred. One shrinks from the thought that so ill-looking a father should have such a delicate son. Yet such things do occur, even in flesh and blood.

H.

Speaking of breeding, we pass at once to a very high bred book indeed, yet one which has experienced a serious fall in fortune, and has been sent wandering around the world in the bindings of other genealogically far less favoured volumes. It bears the letter H, and was written in the sixth century in large well-shaped letters which someone maltreated when they grew old and pale by tracing them anew in a very ugly and careless way. At present forty-one leaves of it are known, but new leaves may any day turn up in old bindings. The greater part of the leaves, twenty-two, are in the National Library at Paris. The Laura of St. Athanasius on Mount Athos has eight leaves. Russia has nine leaves, three of which are in two libraries at Moscow, three at St. Petersburg, and three at Kiev. And, lastly, there are two at Turin. That is in part the result of the work of Makarius, who in the year 1218, in the Laura on Mount Athos, used some of these leaves for bookbinding. They contain fragments from a number of the Epistles of Paul, including Hebrews. These leaves are, I think, the oldest, aside from that subscription to Esther in the Codex Sinaiticus, that carry us back to the great library of Pamphilus at Cæsarea of which we have spoken more than once. Indeed, if Tischendorf was right in dating that subscription as of the seventh century, and if we are right in thinking that this manuscript is of the sixth century, it was written before that collation was made. Henri Omont published the forty-one leaves. But strange as it may seem, there is something more to tell. Omont published one more page than the eighty-two pages, and J. Armitage Robinson and H. S. Cronin published that one more and fifteen more in addition, and yet no more leaves had been found. The secret was that these sixteen pages had printed themselves off on various of the forty-one leaves, and were now with great pains reproduced as though from the thin air by those scholars.

I M N O Q R T.

There is one fragment in two leaves at St. Petersburg which is lettered I and is of the fifth century, and contains a little of First Corinthians and a little of Titus.—In the British Museum there are two leaves, and in the City Library at Hamburg there are two leaves written entirely in red. They are M. They are of the ninth century, and give a part of First and Second Corinthians and of Hebrews. Tischendorf published the four leaves in 1855.—The letter N attaches to a fragment of the ninth century at St. Petersburg with a few verses from Galatians and Hebrews.—The same Imperial Library owns O, with two leaves of the sixth century from Second Corinthians, and Q with five papyrus fragments of the fifth century with scattered bits from First Corinthians.—The library at Grottaferrata has a leaf from the close of the seventh century with ten verses from Second Corinthians. It is lettered R.—The letter T^a stands for two little fragments in the Louvre at Paris, from the fourth to the sixth century, with a few words from First Timothy.—Under the letter T^b are placed two leaves in the National Library at Paris of the ninth or tenth century, with seven verses of First Corinthians.—Seven fragments of papyrus of the fifth century from First Corinthians are at Sinai, and bear in our lists the letter ר[14].

For the Revelation we need only refer to a single manuscript in the Vatican Library which has as its sign the letter B, and is of the tenth century. This manuscript offers an eminent example of the fact emphasised in treating of the canon, namely that the Revelation is, contrary to the custom with other books of the Bible, often found in non-biblical manuscripts. This is not a biblical manuscript. We find in it writings of Basil the Great, of Gregory of Nyssa, and of other Church writers. And the Revelation stands among these books. Tischendorf published the text in 1869.

We have now seen the uncial manuscripts of the New Testament with a hasty glance as if we had passed by them in an express train. They contain among their number the most important witnesses to the text of the New Testament, and the presumption of age lies in their favour. Yet we should not forget that their quantity is by no means so great as the long description of them and the many letters used as signs might seem to indicate. Many of them are mere trifles. Each has, that must be insisted upon, its place and value. A bit of parchment with only a half a dozen words on it and no important reading among them may nevertheless offer some day a key to open the way to a connection between widely scattered texts, or to tell us the secret as to some date or place. But a large part of them only speak as direct authority for a very few interesting readings. We can almost count on our fingers those that range widely through the books outside of the four Gospels. We therefore need to turn our attention to other manuscripts, to the small letter or minuscle manuscripts, and see whether in spite of their youth they may not be of service. The earliest of these overlap the large letter manuscripts.

24

IV.

SMALL LETTER GREEK MANUSCRIPTS.

The ninth century probably saw the first books written in
this small letter. The large letters were too stiff, and in their
several, individual isolation could not be written fast enough to
satisfy the demands of the times which were growing ever more
hasty. A passing observer might suppose that the cursive
writing would have answered all purposes of quickness. That
is true. The ancients wrote this running hand without any
doubt as swiftly as we to-day write our letters and our scrawled
notes. And it may well sometimes have happened that someone
wrote a little of the New Testament text in cursive writing. But
that, so far as we can see, never became a rule. We do not
print our Bibles with our ugliest types. Not only the Bibles, and
in particular the New Testaments or New Testament books, but
also polite and learned literature in general, wished for a change.
The large letters had become unwieldy. Either they were black,
thick, and big, and devoured parchment, ink, and time, or they
were small and delicate, and consumed time both for the writer
and for the reader. The problem was to produce a script that
could be written with tolerable speed and ease, connecting many
of the letters without raising the pen. And this script must be
so legible and so beautiful that it could be applied to works of
literature and to sacred books without detracting from the agreeable impression desirable in the former or from the honourable
treatment due to the latter. This problem was happily solved in
the small letter writing, the minuscule. The word "cursive" is
often applied to this hand, but I think it better to restrict that
designation to the running hand to which it properly belongs.
The cursive is not for these times a literary hand. The words
uncial and minuscule, or large letter and small letter, are in a
manner deceptive for a stranger who should take the terms as
expressing of necessity a larger and smaller number of millimetres
in the height and breadth of the letter used. Many of the large

or uncial letters are much smaller than a great deal of the small or minuscle writing. It is, after all, an arbitrary distinction, and the names give no trouble as soon as it is understood to what script they apply.

The small letter manuscripts are likely some day to give us much information in reference to the history of the text. They are numerous, and range widely through the lands and the centuries. Their lines are likely to close quickly if we succeed in gaining a few certain connections between time and place and handwriting and text form. In general it is to be emphasised that the testimony for the New Testament books which follow the Gospels is particularly in need of the help of the small letter manuscripts. These manuscripts are denoted by Arabic numbers. As there are hundreds of them I shall not pretend to go through the list book by book. It will be enough to describe characteristic points, or to call attention to peculiarities in reference to the manuscripts or to their history.

The very first manuscript, 1, of the tenth century, contains all the books of the New Testament except the Revelation. It is in the University Library at Basel. Historically it is interesting to know that this book was used in the correction of the proofs of Erasmus' New Testament. Its text in the Gospels is good. That New Testament would have been much better in its Gospel text if it had followed this copy.—Unfortunately, 2, of the twelfth century, now in the same library, was handed over to the printers by Erasmus, and 2 has a bad text. It only contains the Gospels.— Number 5, at Paris, is a good manuscript. It is of the fourteenth century, and only lacks the Revelation. It has placed Colossians before Philippians, just as the Codex Claromontanus did. This volume was formerly in Calabria.

13. 69. 124. 346.

The manuscript 13, also in the National Library at Paris, may serve as an introduction to a series of manuscripts. Possibly all of this series came from Southern Italy, from Calabria, or were copied from Calabrian manuscripts. The subscriptions say that Matthew was originally written in Hebrew and Mark in Roman or Latin ῥωμαιστί, but Luke in Greek. The pro-

bably spurious words in Matt. 16[2. 3] are omitted, and so are
in Luke 22, vv.[43] and [44]. Then, too, the interpolation about
the adulteress is not at John 7[53] to 8[11], but is placed directly
after Luke 21[38]. This volume was written in Calabria or Sicily
in the thirteenth century. W. H. Ferrar, of Dublin, observed
that this manuscript was much like those numbered 69, 124,
and 346, and collated them to prove it. Thomas Kingsmill
Abbott completed the valuable work in 1877. Since that time
several more copies have been found to belong to the same
group.—Number 14, of the twelfth century, and at Paris, contains the Gospels, and is peculiar, and shows traces of a most
excellent and ancient tradition in that after Mark 16[8] the words
are written in gold: "In some of the copies, up to this point
the evangelist is finished. But in many this also is added";
and then the usual false ending vv.[9-20] follows. The story of the
adulteress is omitted, properly.

Another Parisian manuscript, it is of the fourteenth century,
was very ingeniously gotten up. The number is 16. The
Hebrew Bible printed in colours, the rainbow Bible, might be
compared to this volume. But in this volume, which contains the Gospels in Greek and Latin, the writing itself is of
the given colour, not the parchment, and that is much better.
The general current of the Gospel narrative is in vermilion.
The words of Jesus, the genealogy of Jesus, and the words of
the angel are in crimson. The words taken from the Old
Testament, the words of the disciples and of Zacharias, Elisabeth,
Mary, Simeon, and John the Baptist, are in blue. And, finally,
the words of the Pharisees, of the people from the multitude,
of Judas Iscariot, of the centurion, of the devil, and of the
scribes, are in black. The words of the shepherds are also
black; but I am inclined to think that that was an oversight.
This manuscript contains beautiful pictures. In one way it has
an interest for a painter or an art-critic who cares to go into the
details and learn how the painters of that day and place worked,
for there are some pictures that are only begun, only have a
few lines laid on. I have no doubt that it was at least in
part the work of an Armenian; there are Armenian as well
as Greek numbers for the quires, and the quires are of five,
not of four, double leaves.

Hermonymos.

Number 17 introduces us again to a series of manuscripts. But these manuscripts are not bound together by the text used, as was the case in the group attaching to manuscript 13, for the centre is the scribe who wrote them. George Hermonymos, born in Sparta, came to Paris in 1472, and taught Greek and copied Greek manuscripts, quite a number in Rome too. I have seen at least a dozen manuscripts written by him. His handwriting was not especially beautiful, but it was characteristic. I think I never saw, certainly I have very rarely seen, other manuscripts, manuscripts written by other scribes, that had a handwriting like his. It is very angular.—Number 33, also at Paris, has all the books except the Revelation, and has a very exceptionally good text. It is of the ninth or tenth century.—In number 38 we come in contact with high personages. This manuscript has the New Testament save Revelation, and was written at the command of the Emperor Michael Palæologus, who presented it in the year 1269 or 1270 to Louis IX. of France.—The manuscript 39 takes our thoughts back to H of the Epistles of Paul, the leaves that are scattered all over. There we see Makarius, a monk, in the year 1218 in the Laura of St. Athanasius on Mount Athos. Now this manuscript was written apparently at Constantinople, and in the patriarchal residence there under the patriarch Sergius the Second, and in the year 1218 Makarius carried it to the Laura on Mount Athos.

Serbopulos.

Number 47 is a fat little book in the Bodleian at Oxford. It was written by John Serbopulos in England in the fifteenth century. He copied it out of number 54. That 54 has the note after John 8^2 "In some copies thus" and adds 8^{3-11}. Serbopulos copied the words "in some copies thus" into the text as if it were a part of the Gospel.—The manuscript 54 was written in the year 1338 by a monk Theodosius "with three fingers." When I first saw this expression I supposed it to refer to a mutilated hand. Now I do not think so. It occurs now and then in manuscripts, and alludes, I take it, to the fact that the pen is held between the thumb and the forefinger and the middle finger. Serbopulos' writing may be seen on the margin of two leaves, where he adds some words left out by Theodosius. At least three other manuscripts besides 47 are in some way related to this one.— One of them is number 56, which Serbopulos also wrote. In this manuscript he copied off some verses that Theodosius had written in number 54, but put his own name Johannes in. The consequence was that it was supposed to be the Apostle John that was meant.

61.

The manuscript numbered 61 is at Dublin in Trinity College, and has a history. It is doubtless related to Serbopulos' group just mentioned. It was probably written in England in the sixteenth century, and we are pretty sure that the text of the Gospels was drawn from number 56. Erasmus, of course, did not have First John $5^{7.8}$, the three heavenly witnesses, in his New Testament, for no one dreamed of putting those words into the Greek text save the Alcalá editors who went before Erasmus. In discussing the matter with a bigoted opponent, Erasmus was so thoughtless as to write that he would put the words in if they could be found in a Greek manuscript. There is every reason to believe that this manuscript was written, with the words added, to compel Erasmus to add them, as he then did, "for his oath's sake," like Herod, to his text. It was a great pity that Erasmus did it. It has taken centuries to get the words out again. The paper on which this volume is written is very thick and is heavily glazed. That does not show in general, because it is so white. The page, however, upon which that spurious text is found has been "pawed" to such an extent by curious visitors, whose acquaintance with soap and its use appears to have been a distant one, that the paper has been well browned, and therefore the glazing is distinctly seen. This deceived a scholar so thoroughly that he printed the statement that this page had been glazed.—Number 69 is like the manuscript Ξ in one thing, it is in the wrong place. It was written in the fifteenth century, and contains the whole New Testament. It should properly be in a great library at

Oxford or Cambridge, or in the British Museum. Instead of that it is up at the top of the Town Hall in Leicester in a sheet-iron box, if I remember aright, along with all kinds of town papers. I hope that the town council will some day give it to the British Museum.

THEODORE HAGIOPETRITIS.

Another group attaching to a scribe must now be mentioned, but it is an older group than those of George Hermonymos and John Serbopulos, and it is not a Western but an Eastern group. It begins with number 74, one of Archbishop Wake's manuscripts in Christ Church, Oxford. This was doubtless written about the end of the thirteenth century. The scribe was Theodore of Agiopetros, a village in Arcadia. A bishop Apollonados Theosteriktos made a present of it to "the monastery of St. Gregory called τῶν πασχάνων, lying on the mountain of the great field." It was later in the monastery Pantokrator on Mount Athos, and was brought from there to England in the year 1727. Theodore Hagiopetritis wrote also number 234 in the year 1278, number 856 in the year 1280, number 484 in the year 1292, number 483 in the year 1295, and number 412 in the year 1301. He also wrote in 1295 a synararion now at Moscow. Number 90 is a late copy of a manuscript that he wrote in 1293.

CONFUSED GENEALOGIES.

Number 80 belongs to Mr. Lesoeuf at Paris. It gives an example of a curious mistake in copying which does not often occur. The genealogy in Luke $3^{23\text{-}38}$ presents a very strange complexion. Upon examination it is clear that this manuscript was copied from one that had twenty-three lines on a page, and, further, that in that manuscript the genealogy was written in . three columns with the names arranged in the order of the columns, not in the order of the lines. Then the scribe of 80 copied the genealogy off in the order of the lines, causing dire confusion, and making everybody the son of some wrong man : τοῦ ἰωράμ· τοῦ καϊνάν· τοῦ ἰωσῆ· τοῦ ἐσρώμ· τοῦ ἐνῶς. One would

have thought that the scribe would have noticed the false family
combinations.   He must have copied very mechanically not to see
the impossibility of the relationship in many cases.—Let us, however, pass at once to number 109.   It is of the year 1326, and is in
the British Museum.   The manuscript from which it was copied
had the genealogy in Luke in two columns of twenty-eight lines
each and following the columns.   The scribe of 109 copied it
then, following the lines.   The conditions of things is much
worse than in 80, and would appear to be blasphemous, were it
not clearly an error of mere stupidity.   It so happened in that
original—for we can reproduce it with mathematical exactness
from these tangled names—that the names, which of course end,
conclude, rise to the apex in God, did not fill the last column.
In consequence the name of God came to stand within the list
instead of at the close of it.   And God is actually said to have
been the son of Aram, and the source of all things is not God
but Phares.   It is hard enough to imagine how a monk could
have written, without observing it, a wrong father for Jesse or
David or Solomon.   But that he should calmly put God as the
son of Aram, passes all fancy.—The next book, 110, does not
belong here at all.   It is of the sixteenth century, and is called
the Codex Ravianus.   It is in the Royal Library at Berlin.
Instead, however, of being a copy of some old manuscript, it is
a copy of the New Testament as it stands in the printed
Complutensian polyglott, and has also a few readings from
Erasmus and Stephens.

THE STORY OF THE ADULTERESS.

Number 129 was written in the twelfth century by Eustathius.
The story of the adulteress was not in the Gospel of John in
the example from which the text was copied.   At the close
of the Gospel, however, on the last leaf of the manuscript,
Eustathius wrote: We have written the chapter about the
adulteress found in many copies.   And then he adds John
8^{3-11}.—Number 145 has the paragraph about the adulteress in
the text, but notes thereby: This chapter is lacking in many
copies.—The manuscript 157 is a very good one.   It is of the
twelfth century, and is in the Vatican Library.   It was written for

John the Second, Porphyrogenitus, who ruled 1118 to 1148.—
In 237, a manuscript of the tenth century at Moscow in the
library of the Synod, the story of the adulteress is at the end of
the Gospel of John as a separate affair, and marked as the lesson
"for one repenting.   Out of the Gospel according to John."
And at the end of the lesson is the remark : "This Gospel [that
means : this lesson] is not found in the more accurate of the
copies."   The way in which the passage is given shows that the
scribe got it out of a manuscript of a book of the lessons from
the Gospels, and that it stood among the so-called "various"
Gospels at the end of that book, not in the regular series of
lessons.—Not very different from that, we find in number 259
at Moscow, also in the library of the Synod, the passage about
the adulteress after the close of the Gospel, with the sentence :
"There is found in some copies also this chapter (some such
chapter) attached to the Gospel according to John."

    Number 288 is one of the books that were cut into several parts,
probably in order to sell them better.   Matthew is in the Bodleian
at Oxford, Luke in the National Library at Paris, and John in the
library of the Institute at Paris.   Where Mark is, if it still exists,
I do not know.   It is on the paper quires 13 to 19, marked in
Greek ιγ΄ to ιθ΄.   George Hermonymos wrote these four Gospels
in his angular hand.—In number 296 we have a specimen of the
writing of Angelo Vergèce of the sixteenth century.   It is in the
National Library at Paris.   The types for Greek in the royal
printing-office at Paris, which was also used by Robert Estienne,
Stephens, are said to have been cut after the writing of this
skilful and artistic scribe.   At the end Vergèce wrote an Amen,
ἀμήν, very much curled up and twisted like a monogram ; and a
scholar who described this manuscript managed to make the
year 1428 out of the word.   That was very ingenious, but
Vergèce must have been born long after that date.

    The manuscript 346 of the twelfth century in the Ambrosiana
at Milan belongs to the group mentioned under number 13.   It
was probably written in Calabria.   This volume presents in
Matt. 1^{16}, a rare reading, and one which would be of much
moment for the development of Christianity, if Christianity
developed upon the lines of scientific research instead of upon
the lines of weak tradition.   This is the reading also found in
some Old-Latin and Old-Syrian manuscripts : "Joseph, to

whom the Virgin Mary was betrothed, begat Jesus called the Christ."

The manuscript 365, the number of the days of the year, is at Florence in the Laurentiana. An amusing thing happened in connection with it. It had been placed in the list of the manuscripts by Scholz. Dean Burgon while at Florence tried to find it. The librarian assured him that no such manuscript ever had existed there, and its appearance in the list was supposed to be a specimen of the most extraordinary carelessness on the part of Scholz, who had even stated that he had collated select passages in this non-existent volume. I had never observed such work on Scholz' part, and was therefore curious to learn how the case might stand. On going to the Laurentiana, of course I examined first of all the catalogues which were on a shelf at the service of all visitors. The great printed catalogue was made by Angelo Maria Bandini, who died in 1800. At the end of the third volume I found on the fly-leaves the description of this, and I think of a few other manuscripts, written there by Bandini himself. I said nothing about it. I simply ordered the book among others, and it was brought to me by the attendant at once without remark. Scholz had not been so careless after all, but only a little more accurate than had been supposed.—Number 418, a manuscript of the fifteenth century at Venice in the Marciana, is of interest for the history of the Lord's Prayer. It is well known that the doxology in that prayer is spurious. This volume gives the doxology in the following form : "And the glory of the Father and of the Son and of the Holy Spirit unto the ages." It is probably the liturgical form to which the scribe who wrote this manuscript was accustomed.—The manuscript numbered 431 may be considered as one raised from the dead. It belongs to the library of the Roman Catholic theological seminary at Strassburg, and is of the twelfth century. Everyone thought that it had perished during the siege and capture of Strassburg by the Germans in 1870. But Albert Ehrhard, now happily again in Strassburg, discovered the manuscript years ago safe and sound.—Fine goods are sometimes said to be done up in small packages. That would fit number 461, which is not more than about seventeen centimetres high and ten broad. It was written by a monk Nicholas in the year 835, and is therefore one of the oldest

Greek manuscripts in small letters that is known. Formerly it was at St. Saba, south-east of Jerusalem.

JOASAPH.

Number 480, written in the year 1366, is one of two concentric groups of manuscripts. It is written in a beautiful hand by the monk Joasaph. The first group is, then, of the manuscripts written by Joasaph. But I find that Joasaph is a member of a widespread school of scribes that did good work through centuries, and this school forms the second group.—Number 565, a manuscript of the ninth or tenth century in the Imperial Library at St. Petersburg, corresponds in its make to the books mentioned by Theonas, for its parchment is purple and the writing is golden. Its text is of high value for the determination of the re-wrought text which we spoke of under the Codex Bezæ.—The manuscript 651, of the eleventh or twelfth century, in Dessau, was one of the first manuscripts, with one in Athens, in which I found the peculiar reading in John 8⁹, where instead of ἀκούσαντες it has ἀναγινώσκοντες, and places before our eyes the dramatic scene in which Jesus writes in the sand ἑνὸς ἑκάστου αὐτῶν τὰς ἁμαρτίας, the sins of each one of the accusing Pharisees who have brought the adulteress before Him. The eldest reads his sin and hurries away, and the rest follow, each after seeing that his sin is known. I have since found this reading in a number of manuscripts, especially upon Mount Athos.—Number 699 is a divided manuscript of the eleventh century, containing, save four small gaps, the whole New Testament. Much of it is in the British Museum, but Ephesians and Revelation are at Highgate, where the manuscripts are, or used to be, most carelessly guarded. Highgate School should give all its manuscripts to, or deposit them in, the British Museum, and at the least give this fragment to the Museum so as to complete the copy of the New Testament. It was Edward A. Guy who discovered that the two manuscripts belonged together.

Number 703 is, so far as I know, a wanderer. It is nevertheless surely resting in somebody's library, and I wish that a reader of these lines would recognise it and write to me about it. I saw it at Quaritch's a number of years ago. It is of the year

1251, and can be further recognised by the circumstance that leaves three and six were cut out of quire 41, $\mu a'$, and new leaves, three, six, and seven, thrust in, containing John 7¹⁸⁻²⁸ and 7⁴⁸⁻ 8¹⁷. That was done in order to insert the story of the adulteress, which was not in the original manuscript. Often we find a single leaf cut out and two put in, in order to add that spurious passage. In John 1²⁸ the word $\beta\eta\theta\alpha\beta\alpha\rho\hat{\alpha}$ was changed by a later hand to $\beta\eta\theta\alpha\nu\iota\alpha$. In 8² it reads $\beta\alpha\theta\epsilon$ος $\hat{\eta}\lambda\theta\epsilon\nu$ $\dot{o}$ $\overline{\iota s}$, and in 8⁵ $\nu\dot{o}\mu\omega$ $\dot{\eta}\mu\hat{\omega}\nu$, $\mu\omega\ddot{\upsilon}\sigma\hat{\eta}s$, and in 8⁷ $\dot{\alpha}\nu\alpha\beta\lambda\dot{\epsilon}\psi\alpha s$. At the beginning are some chronological remarks, in which the scribe put in by mistake the year 1259 instead of 1251.

VULGARIUS.

Number 817 carries us back to Basel, where we found numbers 1 and 2, and to Erasmus' edition of the New Testament. This manuscript is of the fifteenth century, and is in the University Library at Basel, having formerly belonged to the Dominicans there. On the title-page of Erasmus' first edition of the New Testament he named among the old writers from whom he had drawn notes, a Vulgarius. It really seems as if he did not know who this Vulgarius was. But he found out; doubtless someone told him, having seen the name on that title and in his commentary. I did not know where he got the name until in 1885 I examined the manuscripts at Basel, and found on the front cover of this one the word Vulgarius. Then all was clear. This was a copy of the Gospels with the commentary of Theophylact of Bulgaria. In Greek B is pronounced like our V. Long before Erasmus some monk has then written, according to the Greek pronunciation, on this volume Vulgarius as the equivalent of $\text{Bov}\lambda\gamma\dot{\alpha}\rho\iota os$, the Bulgarian. The heading of the commentary inside had been so much defaced as to be for a hasty glance illegible, and Erasmus had been content to use the name found on the cover of the book.

The manuscript 1076, in the Laura of St. Athanasius on Mount Athos, written in the tenth century, places the passage about the adulteress after the close of John with the remark: "There is also something else found in old copies, which we have thought well to write at the end of the same Gospel, which is what follows."—Numbers 1098 to 1109 have probably all perished. They were in the monastery of Simopetra on Mount Athos, where I saw them in passing in 1886. The library was burned in 1891.—It was similarly supposed that the books of the Greek Gymnasium at Saloniki or Thessalonica were destroyed by fire. I had numbered the New Testament volumes in 1886. I think that some of them are still there. Others took wings during the confusion of the fire, and have found a place in another Eastern library.—Number 1194, of the tenth or eleventh century, at Mount Sinai, "was written on the island Patmos, in the cave where the holy John the Theologian saw the Revelation, by the hand of John, a monk, for the head monk Theoktistos." That name is probably a favourite one on Patmos. I saw there a Theoktistos over eighty years of age, living as a hermit away off in a lonely corner of the mountains.—It will be remembered that we spoke of John as dictating his Gospel to Prochorus. Number 1322, in the library of the patriarch of Jerusalem has the picture of John and Prochorus, and gives the hand of the Lord reaching forth from the cloud as I described it ; and John says to Prochorus : " Child Prochorus, what thou hearest from me, that write."—The manuscript 1346, in the patriarchal library at Jerusalem, reminds us of a man who sinned much against the manuscripts, whose memory is noisome not only in his home surroundings, but also through the monasteries of the East. Two leaves of this manuscript of the Gospels are at St. Petersburg. The Imperial Library there contains a large number of fine leaves from valuable manuscripts which Porfiri Uspenski of Kiev cut, tore, stole out of all manner of books in the large Eastern libraries. How coarse and brutal he must have been !

Acts and Catholic Epistles.

The manuscripts of Acts and of the Catholic Epistles begin a new series of numbers. Number 2 among them is, like number 2 in the manuscripts of the Gospels, the volume that Erasmus sent to the printers so that they should set up the Acts and the Catholic Epistles and the Pauline Epistles from it. It is in the University Library at Basel.—The manuscript numbered 162 is of the fourteenth century, and is in the Vatican Library at

Rome. It contains the Acts and all the Epistles, both Greek and Latin, and the Greek text is made to conform to the Vulgate Latin text. Words are put in a different order. Sometimes the division of lines and syllables in the Greek is assimilated to that in the Latin text. It is as if the scribe had foreseen the decree of the Council of Trent, that the Vulgate should be the one authentic text, the measure for the correctness of everything else. This manuscript has a particularly exceptional position. It will be remembered that we saw above the probability that a Dublin manuscript had been written for the purpose of forcing Erasmus according to his promise to put 1 John $5^{7.8}$ into his edition, he having said that he would put it in if it were shown to him in a single Greek manuscript. Now at that time no one knew anything of this manuscript. And if anyone had known of it, it would have given him another shape of the verse. For there can be no reasonable doubt that this interpolation is part and parcel of the assimilation of the Greek text in this manuscript to the Latin text, and that by someone who was not a good Greek scholar. It is therefore not in the least degree a Greek witness for the authenticity of the spurious words.—The manuscript 311 is instructive for this 1 John $5^{7.8}$. At the word "three," $\tau\rho\epsilon\hat{\iota}s$, in 1 John 5^7 is the marginal note: "The Holy Spirit, and the Father, and Himself of Himself."—I referred above to a manuscript of the Gospels written by George Hermonymos, which was partly in three libraries, and partly, Mark, of unknown residence. Number 331 here is made up of James and First and Second Peter in the Vatican Library at Rome, and of the Epistles of Paul in four parts in the National Library at Paris, all of which I connected with each other in 1885 and 1886. The quires 6–9 and 27–31, or $\varsigma'-\theta'$ and $\kappa\zeta'-\lambda a'$, with 2 Pet. 3^{16}–Jude ^{25} and 2 Cor. 13^1– Eph. 6^{24}, are still to be sought for. It was also written by George Hermonymos, and appears to be related to at least two other manuscripts of these books.

It is not necessary to delay over any of the manuscripts which begin with the Epistles of Paul. We have already spoken of many of the manuscripts containing these Epistles, but beginning with the Gospels or the Acts or Catholic Epistles. The manuscript numbered 1 in the Revelation is again a manuscript that was used by Erasmus. It is the only manuscript that he had for Revelation, and the defects of various kinds in these pages have left their stamp upon Erasmus' edition of that book. For centuries this volume lay hidden. Finally, Franz Delitzsch, then at Erlangen, discovered it in the library of the family Öttingen-Wallerstein in Mayhingen. The text is a good text, but it is easy to confuse it at some points with the accompanying commentary of Andrew of Cæsarea, and Erasmus did in one place consider words of commentary to be text. Then again the end of Revelation (22^{16-21}) was lacking, and this as well as trifles elsewhere Erasmus translated from the Latin into mediocre Greek for his text. This manuscript brings before us the one kind of manuscripts of the Revelation, the manuscripts which present the text with the commentary of Andrew or of Arethas of Cæsarea. Of these manuscripts there are a number, and it is to be expected that they will in a large measure be from one or two antitypes, and present but one or two types of text. One type is to be looked for, if it can be proved that Arethas adopted the text used by his acknowledged predecessor Andrew. Should, however, Arethas have made many changes in the text of Andrew, then two types of text would be before us in these commentaries. That is, then, one kind of text for Revelation, whether in one or two types.

The other kind of text is that which is scattered among non-biblical manuscripts. This is likely to be of different types. As specimens of this position of Revelation in non-biblical manuscripts we saw above the manuscript in the Vatican Library denoted as *B*. Here we may mention 18, which is simply the quires 13 to 15 out of a manuscript which will be sure to have been non-biblical,—then number 31, which begins with Dionysius the Areopagite;—number 32 is again probably torn from a general theological manuscript, and has at the end an essay of Theodore Prodromos;—number 49 is in a volume of the orations of Gregory of Nazianzus;—number 50 is combined with lives of the saints;—number 58 contains Job, that is biblical, but also Justin's Exhortation to the Greeks;—number 61 contains various writings of Basil, Theodoret, and Maximus; —number 65 contains works of Basil, Gregory of Nyssa, and Peter of Alexandria;—and 81 contains much from Gregory of Nyssa. That is enough to show the point referred to.

So much for the small letter manuscripts of the continuous text of the books of the New Testament. We now turn to the books which have a liturgical aim.

V.

LESSON-BOOKS.

WHEN treating of the criticism of the canon we had occasion more than once to refer to the reading of the books of the New Testament in church. So long as this reading took place upon the basis of the ordinary manuscripts of the text of these books it will have had no great influence upon the form of the text in one way or the other, in conserving old forms or in introducing changes of any kind whatsoever. Introductory words for these lessons drawn from the manuscripts of the continuous text may have been originally added verbally, and gradually written on the margin at the proper places. This latter habit will have served as a transition to another kind of manuscript. For in time it will have become irksome to take the regularly used lessons from a general text, in which the clergyman will not have been able so quickly or so clearly to catch the proper beginning or the due ending of the passage for the day. The time came at which the clergy, having a fixed series of lessons to read and re-read, placed these lessons in special books, every lesson being supplied with the necessary words of introduction and with such more trifling modifications as might be incident to and necessary in detaching the section from the surrounding text. Thus the Church came to have lesson-books.

These lesson-books, especially those of the Gospels, soon became the chief ornaments of the library of the churches. The Gospel lesson-book was carried through the church at the chief service, was held aloft to the view of all at a solemn moment in the services. It was then necessary that it be ornamented in the highest manner possible. The front cover was set with such precious stones as could be obtained. In the middle of it there was often a heavy silver crucifix. The writing used was, of course, at first the large letter or uncial, and those large letters may have continued to be used in these lesson-books even after they had passed out of fashion in other works, and even in the copies of the scripture with the continuous text. At the beginning of each lesson stood in the better copies a large letter that was at least red, but perhaps painted also with blue and yellow, or was traced in most delicate combinations of colours and of gold. Sometimes these letters were formed into animals or men, perhaps occasionally hinting even at a scene spoken of in the lesson.

The volume which contained the lessons from the Gospels was called a "Gospel," εὐαγγέλιον. We could fancy to ourselves a certain propriety in this name, as though the distinctions of the four evangelists were here to be sunk in the presentation of the one "Gospel" lying at the foundation of all they give. But this fancy does not fit, seeing that a large part of the individuality of the evangelists remains even in the books of lessons, and we know also that at a very early age the four Gospels themselves were designated more than once as "the Gospel."

We find in the reading-books two parts, each of which embraces the whole year. At first it seems strange that the lessons should be given twice for the year, and it might be suggested that there should be but one series of lessons from beginning to end. But that would not be easy. The Church brought over, alas, from Judaism a movable Easter, and we are many of us still bound by this unchristian variable day. The consequence was that the two parts of the Gospel—we shall for the sake of simplicity now speak chiefly of the Gospel—were devoted respectively to the movable and to the fixed year, and thus give the year twice. We shall, however, see that the two years do not begin at the same point of time. Nowadays in the West the church-year begins largely with the first Sunday of advent. That has nothing to do with the Greek Church.

The church-year in the East begins, not with the quiet scene at the manger accompanied by the heavenly strains of angels, but with the blaze of light at the resurrection, with the triumphant return from the dead, with the heralding of the conquest over death itself. Seven weeks bring us to Whitsuntide, where a new section of the book opens. Here in this section one part of the movableness or mutability of the lessons comes into play. For according to the advance or recession of Easter there remains for the time after Whitsuntide a larger or smaller number of weeks before what we call—it is nearly the same thing—Michaelmas,

25

but what the Greeks call New Year. If I am not mistaken this New Year is, like Easter and like the English designation of Sunday or the Lord's day as Sabbath, something borrowed from Judaism, and this therefore is a continuation of the Jewish New Year, Head of the Year, the Seleucidian or Syro-Macedonian year. The book provides for seventeen weeks, but that number rarely or never occurs. Then from September, though sometimes not from the first day of the month but from the Sunday after the festival of the cross on September fourteenth, a new series of lessons begins. The beginning of this series of lessons is the one fixed point, so far as I can see, in the whole movable year, and betrays therefore the presence in the ancient Church of a practical respect for the given New Year, even though we may ask whether all Christians recognised the connection of the year with Jewish habit or not. It was the time of the equal day and night. The lessons that began here were again compelled to suit themselves to the motion of the feasts, and to fill out the time that separated September from Lent. The lenten lessons formed a compact mass by themselves, closing with the evening of Holy Saturday, and giving place anew to the Easter celebration at midnight. This is the movable year.

Of course, the fixed year cannot begin at the same place, cannot depend upon the Passover feast wandering with the Israelites in the desert. The fixed year returns to the Jewish or Syro-Macedonian year, and begins with the first of September. It cleaves to the months and the days. It is called a " month-reckoning " or "month-booking," a menologion. Saint after saint is marshalled before us. Christmas rises to view, and then Epiphany. And it closes its round on the thirty-first of August with the laying away of the girdle of the Virgin Mary in the Chalkopratia at Constantinople.

At the first blush it might seem as if we had with these two divisions, with the movable and with the fixed year, exhausted the possible need for Gospel lessons. That is not the case. One of the greatest festivals in the East, and indeed in Europe as well, is the festal day of the local church. Now that birthday of the church is, of course, not a part of the movable year. It is for each single church a given fixed day. This day varies, however, with the single churches. One may have been dedicated on the tenth of April, another on the twentieth of July, and the lesson appointed for the saints of those particular days may have no possible connection with the dedication of a Church. In the same way there are funeral services that agree with neither year. There are continually earthquakes, and these too refuse to bind themselves to a day and an hour. People repent of their sins—perhaps not quite so often as would be desirable—and they cannot be requested to save up their feelings of a change of heart until a particular day thereunto set. Armies secure victories, and the Church must celebrate them then, and not next Whitsuntide, and not on the eighteenth of the next or any other month. There must therefore, for these and for similarly unmanageable occasions, be still a third and a very short series of lessons for various purposes. Therewith the book closes.

The method in which the ancient Church chose the lessons for all these movable and immovable days leads us far into the unknown regions of the past history of Christianity. There are, so much is plain, at least three different lines of lessons in the movable year, and it is possible that there were still more, only that we can no longer distinguish, or have not yet succeeded in distinguishing, them. It seems to me likely that at an extremely early date the lessons were chosen for the Sundays. At that date, and therefore we must go very far back, the Church still celebrated, certainly not only Sunday but also the Jewish Sabbath, not the false English Sabbath but Saturday. And it seems probable that then the lessons for the Saturdays or Sabbaths were still from the Old Testament. At a later time, but still at an early period, the Gospel lessons for the Saturdays or Sabbaths were chosen.

We must stand still a moment here. The fact that the lessons were chosen for the Saturdays shows us that the Saturday or Sabbath was still especially celebrated, and that forces us to the same conclusion, stated a line or two back, for the preceding period. The celebration of Saturday or Sabbath must have been an original, Jewish-Christian observance, cannot have been a later addition to the Christian Sunday. And the order of time as to the choice of these two lines of lessons is for this reason a necessity, because it would be inconceivable that the Saturday or Sabbath lessons should have been chosen first, and that at that time the Sunday lessons remained Old Testament lessons. A body might be inclined to fancy that the Old Testament lessons were retained for

Sunday as being more certainly sacred, even after the Church had proceeded to choose Saturday or Sabbath lessons from the Gospels. I regard that as totally impossible. It seems to me that the moment that the distinctively exceptional and divine character of the Gospels became clear to the Christian Churches, that at that moment they will have proceeded to set for the Church services for Sunday lessons from the Gospels. The reasons that I do not assume a determination of these lessons for both these neighbouring great days at one single time is that the two lines are independent of each other. For the first the Sabbath or Saturday lessons probably remained the Jewish Old Testament lessons. At a still later period, at one which I at present cannot even approximately fix, the Gospel lessons for the week-days were chosen and formed a line for themselves. So much for the movable year.

The lessons for the fixed year were, I am inclined to think, not chosen at one time, but at first saint by saint and day by day. It would be possible that after the year was tolerably well filled some one should have set about completing it, fitting saints to and into days that had remained saint-less, and assigning Gospels to their memory. Aside from the regular lesson-books, we sometimes find in liturgical manuscripts a set of Gospels for a week, so that any and every day could at once be suited with a lesson. Monday was the day of the angels, Tuesday of John the Baptist, Wednesday of the Virgin, but called in Greek invariably " the bearer of God," Thursday of the holy apostles, and Friday the day of the crucifixion. For Saturday and Sunday nothing was given, because they had the regular lessons, the backbone of the determination of all lessons. It might be queried whether some such set of weekly Gospels or week-day Gospels had preceded the choice of lessons for every single day. I could conceive of such a thing, yet at present I do not think it likely, because I cannot remember finding this week of Gospel lessons in other than comparatively young manuscripts.

It was very fitting that the Greek Church should place at the head of all the Gospels on the opening " holy and great Sunday of Easter," τῇ ἁγίᾳ καὶ μεγάλῃ κυριακῇ τοῦ πάσχα, the beginning of the Gospel of John : In the beginning was the Word. This Gospel, with but one or two exceptions, then fills the Sundays and Saturdays and week-days for the seven weeks until Whitsuntide.

The close is an interesting one both for the textual critic and for the Christian in general. The last lesson, the lesson for Whitsunday, has no trace of the story of the adulteress between John 7^{52} and 8^{12},—that is for the critic. For the general Christian it is a beautiful ending for the lessons which began with: In the beginning was the Word, and the Word was with God: to read Jesus's proclamation of Himself in John 8^{12}: "I am the light of the world. He that followeth Me shall not walk in darkness, but shall have the light of life." At the close of this section it must be observed that by far the greater majority, that almost all of the books of lessons have all the lessons for every day up to this point. From this point, however, until Lent a very great many of the books do not give the daily lessons, but only those for the Saturdays and the Sundays.

With the day after Whitsunday, with Whitmonday, the Gospel according to Matthew comes in, and it supplies the Saturdays and Sundays for seventeen weeks, tentatively, as above explained, thus caring for the weeks between Whitsunday and Michaelmas. In reference to the Gospels for the week-days, Matthew is their source during the first eleven of these seventeen weeks. Now the Gospel of Mark does not, as we shall see, rise to the dignity of having a section for itself in which it furnishes the lessons both for the Saturdays and Sundays and for the week-days. For that reason it is after the eleventh week here put into the Matthew section to give the lessons for Monday, Tuesday, Wednesday, Thursday, and Friday. At Michaelmas, then,—let us say at the beginning or at the middle of September, seeing that it sometimes, in some places, depends upon the Sunday after September fourteenth, a comparatively fixed point as I above called it,—the Gospel according to Luke begins, and is the source of the Saturday and Sunday lessons until Lent. As with Matthew so with Luke, Luke offers the week-day lessons also until the close of the twelfth week—in Matthew it was the eleventh—and then these are drawn from Mark. In Lent the Saturdays and Sundays are dedicated to Mark, but the five week-days are filled by the Old Testament. It strikes one strangely to think that in this great Church the Old Testament is placed in such a comparatively inferior position. Indeed, manuscripts of the Old Testament are rare things, and there are not even many manuscripts of the lesson-books of the Old Testament. As might be expected, the lessons for the passion-week are particularly numerous and long. On Good Friday there are twelve Gospels of the passion and four Gospels of the four hours. There is also a group of eleven morning resurrection lessons.

The monthly register, the fixed part of the Gospel, is very differently treated in different manuscripts, varying perhaps with the money or with the time which those who ordered or he who wrote the book had at command. Some volumes have the few strictly necessary great days, and then very few saints and almost none of less known name. Others have a saint for at least every day in the year, save the great feasts. Certain lessons are often repeated for similar memories. For example, the passage Matthew 11$^{27\text{-}30}$ is used for the memory of a saint in general among the "various" Gospels at the end of the list, and is applied to various special or single saints in the list itself.

The "Apostle," the book containing the lesson from Acts and the Epistles, is far more rare than the "Gospel." It is also arranged in two parts, but in one respect it is more simple than the Gospel, because the lessons after Whitsuntide flow on in a single series of weeks up to Lent. The book of Acts is read on Saturdays and Sundays and week-days between Easter and Whitsuntide, and it is of interest that we know that that was the custom at the time of Chrysostom, who died in 407. It is clear from that circumstance that the lessons are not of a very late date.

In a large number, probably in the majority of the books of lessons, there are red musical signs above or below the words to direct the one who has to read, intone, or sing them before the assembled Christians.

Since the sixteenth century a number of editions of "Gospels" and "Apostles" have been printed, largely in Venice. The oldest Gospel that I know of is the one printed in Venice in 1539. I have never heard of a copy of it in the West, save a single one, and I have not been able to find many copies of it in the East. The fact appears to have been overlooked that in the earlier editions of these books large portions of the Greek text of the New Testament were published in print drawn directly from manuscripts, and without connection with the Western editions of the New Testament.

The manuscripts of these lesson-books have their own Arabic

numerals. Number 13, of the twelfth century, in the National Library at Paris, reminds the reader of a various reading sometimes found in the title of the twelve Gospels of the passion. There I have just written "passion." We say "passion" in the West. In the East, in the Greek Church, they say "passions," or, if you please, "sufferings": τὰ εὐαγγέλια τῶν παθῶν. That is the Greek rule: The Gospels of the passions. But there are a few manuscripts that have: The Gospels of the passion: τὰ εὐαγγέλια τοῦ πάθους. I think that they must be attributed to the West, to the influence of the Latin Church.—The manuscript 46 is of the costly kind, on purple parchment in golden uncial writing. It is of the ninth or tenth century, and is in the Imperial Library at Vienna. Like many a distinguished book, it brings more show than contents, for it only offers us nineteen select lessons.—Number 117 of the twelfth century in the Laurentiana at Florence is also in golden writing, and contains about twenty-two lessons.—In number 280, which lies in the Greek Church of St. George at Venice, and is of the fourteenth century, we find two characteristic subscriptions, showing us how these manuscripts were used for special requests for prayer on the part of those who wrote or who possessed or who made presents of them: "The present holy Gospel was completed by me the worthless priest and first judge (advocate) of the holy metropolis of Lacedæmonia, Nicholas Malotros, and ye priests who in the future open it pray for me the wretched one in your sacred functions, that the Lord may also forgive you your transgressions in the terrible day of His repaying." Doubtless in some such cases the writing of the book was the self-imposed task in expiation of a sin, and the prayer desired was aimed to cover that sin. Nevertheless the expressions worthless and wretched here used are so frequently found in such subscriptions that one is inclined to attribute them to a show of modesty. A later hand wrote the following: "Every one who reads this holy Gospel should pray for and remember in the sacred functions Nicholas the son of Eustathius, who bought it and gave it to me the Spiritual Isaiah, in order that I remember him so long as I remain among the living, and that after my departure hence I leave it to whatsoever monastery I please. I received it in the year from Christ 1462, the eleventh indiction." In general the dates in the manuscripts are in the year of the world. Only a

few late manuscripts write the year of our Lord as this scribe
Isaiah does.—Number 292 is of the tenth century, and is in the
city library at Carpentras in southern France. It is written in
uncial letters. In the year 1091 Epiphanius Magister Paschales
presented it to the monastery of the bearer of God of Alypos.
There are several historical notes on the margins, telling of the
pest on Cyprus in 1438 and in 1575.—In the manuscript 396
Hilarion, who wrote it in Berœa, tells how they had been driven
from Mount Athos by the Turks, and had halted in Berœa.
Having no "Gospel" in the monastery, and there being no
skilled writer, τεχνίτης, he had copied this Gospel: "And ye that
read, if ye find mistakes, forgive and pray to the Lord for me
Hilarion, monk and priest, written in the year 6836, tenth
indiction." That is, 1328.—In number 835 of the Greek
gymnasium at Saloniki, or Thessalonica, the writer makes a new
word to name in one breath the people whom he wished to have
pray for him: "Ye who read this holy volume priestpastor-
deacons, πρεσβυτεροπαπαδοδιάκονοι, pray for me to the Lord."
He wrote in the year 1072.

Herewith we leave the Greek manuscripts of the text of the
New Testament. No other Greek book has anything like the
amount of testimony to its text that the books of the New
Testament have. The only difficulty is that there are not
workers and there is not money enough at command to secure
the collation of these hundreds of manuscripts in all parts of
Europe and of the East. The greater part of them have only
been touched in select passages. Now that is far better than
nothing, and we may be very thankful for what has been done
in that respect. Yet that is not the clear-cut, whole work. For
the text of the New Testament, the right thing, the whole thing,
the very best thing that can be done is just good enough. There
should be a carefully drawn up plan and a systematic inspection of
the whole field, and then the work should be divided up among
collators and finished piece by piece, library after library, and
sent in copy to four or five of the great libraries of the world,
so as to be at the service of every Christian scholar who is
prepared to work upon the subject. Christianity could well
spare the men and the money for this purpose. Every manuscript should also be photographed, and its ornaments and large
section letters should be copied, so that even externally the

comparison of the way in which the books have been prepared
and written may lend its aid to the grouping of kindred manuscripts and to the determination of the time and place of origin
of the manuscripts.   Such a systematic endeavour to work over
this field should receive not merely the interested attention but
also the most active help of all classical philologians who busy
themselves with Greek texts.   For every advance, every new
determination in reference to the Greek manuscripts of the New
Testament, is of peculiar moment for Greek palæography.   No
classical books, and not the whole of the Greek classics combined,
offer such an opportunity as the manuscripts of the New Testament offer, for the decision of palæographical problems from the
fourth century down to the sixteenth.

VI.

TRANSLATIONS.

BEYOND all question the original Greek text of the New Testament has the chief interest for us, and must remain our final
aim.   It is perfectly true that Jesus and His disciples without
doubt commonly spoke Aramaic, an Aramaic that had come
down from the North, though I consider it as possible that He
and they also understood and spoke more or less Greek, seeing
that the tiny province in which the Jews prevailed was so closely
surrounded by and permeated by Greeks.   The words of Jesus,
therefore, which the Gospels have preserved for us are, aside
from a few cases, words that have been translated from the
Aramaic into Greek.   Now it might at first sight seem proper and
desirable that we should in textual criticism be especially glad if
by any chance we came upon and could insert at the given place
in the Gospels any Aramaic words that Jesus spoke instead of
the Greek words which now stand there.   Not in the least.   We
should rejoice with all our hearts to be able to determine
certainly any of those Aramaic words and sentences.   But they
would have nothing directly to do with textual criticism.   The
textual critic must necessarily limit his work to the reconstruction
of, the purifying of, the accurate determination of the original
Greek text of these New Testament books.

In pursuing this aim the critic appeals first to the manuscripts
which in one way or another offer him in its entirety or in large
parts and sections that Greek text, and we have already spoken of
these manuscripts.   As, however, these Greek Gospels with their
translations give us the Aramaic words of Jesus, so is it also
possible that translations of these Greek Gospels be of very great
assistance to us in determining the original Greek text.   These
translations have in one way an extraordinary interest for the connection between the New Testament and Christianity, because
thousands of Christians in the Churches of the respective countries
for centuries have drawn and many still draw much of what they

know about Jesus and His work and His worth from these translations. But their advantage for us lies in another, in the inverse direction. We wish to know their source. We wish to determine the form from which they were taken, the model after which they were drawn, the seal which made this impression. Then we turn back to the early Church and pass beyond the wide circles which the Greek Church embraces, and ask among other languages and peoples for those who used the books of the New Testament in other than the Greek tongue. Everywhere it must then be our effort to ascend the stream of each such tradition to its head, to the point at which it has branched off from the Greek mother tradition in our Gospels.

Of course, we cannot expect to be able to reach in any language the precise point at which the very first translation of any part of the New Testament was made. It would be scarcely possible to imagine that positively nothing of the volume had been transferred to a given language before a definite day upon which some one set himself the aim to translate it, and then in a single effort rendered every part of it from Matthew to Revelation into his native tongue. We should indeed have to ask ourselves, whether no one translated some one book or more than one book into another language even before the collection was gathered together into one whole. And we must in the nature of the case presuppose that many fragments or various single books were here and there translated before the whole was systematically taken in hand.

Our inward inclination would lead us to lay at first and continually the greatest stress upon the translations made in the East. We feel instinctively that they must be of most service to us, because they lie so near to the origin of Christianity. This feeling is natural. Yet two considerations join to combat the preëminence of these Eastern translations, to decrease their practical value for us. On the one hand, the Eastern languages are to such a degree in their nature foreign to the Greek language that it was not easy, indeed in some cases that it was not in the least possible, to render the expressions of the New Testament writers in an adequate manner in the desired tongue. That is one side. And on the other hand, we of the West are so very seldom well, thoroughly, livingly acquainted with those Eastern tongues, that we find it difficult to attain to an even tolerably correct judgment as to the original text from which the Eastern phrases have been drawn. The former of the two difficulties had a curious effect upon the translations, in that the given foreigner at times adopted Greek words into his own language. Sometimes such words were prepositions or conjunctions, but in other cases they were substantives. If in the Syriac translation one meets with a long word, the proper thing to do with it is to spell it in Greek letters, in which case it usually proves to be an old friend. We do not need to say that that was bad translating on the part of the given translator, yet it presents a most excellent result for textual purposes. It may at once be emphasised that in general we may declare that the worse a translation is, as a translation, the more the translator fails to deprive the original of its form and local colouring and to mould it into the distinctive idioms of his own language, the more easily we can recognise under his rough work the Greek text which he had before his eyes. We must, however, take each translation as it comes. The work that was done centuries ago must be brought to bear upon our task as well as the circumstances admit.

The value of the translations attaches especially at first to the localising of texts or of readings, or we may say to the perceiving of the extent to which readings were spread abroad. For it is clear that a reading, whencesoever it may have come, if it be in the Syrian translation, must have been in Syria; if it be in the Coptic translation, must have been in Egypt. Furthermore, in so far as we may succeed in dating a translation approximately, its text offers us a clue to the age of a given form or of given readings.

SYRIAC TRANSLATIONS.

Let us take our stand in Syria. Palestine is almost a Syrian province. It is a continuation of the same mountains and valleys and desert and sea-coast as those that are in Syria. The early Christians who gathered together at Antioch formed, so far as we know, the first important assembly of Christians outside of Palestine. Antioch was the capital of Syria, but as well the second capital of the Roman Empire. It was a Greek city, yet it is impossible that it should not have had a large proportion of

Syrians within its walls. At no very great distance were other large towns. We have already alluded to the fact that Paul's campaign directed against the Christians in or around Damascus assures us that at that extremely early date, probably in the year 30 of our era, there must have been an appreciable, technically an attackable, number of Christians there. And everything, the letters of the chief priests and the elders in Jerusalem to their Jewish brethren in Damascus, points to Aramean not to Greek Christians. Paul would not have dreamt of dragging Greeks bound from Damascus to Jerusalem to have them punished. It must have been genuine Jews whom he had in view. The result of Paul's journey to Damascus, his conversion, his stay there to be instructed in Christianity, and his two years there or in that neighbourhood, must have been a large increase in the number of Christians.

Considering the frequent communication between Damascus and Antioch on the one hand, and Aleppo, Edessa, and Nisibis and Peter's Babylon on the other hand, it would be easy to believe that even during the years before the death of Paul many Christians were to be found in that neighbourhood; it would be hard to believe that there were none there. Given a number of Christians, it is not possible to determine at what precise moment of time they felt it necessary for them to have a translation of the New Testament writings. Let us leave that time for a moment.

Ephraim the Syrian, who was mentioned on occasion of the manuscript at Paris, C, named after him, was born at Nisibis about the year 306, born a heathen, became a pupil of the bishop of Nisibis, lived in or near Edessa, and died there in 378. He is a witness to the fact that in his day the Syriac translation had long been in existence. The point is for the moment, before other possibilities arise, to make an equation of some kind, to calculate how long the Christians of those lands could have waited after the year 30 or the year 60 before they demanded or prepared a translation of the New Testament ; and conversely, how long before Ephraim's day we should think that the translation had been in use. It does not seem to me likely that the Christians in Syria will have waited for a New Testament of their own until the year 150. Having, however, until now no proofs one way or another, I am for the moment inclined to name that year 150 as a date at which the Syrians probably were able to read and hear in their own tongue such New Testament books as they received. In all this exact dating, be it remembered, we are going by necessity upon theory. Testimony is at present not to be found for it. We have in actual parchment and ink a multitude of Syrian manuscripts, and we must look at them and see what they are like, what classes they show among themselves that seem to determine something about their history.

A little before the middle of the nineteenth century, in the year 1842, William Cureton, in the British Museum, found among some manuscripts from the Nitrian desert in Egypt fragments of an old copy of the Syriac Gospels probably written about the year, let us say, 460. And fifty years later, in the year 1892, Mrs. Agnes Smith Lewis and her twin sister Mrs. Margaret Dunlop Gibson, discovered in the monastery of St. Catherine on Mount Sinai a palimpsest manuscript which lacked only about eight pages of the four Gospels. This manuscript is of the fourth or fifth century. The work of these two learned ladies upon this and the other manuscripts, especially Syriac and Arabic, of the Sinaitic monastery forms a peculiar and a brilliant chapter in the scientific achievements in library work during the last decades. Their photographing the whole palimpsest, their researches upon it again at Sinai with a corps of scholars, their edition of it, their repeated examination of it—I saw them at work at Mount Sinai on their sixth visit in February and March 1906—and an edition that they now are preparing, claim for them the warmest thanks of all biblical and Semitic scholars, and have received the highest recognition in learned circles, not only in Great Britain but also in Germany and America.

The age of these two manuscripts is of itself a warrant for the importance of their testimony. The text which they gave us is undoubtedly of a much higher age than the manuscripts themselves, and appears to be of the Re-Wrought Text, the widespread text of the second century. It would, of course, be possible that this text should have been translated during the third century. For myself, if anyone asserts that, I can scarcely prove him wrong. That does not, however, agree with my view of the whole situation, of the probabilities of the case. I assume that this text is essentially the earliest Syriac text, always provided that no one proves, what I myself could without difficulty agree to, that parts of the New Testament were translated at Edessa even during the first century or early in the second century, before the reshaping of the text had taken the cast which it put on by the middle of the second century.

A certain complication of the question, one which may some day help to a better decision as to it, is found in the existence of a Gospel harmony made by Tatian. Some declare that Tatian made his harmony at first in Greek, others that the Syrian text was the original. I have little doubt that the harmony was originally Greek. Tatian was a Syrian—the name Assyrian was also used—by place of birth, but he was a Greek nevertheless, and was brought up as a Greek. It seems to me to be especially worthy of note that the Arabic translation particularly emphasises in the heading the fact that the harmony was the work of Tatian "the Greek." Had he written the harmony in Syrian it can scarcely be doubted that he would there have been called, as he has else often been called, Tatian the Syrian and not Tatian the Greek. So much for that point. It must nevertheless be conceded that, even if Tatian's harmony had been originally composed in Greek, it would have been altogether a possible thing that it should, either by him or by his immediate neighbours, at an early date have been translated into Syrian. He may have prepared the original harmony at once after his separation from the Church in the year 172, or he may have made it several, even ten, years earlier. We do not yet know about it.

It is declared that the Syrian harmony of Tatian was the first, and for a long while, possibly until the year 250, the only written representative of the four Gospels in the Syriac language. I have thus far not been able to see that this statement has been proved. The harmony was very convenient. It was a cheap and handy compendium of the Gospel. I see no difficulty in supposing that, even if a Syriac translation of the four Gospels in their entirety had been made ten or fifty years before Tatian's book appeared, this book should in wide circles have usurped the place which the four Gospels would otherwise have occupied. Were this the case the number of manuscripts of the four Gospels would remain limited, and it would certainly often happen that even scholars would refer to the handy book. We should never forget the practical side, and should never forget that the view of Scripture at that day was several removes from the view held by the strict inspirationists of the nineteenth century, who are now apparently dying out in educated circles. The practical side tells us that those people largely not blessed with very great fortunes, and not given to much reading, seeing that many of them could not read at all, were far more likely on that account to choose a small book when they could buy one instead of a large one. It is further to be remembered that this small book was supposed to contain all that was in the larger book, that only useless or unnecessary repetition was avoided in it. Lastly, the thing at which the Christians then and there aimed was not an amulet but the Gospel. They wished for the sense, the message, the proclamation of good-will to men, and they thought that they had this—and I think too that they had this—in the Diatessaron.

If Tatian wrote his harmony at first in Syrian, and if it appeared before the Syrian translation of the separate four Gospels appeared, then it would be a matter of inevitable necessity that its form should have an important influence upon the form of the four Gospels when they came to be rendered into Syrian, and this would, I concede, account for similarity of readings here and there. Inasmuch, however, as it seems to me in every way more reasonable to suppose that the Syrian translation of the separate four Gospels was in vogue long before, or at least ten years before, Tatian's harmony saw the light in a Syrian form, I insist upon it that in this case that Syrian form of the four Gospels will by just as inevitable a necessity have had a great influence upon the shaping of the Syrian words and sentences in Tatian's Diatessaron or harmony of the four.

Going back to our manuscripts, I take it for granted that the Syrian text represented in the Curetonian and in the Lewis-Gibson manuscripts is the text of the Syrian Gospels as it was in existence in the year 150, little as I should wish to be so obstinate as to say that it had not in the later years experienced one modification or another. This is what I call the Old-Syrian text. It could have been called then Peshitta, but I do not know that that word was used for the text of the New Testament at so early a date. The statement just made as to the Old-Syrian text is sometimes so conceived of as if it necessarily were antagonistic to the high age of the so-called Peshitta Syriac translation. The previous sentence gives, I think, a clue to my thoughts upon that point. I take it that the relation between that Old-Syrian text and the Peshitta is one conditioned by age and experience. I suppose the Old-Syrian to have with time, by means of the work of Syrian scholars in the third and in the fourth century, glided into the form which the centuries that followed used, and which is now found in the editions of the Peshitta.

The word Peshitta, which used to be written Peshito, means "simple," and as applied to a text, especially of a translation it would appear, seems to amount to as much as "usual," "current," "common," and may be compared with the word Vulgate in the Latin Church. The Syrians named their translation of the Old Testament which had been made from the Hebrew "the Peshitta," as distinguished from a later translation made from the Greek text of the Septuagint. Probably the name passed over to the New Testament through the association of the New Testament with that Peshitta Old Testament translation. We shall have occasion to refer to the text of the Peshitta later in connection with the Greek text, and can here leave it. The first edition of the Peshitta was published at the wish of the Jacobite patriarch of Antioch named Ignatius. He sent Moses Marden, a priest from Mesopotamia, to Europe to find someone who would help the poor Church make an edition. Moses tried in vain in Rome and in Venice to find a Mæcenas. He found at last in Vienna, however, a statesman, the imperial chancellor, Johannes Albert Widmanstadt, who actually understood Syriac. The two printed then the edition which was issued in 1555 in four parts, the Gospel, the Epistles of Paul, the Acts, the Catholic Epistles. The Catholic Epistles were but three in number: James, First Peter, First John. That edition was an interesting one. No Second Peter, no Second and Third John, no Jude, no Revelation. Further, it did not contain Luke $22^{17.\,18}$ or John 8^{1-11} the Adulteress, or 1 John 5^7. George Henry Gwilliam published the Gospels of the Peshitta at Oxford in 1901.

The Peshitta is, however, not the only form of the Syrian text. Another form is called the Jerusalem or Palestinian form. We have not very many representatives of this text. It is rougher, less scientific than the Peshitta. The local colouring is much like that of the dialect of the Jerusalem Talmud.

26

Probably it is more nearly conjoined to the Old Syrian than to the later polished form of the Peshitta. The best theory at present is that it was made for the Melkitic Church in Palestine, perhaps in the fourth century, that being the Church of the Syrian tongue which holds to the patriarch of Constantinople.

Another form of the Syrian text is in reality a double form, or consists of two forms. The reason why we do not entirely separate them from each other is that we cannot, that, in spite of the labours of Isaac H. Hall and of John Gwynn, we have not yet come to understand the exact distinction between them throughout the New Testament. The earlier part of these texts, the form that was first evolved, might be named after Philoxenus or Xenaia, who was from 488 to 518 the monophysitic bishop of Mabbogh or Hierapolis, and who seems to have first thought of the plan, or after Polycarp who prepared this translation, in the year 508. Polycarp's name might easily, however, be confused with that of the great Polycarp of Smyrna, who, though he was a friend of Ignatius of Antioch, may not have known Syrian. It is in the nature of the case impossible for Polycarp to have translated the Greek text anew without any reference to the current translation upon which he had been brought up. He could not for the purpose of making a new text go to China and cleanse besides his brains and his tongue from all traces of the existing one. But we cannot yet say so very much about this text. For it was revised, and thus far, as first said, we cannot distinguish clearly between the one and the other of the two forms.

This other form of the twin texts arose a century later, in the year 616, in the "Nine Mile" monastery, that far from Alexandria. This monastery, in the village Enaton, was a monastery of St. Anthony. Thomas of Heraclea, in Syria, that was his birthplace, had been bishop of Hierapolis, but had been compelled to fly from his diocese and take refuge in that monastery, and he took up the task of revising Polycarp's text. For this purpose he used two or three manuscripts of the Gospels, one of Acts and of the seven Catholic Epistles—this text contains seven, and not merely three Catholic Epistles— and two of the Epistles of Paul. We see the result of his work in part with absolute certainty, because the readings are standing on the margin of the text. We perceive at once that he had good manuscripts, manuscripts that agreed largely with the Re-

Wrought Text of the second century as represented in the Greek large letter manuscripts marked D. That we know about. But what else he may have done is not yet perfectly evident. He may have let the text stand without a single change, just as Polycarp had determined it. Or he may have changed it, made it according to his opinion better, in various ways. This translation is an excellent one for the textual critic, in the sense explained a little way back. It does not pay the least attention to the Syrian habits of thought or speech. It settles upon the words to be used, fixes the order of the words, builds the sentences as far as it is possible after the Greek text. It is, humanly speaking, more likely that Thomas should have put many a reading that pleased him into the text. Syrian scholars will doubtless some day unravel the tangled threads of these two forms of the text and assign to each of the two, to Polycarp and to Thomas, what belongs to each. John Gwynn published in 1897 the Revelation in the Philoxenian or Polycarp form. He is the master in this field. May he live to give the Church an edition of the twin-text for the whole New Testament.

It is not possible, nor is it necessary, for us to treat of the Syrian manuscripts in general. But we must glance for an instant at the books of lessons. We have seen that in the Greek Church the movable part of the year began with Easter and the fixed part with September. The Syrian books begin both parts with the fixed date of Epiphany, and close with the Sunday for the Dead. It will be remembered that the sixth of January was the old date for Christmas. Many of the books contain only the lessons for Sunday, with perhaps the week-day lessons for Lent and Easter week. Some books contain only feast-days, and begin with the angel and Zacharias, or with the angel and Mary, or with the birth of John the Baptist, or of Jesus. Moreover, the Syrian books of lessons combine more frequently than the Greek books do Old Testament lessons with those from the second part of the New Testament, from the Apostle.

COPTIC TRANSLATIONS.

In turning to the Egyptian or Coptic translations we again have to consider the question of date. St. Anthony heard the

Gospels read in Church in Coptic when he was a boy. That assures us that there was a Coptic translation in use about the middle of the third century. Now, it must be kept in mind that Egypt was a land of science and of education and of progress, in spite of the pyramids in their stolid calm. In consequence, seeing that as with the Syrian translation we are without direct testimony, I presuppose that the two main Coptic translations were made before the close of the second century. We may name three forms of the Coptic translation or three translations, of which, however, the third is a somewhat uncertain quantity. The dialect of Lower Egypt is represented by a translation which has been called Alexandrian and Memphitic, but is now termed Boheiric. The dialect of Upper Egypt gives us the Thebaïc or Saïdic translation. These two appear to have been made directly from the Greek. The third translation, the Fayyumic, probably, or possibly, flowed from the Saïdic towards the end of the third century. The two great translations have been favoured by fortune, at least from the point of view of textual criticism, so little from other points of view as their experiences could be called desirable. It was a pity that the great Church split, and that Jacobites and Melkites were separated from each other. But this separation of the Coptic Church from Constantinople and the Imperialists prevented the translations from being spoiled by the textual movements and changes in Syria and Asia Minor. Then the Arabs came a century and a half later, and began to thrust the Coptic language aside and to put Arabic in its place, and that tended to keep the old texts pure. And finally, a good and an honourable thing too, the scribes and scholars of the twelfth and the succeeding centuries did all they could to keep the text free from false additions and false changes.

The Boheiric form, to use the Arabic name for the dialect of Lower Egypt, was so wielded by the translator as to represent the Greek text very fairly, different as the languages are. In Boheiric it is not possible to distinguish between a sentence with a participle and one with a finite verb. Nor is there a passive voice. Greek passives are sometimes rendered by a third person plural of the active used impersonally, sometimes by the third personal singular if a singular subject can be brought into play, and sometimes by the qualitative form of the verb. The whole

New Testament was translated into Boheiric, but the Revelation is placed at one side by itself and is not copied with the other books. This treatment of Revelation agrees well with what we have observed in the Greek Church, and with memories of the criticism of Dionysius of Alexandria upon this book, which we referred to in treating above of the canon. The books are arranged in the order: Gospels, Pauline and Catholic Epistles, Acts. George Horner, of Frome and Oxford, has with un-wearying diligence, through years of work, copying and collating from London to Cairo and from Rome to St. Petersburg, placed before the Church a complete edition of this version in four volumes with an abundant critical apparatus.

The Saïdic form in Upper Egypt came later to the hands of Western scholars, and was for an indefinite time very limited in extent of testimony. The translation is of a rougher description than that of the Boheiric dialect. Although the Saïdic translator uses Greek words if possible still more freely than the Boheiric translator, he is less true to the form of the Greek sentence, and he often leaves out conjunctions. George Horner is preparing an edition of this version.

The Fayyumic translation rejoices in several names, unless we please to say that some of the names are the names of relatives and not of this translation itself. It will be enough, under the present ignorance of all concerned as to the qualities of this or of these forms, to say that the names Bashmuric, Ammonic, Elearchic, Oasitic, Akhmimic, Subsaïdic, and Middle Egyptian are all at the command of a scholar who is ready to examine these fragments. If the names continue to multiply I fear we shall soon have as many as there are words in the trans-lation, the fragments are so few and brief.

The lesson-books in the Coptic Church begin with the month Thoth, or on the twenty-eighth of August.

ETHIOPIC TRANSLATION.

Pursuing our way towards the south, we approach the Axumitic Church in Abyssinia, with its Ethiopic translation. Here the question of date is extraordinarily difficult. Two Ethiopic scholars who expressed themselves fully upon the question varied between the fourth and the seventh century, so that we do not yet know how to define a certain period. I accept Dillmann's view that the translation was made from the Greek text between the fourth and the sixth century. The translator does not appear to have been well acquainted with Greek, and therefore to have made many mistakes. A revision, which Dillmann placed in the fourteenth or a later century, corrected the mistakes with the help of Coptic and Arabic translations. At that date, in the fourteenth century, the Ethiopic language was replaced in daily intercourse by the Amharic language. The first edition of the Ethiopic New Testament was made in Rome in two volumes in the years 1548 and 1549. A monk, Tesfa Zion, of the order Takla-Haimanot, who was by birth an Ethiopian from Malhez, came to Rome from the monastery Dabra-Libanos on Mount Lebanon, with two other monks from that monastery named Tank'a Wald and Za-selase. They brought with them Ethiopic manuscripts of the New Testament. Three men whom they met in Italy, one of whom was an archdeacon from Constantinople, helped the Ethiopian monks prepare and print that edition. Thus far we have no scientific edition of the Ethiopic New Testament.

ARMENIAN TRANSLATION.

The Armenians used at first the Syrian Bible. Mesrob and the Armenian patriarch Isaac began in the fifth century to prepare an Armenian Bible from the Syriac. In the year 431, however, two of Mesrob's pupils named John "Ekelensis" and Joseph "Palnensis" were at the Council of Ephesus and brought Greek manuscripts home with them. Mesrob and Isaak recognised at once the greater value of the Greek text, and threw aside the translations that they had already made from the Syriac. John and Joseph were sent to Alexandria to learn Greek thoroughly, and then they translated the whole New Testament from the Greek. Nothing was more natural than that their long use of the Syrian New Testament should have so strongly impressed its forms upon their minds as to cause them here and there to use Syrian readings. The Armenian synod of the year 1662 sent a clergyman named Oskan from the city Erivan near Ararat to the West to try to have the Armenian

Bible printed. Oskan stayed a long while in Rome, but could do nothing there. At last, in the year 1666, he published in Amsterdam the first edition of the Armenian Bible.

We know almost nothing about the Georgian or Grusinian translation. It was printed in 1723 in Moscow.

Persian translations of a late date, two of the fourteenth and one of the eighteenth century, one from the Greek, one from the Syriac, and one from the Latin, do not at all satisfy our wishes. It seems as if the Christians in Persia must have long before the fourteenth century freed themselves from the necessity of using the Syrian translation.

There are a number of Arabic translations, the earliest dating apparently from a time soon after Mohammed. Therewith we may turn from the Eastern to the Western translations.

Latin Translations.

We have passed by the companies and groups of the various Eastern translations. There really were among them different translations of such an age and of such a literary character and at least partially to such an extent accessible that we could make some use of them. In the West and North we have three that we can name. Two of these, however, are not yet of great moment for us. The Slavic translation is still too little known in the West to be thoroughly weighed and proved. And the Gothic translation is only a matter of fragments. The one remaining translation is the Latin. But that is one of eminent importance : One child of the West, but a lion.

The proper way to attack the Latin form of the Bible would, I think, be to divide its history and growth into three parts, and treat of Old-Latin, Middle-Latin, and New-Latin. But the Latin manuscripts are not my province. That belongs to John Wordsworth, the bishop of Salisbury. So we shall only have two parts : Old-Latin and Vulgate, keeping in mind that the name Vulgate for our purposes is a comparatively modern affair. The Old-Latin used to be called the Itala, but that name was wrong and has been shelved. It, the term Old-Latin, belongs in general to such examples of the Latin translation as were written, translated, before the time of Jerome, we might

say roughly before the year 400, seeing that he died in 420.
The rise or origin of the Latin translation gives occasion to many
a disputable question, offers many a problem that we at least
to-day cannot solve.   The statement has been made that there
were at the first a number of separate translations made.   With
like certainty we have been assured that every phenomenon in
the history of this text is to be led back to one single original
translation.   We have already spoken of the probable sporadic,
tentative, partial translation, a thing that in every case is quite
likely to have taken place.   Perhaps such previous work was
more likely in Latin circles than in Syrian or Coptic circles.
The two languages, Greek and Latin, were cognate, and they
were coëxistent in many provinces of the Roman Empire.   The
translation would in this case be so much easier than in the
case of the Eastern translations, that it is likely to have lured
many a priest or deacon or reader to put pen to paper and to
place the Greek text into the known words, which were adapted
to reading before the Church.   But in spite of the existence of
such preliminary work the possibility would remain that, when
the time came, a single complete translation might have been
issued at one place, or that two or three complete translations
might have seen the light at about the same time in different
provinces.

We should bear in mind that the greater part of the literary
phenomena in a case of this kind admit of reduction to
the one or to the other of these origins.   A single translation
would admit of revising in different directions, in different
provinces, and might appear in the end not to be related even
distantly to its own former self.   And a double or triple translation might by the usage of the provinces be so assimilated and
so differentiated as to give the appearance of being forms of a single
original.   In so far, moreover, as one translation should precede
others, its influence, if it were known, could hardly fail to be
yielded to by any succeeding translator.

It is pertinent to ask, where a translation of the Greek text into
Latin would be first to be expected.   One thinks at the word Latin
involuntarily of Rome.   Rome was nevertheless in the second
century still a Greek city in the main, and the Christians in it
seem to have been chiefly Greeks until well into the third century,
so that a translation was not likely to be called for there until after

the beginning of the third century. The districts of Northern Italy may at an early period have been anxious to have a Latin Bible. But the place where the want of the Latin form was probably first felt, and felt most keenly, was Northern Africa. There Greek was not so well known. There were a great many Christians in the province, and few of them understood Greek. Sunday after Sunday the lessons had to be translated, interpreted by word of mouth. That was troublesome for the reader, and surely sometimes unsatisfactory to the hearers. It is then in Northern Africa that a Latin translation was probably first needed and first made. That may have been the only complete first translation. For it will certainly have soon been carried to Rome and to Northern Italy, and if translations did not yet exist there, the clergy of those provinces will doubtless have eagerly taken this North African text and corrected into it their own provincial expressions, at the same time changing anything else that did not agree with the texts which they were accustomed to use.

The African translation lies before our eyes in manifold quotations by a number of African Church writers. It was not a peculiarly polished piece of work. It paid much more respect to the Greek words and to the Greek order of the words than was consistent with a good Latin style. For the textual critic that is a very welcome kind of work. We can tell much better what the original text before the eyes of the translator was.

From one translation, then, or if anyone insist upon it, from two or three independent Latin translations, the manuscripts passed through the provinces to Gaul, to Great Britain, to Ireland. Every province has its own local names for all kinds of things. Every province has its own way of treating the language of Rome. And each province changes the new translation to suit its own tongue and ears and needs, not forgetting to change readings which did not conform to the text they had used up to that time, to the manuscripts that they had in their hands. After the first receipt and adoption of the foreign work the Latin text in each province will usually have begun a life for itself, and will have passed through stages of development peculiar to itself. Undoubtedly the mental activity or dulness of the clergy in given provinces will have influenced the text in one direction or another, seeing that bright, quick thinking and acting men will have more readily taken up their pens for necessary correction, or even for unnecessary and more wilful change, whereas sluggish and thoughtless men will have through carelessness allowed the manuscripts copied to deteriorate. As a result, provincial texts will have been produced: a Gallican, a British, an Italian text. All of these European texts should have a certain relationship to each other from the more active intercourse between the provinces. Perhaps it will be possible finally to determine, as Westcott and Hort said, three types of text,—an African, a European, and an Italian type.

Old Latin Manuscripts.

The first manuscript that we have of the Old-Latin Gospels is called *a*, for we use for these Old-Latin manuscripts the small letters. It appears to have been written in the fourth century, and it may have been written for or even by the hand of Eusebius, the bishop of Vercelli, who died as a martyr in the year 371. It is in the cathedral of Vercelli, where it used to lie in the sacristy, and be shown about and kissed as a relic until it was torn almost to tatters. Now it is carefully guarded in an upper room under a glass case.—The letter *e* is the Codex Palatinus at Vienna. It is of the fifth century. Oddly enough, a leaf from it is in Trinity College at Dublin.—The manuscript *k* of the fifth or sixth century at Turin came from Bobbio, and is said to have belonged to the founder of Bobbio, Columban, who died in the year 615.—In the manuscript *m*, which is at Rome in the monastery of the Holy Cross, and is of the eighth or ninth century, Hort was inclined to think that he had discovered a Spanish form of the text. Its name is Speculum, and it has been, but incorrectly, attributed to Augustine. It contains Church lessons from all the books of the New Testament save Third John, Hebrews, and Philemon. The text in it is much like the text used by Priscillian. The fact that it does not contain the three heavenly witnesses 1 John $5^{7, 8}$ is the more interesting in connection with its Spanish allures, for the newest researches attribute the insertion of those witnesses to Priscillian himself.—At Stockholm in Sweden, in the great library, there lies, I think, the largest known manuscript. It is of the thirteenth century, and contains among other things a Latin Bible. Among the manuscripts of the Old-Latin text for Acts and for Revelation it bears the letter *g*, and is apparently of the Italian type. Only in it do we find a complete Old-Latin Revelation. Formerly it was in Bohemia, and was carried from Prague to Sweden as war booty in the year 1648 at the close of the Thirty Years' War.

We observed above that, however the origin of the Latin form of the text of the New Testament may be conceived of, whether as proceeding from one original or from more, the resulting facts have been such as may be explained from either theory. The various provinces had texts which little by little became more and more corrupt, more and more different from the earliest text, and more and more different from each other. This was a plague for the learned members of the clergy, and Damasus, the bishop of Rome, appears to have asked Jerome the Dalmatian, in the year 382, to produce a new Latin Text. By the year 384 he had finished the Gospels, and handed them over to Damasus. This was his first revision, and he did it very well, taking care as far as possible to change no well-known phrases unless it proved to be positively necessary. He knew very well, and he wrote it in advance, that the people would not like the change. The opposition to his work was, however, so great that he was much more conservative in constituting the text of the rest of the Bible. Dean Burgon's opposition to the English revision of 1881 seemed to us serious, but it was mere child's play beside the antagonism shown in the fourth century. Augustine wrote to Jerome the story of a bishop who had used a reading of Jerome's in Jonah 4[6]. The people of the church raged about it, and insisted upon asking the Jews about it. The Jews said that the Hebrew text supported the reading familiar to the people. And thereupon the bishop was forced to restore that old and false reading in order not to become a shepherd without a flock, a bishop without people. It was centuries before the revision of Jerome was accepted by the Church. When Gregory the Great sat in the chair at Rome both the old and the new translation were there in use. Sometimes the ninth century has been named as the time at which Jerome's work came into general use. Yet the Anglo-Saxons, who copied many manuscripts, kept to the old text. And the manuscript of the Old-Latin text marked *c*, the Codex Colbertinus, was written in the eleventh century, and that Gigas, the gigantic manuscript at Stockholm with the Acts and Revelation in Old-Latin, was written in the thirteenth century.

All the while the manuscripts were being corrected and altered hither and thither, and from the eighth century on every effort was made, now by Charlemagne with Alcuin, now by Theodulf the bishop of Orleans (787 – 821), now by Langfranc, archbishop of Canterbury (1069–1089), now by Stephen II. Harding, bishop of Citeaux († 1134), and now by the Cardinal Nicholas (1150), to reduce the chaos of manuscripts to order, but in vain. In the thirteenth century regular books of corrections were made by the faculty at Paris, by the Dominicans, and by the Franciscans, yet the text grew ever worse. Roger Bacon attacked the corrupted text in strong terms about the year 1266, and berated particularly the Dominicans for vacillation in correction: "As a result their correction is the worst corruption, and the destruction of the text of God." It is often supposed that the name Vulgate attached to Jerome's translation from the first. So far as I have been able to discover, the name was not definitely attached to it until the decree of the Council of Trent on the 8th of April 1546, and was in that decree not at all used as a well-known name, not used as a name at all, but merely as an adjective in the sense of "common" or "current." The council, not having a suspicion of the real facts in the case, called it the "old and current edition." It might almost have been said that the other editions, could the corruptions so far as they were Old-Latin have been gathered together by themselves, were still older and still more current, and that this decree was meant to raise a dam to prevent their further progress. The name Vulgate, then, in our way of using it, is a modern invention. Pope Sixtus V. made an edition of the Latin text of the New Testament, published in the year 1590, and declared his edition to be the Vulgate to which the decree of the Council of Trent had pointed, and that it "must be received and held as true, legitimate, authentic, and undoubted, in all public and private disputations, lectures, sermons, and explanations." Unfortunately, it was at once discovered that Sixtus's edition was extraordinarily bad, and must be as far as that was possible suppressed and replaced by another. It was Bellarmin who suggested the "pious fraud" that they should recall the volumes and correct and re-issue them as if the deceased Sixtus had ordered it. It is a curious combination of laxity and severity when we perceive that, on the one hand, this fraud was carried out, and that, on the other hand, poor Bellarmin was refused canonisation as a saint because he had suggested the trick. The new edition appeared in the year 1592 under Clement VIII., and is called the Clementine Vulgate. It was far better than the bad edition of Sixtus V., but was not so carefully revised as it should have been. It is singular that the great Roman Catholic Church, with its large number of talented and immensely learned scholars, with the vast libraries at its command, with means unlimited for any necessary work, should in the three centuries that have passed by since the issue of the Clementine edition not have made a good edition of the Latin text. We now have a good edition of the Gospels and of the Acts which we owe to thirty years of work on the part of John Wordsworth, the bishop of Salisbury, and his friends, especially William Sanday and Henry Julian White, and may heaven give him and them years and strength to bring it to a happy completion.

Vulgate Manuscripts.

The great manuscript of the Vulgate is the one named after Amiata, where it used to be. The sign for it is *am*, because the Vulgate manuscripts are often designated by a syllable to distinguish them from the Old-Latin manuscripts that only have a letter. But this fine volume, now the pride of the Laurentiana at Florence, is English work. It was written shortly before the year 716 at the order of Ceolfrid, the abbot of Yarrow, who intended to carry it as a gift to Rome. He died at Langres on the way on the 25th of September 716, and his companions probably took the volume to Rome. The text of this Codex Amiatinus is excellent, and contains, as is easily explicable, many Anglo-Saxon and Irish readings.—The La Cava manuscript, marked *cav*, was written by a scribe Danila in the ninth century, and is in the Trinity monastery of the learned Benedictines in La Cava, near Corpo di Cava, not far from Naples. Its text reminds us of the Speculum mentioned above, for it has, indeed, the Vulgate text, but in combination with Spanish readings.—The Royal Library at Munich contains a manuscript of the year 870, the Codex of St. Emmeram, as it is named, *em*, from the monastery to which the Emperor Arnulf gave it. It was written in gold by Berengar and Liuthard at the order of Charles the Bald. It is ornamented with beautiful pictures.

In the library at Fulda, between Eisenach and Frankfurt-on-the-Main, is the Codex Fuldensis, *fuld*, which contains the whole New Testament, but has the four Gospels in a harmony that is often found in different languages. It has a good text. This book was written about the year 540, at the wish of Victor of Capua.—The manuscript *gat* has had a varied history, though now resting quietly in the National Library at Paris. It was written by an Irishman, and was once in St. Gatiens de Tours. The book-thief Libri stole it and sold it to Lord Ashburnham. Now it is once more in France.—In the British Museum is the manuscript *harl*, or Harleianus, of the sixth century, with a very good text. Apparently it was stolen by Jean Aymon from the library at Paris in the year 1707, and sold to Robert Harley.— Very properly we find at Madrid, in the National Library, a manuscript of the eighth century, *tol*, that used to be in Toledo, and that gives us the Vulgate text mingled with Spanish readings.—There is also a *harl*, or Harley manuscript, for the book of Acts, which is of the ninth century, and which like the one of the Gospels just mentioned appeared to have found its way in 1707 under Jean Aymon's auspices to Robert Harley and thus finally to the British Museum. But this manuscript seems to be of the Old Latin and not of the Vulgate form, so that it belongs in the foregoing list, not here.

We now turn to some manuscripts that have a passing Arabic number.—Number 5 belongs to Thomas Irwin in Oswego, New York, and is on purple parchment in golden writing. It seems to have been written in the eighth century.—Number 95 is in the University Library at Cambridge, England, and is of the eighth or ninth century, with an emendated Irish text. It is called the Book of Deer, because it used to be in the monastery of Deer or Deir in Aberdeenshire.—The same library contains my number 102*a* of the eighth century, which offers the passion and the resurrection from the four Gospels. It appears to have been written for Ethelwald, the bishop of Lindisfarne.—Durham cathedral owns a mutilated copy of the Gospels and eleven leaves of another, both of the eighth century and with a good text; in the list they are 115 and 116.—Another mutilated copy of the Gospels, 131, of the eighth or ninth century, belongs to Hereford cathedral. It is of the emendated Irish text.—The Book of Chad, 137, is the property of Lichfield cathedral, is of the seventh or eighth century, and contains the emendated Irish text of Matthew, Mark, and the beginning of Luke.—The Lindisfarne, or St. Cuthbert's gospels, 153, of the eighth century are in the British Museum. They are written in an Anglo-Saxon script, and contain between the lines a series of Northumbrian glosses.

The Coronation Book, 156, of the tenth century, in the British Museum, has many old readings in it.—The same library owns my number 184, of the eighth or ninth century, written in gold, and having a good text,—185, of the ninth century, with a good text, —186, of the ninth or tenth century, in red writing with a late text, —187, of the ninth century, in gold script also with a late text,— 234, of the eighth century, with a fine text, of the British family,— 238, of the ninth century, Wordsworth's Beneventanus with a good text,—239, of the tenth century, with some peculiar readings, from St. Petrocius in Bodmin in Cornwall among the Celts,—240, of the ninth century, with Alcuin's text, called Charlemagne's Bible, from the monastery Moûtier-Grand-Val, near Basel,— 241, of the ninth century, well written and corrected, formerly in the possession of St. Cornelius of Compiègne,—and 254, of the ninth century, from St. Hubert, near Liège, containing parts of the Old Testament, the Gospel, the Epistles of Paul, James, and 1 Peter 1^1–4^3.—The Gospels of Mac Regol, 502, are in the Bodleian at Oxford. They are of the ninth century, and give the emendated Irish text with the series of Northumbrian glosses between the lines.—Stonyhurst owns my number 523, the Gospel of John of the seventh century that was found in the year 1105 in the grave of St. Cuthbert. Its text is very good.—The imperial treasure-room at Vienna has my number 698, which used to be at Aachen (Aix-la-Chapelle), and which is called the Gospels of the Oath or the Gospels of Charlemagne. It is on purple parchment and is written in gold.—Similarly the City Library in Abbeville possesses a manuscript of the eighth century, my 774, written on purple parchment in gold script.

At Tours is number 913, of the ninth century in gold script. Formerly in St. Martin at Tours, it was the copy of the Gospels upon which the French kings from Louis VII. in the year 1137 to Louis XIV. in 1650 took their oath when they were first received as abbots or canons of that church.—The National Library at Paris owns my number 1265, St. Medard's Gospels of the eighth century written in gold script, and Theodulf's Bible of the ninth century, my number 1266, on purple parchment in gold script,—and 1267, of the eighth century, on purple parchment,—and 1269, of the eighth century, the Echternach Gospels, — and 1274, of the ninth century, the Corbey Bible,—and 1278, of the eighth century, on purple parchment in gold script,—and 1285, of the ninth century, the Gospels of Adalbald.—The City Library of Rheims has my number 1289, of the ninth century, a Bible which Hincmar presented to the cathedral there.—Number 1419, of the ninth or tenth century, in the Royal Library at Berlin, is the Codex Witekind.—The University Library at Würzburg possesses seven fine manuscripts formerly in the cathedral there. My number 1606 is a Matthew of the eighth century,—1607 is a copy of the Gospels of the eighth century,—1608 is also a copy of the Gospels of the eighth century,—1609 offers Gospels from the end of the seventh century,—1610, of the sixth century, is supposed to have belonged to St. Burkard of Würzburg ; it contains the Gospels,—1611 is a copy of the Gospels of the ninth century,—and 1612, the Gospels of the sixth century, is reputed to have belonged to St. Kilian the apostle of the Franks.—Quedlinburg owns my number 1859, the Gospels in gold script in uncial letters of the eighth century, possibly from the year 740.

The City Library at Trier owns the Ada Codex of the eighth century, my 1877, written in gold script, and having pictures that are important for the history of art.—In Trinity College at Dublin is the Book of Armagh, my 1968, written in the year 812, containing the New Testament in the emendated Irish text.—An eighth century copy of the Gospels, my 1969, named Domhnach Airgid, is in the Royal Irish Academy at Dublin.—My 1970 is in Trinity College there, and is a copy of the Gospels of the eighth century. —My 1971 is also in Trinity College. It is of the ninth century, and is called the Book of Moling or Mulling. This and 1968 are two of the most important Irish manuscripts.—My 1972, in the same library, the Gospels of the seventh or eighth century, is called the Book of Kells.—Similarly 1973, at the same place, the Gospels of the eighth century, is called the Book of Durrow.—And 1974, also there, of the ninth century, the Gospels, is called the Book of Dimma. These fantastic old names seem to carry us back to the days of the elves and fairies among the oaks of the Druids.—Number 2138, a Bible of the ninth century, is at Rome, in St. Paul Outside the Walls. It was used by the scholars who corrected the text of the Vulgate at the desire of Pius IV.—Number 2225 is in the Royal Library at Stockholm, and is of the sixth or seventh century, partly on purple parchment in gold script. The Gospels in it appear to be of a Vulgate type, but to have been corrected according to an Old-Latin text. It is likely that this book was written by Irishmen in Italy. King Alfred gave it to the Cathedral at Canterbury. The Swedish scholar John Gabriel Sparwenfeldt bought it in Spain in 1690 and gave it to the library at Stockholm.—In Prague, in the Stift Strahov, is a copy of the Gospels of the ninth century which used to belong to St. Martin's on the Mosel. Herewith we leave the Latin translation of the New Testament.

GOTHIC TRANSLATION.

The Gothic translation is due to the Bishop Wulfila, who was born about the year 310 and died about 380. In translating the greater part of the Bible about the middle of the fourth century, he seems to have used for the New Testament a Greek text which was largely of a later type, and which nevertheless contained many old readings. Some scholars, urging that the text of the Gothic was much like the Latin text in certain readings and interpolations, and laying stress on the fact that the four Gospels stood in the Western order: Matthew, John, Luke, Mark, came to the conclusion that this translation of Wulfila's was revised in the fifth century or later, while the Goths were in Italy and Spain, and that not after a Greek text of the New Testament, but after the Italian form of the Old-Latin translation. It must be conceded that such a thing would be conceivable. Yet the

27

circumstances do not call for a supposition of this kind. The similarity of text could be due to the Greek manuscripts used by Wulfila and his correctors. And, moreover, the chapters and the lessons in one of the Gothic manuscripts agree with those of Euthalius. All our discussions about this translation suffer from the fact that we have but little of it to judge by. There is a fragmentary manuscript of the four Gospels, and there are a few further fragments of the Gospels with fragments of the Epistles of Paul. Thus far we have found no manuscripts of the Acts, of the Catholic Epistles, or of Revelation. The one larger manuscript is the Codex Argenteus, of the sixth century, in the University Library at Upsala, on purple parchment in silver letters. It may have been written in Northern Italy. In the sixteenth century it was in the monastery Werden in Westphalia, and at the close of that century at Prague. In 1648 it travelled to Stockholm as booty of war. Perhaps it was given to Isaac Voss, the librarian of Queen Christina, for it was at Voss' in Holland in 1655. In 1662, Count Magnus Gabriele de la Gardie bought it and gave it to the University at Upsala. It was well travelled. The remaining fragments in Milan, Rome, Turin, and Wolfenbüttel are all palimpsest, and all of the sixth century.

SLAVIC TRANSLATION.

The Slavic translation is usually attributed to a Thessalonian named Constantin, but renamed Cyrill, who was called by Rastislav, the Duke of Moravia, in the year 862 to come and preach the gospel in his domains. Cyrill and his brother Methodius went thither, made a Slavic alphabet drawn chiefly from the Greek alphabet, and translated the New Testament into Slavic. Perhaps they translated merely the Church lessons, therefore omitting the Revelation. The Greek manuscripts which they used were apparently chiefly of a later type. There are a great many Slavic manuscripts in Russia, and we certainly shall some day have from a Russian scholar a grand catalogue of them all as a basis for critical work upon them.

VII.

CHURCH WRITERS.

IT might seem to a person approaching this field for the first time that the witnesses to the ancient condition of the text were now exhausted. We have called up the array of the Greek copies of the books of the New Testament, we have seen the full ranks of the volumes containing the lessons to be read in the Greek Church, and we have just left the great corps of the translations of the sacred text. That must be all. It is certainly a great deal, but it is not all. Nor may we stop short of all. Were we concerned with the text of Shakespeare or Dante or Goethe it might be pardonable to pass by some less direct evidences of their utterances or sentences. In the case of the New Testament it would be a crime to fail to approach the last witness, to omit the last question that could be put, in order to gain a ray of light upon its history, in order to solve a problem touching the form of its original text.

In the case of the witnesses thus far called upon the stand, the clerical character of their testimony prevailed, and especially the liturgical character. For although many a book was in old times written for private possession and use, nevertheless a large number of the manuscripts in all the series that we have scanned up to this point were directly written for use in the churches. Many even of the volumes written at private order, at the order of laymen or of laywomen, were ordered solely for the purpose of being given to a cathedral, to a monastery, or to the church of the choice of the one ordering the work. All of the books had but one aim, and this aim was the text of the New Testament itself.

In the books of the New Testament we find that reference is made to previous works, and above all to the Old Testament. We are able to see from these references what the state of the text of the Old Testament then was. In Luke 11^{49} Jesus says : "On this account also the wisdom of God said : I will send to them prophets and apostles, and some of them they will slay and will persecute : in order that the blood of all the prophets, that was shed from the foundation of the world, from the blood of Abel unto the blood of Zachariah, who was slain between the altar of burnt-offering and the temple, should be demanded from this generation." Whence this quotation came, we do not in the least know. It appears to be from some apocryphal book. In Acts 20[35] Paul says to the elders of Ephesus who had met him at Miletus : "And remember the words of the Lord Jesus, that He said : It is more blessed to give than to receive." We do not know whence Paul drew these words. That is to say, we have no clue to the line of oral, word of mouth, tradition which supplied them to Paul, and no clue to the connection of that unknown line of tradition with the written accounts in our Gospels. And Jude [17] writes : "And ye, beloved, remember the words which were spoken before by the apostles of our Lord Jesus Christ, that they said to you : At the end of the age there shall be scoffers walking in the way of ungodliness according to their own lusts." To what passage he refers, or whether he refers to any definite single passage, is not known. The author of the late letter, Second Peter, quotes this all, 2 Pet. 3[3], as if it were his own, but reinforcing and paraphrasing it or spreading it out.

As Jesus quoted, as the apostles quoted from the Old Testament, as Paul quoted Jesus, and as Jude quoted we know not whom, so also the Christians who wrote letters and treatises of Christian contents quoted Jesus and the apostles and the non-apostolic writers of New Testament books. Their quotations, then, may sometimes be of use to us in our attempt to determine the original words of the text of these books. Their use of these books forms for us the last source of testimony to the text we are seeking. When we turned to the translations, I emphasised the fact that those translations gave us a certain localisation of the readings which they contained, and thereby helped determine in the most certain manner the spread of given forms of text in early times. It will be at once apparent that Christian writers who quote the words of the New Testament must in like manner localise readings, give a definite knowledge of the presence of given readings in certain places.

It is, of course, necessary to keep in mind the fact that

writers sometimes journeyed afar, that Irenæus was of Smyrna, but also of Lyons, and visited Rome; that Origen was of Alexandria, but that he visited Rome and Arabia, and that he lived long at Cæsarea; that Gregory of Nazianzus was of Asia Minor, but visited Athens, and Alexandria, and Cæsarea, and Constantinople; that Jerome came from Dalmatia, but visited Rome, and Gaul, and Alexandria, and Antioch, and Constantinople, and spent the last thirty and more years of his life at Bethlehem. But it does not follow that a man changed his text because he changed his residence. It would probably be nearer the truth to place the word text for mind in Horace's verse. When a man had been brought up on a given form of the New Testament, he was likely, other things being equal, to stick to it. Had he the means to make a journey, he had doubtless also the means to buy a copy of the New Testament suited to travel with him. Of course he may have been persuaded to accept a new reading on due evidence in place of an old one, but his general text is likely to have remained the old-accustomed text. And whatever he accepted, so was that reading, if he returned and lived again in his early home, a reading that also was found at that place, and, if he was a man of weight, a reading that may have come to prevail there.

The reading, the cast of text that is found in a Church writer has, however, in one respect a great advantage over the reading found in a translation, namely, that it is by its connection with the author in most cases definitely dated as well as placed. That is very important. It is true that there are drawbacks that lessen the value of the testimony, or we may say lessen the amount of testimony that we can get from the Church writers. One of these drawbacks became very apparent during the discussion of the criticism of the canon, namely, the loose way in which these writers like other writers often quote. In spite of this difficulty we may gain much even from such writers, even from writers who quote in a free way, and it need not be said that there are writers who often quote carefully. Yet even a carelessly presented sentence may assure us of the presence of one or another important element in the readings that the passage offers in various witnesses, and be enough to fix a date and place for it. The very point that the author using it is trying to make, may decide the form of the text to which he is

accustomed.   Another drawback is to be found at times in the
silence of an author.   We observed in the criticism of the canon
that it would not do to lay all too great stress upon the silence in
reference to a questioned fact.   We saw that it was more than
once, humanly speaking, only the merest chance that a passing
sentence occasioned by the most trifling circumstance gave us a
view of the opinion of the writer touching the mooted point.

In one way these Church writers can be of use to us even in respect to passages which they do not directly quote.   We can apply
their testimony indirectly.   In dealing with the witnesses to the
text it is often of great weight to determine the habits of a given
witness, whether that witness be a Greek manuscript or a manuscript of a translation, or even a Church writer.   If we know the
habits, the inclinations, the virtues, and the faults of a witness,
we are in a position to understand, to determine the value of,
and to apply its testimony in a much more certain and more
effectual and more just way, than if we merely consider its
testimony for each single passage in isolation from its further
testimony.   Now a Church writer may by his whole series of
quotations establish in a comparatively definite manner and to a
very great extent the character of a witness of another class.
There are even cases in which it seems almost as if, for example,
a given manuscript in our hands had been the volume from which
the writer concerned had copied out his quotations.   The conclusion at which we are aiming is then clear.   By enabling us to
determine the relations of the text of that other witness, to be
sure of its speaking for a certain time and place, whatever other
times and places it may represent, the writer has given us a
criterion for the decision as to all readings which that witness
offers, even though he himself may not have quoted them.

By themselves, without Greek manuscripts and without translations, the Church writers cannot decide that a reading is genuine.
They are too late and too uncertain for that.   We might say that
they could under the best of circumstances, if all other witnesses
were lacking, only serve to bolster up a conjecture.   The case of
the book of Revelation is peculiar, and is by no means clear to
us.   We have already perceived that a large number of the
manuscripts which contain that book, contain it in combination
with the commentary of Andrew of Cæsarea or of Arethas of
Cæsarea.   It would be conceivable that a man copy some text

of the Revelation that pleased him, and add to it one of those commentaries in spite of their being written in connection with another form of the text. That would be possible, but only barely possible and not in the least likely. Moreover, if I am right in thinking at this moment that the greater number of these commentated texts of Revelation have the text and commentary intimately combined in irregularly measured sentences, but such as follow closely upon one another without appreciable break, then it is all the less probable that scribes or scholars joined the commentary to their own peculiar texts. Therefore these manuscripts should, as a rule, offer to us the text or the texts approved by those two writers.

When I was a student of theology over forty years ago, I spent two years with great profit in the theological seminary of a Church, not my own, in which a warm discussion was being carried on as to the use of hymns and as to the use of organs. During the course of the debate in the journal of the Church, the more progressive members who were for greater freedom appealed to the testimony of the Israelitic scholars who were accessible, appealed to their testimony as to certain facts connected with the Jewish interpretation of some passages of the Old Testament which had been brought into evidence. In the next lecture after the appearance of the article containing the appeal to the testimony of these scholars, the professor who led the opposition referred to the matter, and said among other things as a final and unanswerable rebuttal of that testimony : "The Jews crucified Christ, and therefore the Jews will lie." That was indeed an unanswerable argument, or an argument that needed no answer. The point of the story for the criticism of the text of the New Testament lies in the distinction between opinion and fact, in the necessity of accepting gladly all testimony to facts of textual history, without the least respect to the theological opinions which the witness cherishes. Whether a Marcionite or a Montanist or an Arian or a Pelagian sees and chronicles a reading, or whether Tertullian, who here rides two horses, or Epiphanius, or Athanasius, or Augustine, uses it, is as to the point of the existence of the reading at the given times and places totally indifferent.

The facts are what we are after, not the theology of a witness. Indeed it has happened, and not merely once, that heretics, that men who have dared to think differently from the leaders of the Church, have been accused of tampering with the text and of having used spurious readings; and yet that we can see, not only that they had not in the given cases tampered with the text, but that they, in fact, had really had the right reading, and their churchly accusers the wrong one. The testimony that we draw in such a case from one side is just as good, just as valuable scientifically, as that which we draw from the other. What the men had before their eyes were the hard facts. I need scarcely add that the fact that the heretics have sometimes had the good readings is not in general to be attributed to a higher or better or more critical insight on their part into the then so little known intricacies of textual tradition and of the way in which to unravel them. They had the better readings, because in the given cases they had received in the course of their theological and ecclesiastical training and life the better manuscripts. They had not chosen them, but merely received them in the current of tradition that struck their shore.

The Greek manuscripts of the text of the New Testament were often altered by scribes, who put into them the readings which were familiar to them, and which they held to be the right readings. In a similar manner, words from the New Testament, which a Church writer has used in his works, have been modified by scribes and made to agree with the text in the hand of the copyists. It is sometimes possible to detect the fraud by the fact that the surroundings of the quotation which has been corrupted show it to be false. The commentary, if it stands in a commentary, may treat of totally different words from the ones now put before our eyes. And if it be a treatise of some kind, the application of the words may depend upon a thought not found in the spurious sentence. These reflections lead us to the whole question of the way in which the works of the Church writers have been handed down to us. It is not to be forgotten that they, like the translations, are also so many needy beggars for a special application of criticism to their writings. They stretch out their hands across the centuries to Christian scholars of the twentieth century and entreat them to free them from the corruption and dross that spoil their works. We cannot properly, that is to say, with definite and final certainty, apply their testimony to the criticism of the text until we have accurate scientific editions of them. Yet it is impossible to stand and wait until that great task is done. The New Testament must be furthered as well as the present circumstances admit. The future will stand upon our shoulders, will see further into the past, then men will have new witnesses, and will have better editions of the witnesses than we have. All such tasks intercalate. The work of bettering the text of the Church writers is rendered more easy by every step gained in the understanding of the connections and relations of the various readings of the text of the New Testament. No scholar should pretend to approach the textual work upon a Church writer before he has made himself thoroughly acquainted with the problems in the criticism of the text of the New Testament, seeing that they may often afford him valuable aid in judging of the manuscripts of the writer whom he is editing.

The very earliest of the Christian writers did not make a point of quoting the New Testament with any precision. The New Testament was in a way for them the air in which they lived. They breathed it in. It filled their hearts and their minds. It poured forth from their lips and their pens. What poured forth was not word for word that which had been breathed into their nostrils, sounded into their ears, devoured by their eyes, and digested in their minds. The sense was there, not the form. In many passages we see the New Testament gold glinting among their sentences like the particles of foil that are scattered throughout a solution. When we try to seize a sentence it disperses, it vanishes before our eyes. The moment we read again we see it return.

TATIAN, IRENÆUS.

One book, a book by a man who came to bear the title of heretic, a book which certainly did valiant service in its day and generation, had a less favourable influence upon the text of the first part of the New Testament. This was Tatian's Harmony of the Four Gospels, the book called "Through Four" or Diatessaron. Four Gospels there were, but these four when closely regarded resolved themselves into two Gospels, the first of which had a triple form. The first three Gospels are to such a high degree not merely connected with but interwoven with each other, that their texts must of necessity have been inclined from the first moment of their contemporaneous existence to run together. When, then, Tatian proceeded actually to weld their particles into one coherent whole, it must have been next to impossible to prevent readings from his work from passing over into the texts of the single, separate Gospels. I have already said that I suppose his Harmony to have been originally Greek. We possess it to-day unfortunately neither in Greek nor in Syrian. Wherever it appeared—it also passed over into Armenian and into Arabic—it must have exerted the same confusing and confounding influence. We have, when we are treating the tangled verses of Matthew, Mark, and Luke, to ask ourselves whether they were by accident or of set purpose combined by scribes who simply had these three Gospels in their hands,—or whether the disorder has proceeded from the circumstance that a scribe has transferred to the Gospels themselves phrases which he found ready combined on the pages of the Diatessaron.

The great treatise of Irenæus against heretics is in one respect the object of much longing on the part of the critics of the text of the New Testament. He wrote this treatise in Greek, and he packed it full of quotations from the New Testament. He wrote, it is true, say about the year 185, yet the manuscripts that he used must needs have been representatives of a much older text. The New Testament of that date would stand before our eyes in a very much clearer form could we exchange our Latin translation of Irenæus for his original Greek text. May it soon be found. Should we find it, it will be sure, like every new find, to answer some questions, but also to put a number of new questions. One asks in advance whether we should expect to find in his text the product of Asia Minor or of Lyons. I think that Smyrna, Asia Minor, must be the source of his text. It does not seem to me that the raising of Greek texts is to be supposed to have been a specialty of the Christian husbandmen in the cities of Gaul. They were probably in this respect consumers and not producers. They were heroes, those early Christians in Vienne and Lyons, but I do not think that the heathen around them left them much time for textual criticism.

ORIGEN.

Our thoughts about Origen are not so very different from those that we cherish in regard to the treatise of Irenæus. The reason, however, that the translations of Origen's works, which in many cases is all that we have left of them, are less satisfactory, is that his translators, and in particular Rufinus, were bent upon making him less heretical than he was. Rufinus is quite frank and open about it, and it was undoubtedly, I think, a matter of conscience with him, but it renders the books much less valuable for the purposes of textual criticism. A translator who confessedly changes the commentary wherever his fancy or his orthodoxy leads him to differ from Origen, will, of course, not stick at changing the text from Origen's form to the form that he himself daily used. But Origen does in some passages do a great deal for the textual critic. He was by nature and by practice an exact scholar for that period. His textual researches in reference to the Old Testament have scarcely a parallel in all antiquity, unless it be in the work of the school at Antioch, of which we, however, have scarcely any mention except in Syrian manuscripts.

The question is often asked, whether he did not also treat the text of the New Testament critically. That he treated many a reading critically is not to be doubted. That he systematically revised the text of the whole New Testament is nowhere reported. His commentaries give, nevertheless, many a note about readings, and occasionally full discussion of them. His judgment as to readings is nothing or next to nothing for us. His facts are what we care for. When he found a reading in a number of manuscripts, that meant something, for every one of them was at least a hundred years older than the Sinaitic and the Vatican manuscript. The fame of Origen in all parts of the world, the number of Christian theologians who sat at his feet, must have tended to spread his readings. The hypothesis has been suggested, that some pupil or admirer of Origen made a point of inserting into the text of the New Testament the readings which Origen had approved in his works. This would have been possible. We have, however, no testimony for it.

As the years advance the literature ceases to be so fragmentary as it had been in the second and third and early fourth
century.   The Church came to be openly acknowledged and
favoured.   Chrysostom, the golden mouthed orator, born and
working in Antioch, and at the end living at Constantinople or
in exile, exerted a wide influence as a preacher, an exegete, and
an author.   His writings are numerously represented in the
libraries of Greek manuscripts, whether in the East or in the
West.   But by his day the text had almost completed the round
of its fates, so that he cannot open for us the door to its secret
history in the earlier periods.

The translations of the New Testament into various languages
were found to be of much use for the criticism of the text.   In
like manner the Church writers who used not Greek but Syriac
or Armenian, or Coptic, or Latin, find a place in these studies.
Their testimony applies in most cases first of all to the translation of the New Testament into the language which they used,
and through it to the original text.   Yet a learned man often
used for his studies a Greek manuscript, so that the distance
between the original text and his commentary was not after all
very great.   Thus far we do not know very much about the
works of the ancient Church writers, who used Syriac or Coptic
or Ethiopic.   It is clear that at an early period Antioch paid
great attention to the text, and wrote books of the most exact
critical character, collections of variations, notes as to corrections,
and we may say in general a critical Masora for the New Testament text.   Egypt and Ethiopia must still give us much.
Armenia has given much and will surely give more.   The
Archimandrite Karapet has just published an unknown book,
a book till then known only as a title, that was written by
Irenæus.   Among Latin writers, Tertullian offers much for the
criticism of the text.   There is one curious thing about him,
about his relation to the text.   Imagine how peculiar it is that
a good author, a man of great intelligence, of high education, and of at least some travel, should transpose two petitions
in the Lord's Prayer.   Nor is the transposition a mere passing change, a variation that might be attributed to a scribe's
or to Tertullian's own carelessness, for he is commenting at
length upon the prayer.   Scarcely less strange is the fact that
we find this transposition neither in other writers in his neigh-

bourhood nor anywhere else. Many a book originally written in Greek or another tongue used in the East, is only preserved to us in a Latin translation, and we must be glad that we have that much of the writings in question. Each such translation demands, then, for itself a critical treatment before we can be sure how much we may rely upon its faithfulness to the original, and in scripture quotations how far we may be sure that the translator did not change them to fit his own accustomed form of text.

Julius Africanus, whose name seems to point to his birth in Africa, presents us a case of a Christian who was not unknown to the heathen authorities. He probably lived from about 170 to 240. His home was one of the Palestinian Emmæus towns, but he visited Alexandria, Rome, and Asia Minor. This town Emmæus, about thirty-five kilometres from Jerusalem, was rebuilt by him under the auspices of Heliogabalus (218–222), to whom he went on an embassy asking help, and it was then named Nikopolis. Africanus was one of the most learned Christians of the early Church, and deserves a place beside the great Alexandrians Clement and Origen. Unfortunately his writings are not well preserved. His great work was a chronography. He wrote a letter to Aristides touching the conflicting genealogies of Jesus.—Ammonius, who lived at Alexandria at the time of Origen, was a philosopher, but as well a Christian; and he wrote a harmony of the Gospels that has, unfortunately for us, not unfortunately for the text of the four Gospels, long been lost. The sections that belong to Eusebius used to be attributed erroneously to him.—A Syrian writer, James Aphraates, or Aphrahat, or Farhad, who was bishop in the monastery of Matthew, near Mosul, lived about the middle of the fourth century. His homilies give us much that is important for the history of the text in Syria.—A Latin companion for the commentaries of Andrew and Arethas of Cæsarea would be found in a work written about the year 540, if we only had a complete copy of it. Its author was Aprigius or Apringius, who was bishop of Pax Julia or Beja in Portugal—not of Pax Augusta or Badajoz, in Spain, as that city dreams.—Cyprian is a very good writer for the purposes of textual criticism. It would be convenient to have a Greek writer like him every fifty years from Paul to Eusebius. Thascius Cæcilius Cyprianus was made bishop of Carthage about 248, and died in 258. He quotes scripture constantly, and in large sections or long passages, which he must needs have taken from the roll, and not have written down from memory. Although he is a Latin writer, and although he is so near to Tertullian, he betrays no acquaintance with that curious Lord's Prayer of Tertullian's.

SECOND CENTURY WRITERS.

Let us ask ourselves in land after land what witnesses were to be had during the second century. We begin with Syria. At the opening of the century we find Ignatius, the bishop of Antioch, who was martyred, perhaps about 117. His New Testament will have been a very early one, will have been one that had not yet been compacted together, but was living along in the rolls of the separate books. Next comes Hegesippus, the traveller and writer, whose book we long to have. Justin the martyr follows, and passes from Samaria to Italy, and becomes a teacher of many in Rome. Tatian approaches, possibly from Eastern Syria, but a Greek and raised as a Greek. Theophilus of Antioch quotes much scripture to his heathen friend Autolycus, but chiefly Old Testament passages, because he is urging the antiquity of Christianity. And for a side-light we may name Manes in Persia. Of course, we should like to have more witnesses for Syria for the space of a hundred years, but these would give us at least a slight notion of the state of affairs in textual matters if we had all their writings. To these writers we must then add the Old-Syrian translation. So much for Syria, although we must not forget that some of these witnesses had, like Hegesippus, Justin, and Tatian, connections with the West, with Rome.

If we turn to Egypt, it is probable that we should name first of all the letter of Barnabas. It seems to belong there. Then comes the important writer Clement of Alexandria, from whom we have fair remains. Then we may hypothetically attribute the Teaching of the Apostles to Egypt. The Boheiric and Saïdic translations bring much material for the text. The side-lights here are Apelles and Basilides and Valentinus, who was also at Rome, perhaps Ptolemæus and the Antitactæ, and then Carpo-crates. Of these Clement is in himself a host.

Asia Minor recalls to us the valiant old Polycarp and his letter, and as well the story of his martyrdom. Then comes Papias, whose book will surely some day open new vistas for textual criticism. The presbyter or the presbyters whom Irenæus names, belong here, and so do Polycrates, and Melito of Sardes.

In Greece two apologists come to meet us, Aristides, to whom Julius Africanus wrote the letter about the genealogies of Jesus, and Athenagoras.

In Italy we have two to mention who came from Asia Minor, and who might be attached to that land, namely, Marcion, the daring and reckless critic, and Theodotus. Victor of Rome must be added tentatively.

From North Africa we receive the Acts of Perpetua, which may even have been written by Tertullian himself, and the Old-Latin translation.

In Gaul we are again reminded of Asia Minor, for Irenæus, the bishop of Lyons, came from Smyrna. And in Gaul the Churches of Vienne and Lyons speak in no uncertain tone.

We may give in closing a few names that we do not know precisely how to limit geographically. There is the Letter to Diognetus. Heracleon is an important writer. Hermias the philosopher may belong to this century, but is placed by others at a later point. As side-lights we have the Docetæ, the Encratitæ, the Marcosians, the Naassenes, the Peratæ, and the Valentinians.

Third Century Writers.

The third century offers us, in Syria, Julius Africanus, who might have been connected with the close of the second century. Archelaus follows, who was the bishop of Chascar in Mesopotamia about the year 278. And in Methodius Eubulius, the so-called bishop of Tyre, we have possibly not a Tyrian but the bishop of Olympia in Lycia. He died as a martyr in 311 at Chalcis in Greece, or in Cœle-Syria. Paul of Samosata, bolstered up by royalty, may form a transition to the heathen philosopher .Porphyrius of Tyre, who wrote fifteen books against the Christians, that disappeared long ago.—Egypt supplies us here with the name of the most powerful of the Christian writers, Origen, whom we could well also bring forward for Palestine, because of his long residence at Cæsarea. His successor, Dionysius of Alexandria, was a man who thought for himself, as we saw from his discussion of the Revelation. Ammonius belongs here, whom we mentioned a moment ago. Peter of Alexandria passes over into the fourth century, dying as a martyr in 311. Alexander of Lycopolis wrote against Manichæism, and reaches into the fourth century also. Theognostus followed Pierius as head of the school in Alexandria. He flourished about the year 283. Adimantus was one of the twelve disciples of Manes. He flourished about 277, but his influence would appear to have been lasting, seeing that Augustine wrote a book against him. The Pistis Sophia is a notable book from the Valentinian school, written in Saïdic.—In Asia Minor we may name Firmilian, who was a friend of Origen's, and who was bishop of Cæsarea in Cappadocia in 233; and Gregory the Wonder-Worker, who was born at New Cæsarea in Cappadocia, and who died as bishop there perhaps in 265 or 270.—Italy furnishes the great name of Hippolytus. Would that we had his complete works, and not merely the names of the most of them. Besides him we may point to Callistus, Cornelius, Gaius, and Novatian.—In North Africa we have two names that give us a great deal of help: Tertullian and Cyprian. From Pannonia we have Victorinus, who may have been by birth a Greek. He was bishop of Pettau about the year 290, and died a martyr's death about 303. Apollonius is not certainly to be localised. It may be that he belongs to Asia Minor. The Apostolical Constitutions have varied relations of date and probably of place.

Fourth Century Writers.

The fourth century brings, with the new freedom for the Church, with the dangerous attachment to the royal houses, the closing great movements for the correction of the text. Now the writers multiply apace. In Syria we have Aphraates and Ephraim, and then Jacob or James of Nisibis, and Titus the bishop of Bostra in Arabia. Titus wrote against the Manichæans, and a very common chain for the text of Luke is largely drawn from his writings. On the Greek side of Syrian life stands

Pamphilus whom we know well, and his friend and mourner
Eusebius of Cæsarea.   Then we find Acacius the One-Eyed,
who was a pupil of Eusebius', and became his successor as bishop
of Cæsarea in the year 340.   Cyril of Jerusalem was bishop
from 350 until 386, but he was driven away from Jerusalem three
times.   Chrysostom belongs here, for Constantinople had but
a few years from him.   Diodorus was born in Antioch, and was
bishop of Tarsus from about 379 to 390.   He wrote a great deal,
but we have only trifling fragments of his works, chiefly found
in chains.   From Eusebius of Emesa or Homs, of about the
year 350, we have a few remains.   Eustathius, elected bishop of
Antioch by the Council of Nice, and soon harried out of his chair
by the Arians, is known to us by some few fragments.   We may
add Macarius I., bishop of Jerusalem, and Meletius an Armenian,
bishop of Sebaste, and in the year 360 bishop of Antioch.   The
Latin contribution from Syria is a large one, for it consists of
over thirty years of the life of Jerome the Dalmatian.

If the suppositions of some scholars correspond to the facts
of the past, Egypt gave us the great Sinaitic and Vatican manuscripts during this century.   From Alexander, bishop of Alexandria,
say from 313 until 326, an opponent of Arius', we have two letters,
one touching the heresy of, and the other the deposition of Arius.
Arius himself must be named, and the other side in Athanasius,
and with them Didymus, then a mere boy, who died in 394 or
399, and Evagrius, who was archdeacon in Constantinople, and
then a monk at Scetis in Egypt, and Theophilus, who became
bishop of Alexandria in 385, and died in 412, and Timotheus,
the predecessor of Theophilus.   To these may be added
Macarius Magnes, Marcus Diadochus, who also was at Rome
and in North Africa, Marcus the Monk, Thalassius in Libya,
Isaiah, Serapion, Antonius, Orsiesis, and Phileas.   We join the
Ethiopic translation on to these Egyptian names.

Asia Minor.

In Asia Minor we have Amphilochius, the bishop of Iconium,
about the year 370.   Asterius, by birth a heathen from Cappadocia,
converted in the year 304, afterwards a zealous Arian, and who
wrote commentaries to the Psalms, the Gospels, and Romans,
28

is only known by fragments in the chains. Basil the Great, bishop of Cæsarea in Cappadocia, was born in 329 and died 379. The two Apollinarius were father and son. The father, born in Alexandria, became after the year 335 presbyter of Laodicea. The son was bishop of Laodicea, but turned heretic. He died about 392. Cæsarius of Nazianzus was a brother of Gregory of Nazianzus, and died in 368. Epiphanius, who was born in Palestine, became in 368 bishop of Salamis, later named Constantia, on the island of Cyprus. He died in 402. His works are extremely important for us. Eunomius was born in Dacora near Cæsarea in Cappadocia, and became bishop of Cyzicus in the year 360. He was expelled and exiled as an Arian, and died, very old, at Dacora. His Presentation of Faith was laid before Theodosius in 383. His Apologetic was directed against the Nicene doctrine of the Trinity. Gregory of Nazianzus we have already discussed. He died in 389. Gregory of Nyssa became bishop there about the year 370. Marcellus, the bishop of Ancyra in Galatia, died in 372.

We may mention in Constantinople, Macedonius, who was originally a feather merchant, but who became a priest, and then bishop at Constantinople. He denied the divinity of the Holy Ghost. His opponents disposed of his arguments in a most Christian and highly effectual manner, by killing him in a fight on the street.—In Thrace, at Heraclea on the Sea of Marmora, Theodore of that city became bishop in it in the year 334. He died about the year 358.—Italy gives us in this century the Codex of Vercelli, the manuscript *a* of the Latin Gospels. Ambrose the mayor and bishop belongs here, who flourished from 374 until 397. A not certainly known author, perhaps Faustinus, is associated with Ambrosius as a Pseudo-Ambrosius or Ambrosiaster. His commentaries on the Epistles of Paul were published with the works of Ambrosius. Fortunatianus was bishop of Aquileia about the year 340. Gaudentius was bishop of Brescia, perhaps from the year 387 onwards. Julius, the bishop of Rome from 337 to 352, wrote two letters which Athanasius gives us in the Apology for Flight. Lucifer, the bishop of Cagliari on Sardinia, was exiled four times. He died in 371.

Paulinus reminds us of Ambrosius by his passage from State to Church. His name was Pontius Paulinus Meropius, and he was born in 353 at Bordeaux, having studied under Ausonius;

he later became Senator at Rome. He was baptized in the year 391, made a presbyter in the year 393, and was afterwards bishop of Nola in Campania, on which account he is sometimes named Paulinus Nolanus. He died in 431. Philaster or Philastrius, possibly an Italian, was a great traveller. He became bishop of Brescia. He flourished about the year 380. We have his book about heresies. Siricius was a Roman. He became bishop in 385 and died in 398. Victorinus, Gaius Marius or Marius Fabius Victorinus, was a celebrated teacher of rhetoric at Rome, and taught among others Augustine. He passed from heathenism to Christianity before the year 361. He was a fertile writer. Zeno, from Africa, was bishop of Verona in the middle of the fourth century. We have sixty-seven sermons from him. Perhaps that Faustinus whom we mentioned above as a candidate for the works of Ambrosiaster was the author of Questions of the Old and New Testament, a work that also belongs to this century.

In North Africa the great Augustine looms up before us; born in 354, he died in 430. Faustus the Manichæan belonged to Mileve about the year 400. We can make the acquaintance of his heretical book in Augustine's answer to it. Optatus was bishop of Mileve about the year 368. He wrote against Parmenianus, the bishop of the Donatist heretics at Carthage. Tichonius or Tyconius, who lived towards the close of the fourth century, was perhaps a friend of the Donatists. There is a book on Re-baptizing among the works of Cyprian that may be from Africa, although it has been also assigned to Italy.—In Spain we have Juvencus, who was a poet as well as a presbyter. He wrote four books about the Gospel history in heroic verse, about the year 330. Pacianus was bishop of Barcelona about the year 370. Priscillian, the bishop of the fourth century, who held heretical views and who taught a Panchristism that disposed of the doctrine of the Trinity, is at the present moment especially interesting, because it has been plausibly argued that the spurious verse in 1 John 5[7, 8] is to be attributed to him.

In Gaul, Hilary of Poitiers filled a large place. He was probably born about the year 310. He was a heathen, but became later a Christian. In 354 he was appointed bishop of Poitiers. Two years later, in 356, he was driven from his chair because he had attacked the Arians in Phrygia violently; but he was rein-

stated in 360, and died in 368. He wrote a commentary on
Matthew, and one on the Psalms, and twelve books on the
Trinity. Lactantius, the brilliant writer, the Christian Cicero,
belongs both to Italy and to Gaul and perhaps also to North
Africa. He was born about the year 260 in Italy, it would appear,
though some say in Africa, went to Nicomedia probably soon
after 290, and to Gaul about 307, dying there about 340. He
wrote a book called Divine Institutions, and another On the
Deaths of Persecutors. Phœbadius or Phœgadius was bishop of
Agen in "Aquitania secunda." He was still alive in 392. He
quoted very carefully from the text and not from memory. We
have a book of his against the Arians. The Gothic translation
may have been made on the banks of the Danube. Faustinus is
of uncertain place, yet he may have been a Roman presbyter
about the year 383, at the time of the schism of Lucifer. He
wrote "to Galla Placidia on the Trinity or about Faith against
the Arians." Maternus is also not to be placed definitely.
He flourished about the year 340, it may be, and wrote "about
the errors of profane religions" to Constantius and Constans the
emperors. Maximinus was a bishop of the Arians of unknown
residence, against whom Augustine wrote two books. Therewith
we may leave the review of the Church writers.

VIII.

PRINTED EDITIONS.

THE manuscripts of which we have spoken brought the text of the New Testament down to the sixteenth century. We are in danger of supposing that so soon as the first printed editions of the texts were issued, the manuscripts stopped short. Yet that is not the case. The New Testament of Alcalá and that of Basel did not instantly spread like wildfire through the cities, towns, villages, and monasteries of the East. Many a manuscript was written after that time and even down into the nineteenth century, both of the continuous text and of the Church lessons. Nevertheless, the critic of the text has a good reason for busying himself less with these later volumes. He does not expect to find in them material which he has not at hand in other and earlier manuscripts. He examines each one in passing, so as to establish the connection of its text with other books, but he considers it likely that he has in his hands some nearer or more remote ancestor thereof.

The beginning of the printed editions of the Greek Text of the New Testament was in more than one way different from what might have been anticipated. We pay so much attention to the Greek text and have such a high respect for it, that it is difficult for us to put ourselves in the place of the Christians in Europe at the opening of the printing-offices. To us it would seem as if the Greek Text must at once have been printed the moment that printing was invented. We should indeed not be surprised that the Bible in the various vernacular languages should be sent to the Press. Yet after these, practically valuable volumes, surely the Greek text must have been issued. But no. The West did not care particularly for the Greek Bible. The one great Bible of Western Europe was the Latin Bible. It was therefore the first or about the first object of the printer's skill. It may have appeared in the same year as the German Bible, or it may have been a few years in advance of it, but at any

rate soon after the middle of the fifteenth century. That was
the time at which the fall of Constantinople and the general
inroads of the Turks were driving the educated Greeks to the
West. They taught Greek wherever they settled, in Italy, and
France, and England. But the scholars who were anxious to
learn Greek did not apply it in the first instance to the New
Testament. They were eager to delve into the profane literature
of Greece. It was new to them. The Bible they had.

The Greek immigrants did have to do with the Greek New
Testament now and then, but it was not with the printing of it.
Now and then they copied a Greek manuscript for a Western
scholar. That was the due continuation of their past. They had
nothing to do with printing the New Testament. It may be that
Eastern Greeks, prelates or rich merchants, would have ordered
editions of their sacred books in the forms of the new art, if the
times had been quiet. But in the East all was turmoil and
confusion. Property and life were the first concern of all. The
Christians were happy if they succeeded in saving their old
books from destruction,—and often they could not compass that,
—and they had no time to think of having new books made,
which they perhaps would be unable to protect from the swords
and torches of their barbarous assailants.

The first verses of the New Testament that were printed
in Greek were, so far as we know, the hymns of Mary—or
is it Elisabeth?—and of Zacharias from Luke $1^{46\text{-}55}$ and $^{68\text{-}79}$.
The Greek psalms in the manuscripts had for centuries had
as an appendix, not only the so-called one hundred and fifty-
first Psalm, but also a series of Old Testament hymns, including the hymn of the Three Children, and the above hymns
from the New Testament, to which the words of Simeon
and a non-biblical morning hymn were often added. Now in
the year 1481 a monk named John of Placenta published on
the twentieth of September at Milan an edition of the Psalms
in Greek, and in the appendix he placed those hymns out of the
first chapter of Luke. There was after all a certain poetical
propriety in the fact that those preliminary odes should have
first found their way to the Press. Theologically speaking, the
next fragment that was printed should have been the first, for
it was John $1^{1\text{-}14}$, the opening lesson on the great Easter Sunday,
as we saw. It came out at Venice in the year 1495 in a volume

containing the Questions of Constantine Lascar with a Latin translation. Still there is no Greek New Testament in print.

The next printed fragment I might call larger, yet it was printed in a very fragmentary way, and in a way that speaks with but little favour for the knightly qualities of the printer, and for his appreciation of the value of the text of the New Testament and of the honour due to it. Aldo Manucci was the printer, we might almost say the culprit. In the year 1504 he printed at Venice, as the third volume of his Christian Poets, sixty-six poems of Gregory of Nazianzus. Besides the Greek text, he wished to give also a Latin translation, and that in such a way that it could be added to the Greek text by placing the double leaves within each other, or could be left out altogether if the buyer preferred. Of course, then the two inner middle pages of each Greek sheet had to be left free from the text of Gregory, because there would be no Latin companion for them. There were then fourteen double pages scattered through the whole book which would have to be left empty if the printer could not devise a special plan for filling them, a plan that would not affect the rest of the text. Manucci's plan, which he carried out so far as this book goes, was to print in these gaps the beginning of the Gospel of John. Accordingly we find on these helter-skelter pages John 1^1–6^{58} in Greek and Latin. Under the Greek text in each sheet we read : " Look for the rest in the middle of the next quire." At the close of the table of contents he said that he would continue the Gospel of John in his translation of Nonnus of Panopolis. Probably he was prevented from printing that, for no copy of it from his press is known. That was not a respectful way to treat scripture, to use it as a mere fill-gap.

ALCALÁ-COMPLUTUM.

But at last we shall reach, just ten years later, a printed copy of the Greek New Testament, though no one was able to buy it until long after it was printed. We must go to Spain. Hard as it seems to day to believe it, there was then in Spain a great cardinal and a great scholar. His name was Francis Ximenes de Cisneros, and he was archbishop of Toledo. As early as the year 1502 he began to prepare in the university of Alcalá, with the Latin name Complutum, an edition of the Bible which was to have in the Old Testament the Hebrew original and as well the Greek and Latin translations, and in the New Testament the Greek original and the Latin translation. The volume containing the New Testament was the fifth volume, but it came out first. The editors were James Lopez de Stunica or Astuniga, Fernando Nuñez de Guzman, Demetrius Ducas from Crete, and Antonio from Lebrija near Seville. They finished printing the New Testament on January 10th, 1514. The first four volumes, containing the Old Testament and the sixth volume with its lexicon, were finished by the 10th of July 1517. Still, however, the volumes were not then published. In reference to the Old Testament it is interesting to observe that the editors betray in their preface by a very strong sentence a preparatory step to the egregious overestimation of the Latin text of the Bible uttered by the Council of Trent on April 8th, 1546. For, referring to the fact that they had placed the Latin text in the middle and the Hebrew and Greek at the sides, they said that the Latin text was like Jesus between the two thieves. The Greek types used in the New Testament volume were singular, very thick and stiff, straight up and down. Instead of the usual Greek accents, the editors merely placed an acute accent on the syllable accented. The monosyllables had no accent at all. There were no spiritus. The other volumes had the usual Greek letters with accents and spiritus. Now these six volumes were all done by the year 1517. The pope's, Leo x.'s, approval was not received until March 22nd, 1520, and we can find no traces of the books being in the hands of scholars before the year 1522. There were five short notes in the New Testament, one in Matthew, three in First Corinthians, and one in 1 John $5^{7,8}$. This last passage was taken from the Vulgate. The Greek text was of a late description; it was the ordinary continuation of the written tradition. Our information about the Complutensian edition is meagre. We are much better acquainted with the rival edition made by Erasmus.

Erasmus.

Erasmus began to print his edition on the 11th of September 1515, and it was done by the 1st of March 1516. Froben, the printer and publisher, had heard of the Alcalá edition, and was anxious to get his edition out ahead of it. He was successful enough in this effort, for Erasmus did not get sight of a copy of that other New Testament until after his own third edition of the year 1522 was done. It was not strange that such a hasty edition as Erasmus' first edition was, should have many faults. Erasmus praised his own edition in a letter to the pope, but he elsewhere conceded that it "was done headlong rather than edited." The manuscripts which he followed most closely were younger ones. As for the Revelation, Erasmus had but one mutilated manuscript, and he supplied what was lacking by translating the words from the Vulgate into his imperfect Greek. In one verse, if we may refer to a special one, he omits the article six times, where it should stand. The second edition, of the year 1519, contains Leo x.'s approving letter of September 10th, 1518. The third edition was issued in the year 1522, and it was this edition that, alas! brought the baleful verse 1 John $5^{7.8}$ out of that worthless manuscript at Dublin. The fourth edition of the year 1527 contained not only the Greek text with Erasmus' translation, but also the text of the Vulgate, which the fifth edition of the year 1535 again laid aside.

ESTIENNE STEPHENS, BEZA.

There was a family of printers at Paris and later at Geneva that exercised much influence in theological literature. Robert Estienne (to be pronounced étienne), the son of Henri Estienne the First, published in the year 1546, in two tiny volumes, a Greek New Testament. His son, Henri Estienne the Second, helped him. The text was chiefly taken from the fifth edition of Erasmus of the year 1535, although Estienne also used the Alcalá edition. In the year 1549 he published a second edition, scarcely differing from the first. The year 1550 saw the publication of Robert Estienne's, Stephens', large edition, named the Regia. This was the first edition with a critical apparatus, for the son Henri compared for his father fifteen manuscripts and the Alcalá edition, and the readings were placed on the margin. This fine edition is in general the source of the so-called Textus Receptus for England. In the following year Robert Estienne

printed his last edition of the Greek text of the New Testament.
This was again a small edition in two volumes, and appeared at
Geneva, not at Paris.   In some copies the year was printed by
mistake MDXLI instead of MDLI.   It is extremely rare.   The
great peculiarity of this edition is that it contains for the first
time our verse division.

The next editor whom we have to name is again a Frenchman, Théodore de Bèze, Calvin's successor at Geneva, to
whom we alluded when speaking of the Codex Bezæ and
the Codex Claromontanus which belonged to him.   His four
large-sized editions of the text of the New Testament were published at Geneva, the first three by the Estienne Press, the fourth
by the "heirs of Eustathe Vignon."   With the Greek text Bèze
published also his annotations.   These he had published before
in a volume with the Vulgate New Testament, the third volume
of a Latin Bible that Robert Stephens issued in 1557.   On the
title-page, therefore, of the Greek New Testament of 1565, his
own first Greek edition, he very properly said that the annotations
appeared for the second time.   In consequence of this, careless
scholars have applied "second edition," "hac secunda vice,"
to his Greek text, and have caused confusion that lasted for
years.   Bèze's Greek text was drawn from Estienne's fourth
edition of the year 1551.   His second edition is of the year
1582, his third of the year 1588, or sometimes, in some copies,
1589, and his fourth of the year 1598.   Besides these large-
sized folio editions which were normative, he published five
small editions.

THE POLYGLOTS.

We have now reached the time of the great Polyglots.   The
Complutensian or Alcalá Bible was indeed in a manner a
polyglot, because it had not only the Greek and Latin text of
the whole Bible, but also in the Old Testament the Hebrew
text.   But now we come to something more extensive.   The
first one appeared under the auspices of Philip II. at Antwerp.
The editor was Benedict Arias Montanus.   In this polyglot we
find the Greek text of the New Testament twice over.   In the
fifth volume we find the Syriac text of the New Testament in
Syriac letters, then the Syriac text in Hebrew letters, then the

Latin translation of the Syriac text, and finally the Latin Vulgate and the Greek text. This Greek text agrees in the main with Robert Estienne's edition of the year 1550. In the sixth volume we again have the Greek text with an interlinear Latin translation by Montanus. This Greek text is much like the other. The volume is sometimes numbered seventh or eighth. The name by which this polyglot goes is the Antwerp polyglot or, after its printer Christopher Plantin, the Plantin polyglot. We shall mention at once the other two polyglots. The Paris polyglot contained the New Testament in the fifth of its huge volumes, the first part of which appeared in 1630, the second in 1633. It offers the Syrian text with a Latin translation, the Latin Vulgate, the Greek text taken from the Antwerp polyglot, and the Arabic text with a Latin translation. The London polyglot, often called Walton's polyglot after its editor Brian Walton, appeared in the year 1657. The New Testament is in the fifth volume, and appears in the Syrian text with a Latin translation, the Ethiopic text with a Latin translation, the Arabic text with a Latin translation,—the Gospels are also given in Persian with an Arabic translation,—the Greek text with Montanus' Latin translation between the lines, and the Vulgate Latin text. The Greek text is from Estienne's edition of 1550. The sixth volume contained several collections of various readings, especially from Walton's hand and from James Ussher's.

The Textus Receptus.

Now we must go back to the end of the first quarter of the seventeenth century and the beginning of the second quarter, a time which exercised, critically speaking, a pernicious influence upon the progress of the determination of the Greek text of the New Testament, which fettered all research or all application of the results of research until far into the nineteenth century. It is a case of the wide influence of apparently trifling actions or words. The Elzevir publishers in Leiden and Amsterdam published in 1624 a neat little New Testament in Greek, taking the text chiefly from Bèze's first edition of the year 1565. There was no harm in that. In the year 1633 they issued a second edition. They had corrected it as well as they knew how, doubtless helped by some unknown scholar as corrector, and this time they put into the preface a sentence, which they, of course, in their ignorance supposed to be true, yet which did not correspond to the facts. They wrote: "Therefore thou hast the text now received by all: in which we give nothing altered or corrupt": "Textum ergo habes, nunc ab omnibus receptum: in quo nihil immutatum aut corruptum damus."

These ignorant words are what did the mischief, and led to two centuries of trouble for textual critics. It was not the case that that was the text received by all, and much less was it the text that should have been received by all. But people, even many who should have known better, whose education should have enabled them to free themselves from the limitations of these publishers, clung to these words, busied themselves with the effort to prove them true, and denounced all who did not agree with them at least as blinded, but sometimes as traitors to the truth, destroyers of the New Testament, and it may be as totally immoral and detestable persons. These publishers issued further editions in the years 1641, 1656, 1662, 1670, and 1678, but these have no further interest for us. The text which has been considered the Received Text by theologians of different places and different years has not always been one and the same. One general distinction to be mentioned is that between England and the Continent, inasmuch as the text of Estienne of the Regia edition of 1550 has for the most part prevailed in England, whereas on the Continent the text of Elzevir of the year 1624 has held the chief place. But then the handy editions of the British and Foreign Bible Society have done much to bring the English form into use in other countries. It is, however, to be kept in mind that in a large number of cases theologians have presupposed that the text which some chance wind had brought into their hands, and which was when exactly viewed neither Estienne 1550 nor Elzevir of any date, was the Received Text. The text had doubtless the qualification for such a juxtaposition in being of a late kind, and in not differing materially in its faults from the fancied but not existing commonly received text.

A Geneva scholar, Étienne de Courcelles, who died at Amsterdam in 1659, had much insight into the condition of the text. He published in the Elzevir office at Amsterdam in the year 1658

a Greek New Testament that must be carefully kept separate
from the Elzevir editions just mentioned. It is true that, as
the necessities of that day demanded, he printed for the most
part the Elzevir text of 1633 with but few variations. But he
added a very learned preface and a great many various readings
both from manuscripts and from earlier editions. He placed
the heavenly witnesses, 1 John 5[7. 8], in a parenthesis. The reward
of his labours were attacks made upon him as a favourer of
Arianism. He intended to publish a large Greek and Latin
edition with various readings, but he did not live to finish it.—
In the year 1675, John Fell, who was afterwards bishop of
Oxford, published a Greek New Testament, giving also the
text of Elzevir 1633 and adding various readings from Courcelles
and from the London polyglot and from twelve Oxford
manuscripts. From friends he received further various readings
from Dublin and from France, these out of Greek manuscripts,
and then from the Gothic and the Boheiric translations, the
latter of which was then still called simply Coptic.

John Mill, Wells, Bentley, Mace

Fell's mantle found worthy shoulders in John Mill, who began
an imposing edition of the New Testament in Greek, and had
reached in print the twenty-fourth chapter of Matthew before
Fell, who furthered the work, died. That was in the year 1686.
Then he seems to have lost heart and to have let the book lie.
Finally, he was in the year 1704 made a canon of Canterbury,
and the Queen ordered him to finish his edition as soon as
possible. It appeared in the year 1707, and Mill passed away.
This was one of the great works of the theologians of the
world, and would have done credit to Origen. He used Estienne's
text of the year 1550, but he changed the readings in thirty-one
passages. He gathered various readings from every accessible
quarter. It would at that time have been totally impossible
for him to make a text for himself. No one would have borne
it. But in the preface, which was beyond praise, and in the
notes under the text, he showed what he considered to be the
right readings. Although he had, by retaining in general the
accustomed text, made such concessions to the opinions of the

common run of theologians, he was nevertheless attacked in the most violent manner; I say, he was attacked, but happily, as we have seen, he had gone to his reward; his book was attacked. It was then republished in Amsterdam by Ludolf Küster, but the age was so little inclined to studies of the kind that the sale hung fire. Again and again it was put forth with a new title-page. I think I have seen copies of Leipzig 1723 and Amsterdam 1746.

Edward Wells, who died in the year 1727, published a Greek New Testament in ten parts between 1709 and 1719, which was accompanied by an English translation and paraphrase as well as by critical and exegetical notes and various long essays. Unfortunately I have not yet seen this work. It was the first edition, after Bèze's editions, that changed the text upon the basis of manuscripts. The great philologian Richard Bentley, who died in 1742, wrote to John Mill so early as 1691 about textual criticism. Later he determined to edit a Greek and Latin New Testament. For this purpose he collated himself and caused others, also Wettstein, and especially John Walker, to collate both Latin and Greek manuscripts. His intention was to constitute the text from the oldest manuscripts in the two languages. His propositions for such an edition were published, and were, of course, the object of the antagonism of the men who thought that the salvation of the Church lay in the undisturbed use of the Received Text. Bentley was not the man to be stopped by an attack of that kind. He liked fighting. We can apparently see that Walker was still collating for Bentley in the year 1732. But the edition never was published. The work grew upon him and he grew old. It is also very likely that he came to see that the harmony between the various Greek manuscripts and the Old-Latin manuscripts was not so close as he had supposed when he issued his propositions, and that this tended to retard the work itself or to lengthen the work itself, and as well to decrease his satisfaction in it.

I have tried in vain to find out something about a Presbyterian clergyman named William or perhaps Daniel Mace, who is said to have been a member of Gresham College in London. In the year 1729 he published at London a New Testament in Greek and English in two volumes: "containing the original text corrected from the authority of the most authentic manuscripts." In many cases he has the readings that the modern critics with their vastly enlarged critical apparatus have chosen. It was a most excellent work, and was, as a matter of course, violently denounced. If Scrivener had given due credit to Mace, he would not have needed to complain quite so much about the neglect of critical work in the department of the New Testament text at that time.

BENGEL.

In the year 1734, Johannes Albert Bengel, who died in 1752, published a valuable edition of the Greek New Testament. As we have so often said of others, so we must say of Bengel, that he could not then publish a text of his own. Neither the publisher nor the public would have stood it. Bengel, however, was equal to the occasion. He only ventured, indeed, to put the good readings into the text when he could show that they already had appeared in some good edition. But he divided the various readings on the margin into five classes. The first class contained the genuine readings, and these, of course, should have been in the text and not on the margin. The second class contained the readings that were better than those in the text, and these should in like manner have been in the text instead of on the margin. The third class contained the readings that were just as good as those in the text. The fourth class contained the readings that were not so good as those in the text. And, finally, the fifth class consisted of readings that were to be rejected. In the book of Revelation he altered nineteen passages to suit the manuscripts. So many people railed at his edition that he published a "Defence of the Greek Testament" in German at the end of a harmony of the evangelists, and by itself in Latin at Leiden in 1737. A smaller edition offered only the text and the readings.

WETTSTEIN, SEMLER, GRIESBACH.

Among those who did collation work for Bentley was Johann Jakob Wettstein, who was born at Basel in 1693 and died in 1754. As early as the year 1713 he wrote a dissertation

about the various readings in the New Testament. Then
he visited various cities in Switzerland, France, and England.
In the year 1717 he was made deacon in Basel. Having published in 1718 a specimen of his various readings, he was
at once charged with favouring Socinianism. After a long
battle he was put out of his office in 1730. About then he
published a prefatory word to an edition of the Greek New
Testament, in Amsterdam, in which city he had a professorship
in the philosophical faculty in view. Having vanquished his
antagonists in Basel in 1732, he became a professor at Amsterdam
in 1733. His great edition of the New Testament in two
volumes appeared at Amsterdam in 1751 and 1752. It contained
also the letter of Clement of Rome and the homily of Pseudo-
Clement, in Syriac and Latin, at the close of the second volume.
Of course, he had to print a common text, and his text was in
the main the Elzevir text. His critical apparatus was the first
in which the uncial or large letter manuscripts were regularly
denoted by capital letters and the minuscle or small letter
manuscripts by Arabic numbers. This edition offered by far
the largest critical apparatus for the text of the New Testament
then existing.

Johann Salomo Semler did not edit an edition of the New
Testament, but he treated of the Greek manuscripts thereof in
a most learned manner and at great length in the year 1765
and later. The name of the book in which he discussed the
manuscripts was Hermeneutical Preparation, and no one has
apparently suspected the character of its contents. It may be
that the readers of the title took it for an elementary book and
passed it by. A pupil of Semler was destined to do great
service, and to make for himself a name in this department.
Johann Jakob Griesbach, who was born in 1745 and died in
1812, published from 1774 until 1777 a Greek New Testament.
The way of it was this. In the year 1774 he issued the three
synoptic Gospels in their combination with each other. The
Gospel according to John and the book of Acts followed in
the year 1775, in which year the second volume with the
Epistles and Revelation came out. And then in 1777 the
synoptic Gospels were published at full length. This was a
complicated way of preparing a copy of the New Testament.
Griesbach continued to collate manuscripts and to examine

and use the collations of others. After a number of years he published the first volume of a new edition in the year 1796 and the second volume in 1806. The critical apparatus here was large, but not so large as Griesbach might have made it by drawing more fully upon the stores brought by his predecessors in collating and in editing. David Schulz began to make a new edition of Griesbach's New Testament in the year 1827, but did not get beyond the first volume. If, however, we wish to have the ripe judgment of Griesbach, we should not take the larger edition of 1796–1806, but the small edition of the year 1805. To this small edition attaches, if I am not mistaken, a trifling literary interest in a curious way. Its text was, I understand, used in printing a large and beautiful edition in two fine quarto volumes, and for a half a century this edition was one of the favourite theological gifts in England, especially of wealthy parishioners to their clergymen.

EDWARD HARWOOD, MATTHÄI, BIRCH, SCHOLZ.

We mentioned a moment ago the Englishman Mace. Another Englishman, Edward Harwood, who was born in 1729 and died in 1794, was a Londoner and a theologian. He broke thoroughly out of the bands and bonds of tradition in preparing an edition of the Greek New Testament. A certain preparation for his work had been made by a learned printer in London, named William Bowyer. Johann Jakob Wettstein had not been permitted to print his own text, but had followed therein the Elzevir tradition, and placed below the text the readings which he thought to be the proper ones. The printer Bowyer was so liberal and so undertaking that he seized this opportunity to do a good work. He had already published Mill's edition four times, but Mill had also used a poorer text. Now Bowyer issued a two volume book which contained in the first volume the Greek New Testament almost always with the readings which Wettstein had declared to be the best ones. And the second volume was for that day still more daring, for it brought a collection of the conjectural readings that had been suggested for the text of the New Testament.

Now Harwood went still further in his work. He knew nothing

29

of the future Codex Sinaiticus, and there were then no scholars to tell him how valuable the Codex Vaticanus was, and his keen discernment led him to turn to the Codex Bezæ for the Gospels and for Acts, and to the Codex Claromontanus for the Pauline Epistles. Where these deserted him, he appealed chiefly to the Codex Alexandrinus. Eduard Reuss, who in the year 1891 died at Strassburg, where he had long worked, and who had pursued the most painstaking researches in the line of the printed text of the Greek New Testament, hit upon a good method for comparing the readings or the texts of the editions with each other. He picked out a thousand passages as normal passages and then collated the editions at those points. The freedom of Harwood's edition is plain when we learn that out of Reuss' thousand passages there are seven hundred and eleven, or more than seventy per cent., in which Harwood does not use the Elzevir text. Out of the thousand passages there are six hundred and forty-three in which Harwood agrees with Lachmann. Reuss counted Harwood's new readings, and did not name as new the ones which Griesbach at about the same time had preferred, and yet he found two hundred and three new readings, many of which are approved of by modern critics. That was a very good showing for the year 1776, and was quite worthy of that year with its 4th of July on the other side of the sea.

Alas! the contemporaries of Harwood as well as of Mace and Bowyer did not appreciate the freedom that this edition placed before their eyes. Scrivener called Mace's work "unworthy of serious notice"; and his editor, referring to Bowyer and Harwood, says that Scrivener "looked for greater names." If Mace, and even the learned printer Bowyer, and Harwood had received from the clergy of their own day due respect, and if Scrivener and Burgon had appreciated and commended what these men did in those times that were so perilous for daring scientific work, the three names would be better known, and would attain at least to such greatness as various other names which Scrivener counted fit for approving notice.

A Thuringian, Christian Friedrich Matthäi, who was born in 1744 and died in 1811, and who held professorial chairs successively in Moscow, Meissen, and Wittenberg, a man of very keen parts, though, we regret to say, inaccurate in his views touching the inviolability of library possessions, did a great deal of very valuable collating of manuscripts of Church writers, in particular of Chrysostom, and of manuscripts of the New Testament. He published at Riga during the years 1782 to 1788 the New Testament in Greek and Latin in twelve volumes that are packed full of valuable material drawn from the manuscripts. A guide to the contents of these volumes would not be amiss, seeing that their arrangement is little less than chaotic. The Greek text is of no great importance, because it is drawn chiefly from young and inferior manuscripts. The Latin text is taken from the Demidow manuscript of the Vulgate. In a second edition, published in three volumes at Hof in 1803 and 1805 and at Ronneburg in 1807, he left out the Latin text, but used collations of several new manuscripts. It was much to be regretted that Matthäi attacked some of his predecessors and contemporaries—for example, Semler and Griesbach—in a violent and, from the standpoint of courtesy, outrageous way.

Denmark is like Weimar, a land devoted to art and science. In the second half of the eighteenth century it sent out a number of scholars to search in the libraries of Europe for manuscripts of the Greek New Testament and to collate them. The real leader was Andreas Birch, who was born in 1758 and died in 1829. He published in the year 1788 at Copenhagen the four Gospels in Greek from Estienne 1550, with various readings from Danish, Italian, Austrian, and Spanish libraries, and from three Syriac versions. The government and Birch intended to complete the New Testament in the same stately form, but a fire in the printing-office in the year 1795 destroyed a great many copies, and as well the paper and the types to be used for the edition. After this great loss the large edition was given up, and Birch published the various readings for the Acts and the Epistles in two small volumes, to which he also added one for the four Gospels.

The Roman Catholic Church has thus far not taken an important part in the editing of the text of the New Testament, although the first editions that were printed were done before 1517. Johannes Martin Augustinus Scholz, a professor at Bonn, who was born in 1794 and died in 1852, was a very diligent worker in this department. He travelled in France and Switzerland and Italy and Palestine collating manuscripts most

industriously, and then published at Leipzig in two volumes, in
1830 and 1836, a Greek New Testament. His Greek text
was modelled largely after that of Griesbach, especially in
the second volume. His critical apparatus then gave his
collations of the Greek manuscripts as well as some readings
from the translations of the text, and from church writers. This
collection of various readings was and is still to-day very
important. The habit of decrying Scholz's carefulness in
collation appears to me to be unjustifiable. I have repeatedly
compared his collations with the originals, and found them to be
very good.

CARL LACHMANN.

We now come to a man who bears in one respect a certain
resemblance to Bentley, in that he was a great philologian.
Bentley was, however, also a theologian, as every professor at
Cambridge and Oxford was of necessity until after the middle
of the nineteenth century. I know of no previous connection
between Carl Lachmann, of whom we now have to speak,
and theology. He was a classical scholar of the highest rank,
and as well one of the first German philologians, so that his
edition of Lessing is still valuable. He began his work upon
the New Testament by a small edition issued at Berlin in
1831. The putting forth of this little book was effected in
the most unfortunate way. It was an unusual example of the
way not to issue a book. Either Lachmann had not reflected
carefully upon the possibilities of the reception of the book,
or he had overrated the influence that his name upon the
title-page would have as a commendation of the text offered, or
he had underrated the conservative inclinations of theologians
and the power that they could exert to hinder a judicial reception
of his efforts. Be that as it may, he published the book in
the following way. In the most important scientific theological
quarterly for 1830, he published an article of about twenty-eight
pages describing his edition. Now that was all very well. A
number of thinking men will there have read his words, and
have known what his intentions were. When the volume itself
came out in 1831 it had no sign of a preface at the beginning.
At the close of Revelation the reader found a few lines that said

in effect this : (*a*) I have told of my plan in a more convenient place, namely, in that journal. (*b*) I have followed the custom of the oldest Eastern Churches. (*c*) Where that was uncertain I have laid weight upon the agreement of Italy and Africa. (*d*) Where all was uncertain, the margin says so. (*e*) Therefore I had no use for the Textus Receptus, but I now add its readings here. Accordingly the closing pages contained the readings of the Textus Receptus.

That was not the way to publish a book. He could not compel everyone who bought his New Testament to go buy a copy of that number of that journal and cut out the twenty-eight pages as a preface to his book. The text differed from the commonly used texts, and it brought with it no adequate explanation of its reason for existence. Why should the theologians assume that this philologian, who had taken a fancy to make an excursion into their domains and to lay hands upon their sacred text, must necessarily have done so with very good judgment ? The probabilities were for them all upon the other side, and they said so, many of them in strong terms. And even the scholars who read that article in the journal were by no means all of them prepared to agree with him. To us to-day what he says is much more palatable, because we stand at a very different point in the development of critical science.

Lachmann did not give up his new line of work. In the years 1842 and 1850 he published in two volumes a large edition both of the Greek and of the Latin text of the New Testament. Philipp Buttmann, the son of the great Philipp Buttmann, attended to the Greek part of the critical apparatus. All the rest Lachmann did. The text was much the same as in the first, the small edition. One of the difficulties in the way of the reception of Lachmann's text was that from Lachmann's point of view, as a matter of fact, it was neither intended for nor adapted to reception in the common use of that word, and in the way in which an edition of the New Testament was applied by the average owners thereof. Almost all the copies of the Greek New Testament that were sold were bought either by students of theology to be used in following the daily lectures, or by pastors to be used in preparing their sermons and their theological essays. Lachmann's edition was in itself, according to his express purpose, what we might call a scientific tool. It might perhaps be called a bridge that was to be thrown across the gap separating us from the true text. What the ordinary buyer of a Greek New Testament wanted, what the student needed for the current exercises of the university, the pastor for his daily work, was the true, real, good text, the very best text that was attainable.

When, then, Lachmann said: "I am not yet trying to find the true reading,—which indeed is often still in existence in some single source, but just as often has been totally lost,—but only the oldest one among those that are evidently widely spread,"—when Lachmann said that, he puzzled and displeased his buyers. So far as that was his purpose, Lachmann should have had a good friend who could have heard his plan and then said: "My dear Lachmann, that is a very fine plan. I do not doubt that you will finally succeed in making a very good text of the New Testament. But, as you say, you are not yet trying to get the true text. You are searching for a middle text which will lead you over to the true text. Now, you must not publish this middle text. Nobody wants it. It is worth nothing to these people who buy the Greek New Testaments. Keep this middle text in your portfolio, and use it as well as you can to help you in the determination of the true text. When you have found the true text, or when you have gotten as near to the true text as you can get, then publish that." That is the way in which a good friend might have saved Lachmann and his opponents much trouble. Lachmann thought that he could get back, for this present bridging purpose, at least as far as the last years of the fourth century, to the time at which Jerome revised the Latin text.

After all, however, we must ask what Lachmann really did, or first of all, what he could do. The answer is, that the witnesses that he had in his hands were not numerous or complete enough, and not adapted to give him the text of the end of the fourth century. Fancy, for example, the wild impropriety of using Origen as a witness for such a purpose. And the other auxiliary troops, Italy and Africa, were as little then to be used for the service for which Lachmann needed them. That is one thing: Lachmann could not do what he proposed to do. Strangely enough, I now have to state something that seems to be directly opposed to much of what I have said of Lachmann's work. It is all right nevertheless. What we have just said aimed at Lachmann's plan and purpose. His plan was not the right one for a New Testament that was to be sold, and his plan was not possible of being carried out. And, in spite of all that, Lachmann's text, the text that he actually published, was a very good one, and was for that day very well fitted to be used not only by students but also by pastors. Lachmann was an exceptionally good philologian, and his skilful hands formed the good text in spite of him, so that instead of constituting a bridge he did much towards—what shall I say?—rebuilding or unearthing that which was on the farther side of the stream of forgetfulness across which the bridge was to be thrown. His art and his insight led him to determine a text which largely belongs to the second century, and modern criticism accepts a great many of the readings which he approved. Lachmann was better than he had in that article declared that he would be. His name will long be held in honour in textual criticism, even though neither he nor anyone else ever used his text as a means of passing on to the true text.

CONSTANTIN TISCHENDORF.

It was above observed that a note of Lachmann's in that article in the journal of 1830 had given Tischendorf the idea of going to Paris and preparing editions of the Codex Ephræmi and of the Codex Claromontanus. In that way Tischendorf really owed his first manuscript work to Lachmann's indirect advice, to the words that Lachmann addressed to the scholars at Paris. This circumstance might have led to an attachment between the two that would certainly have been an advantage to the younger man. But a quick word of Lachmann's barred any such connection, and excited in Tischendorf bitter feelings that only passed away after a long series of years. The way of it was this. Tischendorf finished at the beginning of October in the year 1840 a small edition of the New Testament dated 1841, and, habilitating at once as privatdozent at Leipzig, started off on that journey to Paris. His New Testament, which was provided with a fairly large critical apparatus, was kindly received in general, and David Schulz, the professor at Breslau, who had published one volume of a renewed edition of Griesbach's Greek New Testament, was particularly friendly.

Lachmann, on the contrary, took an unfavourable view of Tischendorf's youthful efforts, and apparently did not suspect in the least that the young editor had set out to do much and good work in this line. Accordingly, in the preface to the first volume of his large edition, which appeared while Tischendorf was still working in the libraries of the West, Lachmann disposed of Tischendorf's New Testament with the curt remark: "For that edition, if the truth is to be spoken, is from cover to cover a mistake"—"tota peccatum est." It will be conceded by everyone that those words were not calculated to awaken agreeable feelings in Tischendorf's mind. He returned the compliment, as was quite natural, by writing some very sharp things about Lachmann's edition, especially laying stress upon the fact, which was undeniable, that Lachmann did not carry out his own principles with any accuracy. I am glad to say that before his death he came to feel and write more kindly with respect to Lachmann's merits.

In that very year, 1842, Tischendorf, who was at Paris, made an edition that I really think was a total mistake, and Lachmann's words, if they had been aimed at the edition I now have in view, would have hit the nail on the head. At Paris, Tischendorf published in a French publishing house a Greek text of the New Testament which corresponded in the main to his Greek text at Leipzig dated a year earlier. No one could object to that, if his Leipzig publisher did not. It was dedicated to the well-known scholar and statesman François Pierre Guillaume Guizot. That was an edition that did no harm. Probably, as the result of some scientific conversations with Roman Catholic clergymen at Paris, the plan was formed of constructing a Greek text which should correspond so far as possible to the Latin text of the Vulgate. Following that plan, Tischendorf published such an edition and dedicated it to the archbishop of Paris, Denis Auguste Affrey. Now, it seems to me that that was a mistake. Tischendorf was bent on doing good scientific work, on finding out as well as he could, by going back to the earliest attainable period, what was the best text of the New Testament. He should therefore not have put his name on a book of this kind. The thing had an almost ludicrous issue. Tischendorf was forced to say on the title-page that he had taken advantage of the help of a Roman Catholic clergyman named Jager. It was not very long before Tischendorf's name was remanded to the second place on the title-page, and Jager took the credit of the edition to himself. I wish he had had it from the first. Happily, that edition was only a parenthesis in Tischendorf's scientific work.

The three editions thus far named were not numbered, but when Tischendorf seventeen years later came to numbering his large editions he regarded these three as the first, second, and third in the order in which I have spoken of them. No one of these editions was of great importance. The next edition was an important one. It is the one which he afterwards counted as the fourth. It was published at Leipzig in the year 1849, and named on the title-page as the second Leipzig edition. The preface filled sixty-nine pages, and the critical apparatus was a very full one. In the following year, 1850, Tischendorf published a handy edition of the text in the Bernhard Tauchnitz publishing-house, afterwards called the fifth edition. This was issued not only alone, but also in union with the Hebrew Old Testament of Theile. It contained almost exactly the same text as the edition of 1849, and had the Elzevir readings below the text. It was reprinted in the year 1862 with the same text but with a new preface, and in the year 1873 the text of the eighth great edition was inserted in it and the readings of the Sinaitic manuscript. Oskar von Gebhardt took up this edition and corrected it with his scrupulous care, adding in a larger form the readings of Tregelles and of Westcott and Hort, and in a smaller form those of Westcott and Hort alone. In the larger form he also combined it with Luther's German text. The edition that Tischendorf afterwards counted as the sixth was one that he published at first as a triglot with a Latin and a German text in the year 1854, and then alone in the year 1855. This became the favourite edition for students, and was called the "academic" edition. In the year 1873 the text of the eighth great edition was inserted in it. These editions of the years 1850 and 1854 were of no moment for the development of textual criticism, save in so far as they contributed to spread the text which the edition of 1849 had determined, and at a later period the text of the eighth edition.   The edition of the four Gospels in the form of a synoptical or combined text which was issued in 1851 need not be described at length.   Tischendorf had done much for the spread of the Greek New Testament, having published before he came to the seventh edition more than fifteen thousand copies of it.

In the year 1859 his first very large edition appeared, and that with the name "The seventh larger critical edition," while a smaller form with a much shortened critical apparatus was called "The seventh smaller critical edition."   It must be kept in mind that Tischendorf at that time had neither the Codex Sinaiticus nor the more exact readings of the Codex Vaticanus.   In the earlier part of the text, in the four Gospels he seems to have doubted whether he had done right to follow, to such an extent as he had done in the year 1849, the so scantily supported ancient text.   The Gospels, therefore, in this seventh edition, show a closer affinity to the so-called Received Text than they did in the fourth edition of the year 1849.   But in the Epistles it is clear that the ancient text had regained its supremacy in his mind, and they are further removed from the Received Text than they had been in the year 1849.   The fact that this seventh edition in the Gospels agreed to so great an extent with the Received Text caused it to be much sought in England.   Long after the issue of the eighth edition many British theologians clung tenaciously to the seventh.   This seventh edition brought out the fullest critical apparatus that had ever been printed.   The prolegomena bore no proportion to the text and to the apparatus.   A slight comparison shows that they were for the most part merely taken over from the edition of 1849, which was much more limited in its scope.   Bentley's proposals were evidently inserted to fill up the pages.   The fact was that at the close of the printing of the text, at which point of time Tischendorf should have properly had at least a year free for the preparation of the prolegomena, he received from the Emperor of Russia the desired pecuniary and moral support necessary for a new journey to Mount Sinai. Under such circumstances it was not strange that he simply reprinted the no longer sufficient prolegomena of the fourth edition, with trifling alterations and additions, and hurried away to the East.

The eighth larger critical edition was published, the Gospels in 1864 and the rest of the text in 1872.   For this edition

Tischendorf had received a strong impulse towards the ancient text. He had found and edited the Codex Sinaiticus, and had secured much more accurate and full knowledge of the text of the Codex Vaticanus, to say nothing of less important witnesses. He felt that he was now fully justified in returning to his earlier predilections, and he declared openly his substantial agreement with the principles of Bentley and Lachmann and his conviction that it was necessary: "to turn away entirely from the text that tradition has placed in our hands, from the Byzantine text which has been unconditionally preferred since the time of Erasmus, and instead of that to constitute the text of the second century as it is witnessed to by the documents, with all possible putting aside of one's own opinion." Thus the text of this eighth edition departed still more widely from the Received Text. It has been complained that Tischendorf paid in this edition far too great respect to the text of the Codex Sinaiticus. If anyone turns to the years 1859 to 1863, during which Tischendorf was busy publishing two editions of this manuscript, and during which his eyes and mind were to such a great extent bent upon the text of this manuscript, the high character of which can only be doubted by those who are not acquainted with it,—if anyone consider these circumstances it will, I think, be plain to him that Tischendorf must have been, would have had to be, more than human not to feel a special liking for this text found by him and thus almost learned by heart. And nevertheless it is not the case that he follows this manuscript blindly. He has, on the contrary, often not followed its first hand, and that in places in which others would have followed it. There should, moreover, be a further word added in justice to Tischendorf. He was always ready to learn, always ready to ask to have the faults of previous publications corrected, always ready to consider testimony judicially. It will be remembered that he was struck with palsy soon after the publication of the second volume of this edition, and passed away a little over a year later without having been able to resume work. For myself, I do not doubt in the least that if Tischendorf had lived a few years longer he would himself have changed some of the readings of which complaint has been made. I have perhaps said more about Tischendorf than the plan of this book would warrant, but I feel sure that many will wish to have this information about him.

SAMUEL PRIDEAUX TREGELLES, SCRIVENER.

England has a special interest in the next editor whom we have
to mention, Samuel Prideaux Tregelles, whose life and works show
what can be effected under all manner of untoward circumstances,
in spite of poverty, opposition, obloquy, and ill-health, if a man
has an iron will and feels sure that God is backing him. He
was born in 1813, two years before Tischendorf, and died a year
later than he, in 1875, so that the two were strictly contemporaries.
But their lives were only alike in the years that they covered and
in the kind of work that they did. All else was different.
Tischendorf lived and worked in the sunshine of good fortune,
success, and praise. Tregelles, lived and worked under a cloud
of difficulties, reviled and hindered, and when at the last his work
began to receive the long merited acknowledgment his health
was so much shattered that he could not finish his one great
edition.

Tregelles should have somewhere in England a monument as
rare as his devotion to the New Testament was. He it was who
almost alone in England fought for the displacement of the
Received Text. Before his death, Alford and Westcott and
Hort took up the battle. It is in a scientific way interesting to
observe that Tischendorf seems to have in some cases delayed
his parts of the eighth edition until he could see the corresponding part of Tregelles' New Testament. Tregelles published in
1844 the Revelation in Greek with a new English translation and
with various readings, he having determined the text according
to ancient authorities. Four years later he published his proposals for an edition of the New Testament in Greek and Latin,
the Greek text to be drawn from ancient authorities, the Latin
text of Jerome from the Codex Amiatinus. The text with the
critical apparatus came out in six parts between 1857 and 1872.
In the meantime, however, a stroke of paralysis had in the year
1861 impeded his work, a second stroke following in the year
1870. B. W. Newton helped him with the Revelation, and
A. W. Streane published select passages from his previous works
as a preface, and copious additions to the critical apparatus. In
preparing this edition Tregelles had worked enormously, visiting
the continent three times and collating numerous manuscripts in

various languages, Greek, Latin, and Syriac. He also published the Codex Zacynthius in 1861, and wrote two most excellent books about the text, one of which formed the fourth volume of Horne's Introduction in the tenth edition in 1856, and the eleventh in 1863,—the other was An Account of the Printed Text which appeared in 1854. He was not only industrious, but also accurate and careful. His judgment was sound. Unfortunately his text of the Gospels was completed before the Codex Sinaiticus was published, and before the Codex Vaticanus was better known. Had this not been the case he would certainly in his text have agreed to a still greater extent with the eighth edition of Tischendorf. This circumstance, and the further consideration that the latter part of his work was often less accurate than it would have been had he been well, deprive his text as text of a permanent value. He would at the time of his death have read the text differently in a multitude of passages. That, however, should not diminish the gratitude of theologians towards him for his faithful labours.

Henry Alford published at London in the years 1849 to 1861 a Greek New Testament in four volumes, with some various readings and with a commentary. It was his purpose at first, when he issued the Gospels in 1849, only to set forth a text for the moment, but he gave up that thought in the second volume which came out in the year 1852. Now and then he made himself, or he obtained from friends, new collations of manuscripts. His text is nearer to that of Tregelles than to Tischendorf's.

Frederick Henry Ambrose Scrivener, teacher and clergyman in Cornwall, and then vicar of Hendon near London, published Estienne's text again and again from the year 1859 onwards in handy volumes with readings from Elzevir (*not* from Beza), Lachmann, Tischendorf, and Tregelles. I say: not from Beza. What he called Beza's New Testament was clearly something else, but something that he later could tell nothing about. He said to me personally that he wished that he had never seen the book. He also published in 1881 the Greek text used by the English revisers of 1611, with the readings which commended themselves to the revisers of 1881. His Plain Introduction to the Criticism of the New Testament in four editions, from 1861 to 1894, was the English handbook of textual criticism. In the year 1859 he published the Codex Augiensis. He also published the Codex Bezæ in 1864. In the same year he issued a collation of the Codex Sinaiticus, and in 1875 Six Lectures on the Text of the New Testament. But his great industry was turned largely to the collation of manuscripts. The collation of twenty came out in 1853, and fifty more appeared in the edition of the Codex Augiensis. A few further collations appeared in Adversaria Critica Sacra, issued two years after his death, but as if he still were alive; it should have remained in manuscript. Scrivener came to see before he passed away that the Received Text could not be supported so unconditionally as he had once thought. But he expressed himself less distinctly in public, moved, I think, largely by a kind consideration for his friend and staunch adherent John William Burgon, whose devotion to that text scarcely knew any bounds. Burgon did a great deal of work in searching out manuscripts, and he published a very learned treatise upon the closing verses attached to the Gospel of Mark. It was a pity that he only published his notes about manuscripts in *The Guardian* newspaper. Would that more of the clergy could be induced to work as Scrivener and Burgon worked in furthering the text of the New Testament.

Thomas Sheldon Green, once a fellow of Christ's College at Cambridge, was of a liberal mind. He published a Course of Developed Criticism in 1856, treating more than two hundred passages in a very judicious manner. The Twofold New Testament appeared in 1865 and its Appendix about 1871. William Kelley published the Greek text of Revelation with a new English translation and with a critical apparatus in 1860. It is interesting to find that John Brown McClellan, who published in 1875 the first volume of a new English translation of the New Testament from a new Greek text, regarded the Codex Sinaiticus and the Codex Vaticanus as very bad manuscripts. In America one of the men who occupied himself most intensely with the Greek text of the New Testament was Ezra Abbot, but he expended his efforts largely upon the books and essays of other people, and published only a few short essays himself. It was he who was the chief representative of textual criticism in the New Testament Company of Revisers in America in the years 1872–1881.

WESTCOTT AND HORT.

Brooke Foss Westcott and Fenton John Anthony Hort, both members of the University of Cambridge, Westcott later bishop of Durham, did more than anyone else ever did to place the history of the text of the New Testament on a sound basis. Hort passed away in 1892, and Westcott in 1901. Westcott published a book introductory to the study of the Gospels in 1851, and a book upon the canon of the New Testament that will long remain standards. For twenty-eight years they worked together upon an edition of the New Testament. With an openness and a modesty which has seldom or never been equalled they sent out their edition in a preliminary form in parts, in the years 1871 to 1876, to a number of scholars asking for comments. Finally, in the year 1881 they published their work in two volumes, one containing the text, the other the introduction. In the text they agree to a large extent with Tregelles and with Tischendorf. The text of Tregelles would have been much nearer theirs if Tregelles had had the readings of the Sinaiticus and of the Vaticanus for the Gospels. And their nearness to Tischendorf would have been clearer if Tischendorf had in some way indicated the readings which were almost as good as the ones which he actually put in the text, or, we may say, if he had explained to us how the case stood in such passages as he was scarcely able to settle with satisfaction, and in which he therefore took one of the readings, seeing that he could not take two at once, and let the other one go. Westcott and Hort give such readings in their margin. Had Tischendorf done likewise we should have seen more distinctly how near the two editions are to each other. These editors hesitated to place in a popular edition readings that were not found in witnesses to the text, but that proceeded alone from conjecture. They insisted, however, rightly upon the necessity of conjecture, and pointed out in their edition the places which in their judgment allowed of no solution by refer-ence to the manuscripts and other sources, and which therefore demanded conjectural emendation. It is not necessary for me to say here what Westcott and Hort thought about the history of the text, seeing that I have good sense enough for the present to accept their conclusions and to work upon them until something better comes, and that I shall therefore give their views essentially when I later give my own. Thus far the larger part of the objections made to their conclusions may be found in their own book.

Bernhard Weiss, of Berlin, who has for more than half a century been studying the New Testament and publishing works upon its different parts, viewing it from various standpoints, has in many of these works, in the commentaries and in the discussions of synoptical questions in particular, treated of textual questions. During all the years he continually busied himself with the text. Finally, in the years 1893 to 1900 he published Researches in Textual Criticism, with the determination of the text, and in the year 1902 the text was again issued in another form with a short commentary. It has often been said that the critics of the text would in certain cases have settled upon other readings than those chosen by them if they had been exegetes. It may be a question how far the exegete should dominate the critic of the text, even when they are combined in one person. But in any case it is of exceedingly great value that a scholar who has for years been commenting upon the text of the New Testament should give us his mature views as to the determination of the true text thereof.

Eberhard Nestle, of Maulbronn, who published an interesting Introduction to the Greek New Testament in 1897, has done something incredible in the field of the textual criticism of the New Testament. The British and Foreign Bible Society has for years held with the utmost tenacity to the Received Text of the New Testament. It did finally allow Franz Delitzsch some years ago, in his Hebrew New Testament, to encroach upon the Received Text, but that was in Hebrew and was little noticed. Years and years ago I planned an appeal to that society to urge upon it a timely change. But I never sent it off. So far as I can remember, everyone to whom I then mentioned it considered the case hopeless. It was desirable for the cause of the Bible, of the Church, and of science that the great apparatus of that society should cease to deluge Europe with this imperfect text. Nestle has effected the change. He, with the self-denying help especially of Paul Wilhelm Schmiedel, of Zurich, published in Stuttgart an edition of the Greek New Testament in the year 1898, and he won the British and Foreign

Bible Society over to take this edition into its own hands. I do not like the way in which he decides upon the text in his edition, but that is a matter of little moment compared with the successful breaking of the dominion of the Received Text. The plan that I wished to suggest to the society was to have as soon as feasible the best possible text prepared, and to name that text on the title-page the text of—say 1905 or 1910, or whatever the year may be —and to keep to that text with that year on the title-page, of course on the upper part of the page, because the year of publication must be in its usual place below, until it was clear that new discoveries or new researches made a change in the text desirable. Then the new text should have been put in as the text of the new year and again retained till a change became necessary. In this way the society and the world would have the state of the text before its eyes, and would have the necessity of occasional change in mind. I need not say that there is no reason to suppose that changes of importance would frequently have to be made after the determination of a good text at the beginning. A see-saw hither and thither at the beck of every edition does not seem to me to be in any wise proper. But I am deeply thankful to Nestle for his deed.

The latest work in textual criticism is that which is in process of issue at the hands of Hermann von Soden in Berlin, who by the laudable great heartedness of Fräulein Elise Koenigs was enabled to send out a number of scholars to examine manuscripts in various libraries. The material gathered together must be immense. Thus far two large volumes of discussions have appeared, containing also a list of the Greek manuscripts. What the text will be no one yet knows. The author's prospectus showed that he either had not read or had not—appreciated— what Tischendorf and what Westcott and Hort had written about their texts. The conclusion or the probability would seem to be, that if the fairly intelligible statements of two contemporary or nearly contemporary scholars of the nineteenth century proved so impossible of comprehension as to be misstated by two centuries in the proclamation of the merits of the coming edition, the difficult entanglements of textual tradition in the first, second, third, and fourth centuries would in the end scarcely prove to the editor so clear as they seemed to him at the first blush to be. Everyone is awaiting the issue with great

30

interest. In the meantime all are astounded at the unbounded working power of the author. Those who are acquainted with the text of the New Testament, or at least many of them, regret that much of the energy of the editor thus far has been expended in operating with the story of the adulteress in John 7^{53}–8^{11}, seeing that the history, the fortunes, and the vicissitudes of these verses, which have only the most frail connection with the text of the New Testament, cannot in any wise offer a norm or an example for the history of the text proper. It is like arguing as to the growth of the oak from the consideration of a twig of mistletoe. May the author and editor reach an end and a clearness and a certainty as to the difficult problems of textual history far beyond what his present words lead textual critics to look for, and somewhere near what his extraordinary labours deserve.

IX.

THE EXTERNALS OF THE TEXT.

IF we could suppose ourselves appointed as a committee to print for the first time the books of our New Testament, one of the questions that would meet us might be the general title. That would be the very tip end of the beginning of textual criticism, in criticising the external addition to the text which stands at the greatest distance from it. In Exodus 24[7] we find "the book of the covenant," which can then have been but a very short book indeed. By the time we reach 2 Kings 23[2, 3] "the book of the covenant" will have been much larger. At that day the Israelites might well have spoken of the book of the Old Covenant, of the covenant from ancient centuries. When Jesus preached and when the apostles went out to the world with His message to men, it was quite natural that the thought of a New Covenant should arise, as in Hebrews 9[15]. The Greek word for covenant, $\delta\iota\alpha\theta\dot{\eta}\kappa\eta$, meant also "testament." The Latin lawyer of Carthage called such a legal document an "instrument," using his technical word. In the early Church the Christians gradually came to transfer the name of the covenant to the book which told of the covenant. And with the other word they spoke of the Old Testament and of the New Testament. In the New Testament the first part consisted of "the Gospels" or "the Gospel Instrument," and the latter part of "the Apostle" or "the Apostolic Instrument."

ORDER OF BOOKS.

The order in which we place the books of the New Testament is not a matter of indifference. Every Christian should be familiar with these books, and should know precisely where to find each book. Every New Testament should have the books in precisely the same order, the order of the Greek Church, which in this case is of right the guardian of this ancient literature. The proper order is, I think : First, the Four Gospels : Matthew, Mark, Luke, and John.   Second, the Book of Acts.   Third, the Catholic Epistles : James, First and Second Peter, First, Second, and Third John, and Jude.   Fourth, the Epistles of Paul : Romans, First and Second Corinthians, Galatians, Ephesians, Philippians, Colossians, First and Second Thessalonians, Hebrews, First and Second Timothy, Titus, and Philemon. And fifth, the book of Revelation.   The order of the four Gospels to which we are used is by far the prevailing order. Sometimes, however, especially in connection with a Latin tradition, we find the order Matthew, John, Luke, Mark.   This order seems to proceed from the wish to give the two apostles the leading place, and then to give the larger Gospel according to Luke the preference before Mark.   That last order of Luke and Mark would point to the early period at which Paul, and therefore his companion Luke, were especially cherished.   The reason given in a Latin manuscript for having John after Matthew is found in the closing perfection of his book.   Druthmar of the ninth century offers a reason for each way of arranging the Gospels.   The usual order places, according to him, one apostle at the beginning and the other at the end, so that the two non-apostles in between them may take their authority from the two apostles who encase them.   And as for the two apostles in front, he asked Euphemius, a Greek, why they were put there, and he replied, "Like a good farmer who yokes his best oxen in front."   Once or twice the order John, Matthew, Luke, Mark occurs.   That looks as if it might have been taken from the books of Gospel lessons, with John at Easter, Matthew at Whitsuntide, Luke at Michaelmas, and Mark in Lent.

The current order of the Catholic Epistles is the usual one in the ancient Church.   Occasionally, however, we find a different order.   Most frequently the change has been made to place Peter in front, and then the order of the other three varies according to the fancy of the scribe.   We have Peter, James, John, Jude ; and Peter, James, Jude, John ; and Peter, John, Jude, James ; and Peter, John, James, Jude ; and Peter, Jude, James, John.

In the Epistles of Paul, with which the Epistle to the Hebrews is closely united, the place of precisely this Epistle is almost the only thing that varies. The Greek order is that which places the Epistle to the Hebrews between Thessalonians and Timothy, and that is the order to which we should hold. The Latin order places Hebrews after Philemon. It would, of course, be a satisfaction to us, in our firm conviction that the Epistle is not from Paul, to put it after his Epistles. But we must keep to the old order or we shall have the New Testament turned upside down in connection with every fancied discovery as to authorship and date of books.

CHAPTERS.

When we approach the single books we meet the question as to the division into chapters. We do not know who determined the large chapters found in the Greek manuscripts, but the very lack of remarks about them leads to the supposition that they were the work of an early age. These larger chapters in the Gospels are of an altogether phenomenal oneness and steadfastness. There are 68 in Matthew, 48 in Mark, 83 in Luke, and 18 in John. They may be left out in a manuscript, especially if the manuscript be intended rather for liturgical use, for then it is desirable that there shall be no divisions and no headings to catch the eye save those that are strictly needed for the lessons to be read. In general the number of the chapter is put in the margin opposite the beginning of the chapter, where also a larger, perhaps a coloured, letter may be found. Then the inscription giving the contents of the chapter is placed in the upper or in the lower margin. These inscriptions usually begin with the word "about" or "concerning,"—for example, the second chapter in Matthew is "About the children who were murdered," περὶ τῶν ἀναιρεθέντων παιδίων. We can see at once that these chapters have their textual character, when I observe that this very chapter has three main readings ; for we may find instead of παιδίων the word παίδων or the word νηπίων, and I have also seen βρέφων. These chapters are of very different lengths. Take, for example, two chapters in Matthew. Chapter 55 contains a dozen lines only, and chapter 56 over ninety.

Eusebius' Harmony of Gospels.

The Jews were in the habit of comparing scripture with
scripture, and the Christians who found in their four Gospels four
accounts of Jesus as a teacher were forced to compare these
accounts with each other and to note their agreement or their
failure to agree with each other.   Ammonius tried to write the
parallel sections alongside of each other.   Eusebius invented a
better plan.   He left the four Gospels each in its own proper
shape.   But he proceeded to mark off in each certain sections
or, as they were called, chapters.   The reason for the length of
the chapters was found in the relation of the four Gospels to
each other.   Let us suppose, for example, that we are reading a
verse which is found alike in all four Gospels.   Now, the
"chapter" in which that verse is will continue until something
comes up that is not in all four Gospels.   Should the new
"chapter" happen to contain material found alone in the Gospel
in question, very good, this "chapter" will continue just so
long as the words are found nowhere else.   The moment that
something occurs that is found, let us say, in two Gospels, in this
one and any other one, there that "chapter" stops and a new
one begins.   In this way Eusebius divided up sections or little
chapters in all four Gospels, making in Matthew 355, in Mark
233, in Luke 342, and in John 232.   Some are very short, once
there are three in a single one of our verses.   And some are
very long, especially the sections in John which have no parallel.
This division is the basis of the work of Eusebius.

Then he prepared lists, canons, of the various possible or
actual combinations of these chapters, and thus of the Gospels
with each other.   There were ten of them.   The first list contained the numbers of the sections in which all four Gospels
agreed with each other.   The second list or canon gave the
numbers of the sections in which Matthew, Mark, and Luke
coincided with each other.   The third canon offered the sections
in which Matthew, Luke, and John agreed.   The fourth canon
has the sections in which Matthew, Mark, and John go together.
The fifth canon is occupied by the sections in which only Matthew
and Luke agree.   The sixth canon is devoted to the sections in
which Matthew and Mark are alike.   The seventh canon shows

in which sections Matthew and John are of one mind. The eighth canon numbers the sections in which Luke and Mark unite. The ninth canon tells us in which sections Luke and John alone are found. And finally, the tenth canon recounts the sections in which each Gospel stands totally alone. We have now the chapters or sections numbered in each Gospel from one up to the last section in that Gospel, and the numbers standing on the margin, so that we can find any section in any Gospel in a moment. And then we have those ten canons.

The way Eusebius brought the two together and completed his system was this. He put on the margin in red ink under every number of a section the number of the canon in which it belonged. Thereby he effected at once two desirable things. The reader saw instantly whether the section was in any other Gospel or not. And if it was in any other Gospel or Gospels he saw at once which, for, of course, every reader soon knew by heart which Gospels were represented in each canon. That was the one good thing effected. The second thing was that by turning to that canon at the front of the volume the reader could at once find the number of the section he had just read in the one Gospel, and would find alongside of it the numbers of the like sections in the other Gospels in which it was found. Turning to these sections, he could compare all most accurately. Here is the first line of the first canon:

Mt	Mk	Lk	Joh
8	2	7	10

and that means that the eighth section in Matthew corresponds to the second in Mark, to the seventh in Luke, and to the tenth in John. This was a most ingenious contrivance, and quite worthy of a place in modern copies of the Gospels. In some manuscripts the matter was made much easier for the reader, and the lists of canons were left for more general comparisons. For in these books the parallel sections, for the sections which occurred upon any given page, were given on the lower margin of the page, so that one could turn at once to the companion sections in the other Gospels. This arrangement is often found in Armenian manuscripts. Eusebius explained his system in a letter to Carpianus, and this letter forms the opening part of many of the manuscripts of the Gospels. Of course, the canons follow upon the letter, and the frames in which the canons are written are often beautifully ornamented in colours, with pillars and arches, and above the arches birds of various feather.

EUTHALIUS.

For the other books of the New Testament there was no need of any arrangement of that kind, for they contained no like accounts, no chapters that needed to be compared with each other. There is for the Acts, the Catholic Epistles, and the Pauline Epistles a whole series of accompaniments to make the use of their text easier. We find chapters with descriptive headings. Sometimes there are under-divisions in these chapters, which again have headings to designate their contents. Then these chapters are not only found on the margin, but they are also collected in lists at the beginning of each book, affording an easy view of its contents. The Church lessons are divided off. The days to which they belong are added. The necessary introductory words for each lesson are put into the margin beside the place where it begins. And the quotations or "testimonies," as they are called, are numbered, have their source set on the margin at the side of the number, and are gathered in lists at the beginning of the books. Add to all this a preface for each book, a preface for the Pauline Epistles in general, a discussion of Paul's journeys and his martyrdom, and it will be apparent that this matter is of considerable extent. The name connected with all this is Euthalius, who is also called in some manuscripts the bishop of Sulke. But Euthalius does not pretend to have done all the work himself. Parts of it were probably at his date, say before the end of the fourth century, already parts of a long forgotten past, parts were done by a previous writer whom he avoids naming and who may have been Theodore of Mopsuestia, then much eschewed as a dangerous heretic; many things were done by Euthalius himself, and some things may well have been added or changed by one or more later hands. As for the text itself, Euthalius marked it off in a careful way for the lessons, that is to say for reading purposes, adding the accents. Perhaps he wrote the text also in sense lines, lines that served to show the subdivisions of thought, as our punctuation does.

The book of Revelation, which was so diligently read in the earliest period of the Church, and later so carefully kept out of the books of lessons and so much pushed aside, received, so far as we know, no chapter division save that which its commentator Andrew of Cæsarea in Cappadocia made. He went about this division in a sentimental way. Instead of asking what material was in the book, and into how many parts it could be most properly divided, he took the number of the elders sitting on the twenty-four thrones around the throne in Rev. 4^4 and divided Revelation into twenty-four words or discourses. He further reflected then that the person of each of the twenty-four elders was properly threefold, for Andrew was a trichotomist, and that each consisted of body and soul and spirit. With these three divisions of the discourses he made then of the whole book seventy-two chapters, three times twenty-four. There is nothing like mathematics for a dreamer.

Modern Chapters.

All of those chapters are different from our chapters. The origin of our chapters has been assigned to Hugo of St. Caro. The real divider appears to have been the cardinal Stephen Langton, the archbishop of Canterbury, who died in 1228. Probably he made the division in the year 1204 or 1205. This division never came regularly into the Greek manuscripts of the New Testament. It is, so far as I can remember, only rarely added in late manuscripts written in the West. But many of the manuscripts written in the West have only the regular Greek chapters, while some have both the Greek chapters and these Latin chapters. When those chapters had been made the theologians wished for a still smaller division so as to be able to refer more accurately to passages which they needed to quote. About the year 1243 a number of learned men under Hugo of St. Caro made a concordance to the Bible, and Hugo divided each chapter into smaller sections by using the capital letters A B C D E F G, although he did not insist upon having all the seven sections if the chapter was not very long. A Latin Bible, the translation of Santes Pagnini, was printed at Lyons in 1528, and divided into verses, but these verses were in the New Testament very different from ours.

VERSES.

Our verses of to-day did not appear in the first printed editions of the Greek New Testament, but they did first appear in a Greek New Testament. The way that these verses came to be made reminds us of Hugo of St. Caro, who made those A B C D sections for his concordance. Robert Estienne was about to make a concordance of the New Testament,—his son Henri published it finally in 1594,—and therefore wished for a small division of the text. He set about the work, and did the most of it, as his son tells us, on a journey on horseback between Paris and Lyons. Henri uses the words "while riding," "inter equitandum," and it has sometimes been supposed that he actually did it while jogging and joggling along the road upon the back of his steed. It may be that he had a very quiet horse, and that he could sometimes have marked divisions while the horse was walking leisurely along. Yet I do not think that he did that, or that his son Henri says that he did that. It seems to me to be more likely that the words "while riding" simply mean that he did it in the breaks of this long ride. When he got up in the morning he may have done something before he set out. During the morning he may have rested a while at a wayside inn, and certainly at noon he will have done so. And again at night he doubtless drew out his little pocket edition and "divided" away until it was time to sleep. This verse division was first printed in Robert Estienne's fourth edition of the Greek New Testament, which appeared in two small volumes in the year 1551 at Geneva. In this edition the Greek text was in the middle column, while Erasmus' Latin translation was on one side and Jerome's Vulgate on the other. Robert Estienne had in mind, as he tells us in the preface, not only the coming concordance, but also the convenience of this edition. That was in showing easily and clearly what words of each of those two translations corresponded to given words of the Greek text.

The first whole Bible with our verses in it was an octavo Latin Bible, a Vulgate, that Robert Estienne published at Geneva in the year 1555. The earliest New Testament in English that was divided into our verses was William Whittingham's translation issued at Geneva in 1557. A very different text of the New Testament came out in the first complete Bible in English with our verses, which was the Geneva Bible, the Geneva translation, finished in the year 1560. The first edition of the Greek New Testament that had the verses divided up in the text was the regrettable "Textus Receptus" Elzevir edition of 1633. The verses have gradually here and there been changed in various editions. That is much to be deplored, and it is much to be wished that in continuation of the work of Ezra Abbot, showing where false divisions have crept in, all theologians would correct their New Testaments in whatever language according to the one standard of Estienne's edition of 1551.

PUNCTUATION.

In the oldest manuscripts there was very little punctuation. In the more carefully written manuscripts an occasional period was about all. Even the words were all written together, just as they are all spoken together. Now and then a sentence began a new line. That was all. Gradually more signs crept in; the comma, and the double point or colon were used more frequently. Sometimes a single point was used in three positions startlingly separated from each other. The greatest distinction was the point high up' The next, but less strong, was in the middle• And the third and weakest, about of the effect of a comma, was low down. A sign of interrogation is, I think, rarely found before the ninth century. Of course, we cannot count the points between every two words in the Codex Augiensis, and sometimes in the Codex Bornerianus, as being precisely punctuation, very much pointed, punctured, and punctuated as those texts are.

It is often said that we cannot use the Greek manuscripts of the New Testament as a norm, a rule, or as a special help in deciding about the proper punctuation of the text. It seems to me that this is going a little too far. There is a fair connection between Greek and Latin and English and German punctuation. Yet there is, if I am not altogether mistaken, at least a shade of nationality and of language in the mere technical signs and in the method of using them, and I do not feel sure that it would be doing justice to the original dress of the New Testament for European scholars to punctuate without reference to Greek tradition. It is true that many manuscripts are badly punctuated, just as they are badly spelled. But there are manuscripts that are carefully punctuated, and I think that their testimony should be used, and used expressly. They are, in fact, the only guides that we have as to the original views of the disposition of the words.

To my mind it is not a sufficient reply to this to say that, owing to the point-lessness of, the lack of punctuation in, the earlier manuscripts, these later manuscripts which have a punctuation have no hold in their own past. That reply appears to overlook the fact that the "traditional" reading of the given passages never ceased to be practised, that is to say, that the reading which was continual was exercised in the traditional way, giving to the passages the force and the direction and the connection that earlier times gave to them, and that this traditional reading, this punctuation by word of mouth, was then brought into a permanent form in the written punctuation of the manuscripts, and should be at least looked into and respectfully considered in the constitution of our texts. The circumstance that this will call for some careful collation of certain manuscripts that were long since thought to be disposed of cannot be considered a reason for neglecting the point. Difficulty of doing a thing is not what decides whether it should be done or not. It would be of value, I think, if someone should be so self-denying as to give a large amount of special attention to this matter. If he prove what I have here said to be all wrong, that is at least a gain. The field will then be clearer.

Spelling.

The care of the text brings with it the question of spelling. When the form of the words is brought under consideration a similar objection to that referred to a moment ago is often made.

We are told that the spelling in the manuscripts was altogether arbitrary, and determined by the wisdom, sense, ignorance, or caprice of the scribes during the centuries of transmission. Granting that there is a certain truth in the uncertain tradition as to forms of words, I should reply again that we have nothing else by which to go, no other due and proper basis for theories about the original spelling of Paul's Epistles, for example, to take a special case, than what we find in the oldest manuscripts in our hands. We are constantly receiving older documents. It would be an interesting inquiry as to whether some day we shall be able to see so clearly into the early conditions as to distinguish between the spelling of the different scribes who wrote at Paul's dictation. In the other direction it might be asked whether we could find such traces of a uniform and early spelling as to decide that Paul had always himself looked through the Epistles written at his dictation and had corrected the spelling, conforming it to his own standard. Then arises the question as to the spelling which the writer of the Epistle to the Hebrews favoured. Paul and Luke were probably much together. It would be possible that the like measure of education which they appear to have enjoyed should have led them to use the same spelling, the same forms of the words applied to their Christian work or to common life.

Even if textual critics should declare positively that no trace of the original spelling could now be detected, or ever would be likely to be discovered, it would be necessary to ask how the spelling should be settled. Given witnesses contain forms that certainly are old, and that do not agree with the spelling of the Attic National Academy. Conceding that these are necessarily not Pauline, or Johannean, or Lucan, they nevertheless may carry with them a local and a temporal colouring that we should do wrong to deprive the New Testament of. It might not always be easy to decide what forms to sanction in special cases, but the difficulty in deciding is no reason for refusing to consider these forms.

Not as a logical sequence to the foregoing, but as a neighbouring problem, we should have to determine whether any editor has a right to say that the New Testament is in so great a measure one book, and emerges within so brief a period of time from so limited an area, and from circles of such homogeneous composition that it would be absurd to pay the least attention to differences of spelling in different parts thereof, even if they should be proved to be original. It must be remembered that in the Greek New Testament there can be no question as to confusing ill-educated persons by lack of uniformity in the spelling, seeing that only educated people take the volume in hand. It seems to be the most reasonable and the most modest course to follow, so far as any thing of the kind can be found, the habits of the best, the earliest, the most unbiassed manuscripts.

X.

EARLY HISTORY OF TEXT.

FOR the textual critic who sets about making an edition of the text the method of constituting that text is one of the weightiest possible things about which he has to decide. A philologian comes to him and declares the decision to be a very simple one. The critic of the text has but to take the best manuscript—and which is the best manuscript is not difficult to say—and to print its text, adding from other manuscripts an occasional various reading. In the case of many of the authors with which the classical philologian has to do, such a course is the only one open to a scholar, inasmuch as there are often but few manuscripts in existence, and inasmuch as these few are usually so related to each other as to make the choice of the best one an easy matter. A lazy man might say: Unfortunately, that is not the case with the New Testament. The textual critic says: Thank God, our sacred volume has a far different testimony from that, and a better one. We have already seen what the kinds of witnesses are and how numerous they are, the thousands of Greek manuscripts, the thousands of manuscripts of the translations, the hundreds or perhaps thousands of manuscripts of the church writers. We cannot throw that testimony all or almost all away, and say that half a dozen of the manuscripts are enough for us. We are bound in duty to make as good a use as possible of the talent given to us, and neither to bury it nor to throw it away. Yet such a myriad of witnesses is puzzling and overwhelming. No one person can command them all or force them all to yield their treasures up to him. Combined work is necessary. Work must follow upon work. Succeeding scholars must stand on the shoulders of preceding scholars. Yet we cannot put off constituting the text until centuries of combined effort have exhausted the materials in our hands. We must be reading the New Testament and preaching from it and explaining it, and we need for that purpose a text, and always at each moment the best text available. The textual critic must be ever settling texts as he goes along. It is, like all human work, but temporary. A later time will make a better text, and a still later time a still better one.

CLASSES OF TEXT.

In the effort to cope with these multitudes of witnesses, whether for the purpose of deciding instantly upon a text for the present, or for the purpose of preparing the gradual complete exhaustion of the testimony, it is necessary to do upon a large scale the very thing that the classical philologian did with his more limited material upon a small scale. We must try to classify. Every scholar who combines two manuscripts and thereby makes one out of them advances the work to be done. Every group of manuscripts that we know thoroughly forms a kilometre stone that marks progress in the long journey. Such combination of witnesses, beginning at the single witnesses and aiming at their unification and simplification, is the basis of all good work in textual criticism. It forms, even strange as that may seem, the basis for the work at the precisely opposite end of the line of research and of combinative reflection. Glad as we are to see individual manuscripts dissolving into each other, our gaze also goes out towards the great masses of witnesses, and wishes to see them gather together into a few great societies of known character from which we may look to receive such and such testimony.

KINDS OF CLASSES.

It would indeed seem to the untutored mind at the first glance as if such inquiries must be unnecessary. We spoke at the outset of the copying of manuscripts. Should we assume that the early Christians in the to them most natural following up of Jewish copying habits, of the Jewish rules for copying the law in particular, copied every word most cautiously and counted its letters, it would appear next to impossible that classes of text should arise, and most of all that they should arise in that earliest period during which the connection with Judaism was still so near. This view overlooks two important considerations. The one touches Judaism, and we can be brief with it. The extraordinary pains of the Masora with the copying of the law was probably a thing of a much later date than the earliest copies of the manuscripts of the books of the New Testament. Therefore we cannot presuppose that this painful exactness had any effect upon the earliest Christian copyists or scribes. The other consideration, however, touches the Christian side, and goes to preclude all such thoughts of Masoretical accuracy. In the first place, the most of the early Christian copyists were probably not particularly well versed in the art of writing and copying. And in the second place, the books of the New Testament were not recognised at the first moment as sacred books. This we saw above in treating of the criticism of the canon. And in consequence, even had the Christians had a prevision of that later Masoretic accuracy, they would have had no occasion to apply it to the books which had not yet become sacred.

Let us then again attack the matter of the classes of text, and ask ourselves in what way differences in the words and sentences could arise. We must not lose ourselves in the woods of the consideration of the merely external side of the matter, and we may say briefly that differences might have arisen, and certainly did arise, without any intention on the part of the copyist to make any change, and as well, on the contrary, as the result of the direct purpose of a scribe or theologian. Variations were unintentional and intentional. It is, I think, important before we go to the question of the classes in detail to make one or two observations here in reference to the probable origin of these classes. It is the habit in philology to call the classes of manuscripts the genealogy or the genealogical classes of the text, and the term is a fit one. One manuscript is the son of an older one, the father of a younger one. In philology the classes differ in general from each other chiefly in the continuation, the propagation, of faults which have not been conscious ones, of changes which were not the results of will but of human frailty. The sources of error may have been in the vision. The eye may in its haste have taken a dim N for an H, or an H for a Π, or an Є for an O, or for a C, or a Γ for a T. It may have mistaken a whole word for another that had about the same general form. The eye may have returned from the page that was being written and caught the same word as the one just copied, but at another part of the column or in another column, and therefore in continuing the copy have omitted all that was between those two occurrences of the same word. Or the error may have arisen in the ear. The text may have been read in the hearing of several scribes, each of whom wrote without seeing the text, and exhibited faults of hearing. Enough of that. These mistakes are purely accidental and unintentional. In general we may, I think, say that the errors in the ordinary run of classical or of profane texts are of this kind.

It is unnecessary to say that the scribes, the copyists of the Greek manuscripts of the New Testament, were also men, also fallible, and that they committed in like manner faults or made mistakes which were in no way connected with their will. Now the classes in the majority of the texts of the profane authors, who for the most part have but few documents, rest largely upon such errors in their cumulative and accumulated propagation. It is natural that philologians and philologically trained theologians should at the first blush take it for granted that the classes in the text of the New Testament originated in the same way. A result of this, if I am not mistaken, false conception and assumption was the presentation in the prefaces to the Greek New Testament of the ordinary, well-established canons of philological criticism as if these were the special principles of the given editor for the determination of the text of his edition. And such prefaces then only propagated further the false conception. It was a matter of course that the critic of the text of the New Testament should use these rules in handling his sources, as much a matter of course as that a cabinetmaker or a smith treat wood and metal according to the rules for treating wood and metal even when making an altar or a reading-desk, or a chancel railing or a bronze lectern. Were these the only sources of change in the text of the New Testament we should, I opine, have a very different task before us, and a very much simpler one. Classes of New Testament manuscripts arising in this way may be met with at almost every turning, to speak with a slight exaggeration.

But these classes, such classes, have scarcely a distant relationship to the classes of the tradition of the New Testa-

ment text properly so called.   This is the reason which renders
the criticism of the text of this New Testament such an absurd
thing to the mind of the ordinary philologian before he has
examined closely into the state of the case.   I should even
venture the hypothesis that a confusion of these classes or a
mistaking of these classes for the sources of the classes of the
New Testament text was the cause for the original hopes of the
greatest philologian the world has ever seen, Richard Bentley, of
a speedy solution of the difficult problems of this text.   At that
day neither he nor anyone else could see through the maze.
Gradually Griesbach and Hug and Lachmann caught glimpses
of the relations that were in existence.   Neither Tregelles nor
Tischendorf occupied himself deeply with the matter.   And it
was left again to two Englishmen, again to Cambridge, to
Westcott, who was Bentley's distant successor in the chair, and to
his friend Hort, to set forth these classes for the first time in an
intelligible clearness.   Their work was initiative work.   They
knew that others would go beyond them.   But they broke a way
through the wilderness, or, to change the figure, they disentangled
the mass of the apparently hopelessly knotted threads of this
tradition.   This practical example has brought me unawares to
the point that must here follow.   I shall for the moment leave
this part of the discussion and, returning to what we said when
beginning with the criticism of the text, speak of what seems to
have been the course of events in the early days of the textual
tradition.   What I have to say is the view of Westcott and Hort
with some slight and external modifications, modifications which
they would in part probably have made themselves had they
been less cautious, less prudent, and less modest than they were.

THE ORIGINAL TEXT.

The books of the New Testament, the Epistles—are they
read first in the church services because they were first written
and because they therefore are prefaces for the Gospels?—the
Gospels, the Acts, Revelation have been written.   As I think
for the moment of about the year 100, I must remind myself that
Second Peter probably was not yet written, but Jude gives us
some of it in a much more concise form.   The most of them

have already been copied off a large number of times, copied partly because worn out and needing to be replaced for the same church, and partly because new churches or other churches far and near asked to have them sent to them. We must assume that these very first copies were really among the best, I mean, the most accurate copies that ever were made. Not that they were pretty or very well written, although those made at Rome may have been that too. They were probably the most accurate because copied simply and naively. I conceive of the early years as by far the best years until the passage of a couple of centuries. The copying before the year 100 will have, as a rule, been better than the copying that was done in general up to the year—to name a totally unfixable year—350. Of the later years we have to speak afterwards. Let us hold for the moment to the years before 100.

And I begin by at once retrenching the statement above. There is, I think, one large or determined exception to be made. I beg, however, to emphasise the fact that this exception is pure theory on my part. I have no proof for it. It only appears to me to be the best explanation for the facts which we afterwards observe. And, of course, I think—others will think differently—that the theory agrees with the conceivable or probable course of Christian life and habit at that day. The exception is the book of Revelation. At present I still cling to the supposition that it was written before the year 70, though I confess that the later date, say the year 90, has something to say for itself. Owing to the inclination of that age towards all manner of apocalyptic visions, owing to the longings for a future suited to make good all that the Christians—as well as the Jews—had suffered and were then suffering, this book was probably far more frequently sought for, read, and copied during the years of which we are speaking, the years up to 100, than any other Christian book. It seems likely that it was originally a Jewish book, and that a Christian re-wrought it. Now, my theory is that this book was during these years the object of an active, not cannonade, but infantry fire. This, however, must not be taken in a hostile sense, save so far as it was hostile to the purity of the text. The people liked the book. They revelled in its dreams and they dreamed its dreams and they embellished its dreams. That was a time of simplicity.

The book was not yet scripture.   It was a dream-book.   Everyone could dream.   Everyone could add another trait here and
there to enliven the story.   Enough of the theory.   That seems
to me to be the probable exception to the plain and simple
copying of the books of the New Testament during the closing
years of the first century.

These early copyists will have made the mistakes that are
the first objects of the philological canons of criticism.   They
will have written words wrong or left words out.   But they
will not have changed the text willingly.   It will not have
occurred to them to change it.   The result will have been that
we may conceive of a large number of copies having already
been made of pretty much all the books of the New Testament, save of the then lately issued Gospel of John, which,
however, will rapidly have caught up to the other Gospels in
its course through the churches.   These copies were doubtless
for the most part still copies of single rolls, although here and
there several of the Epistles of Paul may have been put into one
roll.   Now, the text found in these early copies will have been
essentially the original text.   The errors to which we have
referred were doubtless in the main as usual of a minor character,
and have in their unintentional kind done nothing to change the
form of the text as a whole.   Before leaving this text to consider
all that happens to it to modify it, and all that follows upon it, I
wish to emphasise the fact that single copies of it, especially of
books that had been re-copied on parchment, may have lasted
well on into the second century, the parchment books or rolls,
at least till the fourth century.   This text I name boldly the
Original Text.   It is the text which Westcott and Hort in their
shrinking modesty called Pre-Syrian and of no family.   But it is
to all intents and purposes the Original Text.   No one has been
doctoring it.   No one has set about changing it.   Only the book
of Revelation has, at least theoretically, had a different fate, and
has, not by the premeditated work of a single Christian but by
the fitful and sympathetic attentions of many a pen backed by
many a fancy, been turned into a piebald representative of its
former self.   Of course, we do not call that the original text of
Revelation.   We shall name it in a moment.

The Re-Wrought Text.

We pass on to the second century. No one will, I trust, imagine that I conceive of these living processes as being limitable thus by sharp dates, because for the sake of a certain definiteness I put in dates and give to shadowy thoughts a local habitation and a name. Textual traditions can no more be cut across with a knife into living sections than an arm can. I said a moment ago that the Original Text named lived on in a private way, did not halt and cease at the year 100, and as well must I say here that the process now to be described also had roots and preceding stages and beginnings before the year 100. The second century is a middle ground. It was neither the early day of unbounded enthusiasm nor was it the later day of calm and definite science. It was neither Peter and John, nor Origen and Hippolytus. Should it at times appear to be chaotic, its chaos is one of life, not of death. If heresies begin in it, the heresies proper are noble, self-denying heresies and not self-seeking ones. Let us look at the text and its treatment during this century. The books of the New Testament are already widely spread. The number of Christian churches is rapidly increasing. The apostle, as the wandering preacher is called, the missionary we should say to-day, is kept moving. It is forbidden to him to stay in one place more than a day, possibly two days, at most three days. He must go on and on, and carry the word farther. And where the word takes root, and a group of Christians is formed, there a book of the New Testament may soon be desired. The means of the Christians and the books to be found in the neighbourhood will have decided how many and what books they first got. This process of rapid increase may well have lasted, with many a break and many a standstill and many a reverse in single districts, on into the fourth century, or at least until the middle of the third.

Let me say at once that in general it is not to be supposed that the new additions to the number of the faithful occupied themselves with the text in any other sense than as diligent readers and ponderers of it. The reason that I have thus pressed at length upon the spread of Christianity, is to show and to urge the call for copies thereby created, and the consequent ever-increasing carrying into new districts of whatever text the older churches used.   In the wide fields in which the Church had taken a firm stand, and won a definite place from the first, the text was the object of the most diligent attention.   Our eyes must turn to the churches in Palestine, and remember Cæsarea and Antioch ; to the churches in Asia Minor, and think of Ephesus and Smyrna with their sister cities ; to the churches in Greece, and recall Corinth ; to the churches in Italy, and behold Rome ; to the churches in Africa, and fancy the forerunners of Tertullian in the West and of Pantænus in the East.   In the domain of these churches there were still in the earlier part of the second century many who had near traditional bonds with the time of the apostles, as we saw in the criticism of the canon (pp. 75, 102).   Now for such persons the inclination to put pen to the margin of the books of the New Testament must often have been very strong.   The very external circumstance that the rolls were written, so that the addition was and looked much more normal and fitting than an addition to our printed texts, must have made the thought of addition and of change more easy.

Precisely what was changed or added depended upon the special case.   Here was an old man who had seen, known, heard Paul ; here was a man whose father had known and heard other apostles ; here was a man with some fragmentary roll of an earlier evangelical story, an earlier tradition about words of Jesus.   One was sure that when the given Epistle came from Paul the sentence read thus and thus.   Another had heard that Jesus at that point had used these precise words, which were not in the text before him.   Another had a beautiful story, let us say the account of the Adulteress, and was ready to put it into the Gospels somewhere.   Another one was sure that Jesus would not have spoken thus, but must have spoken thus.   Another, even without traditional hold, was ready to add, to strike out, to change because it seemed to him that at the given point he could make the New Testament books better than they were.   It was all in the Church.   These were books of the Church.   He was a member of the Church.   Of course he had a right to improve these books.

We must herewith again urge a previous observation.   These books were at the first moment not sacred in the same sense as the writings of the Old Testament. They were books of the day. They came from a valued preacher, from that little shrivelled up missionary Paul who went about from place to place with his loom packed together on his back. They were Gospels, it may be, a written form of what the apostles and wandering evangelists were saying by word of mouth. For the future of this literature there was no thought. The literature would have no future. The future would bring, and that right soon, the return of Jesus. The Messiah and King must soon appear. And so one and another used his pen on the margin and between the lines of these books without feeling any compunction. Two points are not to be lost sight of in this connection. In the first place, the general remarks just made are not to be understood in the sense that positively everyone, every Christian who could read and write, felt an inclination to modify in this way the text, or even that the majority of the Christians wrote in the manuscripts. The aim of these remarks is to show the thoughts of those who really did use their pens in this way. And, in the second place, the alterations or additions made by these hands were by the necessity of life locally different, and therefore the changes made in one place were more noticeable than those made in another. The gifts and the experiences of one Christian who changed the text were not the same as the gifts and experiences of another.

The necessary consequence was that these texts then took gradually a somewhat different form in different provinces. Many a change was made early and and then passed by the process of manuscript transmission and tradition, or by the verbal communication of member to member, into other districts. Yet each district kept adding or changing for itself. This brought a difference of character from that of the Original Text which remained in general, so far as it remained untouched, of one and the same cast. This text was, strictly speaking, alike in no two provinces. It proceeded from no single source. It pursued no single aim. In fact, at the first instant the observer would be quite right in declaring that it was not a text, was not a clear-cut revision or correction of the former text, but that it was a series of varying experiences of the earlier text in various places. One could deny that we were justified in individualising it, in calling it "it." As time passed this process, however, ceased.   It did not cease as if an express-train brake had stopped it.   It was not cut off at midnight on the last day of the year 200.

In most districts it had come to an end fifty years before that point of time.   We shall nevertheless, for the sake of clearness, in order to fix the thought, name the year 200 as the close of this process.   What has been said makes it apparent, not only that we must see in the witnesses of that period which are in our hands, traces of different phases of this second kind of text, but also that we must be prepared to meet with, must expect to meet with, still further phases of it in any new records of the period which the future may bestow upon us.   But in all its phases this text will have two characteristics which merge into each other.   It will in the first place be old.   Be the alterations in it, the additions to it, what they may, none of them will recall to us the characteristics of a later period in the life of the Church or in the fortunes of the text.   Wherever we light upon them they will meet us with the lavender-freighted air of the ancestral chest.   And it will, in the second place, precisely with this age, preserve for us large quantities of the Original Text.   It is not another text re-wrought, but the Original Text re-wrought.   And that in it which is not changed, which, of course, will be by far the greater part of it, that is original text.

When we spoke a moment ago of the many phases of this text, some persons may have had a feeling of mistrust towards it, and an inclination to shrink away from its uncertainty and intangibility.   A moment's reflection shows, however, that in this very respect it is of great value to us.   In the different phases and different modifications, the parts of the original text that were modified, or that were left untouched, become clearer to our view.   Two modifications of the same words permit a more certain conclusion as to what the original words were, than a single modification does.   And words modified by one province may in another have been left as they were.

The name of this text is the Re-Wrought Text.   This is the plain everyday name for the fact that is observed.   Westcott and Hort used the old name Western Text, though they conceded that, or better, asserted that the word Western was wrong, that it was not a Western text.   It was their inborn and scientific modesty that led them to use the old name.   But a name has its influence upon the thoughts, ard if we recognise that a name is one that leads the thoughts astray in spite of themselves, the sooner we change it the better. To call this Re-Wrought Text the Western Text, pulls the mind awry, and compels a constant astigmatism of view. That figure is doubtless all wrong, for I am no oculist, but I mean that the eye of the mind sees Western and does not see Western, and that the rays refuse to centre.

This Re-Wrought Text was the text which at the close of the second century was to be found almost everywhere. It was not to be found wherever by some happy provision of providence, bearing upon the clearness of mind or on the comparative freedom from mental action—here is an argument for the people who deprecate general education—of a given community, the Original Text was to be found. But it was to be found everywhere else. There were then but these two kinds of texts. We see here again how little it will do to deal rashly with dates. Lachmann thought he could get a text of the fourth century or the text of the fourth century. What he really got was something far better. He did not know, as we now know, that the text of the fourth century was the worst text there is. Now, if a good Christian should say : Give me the text of the second century, and I will ask for nothing better, he would be wide of the mark. He would find in this Re-Wrought Text a better text than that text of the fourth century, but it would still not be the right, the Original Text. This text had in the second century a certain fascination for the Christian gaze. It retains some of that power to-day. Alongside of the Original Text it was more juicy, more popular, and more full. It left almost nothing out. It added almost all it could lay hands upon.

Many a scholar looks at it to-day and finds in it a charm that the other old text does not possess. One part of its charm for some scholars lay with justice, though not a justice that they recognised, in the measure of its preservation of the original text. They then proceeded to claim for it the excellence that belonged not to it but to the Original Text, so far as that was still to be found within the witnesses for the Re-Wrought Text. In consequence of this preservation of its source it plays everywhere into the hands of the Original Text. Its witnesses are of necessity among the most important witnesses for that text. What we need to do is to distinguish between what is original and what is re-wrought.

There must, of course, be something chameleon-like in such a text, in that it varies in the many shadings of local alteration. That does not matter.   And, at any rate, we must take our text as we find it.   We must use the witnesses that tradition has given us.   We cannot have them made to order.   This Re-Wrought Text has given us no tokens of scientific operations to which the text was subjected.   It has shown us people who acted naively rather than of set purpose.   They were practical, not theoretical people.   They were not thinking of the text as a text or as a book.   They were full of the thing, the thoughts, the story, the exhortation, the vision.   And here we see that the process which we have described is the same as that to which we pointed when speaking of the book of Revelation and its text during the former period.   Special reasons led the Christians to work over, to impress themselves upon the text of Revelation at that early time, and the special character of that book called for that treatment of its text, guided and made easy that treatment, and prevented the all too speedy application of a similar treatment to the other books.   But here I shall say something against myself.   It was one of the difficulties with Westcott and Hort that they knew so very much, that it was hard for them not to know and not to recognize the justice of the "other side."   With less knowledge I should like to emulate their modesty.   Here, therefore, I observe, that if anyone prefer to suppose that the working over of the various books of the New Testament did not tarry for the year 100, did not merely have roots and inceptions before that date, but vigorous action, I shall not quarrel with him.

The Polished Text.

The first inclinations of the early Christians were not scientific inclinations.   That was no wonder.   But science came with time.   Scholars were converted and became Christians, and Christians were trained and became scholars.   It is usual to point for the earliest Christian scholarship to Alexandria and to the beginnings of the theological school that threads upon its necklace the names of Pantænus, Clement, Origen, and Dionysius. I do not wish to detract in the least from the merits of that school. Yet with that persistent bent towards theorising under which these pages have so often suffered, I should like to break a lance for Antioch again, and to say here in connection with the text, that I would fain think that at a very early date, long before the definite knowledge we have of it, there existed at Antioch a theological school.

The moment that Christian science existed, that moment it busied itself with the text of the New Testament. There is no help for that. Whether at Alexandria, or at Antioch, or at Cæsarea, when men who had had an accurate training in grammar came to examine closely the text, they found many a trifle that did not agree with the rules then long recognised for the use of the Greek language. They were acquainted with the dangers of manuscript tradition, and had at least some vague conception of the comparatively unlearned character of the early Christian communities. When, then, they found in the text of the books of the New Testament what seemed to them to be or what actually were faults of one kind and another, two ways of accounting for these faults were open to them. It was possible to say that the writers of these books had been guided and protected from faults by the Holy Spirit, that the original form of their writings must have been in every respect all that could be desired, and that if in the copies in hand there were found errors or faults, these must necessarily be attributed to the carelessness or ignorance of the Christians who had from time to time copied the rolls. There is, then, no need to say that Christian scholars, detecting these faults, corrected them without hesitation ; and considered themselves not merely justified in so doing, but as forced by duty to do so. That was the one view.

It was possible also to say that these writers of the New Testament were most of them by no means so well at home in the Greek language as to be able to use it skilfully, to write it correctly. They were guided by the Spirit of God in the sense of their utterances. But this Spirit of God did not occupy itself with the external form of the language. In consequence, the sacred writers had written less elegantly and less correctly than was really to be desired in a book of so great moment. That had not been a serious detriment to the spread of Christianity during those earlier years of plain preaching. Now, however, that cultured men began to interest themselves for Christianity, now that the reading of these writings formed so important a part in the services of the churches, it was necessary that a skilful hand smooth away the linguistic roughnesses and make the text, if not good, at least better than it had been.   We may imagine that the scholars of Alexandria and Antioch and Cæsarea viewed the matter from the one or the other of these two points of view.

There does not appear to have been any concerted action in reference to the text.   So far as our documents go, no one seems to have set about a regular revision of the whole New Testament, or even of one or more books.   Whether these scholars did not venture to do the thing thoroughly, and whether they supposed that if they did but change a little here and there for the better it would never be noticed, or whether the rolls in which they made their complete correction of the text have failed to be handed down to us, we cannot with certainty determine.   What we find in the documents, and particularly in documents and in the writings of theologians connected with Egypt, is that in a number of passages, readings have been produced which have certainly been after-thoughts and not the original readings, and which betray the moulding hand of the trained scholar which has been making the text more presentable to, more agreeable for learned and for educated eyes and ears.

Seeing that this correction of the text either did not extend to the whole New Testament or has at least not reached our hands in its entirety, we perhaps should speak only of "readings" and not of a "text."   Yet we give it for the present the benefit of the doubt and call it a text.   If complete manuscripts be one day found, they can at once pass into their place.   This text I name the Polished Text.   This name is again one that simply puts the fact on record.   The corrector wished to file the text off, to give to it as nearly as possible the smooth surface of polite diction.   Westcott and Hort called it, and that with geographical propriety, the Alexandrian Text.   The documents for it thus far known agree with that name.   Nevertheless, I have taken the matter of fact name, partly led perhaps by a less matter of fact and rather sentimental desire to keep the door open for the possible participation of a dreamed of early Antiochian school in this learned care for the text.

Since this text is, as has been seen, of a fragmentary character or of an ethereal existence, it is less easy to determine definitely at what time it probably arose. It seems most likely to have been the work of the early third century or of the late second century, and it will be the most prudent thing for us for the present to date it simply with the year ± 200. The scholar may comfort himself with the thought that his predecessors at that day tried to do their duty towards the text, even though we to-day do not think that what they did was after all the right thing to do. It is in connection with this text that we can apparently in some places see that Clement of Alexandria used different rolls of scripture when writing different works.

Herewith we close the short list of the old text. We might in one way term these three texts single-eyed texts. The Original Text, the Re-Wrought Text, and the Polished Text were all simple texts. For the Original Text that is a matter of course. For the Re-Wrought it is the result of the fact that the application of the foreign material to the Original Text takes place more in the way of accretion than in that of combination. I hope that is as sensible and as intelligible as it sounds. What I mean is that the additions to the Original Text which were made in the Re-Wrought Text seldom took the form of interweaving parts of sentences of the old text with similar parts from other sources, but were clear additions of new matter, whether long or short ones. The Polished Text is again altogether single. There is little or no question in it of the gathering together of previous material. The two older texts, and especially the Original Text, are its only basis, but not its basis in such a sense as that the corrector regards them as two sources which he must write into one, not even its basis in such a sense that this corrector recognises them as two distinct things.

The Syrian Revisions.

Should we call upon a good bishop in Antioch in the year 230, supposing that that year and the bishop were still accessible, we might find him puzzling his brains over the three texts that we have just named. A parish clergyman from a village off towards Aleppo had come in to this great city to ask the advice of the learned bishop about a text which had given rise to some difficulties for him and the clergy near him.   The bishop found that the clergyman had a very old manuscript, and we know when we look at it, what the bishop did not know, that this roll represented quite fairly the Original Text.   The verse struck the bishop as strange, and on taking his own roll of the book down from the case above his desk, he found that his text was not the same.   Now his roll was one of the Re-Wrought Text.   While the bishop and the priest were pondering over the matter, a young clergyman from Asia Minor came into the room.   He had been studying for a time at Alexandria, as we know that Gregory of Nazianzus did, and was now on his way home, but resting for a few days at Antioch.   The bishop spoke of the text, and the Asia Minorite drew out of his bosom a new roll of the book which he had copied at Alexandria, and showed a still different reading, one that was clearer and in better Greek than the other two, the reading of the Polished Text.

Now I cannot give the hour of the day at which, nor the day of the month on which, this happened, nor do I feel sure of the precise text which had plagued the group of village pastors and caused the journey of their representative to consult the bishop. But one thing is sure, and that is that such difficulties were rife, and rife in more than one place.   The fact that Syria formed a middle ground, may have led the clergy there to feel the difficulty the more keenly.   Into Antioch came from the west not only now and then more distant theologians from Rome and Athens, but also and especially the mentally active Greeks from Asia Minor. From the east came the Greeks living among the Syriac-speaking population, and compelled to know and to explain the readings of the Syrian manuscripts, and to compare them with their own Greek manuscripts.   And from the south came the men who had sat at the feet of Origen at Cæsarea, or who had been spending, like the above-mentioned clergyman, some time at Alexandria for the purpose of study.   No other point in all Christendom was in such a respect and to such an extent central. Further, however, the subsequent history of Antioch offers the apparently correct sequence for the previous scholarly inclinations and learned practices of Antioch.

In the earlier times there had been no leisure for, and no one had felt the need of, textual researches, or of efforts to correct the text.   Then the Christians had lived and preached and fought a good fight, but had not bothered themselves much about various readings. But the time seems now to have come for the consideration of the text. We are not perfectly clear about the matter. Much remains to be cleared up or to be cleared away and changed by future inquiries. Yet the most likely course of events from our present position and with our present power of reading in the dark mirror of the past is the following.

THE FIRST SYRIAN REVISION.

Someone in Antioch—it might have been a company of scholars, but it was probably a single one—at the request of the bishop or feeling himself the difficulty of the described state of affairs, determined to revise the text, to bring the text into a good and practical shape. We may name for him as a date the middle of the second century, though it may have been somewhat earlier, but was probably somewhat later. The precise year is of no great moment, seeing that we do not have to compare it again with a definitely fixed year in the neighbouring decades. The material that he had at command we have already mentioned.

Now we may question whether the task that placed itself before the mind of this theologian was just the one that a modern critic of the text would appoint for him if he could project himself back through the centuries and assume the position of guide and mentor for the Antiochian scholar. I do not think it likely that the problem before the mind of that Syrian Greek scholar was devoid of reference to the original text, but I do think it likely that the question of the genuine words filled a much narrower space in his deliberations than it would in our minds to-day. He will probably have bent his thoughts more upon two or rather upon three things.

In the first place, it will have been his wish to have in his text everything that was in the manuscripts before him that he could conscientiously bring into it. Just as the ordinary author or editor to-day desires, if possible, in making a new edition to be able to say that it is "revised and enlarged," so the natural wish of that reviser in Syria will have been to make each book as full and complete as the texts in his hands permitted. Feeling sure of this principle in his mind, we shall at least have in the text which he constructs a clue to the more exact contents of the manuscripts which he had in his hands. In general, we have to reckon with the established and acknowledged habit both of tradition by word of mouth and of written tradition to increase and not to decrease the thing, the statement, the history, the argument, the explanation, which has been received and which is passed on to the next persons in the order of place and especially in the order of time. That was the first aim.

In the second place, our reviser will have been intent upon relieving any difficulties which were found in one or in all of the texts in his hands. One of the main reasons for going at the work, for undertaking to reconstitute or to redetermine the text of the books of the New Testament, was that in the single manuscripts difficulties were found, the solution of which gave the keenest exegetes trouble. And there was coupled with this the difficulty that arose when two different witnesses gave different and clashing testimony. The reviser will, in judging of different readings before him, have been sure not, for example, in this point to have been led, by the consideration of the necessity of reaching the original text, to press the well-known canon, of all textual criticism in whatever language and with respect to whatever book, that the harder reading is the truer reading. He will have had his daily life in mind, and the need of leaving as few problems as possible unsolved, and he will have chosen the easier reading. In pursuance of the same thought, in the case of difficult readings which did not differ in the documents before him, he will have been inclined, when it proved possible by a trifling or apparently trifling change to render the sense clear and unquestionable, to make such a change and to have more unconsciously than consciously thereby presupposed that he in this way attained either the original text or the text that the original writer would have written, had his attention been called to this difficulty. That was the second aim.

The third aim reminds us in part of the very last remark and in part and particularly of the Polished Text. For, in the third place, the reviser will have desired to make a smooth text, a text free from less elegant expressions, a text that contained no odd or obsolete grammatical forms, a text that would not excite the disdain of scholarly men who heard it read. And here again

32

the question of authenticity of the words and phrases will certainly not have stood in the foreground of his thoughts. He
will have thought of the beauty and not of the rightness, the
correctness of the sentences in reference to originality as having
been the words of the author.

Such we suppose to have been the work of an Antiochian
theologian somewhere near the middle of the third century.
It has sometimes been suggested that an Egyptian theologian
may have shared in the work. It must be conceded that we are
totally ignorant of all details, and that the co-operation of an
Alexandrian scholar would be quite conceivable. The Alexandrian critic might have remained at home and sent his
thoughts about the text to Antioch by a messenger, receiving
in return the suggestions of his colleague at Antioch by the same
messenger. Or the Alexandrian might have made the journey to
Antioch and there have contributed to the revision. I confess,
however, that this common work does not seem to me to be
very likely. It reminds me more of modern times. The English
revisers with their American colleagues across the Atlantic have
so far as I can remember no parallel in antiquity. It would be
far less difficult for me to suppose that an Egyptian revision of
the text preceded or succeeded the revision in Antioch.

We have a definite reason for placing this work at Antioch or
at least in Syria. And if we go to Syria, Antioch is the place that
most commends itself to us. The reason is this. The Syrian
translation of the New Testament appears to have been revised
soon after the same time and in the same sense, that is to say,
so as to present in general a newly determined text, even though
perhaps not precisely the same text as that found in the Greek
form. Now this circumstance points to the work of revision as
done in Syria. Without doubt the difficulties found in the
Syrian version had also contributed to hasten the necessity of the
revision. And the moment that the Greek text was done, or
even perhaps step by step as the revision advanced, the Syrian
translation was made to correspond to it. Had the revision been
made in Alexandria it would have been possible that the Coptic
texts, the Boheiric and the Saïdic, would have been made to
correspond to the Greek. I remember no such change in them.
The theologian who made this revision probably did it, probably
was fitted to do it and was appointed to do it, because he was

known as one of the most learned men of his day at Antioch. He is likely to have been asked to do it by the bishop of Antioch, and may even well have done it in the "palace" of the bishop, if we could imagine that by that time the bishop there ventured to have a larger house or series of houses for himself and his clergy and our hypothetical school.

We should, of course, like very much to know what became of this revision, that is to say, what success it met with as a literary and ecclesiastical effort. We should be inclined to think that in view of the generally or often acknowledged differences in the current texts, and of the disagreeable consequences that resulted from them, all Christians who heard of this work, at least all theologians, would at once have ordered copies of it for themselves. At present we are not able to say just how far that took place. There are, however, two circumstances to be brought into view which help to make the surroundings clearer.

That revision of the Syrian text, to make it agree with the revised Greek text, may have been cared for in Antioch or, it may be, in one of the more definitely Syrian centres, centres of Syrian speech, Nisibis and Edessa. We have a fairly definite proof that this revision of the Syrian text was made and backed up by the Church authorities. For the Syriac manuscripts of the older text disappeared almost as if by magic, and only the newer text was copied off. That was possible with the Syrian manuscripts. They were in comparison of limited range. They were to be reached by the authorities from that one great Syrian centre. The Greek text was in a different position. It was scattered over wider fields, and was not at that time to be commanded by any single authority. This Greek text—I refer in this sentence to the revised Greek text—does not seem to have gone very far. We might imagine that it passed from Antioch to one church and another in Asia Minor to the north-west and in Palestine to the south. But the previous texts, and that means, of course, especially the Re-Wrought Text which had by all odds the wider sway, continued to be used. I spoke above of all this Syrian revision as perhaps done about the middle of the third century. Nevertheless, it is not altogether impossible that it was done later than that, towards the end of the century. The name of Lucian, who died as a martyr in the year 312, has been mentioned in connection with the revision

of the text.   Perhaps it was he who made the revision of which
I have just spoken.

THE SECOND SYRIAN REVISION;

OR,

THE OFFICIAL TEXT.

As the fourth century moved on, there befell the Church a
great change.   The conversion of Constantine brought into
Christianity the element of authority in a totally new sense, and
that in two ways.   On the one hand, this authority was not, like
all sympathetic authority up to that time, an ecclesiastical
authority, but a civil authority.   To-day that would make a great
difference in the valuation of that authority, and in the respect
paid to it or not paid to it.   At that time it made little difference,
save in a favourable direction.   The Christians were only too
glad to forget the persecutions, and were ready to welcome in
obedience the Christian emperor.   And, on the other hand, this
authority was of wide domain.   Until then the bishop had been
the highest official for them.   Single bishops sometimes attained
to a wider authority by courtesy, reverence, and affection, as we
saw in the case of Dionysius of Corinth.   But here we have the
emperor.   Now the Christians have in Constantinople a new
hold, and they are conversely under a new authority.   This new
authority attached to the new centre gives to Christianity a
new impulse.   It does not concern us here whether this novelty
was a blessing or a curse in general.   We have to do with its
influence upon the text.

The Greek revision of the text of the New Testament of
which we have just spoken, appears to have failed to impress
itself upon distant circles, upon Christian churches far from
Antioch, though it doubtless was sometimes copied for various
churches.   So long as this revision did not prevail, the tendency
of its existence was to make matters worse.   If it did not replace
or supplant the other texts, it made a fourth text that only
increased the confusion.

Now, however, the Church grows and flourishes in the sunshine of imperial favour.   The Council of Nice tends to make
it feel its oneness and its power.   It was probably towards the

middle of the fourth century that the text was again revised, and again at Antioch. For this revision, Antioch had become all the more probable, appropriate, and practically desirable because of its geographical nearness to, and because of its political as well as religious connection with, Constantinople. We do not need to discuss at length the possibilities and the probabilities of the process of revision at this time, for they do not differ materially from the conditions considered on the occasion of that preceding revision, save in so far that a revised Greek text, the work of that former revision, was a fourth source of material.

This revision contributed still further to make the text of the New Testament complete in the sense that the reviser packed into it all the words of the preceding texts that he could well stow away in it. At the same time it made the text still smoother and weaker. The text reached herewith, in this Church text, its greatest distance from the original text. This text is the worst text in existence. But it was born under a lucky constellation. Now, there was a central authority that extended farther than any bishopric. And the bishops who enveloped themselves in this authority seem to have at once taken hold of this new revision and to have spread it broadcast. Now, the manuscripts of the older texts vanish, just as the Syrian manuscripts vanished when their text had been revised at that earlier period. Therefore we may term this last and worst of texts the Official Text.

Here the history of the Greek text in the manuscripts closes. I say history in the pragmatic sense. From this time onwards the Greek text of the New Testament, having been reduced to its lowest estate, simply lived along. It had no more experiences than an oyster has in its rocky bed. History for the Greek text begins again when Fell and Mill and Bentley and Bengel and Wettstein and Griesbach and Hug and Lachmann and Tischendorf and Tregelles and Westcott and Hort draw it forth from the Slough of Despond and place it upon the high road leading to its pristine purity. That worst text is, so far as the Textus Receptus, the Received Text, is made fast and sure in Estienne's and the Elzevir Texts, the text for which so many theologians fought for long years. If Lachmann had taken that, instead of doing the good critical work that he did do, he would have had the text of the fourth century at which he in name aimed his efforts.

Origin of Classes of Texts.

We can now return to a matter that has already been briefly mentioned, but which we are now prepared to treat more fully. I refer to the way in which classes of texts have arisen in the New Testament. In old days it was the custom to say and to believe that the classes of texts in the New Testament arose from the errors of scribes, that they were the usual classes known in classical philology, and that intentional change had nothing to do with them. It has more than once been asserted, that aside from an exceedingly small number of possibly intentional changes, perhaps two or three, the New Testament enjoyed the pre-eminence of having a text that no one had changed of set purpose, that the will of man had as good as not entered into the realm of this textual treasure.

Having passed by the classes of the text in rapid review, we are in a position now to say that precisely the contrary is the case. It is true that the scribes who copied the manuscripts of the New Testament remained men and made their usual mistakes. And it is likewise true that we can repeatedly with their errors prove the existence of groups of manuscripts, just as in the documents for the works of classical authors. But with the thousands of manuscripts at our command, such groups are in the textual criticism of the New Testament a very subsidiary matter. We are glad to observe them and to apply them as a means of reducing the number of manuscripts in our hands, by leading half a dozen manuscripts back to their one source. For determining the text they are much too far from the centre of observation. These groups are not formed by acts of intention, but by unintentional mistakes. These groups have not the least in the world to do with the formation of the four or five classes of text of which we have here treated.

In the face of all that has been repeated for many years, the classes of which we have spoken have nothing to do with unintentional change. They are the results of the purpose of many persons. Advancing from the Original Text we come first of all to the Re-Wrought Text, and see in it the results of the action of the wills of various men at various times in various countries. These men did not just by accident, without seeing what they were about, add here a word and there a word. They had their eyes open and their heads clear, and they wished to make the text before them better, and to their way of thinking they did make it better. What they did they willed to do. Precisely the same was the case with the scholars who prepared the Polished Text. They filed here and altered there, and used their philological acumen in order to secure the best results. It was all the work of will, not of accident. It is not necessary to follow up the two texts that were last produced. For they were directly the product, as we saw, of the effort to make things better. The fact that the chance mistakes of the scribes do not cause classes of this kind is then made clear by a view of the history of the texts.

A mathematician might make for us some equations or solve some problems for us. If the unintentional errors of the early Christians produced within a century or a century and a half the text we name the Re-Wrought Text, and if further unintentional errors in a further century and a half produced the Official Text, what must unintentional errors have produced in the way of change, disorder, and confusion in the course of the following eleven centuries before the text of the New Testament was printed? And then we perceive that at the end of the eleven centuries the text is to all intents and purposes precisely where it was and in the condition in which it was at the beginning of the eleven centuries. It is of no avail to say that Greek had become a "dead" language, and that the scribes therefore were ignorant and kept slavishly to their text during the eleven centuries. In the first place, the Greek language is not yet dead, as anyone can settle for himself by a journey from Messina, or Trieste, around the Mediterranean, including the Ægean and the Black Sea, to Alexandria. In the second place, the "death" of the language and the ignorance of scribes would only have heightened, in no case lessened, the number, the pernicious effect, and the class-making influence of unintentional mistakes.

What unintentional errors and faults did not do in eleven centuries they certainly could not have done in either one of the periods of a century and a half before the eleven centuries. The classes of text in the New Testament are solely the result of arbitrary, that is, willed action.

If those who wish to find in the history of the New Testament text excellent care, and who in pursuance of that wish have urged the lack of wilful change, would formulate their statement more guardedly, there would be less difficulty in accepting their contention. There are a few cases in the New Testament in which, as we may see, for example, in John 7[8], changes have been made for a definite purpose which we might call dogmatical or even apologetical. In the verse mentioned Jesus says: "I go not up to this feast," using the phrase which was rendered in Greek by οὐκ ἀναβαίνω. Some good Christian in early times, reading this and finding two verses later that Jesus actually did go up to that feast, said to himself apparently: "That cannot be. Jesus cannot have said that He was not going up to the feast. He can only have said that He did not intend to go at that moment. He must have left room open for His later going up to Jerusalem." And therefore this Christian wrote over the οὐκ or on the margin beside οὐκ the word οὔπω, "not yet," and caused Jesus to say: "I am not going up to this feast yet." There are, in my opinion, not many cases of this kind in the New Testament. And if therefore those who have wished to exclude intentional change altogether from the fortunes of the text of the New Testament would but limit their statement to the observation that changes of such a dogmatical or apologetical character are rare in that text, it would not be hard to agree with them.

Pondering over the presentation of the course of the history of the text here given, it would be possible for a thinking, an active mind to ask what the explanation is for the circumstance that four or five classes of text were made during the first four centuries, or about within the years from 100 to 350, and that absolutely none were thereafter produced. The answer is not far to seek. Each of those classes of the text had its reason for being made. The Re-Wrought Text applied the then still flourishing written and oral tradition of the apostolic age to the enriching and the embellishing of the text. The Polished Text sought to remove the comparative uncouthness of the primitive form for polite ears. And the two revisions which culminated in the Official Text had for their purpose the unifying of the contradictory or varying forms of the text, as well as the simplifying and smoothing off of its language. Everyone of these reasons attaches to an early date in the life of, or in the development of, a text. No such reason could arise to demand a new class of text, after the whole Greek Church had at the beck of authority acquiesced in the weak and poor text of the revision of the fourth century. It was left for the impulse of modern science to discover by a long series of efforts the probable sources and causes and courses of the movements in and changes in the text, and to endeavour by reversing the wheel of time to undo the false development, and to reach in skilful unravelling of the lines of tradition the Original Text.

Should this action of modern science prove even but to a certain extent successful, it will have great value. If the researches into the earlier years of Christianity receive in the future as in the past, as I confidently expect, many new documents for the period from 90 to 200 A.D., and if these documents sustain the theory as to the early facts of the text that Westcott and Hort framed, then we shall be able to develop it in a more complete manner, particularly in the direction of new editions of the early writers. I have written: "sustain the theory." That does not mean that I look for, or that Westcott and Hort looked for, a precise corroboration of every suggestion in, of every ramification of, their hypothesis. What they gave us was a hypothesis to work upon, the best they then could make. Had they lived they would have modified the hypothesis with new discoveries. We must modify it for them, when the new discoveries come. The sustaining of their theory to which I allude is then a general one, and not necessarily one that goes into all details.

So far as I can judge of a number of the efforts that have been made since the year 1881 to do something new in the field of textual criticism, these efforts have laboured under three disadvantages which have impaired their effect or have rendered them comparatively fruitless.

In the first place, these efforts were partial, not general. That was not singular. The great knowledge of the Church writers and of the ins and outs of Christian literature that Westcott and Hort possessed cannot be matched in a couple of years of desultory reading that dips here or there into the field. It was further not singular, because these efforts were sometimes the happy thoughts of specialists in limited fields who had neither inclination nor time to occupy themselves with the whole subject. Yet precisely such researches, such contributions of men who were masters of a circumscribed domain, were and remain desirable.

But in the second place, if I do not err, these partial efforts, every one of which, like every careful bit of work in any department, was welcome, failed partly to have the desired effect because of their antagonistic attitude over against the hypothesis which Westcott and Hort had presented. To be very plain, the scholars who made these partial researches did not say: "I have observed these facts. Let us see whether we can range them under the given theory or whether they demand a change in the theory." On the contrary, they said: "This theory is all wrong. For I have observed here a trifle which I cannot make square with the theory."

And in the third place, this antagonism against the theory and the failure to recognise the coincidence between the newly found facts and the theory has, I think, in several instances been due to an imperfect conception of the theory. The hypothesis of Westcott and Hort is given in Hort's book, the introductory volume to their edition, in an exceedingly cautious manner, so that it is not easy, I think, for a hurried reader to be sure of their full intention. I remember one page which I wished to have made more clear, but which seemed to the editor to leave nothing to be desired. At a later date, after the book had been issued, I made two columns on a page of paper and wrote in one column the text of the given paragraph. In the other column I re-wrote the sense in my own words up to the point at which I could not tell what to write. Then the editor gave me the clue. I refer to this simply to show that in a field that contains so many and such different parts a theory dealing with the whole may fail to be easy of comprehension for one whose time does not allow him to consider it at length. This refers, as is evident, to those who have gained their knowledge of the theory from Hort's own book.

Apparently, however, some have taken their view of the theory from brief, tabular statements made about it. It is therefore desirable to remind scholars of Hort's thoughts upon this subject. I had asked him, urged him, to make in his volume a short and skeleton-like review of what the two editors aimed at, and of the facts of early textual history as they presented themselves to the eyes of the editors. He replied that he, and I think Westcott also, had tried to make such a summary presentation, but had not succeeded. This was, I think, to a large extent the result of their great knowledge and their great modesty. Every curt, combining, crystallising sentence that they formulated met at once in their brains such a multitude of contrary or divergent considerations as to be impossible for them. It is the man who knows little who is "absolutely certain." He does not know the limits of his knowledge. I succeeded in getting from them what I suppose to be the only existing brief, authentic exposition of their theory. But even this short statement, this authentic one, can in no wise replace the study of their book for anyone who makes the most distant pretensions to form a judgment as to the correctness or the faultiness or the worthlessness of their theory. If those who combat the hypothesis of Westcott and Hort would first be willing to take the pains to read Hort's book carefully, we should less frequently find them urging as new objections to that hypothesis considerations which Westcott and Hort themselves presented to the public.

We have dwelt long enough upon the theory of the origin and early history of the text. No one can tell how long it will be before we are sure of the correctness of that theory, or are able to replace it by a better one. In the meantime the Church, Christianity, Christian theologians need a Greek New Testament. There is no danger of anyone's trying to stop all preaching until the text of the New Testament is finally settled. That would be absurd. For preaching did not begin with the New Testament. Preaching, vivid work in the Church, preceded by years the New Testament. And no one can venture to say that the theological study of the New Testament must halt until the text has been made absolutely perfect. Theology must be moving on with its other tasks as well as with those in textual criticism. We are bound to make to-day the best text we can, and to use that text diligently and undoubtingly. If that be the case, Christians have a right to ask textual critics whether the text that can be determined to-day is in the main a reliable text.

We can divide the consideration of this thought into two parts, a more negative and a more positive one. It is on the one hand of first importance for Christian theologians to be assured that what they have before them in the New Testament is really in the main New Testament, really is a part of the books to which it is alleged to belong. Should we be compelled when commenting upon the text of the New Testament, or when trying to draw from its pages arguments for our views, or when seeking comfort and counsel in it—should we be compelled at every instant to bear in mind the possibility that the whole paragraph upon which we have fixed our thoughts might as a matter of fact not be a part of the book in which it stood, might be a spurious interpolation, our thoughts would be confused and lamed. It is therefore of cardinal importance that textual criticism place before Christians one result of the work of the past two centuries. That result is, that we have no ground for assuming that, no ground to suspect that, no ground to fear that any large sections that we consider to-day to be a part of the text of the New Testament will ever be proved not to belong to it. Textual criticism has determined, I think finally and irrevocably, that three passages form no part of the text. Aside from an omission or two of verses that have crept in from parallel passages and have no interest for us, there are three other passages, of not more than two verses each, that are probably spurious. Aside from these, I think we may say that the text of the New Testament is in the main assured. We have succeeded in gaining such a control of the realm of testimony and such a comprehensive view of it, that surprises in this direction seem to be excluded. Textual criticism will not again be called upon to decide whether a whole series of verses belong to a New Testament book or not. That is the way in which the case presents itself to us to-day. Are we deceived, will textual criticism at some future day have to cut out parts of, say Second Corinthians, and recombine the remnants,—I at least do not now know that, nor do I in the least anticipate it. In this respect, in respect to the future excision of larger portions of the text, the New Testament is safe.

INTERESTING PASSAGES.—FIRST JOHN $5^{7.8}$.

It will not be uninteresting to cast a glance at the passages referred to, to the three that beyond all doubt form no part of the New Testament, and to the other three that probably do not

belong to it.   They are for the most part of a character foreign
to the rest of the text, so that we can easily let them go.   The
one passage in the New Testament of our ancestors which had
not the slightest claim to a place in it was the passage, to which
I alluded a while back, in the First Epistle of John.   In First
John 5⁷·⁸ the text of the New Testament reads : " For there
are three that bear witness, the spirit and the water and the
blood, and the three are one."   There is a corrupt Latin text
which says : "There are three that bear witness on earth, the
spirit, water, and blood, and these three are one in Christ Jesus.
And there are three that speak testimony in heaven, the Father,
the Word, and the Spirit."   That corrupt text put in the words
"in earth" and "in Christ Jesus" and the whole sentence about
the heavenly witnesses.   Now, these words have not the least
shadow of a right to a place in the text of the New Testament.
We may begin with the latest treatment of the question.   Karl
Künstle argues with great learning and apparently with great
justice that this passage is to be attributed to Priscillian.   Let
me observe by way of parenthesis that the passage has a number
of quite different forms.   Priscillian was a heretical Spanish
bishop of the fourth century.   It is one of the curious contrasts
of life and history that this text should be traced back to this
heretic.   Since the printing of the New Testament, and Erasmus'
fatal promise to insert the verse if it should be found in a Greek
manuscript, it has been the habit of the friends of the verse to
claim it as the great proof-text of the New Testament for the
doctrine of the Trinity.   What would Priscillian say to that!
For Priscillian did not hold to the doctrine of the Trinity.   He
was very much of a Manichæan.   His views were, we may say,
a Gnostic Dualism.   He taught not pantheism, but Pan-Christism.
And the text that came from him is claimed for the Trinity.
That is very odd.   But it does not belong in the New Testament,
as we have said.

It has been said to be in three Greek manuscripts.   Now,
one of the three is that Codex Montfortianus at Dublin, of
which I spoke above (see page 374).   The two points to be
emphasised about it are, in the first place, that the Greek
text here was changed so as to conform to the Latin text of
the passage ; and in the second place, that the Epistles in this
manuscript were written about the time at which Erasmus, after

printing two editions of his Greek New Testament without the
verse, had promised to put the verse in if it were found in
a Greek manuscript. Thus far no positive proof thereof has
been found, but it is in every way probable that this copy of the
Epistles was written, and that these words were here put in, in
less correct or less fitting Greek as drawn from the Latin, for the
purpose of forcing Erasmus to print the verses, as he then did.
In no case has this manuscript of the sixteenth century a particle
of value for the Greek text in general, let alone for a verse which
its scribe evidently took from the Latin.

The second Greek manuscript which is cited for these three
heavenly witnesses is a manuscript of the fourteenth century in
the Vatican Library at Rome. We can here see plainly that
the words are taken from the Latin. The manuscript is in two
columns. Here the left-hand column is Latin and the right-
hand Greek, and the text in the two languages corresponds
as nearly as may be line for line. Therefore the scribe has
translated the Latin words for those lines into Greek. He
agrees with the man who made the bad translation in the Codex
Montfortianus in leaving out the article in the case of the
heavenly witnesses, but he gives it, as he will have found it in
his Greek text, for the witnesses on earth. The scribe of the
Montfortianus left it out there too. But the translation is a
different one.

And finally, the third Greek manuscript is one at Naples,
which, however, has the usual Greek text without the heavenly
witnesses. Some modern hand has written the heavenly witnesses on the margin. So we see that these three alleged
witnesses in favour of the three heavenly witnesses prove to
be nothing but witnesses against the authenticity of the text.
The facts which I have here stated are nothing new. Yet a
Roman Catholic edition of the Greek New Testament which
claims to be constituted according to the ancient manuscripts
has just been issued, for I think the third time, containing this
verse without note or comment and with no allusion to it in
the critical notes. Such an edition is insupportable when we
consider the learning of the Roman Catholic theologians. Why,
it is precisely a Roman Catholic professor of theology who has
shown that these words come from a heretic. And nevertheless
Brandscheid ventured to publish them as good scripture with

episcopal approbation.   No one can to-day complain that textual criticism has done wrong in thrusting these spurious words out of the text of the New Testament.   The pity is only that they have been allowed for so long a time to usurp a place upon the pages of the New Testament, and that a theologian could in the twentieth century still be found so devoid of critical insight as to publish them as a part of the sacred text.

MARK 16⁹⁻²⁰.

Another passage that textual criticism has shown to have no right to a place in the text of the New Testament is the close of the Gospel according to Mark as it stands in the common editions.   Mark 16⁹⁻²⁰ is neither part nor parcel of that Gospel. Many a question suggests itself to the textual critic when he looks at these verses.   We cannot tell what happened to this Gospel. What we now have left of the original Gospel stops off short with the Greek word γάρ, " for ": " For they were afraid."   The first supposition would appear to be that Mark had been interrupted in writing, but on second thoughts we cannot approve of that view.   Mark doubtless lived longer, and could have continued and closed his book again before publishing it.   Another supposition would be that the last sentence we have of the original was at the foot of one of the columns towards the end of the roll, and that the last columns had been lost from the first or from a very early copy, and that all subsequent copies came from the imperfect volume.

And taking up the other side, the question arises, whence the present verses ⁹⁻²⁰ came.   A few years ago no one could answer that question.   Now we can answer it, for Frederick Cornwallis Conybeare found an old Armenian manuscript that named these verses as from the Presbyter Aristion, and thus far no good reason has been found for doubting his authorship.   Aristion is called by Papias a disciple of the Lord, and his words are every whit as good as Mark's words.   But they do not belong here.   They are not a part of the New Testament, and they were probably added at this ninth verse in Asia Minor at the close of the first or the beginning of the second century.   It has been suggested that the real end of Mark was purposely cut off by a man who did

not like it, and who chose to replace it by the passage from
Aristion.   That does not seem to me to be probable, and for
a very commonplace practical reason.   If a chance critic should
have cut away the end and replaced it thus, one of two things
would have happened.   Either we should have had manuscripts
with the proper ending, the manuscripts, that is to say, which that
critic could not reach, and the manuscripts which we have with
this Aristion ending ; or, if the critic had all in his hand, we
should only have had manuscripts with this Aristion ending.

Now neither of these things is the actual case.   We have
very old manuscripts which close blankly with that word γάρ, as
if their scribes had never thought or heard of anything after it.
Then, of course, we have manuscripts with this common Aristion
ending.   And—here is the still stranger thing, but as it seems to
me the proof that the Gospel was wandering about without a
close—we have in the manuscripts a totally different ending.   A
manuscript I found at Mount Athos twenty years ago continues
after the γάρ: "And all the things announced to those about
Peter briefly, they spread abroad.   And after that Jesus also
Himself appeared from east, and up to west He sent out by them
the sacred and incorrupted preaching of the eternal salvation.
Amen.   And this also is found after the 'For they were afraid,'"
and then follows the Aristion ending.   Now, that seems to me
to show conclusively the same thing that our old manuscripts
show, namely, that this Gospel was spread abroad in ancient
times without the proper ending.   Seeing the wide prevalence
of the Gospel without an ending or with one of the false endings,
the necessary conclusion is that the curtailing took place at an
extremely early date.   I regard it nevertheless as one of the
possibilities of future finds that we receive this Gospel with its
own authentic finish.   Mark has been connected with Alexandria.
May Grenfell and Hunt add to their numerous gifts the close
of the original Mark from an Egyptian papyrus.

What I said a moment ago must, however, now be repeated
and emphasised.   It sometimes seems to Christian laymen as if
textual critics warred upon the New Testament.   If the textual
critics did not like the New Testament they would surely find no
difficulty in discovering other objects of study that they liked.
They work upon the New Testament because it appears to them
to be in an especial manner worthy of their highest efforts.   Here

is a case. These closing verses of Mark positively do not belong
to this Gospel, positively have no right to be in the New Testament. If I said that they did belong to this Gospel I should speak
as direct an untruth as if I should insist upon it that Moscow was
a city in Spain. The kind of assertion would be different, the
untruth would be equal or even greater. But in spite of all that,
I insist upon the words above. These words of Aristion's are as
good as or, if you please, better than Mark's words ; for all that
they are not a part of Mark's Gospel. A Christian may read,
enjoy, ponder them, and be thankful for them as much as he
pleases. The textual critic will in no wise hinder him. The
critic has but to study the question of belonging or not belonging
to the text. No one thing in reference to the Gospel of Mark
could afford the textual critic greater pleasure than the finding
of the words with which Mark continued the text after γάρ and
finished his Gospel.

JOHN 7⁵³–8¹¹.

The third of the passages that are beyond all doubt proven
not to belong to the New Testament is just about of the same
length as the verses Mark 16⁹⁻²⁰, or about of one hundred and
sixty-six words, varying according to the readings chosen. I
refer to John 7⁵³–8¹¹, the story of the Adulteress, a story that
has for centuries been a comfort to repentant sinners, whether
men or women, and whatever the sin was of which they had
been guilty. I do not doubt that this story is a true story,
and that it has exercised its charm in oral and then in written
tradition since the day on which the woman stood before Jesus.
The only reason I could think of for questioning its historical
accuracy is the circumstance that no one of the four evangelists
relates it. And yet we must remember how much there was to
be told. The world itself would not have contained the books
if all were to have been written down. And our view of the most
beautiful or the most striking or the most touching scene may
in some cases be different from that of the evangelists. This
story, these verses, have had a most singular fate in the life of
Christianity, so that one scarcely knows where to begin or where
to end about them. The verses 7⁵³ and 8¹, and in part 8², have
to a great extent been kept separate from the verses 8² or ³ to ¹¹,

33

seeing that the lesson containing this story usually began with 8^2 or ^{3}. It is further to be observed that there is a certain likeness between the verses 7^{53}–8^2 and Luke $21^{37, 38}$, which perhaps was one reason for the insertion of the story at the latter point in a group of Calabrian manuscripts.

In one respect there seems to be a similarity in the textual fortunes of this section and of the book of Revelation. The great favour that that book found in the eyes of the earliest Church led, I think, to its being at that time altered in its text more than any other book of the whole New Testament. This section about the Adulteress was probably the most read single section in the whole history of the Church. We learn from Eusebius that it was in the Gospel according to the Hebrews. Yet his reference to its being there seems to indicate that that was but one of the places in which it was found. If I am not mistaken, there are in the whole New Testament no other dozen verses that exhibit such a manifold variation of reading. It is a section that in reference to its textual history and textual character stands totally alone. This multifariousness of form I am inclined to connect with its having been so very often read, and especially at a very early time. It would, I confess also, be possible to argue that its readings were the more readily changed because it often stood outside of the frame of the Gospel. Many a hand seems to have changed trifles in the wording here and there.

One of the forms of change in the eighth and ninth verses makes the narrative in the highest degree dramatic, and places what we might call the possibilities of the scene in the most living and moving manner before our eyes. It is scarcely conceivable that this peculiar change of which I am speaking go back to a more correct form of the Aramaic oral tradition. It is therefore probably a late invention. It is found chiefly in manuscripts now on Mount Athos, and may have started there. This most radical of all the changes is the following. At the close of the eighth verse, when Jesus again turns away from the Pharisees and again writes on the ground, we are told what He wrote. For the sentence is made to say: He wrote upon the ground the sins of each single one of them. Of course, that is aimed at these accusing Pharisees. We see the people crowding around Jesus. In the midst of the group are a half a dozen or more scribes and Pharisees, who have brought the woman to Jesus and have stated

her sin.   They think to lay a snare for Him.   They have no fear
for themselves.   The ninth verse completes the change that
turns the tables upon the Pharisees.   It does not read : And
they when they heard it.   It reads : And they when they read
it.   The Pharisees accused the woman.   Jesus wrote on the
ground, affecting not to hear them, as also an old reading
suggests.   They badger Him until He looks up at them and
curtly says : He that is without sin among you let him first cast
a stone at her.   And then He stoops down and again writes
upon the ground.   What is He writing there ?   The foremost
Pharisee is of course the oldest.   It was his right to be in front.
He looks down at the sand at the word that Jesus has just
written, and sees there the name of a great sin that he has
done, but which he thinks is known to no one.   Like a flash
his conscience wakens.   Verse ninth says : And they, when they
read it, being convicted by their conscience, went out one by one,
beginning from the eldest unto the last.   This oldest Pharisee
has turned and edged his way out of the crowd as fast as he
could.   Jesus has swept His hand across the sand to smoothe
it over, and has again written something.   This word the next
Pharisee reads, and recognising a hidden sin of his own he too
flees.   And thus it goes on till the accusers are all away.   And
Jesus is left alone with the woman in the centre of the group of
people.   Jesus looks up at her and asks her—we can hear the
scathing irony of the words—Where are they ?   Doth no man
condemn thee ?   Yes, indeed, He may well ask where they are.
They have gone off, thinking of their own sins.   Their own
thoughts are now accusing and perhaps weakly excusing them,
but chiefly condemning them.   And the woman answers : No
man, Lord.   And Jesus said : Neither do I condemn thee.   Go
thy way, and from henceforth sin no more.   That is a wonderful
scene.   The whole process might have taken place precisely as
this form of the text places it before our eyes.   But thus far the
witnesses for that word " read " are not important enough to
admit of our putting it into the text instead of " heard."

In the Greek Church this section was used as the lesson for
people who repented and confessed their sins, whether men or
women, and it is not hard to imagine how often it must have
been read, and what grateful ears it fell upon.   It was read and
re-read, but it was very rarely found at this place in the Gospel

of John.   In many manuscripts it stands after the end of John
as an extra piece all by itself.   There is an interesting external
proof that it was not a part of the original Gospel.   We spoke
some time ago of the chapters in the Gospels, the large chapters
with their headings.   These large chapters call attention to every
remarkable narrative in the text, and it is a matter of course that
if the story of the Adulteress had been in John it would have
formed a chapter and had its heading.   But it is very rarely
found in the list of the chapters of John.   There are eighteen
chapters in John in almost all the manuscripts, and the tenth
chapter is "about the man blind from birth."   Even in many of
the manuscripts in which the section has been inserted into the
Gospel the list of the eighteen chapters remains as usual.   Then
in a number of copies the scribes have felt that that was not
fitting, have thought that the story must appear also in the
chapter list, and they have put it in as chapter tenth "about
the Adulteress," thus making in all nineteen chapters.   There it
would have been from the first had it been part of the Gospel,
and its failure to appear there proves that it was not in the
Gospel.   Thus such a thing as a list of chapters can, after all,
tell us something of importance for the text.

I have said that this section is not found in a large number of
manuscripts.   It is the only section which in no small number of
manuscripts has been put into the text by force.   In many a copy
it has been merely added, often in a small hand, on the margin.
But in many, when we reach that point in the Gospel, we see
of a sudden two newer leaves, written also of course in a newer
hand.   The moment such leaves appear the textual critic knows
what is up.   The manuscript did not originally contain the story
of the Adulteress.   Thereupon the owner of the manuscript tore
or cut out the leaf upon which the surrounding verses were
written and put in two new leaves, on which he wrote those
surrounding verses which he had removed, and in the midst of
them the section about the Adulteress.   There is no help for it.
These verses do not belong to the Gospel of John.   They form
no part of the New Testament.   That is, however, no reason
why we should not gladly read them.   In the case of Mark 16$^{9\text{-}20}$
we have learned from whom the verse came—from Aristion.
In the case of this section we do not know from whom it came.
But it may well be older, not younger, than the Gospel of John.

Textual criticism knows that it is not, however, a proper part of that Gospel.

We have said that neither Mark 16$^{9\text{-}20}$ nor John 7^{53}–8^{11} belongs to the New Testament. The problem at once arises, what should be done with these verses? Here are two sections, each about of a hundred and sixty-six words, which have almost from the outset been more or less closely joined to the New Testament. One of them is from a disciple of Jesus named Aristion; the other is, I take it, also originally from a disciple of Jesus, though I do not know his name. Textual criticism having now shown that neither the one nor the other of the two is by rights a part of the New Testament, some persons might think that the only proper conclusion would be to cast them both altogether away, not to allow them to appear in the New Testament in any form. Should that be done, should they no longer be printed in the New Testament, should they be left to casual collections of early Christian writings, the one, the Aristion passage, would probably soon be forgotten. That would be of less consequence, owing to the fact that its contents are pretty much all in our hands in other passages. The other passage, the story of the Adulteress, would not be forgotten. It would, however, on the one hand certainly fail to be seen so often, fail to be read so often as it is now read in the New Testament; and on the other hand, it would in all likelihood be the object of many changes and of many interpolations in the course of time.

It seems to me that these two passages have a thoroughly different standing from the first passage mentioned, 1 John 5$^{7,\,8}$. That passage never was a part of the Greek New Testament, and should be omitted from it as if Erasmus had never been brought to print it. It should be left out without word or sign that any false words ever had been there. But these two passages should on the contrary remain in the New Testament. Should the real end of Mark some day be found, it might then be well to let the present verses 16$^{9\text{-}20}$ go. Yet even then, as I think should be the method of proceeding now, these lines from Aristion might be printed after the Gospel as the long-used close of it. It is only desirable that they should be distinctly separated from 16^8. There should be a slight space between verse eighth and verse ninth, and the passage should be in brackets and have Aristion's name attached to it. It is very convenient that this passage takes its place in the course of nature at the end of the Gospel where it occasions no difficulty. As for the story of the Adulteress, three courses are open. It could be left in the text, but be separated from the rest by a gap before and after it, and by double brackets. This does not seem to me to be advisable. It could be placed at the foot of the page on which John 7⁵³ occurs, as if it were a note. It seems to me, however, that the best way of all to dispose of it would be to follow some of the manuscripts and to print it after the close of the Gospel of John as a separate piece. It could then be found even more readily than now. These are the three passages about which textual criticism gives us clear and definite information.

LUKE 22⁴³.⁴⁴.

The three passages that probably should be left out, but about which the verdict of textual criticism is not so clear as in the three passages named above, are the following. In Luke 22⁴³.⁴⁴ the vision of the angel and the narrative touching bloody sweat are lacking in some documents, and are in others marked as spurious. They should at least be placed in brackets or be put on the margin. There is in that passage perhaps an element of exaggeration or of fable that helps condemn it. In the next passage there is nothing of that kind, but only the plainest everyday matter of fact.

MATTHEW 16².³.

It is in Matthew 16².³: "When it is evening ye say: Fair weather. For the sky is growing red. And in the morning: A storm to-day. For the sky is growing red and lowering. Ye know how to tell the face of the sky, but the signs of the times ye cannot." Nevertheless, so little reason there would seem to be to object to these words, the documents are against them. One would naturally ask, how the presence of such indifferent phrases could be accounted for if they were not genuine, if they had not been there from the first moment. For it is clear that we do not find such things, such phrases thrust in at other places in the New Testament. It is possible that Jesus spoke these words at some other time. The somewhat sarcastic turn, that they could tell what the weather will be, but not what the evident course of affairs would be, might easily have been used against the Pharisees. We could then suppose that some one who had heard these words from Jesus' lips, or who had caught them up from oral or even from some written tradition, placed them here as fitting nicely in where the Pharisees and Sadducees asked for a sign. We might even go so far in theorising as to conceive that Jesus actually said them at this time, but that the evangelist had not happened to have them, and that they were then supplied as just suggested. They probably should be omitted here as not a part of the original text. And we may freely say, that although they may have been spoken by Jesus, and although we should wish to preserve every thought uttered by Him, there is, nevertheless, nothing in these words that would make us greatly mourn their loss. They can be bracketed or put in a footnote. Our conception of Jesus and of His teaching will not be altered by the omission.

JOHN 5³·⁴.

The third passage reminds us of the verses in Luke 22⁴³·⁴⁴, for an angel comes in again. This is in the Gospel according to John 5³·⁴. The words which represent the multitude that is seeking healing as waiting for an angel to trouble the water, and the narrative of the descent of the angel and of the surety that the first one who stepped into the pool after the troubling would be healed, no matter what disease he had, —those words are not supported by the best witnesses, and they should be placed in a footnote. It is less difficult to account for their presence than it was to account for the presence of the words in the passage last discussed. For it was quite natural for someone who read the Gospel at an early date to put in just such an explanation. We have so little inclination to-day to look to the intervention of angels, we are so much accustomed to think of God as Himself near us and Himself caring for us, that we should not regret at all to lose the story of the angel here. But in the early years of Christianity the case was different. Then, perhaps largely in connection with

Persian fancies or as a result of some other heathen dreams about half-divine beings, whom we might call little gods, nothing was more natural or more attractive to the imagination than such a mediating personification of the power of God.

With these three passages following upon the three discussed before them we have had a glimpse of the problems of textual criticism which have to deal with a greater number of words, and we have also learned that, aside from these passages, which are to be switched, shunted out of the direct lines of the text of the New Testament, there are no larger passages which are called in doubt textually.

ROMANS 9⁵.

As a contrast to these more comprehensive or externally extensive problems, I shall touch next one of the questions which turns upon a single point, or we might in view of old Greek punctuation even say, upon the position of a single point as either at the upper part or the lower part of the last letter of the word after which it stood. The passage is in the Epistle to the Romans 9⁵. In order to understand this passage we must go back to an old habit of the Jews. They had a great way of breaking out anywhere and everywhere with a doxology. We can see the same thing to-day if we take up a Jewish prayer-book. Indeed, we may find the same thing in more than one place in the New Testament. Nor is the history of the Church lacking in similar phenomena. Certainly thirty years ago in America it was not uncommon in some Church services to hear in the midst of a prayer or a sermon one Christian and another ejaculate loudly : "Glory be to God !" —or "Hallelujah !"—or "Blessed be the Lord!"—or "The Lord's name be praised !" Paul was in the first verses here speaking of the glorious privileges of Israel. He was about to discuss Israel's sins, and he wished in advance to put on record his high respect for, and his devotion to his race. The Israelites have the adoption, and the glory, and the covenants, and the lawgiving, and the service, and the promises, and the fathers, and from them is Christ according to the flesh. In the third verse of the first chapter he had said that the Son of God was of the seed of David according to the flesh. And now, having summed up these glories of Israel, he says like a genuine Jew : "Thank God !"

That is to say, just as in Rom. 1²⁵, so here he declares God blessed: "God who is over all be blessed for ever. Amen." The whole problem lies in the punctuation after the word "flesh." In my opinion there is no doubt that a full stop must follow that word. I have examined a great many manuscripts in many different libraries, and almost all of them have their largest stop after σάρκα, "flesh."

Romans 15 and 16.

Questions of textual criticism may have a bearing upon questions that belong partly to the criticism of the canon in a certain way and partly to the criticism of the writings. A very striking case to which we alluded above is found at the close of the Epistle to the Romans. In our editions the Epistle closes (16²⁵⁻²⁷) with a doxology: "To him that is able to confirm you according to my gospel and the preaching of Jesus Christ, according to the revelation of a mystery that had been kept silent from eternal times, but now has been revealed and also made known by prophetic writings according to the command of the eternal God unto all the nations unto obedience of faith, to the only wise God, through Jesus Christ, to whom be glory unto the ages of the ages. Amen." These majestic words make a fitting close for this grand Epistle. But do they belong here? For in the documents we find that they are sometimes omitted. We shall see that they were omitted largely in Western documents, but that the omission was known in the East.

A slight, a passing testimony against these verses was offered by a Greek, who probably in the ninth century corrected the Greek text in the Codex Claromontanus, D^paul. This Greek added the spiritus and accents to the text, but left them out in the case of words which he did not approve. Here he accented the first four words as it were by chance, and then, seeing what the text was, added no more. That was a Greek testimony in the West, for this Codex Claromontanus is a Western manuscript. The Greek text of the Codex Augiensis, F^paul, also leaves these words out, but it leaves room for them in the Greek text here at the close of the sixteenth chapter. The other Greek-Latin manuscript of the Epistles of Paul, the Codex Boernerianus at Dresden, G^paul, omits these words in like manner, but differs

nevertheless from the Codex Augiensis, because it leaves room
for them not here, but at the close of the fourteenth chapter, after
14^{23}, and that both in the Greek and in the Latin text.   It is a
curious circumstance, and shows how trifling a thing may throw
light upon the history of a reading, that we find traces of this
omission in Jerome's commentary to the Ephesians.   He is
discussing Eph. 3^5, and refers to those who think that the
prophets did not understand what they spoke, but made their
utterances in an unwitting ecstasy.   He declares that they use
as a proof of their view not only Eph. 3^5, but also this
passage: "To him that is able," etc., which he says "is found in
the most manuscripts to the Romans."   When he says it is in
the "most" manuscripts, he shows that in some this passage is
not found.   Thus we have word of the omission of this doxology
in the fourth century.

But we can go back to the second century, for Origen
relates that Marcion took this passage out of Romans.   We shall
return to Origen's further testimony later.   Here a word is
necessary as to this statement.   In spite of the fact that Origen
lived not far from Marcion's day, and in spite of the fact that
Marcion did use a sharp dissecting knife upon the books of
the New Testament, we do not feel perfectly sure that the
excision of the words, or, to speak more cautiously, that the
absence of these words, was due to Marcion.   The fact remains,
however, that they were wanting in Marcion's manuscripts, and
therefore in the manuscripts of his followers in the second
century, scarcely a hundred years after Paul dictated the Epistle
to Tertius, to Tertius if the sixteenth chapter belongs here.

There certainly is, nevertheless, a fair amount of documentary
evidence for the existence of these words as a part of this Epistle.
But strangely enough this evidence is of a double nature.   The
French would say that it was cross-eyed.   It looks towards two
places at once.

We saw a moment ago that the Codex Augiensis left a
blank space for these words after Rom. 14^{23}.   Now there is an
uncial manuscript of the ninth century in the Angelica Library
at Rome which has these words at that point, after 14^{23} and
not after 16^{24}.   They are found at that same place in a couple
of hundred of the younger manuscripts in small writing.   The
later Syrian translation also has them there.   The Arabic trans-

lation that was printed in the Paris polyglot has them there. They seem to have been in the same place in the Gothic translation. And Origen, whom we named above, says that in some of his manuscripts these words stood after 14^{23}. Origen's manuscripts stretched, we may be sure, far back into the second century. Chrysostom, the golden-mouthed orator, had them there in his text, and so had Cyril of Alexandria of the early fifth century, and Theodoret an opponent of Cyril and a friend of Nestorius, and John Damascenus who died after the middle of the eighth century, and Theophylact the Bulgarian bishop, and Oecumenius. All these have this passage not at the end of the Epistle, but at the end of the fourteenth chapter.

Then there are a few documents that have the words at both places, both at the close of the sixteenth and at the close of the fourteenth chapter. Even the great Codex Alexandrinus of the fifth century has them thus twice, and so has a ninth century large letter manuscript at St. Petersburg, P, and so have some younger manuscripts and some Armenian witnesses.

And, finally, they stand at the end of the Epistle, as in our editions, in the Codex Sinaiticus and the Codex Vaticanus both of the fourth century, in the Codex Ephraim of the fifth century, and in the first hand of the Codex Claromontanus of the sixth century. Besides that there are some small-letter manuscripts that have them there; and Origen says that they were there in some manuscripts that were before him, which will have been doubtless of the second century. Three Old-Latin manuscripts have them there, and so does the Vulgate. And the Syrian translation joins with the Boheiric and the Ethiopic in placing them there. Origen and Ambrosiaster are of the same mind.

I feel sure that many a reader will by this time begin to think that this passage is a piece of textual fireworks. The reason I have here called attention to it is because it seems to me to be uncommonly full of instruction. It involves all manner of questions, and insinuates itself into several departments of New Testament study. We may find a clue to the difficulties and intricacies of the whole matter in the possibilities of the earliest history of this Epistle, we might say, both in Paul's hands and in the hands of the church at Rome. The textual doubtfulness is probably a token of certain things that have left no other traces behind them.

To try to put the matter plainly, we must, first, insist upon the purely theoretical character of the explanation that we have in mind, and then, second, speak definitely as if we knew all about it. If we look at the sixteenth chapter and see what a number of persons Paul salutes in it intimately, it will give us food for thought.   Prisca or Priscilla and Aquila are old friends and fellow-workers of Paul.   They had to leave Rome.   They were with Paul at Corinth.   They formed a theological training school then for Apollos at Ephesus, and sent him to Corinth to follow up Paul's work.   Now they might by this time be again in Rome, but we knew of them last at Ephesus.   Then comes Epainetus, "the first-fruits of Asia unto Christ."   He might have been at Rome, but Asia is nearer Ephesus.   Paul knows about Mariam's work for the Christians to whom he is writing.   Andronicus and Junias were relatives and fellow-prisoners of Paul's, and were notable among the apostles, and had been Christians before Paul was.   And the list runs on and on, and includes households or churches in special houses, as in Prisca's and Aquila's at the beginning, and even includes Rufus' mother, who had filled a mother's place towards the old bachelor Paul.   Look at the list carefully. Write down the number of people mentioned, counting as few as may be admissible for the anonymous groups.   We shall probably reach at least fifty people whom Paul knows intimately.   And then reflect that the Epistle to the Romans is written to a church that Paul has not yet visited.   It is hard to account for the fact that Paul should know so many people well in a still unvisited church, and almost as hard to understand how he could speak as if he did not know the church if he knew fifty of the certainly then not very large group of Christians at Rome.   If these salutations should have been written to the church at Ephesus where Paul had spent a couple of years, they would be in every way at once to be accounted for.   No single name would appear to be singular.

If, however, this letter, that is to say, this sixteenth chapter in the main, had been written to Ephesus, and if that fact were to be reflected in the documents which contain the text, the doxology would not be moved from the end of the sixteenth chapter to the end of the fourteenth, but to the end of the fifteenth chapter.   But no single document puts the doxology there.

Here a word comes in that Origen speaks. He really said a great deal about this passage in a very few words. He not only says that Marcion omitted the doxology, but he also says that Marcion cut out the whole of the last two chapters. I said a while ago that heretics were sometimes accused of corrupting or curtailing the text, when it is apparent to us that they are merely using the manuscripts which the ordinary course of their life had placed in their hands. And those manuscripts may have been better than the manuscripts of the men who attacked them. Marcion, who came from the East, from Pontus, to Rome in the year 138 or 139, perhaps, only about eighty-five years after Romans was written, may have had in Rome, and copied, a roll of Romans which did actually stop at 14^{23}. The doxology might have been there or not. If it were there, Marcion may have cut it off because he did not like the favourable allusion to the prophetic writings.

It would be possible that Paul's original letter to the Romans had closed at 14^{23} with the doxology, and without a long series of intimate greetings to people whom he did not know. The fifteenth chapter might then have been a letter written by Paul at a later date, and written to the Romans. The sixteenth chapter could well have been a letter of recommendation written for Phœbe to the church at Ephesus. Phœbe might even have received the Epistle to the Romans from Paul at Cenchrea, and have taken a ship which was going to sail from Cenchrea to Ephesus and then westward to Rome. It may have been the ship of a Christian owner who gave her a free passage. Such a roundabout voyage would not have been strange at that day, and might occur even to-day. All ships do not touch at all ports. Pursuing the thought, Phœbe having delivered the letter at Ephesus, will then have begged it off or have copied it for herself as a recommendation for Rome, and all the good people so kindly named by Paul will have been glad to let their praises be carried by Phœbe to the capital city. Then at some later day, the short letter composing the fifteenth chapter and Phœbe's Ephesian letter were (see p. 320) by accident, or even on purpose as Pauline, copied at the end of a new roll on which Romans was written, and the doxology was moved from after 14^{23} to after 16^{24}.

Should, however, anyone choose to reject as pure fancy the theory of the main part of the sixteenth chapter as sent first to

Ephesus and then reaching Rome, I have only to say that I should have no objections to offer to another thought. If, namely, the greetings in the sixteenth chapter, naturally as many of them seem to appertain to Ephesus, should be conceived of as written in a brief note by Paul at some later day, after he had spent the first two years at Rome and had become, though a prisoner, well acquainted with the Christians there,—as written then to the Romans, they would offer no further difficulty. The addition of the two notes to the Epistle and the transfer of the doxology would remain the same.

*   *   *   *   *   *   *

Oneness of Modern Text.

Before taking up the consideration of these various passages, I referred (p. 508) to the negative comfort that may be drawn from the thought that we need not look for a future cutting out of larger portions of text. We may close our view of the criticism of the text by the positive comfort to be found in the oneness of modern textual criticism, and in the proportionally large amount of text that seems to be well settled.

It has sometimes been thought that textual critics endangered and damaged the text, and it has been imagined that their collections of various readings from the manuscripts were so many signs of the disintegration of the text at their hands. But those who have such fears forget that the critics do not invent the various readings. They only take the trouble to compare texts, and to say what the testimony to the various forms of the text is. And it is further alleged that every text determined upon is different from the preceding text, and that there is no progress in textual criticism, but that all is growing worse. The aim of all these complaints is to say that we should throw all textual criticism and all textual critics overboard, and live along in blissful ignorance of right or wrong readings, or of goodness and badness in texts, not taking as much interest in the texts of our New Testament as the Shakespeare scholars take in the text of Shakespeare, the Dante scholars in that of Dante, or the classical philologians in that of Homer.

So far from its being the case that the great textual critics have made no progress in determining the text, we can see by a single example in what a high degree they have succeeded in fixing it. If we turn to the Epistle to the Hebrews we find in a single chapter, in the twelfth, besides a number of other places in which the so-çalled Received Text was wrong, five places in which the readings which it contained either have no known documentary support or such as is in no wise to be compared to the support given by the better witnesses to the readings of the great critics. That by the bye.

As to the agreement of the three editions of Tregelles, Westcott and Hort, and Tischendorf, we may take into account the whole of the Epistle to the Hebrews. Tregelles did not have at his command all that the other editions had, and nevertheless he only stands alone in ten places, two of which are omissions, in that he once leaves out "the" and once leaves out "and,"— three are additions, in that he adds the word "the" twice in one verse, and in another verse the word "work," and at the end of the Epistle "Amen,"—and three are grammatical differences. Westcott and Hort are found alone seven times. They make two additions, once of "as a garment," and once of "and." They put the word "roll up" instead of the word "change," which in the Greek only alters three letters. They move a comma from after the word "assembly" to before that word. And they make three grammatical changes. And, finally, Tischendorf, of whom people often speak as if he treated the text inconsiderately, arbitrarily, and rashly, is found to stand alone only four times. He has "injustice" instead of "lawlessness," a difference of three letters in Greek ; he leaves out an article ; he has "to the" instead of "the" ; and he has a different tense of the same verb in a quotation from the Old Testament.

From that we can see that the tendency of these scholars was not altogether so centrifugal and destructive as has at times been supposed. Those who decry textual criticism as dangerous and destructive, are usually not aware of the comparatively limited extent of the text of the New Testament, which is subject to doubt. And the work of the editors whom we have just mentioned has gone far towards circumscribing still more narrowly the field. They have in so many cases cleared up difficulties, solved doubts, and settled readings apparently for good, that much less is left as debatable ground. The second page of Hort's Introduction to the edition of Westcott and Hort should be learned by heart by everyone who fears that the New Testament will vanish into thin air under the chemical processes of textual criticism.   Hort presents first of all as the result of a rough computation the proportion of words that are generally accepted as well established and beyond doubt, as not less than seven-eighths of the whole New Testament. Then, however, he takes up the remaining eighth, the due field of the textual critic, and reminds us that it is very largely made up of trifling differences ; for example, among other things, of the mere order of the words, and of differences of spelling.   In consequence, he reckons that the words still subject to doubt do not make up more than about one-sixtieth of the New Testament. This might seem to be enough to calm the troubled minds of those who tremble before or are indignantly hostile to the criticism of the text.   Yet that is not enough.

The examination of the variations still left shows that a large majority of them are of comparatively slight importance. Hort's final judgment is that the field covered by substantial variations " can hardly form more than a thousandth part of the entire text."   In order to gain an idea of what that means, we can be very plain.   A Greek New Testament lying at my side contains five hundred and sixty pages not as large as my hand, and there are a couple of lines of various readings on most of the pages.   A thousandth part of that would then after all be in the neighbourhood of a half a page or fifteen or sixteen of these small lines.   Really that is not very much.   And the great point for a Christian is that he must wish to have his one great book brought into the very best condition possible.   It would be strange if a Christian should take pains to have a well-built church, and wish to have a well-prepared pastor, and be anxious that a good choir be at command, but should say : " It is no matter about the New Testament.   The edition that Estienne printed three centuries and a half ago, when but little was known about the text, is quite good enough for me."   It is singular to see a man anxious to have the latest and best thing in electric lights, but totally indifferent as to having the best text in his New Testament.

INDEX

A

B

Bacchylides, 134.
Bacon, Roger, 412.
Bandini, Angelo Maria, 378.
Barnabas, letter of, 77, 204, 209, 239, 240, 430.
Barrett, John, 357.
Bashmuric translation, 405.
Basil the Great of Cæsarea in Cappadocia, 274, 275, 434.
Basilides, 69, 70, 116, 133, 171, 187, 203, 207, 209, 430.
Batiffol, Pierre, 362, 364.
Bede, the venerable, 251, 363.
Bellarmin, 412, 413.
Bengel, Johannes Albrecht, 447.
Bentley, Richard, 353, 446.
Berengar, 414.
Bessarion, Cardinal, 345.
Bèze, Théodore de, 350, 351, 442.
Birch, Andreas, 451.
Blandina, a martyr, 143.
Boheiric translation, 404, 405, 430.
Boniface of Rome, 278.

Book of the Dead, 21.
Book of Armagh, 416.
    Chad, 415.
    Deer, 414.
    Dimma, 417.
    Durrow, 417.
    Kells, 417.
    Moling, \
    Mulling, ⌡ 417.
Bookmaking, 32.
Books outside of New Testament, 40 41.
"born again," 93, 94.
Bowyer, William, 449, 450.
Brahmans, 21.
Brandscheid, 510.
British and Foreign Bible Society, 361, 464.
Buddhists, 21.
Burgon, John William, 339, 378, 411, 462.
Burkard, St., of Würzburg, 416.
Buttmann, Philipp, 453.

C

Cæsar on journey, 29.
Cæsarea and manuscripts, 35.
Cæsarius, 434.
Callistus, 432.
Canon in Egypt, 21.
Canon, history of, 7, 8.
Canon, Jewish, 21.
Canon, the word, 15.
Carpocrates, 163, 430.
Carpocratians, 116.
Carthage, Synod of, in 397, 278.
Cassiodorius, 221, 281.
Cassius of Tyre, 158.
Cataphrygians, 133.
Catholic Epistles, 184–186.
Catholic Epistles of Dionysius of Corinth, 134.
Celsus, 111, 145, 146.
Ceolfrid, abbot of Yarrow, 413.
Cerinthus, 68, 163, 211, 229, 250.
Chalkopratia, 386.
Chapters, 469.
Charlemagne, 412.
Charlemagne's Bible, 415.
Charles the Bald, 414.
Charles I., 341.

Cherubim and Gospels, 149.
Christians and scribes, 34.
Christina, Queen, 418.
Chrysophora, 136.
Chrysostom, 279, 280, 390, 428, 433.
Church Writers, 419–436.
Claromontanus, Codex, 282, 350.
Clarus of Ptolemæis, 158.
Classes of text, 480.
    their origin, 481, 502, 503.
    in profane books, 481.
Clement of Alexandria, 17, 21, 79, 165, 169, 172, 187, 199, 219–222, 238, 250, 430.
Clement of Rome, 16, 42, 62–67, 116, 135, 186, 192, 195, 203, 209, 210, 236–239.
Clement VIII., Pope, 413.
Cleobios, 116.
Clermont, 351.
Clopas, 120, 159.
Cnossians, 134, 135.
Codex Alexandrinus, 340–343.
    Amiatinus, 413.
    Argenteus, 418.

F

G

H

I

J

Q

R

S

T